Here's What the Reviewers Say...

"This book will be the one you'll want in your library and to carry with you on your next trip to Costa Rica... The references are excellent and good reading. If you want to expand your knowledge about Costa Rica, then buy a copy of this book and READ it! You'll enjoy the light writing style." Shirley Miller, *Costa Rica Outlook*.

"Each title in this fine series shares a similar format: extensive background on the island's history, economics, and politics, flora and fauna, and culture and religion; the daily practicalities of life (e.g., recycling requirements, boating conduct, buying land); what to see and do." *Library Journal*

"... straightforward, easy to use... valuable practical tips..." Gypsy Cole, *Tico Times*

"A good combination of practical travel information, background, and descriptions of sights and activities.... Travelers will find all the information they need to prepare for a trip in the book. For its mix of practical information and the range of travel activities described, the book is difficult to beat." *Travel Library*

"This extensive, up-to-date guide for Costa Rica is a welcome sight. Selected accommodations and restaurants span the scale from luxury to low budget, while the author's respectful, ecologically aware perspective contributes a progressive view of the sights and scenes." *American Library Association Booklist*

"Pariser's book may be the best-balanced, most comprehensive guide of the entire Tico bunch. Excellent sections on the national parks, flora and fauna, and Costa Rica's history. This is the one to take with you...." Lan Sluder, *Great Expeditions*

S0-ARK-255

*A*dventure Guide to

CostaRica

3rd Edition

Harry S. Pariser

HUNTER
PUBLISHING

Hunter Publishing, Inc.
300 Raritan Center Parkway
Edison NJ 08818
(908) 225 1900 Fax (908) 417 0482

ISBN 1-55650-722-4

© 1996 Hunter Publishing, Inc. (3rd Edition)

Maps by Kim André
All photographs by author, except as indicated.
Cover: *Red-eyed Tree Frog*, Renée Lynn (Davis/Lynn Photography)

Acknowledgments

Thanks go out to my publisher Michael Hunter and his staff, Harvey Haber, Pat Bliss, Woody, Eva Pedino, Alex Grant, Peter, Shirley Miller, Rudi Hessel, Diana Hare, Michael Medill, Marucio Jurado Fernández, Milvia E. Comacchia Grossi, Luz Elena, Sandra Leitón, Rick Dillon, Jeffrey De Vito, Denise Richards and Michael Holm, Xiomara Rivera López, Raymond Johnson, Al and Jean Bair, Laura Owens, Laura Wedmore, Miguel Gomez Doninelli, Frank Healy, Nina M. Rach, Ron Lippert, Michael Kaye, Gisele Mendez, Sergio Miranda T., Maria Pinagel, Bob Grey, Gordon Slack, Linda Holland, Jack Ewing, Richard Krug, Milton and Diana Lieberman, and to many others. A final thank you goes out to my mother who always worries about me.

Contents

Charts

Maps

A Note on Prices

For the reader's convenience prices (generally inclusive of 15.4% tax) are listed in US dollars. They are subject to fluctuation and should be used only as a guideline. Wherever you go, there are likely to be one or more newer places not listed in this guide. Per person prices for *cabinas* are generally highest for just one person, cheaper for two, and lower thereafter. Local hotels either charge double the single price for a couple or reduce the price slightly. Establishments for which no prices are listed are classified as follows: **low budget** (under $20 d), **inexpensive** ($21-30 d), **moderate** ($31-50 d), **expensive** ($51-90 d), **luxury** ($90-120 d) and **ultra-luxury** (over $120 d). Prices are approximate and may vary with the season.

Abbreviations

AID – Agency for International Development
Av. – Avenida (avenue)
C – centigrade
C. – Calle (street)
d – double
E – east, eastern
ha – hectare

km – kilometer
m – meter
N – north, northern
OW – one way
pp – per person
s – single
S – south, southern
W – west, western

About the Author

After graduating from Boston University with a B.S. in Public Communications in 1975, Harry S. Pariser hitched and camped his way through Europe, traveled down the Nile by steamer, and by train through Sudan. Visiting Uganda, Rwanda, and Tanzania, he then traveled by ship from Mombasa to Bombay, and on through South and Southeast Asia before settling down in Kyoto, Japan. There he studied Japanese and ceramics while teaching English to everyone from tiny tots to Buddhist priests. Using Japan as a base, he travelled through other parts of Asia: trekking to the vicinity of Mt. Everest in Nepal, taking tramp steamers to Indonesian islands like Adonara and Ternate, and visiting rural China. He returned to the United States in 1984 via the Caribbean, where he researched two travel guides: *Guide to Jamaica* and *Guide to Puerto Rico and the Virgin Islands*, published in 1986. He currently lives in San Francisco and can be contacted by e-mail at salsa@catch22.com or can be visited on the Internet at http://www.catch22.com/~vudu.

Reader's Response Form

Adventure Guide to Costa Rica, 3rd Edition

I found your book rewarding because:

Your book could be improved by:

The best places I stayed in were (explain why):

I found the best food at:

Some good and bad experiences I had were:

Will you return to Costa Rica?

If so, where do you plan to go? If not, why not?

I purchased this book at:

Please include any other comments on a separate sheet and mail completed form to Harry S. Pariser, c/o Hunter Publishing, 300 Raritan Center Parkway, Edison, NJ 08818. Fax to 908-417-0482 or e-mail: salsa@catch22.com.

We Love to Get Mail!

Things change so rapidly that it's impossible to keep up with everything. Like automobiles, travel books require constant fine tuning if they are to stay in top condition. We need input from readers so that we can continue to provide the best, most current information possible. Please write to let us know about any inaccuracies or new information. Although we try to make our maps as accurate as possible, errors can occur. If you have suggestions for improvement or places that should be included, please let us know.

Introduction

The nation of Costa Rica, encompassing an area half the size of Ireland, brings together pronounced geographical extremes ranging from spectacular beaches to majestic volcanoes, from swampy lowlands with swarms of birds to highlands that turn frigid at night. Although smaller than most US states and Canadian provinces, it is larger than Holland, Denmark, Belgium, and Switzerland. In addition to traditional Tico hospitality, Costa Rica offers hiking and water sports, casinos and discos. A wealth of wildlife makes it a paradise for naturalists and birdwatchers.

The Central American isthmus is the only region in the world that is both interoceanic and intercontinental. Bordered by Mexico to the N and Colombia to the S, the region comprises seven nations: Belize, Guatemala, El Salvador, Honduras, Nicaragua, Costa Rica, and Panama. All of the nations except Belize are former members of the Spanish Empire, although some contain large indigenous populations. They share a similar cultural base that includes the Spanish language and the Catholic religion. Despite their surface similarities, each has evolved its own national character, making union unlikely.

The Land

Geography

Covering 19,653 sq miles (50,900 sq km), an area a bit smaller than West Virginia, Costa Rica lies on a NW-SE axis between Nicaragua to the N and Panama to the S. Its unoffical border with Nicaragua, accepted provisionally by both sides, extends for 186 miles (300 km). Definitively delineated only in 1941 after a century-long dispute, its border with Panama is 226 miles (363 km) long. It extends 288 miles (464 km) N to S and 170 miles (274 km) E to W, and no part of the country is more than 300 miles (200 km) from the sea. A series of *cordilleras* (mountain ranges), ridges, and valleys traverse its length.

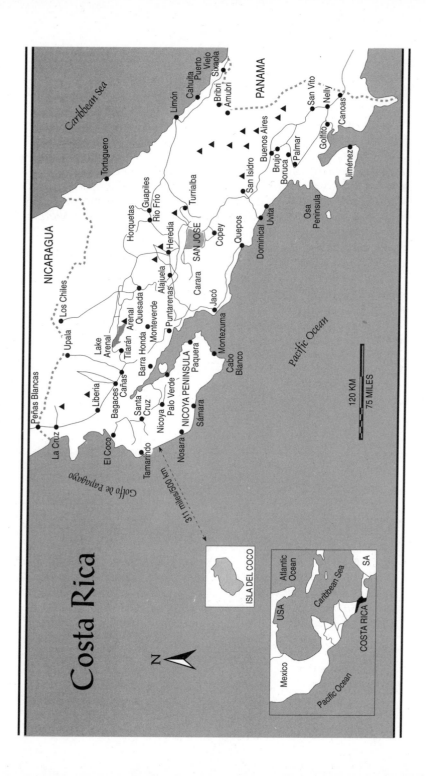

Costa Rica

Caribbean Sea

NICARAGUA

Pacific Ocean

PANAMA

Peñas Blancas
La Cruz
El Coco
Tamarindo
Nosara
Sámara
Nicoya
Palo Verde
Santa Cruz
NICOYA PENINSULA
Paquera
Cabo Blanco
Montezuma
Liberia
Bagaces
Cañas
Barra Honda
Tilarán
Lake Arenal
Arenal
Monteverde
Puntarenas
Upala
Los Chiles
Quesada
Alajuela
Carara
Jacó
SAN JOSE
Heredia
Copey
Quepos
Turrialba
Río Frío
Guápiles
Horquetas
Tortuguero
Limón
San Isidro
Dominical
Uvita
Brujo
Boruca
Buenos Aires
Palmar
Osa Peninsula
Golfito
Jiménez
San Vito
Nelly
Canoas
Amubri
Bribrí
Sixaola
Puerto Viejo
Cahuita
San Ramón

Golfo de Papagayo

311 miles/500 km

ISLA DEL COCO

120 KM
75 MILES

N

Atlantic Ocean
Caribbean Sea
USA
Mexico
Pacific Ocean
COSTA RICA
SA

MOUNTAINS: The nation has four principal mountain ranges. The Cordillera Volcanía de Guanacaste lies in the far NW; to the S rises the lower and smaller Cordillera de Tilarán. Farther S still are the Cordillera Central followed by the Cordillera de Talamanca. Although the last is of non-volcanic origin, the latter two sets of ranges contain several volcanoes. Two mountains, Poás and Arenal in the Cordillera Central, are active. The Cordillera de Talamanca has 10 peaks above 10,000 ft (3,000 m), including 12,500-ft (3,810-m) Cerro Chirripó, the nation's highest point, which is located inside the national park of the same name. A geographical continuation of the plains (*llano*) found in Nicaragua, lowland covers most of the N and stretches along the Caribbean coast.

Geothermal Power

Set at Volcán Miravalles in Guanacaste, a geothermal plant produces 5% of the nation's electricity; capacity will expand to 10% when a second plant opens in 1997-98. The plant is powered by underground vapor; the humidity is separated from the vapor and the dry gas powers the turbines. *Miratur* (☎ 673-0260) offers tours here, which include a walk through the plant and a dip in the hot springs.

VOLCANOES: Perhaps the most spectacular features of Costa Rica's landscape are its volcanoes. These are Poás, Irazú, Rincón de la Vieja, Arenal, Tenorio, Turrialba, and Barua. Around volcanoes you're certain to notice volcanic sand, which is either black or light grey. While the light-colored sand is from obsidian, the black sand comes from pumice. The term volcano (*volcán* in Spanish) derives from Vulcano, an active volcanic island off the N tip of Sicily, which was believed to be the entrance to the nether world and the domain of Vulcan. He was the Roman deity who forged Jupiter's thunderbolts. Universally, volcanoes have been linked with hell, gods, and demons. *Magma*, molten rock from the crust and upper mantle of the Earth, is less dense than solid rock. Its bouyancy causes it to rise through cracks. A volcano allows magma to rise to the surface and a hill or mountain results as the magma cools and accumulates. The three types of magma (rhyolitic or granitic, basaltic, and andesitic) produce the majority of volcanic rock.

Although there are various types of volcanoes, Costa Rica's major volcanic peaks are all *strato-volcanoes* or composite volcanoes – so called because they build up through eruptions stemming from a vent and comprise interbedded cinder, ash, and lava in varying proportions. Generally conical, irregular shapes result from landsides, streams carv-

Volcanoes, Parks, Refuges, Reserves, and Gardens

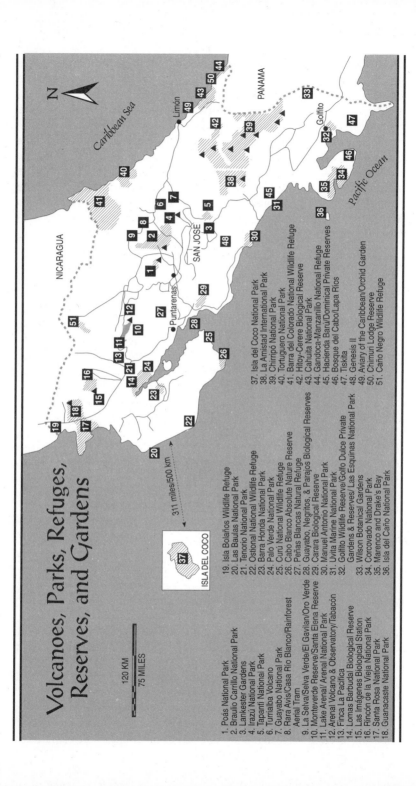

1. Poás National Park
2. Braulio Carrillo National Park
3. Lankester Gardens
4. Irazú National Park
5. Tapantí National Park
6. Turrialba Volcano
7. Guayabo National Park
8. Rara Avis/Casa Río Blanco/Rainforest Aerial Tram
9. La Selva/Selva Verde/El Gavilan/Oro Verde
10. Monteverde Reserve/Santa Elena Reserve
11. Lake Arenal/ Arenal National Park
12. Arenal Volcano & Observatory/Tabacón
13. Finca La Pacifica
14. Lomas Barbudal Biological Reserve
15. Las Imágenes Biological Station
16. Rincón de la Vieja National Park
17. Santa Rosa National Park
18. Guanacaste National Park

19. Isla Bolaños Wildlife Refuge
20. Las Baulas National Park
21. Tenorio National Park
22. Ostional National Wildlife Refuge
23. Barra Honda National Park
24. Palo Verde National Park
25. Curú National Wildlife Refuge
26. Cabo Blanco Absolute Nature Reserve
27. Peñas Blancas Natural Refuge
28. Guayabo, Negritos, & Parajos Biological Reserves
29. Carara Biological Reserve
30. Manuel Antonio National Park
31. Uvita Marine National Park
32. Golfito Wildlife Reserve/Golfo Dulce Private Gardens & Reserves/ Las Esquinas National Park
33. Wilson Botanical Gardens
34. Corcovado National Park
35. Marenco and Drake's Bay
36. Isla del Caño National Park

37. Isla del Coco National Park
38. La Amistad International Park
39. Chirripó National Park
40. Tortuguero National Park
41. Barra del Colorado National Wildlife Refuge
42. Hitoy-Cerere Biological Reserve
43. Cahuita National Park
44. Gandoca-Manzanillo National Refuge
45. Hacienda Baru/Dominical Private Reserves
46. Bosque del Cabo/Lapa Rios
47. Tiskita
48. Genesis II
49. Aviary of the Caribbean/Orchid Garden
50. Chimuri Lodge Reserve
51. Caño Negro Wildlife Refuge

ing eroded paths, major explosions, and a shift in position of the summit's vent. The remnants of lava flows can be seen draping their sides. Volcanoes are classifed as "active," "extinct" and "dormant," but whether a given peak is dormant or extinct is often difficult to ascertain. The most active peak in Costa Rica is Arenal.

When magma reaches the earth's surface, it is known as *lava*. *Fumaroles* (from the Latin word *fumus*, meaning "smoke") are vents that emit gases and vapors. They are commonly seen at the top of active volcanoes, as well as in Rincón de la Vieja National Park. Hot springs, undoubtedly the most delightful feature of volcanoes, stem from circulating groundwater which contacts hot volcanic rock and then finds its way to the surface. The water's mineral content gives it the characteristic smell and its medicinal properties. Most of Costa Rica's hot springs center around the Arenal and Rincón de la Vieja areas NW of San José. Similarly, mud pools contain a mix of water, volcanic mud, and minerals that is kept bubbling through volcanic heat.

Eruptions are both the up and down side of volcanoes. While they cause devastation, they also lay down fertile soil. Lightning is a frequent companion of eruptions, and they are almost always preceded by earthquakes. *Tsunamis*, like the one that devastated the SW coast of Nicaragua in Aug. 1992, are seismic sea waves traveling at a speed of 500 mph (800 kph) and generated by movements of the earth's crust or by underwater volcanic explosions. **information:** Volcanologists can contact the Escuela Centroamericana de Geología, Universidad de Costa Rica, Apdo. 35 UCR, San José; the Observatorio Vulcanológico y Sismológico de Costa Rica, Escuela de Ciencias Geográfricas, Universidad Nacional, Heredia; and the Instituto Costarricense de Electricidad, Apdo. 10032, San José.

☞ **Traveler's Tip**. When visiting Irazú or Póas volcanoes, be sure to get an early start! Clouds move in early, and it may be impossible to see anything after 10 AM.

RIVERS: Innumerable rivers and streams originate in the interior highlands and flow either to the Pacific or the Caribbean. Sadly, many have become polluted and others are slated for damming in order to generate electricity. In 1991, the owner of Ríos Tropicales and his brother kayaked along the Río Torres, which runs through metropolitan San José. In order to bring attention to the pollution, they equipped themselves with wet suits, gloves, and gas masks.

The most famous whitewater rafting river is the Reventazón. The Río San Juan collects water from streams in the northern lowlands and then flows through Nicaragua until it reaches its mouth, a delta region formed in conjunction with the Río Colorado lying almost entirely within Costa Rica. (This is a popular excursion.) The Río Tortuguero flows directly to the Tortuguero waterway, which parallels the Caribbean coast, stretching from the mouth of the Río Colorado to a point just N of Limón. The rivers that empty into the Pacific are mostly fewer, shorter, and steeper.

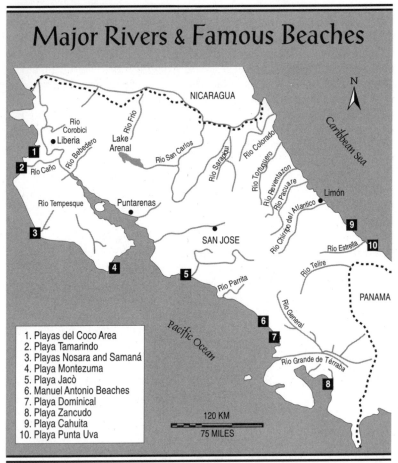

Major Rivers & Famous Beaches

1. Playas del Coco Area
2. Playa Tamarindo
3. Playas Nosara and Samaná
4. Playa Montezuma
5. Playa Jacò
6. Manuel Antonio Beaches
7. Playa Dominical
8. Playa Zancudo
9. Playa Cahuita
10. Playa Punta Uva

120 KM
75 MILES

VALLEYS: The Meseta Central is nestled in the Central Highlands, a temperate area, at an elevation of 3,280-4,920 ft (1-1,500 m). It makes up the major part of the Valle Central and consists of two basins separated by low hills. Taken together, these encompass nearly 3,861 sq miles (10,000 sq km). The Cartago Basin gets more rain and is more humid than its San José neighbor to the W, and is smaller and higher (4,920 ft, 1,500 m). Situated between the Cordillera de Talamanca and the mountains bordering the Pacific, the low-lying Valle de General lies to the S. Settlement began here only in the 1920s.

The Land

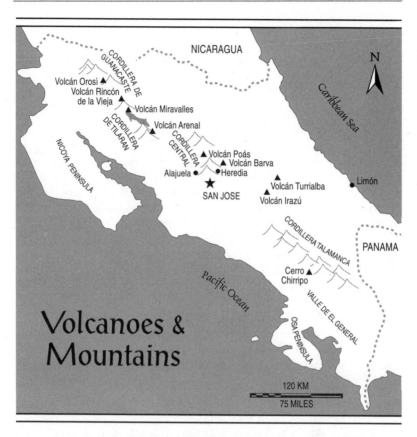

Volcanoes & Mountains

THE COASTS: The Pacific coast, marked by steep cliffs and numerous narrow beaches, stretches 631 miles (1,016 km) and contains three peninsulas: Buriya, Osa, and Nicoya. Although it is not entirely continuous – being separated in stretches by low-lying coastal mountains – a narrow alluvial coastal plain extends from the Peninsula de Osa in the S up to the port of Puntarenas, where it widens, merging with the Valle de Tempisque. The Palmer lowland complex to the SW includes rainforests. Widest along the Nicaraguan border, the swampy, heavily forested Caribbean lowland comprises about 20% of the land area. Received after a boundary dispute with Panama was settled in 1900, the 9.3-sq-mile (24-sq-km) Isla de Coco, situated 311 miles (500 km) SW of the Peninsula de Osa, is a national park.

Climate

As holds true for the rest of Central America, Costa Rica has a delightful climate, especially in its highland areas. Its mild, subtropical weather varies little throughout the year; most of the variation in temperature comes from differences in elevation. The E and SE coasts cool down delightfully at night during the winter. Rain, which usually consists of short showers, is most likely to occur from July through the end of November; the driest months are February and March. Although the average rainfall is 150-200 inches (3,807-5,076 mm), annual precipitation totals actually vary from 59 inches (1,500 mm) in the NW to 197 inches (5,000 mm) in the S. Although no area is drought-stricken, there is a considerable variety in both rainfall and the length of the dry and wet seasons. Winds prevail from the N in the winter and early spring months and come in from the SE during the rest of the year. The Caribbean coast, receiving the heaviest rainfall, has no dry season and its mean annual total exceeds 2,000 mm (79 inches). During the rainy season along the drier NW coast, rain falls in late afternoon or evening.

Seasons & Climatic Zones

What residents of the Northern temperate zones know as "summer" and "winter" are reversed for the Costa Ricans. As arriving Spaniards acclimatized, they associated their Mediterranean regimen of hot, dry summers and cool, wet winters with their new abode, disregarding the actual time of year. Thus, while *verano* (summer) refers to the dry season between December and May, *invierno* (winter) designates the wet season which, running from May through Nov., corresponds with the Northern Hemisphere's summer and fall. In some years the Pacific coast has a third period, *veranillo* (little summer) – a short dry season that sometimes emerges during July and August. Short rainstorms that cover a small area are known as *aguaceros*; less intense storms, more widely distributed and of longer duration, are known as *temporales*. *Temporales del Atlantico* and *temporales de Pacifico* are the two types. Both are the result of laterally moving air masses reaching mountains, rising, and cooling. More and more, as a result of widespread deforestation, *temporales* result in flooding. March showers are known as *"aquaceros de los cafetaleros"* (the coffee grower's showers), while the mid-Dec. rains are known as *"las lagrimas de Mary"* (Mary's tears). Between November and January, *nortes* – cold polar air fronts channeled southward between N American mountain ranges – reach

Costa Rica, one of the few places in the world where polar air travels so close to the equator. When they blow inland from the Pacific Ocean, these winds bring fine weather to the Pacific coast, where this type of breeze is known as *papagayo*.

CLIMATIC ZONES: Costa Rica has three distinct climates. The *tierra caliente* (torrid zone) encompasses the two coastal plains that rise up to 1,500 ft (450 m), with a corresponding temperature range of 85°-90°F (29.4°-32.2°C); the *tierra templada* contains the Meseta Central as well as other regions from 1,500-5,000 ft (450-1500 m), with temperatures of 75°-80°F (23.9°-26.7°C); the *tierra fria* (frigid zone) includes areas over 5,000 ft (1,524 m), with temperatures ranging from 41°-59°F (5°-15°C). On lower slopes and intermontane depressions, mean annual temperatures range from 52°-78°F (12°-24°C). Up in the higher regions of the Cordillera de Talamanca and the Cordillera Central, the annual average is less than 52°F (12°C), and may reach 32°F (0°C) on occasion. Variation in temperatures is greatest during the dry season, when the nights are cool in the highlands.

WEATHER INFORMATION: Check the inside front page of the daily *La Nación* for the national weather forecast.

Earthquakes

Other than crazy drivers, the major environmental hazards to which Costa Rica is subject are volcanic eruptions and earthquakes. Most of Cartago was destroyed by a volcanic eruption in 1910; it was devastated by others in 1620 and 1841. Limón was heavily damaged in 1935 and again, to a lesser extent, on April 22, 1991. Three of the most recent earthquakes were in 1973 in Tilarán and two in 1983. An April quake based off the tip of Osa Peninsula left one dead and 500 homeless, and a second quake in July, based 60 km S of San José, left 3,000 homeless, two dead, and 13 seriously injured. A quake measuring 5.5 on the Richter scale struck in March 1990, creating landslides on the San Juan-Atlantic Coast Highway and causing extensive damage in Puntarenas. A series of frequent, smaller tremors followed during the ensuing months. The latest quake was in April 1991 and mostly caused damage along the east coast. It registered 7.1 on the Richter scale.

Positioned atop a series of faults, Costa Rica is second only to Guatemala in Central America as a center of seismic activity. But Costa Rica has so far not experienced quakes as catastrophic as those that hit Nicaragua in 1972, Guatemala in 1976, and El Salvador in 1986. If you should experience tremors during your visit, remember that they have been going on for millions of years and will continue until the planet's demise. If a tremor should occur, don't rush outside. Get to a doorway, an inside corner wall or crawl under a desk or table for protection.

Flora & Fauna

Straddling an area from 8° to 11° N of the equator, Costa Rica has an unusual variety of ecosystems. Its high, rugged, and youthful cordilleras contain a complex ecological mosaic, as do its plains, rivers, and coasts – an ecological diversity matched in Central America only by Guatemala. There are 12 life zones in Costa Rica, as defined by L.R. Holdridge, based on seasonal distribution and variation of rainfall and temperature. There are four major zones (tropical dry, moist, wet, and rainforest), each of which is further subdivided into premontane and lower montane divisions. There's also the tropical subalpine rain *páramo* (flat, barren cold plain), though that occupies only a small area in Costa Rica.

NATURE WATCHING: The land is very much alive and nature abounds outside of crowded, polluted San José. Many species are nocturnal; they tend to gather in early evening or morning at water holes. Don't be disappointed if you fail to see many animals; the dense underbrush frequently makes viewing difficult. Many of the smaller animals are strictly nocturnal; others are wary of humans. However, such animals as the monkeys, peccaries, and coatis are highly visible. Try to develop a sense of the forest's "musicality," responding to it as you would to a complex interplay of musical instruments. Only by attuning yourself to its rhythms can you truly experience the rainforest's wonders. **opportunities:** Rather than winging it, consider a tour. See Nature and Adventure Tours, page 149. The best way to see a lot of wildlife is to stay in a lodge near a tropical forest or camp within the forest itself. The latter, while preferable, requires equipment and preparation. Orchid lovers can visit the University of Costa Rica's Lankester Gardens.

What Once Was

Costa Rica has a phantasmogorical variety of flora. There are over 800 species of ferns, 1,200 different orchids, and 2,000 types of trees. To appreciate what still exists and understand today's problems, it's necessary to examine the past.

Costa Rican Flora: A to Z

Aguacate - avocado
Almendro - wild almond
Cacao silvestre - wild cocoa
Caña de Indio - Indian cane
Caoba - mahogany
Carambola - star fruit
Ceiba - kapok
Chaperno - dogwood
Cocobolo - rosewood
Cocotero - coconut palm
Fruta dorada - golden nutmeg
Guanacaste - ear tree
Guanábana - soursop
Guarumo - trumpet tree
Guatusa - paca palm
Guayabo - guava

Guácimo - bastard cedar
Higuerón - wild strangler fig
Icacos - sea grape
Lirio de Agua - water hyacinth
Mangle - mangrove
Manzanillo - machineel
Mapola - hibiscus
Naranja - orange
Níspero - chicle tree
Palma real - royal palm
Palma de sombrero - hat palm
Panama - Panama wood
Papayo de monte - wild papaya
Pochote - spiny cedar
Toronja - grapefruit

Flora & Fauna

Arriving Spaniards found a covering of virgin forest, mostly rainforest made up of broadleaf evergreens. Deciduous forests abounded in the NW; mangrove forests lined the coasts. A dense growth of palms stretched along the Caribbean coast from Puerto Limón N to the Nicaraguan border. Although the indigenous people had practiced slash-and-burn cultivation, they were so few in number that they had little impact on the natural vegetation. During the 19th C., much land was stripped of its primeval growth in the Meseta Central, to be used for agriculture and, along the Caribbean coast, for bananas. Due to the dearth of sawmills and the lack of transportation, nearly all of the timber was either burned or left to rot on the ground – a process that virtually exterminated a number of species. By the 1940s only scattered stands of timber remained in the Meseta Central. Still, it was estimated that 78% of Costa Rica remained covered by largely virgin growth forest as of 1942.

The Costa Rican segment of the Interamerican Highway opened up the valley area of the Río General, along with other areas for cultivation. The expansion of agriculture in general and cattle ranching in particular also took its toll. Between 1950 and 1960, an estimated 108,000 acres (44,000 ha) were cut annually, a figure that increased to more than 148,000 acres (60,000 ha) during the 1961-67 period. As during the homesteading era in the US, the forests were viewed simply as impediments to economic progress. Also, by cutting down the trees, the *campesino* obtained squatter's rights because he had "improved" the acreage. According to 1977 government figures, some 12,000 sq miles (20,000 sq km) – about 39% of the total land area – was wooded.

Despite the protection afforded by the government, the remaining forests are threatened by the estimated 100-200,000 *precarista* (squatter) families and by the estimated 200,000 refugees in the country, to whom forest reserves and private forested tracts represent idle land waiting to be claimed. In their eyes, although farmland is easier to squat initially, forested land is a better long-term bet. A study of satellite photos taken in 1983 showed only 17% of the country was still covered by virgin forest. Ironically, owing to the nature of its soil composition and topography, more than half of the land is judged unsuitable for growing permanent crops or for anything other than trees. Although the nation contains a dozen ecological zones and 8-12,000 species of plants, its forests are still falling at a rate nine times faster than Brazil's.

Things You Can Do to Save the Forests

☐ Start at home. Much of North America's old growth forest is under threat from the timber industry. It is unrealistic to expect nations like Indonesia, Brazil, and Costa Rica to save their forests if the US and Canada cut theirs down. In particular, the government-subsidized rape of the US National Forests and the destruction of British Columbia's old growth must be halted.

☐ Visit the rainforests. Showing an interest in them reinforces pride in the forests and instills a sense of value in local people. When you return, tell your friends and relatives about what you've seen.

☐ Boycott tropical products. Don't purchase imported tropical birds, snakes, or animal hides. Avoid buying products made of teak, mahogany, or other tropical woods unless you are positive that they come from tree farms and not from virgin rainforest. Encourage retailers to question the source of their products.

☐ Organize. If you live in a major city such as New York, there is likely to be an environmental organization for whom you can volunteer. If not, start your own! For maximum effectiveness, coordinate your efforts with groups operating in tropical nations.

☐ Educate yourself. The most important hope for the human race is education. Read as much as yotu can, see as much as you can, and write to your political leaders and to newspapers to inform people of what you have seen.

Rainforests

Rainforests, containing the planet's most complex ecosystem, have a richer animal and plant life than any other type of forest. Unlike other areas where life struggles to survive against a hostile climate, here organisms struggle primarily against each other. Each being – whether plant, animal, insect, or microbe – has been able to develop its niche. Rainforests occur in regions without major seasonal variation (although rainfall does vary during the year) and where more than 70 inches (1,800 mm) of rain fall annually.

How Old Are the Rainforests?

The rainforests were once believed to be stable environments lasting 60 million years or more, but thinking on this point has shifted. As the northern temperate zone underwent radical shifts in temperature during glacial and interglacial periods (with a resulting movement of ice sheets and shifts in vegetation and fauna), the tropics saw equally radical alterations known as pluvials (wet, warm periods) and interpluvials (dry, cold periods). As the glaciers would descend, the tropics would enter an interpluvial. Much of the Amazon had dry, scrub vegetation as recently as 6,000 years ago.

How old are the nation's ecosystems? Quite young. The land mass was not even in place in Central America – along with the connections to Columbia and Mexico – until about three million years ago. This region is believed to have had its origins in the "Galapagos Hot Spot," an active area of sea-floor spreading which drifted slowly until reaching its present position. An earlier instance of this spreading formed Cuba and the Antilles.

The rainforests are dynamic ecosystems. The vegetation shifts as climates change; species colonize new areas as they become available and accessible to seeds. They are diverse because most times of the year are reasonably suitable for plant growth and animal activity. In contrast, the temperate zone not only has a winter – which weeds out weaker species – but the northern hemisphere was also largely covered with glaciers (or affected by ice sheets) until recently. Consequently, vegetation is still recolonizing habitats there; recent studies of fossil pollen indicate that forest composition has undergone striking changes in the past 5,000 years. Another reason why the tropics have more species than other areas is that many had their origins here and this is where they remain concentrated. (From information supplied by Drs. Diana and Milton Lieberman.)

Flora & Fauna

VARIETIES: There is no single "true rainforest," and forest botanists have varying definitions of the term. It may be argued that there are some 30 types, including such categories as semi-deciduous forests, tropical evergreen alluvial forests, and evergreen lowland forests – each of which can be further subdivided into three or four more categories. Equatorial evergreen rainforests comprise two-thirds of the total. As you move away from the equator on either side, the forests develop marked wet and dry seasons. **other rainforests:** Cloud forest is another name for montane rainforest, characterized by heavy rainfall and persistent condensation due to the upward deflection of moisture-laden air currents by mountains. Trees here are typically short and gnarled. Costa Rica's most famous cloud forest is at Monteverde in the NW. The so-called elfin woodland or forest is so named because of its stunted, moss-covered trees. Rainforests without as much rain, the tropical dry forests, once covered Pacific coastal lowlands stretching from Panama to Mexico, covering an area the size of France. Today, they have shrunk to a mere 2% of the total area and only part of this is under protection; surviving sections are found in Guanacaste and Santa Rosa national parks, among other places.

LAYERS: Life in the rainforest is stratified in vertical layers. The upper canopy contains animals which are mainly herbivorous and, in Costa Rica, have prehensile tails. They rarely descend to earth. Typically more than 100 feet in height (30 m), these canopy trees generally lack the girth associated with tall trees of the temperate forest, perhaps because there are fewer strong winds to combat and each tree must compete with the others for sunlight. The next lower layer is filled with small trees, lianas, and epiphytes. Some of the plants are parasitic, others use trees solely for support purposes. The ground surface layer is littered with branches, twigs, and foliage. Most animals here live on insects and fruit; others are carnivorous. Contrary to popular opinion, the ground cover is thick only where sunlight filters through sufficiently to allow such vegetation; secondary forest growth is generally much more impenetrable than old growth forest. The extensive root system of the trees and associated fungi (*mycorrhizae*) forms a thick mat that holds thin topsoils in place when it rains. If these are cut, the soil will wash away; the steeper the slope, the faster the rate of runoff. As most of the nutrients are regenerated via the ecosystem, the land soon deteriorates after cutting. As the sun beats down on the soil, sometimes baking it hard as a sidewalk, the crucial fungal mat and other organic life die off. It may take hundreds, if not thousands, of years to replace important nutrients through weathering, rainfall, or volcanic eruption, and such forests may never recover.

Exploring the Canopy

In recent years, biologist Don Perry's exploits along with a number of television specials have focussed attention on the canopy – a realm of the earth heretofore restricted to our arboreal relatives and other creatures. Now it's possible for mere mortals to ascend to the canopy layer. Methods include being hoisted up and down in a harness, having yourself hoisted up and rappelling yourself down, or cruising by the canopy in a glorified ski lift. Fees are typically high, both because material and labor costs are expensive and promoters hope to turn a buck. If you're heading up in the canopy, prepare yourself for the fact that you may not see a whole lot of wildlife.

Both the Rainforest Aerial Tram as well as many of the nation's various platforms are described in the text below. Some of the platforms are designed to be used by serious researchers. All involve the use of ropes and are not for the timid or agoraphobic. The Rainforest Aerial Tram offers a much safer and more comfortable experience. It is modeled on a device that Don Perry used to explore the canopy.

Another type of device, the construction crane, has been used together with a gondola to explore the rainforest canopy in Panama and in Venezuela. In 1995, a $1 million, 260-foot (80-m) version was completed near the scenic Columbia River Gorge in Carson, WA. An endeavor financed by the University of Washington in Seattle and the US Forest Service, it aims to study the temperate canopy. Owing to the comparative paucity of species found here, the focus will be on interactions between the air, soil, trees, animals, and parasites, as opposed to simply cataloging biodiversity. The program's director is Jerry Franklin, a proponent of "New Forestry." It aims to find sustainable logging practices that will allow the forest to regrow. The crane was originally slated to be erected in the Olympic peninsula but was stymied by protesting locals who feared research might lead to more prohibitions on logging.

Another device – described in the marvelous book, *The High Frontier* by Mark Moffett – is a colorful dirigible balloon which has been used to explore the canopy in Cameroon.

Flora & Fauna

INTERACTIONS: As the name implies, rainforests receive ample rain, which promotes a rich variety of vegetation. Animals and insects, in turn, must adapt to that variety. Lowland rainforests receive at least 100 inches (2,540 mm) of rain. Although some rainforests get almost no rain during certain parts of the year, they are generally cloaked in clouds, from which they draw moisture. The high level of plant-animal interaction – taking forms such as predation, parasitism, hyperparasitism, symbiosis, and mutualism – is believed by many biologists to be one major factor promoting diversity. The interactions are innumerable and highly complex: strangler figs steal sunlight from canopy trees; wasps may pollinate figs; bats and birds transport seeds and pollinate flowers. When a species of bird, for example, becomes rare or extinct, it may have an effect on a tree that depends heavily upon it to distribute its seeds. There is no such thing as self-sufficiency in a rainforest; all life is interdependent.

INBio & Preservation of Biodiversity

Dedicated to the preservation of biodiversity, INBio is among the most dynamic of Costa Rica's foundations. Created in 1989, INBio employs 40 parataxonimists who have collected some 2.5 million specimens. The institute's highy ambitious long-term goal is to catalog every species of life in the nation. A revolutionary agreement with Merck has cast a spotlight on this organization. It signed a two-year pact with Merck in 1991, according to which INBio was intended to supply the drug company with samples in exchange for funds and training. Merck contracted to pay a royalty on drugs developed; any revenues will be split between INBio and the Ministry of Natural Resources.

This agreement incited controversy because some accused the organization of selling the nation's resources too cheaply and of negotiating improperly on behalf of the entire nation. Despite the controversy, INBio has signed cooperative agreements with Kenya, Indonesia, and the Philippines, and its contract with Merck was renewed.

A second agreement has been signed with the Intergraph Corporation, another Fortune 500 company, who agreed to donate some $750,000 worth of equipment and software in exchange for publicity. The organization is intent on screening its own samples. It is also working on a number of projects aimed at discovering products of agicultural, industrial, or pharmaceutical value. For example, INBio is prospecting for insect species in Guanacaste, hoping to discover significant chemicals; a second project involves research on how a certain tropical dry forest tree kills nematodes, pests that also destroy bananas. It's funded by the National Banana Corporation along with a British biotech company.

GREENERY AND THE GREENHOUSE EFFECT: Biodiversity is only one of many reasons to preserve the forest. They also act as watersheds, and cutting can result in flooding and erosion as well as increased aridity. Much rain is produced through the transpiration of trees, which helps keep the air saturated with moisture. Although it is commonly believed that rainforests produce much of the earth's oxygen, in fact there is an equilibrium between the amount mature forests consume through the decay of organic matter and the amount they produce via photosynthesis. However, many scientists believe that widespread burning of tropical forests releases large amounts of carbon dioxide into the atmosphere. The amount of carbon dioxide in the atmosphere has risen by 15% in the past century (with about half of this occurring since 1958), and forest clearance may account for half of that gain. As carbon dioxide, along with other atmospheric elements, traps heat that would otherwise escape into space, temperatures may rise. Rainfall patterns would change and ocean levels would rise as the polar ice packs melt. In many areas, deforestation has already had an adverse effect on the environment. Although many uncertainties remain about the "greenhouse effect," one certainty is that by the time the effects are apparent they will be irreversible.

USEFUL PLANTS: Those who are unfamiliar with the rainforest tend to undervalue it. Tropical deforestation is one of the great tragedies of our time. We are far from cataloging all the species inhabiting the rainforests, and when the forests are cut down, many species can be lost forever. More than 70% of the plants known to produce compounds with anti-cancerous properties are tropical, and there may be many cures waiting to be found. One survey of Costa Rican plants found that 15% had potential as anti-cancer agents. Cures for malaria and dysentery have been found in the forests. Louis XIV was cured of amoebic dysentery by ipecac, a South American plant that remains the most effective cure. Cortisone and diosgenin, the active agents in birth control pills, were developed from Guatemalan and Mexican wild yams. These are some of the 3,000 plants that tribal peoples use worldwide as contraceptives. Continued research could yield yet other methods of birth control. Not all rainforest products are medicinal. Rice, corn, and most spices – including vanilla, the unripe fermented stick-like fruits of the Central American orchid, *vanilla fragrans* – are also medicinal. Other products native people have extracted from the rainforest include latex, resins, starch, sugar, thatch, dyes, and fatty oils. The rainforest also acts as a genetic pool, and when disease strikes a monoculture such as bananas, it's possible to hybridize it with rainforest varieties to see if this produces an immunity to pests or fungus.

Flora & Fauna

Common Misperceptions About Rainforests

❏ Rainforests are not "the lungs of the planet." Mature trees produce as much oxygen as they consume. The danger in destroying rainforests lies with the effects on rainfall, flooding, and global warming resulting from increasing amounts of carbon dioxide being released into the atmosphere.

❏ The rainforests are not bursting at the seams with colorful plants, wild orchids, and animals. The overwhelming color is green; flowers are few; and the animal you're most likely to see is the ant.

❏ Rainforests are not a renewable resource. It is impossible to cut trees without destroying other plants and affecting the environment.

❏ Rainforests are not merely a source of wood. They have other values, particularly medicinal, which must be considered.

❏ Once damaged, rainforest does not simply grow back as it once was. It may take centuries for the complex ecosystem to regenerate. Reforestation cannot restore the environment.

❏ Despite its rich appearance, rainforest soil may not be fertile. Most of the nutrients are contained in the biomass.

❏ There is no need to "manage" a rainforest. They've been doing just fine for eons on their own. Everything in the rainforest is recycled, and anything removed has an effect.

❏ "Selective" cutting has detrimental consequences because it affects the surrounding soil quality and weakens the forest as the strongest specimens are removed. No way has yet been found to exploit a rainforest so that all species may be preserved.

❏ One "endangered" species cannot be effectively protected without safeguarding its ecosystem as well. Botanical gardens or seed banks cannot save important species. These are too numerous in quantity, seeds have too short a lifespan, and the species depend upon animals for their lifecycle equilibrium.

❏ Reduction in consumption of tropical hardwoods will not preserve rainforests. The only effective method is to protect the forests in reserves and parks. The forests are falling at too fast a rate for any other methods to be effective.

FATE OF THE FORESTS: Just a few thousand years ago, a belt of rainforests covering some five billion acres (14% of the planet's surface) stretched around the equator. Wherever there was sufficient rainfall and high enough temperatures, there was rainforest. Over half that forest has now been destroyed, much of it in the past few hundred years, with the rate accelerating after the end of WWII. Squatters and logging continue to cause deforestation throughout the region. At current rates, much of the remaining forest will vanish by the end of the century. One reason for expansion into the forests is the need for arable land in areas where land ownership is concentrated in a few hands and most peasants are landless. Cattle ranching, logging, mining, and industry are other reasons to cut the forests. Forests do not recover easily.

EDUCATING YOURSELF: Don't miss an opportunity to visit the rainforest while you are in Costa Rica. When you return home, one of the best organizations to join is **Rainforest Action Network** (☎ 415-398-4404, fax 398-2732). Write Ste 700, 450 Sansome, San Francisco, CA 94111. Another is **Earth Island Institute** (☎ 415-788-3666, fax 788-7324), which was founded by longtime environmental activist, David Brower. Write Ste. 28, 300 Broadway, San Francisco, CA 94133. A third is the **Rainforest Alliance** (☎ 212-941-1900, fax 941-4986). Write 270 Lafayette St., #512, NY NY 10012. **Greenpeace** (☎ 202-462-1177) also has a rainforest program. Write 1436 U St. NW, Washington DC 20009. Other specifically Costa Rican-orientated organizations are listed under "foundations." Some books about the rainforest are listed in the booklist in the back. If you want to inform yourself about the state of US National Forests, join the **Native Forest Council** (PO Box 2171, Eugene OR 97402). A donation of $25 or more gives you a subscription to their informative newspaper, *Forest Voice*. If you're planning a visit to the Pacific Northwest and would like a guided tour, **Ancient Forest Adventures** offers both resort-based trips and less expensive backpacking trips. Call Mary Vogel at ☎ 503-385-8633 or write AFA, 16 NW Kansas Ave., Bend OR 97701-1202.

Flora & Fauna

Trees & Tropical Vegetation

The hallmark of the rainforest is diversity, and trees are no exception to that rule. While temperate forests contain only an average of four species per acre, tropical forests may have from 20 to 86. Rainforest trees often have shallow root systems and they may be physically supported by basal buttressing or stilt roots. These root systems are bound together in mutually beneficial relationships with the lowly fungi. If you look carefully, you can spot a link between the white threads of fungi, as it decomposes a leaf or fruit, with a rootlet of a tree. Fungi are able to feed 20 times as much potassium and phosphorus to a tree as it will lose in the rains. The rainforest's high humidity and relatively uniform temperatures allow fungi to flourish. Perhaps in a largely unsuccessful evolutionary attempt by nature to combat strangler vines and other plants, the trees are generally smooth-barked.

CHARACTERISTICS: Tree buttresses are triangular when viewed from the side and, when viewed in cross-section, buttresses may resemble an irregular two- , five- or occasionally up to 10-armed star. They function much like the guy ropes on a tent: hitting them with the blunt side of a machete will produce a "bong," showing that they are under tension. There are three types of buttresses: *plank* (resembling giant wedges), *flying* (of the stilt-root type), and *serpentine* (often looped or undulating from side to side, these extend for some distance from the tree). Many trees have buttresses of more than one type. A special characteristic of rainforest trees are the drip-tip leaves, which are elongated at the end by an inch. This allows them to shed water after a shower more quickly and resume assimilating and transpiring. An additional advantage is that the quick passage of water may act to deter the growth of mosses and lichen. Another feature of tropical trees is *cauliflory* or flowering from the trunk. Southeast Asian examples of fruit produced in this fashion are jackfruit and durian. Neotropical examples include *cacao* and calabash.

VARIETIES: The tropical dry forest contains more than 30 species of hardwood. Found only in the NW, two of the three species of *caoba* (mahogany) are indigenous. Attempts to grow it commercially have been stymied by the mahogany shootborer, which thrives in mahogany groves. Another giant that lives well in Guanacaste, the evergreen *cenízero*'s (raintree's) English name derives from the aphids who, residing in its branches, extract large quantities of sap, drain it of nitrogen-rich compounds, then defecate diligently. The *pilón* or *zapatero* tree, used for furniture, walls, beams, and counters, is large, with serpentine buttresses. The *manú* (manwood) tree, termite-resistant and heavy, now virtually extinct in unprotected forests, was commonly used for dock construction, posts, beams, and large columns. Another favorite is the *Ira Roosa*, which is primarily used to build furniture or do interiors. The *fruta dorada* (wild nutmeg), growing up to 40 m (128 ft) in height, abounds in moist forests. One of the largest trees, the deciduous and corpulent *calyptrogyne* or "dovetail" tree has a well-formed straight and smooth trunk. Seen on coffee plantations, the *poro* tree's function is not only to shade coffee but also to fix nitrogen into the soil; its prunings provide feed for animals as well as firewood. The *jícaro* (calabash) tree is identifiable by its hanging, balloon-like gourds.

FORBIDDEN FRUIT: The **manchineel** (*manzanillo*) grows near the sea. It is small, with a short trunk and numerous branches. The tree's elliptical leaves possess a strange bright green sheen. The manchineel secretes an acid that can be deadly. Biting into this innocuous-looking, yet highly poisonous fruit, said to be the original apple in the Garden of Eden, will cause your mouth to burn and your tongue to swell. In fact, all parts of this tree are potentially deadly. Cattle, standing under the tree after a torrential tropical downpour, have been said to lose their hides as drops fall from leaves. Other tales tell of people going blind after a leaf touched an eye. Slaves (in the Virgin Islands to the NE), wishing to do away with a particularly despicable master, would insert minute quantities of juice into an uncooked potato. Cooked, these small doses were undetectable, but always fatal if served to the victim over a long period of time. If you should spot one of these trees – which are particularly prevalent along Manuel Antonio's beaches – stay well away!

EPIPHYTES: The name is taken from the Greek words meaning "upon plants." The luxuriant verdancy commonly associated with rainforests depends upon these hangers on. Although they may be found in temperate and drier tropical forests as well, the combination of rain and warmth unique to the rainforest helps them flourish here. Treetop life has many advantages. Birds and bats arrive to pollinate and deposit nutrient-rich dung, and it is more likely that their seeds will be dispersed by the wind. Water may be harder to come by and evaporation is a problem, so many bromeliads have evolved tanks to hold up to two gallons (eight liters) of water, along with other adaptations. Don't make the mistake of thinking that these plants are parasitic. Although they are perhaps unwelcome guests, most do not feed on their hosts. Generally, they arrive in the form of tiny dustlike seeds. These establish themselves on moss or lichen, which serves as a starter. All told, there are 247 species of epiphytes found in Costa Rica.

An epiphytic, tree-dwelling cactus, the *pitahaya silvestre* thrives in the NW. Its flowers, some 12 inches (30 cm) long and weighing up to 100 g (four oz), are among the world's largest. They open only at night, releasing a potent, moth-attracting, jasmine-like fragrance that can be smelled as far as 1,000 ft downwind. Tiny epiphytes residing on leaf surfaces, epiphylls (algae, liverworts, lichens, and mosses) are generally found on lower plants. **Bromeliads** are ground-dwelling epiphytes, the most famous of which is the *piña* (pineapple). They are named after Swedish botanist Olaf Bromel. *Piñuelas*, one species of bromeliad typically found in Guanacaste, are equipped with large (100-140 cm, 39-55 inches), jagged aloe-like leaves.

ORCHIDS: Costa Rica's extraordinary natural wealth includes 1,200 varieties of *orquídeas* (orchids), the grandest collection in all of Central America. The *guaria morada*, a commonly seen orchid, is the national flower. Although they grow all over the country, orchids are most diverse in the humid forests at 2,625-6,562 ft elevation (800-2,000 m). Not all are epiphytic (i.e., growing on other plants). The ones that are generally possess thicker leaves and keep their stomata – tiny pores on their leaves that absorb carbon dioxide – shut during the day, storing carbon dioxide for the next day's use. Nearly all orchids are pollinated by insects or hummingbirds and it is believed that many may only be pollinated by a single specific species. Certain orchid blooms even bear an amazing resemblance to specific bees or wasps. Despite their aesthetic value, orchids are of little economic importance. They were once thought to have medicinal properties, but these claims have largely proven false and not a single species is currently used in modern medicine. Their only valuable product is vanilla, an extract obtained from the cured unripened pods of various species belonging to the genus *Vanilla*. Orchids were named by Dioscorides, a Greek physician who, noting the similarity of the tubers of one species he was examining to male genitals, named the species "orches" (testicles).

VINES AND COMPANY: Woody vines, lianas, bush ropes and herbaceous climbers are rainforest landmarks. Vines use trees as trellises, crawling up from the ground to reach the light. Scramblers grow in gaps in the rainforest. Over 90% of liana species are found in the tropics, where they commonly grow as long as 230 ft (70 m) and as wide as six inches (15 cm) or more. Lianas twine around the tree and also use tendrils or hooks to secure themselves. Like vines, they drop their shaded understory leaves as they reach maturity. To guard against damage from kinking as trees sway, lianas have evolved bends, coils, and twists. One of the most remarkable of these is the *uña de gato* (cat-claw bignone). In the juvenile form, it grows leaves and tendrils bearing a remarkable, almost haunting resemblance to cat claws. It almost looks as if the plant could walk! The longest lianas are rattans – one of the rainforest's harvestable products – which may grow to more than 500 ft. In addition to closing the canopy, thus stabilizing the microclimate, lianas also offer protection to animals such as sloths. By sleeping in a mass of lianas, sloths tie in to a tensile network of vines that will alert them to the presence of an arboreal predator.

STRANGLER FIGS: Beginning life as epiphytes, some species of *Ficus* (fig) and *Clusia* (non-fig species) send down woody, clasping roots that wind themselves around the trunk as they reach for the earth. As the roots grow in size, they meld and develop into a trunk that surrounds the tree. These "strangler figs" most likely kill the tree, not through strangulation, but by robbing it of canopy space. They can grow in the ruins of buildings as well. Known locally as *matapalos* or "tree killers," strangler figs are often the only trees left in an otherwise cleared tract of forest. There is little incentive to use their poor quality wood, and their spreading branches provide shade. The holes, cracks and turns in their trunks host geckos, anoles, ants, stingless bees, scorpions, and other life – each inhabiting its ecological niche. Bats, birds, and other fruit eaters flock around the trees, attracting ornithologists in the process. Even peccaries and other ground dwellers arrive to share in the bounty that falls to the ground. These creatures all help distribute the seeds when they defecate.

Heliconias

The heliconia (*platanillo*) is famous as an ornamental. It lends an infusion of bizarre color and shape to the tropical landscape. It's represented here by some 30 species. The heliconia thrives in secondary forests, so it's very common. The plant is cultivated for sale at places such as Costa Flores near Guapiles. These large herbs are named for Helicon, a mountain in southern Greece believed to have been the home of the muses. They belong to the order known as the *Zingiberales* and there are thought to be 200-250 species. Relatives within this category include bananas, birds-of-paradise, gingers, and prayer plants. The name *Zingiberales* comes from the Sanskrit word *sringavera*, meaning "horn shaped," which describes the appearance of the rhizomes or root runners. Each erect shoot has a stem and leaves that are frequently topped by an infloresence with yellow or red bracts. Each infloresence may produce up to 50 hermaphroditic flowers. Leaves are composed of stalk and blade and resemble banana leaves. The flowers produce a blue fruit with three seeds.

In Costa Rica you're most likely to find heliconias near rivers and along roads; they thrive in light gaps. Most are found in the tropical lowlands or in middle-elevation or cloud forest habitats.

Hummingbirds, lured by the bright colored flowers and bracts, arrive to pollinate the blooms. They spread pollen as they fly from flower to flower in search of nectar.

Flora & Fauna

UNIQUE NATIVES: The *pejibaye* palm is well known for its fruit and edible palm heart. Found mainly in dry forest environments, *Indio desnudo* (naked Indian) uses chloroplasts under its orange bark to continue photosynthesis from November to May when it is leafless. The *ceiba* or **kapok** tree, noted for its eye-catching "plank" root buttresses, has conical spines on its trunk. The silky quality of the fibers surrounding the seed in its fruit have given it the English name of silk cotton tree. The *guanacaste* or **ear fruit** receives its English name from the unique shape of its fruits. Although the province of Guanacaste gets its name from the tree, they may well be extinct in the area 100 years from now, since they need an enclosed, noncompetitive tropical forest to thrive. The *encino* or *roble* (oak) is distinguished by a hard-covered dark bark and acorns that can take two growing seasons to mature. Another variety is the *roble encino*, an evergreen that thrives in upland dry forest. While some palms have adapted to brackish tidal swamps and dune swales, the **coconut palm** (*coco*) is the only one that makes these areas its sole habitat. It may have originated in the Indian Ocean. While those on the Pacific coast are related to Asian varieties, the ones on the Caribbean side are of the Jamaican tall variety found in W Africa and in the W Indian Ocean. The *guapinol* (stinking toe) tree bears large, toe-shaped pods. It produces a resin that, when fossilized, is the source for amber. A cousin of the tree (the *jícaro* or monkey pot), produces the Brazil nut. It bears large woody fruits that hang upside down. Upon ripening, the lid drops off, revealing 20-50 seeds, which are favored by hungry bats. Lightest of the commercial woods, **balsa** (Spanish for "raft") is native to humid subtropical and tropical areas; it has had a variety of uses through the centuries. The latest is to deter supertankers from building up static charges owing to wave action which can result in explosions. The **sandbox tree's** (*jabillo's*) English name comes from its fruit; the ribbed peel, when seeded and flattened, was used to sprinkle sand used for blotting ink spilt on parchment. The tree is large, symmetrical and stout.

OTHERS: Tree ferns make a strong impression on the imagination of most visitors. They abound in high-rainfall forests. In Costa Rica, they are labeled *rabo de mica* (monkey tail) ferns from the shape of their uncurling young fronds. *Zamia* (cycads) are sometimes called living fossils because they were among the earliest plants to evolve. They superficially resemble small palms and have conelike flowers that emerge from the base of their fronds. The *jacinto de agua* (water hyacinth), A free-floating aquatic perennial, has spread during this century from its South American homeland to become one of the most troublesome and widespread aquatic weeds. Members of the three existing species can be seen everywhere from Carara to Tortuguero. The red spots on the underside of the *sangre de Cristo's* ("blood of Christ") leaves resemble stained glass windows. Jaráguá, of African origin, is the most common cultivated pasture grass and it is especially abundant in Guanacaste where, owing to its remarkable regenerative abilities after a fire, it has been supplanting other indigenous grasses. They are more adept than the native varieties in converting croplands into pastures. The *sombrilla de pobre* ("poor person's umbrella") has enormous leaves (up to two m or 6.5 ft) and is common in verdant, elevated areas; locals cut them for use as umbrellas. By producing nectar both deep in their flowers (for bees and hummingbirds) and also at nectaries on petals, stems, and leaves (for aggressive ants and wasps), **passion flowers** provide themselves with both pollination and protection. *Labios ardientes* ("ardent lips") or *labios de puta* (hooker's lips) lend color to the rainforest landscape.

Mangrove Preservation in Sierpe

One major problem environmental conservationists continually confront is the challenge of maintaining balance between a community and its lifestyle with the needs of the area's other living residents – the plants and animals. Coopemangle is a cooperative aimed at solving that conflict in the community of Coronado, just outside of the 40,247-acre (16,700-ha) Reserva Forestal Terraba-Sierpe. In former times, locals cut down mangroves for charcoal production and sold the trees' bark (which contains tannin) to factories for use in dying leather. Today, the community is cutting the forest only selectively and uses a solar-powered plant to process the bark. They now have a truck, which allows them to sell their products for twice what they might get locally. Sales provide each member with $150 per month and extraction has been limited to a 482-acre (200-ha) area. There are hopes for nature tourism here in the future.

MANGROVES: Mangrove (*mangle*) forests are found along the coasts. These water-rooted trees serve to shelter sponges, corals, oysters, and other members of the marine community around its roots. These organisms, in turn, attract a variety of other sealife. Some live out their lives in the mangroves, and many fish use the roots as a shelter or feeding ground; lobsters use the mangrove environs as a nursery for their young. Above the water level, mangroves shelter seabirds and are important nesting sites. Their organic detritus, exported to the reef by the tides, is consumed by its inhabitants, providing the base of an extensive food web. Mangroves also dampen high waves and winds generated by tropical storms. By trapping silt in their roots and catching leaves and other debris which decompose to form soil, the red mangroves act as land builders and stave off erosion. Eventually, the red mangroves kill themselves off by building up too much soil, and the black and white mangroves take over. Meanwhile, the red mangroves have sent out progeny in the form of floating seedlings – bottom-heavy youngsters that grow on the tree until reaching six inches to a foot in length. If they drop in shallow water, the seeds touch bottom and implant themselves. In deeper water they float and, crossing a shoal, drag until they lodge. The white mangroves, named for their light-colored bark, are highly salt-tolerant. If growing in a swampy area, they produce pneumatophores, root system extensions that allow them to stay above the water during flooding or tides and

Flora & Fauna

that carry on gaseous exchange. The black mangrove, producing a useful wood, also generates pneumatophores. The buttonwood, smaller than the others, is not a true mangrove, and is found on the coasts where no other varieties occur.

Animal Life

As with the plants, the Animal Kingdom is also wonderfully diverse. Many of the indigenous species are in danger of extinction, largely from loss of their traditional habitats through deforestation. Sea turtles, though, are threatened by overhunting and beach development. The panoply of species includes manatees, ocelots, sloths, deer, capuchin and spider monkeys, coatimundis, coyotes, jaguars, margays, peccaries, tapirs, and squirrels. Unlike their temperate counterparts, they are relatively difficult to spot. You need to keep still, have a keen eye, and – best of all – have a local friend or guide along. A fascinating book to peruse before your arrival is *Costa Rican Natural History*, edited by the eminent biologist and conservationist, Daniel Janzen.

DOMESTICATED ANIMALS: Today's barnyard animals – cows, pigs, horses, donkeys, goats, and chickens – come from a lineage stretching back to the 1560-70s, when the *conquistadores* brought them in from Nicaragua. There are also fine but rare examples of Paso Fino and Andalusian horses. Even a herd of water buffalo was imported from Trinidad in 1975 and resides near Limón.

Mammals

PRIMATES: New World monkeys differ from their Old World and ape cousins in many respects. Their nostrils are wide apart and point sideways, rather than being close-set and pointing downward. In addition, they are primarily arboreal and they show a greater variation in color patterns.

Actually sounding more like a "growler" than a howler, the mantled **howler monkey** (*mono congo*) can be heard up to several km away. The unusual sound results from a special bone in its throat which acts as an amplifier. There are numerous local explanations as to why howlers roar. Some say it is when rain is approaching or when other animals are feeding. Actually, they react to loud noises and to rain; they roar more at midday. The cacophonous howling begins with an accelerating series of low-pitched grunts by the male, which change to a series of long, deep roars; the females join the fun with higher-pitched roars. Another unique characteristic of the howler is its prehensile tail, which features a dermatoglyph or fingerprint. Living in groups of up to 20 led by a senior male, they dine on flowers, fruits, and tender leaves. The howler is entirely black, except for its sides, which have a pale fringed mantle. Its robust shoulders contrast with its comparatively diminutive hindquarters. If you should see a colony, don't get underneath it: A favorite pastime is to urinate on *homo sapiens*.

Moving rapidly through the trees, the **black-handed spider monkey** (*mono araña, mono colorado*) has a very complex language and lives in bands of about 20, which frequently subdivide into smaller groupings.

The **white-throated capuchin** (*mono cara blanca*) has white shoulders, upper chest, and face. It dines on fruit and insects. The name comes from the resemblance of its head and shoulder covering to a monk's hood. This noisy forager, both extremely curious and agile, lives in groups of five to 15; its varied diet includes birds, fruits, tender leaves, eggs, and honey. It barks, screams, yips, and whistles.

The **Central American squirrel monkey** (*mono tití, mono ardilla*) dwells only in the country's SW corner, confined to lowland rainforest, where it lives in small groups. Its miniscule geographical range may indicate that it was introduced by man. It is identified by its black-capped head, olive green shoulders and hips, and orange-gold hands, feet, back, and lower legs.

RACCOON FAMILY: The northern **raccoon** (*mapache*) is omnivorous, solitary, nocturnal, crafty, and clean. It will dine on anything from frogs and fish to fruit and vegetables. The mischievous and sociable **coati** (*pizote*) is nimble, omnivorous, and solitary in old age; it hunts at dawn and dusk – resting in treetops or in hollow trunks the rest of the time. The term coati-mundi refers only to solitary coatis, adult males over two years old. The gregarious **kinkajou** (*martilla*) dines on small animals, birds, eggs, and honey. It has short, woolly fur, large soulful eyes, small ears, and a long prehensile tail. Kinkajous use their tails to anchor themselves as they move from tree to tree, mainly at night. During the day, they nap in a tree hollow. Smaller and lacking the prehensile tail, the agile **olingo** or pale-faced kinkajou is a close relative. It journeys high in the rainforest canopy. A third related species is the **cacomistle**, a nocturnal and solitary tawny-brown creature that barks and has a tail longer than its head and body combined.

WEASEL FAMILY: The long-tailed **weasel**'s (*comadreja's*) slim frame allows it to slither into the burrows of mice. It also feeds on rabbits, birds, and reptiles. Its attractive fur is short and thick, but soft. A nervous, nocturnal, and solitary creature, the weasel is hard to spot. The **grison** or **huron** (*grisón*) resembles a large weasel with extremely short legs and tail and a long neck and back. The **striped hog-nosed skunk**

Flora & Fauna

(*zorro hediondo*), perhaps the nation's least popular mammal, is probably better left unseen and unsmelled. Although it is not a true rainforest creature, you will sometimes encounter one there. The **southern river otter** (*nutria, perro de agua*), an excellent swimmer, eats fish, shrimp, and turtles. This graceful creature in water waddles awkwardly on land. The **tayra** (*tolumuco*) resides in an underground burrow and resembles a lanky mink with a long-haired tail; it feeds on grubs, bird nests, fruit, eggs, and chicken and goat meat.

CAT FAMILY: The cat's physique suits its killer lifestyle. It is the principal predator in rainforests worldwide, with teeth designed for killing and meat eating, excellent sight and hearing, strong shoulders, and sharp claws. Some are territorial, most are solitary, and all prey on anything that comes their way – from large insects to small mammals. The best time to see one is after nightfall, when they take to trails and their bright eyeshine makes them visible. Should you come across a den with kittens, leave them alone. They have not been abandoned: the mother has gone off to search for food.

The graceful, nocturnal and diurnal "king of the tropical rainforest," the **jaguar** (*tigre*) is this hemisphere's largest cat. It may reach six ft (two m) in length and three ft (one m) in height at shoulder level. It dines on peccaries, deer, monkeys, sloths, and even fish. The only large, spotted cat in the Americas, the jaguar is easily identifiable. You might hear one roar at night – a series of hoarse, deep grunts. Although an encounter is unlikely, if you see one, walk toward it shouting and clapping your hands. If you run, it may pursue you, and you'll regret it!

The **puma**, sometimes called a cougar or mountain lion, ranks second in size. Slightly smaller than a jaguar, it has an unspotted tan or dark brown hide, a leaner, lower-slung frame, and a longer, thicker tail. It is the only large, uniformly colored cat. Although pumas may tag along behind humans out of curiosity, few attacks on *homo sapiens* have ever been documented.

The **ocelot** (*manigordo*), resembling a miniaturized jaguar, feeds on anything from rabbits to insects. Unlike a jaguar, it has stripes, not spots, on its neck. The ocelot captures its game on the ground and may be encountered walking on man-made trails at night. A smaller version, the **tiger cat** (*tigrillo*) has a combination of spots and stripes. Ranging between 33 and 51 inches (85-130 cm), it may weigh up to 22 lbs (10 kg). Rarely sighted, it survives in the Tortuguero, Santa Rosa, and Corcovado national parks, the Reserva Forestal Río Macho, and on the lower slopes of the Cordillera Talamanca.

More solitary and nocturnal than the ocelot, the **margay** (*caucel, tigrillo*) is the size of a large house cat, weighing six-10 lbs. It has a somewhat bushy tail, which runs well over half the extended length of its head and black-spotted body. This magnificent feline, once wide-spread and currently endangered more by habitat loss than by hunting, abounds now only in Corcovado and Santa Rosa. It may easily be confused with an ocelot. The **oncilla**, also known locally as a *caucel*, has the shape of a slender house cat.

The **jaguarundi** (*león breñero*), with unspotted blackish-brown or chestnut-to-red fur, has a small flattened head, long sleek body, and short legs – all of which make it appear to be a cross between a cat and a weasel.

MARSUPIALS: Opossums have short legs, long tails, large and delicate ears. They have five toes and their first hindfoot toe functions as an opposable "thumb," used to clutch thin branches when climbing. Born only eight days after fertilization, opossum infants follow a trail of their mother's saliva from the cloaca to her pouch, where they secure themselves to their mother's nipples for the next 60 days. These malodorous creatures – which feed on small animals and fruits – enjoy rolling in fresh dung. When handled, they are aggressive, defecating and squirting evil-smelling urine with a twist of their tail. Among the species of opossum (*zorro*) found here are "four-eyed," "woody," and "regular." The *zorro* is an omnivore, living in the trees and active only at night. The woolly mouse and slaty slender mouse opossum (*zorra, zorrici*) are also found here.

EDENTATAS: This order, indigenous to the Americas, includes ant-eaters, sloths, and armadillos. The name refers to the few teeth found in the latter two and their complete absence in the anteaters. They represent the last remnant of an order that evolved during the period when South America was an isolated island continent. Sloths and ant-eaters are both arboreal, soft-furred creatures.

The distantly related, brown-throated **three-toed sloth** (*perezoso de tres dedos*) and the rarer **two-toed sloth** (*perezoso de dos dedos*) reside in the highest tree tops and live off plants and leaves. Their Spanish name (*perezoso*) means "lazy," which perfectly fits their somnolent attitude, slow movements, and propensity for hanging upside down over long periods without moving. A sloth differs from other edentates in that it has well-developed crushing teeth and a digestive tract akin to a grazing ruminant (cud chewer). It uses its many-chambered stomach to digest leaves through bacterial fermentation. Long-limbed and clawed creatures, sloths are camouflaged by the blue-green and green single-cell algae that grow on microscopic grooves and notches on its fur. Some species of moths feed on this algae. Cecropia (*guarumo*) trees are a particular favorite of sloths and can be one of the best places to see them. They descend every week or so to defecate, carefully digging a hole with their stubby tails and burying their feces; one explanation

Flora & Fauna

for their descent, which exposes them to predators, is that the decomposition of their feces at the tree's base helps provide them with a higher quality food supply. Sloth pellets apparently return to the tree half the nutrients that the beast has taken through eating its leaves. As sloths generally feed on only 15 to 40 trees in the period of a few months and have a single tree they return to frequently, this seems to be an intelligent investment. But this is not the only way they contribute to the ecosystem. Beetles, moths, and mites live on sloths and deposit their eggs in the sloth's dung.

The strictly nocturnal **silky anteater** (*ceibita, tapacara, serafin de planar*) has a prehensile tail and a long retractile tongue. It breaks open ant and termite nests to feed. The best way to find one is to gaze into clumps of lianas up to 33 ft (10 m) above the jungle floor for something resembling a golden tennis ball – in reality a sleeping anteater. Another species is the banded or **lesser anteater** (*oso jaceta, oso hormiguero*), distinguished by the black V-shaped mark across its back, resembling a vest worn backwards. The **northern tamandua** (*oso mielero*) is black-vested and nocturnal. During the day, you will see them accompanied by a dense halo of flies and mosquitoes, which they brush away with a forepaw. The **giant anteater** (*oso caballo*) is a large shaggy creature that ambles about on its knuckles.

Armadillos, mainly insectivorous and nocturnal, are protected by banded and bony plates. The plates are separated by soft skin, which permits the creature to bend. Resembling a trotting windup toy, an armadillo may run right into you. Their burrows can be recognized by the smooth, dome-shaped roof. Each litter born in the burrow is a set of four identical quadruplets hatched from a single egg. The **nine-banded long-nosed armadillo** (*cusuco*) eats beetles, ants, termites, fungi, berries, slugs, centipedes, millipedes, and other such exotic cuisine. Chiefly nocturnal, it is the most commonly seen variety. The rare northern **naked-tail armadillo** (*armado de zopilote*) walks about on the tips of its foreclaws. You might catch a glimpse of its naked tail disappearing under a log.

PERISODACTYLES: This group, which includes horses and the African and Asian rhinoceroses, is characterized by two unmatched or unequal hoof-covered toes. **Baird's tapir** (*danto, danta, macho de monte*) is one of the Americas' largest mammals and the rainforest's largest terrestrial mammal. It weighs as much as 550 lbs (250 kg) and may grow to six ft (two m) long and three ft (one m) high. A tapir devotes 90% of its waking time to foraging for food – seeds, leaves, twigs, and fruit – because the microorganisms that live in its stomach and digest its plant material through fermentation are not very efficient. Its excellent hearing and sense of smell compensate for this ungainly creature's poor eyesight. Tapirs are solitary and nocturnal, often living in marshy areas. They bolt when frightened, flattening everything in their wake! Despite the fact that they are the mammalian equivalent of the all-terrain vehicle, tapirs are shy creatures and difficult to see. However, hunters can easily locate them through dogs and calls, and their meat is considered a delicacy.

PECCARIES AND DEER: These are the two families of *Artiocactyla* (even-toed hoofed animals) found in the rainforest. Resembling a gigantic pig, the **collared peccary** (*saino, javelina, chancho de monte*) lives in a group of two to 15, whose members recognize each other by their pungent, musky body odor reminiscent of chicken soup or cheese. A peccary may be identified by a faint but nevertheless distinct collar of pale yellow hairs running from its lower cheek down to the top of its shoulder. They are most often found at salt licks or mud wallows. Another species is the *cariblanco* or **white-lipped peccary**. Generally black in the rainforest environs, it may also be brownish or red. There's always at least a sprinkling of white hair on its jaws and body and some are even snow white. White-lipped peccaries cover a wide area daily, feeding in large herds on fruits, palm nuts, and the like. They leave the ground churned and pocked in their wake. The noise coming from big groups (tooth clacking, screaming, bellowing) has given them a greatly exaggerated reputation for aggressiveness. They generally retreat in the face of humans, although one might rumble past without seeing you.

Male deer have antlers that are shed and regrown annually. The **white-tailed deer** (*venado, venado cola blanco*) was almost exterminated during the 1940s, when the harvest of 10,000-40,000 animals was used for leather goods manufacture and for dog food. They are identical to, but smaller than, the white-tailed deer found in the US. Not rainforest animals, they are generally found out in the open. Another variety is the **red brocket deer** or *cabra de monte*. Its tapered shape is ideal for pushing through rainforest. It feeds on fallen fruits, flowers, and on other vegetation, living a solitary life.

MANATEES: Popularly known as the sea cow, the manatee (*manatí, sirena*) has been sighted in Tortuguero and off Gandoca on rare occasions. Once ranging from S America up to N Carolina, their numbers have dwindled dramatically. Manatees move along the ocean floor (at a maximum pace of six mph) searching for food, surfacing every four or five minutes to breathe. Surprisingly, as the manatee's nearest living relative is the elephant, the creature was thought to be the model for the legend of the mermaid – perhaps because of the mother's habit of sheltering her offspring with her flipper as the infant feeds. The pudgy creature weighs 400-1,300 lbs and its finely wrinkled grey or brown skin is decorated with barnacles and algae. A manatee may reach 12 ft in length. Although to you they may appear ugly, with their small eyes, thick lips, bristly muzzles, and wrinkled necks, they are affectionate, kissing each other and sometimes swimming flipper-to-flipper. They dwell in lagoons and in brackish water, eating as much as 100 lbs of aquatic vegetables per day. Their only enemy is man, who has hunted them for the hide, oil, and meat.

RODENTS: The trademark of rodents is their sharp and versatile front incisors. Those teeth are supported by several different complex muscle systems. They may be used to slice, dig, pry, and cut. Some can even fell trees and kill animals. These differences allow them to be separated into three groups: Squirrel-like (*Sciuoromorpha*), cavy-like (*Caviomorpha*), and mouse-like (*Myomorpha*). By far the most diverse order of mammals, there are some 1,750 species worldwide – a number which nearly equals the 2,300 other species of mammals.

The cavy-like rodents all have four toes on their front feet. The edgy brown Central American **agouti** (*guatusa*) lives near rivers and dines on tender shoots, fruits, and seeds. They are active during the day and, largely solitary, they are frequently seen in protected areas, especially in late afternoon. Newborn young stay apart in their own burrow; mama calls them out for nursing and care. Living in a burrow, its cousin, the nocturnal and solitary **paca** (*tepezcuintle*) is larger and twice as heavy. It has horizontal rows of cream-colored spots along its flanks and a pig-like body.

Squirrels found in the rainforest may feed on palm nuts as well as fruits, insects, fungi, and even leaves, bark, and flowers. The red-tailed squirrel (*ardilla roja, ardilla chisa*) is widespread in some parts and may commonly be observed scurrying up a tree. Other species include the variegated squirrel, Deppe's squirrel, Richmond's squirrel, the Central American dwarf squirrel, and the montane squirrel.

The **porcupine** (*puercoespín*) forages at night for fruits and seeds. It is covered with short, strong quills and has a skinny prehensile-tail. The barb-tipped spines detach readily, and work their way inward in the flesh of an attacker. Rothschild's porcupine is entirely spiney and mostly black. The spines of the Mexican hairy porcupine are largely covered with dark fur. Another common rodent is the **gopher** (*taltusa*). There are also a variety of rats and mice in Costa Rica.

RABBITS: Cottontail rabbits (*conejos*) eat grass and tree bark. They dwell in thickets and forests and may have up to five litters per year. The only other species found here is the Brazilian; it is small, reddish, and has only a small tail.

BATS: Bats are the most important animals, judging by sheer number of species, in most New World tropical rainforests. The only flying mammals, bats have wings made of amazingly elastic skin, which contracts rather than folds when the wings are closed. Emitting high-frequency sounds through their nose or mouth, bats plot their route by calibrating distances to solid objects based on returning echoes. Contrary to popular belief, they will not become tangled in your hair, nor will they bite – except in self-defense. In addition to consuming huge quantities of insects, bats benefit the environment through pollination of many important plants and by seed dispersal. Costa Rica has over 100 bat species, as compared to only 40 in the US. Some feed on nectar, some on frogs, others on fish, and still others on sleeping birds and lizards. Hiding out in caves, their harems guarded by a single male, the **short-tailed fruit bat** (*murciélago*) emerges at night. It resides in the rainforest understory and is an important seed disperser.

The infamous **vampire bat** (*vampiro*) also lives in Costa Rica. Stealthily landing on a horse or cow, it makes an incision, a process which may take up to 20 minutes. The bat exudes an anticoagulant and quietly laps up the blood. It may run and hop with agility on all fours, using its thickened thumb as a foot. Its feces contain a fungus which causes histoplasmosis, a debilitating disease. The **fishing** or **bulldog bat** (*murciélago pescador*) skims water as it flies and feeds on insects and fish, which it grasps with its enormous feet. **Nectar-feeding** or **long-tongued bats** are important pollinators, often attracted by plants with large flowers that open at night. Other species include the **Jamaican fruit bat**, the **lesser short-tailed fruit bat**, the **black myotis**, the **sac-wing bat**, and the **false vampire**.

Reptiles & Amphibians

Reptiles and amphibians thrive in the rainforest, where they blend in very well. Although many species of lizards and frogs are found, there are only 26 species of salamanders – mostly found in montane rainforests. Snakes are definitely around, but they are secretive, mostly nocturnal, and tend to be small.

TURTLES: There are a large variety. Smaller turtles include the *tortuga bocado* or **snapping turtle** and the semiaquatic *tortuga jicóte* or **mud turtle**. The large-finned, herbivorous *tortuga blanca* or *tortuga verde* (**green turtle**) is about a meter long and weighs 165-440 lbs (75-200 kg). It lays eggs every two to three years, storming the beaches in massive groups called *barricadas*. Dining only on marine plants like turtle grass, it has a short rounded head and occurs on both coasts. The *tortuga carey* (**hawksbill**) is one of the smallest sea turtles at 35 inches (90 cm) or less. It has a spindle-shaped shell and weighs around 220 lbs (100 kg). Because of its tortoise shell – a brown translucent layer of corneous gelatin that covers it and peels off the shell when processed – the hawksbill has been pursued and slaughtered throughout the world. It eats largely mollusks, sponges, and seaweed. Its shell, worth a fortune in Japan, appears to have condemned it to extinction. While the loggerhead is found mainly in the Caribbean, it is also occasionally seen in the Pacific. The short-finned *tortuga cabezona* (**loggerhead turtle**) is rarely longer than four ft (1.20 m). Its narrow head, the mouth shaped like a bird's beak, is twice the size of the green turtle's. It feeds on sea urchins, jellyfish, starfish, and crabs. The loggerhead is threatened with extinction by coastal development, egg gathering, and from hunting by raccoons. The **leatherback** (*baula*) – black, with very narrow fins – gets its name from the black leathery hide that covers its back in lieu of a shell. It reaches up to seven ft (two m) and weighs as much as 1,500 lbs (700 kg), with its chief predator the poacher. In Costa Rica, poachers traditionally lie in wait for the turtles. Flipping the latest arrival on her back, they stab it with long knives, slicing down to the lower shell, which is torn off. After extracting the calipee (a gelatinous substance next to the lower shield used to make turtle soup), a poacher will run to the next turtle – leaving his helpless victim flailing, with her intestines exposed. Arriving the next morning, vultures circle the still-living turtle, then descend to feast on her entrails. Dogs also pose a threat: they love to dig up eggs. Most abundant but least understood of the sea turtles, the **Pacific ridley** (*lora, carpintera*) is endangered by its nesting habits. Although restrictions have been put in force since then, in 1968 alone the Mexicans slaughtered over a million for use in the leather industry. And, as beachside development continues worldwide, their future appears in doubt. A final species is the **Pacific green turtle** (*tortuga negra*) which, like the green, hawksbill, and leatherback, are found on both coasts; the ridley is found only on the Pacific side.

NESTING SITES AND TIMES: Green turtles generally nest at Tortuguero and Barra de Matina during early July into October, peaking in August. Leatherbacks nest from February to July, peaking in April and May, at Barra de Matina and from October to March at Playa Grande. They also nest at Nacite and Playa Naranjo. Pacific ridleys arrive in barricadas of up to 120,000 to lay eggs on Playa Nancite and in Ostional along the Pacific side during periods of four to eight days from July to December. Pacific greens nest at Nancite and Playa Naranjo; hawksbills nest on both coasts all year round, but they can be seen most easily at Tortuguero from July to October. For information on egglaying, see the description in the Tortuguero section.

FROGS AND TOADS: The glands of the **marine toad** (*bufo marinus*) contain toxins. Don't try to pick one up: it will urinate on you! The predominantly nocturnal marine toad exercises control over its paratoid gland, and it can direct its poison in a fine spray, one that can prove fatal to dogs and cats if they pick it up in their mouths. An equal-opportunity eater, it will snack on anything from wasps to dog and cat food set out for pets. The aggressive **smoky frog** (*rana tenero*) is second only to marine toads in size, growing to at least six inches (160 mm), and has been known to eat snakes up to 20 inches (500 mm) long. The **burrowing toad** (*sapo borracho*) resembles an amorphous blob of jelly. It dries up completely while underground; when disturbed, the toad excretes a sticky white substance that causes an acute allergic reaction in some people. The small **glass frog** (*ranita de vidrio*), so translucent that it barely casts a shadow, has green veins and a visible red vein leading to its heart. The **poisonous true toad** (*sapo*) is smooth-skinned and lacks warts, dwelling in mid-elevation wet forests. The gaudy **leaf frog** (*rana calzonudo*) is Central America's most colorful. It has a bright, leaf-green dorsum, creamy-white throat and belly, orange hands and feet, dark blue side markings, and blood-red irises. Named after its sharp call, incredibly powerful for a frog less than an inch (25 mm) long, the **tink frog** (*martillito*) exercises remarkable agility and can run like a mouse on its stubby legs.

POISON DART FROGS: Dendrobatids are the genus of poison dart frogs (*ranita roja, ranita venerosa*) which are aspomatic – possessing a warning coloration that advertises their toxicity. Their natural danskins, coming in bright red and blue decorator colors, broadcast a message geared chiefly toward predatory birds. Many other frogs also have these "flash" colors, primary coloring on their undersides and groins, which are flashed at predators, causing confusion. The frog's English name refers to Western Colombia's Chocó tribesmen, who extracted an alkaloid-based poison from the skin glands which they use on the tips of their blowgun darts. The frogs are harmless to handle as long as your skin is unbroken. **mating practices:** Male frogs perch in mushrooms, calling out for a mate. After a female arrives, he scouts for the proper site. When she lags behind, he calls and waits. The female rubs the male's head and chin with her head. Facing back to back, she lays a few eggs, which the male fertilizes and guards for a two-week period, after which the female returns. She takes one of the newly hatched tadpoles on her back, then deposits it in a suitably isolated pool of water (often the leaf axil of a bromeliad). She may have to climb up a tree in order to do this. As the water lacks nutrients, the female returns later repeatedly to lay unfertilized eggs, which the embryo feeds on. Each tadpole is deposited in a different location so as to prevent a damselfly larva from decimating her brood. When the female approaches a bromeliad that is already occupied, the tadpole

Costa Rican Wildlife: A to Z

Ardilla - squirrel
Ave - bird
Baula - leatherback turtle
Buchón - pelican
Cabra de monte - brocket deer
Caimán - caiman
Cariblanco - white-lipped peccary
Caucel - margay
Chiza - squirrel
Cocodrilo - crocodile
Colibrí - hummingbird
Culebra - snake
Cuzuco - armadillo
Danta - tapir
Gallito de agua - northern jacana
Garcilla bueyara - cattle egret, common white heron
Gavilán - roadside hawk
Gaviota - gull
Guatusa - agouti
Hormiguero - antbird
Lapa - scarlet macaw
León breñero - jaguarundi
Loro - parrot
Manigordo - ocelot
Mapachín - raccoon
Mariposa - butterfly
Martilla - kinkajou
Martín pescador - kingfisher
Mono araña, mono colorado - spider monkey
Mono ardilla, mono tití - squirrel monkey
Mono cara blanca - white-faced Capuchin monkey
Mono congo - howler monkey
Murciélago - bat
Nutria - river otter
Oso hormiguero - lesser anteater, tamandua
Paloma - pigeon or dove

Pájaro - bird
Pelicano - pelican
Perezoso - sloth
Perica - three-toed sloth
Perro de agua - river otter
Pizote - coati
Puerco espín - porcupine
Puma - cougar, mountain lion
Quioro - chestnut mandibled toucan
Rana - frog
Saíno - collared peccary
Sapo - toad
Serafín - silky anteater
Serpiente - snake
Taltusa - gopher
Tepezcuintle - paca
Terciopelo - fer-de-lance
Tigre - jaguar
Tigrillo - tiger cat
Tijereta del mar - magnificent frigatebird
Tijo - smooth- or groove-billed ani
Tolomuco - tayra
Tortuga - turtle
Tortuga blanca - green turtle
Tortuga bocado - snapping turtle
Tortuga cabezona - loggerhead turtle
Tortuga carey - hawksbill
Tortuga jicóte - mud turtle
Tortuga negra - Pacific green turtle
Tortuga verde - green turtle
Venado coliblanco - white-tailed deer
Zompopas - farmer ants
Zorro hediondo - skunk
Zorro - opossum

makes its presence known by aiming its head towards the center, holding itself rigid, and rapidly vibrating its tail.

LIZARDS: The **basilisk** or "Jesus Christ lizard" (*Basiliscus basiliscus*) is so named because, while fleeing predators or pursuing prey, it may dart across the surface of a stream, balancing itself with its tail. You'll undoubtedly see these lowland dwellers scurrying across your path, resembling miniature sailfin dinosaurs. There are also a wide variety of **anoles**, small sit-and-wait predators that many North Americans mistakenly call chameleons. The territorial, primarily vegetarian *garobo* or *iguana negra* (**ctenosaur**) occurs in the drier lowlands. The **iguana** is distinguished from its cousin by green coloration, a longer tail, and a large scale on the side of the head just behind the lower jaw. Other lizards include the **skink** and the **spiny lizard**. There are two species of crocodilians: the occasionally cannibalistic **caimán**, which grows up to eight ft (2.5 m), inhabiting lowland swamps and slow-moving streams; and the larger, coastal **crocodile** (*cocodrila*). To tell the difference between them you must look at the brow, snout and back. While the caimán's brow slopes down to the base of its snout, the crocodile is flat-headed. The caimán has a shorter and wider snout than the crocodile. Finally, the crocodile's back is spiky and ridged, unlike the caimán.

SNAKES: Despite what you may think, there is a much greater chance of your dying crossing the street in San José than from receiving a poisonous snakebite here. Of the 162 species, 22 are poisonous. The most infamous is the **fer-de-lance** (terciopelo, "velvet snake"), which is colored olive green to dark brown with yellow, V-shaped markings along the sides. This lowland-dwelling snake reaches lengths up to seven ft or more and dines on mammals, especially opossums, with an occasional bird thrown in for variety. If you leave it alone, the *terciopelo* won't bother you. Its natural foe is the snake-feeding *zopilota*, which is immune to its venom. Another similar variety, but stockier and more aggressive, is the *mano de piedra* ("stone fist," **hognose viper**, *Bothreicheis nasutus*). The small (20 inches, 50 cm), strictly arboreal *bocaracá* (**eyelash viper**) is quite poisonous. It has what appear to be small horns above its eyes and tends to thrive in the tropical lowlands. Another arboreal poisonous snake is the *víbora de árbol* or *arboicola*, which is found at the 4,260-8,200-ft (1,300-2,500-m) level. The deadliest snake is the rare **cascabel muda** ("silent rattler"), which may reach up to six ft (two m). There's also the **cascabel**, the tropical rattler, which has been known to bite cows on their tongues as they graze. It's found only in Guanacaste. Another serpent to watch out for is *la coral* (the **coral snake**), which does not bother humans unless handled. It comes in a number of varieties: one colored red, yellow and black, and others variously striped black and red, black and orange, or black and white. The harmless *sabanera* (**grassnake**) has a dull brown color and a distinctive red or orange underbelly. There's also the *bejuquilla* ("**little vine**"), a vine snake living in arid areas. The large, non-venomous boa (**boa constrictor**), a climber par excellence, devours everything from lizards to dogs. After striking its prey, the boa coils around it and swallows the animal head first. The most frightening snake is the **pelagic sea snake** (*culebra del mar*), for which there is no serum available; it's found 1-20 km offshore along the Pacific coast from California to Chile. Fortunately, only 10 people have been bitten by it during the past decade.

Birds

Costa Rica's geographical location as a land bridge between two continents makes it a meeting ground for a huge variety of American birds. A full tenth of the world's flighted species visit or permanently reside here. There are over 850 species of birds, more than in all of North America above Mexico – a population that includes brightly colored wild parakeets, an assortment of trogons and macaws, hummingbirds, pelicans, antshrikes, swallows, wrens, thrushes, warblers, ovenbirds, cuckoos, hawks, swifts, owls, egrets, and others.

WHERE TO FIND BIRDS: One of the reasons birdwatchers flock to Costa Rica is the number and variety of its species. Even if you aren't a diehard, be *sure* to bring binoculars. Everyone has a favorite spot. It may be around your hotel or at a nature preserve. The parks and reserves – public or private – are sure bets, and one of Costa Rica's great outdoor aviaries is the area surrounding the mouth of the Río Tempisque inside the Palo Verde National Park. Birdwatchers will want to pick up a copy of *The Birds of Costa Rica* by F. Gary Stiles and Alexander Skutch, the most authoritative guide available. Buy it before you arrive. It is very expensive in Costa Rica. Another useful book is a *Birder's Guide to Costa Rica* by Keith Taylor, which provides checklists and directions to birding sites. It can be difficult to obtain and is out-of-date in terms of prices and hotels. One possibility might be the LA Audubon Bookstore (☎ 213-876-0202).

> ☞ **Traveler's Tip.** Serious birders will want to pick up a copy ($5) of *An Annotated Checklist of the Birds of Monteverde and Peñas Blancas* by Michael Fogden. Published in 1993, it includes a list of 452 species, about 330 of which breed in the area.

THE BEST SPOTS: The first includes the province of Guanacaste. Northern birds predominate here. Santa Rosa and Palo Verde both are outstanding birding spots, as are other parks and reserves in the region. Many migratory birds are found in Palo Verde's Tempisque River basin. The cloud forests in the highlands contain a large number of endemic species as well as Andean or southern varieties. The southern Pacific area boasts Corcovado, one of the best all-around places to see birds. The Caribbean coast also provides fine birding in its lowlands. Many South American species are found here.

SEASONAL MIGRANTS: There is a remarkable influx of long-distance migrants from North America. **Warblers** predominate – both in their numbers and in the variety of different species that appear. Other species include **thrushes, vireos, tanagers, cuckoos, kingfishers, raptors, swallows,** and **flycatchers.** Birds first start arriving along the Caribbean coast in August; their numbers swell throughout the country in September and October. Prominent winter residents are the small **yellow-throated vireo,** the *sargento* or **scarlet-rumped tanager,** the **red-winged blackbird** (*tordo sargento*), the **sanderling,** and the **Tennessee warbler.** Others are not true migrants but tropical birds that go north to breed, spending more than half the year in Costa Rica. Birds that migrate in spectacular flocks include **Swainson's hawks, turkey vultures,** and **barn, bank,** and **cliff swallows.**

BIRDS WITH CHARACTER: The **cattle egret** (*garcilla bueyara*), having first arrived in the New World from Africa around 1877, follows cattle and eats the insects disturbed as they move about. The sedentary **roadside hawk** (*gavilán*) thrives in deforested territory and abounds in Guanacaste, preying on lizards, snakes, rodents, and large insects. The enormous *rey de zopilote* (**king vulture**) has creamy white and black on its wings, along with a red and orange head. The mostly black **frigate bird** (*rabihorcado magno*), found in the waters near Puntarenas, swoops ominously overhead, occasionally veering down to the water to make a capture. Dark-colored **antbirds** (*hormigueros*) are best seen if you are on a solitary excursion into one of the primary forests. The omnivorous *oropendola* is mostly black with yellow outer tail feathers. It is related to the oriole and the grackle. The female constructs her sagging sac-like nests on the ends of tree branches. "Motmot, motmot" is the cry of the blue-crowned **motmot** (*pajaro bobo*), which numbers among the most beautiful of the nation's birds. The **chestnut-mandibled toucan** (*dios tede*) is the largest toucan in Central America and one of the forest's biggest fruit eaters. A piercing call and brown and yellow bill are its trademarks. The *perico* (**orange-chinned parakeet**) is bright green, with an orange patch just below its bill. The **three-wattled bellbird** (*pajaro campana, campanero tricarunculado*) has a metallic call much like a bell. The male is chestnut with white chest, neck, and head; it has three wattles. The female is olive-green and has fine yellow stripes on her upper chest and on the sides of her head. Her bill is also black but lacks the wattles.

COWBIRDS: In Costa Rica there are two varieties: giant (*vaquero grande*) and bronzed (*vaquero ojirrojo*). These birds, members of the oriole family, are celebrated for their breeding practices, which some biologists have regarded with moral indignation. Either too lazy or too enlightened to build nests and nurture offspring, cowbirds indulge in a practice known as brood parasitism. After locating a suitable nest, the female sneaks in and deposits her egg among those of the builder. Whereas giant cowbirds chiefly choose the nests of *oropendolas* and *caciques* to victimize, the bronzed cowbirds seek out sparrow, finch, and other nests. Baby cowbirds hatch a week earlier than their nestmates and develop more quickly. They are thus able to dominate the others. Working in Panama, researcher Neal Smith discovered that the birds exhibit two types of behavior. In one, a cowbird sneaks around an oropendola nest and stealthily lays an egg or two. The eggs resemble oropendola eggs but, should the female *oropendola* suspect something is up, she will not hesitate to roll the egg out of the nest. In other cases, the cowbird brazenly lays up to five eggs, which do not resemble *oropendola* eggs, in the presence of the female oropendola. In these instances, he found that the aggressive cowbird hatchlings protected the nest from botflies by swiftly swallowing the flies and their larva as well. In nests where the cowbirds practiced their usual behavior, Smith noted that the nest was protected from the botflies through the proximity of a bee or wasp nest.

THE SCARLET MACAW: Residing on the Pacific side, this spectacularly plumaged parrot is perhaps the nation's most beautiful bird. You are likely to see it flying overhead and sounding off raucously. Its bright red-orange plumage has touches of yellow and blue and does not vary with age or between sexes. Scarlet macaws (*lapas*) apparently mate for life, which is one reason they are in danger of extinction. Another is their black market value – up to $500 per bird. A third is habitat destruction: they generally nest in large trees. You'll commonly see them in fruit trees, where they may be found pecking through the pulp of fruits and cracking open the seeds, the contents of which they devour. They may also consume the pulp, as well as some leaves and flowers, but the seeds are their bread and butter. In pursuing fruit, the birds can perform gymnastics that would be the envy of any Olympic acrobat. Their four-taloned feet – two of which face backwards – enable them to accomplish these feats. Another tool is their remarkable hooked beak, which can be used for climbing. Macaws have also been known to consume riverbank clay, which may serve to counter the effects of poisonous seeds high in alkaloids and tannins. Since 1992, it's been illegal to import macaws to the US.

The birds generally mate in December; the female lays two eggs. During the month-long incubation, her partner brings her delicacies, which he has previously swallowed and stored in a throat pouch. Regurgitating, he feeds his mate, and they both feed the chicks this way. Chicks fledge at three to four months. Male and female are distinguishable only during breeding and nesting. You may commonly see them preening each other. Macaws may live for as long as 45 years. The only reliable places to see macaws are in the Corcovado and Carara national parks.

A related species, the green macaw (buffon) is found on the Caribbean coast but rarely seen.

THE QUETZAL: The resplendent quetzal (pronounced "ket-ZAL") is the nation's most famous animal, period. It lives in the cool cloud forests of Monteverde, Braulio Carrillo, and Chirripó, among other places. Costa Rica is the easiest place to see a quetzal, and you can find them in damp, epiphyte-laden mountain forests between 4,000 and 10,000 ft (1,200-3,000 m), particularly along edges and canopies. The bird usually keeps the highest profile during breeding season between March and June, when they nest in high hollows of decaying tree trunks. Because they subsist on fruit and insects, the easiest place to spot them is around fruiting trees. Males and females take turns sitting on the pale blue eggs, which are laid directly atop the sawdust-like material that covers the floor of the hole. They are readily identifiable by their red underbelly, iridescent green back, and trailing green plumes. The short yellow bill is ideal for drilling in soft, dead wood. Usually found alone or in pairs, they sound with a sharp cackling "perwicka" when disturbed or taking off. The male sounds a strikingly melodious or whining "keow kowee keow k'loo keow k'loo keeloo." It also cries "very good, very good" in rising display flight. In flight, it resembles a woodpecker – flying in short, undulating dips and rises, plumes rolling at its rear. The tail length of the male ranges from 14 to 25 inches (36-64 cm). Only the male of the species grows a long tail. The plainer female sports barred tail feathers and only a touch of red.

The Aztecs borrowed the bird's image for Quetzalcóatl, their feathered serpent god; its name is derived from *quetzalli*, an early Aztec word for its tail feathers, which also means "precious" or "beautiful." Native American kings and priests used the bird's feathers for adornment. Decreed sacred, males were caught, plucked, and released. Unfortunately, quetzals by the thousands were slaughtered for export to Europe during the mid-19th C., and the carnage continues to this day.

Flora & Fauna

The Guatemalans named the quetzal their national bird in the mistaken belief that it could not live in captivity. The first part of its scientific name, *Pharomarchrus mocinno*, derives from the Greek words for "long mantle" and the second immortalizes the 19th-C. naturalist who helped bring the first scientific specimens to Europe. Nine other species of trogons, the group to which the quetzal belongs, also reside in Costa Rica.

HUMMINGBIRDS: Bold and strikingly beautiful, the **fiery-throated hummingbird** (*colibrí garganta de fuego*) hovers above flowers. Colored a glossy green, it has iridescent patterning, which is only visible from above and at close range. Its dull-colored relative is the **long-tailed hermit** (*ermitaño colilargo*). Hummingbirds are attracted to colorful flowers and, should you wear bright red, you may find yourself a target! Despite what you might think, these enchanting creatures are nourished not by nectar but by insects. They are thought to use the low-nutrient nectar, which has a high sugar content, for an energy boost. The flowers, which have evolved to cater to this addiction, are often tubular and suspended away from their branches, allowing the birds space to probe with their long tongues.

LONG-TAILED MANAKINS: Commonly found in the forests of the NW, these chickadee-sized birds are noted for both their large size and their behavior. Blue-black in color, males have azure backs and scarlet crowns and legs. Two slender plumes fork from their tails. The females are greenish, with short tails. Perhaps because they dine mainly on abundantly available fruit, manakins have evolved their own eccentric mating behavior. Males partner with each other in a dynamic singing duo. One tweets "to-de-lo" and the other responds with a noisy, less melodic reply. The two birds dance in tandem in a kind of cartwheel with rotating positions. While the birds are going at it, a female may be attracted. The dominant male mates with her and then resumes dancing with his partner.

GREAT CURRASOW: An unforgettable resident of the forest, the 36-inch (91 cm) great currasow (*pavón grande, granadera*) is black, with a long tail, a curly erectile crest and a bright yellow knob at the base of its bill. The smaller female lacks this knob and is grey. The bird spends its days scratching the ground in search of fallen fruit and small animals. If frightened, it generally runs away, emitting a high-pitched yip like a dog. Endangered, it is now most easily spotted in Santa Rosa, Rincón de la Vieja, and in Corcovado.

OTHER BIRDS: Other indigenous species of note include the Muscovy duck, a variety of woodpeckers, the rufous-naped hen, the turkey vulture and its relatives, the green kingfisher, the boat-billed heron, the bananaquit, the groove-billed ani, five species of tinamou, the brown jay, the white-collared swift, the rufous-tailed jacamar, the laughing falcon, the mangrove swallow, the jacana, and the ochre-bellied flycatcher. You may also see the white-fronted nunbird, the pauraque, the tropical screech owl, the spotted barbtail, the great-tailed grackle, western and spotted sandpipers, the variable seedeater, ruddy-tailed and common-tody flycatchers, the barred antshrike, the tropical kingbird, the wrenthrush, and the rufous-colored sparrow.

Insects

Insect life is both varied and abundant. In the 89,000 acres (36,000 ha) of Corcovado National Park, there are at least 220 species of butter flies. In mountainous Chirippó, only 70 km away, there are 30 species, with less than 5% overlap. There are more cicada species than found E of the Mississippi River in the US. There may be more than 20 million different insect species in tropical rainforests worldwide. A study by Terry Erwin of the Smithsonian estimated that each tree supports 405 unique insect species.

Lest you be tempted to view insects as uninteresting, remember that they have been around for at least 400 million years and butterflies are believed to have evolved around 200 million years ago during the Triassic period. Tropical forests have evolved in tandem with insects, and some of the most fascinating interactions involve flora and insects. Many are masters of disguise and blend in with their surroundings. Katydids take on the colors of moss and lichens; caterpillars craftily masquerade as bird droppings; moths masterfully imitate dead leaves. Take time to watch the bugs!

BUTTERFLIES: All told, there are 1,239 species, but few are unusual or spectacular. Possibly the world's most beautiful butterfly, the **morpho** (*celeste común*) is common in forests from sea level to 4,500 ft (1,400 m). The most colorful of the two forms found, which has almost completely iridescent blue upper wings, is most plentiful on the Caribbean coast. The **cream owl butterfly** (*buhito pardo*) has two glaring eyes on its underside. Various theories suggest that these serve as 1) mimicry of a vertebrate so as to ward off attacks, 2) mimicry of a large, distasteful tree frog that clings to the sides of trees, or 3) target spots for predators that, because of their position, allow the butterfly to escape relatively unscathed. Other butterfly species of note include the **common calico**, the **zebra**, the **Saturnia, skipper, hecale, orión, giant swallowtail,** and the **orange-barred sulfur.**

lifestyle: As they have no jaws, butterflies must take all nutrients in liquid form. They feed on water suffused with mineral salts found in the earth, nectar, juice from decaying fruit, juices from carrion, honeydew secretions from aphids, and other such delicacies. While you may find them warming up in the sun or drinking water at mud banks, they rest on the undersides of leaves to protect themselves during rainstorms.

guides: Be sure to check out Philip J. de Vries' fine guide, *Butterflies of Costa Rica.*

MEMORABLE VIEWING: The pencil-thin **helicopter damselfly** (*gallito azul*) beats each of its four wings independently, resembling a slow-motion windmill. Its wing movement renders it invisible to spiders, upon whom it launches a single attack burst, snipping and capturing the succulent abdomen as the rest falls. The pit-making **ant lion** (*hormiga león*) is actually the larval form of a beautiful fly similar to a damselfly. It spends its childhood digging a pit, heaping up loosened particles on its head and tossing them clear. Then burying itself – only its jaws project – it awaits the prey. Any captured game has its contents sucked out and the empty skin tossed out of the pit. After it has stored up enough food to support its next incarnation, it enters a cocoon, re-emerging as a sexually mature adult. A pretty good handful, the male **rhinoceros beetle** (*cornizuelo*) sports a long upward-curved horn, but the females are hornless; they are endangered by habitat destruction. The **frangipani sphinx** (*oruga, falso coral*), the most conspicuous moth larva found in Guanacaste, appears to mimic the coral snake, both with its bright yellow coloring and red-orange head and in the way it thrashes back and forth when touched; it also bites viciously! The *machaca* (peanut-head bug, lantern fly) is one of Latin America's best known insects. Its color harmonizes perfectly with the large branches and logs on which they rest. Its enormous hind wing eye-spots and lizard-shaped head are probably designed to confuse predators. If pestered it will release a fetid skunk-like spray or drum its grotesque head against a tree trunk. A popular Latin American folk saying maintains that if a young girl is stung by a machaca, she must have sex with her boyfriend within 24 hours or die. In many parts of Latin America, locals are terrified of this harmless insect.

Other intriguing bugs include the **tarantula, paper wasp,** the local version of the **praying mantis,** and the **Guanacaste stick insect** (*palito andando*).

ANTS: This is one resident of the rainforest you'll undoubtedly encounter. If you sit down, you may well have some unpleasant bites to contend with. Shake a bush and ants will scurry out. In many tracts, they may outweigh all of the vertebrates present. You may see the large black **bullet ant** (*hormiga bala*) along the trail. Be wary; it has a nasty bite. **Leaf-cutting** or **farmer ants** (*zompopas*) are commonly seen marching along a forest trail holding aloft cut pieces of leaves and flowers. They chew leaves into shreds and carry them off to their nests, where they then clear the leaves of unwanted fungal spores and chew the plant material, mixing it with a combination of saliva and excrement. On this they cultivate a spongy, breadlike fungus (*Rhozites gongylophora*), which they consume. This fungus no longer produces sexual spores and has come to rely solely upon the ants for propagation. Each colony, ranking among the largest and most complex societies in the world, may have a million members, each with a role to play. The smallest tend to the eggs and larvae, larger ones forage, and the even larger soldiers defend the nest. Watch them as they meet, stroke antennae, and exchange chemical cues.

The **acacia ant** (*hormiga de cornizuelo*) is joined in a symbiotic relationship with the acacia tree. It wards off herbivores, while the tree supplies the ants with nectar, protein and protection in return. The ants produce an alarm pheromone that can be detected some six ft (two m) downwind. You can easily recognize acacia trees by their hollow swollen horns, resembling those of cattle.

Another example of mutualism is found between the *Azteca* or *cecropia* **ants** and their namesake plant. In order to ward off herbivores, the *cecropia* attracts the ants, which it provides with specialized food called Beltian bodies. These are budlike leaflet tips, which the ants harvest and use to nourish their larvae. These are raised inside the tree's thorns. In return, the ants defend the tree. Although stingless, they bite with their tough jaws and secrete caustic chemicals, which they rub into bites.

Semi-nomadic **army ants** may travel in packs of up to 20 million members, foraging along a 20-foot-wide front. They bring back bits of twigs, lichen, leaves and other insects to feed their queen; the detritus also feeds the roots of nearby plants and helps a number of species – from birds to flies to millipedes – in their feeding. The rarely seen red-colored **trapdoor ant** thrusts her abdomen forward, injecting venom with her stinger. Other species include the **giant tropical ants**.

TERMITES: Resembling gigantic wasp nests and found on trees, dark brown or black termite nests are a frequent feature of the forested landscape. The nest is made of "carton," wood chewed up by workers and cemented with fecal "glue." It has one reproductive king and queen commanding hordes of up to 100,000 attending workers and soldiers. Termites digest raw cellulose, a substance low in nutritional value, with the aid of protozoa dwelling in their guts. The **assassin bug** (*reduvio*), camouflaging itself with bits and pieces of termite nest, preys at the entrance. In death as in life, termites contribute to the rainforest ecosystem. Their defecated roughage is a feast for fungi, which also grow on their carcasses.

LOATHED BY HUMANS: Nearly invisible, **chiggers** (*coloradillas*) thrive in locations ranging from lowland cattle pastures to rainforests. They are a form of mite larva that insert the tips of their well-developed mouthparts into your skin. They love to squeeze into protected places such as bra and belt lines and the genital area, where they bite and deposit a histamine that makes the surrounding area itch like hell for up to 10 days! **Purrujas** (no-see-ums, biting midges) are small gnats that favor the tender skin of the ears and neck. They are almost invisible and are most active on warm days and windless evenings. Only the females bite humans. In the forest, you'll also find an abundance of **ticks** (*garrapatas*). With 20 body segments, the forest-floor **millipede** (*milpies*) is readily identifiable both by its movements and its dull whitish-yellow color. Its ability to curl up in a spiral and violently expel a solution of hydrogen cyanide and benzaldehyde as far as 12 inches (30 cm) discourages predators. In copulation the males (26-35 inches, 65-90 cm long) have a habit of "riding" the larger females (28-39 inches, 70-100 cm long) for periods of five days or more. Unescorted females are rare in millipedal society, but bachelor millipedes may remain sexually unfulfilled for long periods. Since copulation generally occurs within the first few hours after mounting, it is thought that the natural selective purpose of this "riding" behavior is to discourage the females from mating again. Otherwise, rivalry among sperm would result, since the sperm is utilized only after oviposition and a female will mate with many others if left alone. If faced with a sexual competitor, the male will flex the rear of his body to force a female's head and rear over her genital openings, thus barring access. Their relative, the **scorpion** (*alacrán, escorpión*) stings only in self-defense; scorpions prey at night on insects and spiders.

flies: Biting flies can be a problem in season, and the most loathesome insect of all is the **botfly** (*Dermatobia hominis*), whose larvae mature inside flesh. An egg-laden female botfly captures a night-flying female mosquito and glues her eggs on to it. When the mosquito is released and bites a victim, the host's body heat triggers an egg to hatch. It falls off and burrows in. The larva secures itself with two anal hooks, secreting an antibiotic into its burrow, which staves off competing bacteria and fungi. Its spiracle pokes out of the tiny hole, and a small mound forms which will grow to the size of a goose egg before the mature larva falls out. Should you be unfortunate enough to fall prey to a larva – an extremely unlikely occurrence for the average visitor – you have three cures available. One is to use the acrid white sap of the *matatorsalo* (bot killer), which kills the larva but leaves its corpse intact. Another is to apply a piece of soft, raw meat to the top of the airhole. As the maggot must breathe, it burrows upward into the meat. A third is to apply a generous helping of Elmer's glue or cement to the hole. Cover this with a circular patch of adhesive tape; seal this tape with a final application of glue. Squeeze out the dead larva the next morning. The only other alternative is to leave it to grow to maturity, giving you an opportunity to experience the transmogrification of part of yourself into another creature. It only hurts when the maggot squirms and if you swim, presumably because you are cutting off its air supply. Don't try to pull it out because it will burst. Part of its body will remain inside and cause an infection.

    Horseflies are an annoyance during May at 1,800-4,800 ft (600-1,600 m), and another biting fly is the hardy but hunchbacked **black fly** (*mosca de café*).

OTHER NUISANCES: Coming in a number of species, the **mosquito** (*zancudo*) needs no introduction, nor does the **giant cockroach** (*cucaracha*). Finally, although they should not be a problem for visitors, Africanized **"killer" bees** are proving a menace. Since their arrival in 1983, they have attacked more than 500 people, resulting in nine deaths.

Sealife

ECHINODERMATA: This large division of the animal kingdom, named from the Greek words for *echinos* (hedgehog) and *derma* (skin), includes sea urchins, sea cucumbers, and starfish. They have in common the fact that they all move with the help of tube feet or spines. **Starfish** (*estrella de mar*) are five-footed carnivorous creatures that use their modified "tube-feet" to burrow into the seabed. Sluggish **sea cucumbers** ingest large quantities of sand, extract the organic matter, and excrete the rest. Crustaceans and fish reside in the larger ones.

    Avoid trampling on that armed knight of the underwater sand dunes, the **sea urchin**. The sea urchin consists of a semi-circular calcareous (calcium carbonate) shell, protected by brown, jointed barbs. It uses its mouth, protected on its underside, to graze by scraping algae from rocks. Surprisingly to those uninitiated in its lore, sea urchins are considered a gastronomic delicacy in many countries. The ancient Greeks believed they had aphrodisiacal and other properties beneficial to health. They are prized by the French and fetch four times the price of oysters in Paris. The Spanish consume them raw, boiled, in *gratinés*, or in soups. In Barbados they are called "sea eggs" and the Japanese eat them as sushi. If a sea urchin spine breaks off inside your finger or toe, don't try to remove it: you won't be able to! You might try the cure people use in New Guinea. With a blunt object mash up the spine under your skin so that it will be absorbed naturally. Then dip the area in urine; the ammonia helps to trigger the process of disintegration. Sea urchins hide underneath corals, and wounds often occur when you lose your footing and scrape against one.

SPONGES: Reddish or brown sponges found in the ocean depths are among the simplest forms of multicellular life and have been around for more than a half-billion years. They pump large amounts of water between their internal filters and extract plankton. There are numerous sizes, shapes, and colors, but they all may be recognized by their large, distinctive excurrent openings. Unlike other animals, they exhibit no reaction when disturbed.

CNIDARIANS: The members of this phylum – hydroids, anemones, corals, and jellyfish – are distingushed by their simple structure: a cup-shaped body terminating in a combination mouth-anus which, in turn, is encircled by tentacles. While hydroids and corals (covered later in this section) are colonial, jellyfish and anemones are individual. This phylum's name comes from another identifying characteristic: nematocysts, stinging capsules primarily used for defense and capturing prey. Hydroids ("water form" in Greek) grow in skeletal colonies resembling ferns or feathers. They spend their youth as solitary medusas before settling down in old age. Some will sting, and the most famous hydroid is undoubtedly the floating **Portuguese Man-Of-War**. Its stinging tentacles can be extended or retracted; wordwide, there have been reports of trailing tentacles reaching 50 feet! It belongs to the family of siphonophores, free-floating hydroid colonies that control their depth by means of a gas-filled float. The true **jellyfish** are identifiable by their domes, which vary in shape. Nematocysts reside in both the feeding tube and in their tentacles. Box jellies, also known as sea wasps, may be identifed by their cuboidal body, from each corner of which a single tentacle extends. Many of them can sting fiercely; keep well away.

If you should get stung by any of the above, get out of the water and peel off any tentacles. Avoid rubbing the injured area. Wash the wound with alcohol and apply meat tenderizer for five to 10 minutes. The jellyfish season is August to October. **Sea anemones** are solitary bottom-dwellers, polyps that lack a skeleton, using their tentacles to stun prey and force them to their mouth. They often protect shrimp and crabs who, immune to their sting, reside right by them. Their tentacles may retract for protection when disturbed. One type of anemone lives in tubes that are buried in the muck or sand. Their tentacles only come out to play at night.

CRUSTACEANS: The **ghost crab** (*Ocypode*) abounds on the beaches, tunneling down beneath the sand and emerging to feed at night. It can survive for 48 hours without contacting water. However, it must return to the sea to moisten its gill chambers as well as to lay eggs, which hatch into plankton larvae. The **hermit crab** carries a discarded mollusc shell to protect its vulnerable abdomen. As it grows, it must find a larger home, and you may see two struggling over the same shell.

Save the Dolphins!

Over the course of the past three decades more than 6.5 million dolphins have been killed through activities associated with tuna fishing. Dolphins are often found near yellowfin tuna, which swim below them. Regrettably, Costa Rica does not afford protection for these dolphins. One organization working to save them is **APROCA** (☎ 255-3365; Apdo. 1863-1002, San José).

Coral Reefs

One of the least appreciated of the world's innumerable wonders is the coral reef. This is in part because little has been known about it until recent decades. A coral reef is the only geological feature fashioned by living creatures, and it is a delicate environment. Many of the world's reefs – which took millions of years to form – have already suffered adverse effects from human activities. One of the greatest opportunities the tropics offer is to explore this wondrous environment, one that, in many ways, goes beyond the limits of the wildest fantasy.

Corals produce the calcium carbonate (limestone) responsible for the buildup of offlying cays and islets as well as most sand on the beaches. Bearing the brunt of waves, they also conserve the shoreline. The reefs began forming millenia ago, but they are in a constant state of flux. They depend upon a delicate ecological balance to survive. Deforestation, dredging, temperature change, an increase or decrease in salinity, silt, or sewage discharge may kill them. Because temperature ranges must remain between 68°and 95°F, they are only found in the tropics and, because they require light to grow, only in shallow water. They are also intolerant of fresh water, so reefs can't survive where rivers empty into the sea.

THE CORAL POLYP: While corals are actually animals, botanists view them as being mostly plant, and geologists dub them "honorary rocks." Corals act more like plants than animals, surviving through photosynthesis: the algae inside the coral polyps do the work, while the polyps themselves secrete calcium carbonate and stick together for protection from waves and boring sponges. Bearing a close structural resemblance to its relative the anemone, a polyp feeds at night by using the ring or rings of tentacles surrounding its mouth to capture prey (such as plankton) with nematocysts, small stinging darts.

The coral polyps appear able to survive in such packed surroundings through their symbiotic relationship with the algae in their tissues. Coral polyps exhale carbon dioxide and the algae consume it, producing needed oxygen. Although only half of the world's coral species possess this type of relationship with these single-celled captive species of dinoflagellates (*Gymnodinium microdriaticum*), these "hermatypic" corals, as they are called, are the ones that build the reef. The nutritional benefits gained from their relationship with the algae enable them to grow a larger skeleton and to do so more rapidly than would otherwise be possible. Polyps have the ability to regulate the density of these cells in their tissues and can expel some of them in a spew of mucus should they multiply too quickly. When you see a coral garden through your mask, the brownish algal cells show through transparent tissues; you are actually viewing a field of captive single-celled algae.

A vital, though invisible, component of the reef ecosystem is bacteria, microorganisms that decompose and recycle all matter on which everything from worms to coral polyps feed. Inhabitants of the reef range from crabs to barnacles, sea squirts to multicolored tropical fish. Remarkably, the polyps themselves are consumed by only a small percentage of the reef's inabitants. They often contain high levels of toxic substances and are also thought to sting fish and other animals that attempt to consume them. Corals also retract their polyps during daylight hours when the fish can see them. Reefs originate as the polyps develop, and the calcium secretions form a base as they grow. One polyp can have a 1,000-year lifespan.

CORAL TYPES: Corals may be divided into three groups. The **hard** or **stony corals** (such as staghorn, brain, star, or rose) secrete a limey skeleton. The **horny corals** (sea plumes, sea whips, sea fans, and gorgonians) have a supporting skeleton-like structure known as a gorgonin (after the head of Medusa). The shapes of these corals result from the way in which the polyps and their connecting tissues excrete calcium carbonate; there are over a thousand different patterns – one specific to each species. Each also has its own method of budding. Giant elk-horn corals found in the Caribbean may contain over a million polyps and live for several hundred years or longer. And then there are the **soft corals**. While these too are colonies of polyps, their skeletons are composed of soft organic material, and their polyps always have eight tentacles instead of the six or multiples of six found in the stony corals. Unlike the hard corals, soft corals disintegrate after death and do not add to the reef's stony structure. Instead of depositing limestone crystals, they excrete a jelly-like matrix imbued with spicules (diminutive spikes) of stony material; the jelly-like substance gives these corals their flexibility. Sea fans and sea whips exhibit similar patterns. The precious black coral is a type of soft coral. Prized by jewelers because its branches may be cleaned and polished to high gloss ebony-black, it resembles a bush of fine grey-black twigs.

COMPETITION: To the snorkeler, the reef appears to be a peaceful haven. The reality is that, because the reef is a comparatively benign environment, the fiercest competition has developed here. Although the corals appear static to the onlooker, they are continually competing with each other for space. Some have developed sweeper tentacles with an especially high concentration of stinging cells. Reaching out to a competing coral, they stick and execute it. Other species dispatch digestive filaments that eat their prey. Soft corals are thought to leach out toxic chemicals called terpines that kill nearby organisms. Because predation is such a problem, two-thirds of reef species are toxic. Others hide in stony outcrops or have formed protective relationships with other organisms. The banded clown fish, for example, lives among sea anemones whose stingers protect it. The cleaner fish protect themselves from the larger fish by setting up stations where they pick parasites off their carnivorous customers. The sabre-toothed blenny is a false cleaner fish. It mimics the coloration and shape of the feeder fish, approaches, then takes a chunk out of the larger fish and runs off!

CORAL LOVE AFFAIRS: Not prone to celibacy or sexual prudery, coral polyps reproduce sexually and asexually through budding, and a polyp joins together with thousands and even millions of its neighbors to form a coral. (In a few cases, only one polyp forms a single coral.) During sexual reproduction polyps release millions of their spermatozoa into the water. Many species are dimorphic – with both male and female polyps. Some species have internal, others external, fertilization. As larvae develop, their "mother" expells them and they float off to form a new coral.

EXPLORING REEFS: Coral reefs are extremely fragile environments. Much damage has been done to reefs worldwide through the carelessness of humans. Despite their size, reefs grow very slowly, and it can take decades or even hundreds of years to repair the effects of a few moments.

Flora & Fauna

COSTA RICAN REEFS: Endangered by runoff from banana planta tions, the nation's largest coral reef is found off Cahuita on the Atlantic coast and is a national park. Much smaller ones are found off the Pacific coast and in the Gandoca-Manzanillo Reserve, also facing the Caribbean.

ORGANIZATIONS: If you're interested in working to preserve coral reefs worldwide, contact **Coral Forest** (☎ 415-291-9877) at 300 Broadway, Suite 39, San Francisco CA 94133.

UNDERWATER FLORA: Most of the plants you see underwater are algae, primitive plants that can survive only underwater because they are unable to prevent themselves from drying out. Lacking roots, algae draw their minerals and water directly from the sea. Calcareous red algae are very important for reef formation. Resembling rounded stones, they are 95% rock and only 5% living tissue. Seagrasses, plants returned to live in the sea, are found in relatively shallow water in sandy and muddy bays and flats; they have roots and small flowers. One species, dubbed "turtle grass," provides food for turtles. In addition, seagrasses help to stabilize the sea floor, maintain water clarity by trapping fine sediments from upland soil erosion, stave off beach erosion, and provide living space for numerous fish, crustaceans, and shellfish.

History

Through the 19th Century

THE START: The area now known as the nation of Costa Rica was, before the Spaniards' arrival, a sparsely settled chunk of the extended isthmus linking two enormous continents – a region where the northern Mesoamerican cultures met the southern Andean cultures. Arriving in the 16th C., Spaniards estimated there to be 25,000 indigenous people divided into five major tribal groups. The Mayan Chorotegas, residing in the Península de Nicoya, accounted for approximately half the total number. They had arrived from Chiapas, Mexico in the 13th C. The warlike, nomadic Caribs roamed the Caribbean coast. The fierce Boricua lived in the Talamanca region along the Pacific. They dwelt in fortified villages comprised of enormous cone-shaped huts that could contain up to several hundred people. Their dialect belonged to the Chibchan language group, common throughout Central

America and the Andes. Little is known about the matriarchal Coro-
bicis. The group thought to be the oldest indigenous tribe, the Aztec-
influenced Nahuas, were grouped into two small, widely separated
settlements. They are credited with having introduced cacao into the
region.

COLUMBUS INTRUDES: During his fourth and final voyage of
1502, Christopher Columbus anchored at the present-day port of
Puerto Limón. He bartered for the gold disks the Caribs wore as pen-
dants. His brother Bartolomé remained behind to explore, only to flee
when his party was attacked. Every attempt to conquer the isthmus in
the early 1500s, from the very first one by Diego de Nicuesa, ended in
failure, with *conquistadores* retreating in the face of hunger, disease,
and armed resistance. Unlike the Mayan and Aztec regions, here there
was no single Native American empire to conquer; each tribe had to
be fought anew. The Native Americans would burn their crops rather
than allow the invaders to take them. And the would-be conquerers
expended a great deal of their time and energy contending with one
another. Between 1511 and 1517, many Native Americans were seized
and shipped off to slavery in Cuba; others fell victim to smallpox. Anthropologists estimate their numbers at 400,000; many of them
dropped dead of the newly introduced communicable diseases without even so much as seeing one of the intruders.

THE FIRST CONQUESTS: The first successful expedition was led by
Gil González Dávila who traded with Chorotegas on the Peninsula de
Nicoya. His compadre, Diego de Aguero, baptized thousands – at
least according to the official version. This settlement ended when
González Dávila was arrested in Panama by Pedrarias Dávila, the
Governor of Veragua, for trespassing on his jurisdiction. Likewise, a
small settlement by Francisco Fernando de Cordova in 1524 ended under threats from Pedrarias. Appointed by the family of Christopher
Columbus, who had died in 1506, an expedition in 1534 by Felipe Gutierrez ended in disaster, with some of its members resorting to canni-
balism. In 1540 Hernan Sanchez de Badajoz founded the settlement of
Badajoz at the mouth of the Río Sixaola. He was driven out by Rodrigo
de Contreras, the new governor of Nicaragua. Contreras, in turn, was
routed by the Native Americans who rebelled at his cruelty. Other
conquistadors followed but none enjoyed success.

EARLY COLONIZATION: In 1539 Costa Rica was separated from
Veragua and was organized as a *gobernación* in 1542. In 1561 Juan de
Cavallon established the first settlement at Garcimuñoz, a point where
the Río Cirueas meets the Pacific. Disheartened at the lack of gold in
the area, Cavallon deserted the colony in 1562 and was replaced by

Juan Vasquez de Coronado, who moved the settlement into the Meseta Central in 1564. From the new town of Cartago, Coronado explored the area, surveying Costa Rica's boundaries. Lost at sea during a return visit to Spain, he was replaced by Perafín de Ribera in 1568. That same year Costa Rica was subsumed in the newly established kingdom of Guatemala. Ribera fought against the indigenous people of the Talamanca region from 1570-72, a costly campaign that again produced no gold. By the time of his departure in 1573, two small settlements had sprung up: Cartago and Aranuez.

EARLY SOCIETY: The Native Americans were decimated by introduced diseases, intertribal warfare, and by conquest. Many starved to death after they had been driven from their land. By 1569, their numbers in Nicoya had declined to 3,300. Others, such as many of the Chorotega tribe, intermarried with Spaniards, producing a *mestizo* population that viewed itself as Spanish, not Native American. Other Native Americans, such as the Changuenes, were captured by the Zambos Miskitos (descendants of unions between Miskito Native Americans and shipwrecked African slaves). They were then sold to Jamaica in conspiracy with English pirates. Other than in such areas as isolated Talamanca, the Native Americans died out. Black slaves were also integrated through intermarriage. Increasingly, the colony came to be seen as a backwater – its lack of gold exposed. The census of 1700 counted 20,000 inhabitants, includng 2,500 Spaniards. Owing to the area's limited natural resources, *hidalgos* (gentry) and *plebeyos* (commoners) alike were impoverished. The system of *repartimientos* (allotments), under which Native Americans were forced into labor on estates, was enforced throughout the Americas; in other Central American nations it resulted in sharp class divisions, with a subservient Native American and *mestizo* class at the bottom. In the case of Costa Rica, although 20,000 Indians were pressed into servitude, the system was a failure, and the captives either died or were assimilated. In lieu of the plantation-style estates that developed elsewhere in Latin America, small family-run farms emerged.

Well into the 18th C., the economy continued to be based on subsistence agriculture and barter transactions. Money had become so scarce that cacao beans were designated the official currency in 1709. The Talamanca highlands remained unvanquished and, in the early 17th C., the *zambos* (bandits of Native American-Black heritage) along with the Miskito Native Americans continually raided the Matina Valley in the Meseta Central. In order to halt the raids, a tribute was paid to the Miskito King from 1779 to 1841. Pirates also plagued the colony, resulting in closure of all of the ports and the collapse of exports. The pirate Henry Morgan and his brigands were turned back in 1666 from their attempt to sack Cartago by an outnumbered band of colonial militia – thought to be the result of divine intervention by the Virgin of Ujarrás, the saint whose image they had carried into battle. Things began to improve with the administration of Diego de la Haya Fernández (1718-27). Under his tenure, the port of Caldera was re-opened, the Matina Valley was fortified against Miskitos, and cacao plantations were developed. He oversaw the rebuilding of Cartago on a grander scale after it was destroyed by a volcanic eruption in 1723. Lacking a resident bishop, the Catholic Church here was not as strong as in other nations. However, the church encouraged farmers to settle near parishes and, in this fashion, Heredia (as Cubujuquí in 1706), Alajuela (as Villa Hermosa in 1782), and San José (as Villaneuva de la Boca del Monte in 1736) were founded.

INDEPENDENCE: In September 1821, the captain general of Guatemala proclaimed the independence of the Central American provinces without consulting Costa Rica. After meeting, the municipal councils of the four major towns (Cartago, San José, Heredia, and Alajuela) formed a junta to draft a provisional constitution. In May of 1822, the newly crowned Emperor of Mexico, Augustin de Iturbide, declared his authority over the Central American provinces. While Cartago and Heredia, out of the four main settlements, favored union with Mexico, San José and Alajuela favored either independence or union with the rest of Central America. Civil war erupted as Mexican supporters from Cartago and Heredia marched on San José, only to be defeated at Ochomongo. In March 1823, a provincial congress in Cartago declared independence from Spain and applied for union with Colombia, in an attempt to forestall an attack from Mexico. After Iturbide was over-thrown around the same time, however, opinion shifted, and the Costa Rican Congress voted in August 1823 to join the newly formed United Provinces of Central America (commonly referred to as the Central American Federation). It included Guatemala, Honduras, Nicaragua, and El Salvador. The first Jefe Supremo of the Free State of Costa Rica served from 1824-33. In 1824, the inhabitants of Guanacaste seceded from Nicaragua and elected to join Costa Rica. The unstable federation collapsed, and Costa Ricans thereafter were wary of attempts to unite Central America, believing themselves to have little in common with their neighbors in the region.

CIVIL WAR: In the early 1830s, geopolitical conflict erupted over the decision of where to base the capital. Heretofore, each of the four major cities had operated administratively as city states rather than as parts of the same nation. Under the Law of Movement enacted in 1834 under José Rafael de Gallegos, the capital was to be rotated from town to town every four years. This failed to resolve the conflict and, after the new head of state Braulio Carrillo Colina established the capital at

History

San José, the three rival towns formed the League of Cities under Nicolas Ulloa to oppose Carrillo. Crushing the revolt decisively that October, Carrillo went on largely to disregard the constitution. He seized dictatorial power after being defeated in an 1838 reelection bid. In 1841 he gave squatters title to government-owned agricultural land, abolished the constitution, and declared himself dictator for life. Carrillo was driven out of power by an alliance between one of his generals, Vincente Villasor, and Honduran Central American Federation proponent, Morazán. Shortly after their accession to power, these two also fell into disfavor and were executed.

THE FIRST PRESIDENT: In 1847 José María Castro Madriz, a 29-year-old editor and publisher, was named the nation's first president by the Congress. His wife, Doña Pacifica, designed the national flag. Declaring Costa Rica an independent republic the next year, he instituted a headstrong program of reforms – including constitutional changes and replacement of the army with a national guard – which resulted in his replacement by more conservative coffee baron Juan Rafael Mora Porras. Mora Porras encouraged the cultivation of coffee for export, an idea in harmony with the liberal laissez faire capitalism espoused in Europe at the time. Politics during this era consisted of rivalries between families. Suffrage was restricted by property and literacy qualifications to a small minority.

WAR WITH WILLIAM WALKER: In 1855 Tennesseean William Walker was deployed by Nicaraguan liberals at the head of a group of European and American mercenaries and given the mission of overthrowing the conservative government. Instead of handing power over to the liberals as had been originally agreed upon contractually, Walker installed himself as dictator and reintroduced slavery. Prodded on by business competitors of Cornelius Vanderbilt, he nationalized Vanderbilt's transport firm which carried gold seekers bound for California across Nicaragua. Vanderbilt retaliated by encouraging Mora Porras to declare war in February 1856. Walker invaded Guanacaste but, in April, the Costa Ricans attacked Rivas across the border. Drummer boy Juan Santamaría set fire to the town, driving out Walker's forces and setting himself up as Costa Rica's first and only national hero. Walker was decisively defeated by a coalition of Costa Rica and other Central American forces during the second battle of Rivas in April 1857. This war has been credited with giving the new nation's people their first sense of national unity. A border conflict with Nicaragua came on the heels of the war's finale. Under the Cañas-Juarez treaty of April 1858, Costa Rica's title to Guanacaste was confirmed and, while Nicaragua's right to the Río San Juan was acknowledged, Costa Rica was granted navigation rights.

THE MONTEALEGRES: After the war, Mora Porras was replaced by coffee baron José María Montealegre in a military coup. A new constitution, providing for limited suffrage as well as indirect election of the president via the Congress, was promulgated in 1859. Although "elections" continued, the army elite and the Montealegre family wielded the real power. In 1870, their chosen president, Jiménez Zamora, was ousted in the aftermath of a coup led by populist General Tomás Guardia Gutiérrez. His new constitution of 1871 was destined to last until 1949, and Guardia was formally elected in 1872. Although the constitution specified a one-term limit for presidential office holders, Guardia dismissed the new president in 1876 and ruled with an iron fist straight through from 1877 until his death in 1882. Although his avowed aim was to break the hold of the coffee barons – by redistributing land and imposing heavy taxes – what he in fact achieved was to replace this elite with another composed of his family and friends. Guardia encouraged public education, improved urban sanitation, abolished capital punishment, and provided trade incentives, but his foremost achievement was the laying of a railway line from the Caribbean coast to the Meseta Central. The line cost US$8 million and 4,000 lives. All of this development came at an additional cost, however, and the nation was saddled with a massive debt, which still had repercussions 40 years later.

POST-GUARDIA: Guardia was succeeded in office by his brother-in-law, army commmander Fernández Oreamuno. After his death in 1885, power passed to Bernardo Soto Alfaro, who created the nation's first free, compulsory public school system. Soto stepped down in 1889, and ushered in a new era when the first election with an unrestricted press, free debates, and an honest tally was held.

The election of José Joaquin Rodriguez Zeledón marked the first peaceful transition from those in power to the opposition. It also brought in members of the "Generation of '89," the young liberals who were to govern the nation and control its political life for all but a brief period over the next half-century. Although he came from a long liberal lineage, Rodriguez revealed himself to be yet another despot. Refusing to work together with the Congress, he dismissed it in 1892. That same year saw the formation of the Partido Union Catolica. The nation's first genuine political party, the PUC was organized by German-born bishop, Bernard August Thiel. Although the party was organized in reaction to the severe governmental curbs on the church's power (that had begun under Guardia and had continued to grow), it focused on criticizing the nation's economic inequities.

Political Parties

Workers' and Peasants Bloc	BOC
Center for the Study of National Problems	CEPN
Democratic Party	PD
Party of National Liberation	PLN
Communist Part	PC
National Republican Party	PRN
Catholic Union Party	PUC
National Union Party	PUN
Popular Vanguard Party	PVP
Social Christian Unity Party	PUSC
Social Democratic Party	PSD

The 20th Century

INTO THE 1900s: While Rodriguez picked Rafael Yglesias Castro to succeed him, the PUC fronted José Gregorio Trejos Gutierrez in the 1894 elections. Trejos Gutierrez won a plurality in spite of governmental fraud, but the Congress chose Yglesias, and a revolt in the countryside ended in the PUC's dissolution. Another in what was becoming a long line of authoritarian presidents, Yglesias arranged to have the constitution amended so that he might succeed himself in 1898. Ascensión Esquivel Ibarra, a compromise candidate agreeable to both the government and opposition, was selected in 1902. Esquivel was instrumental in fostering new democratic reforms and advancements in education, policies continued by his successor Cleto González Viquez. González was elected in 1906 in a five-way race. Although he had received the highest number of votes, his election was secured only after Esquivel had exiled the three candidates with the lowest count!

Ricardo Jiménez Oreamuno, who succeeded him in 1910, successfully pushed for a constitutional amendment, ratified in 1913. It established direct presidential election and, although the numbers remained small, it expanded voter franchise. Despite these improvements, the politics of *personalismo* still prevailed, and parties remained dormant until election time, when they awakened from hibernation to support their "liberal" candidate. Costa Rica's population had tripled from 1860 to 1913 and was now 360,000. A large number of immigrants had arrived from Spain, Germany, and Italy, and a new rural elite, comprising small farmers, was now making its presence felt in local government.

THE TINOCO DICTATORSHIP: Alfredo Gonzales Flores, picked as a compromise candidate by the Congress in 1914, followed Oreamuno. He faced a severe economic crisis brought on largely by falling coffee prices and the closure of the European markets due to the onset of WWI. Gonzales Flores attempted – through higher export levies on coffee and by proposing increased taxation of the upper classes – to prevent capital flight to the US. These moves lost him the elite's support. His cuts in government expenditures and civil service salaries proved unpopular among local politicians and governmental corruption lost him his popular backing. His government was overthrown in a January 1917 military coup led by his own secretary of war, General Federico Tinoco Granados.

Tinoco, too, soon lost his own widespread support. Woodrow Wilson had announced a policy of nonrecognition for governments that had not been democratically elected. This curtailed trade with the US. In August 1919, Tinoco handed over command to his vice president, Juan Batista Quiros Segura. The American Government, however, was still insistent on new elections. The US positioned the cruiser *USS Denver* off the coast, thus forcing Quiros's resignation. A former vice president under Gonzales Flores assumed command until Juan Acosta Garcia, who had been Gonzales Flores' foreign minister, was elected in 1920. Meanwhile, in 1916 Costa Rica had filed suit in the Central American Court, protesting the perpetual rights granted the US to build a trans-isthmian canal through Nicaragua. The canal would use a portion of the hotly contested Río San Juan. Although the court ruled against Nicaragua and the US in 1918, the defendants ignored the decision, and the discredited court subsequently disbanded. The southern border with Panama had been disputed since the days when that nation was part of Colombia. A conflict in 1921 between the two nations was settled only after US intervention.

"DEMOCRACY" RESTORED: In 1919 Julio Acosta Garcia was elected, taking office the following year. For the next three four-year terms, the presidency alternated between "liberal" past presidents Jiménez Oreamuno (Don Ricardo) and Gonzalez Viquez (Don Cleto). Despite the lack of any substantive differences between candidates in the 20s and 30s, campaigns were hotly contested, with frequent charges on both sides of voter manipulation and fraud. Secret ballots and yet wider suffrage were introduced during the 20s. Jiménez Oreamuno, under pressure from discontented laborers, pioneered minimum wage legislation, underwrote the establishment of a government-owned insurance monopoly offering low-cost coverage, and purchased untilled acreage from the United Fruit Company – out of which plots were distributed to landless farmers.

History

Over the course of time, the efficacy of the educational system had produced political awareness that gave rise to social dissent. During the 1930s, workers organized themselves, farmers became increasingly vocal, and the educated urban upper middle class complained about deficiencies in health care, housing, and transportation. Discontent focused on the prevailing system of liberal elite rule, concentrated in the hands of only a few families, and on its symbiotic relationship with a bureaucracy selected by patronage.

Returning from theological studies in Europe in 1912, Jorge Volio Jiménez published a journal propounding "Social Christianity," rooted in recent Catholic thought. Mercurial, often demagogic and enigmatic, Volio was politician, priest, scholar, and soldier – possibly the most original thinker and theorist of his era. He founded the Partido Reformista and entered the 1923 election on a platform calling for union legalization, taxes on the ruling class, and other broad social reforms. Coming in third, he became second vice president in the Jiménez Oreamuno administration, a position that compromised him in the eyes of his supporters, marking the end of his party. When he was implicated in a coup attempt, President Oreamuno explained that he had suffered a mental breakdown and shipped him off to Europe for an extended treatment. Volio continued to fight with his church superiors and was eventually defrocked.

THE LEFT EMERGES: Organized by 19-year-old student Manuel Mora Valverde in 1929, Bloque Obreros y Campesinos (Workers and Peasants Bloc) fielded candidates in the 1932 election. By the late 1930s, the BOC had gained control over important sectors of the labor movement, including Spanish-speaking banana plantation laborers. The party organized a 1934 strike that shut down the nation's banana production and forced United Fruit to equalize wages paid to Jamaican and Costa Rican workers.

León Cortés Castro, the PRN (National Republican Party) candidate, followed Jiménez Oreamuno in power in 1936. Like Oreamuno, Cortés intervened in order to stabilize prices and to encourage the growth of the banana industry, approving an extension of the Pacific railway. Suspected of being a Nazi sympathizer because of his ties to rich German expatriates, Cortés appointed a native German immigration official to prevent entry by Jews. He cracked down hard on the left, and his political opponents' civil rights were frequently curtailed.

In order to challenge Cortés in the 1940 election, Jiménez Oreamuno formed the Alianza Democratica (Democratic Alliance), which included the BOC. But he was forced to resign as its leader after obstructive pressure from Cortés. Cortés handpicked physician Rafael Angel Calderón Guardia to represent him until he could legally run for office again. Facing only token opposition, he won by a landslide.

THE CALDERON ERA: Surprisingly to Cortés, Calderón proved to be independent. Relying on patronage and *personalismo* for his support, the new president was the first to stress social and economic reforms as a priority. A staunch Catholic, he sought rapprochement with the Catholic church. He dictated reforms from above, reforms which made others in his social stratum view him as a traitor to his class. In 1941 Cortés broke with Calderón to form the Partido Demócrata.

While the PD opposed Calderón's proposed reforms, other critics charged that government inefficiency and corruption, rather than constitutional restrictions, stood in the way of their implementation. Other harsh critics were the Acción Demócrata, an organization formed by Francisco Orlich Bolmarcich and Alberto Marten, and the Centro para el Estudio de Problemas Nacionales (CEPN), which produced critiques and studies.

On December 8, 1941, Costa Rica declared war against Japan – largely a symbolic gesture since the nation had no men or other resources to offer. After the United Fruit Company's merchant vessel, the *S.S. San Pablo*, was torpedoed by a German submarine killing 27 and seriously hampering exports, Calderón enacted an alien property act. This enabled him to seize the property and assets of wealthy resident German and Italian families. Largely unknown landowner José Figueres Ferrer, encouraged by the CEPN, purchased airtime, using it to make a speech highly critical of governmental policy. Figueres was later arrested and sent into exile.

A series of 15 constitutional amendments, known collectively as the Social Guarantees, passed in 1943. These gave the Congress wider authority, paving the way for the administration's agenda of interventionist legislation. The bills encompassed social security legislation that included health insurance, a law allowing squatters title to land, and a comprehensive labor code – one that guaranteed some types of workers a minimum wage, ensured job security, mandated collective bargaining, and legalized strikes.

Calderón, together with the church under the leadership of Archbishop Sanabria, permitted the communists participation in the civil service, police, and government in exchange for their support. The PC (Communist Party) changed its name to the Partido Vanguardia Popular and included other leftist organizations, and Sanabria allowed Catholics to join the PVP. At the same time he encouraged Father Benjamin Nuñez Vargas to form the Confederacion Costarricense de Trabajo Rerum Novarum (Costa Rican Confederation of Labor Rerum Novarum), a Catholic-run labor union that would compete with the other, communist-led ones. In order to back Teodoro Picado Michalski, Calderón's handpicked successor, the PRN and PVP formed the Bloque de la Victoria (Victory Block). Anti-communist conservative Picado accepted the PVP's participation as necessary in order to defeat

Cortés. In what was a record turnout of 137,000 voters, Picado defeated Cortés two-to-one in the February 1944 election and also scored a similar victory in the legislature.

THE PICADO ADMINISTRATION: The Partido Social Democrata, PSD, was formed several months later, merging the Acción Democrata with the CEPN. This left-of-center, anti-communist party's platform advocated systematic progressive reform based on the prewar European social democratic party model. Decrying both present and past corruption and election manipulation, the PSD sought a complete overhaul for the system.

Figueres returned from exile in May 1944 and joined the party leadership. But, in spite of its staunch middle class backing, the PSD remained a marginal force. After Cortés' sudden death in 1946, Figueres joined the PD. His hopes were dashed, however, when he was defeated in his bid for leadership by conservative businessman Fernando Castro Cervantes. He then went on to form a splinter party with Cortés' son. Venerated conservative newspaper editor Otilio Ulate Blanco entered the 1948 election as the party's standard bearer. He revived the party name, Partido Unión Nacional (PUN), and was backed by business interests who feared Calderón's return to power.

In the meanwhile, the violence that had scarred the 1944 election campaign continued to escalate. Demonstrations, strikes, and coup attempts plagued the Picado administration, leaving it increasingly dependent on the communist-controlled worker's militia to provide security. Governmental opponents were periodically abducted and questioned without regard for their civil rights. Some were forced into exile. In 1946, after troops fired into a crowd protesting irregularities in off-year congressional elections, killing two and wounding several, Picado disavowed all responsibility. The Huelga de Brazo Caídos (Strike of the Fallen Arms) – which brought the nation to a virtual standstill for two weeks – was staged by merchants and managers in major cities. The communist militia attempted to break the strike by looting shops and distributing merchandise. But Picado was forced to capitulate, signing an agreement to place controls on the security forces and pledging that the next election would be fair.

While in exile, Figueres had plotted to overthrow the Calderón government, forming the Caribbean Legion, which was supported by Guatemala and Cuba. At Lucha Sin Fin (Struggle without End), his farmhouse base S of Cartago, Figueres continued to build his militia. Negotiating in Guatemala with other exile groups in 1947, he signed the Pact of the Caribbean in which he pledged to use Costa Rica as a base for liberating other countries struggling under dictatorships – including Honduras, the Dominican Republic, Venezuela, and Nicaragua – if they helped him to overthrow the Picado/Calderón regime.

Calderón still commanded working class backing, supported by both the PRN and the PVP, when he ran again in 1948. He also had the bureaucracy and the government apparatus to support him. Castro Cervantes and the PD opted to support Ulate. The reformist PSD also threw in its support. All denounced the violations of civil liberties and the governmental inefficiency that hallmarked the regime. Despite Picado's pledge, the security forces disrupted meetings and attempted to intimidate voters. With 100,000 votes counted on February 8, preliminary results showed that Ulate had won by a 10,000-vote margin. Both parties claimed that election irregularities had adversely affected balloting. After examination, the election commission upheld the results by two to one. The Picado administration maintained that the one dissenting member had invalidated its decision and insisted that the president be selected by the Calderón-controlled current legislature. The legislature voted 28 to 18 for annulment – leaving them free to name Calderón as the new president. Ulate was arrested and released the next day, an indication that the government was committed to holding power by whatever means necessary. Over the next two weeks Archbishop Sanabria attempted to mediate as Figueres assembled a 600-man volunteer army at La Lucha. The rebels were up against a small army and police force, the PRN-armed *calderonistas*, and the communist-run 3,000-man militia. Shortly after capturing an airfield and blocking the Interamerican Highway, Figueres was forced to retreat into the nearby mountains, leaving forces behind to cover the airfield. Capturing Puerto Limón and Cartago, Figueres forced the government's fall.

On April 19th, Picado and his lieutenant, Nuñez, signed a pact allowing for the government's conditional surrender at the Mexican Embassy in San José. Amnesty was granted to all those fighting on the government side. No one would be responsible for property that had been damaged or lost during the conflict, and the PVP as well as the communist-controlled labor union were guaranteed continued legality. Finally, it was agreed that the Social Guarantees would not be repealed. Calderón and Picado were exiled to Nicaragua and 74-year-old Santos León Herrera, who had been completing his third term as vice president, was appointed caretaker president. Known as the "War of National Liberation," this short-lived but brutal and divisive civil war left bitter after-effects. More than 2,000 died – mostly on the government side – and many more were wounded. Intervention by Nicaragua, which sent troops in to Guanacaste to buttress the government, was insufficient and arrived too late.

THE ULATE-FIGUERES ERA: Cognizant of the difficult realities facing the nation, Figueres and president-elect Ulate suppressed their differences of opinion for the common good. They both agreed to give power to an interim government for an 18-month period in which a constituent assembly would be elected and would prepare a new constitution. On May 8 Figueres became the president of the Junta Fundadora de la Segunda Republica (Founding Junta of the Second Republic), whose members were Marten, Orlich, and Nuñez. During the first 18 months the junta passed 834 decree-laws, many of which violated the suspended constitution as well as the cease fire agreements. One of the more notable of these was the law granting suffrage to women. Meanwhile, hundreds of *calderonistas* remained across the border in Nicaragua. The exposure of a counter-revolutionary plot as well as a large weapons cache enabled Figueres to renege on his pact with the former government. The PVP was outlawed, the communist-run unions banned, critics were purged from governmental posts and teaching positions, and over 200 communists were arrested. The Court of Immediate Sanctions, a special tribunal, was set up to punish retroactively alleged crimes committed during the previous administration and the civil war. Operating outside of the regular court system, no appeals were permitted. Astutely, Figueres abolished the army – a force not loyal to him – in December 1948, replacing it with a 1,500-man Guardia Civil. His Caribbean Legion, however, continued to operate independently.

At the beginning of that same month Costa Rica had ratified the Interamerican Treaty of Reciprocal Assistance (Rio Treaty), a mutual defense pact between Central American nations in which the US served as guarantor. On December 10, a week after its ratification, 800 well-equipped *calderonistas* poured in from Nicaragua. When the envisioned general revolution failed to materialize, the insurgents pulled back. While the OAS (Organization of American States) harshly criticized Nicaragua for its support of the invasion, it also rebuked Costa Rica for permitting Nicaraguan exiles to train on its territory and advised that the Caribbean Legion be disbanded. In April 1949, the minister of public security, Colónel Edgar Cardona Quirós, attempted a coup, which garnered no support.

The youthful PSD activists, who were in charge of drawing up proposals for the new constitution, had their radical recommendations largely rejected by the mostly-PUN constituted assembly. The body even omitted the term "Second Republic" from the constitution's final version. The 1949 constitution, Costa Rica's eighth since 1825, established separation of powers and embodied the substance of the Social Guarantees. The function of the Figueres-devised Tribuno Supremo de Eleciones (TSE) was to supervise elections.

On November 8, 1949 Ulate and the Legislative Assembly took power. Most of Figueres changes were left intact by the Ulate government. The high price of coffee and the reopening of the banana plantations brought revenues in, and the external debt left by the junta was reduced by US$30 million during the first two years. The World Bank financed construction of a new airport as well as the purchase of agricultural and industrial equipment. The US aided in financing the building of a dam and power plant on the Río Reventazón.

In late 1951 Figueres formed the Partido Liberación Nacional and announced his candidacy for the July 1953 election. Incorporating the PSD, the broader-based social democratic PLN identified itself with the Figueres-led victory and the as-yet-unfulfilled promise of a Second Republic. Its platform stressed that institutional reform and modernization were prerequisites to substantive social reform. This could be achieved through improved efficiency, advanced technology, and long-term planning. Despite the party's pro-American stance, it advocated monitoring and regulation of foreign companies and investment. Although Figueres designed the party as a permanent organization – one that would operate independently of any specific individual – it came to revolve, nevertheless, around "Don Pepe," as Figueres was known to his followers.

FIGUERES SECOND TERM: In the 1954 elections the PUN candidate withdrew, and both the PUN and the PD united behind the candidacy of conservative businessman, Fernando Castro Cervantes. Figueres promises to end poverty and improve the standard of living for all classes contrasted sharply with Castro Cervantes, who put forward no program other than opposition to Figueres. Figueres was elected by a two-to-one margin in July. His controversial administration renegotiated its contract with United Fruit, doubled income taxes imposed on the wealthy, financed agricultural development and food processing projects with revenue generated by the governmental alcohol monopoly, and hiked import duties to shelter fledgling industries. Critics charged that these expansive, expensive policies increased inflation, indebtedness, and economic instability. In pushing through his legislative agenda, Figueres had faced bitter opposition in the Legislative Assembly from both the PLN and the conservative opposition. Nor was any love lost between Nicaragua's dictator Somoza Garcia and Figueres. They hated each other's guts and actively plotted one another's demise. After captured members of a coup attempt revealed that they were Costa Rican-trained, Somoza Garcia challenged Figueres to a duel. Figueres responded by advising him to "grow up." Figueres also sheltered opponents of dictators ruling in the Dominican Republic and Venezuela.

INSURGENTS INVADE: On January 11, 1955, several hundred *calderonistas* – well armed and equipped – poured across the border from Nicaragua. Moving swiftly, this self-proclaimed "Authentic Anti-Communist Revolutionary Army" captured Quesada, lying about 50 km

NW of San José, and took over sections of Guanacaste. One of their aircraft strafed San José. Two days later an OAS fact-finding mission decided that, despite Nicaragua's denials, the forces had come from Nicaragua, and Nicaragua was told to capture the insurgents operating from its territory. Fulfilling the terms of the Río treaty, the US sold Costa Rica four fighter aircraft for US$1, which served to deter any additional air attacks. Somoza Garcia, protesting the shipment, claimed that the US was "putting dangerous toys in the hands of a lunatic." Quesada was retaken on January 21, and the two nations agreed on a demilitarized zone. The OAS-recommended formal treaty of friendship remained unsigned until December 1956, three months after Somoza Garcia's assassination.

ECHANDI'S ADMINISTRATION: In the 1958 election Ulate was still ineligible to run again under the constitution, so Echandi was again selected as the PUN's candidate. The PLN's choice was Francisco Orlich Bolmarich. A close friend of Figueres, he had served as party leader in the Legislative Assembly. Late in 1956, after a disagreement on financial policy, Figueres' finance minister, Jorge Rossi Chavarria, broke away – along with many of the party's moderates – to form the Partido Independiente. Rossi split the PLN vote, ensuring Echandi's victory. The PLN now held 20 seats in the Legislative Assembly, as opposed to the PR's 11, the PUN's 10, and the PI's three. The PR's strong showing was evidence that Calderón's support base, even after a decade in exile, was still considerable. Lacking a majority in the legislature, free enterprise advocate Echandi was unable to alter Figueres's basic programs and policies. After coffee prices plummeted in 1957, Echandi was forced to borrow money abroad, and the national debt mounted further.

THE 1960s: Two former presidents, Ulate for the PUN and a newly returned Calderón heading the PR slate, contended in the 1962 election. But a healed PLN, with Francisco Orlich Bolmarich again its candidate, won half the vote. Calderón ran a distant second, Ulate a poor third, and a pro-Cuban Marxist party candidate received fewer than 3,000 votes. Although the administration expropriated unused United Fruit Company land as well as large individually owned estates for redistribution to landless farmers, support waned as the economy plummeted headlong into a recession. Striking banana plantation workers blamed Orlich for the industry's decline.

Irazú's untimely March 1963 eruption, which coincided with US President Kennedy's visit, devastated the vital agricultural region surrounding San José. The right wing assaulted the cancerous growth in the public sector which, according to some estimates, consumed half of the GNP.

Despite their past roles as opponents in the civil war, Ulate and Calderón swallowed their differences and, together with former president Echandi, formed the conservative Unificacion Nacional. For the 1966 presidential election, they threw their support behind anti-PLN candidate Trejos Fernandez, a little-known university professor. Figueres, although now constitutionally eligible once more, decided not to run. Accordingly, the PLN selected the party's aggressive left wing leader Daniel Oduber Quiros, who had challenged Orlich for the nomination four years earlier. Trejos's "neo-liberal" candidacy promised an administration attentive to the needs of the private sector. His influential backers propagated fears that another PLN victory would lead to a one-party state. Backing given Oduber by the communist Alianza Socialista Popular, an organization found constitutionally ineligible to field its own candidate, did him more harm than good. In the end, Trejos won 222,800 votes to Oduber's 218,000. Introducing a sales and import tax, Trejos worked to slash public sector expenditures. His grant of a strip mining concession to ALCOA aroused ire.

FIGUERES RETURNS: Representing himself as a candidate of the "democratic left," Figueres handily triumphed over Echandi in the 1970 presidential contest, harvesting 55% of the vote. His second administration concerned itself with improving and extending past PLN-initiated programs, rather than breaking new ground. Attempts were made to diversify the economy in order to loosen its dependence on bananas and coffee. Just before his inauguration in April 1970, student and non-student demonstrators stormed the legislature buildings to protest approval of ALCOA's strip mining concession. This and subsequent disturbances were blamed on communist agitation.

Figueres was tainted by his association with Robert Vesco. When Vesco – who had invested heavily in the country and applied for citizenship – was indicted in the US, a Costa Rican judge refused to issue extradition papers, claiming that its extra dition treaty with the US failed to cover the charges against him. Allegations in the US linked Figueres with this white collar criminal, claiming that Vesco had showered him with campaign contributions, personal gifts, and investment capital for one of his businesses.

THE MID 70s: In 1974 Oduber broke with the nation's informal different-party-each-term tradition by securing 42% of the vote in a field of eight candidates. During the campaign, the issue of alleged communist subversion had been so intense that the election tribunal banned the use of the words "Marxist" and "communist" from the campaign. Oduber called for nationalization, higher taxes, land redistribution, and strengthening of the public sector to increase employment and raise the standard of living. After the party's proscription had been lifted by a constitutional amendment, Mora Valverde revived the PVP.

Oduber reopened trade with Cuba and reestablished diplomatic relations, broken under the Orlich administration in 1962. After the tax on banana exports was raised by more than a third in May 1975, Oduber had to threaten the multinational fruit companies with expropriation in order to force them to pay the tax. He encouraged export-oriented agricultural production at the expense of local industries that produced goods for local consumption. In mid-1976, a party crisis arose when Figueres pressed for a constitutional amendment that would allow the president to succeed himself. To add to the tense atmosphere, electrical workers went on strike, and a plot to overthrow the government was unveiled.

As Oduber's administration reached its finale, Figueres withdrew from party activities, the economy continued to worsen, and the Sandinista struggle against dictator Anastasio Somoza Debayle in neighboring Nicaragua threatened to suck Costa Rica in. In the 1978 election, Figueres decided not to campaign for Monge, the PLN's candidate.

The greater part of the opposition, composed of right-of-center groups, organized the Unidad Opositora (Unity Opposition) which fielded businessman and former PLN-member, Rodrigo Carazo Odio. Taking a firm anti-communist line, Carazo pledged to recall the Costa Rican ambassador in Moscow. He also promised to expel Robert Vesco. As head of his own party in 1974, Carazo had won only 10% of the vote. But this time he took 49% in the five-candidate race to Monge's 42%. Unidad secured 27 seats in the Legislative Assembly, the PLN took 25, and the Pueblo Unido, a leftist coalition, won three.

THE TURBULENT 1980s: Relations with Nicaragua had deteriorated throughout the end of the 70s, culminating with Costa Rica's breaking relations in November 1978, and calling for Nicaragua's expulsion from the OAS. Costa Rica actively supported the Sandinistas in their struggle, serving as a conduit for supplies and arms – a very profitable business – to the 5,000 Costa Rican-based troops under Eden Pastora Gomez. After Somoza fled in July 1979, Costa Rica recognized Nicaragua's provisional junta.

Banana plantation workers struck again in 1979 and in 1980. In March of 1981, three USMC American Embassy guards were wounded when Costa Ricans attacked their vehicles. A San José shootout with terrorists in June left three Civil Guardsmen dead. A public rally in San José, called to protest the government's perceived lack of effectiveness in dealing with violence, turned violent itself when guardsmen, attempting to intervene as the crowd called for Carazo's resignation, were stoned. Relations with Cuba were again severed that May.

As Unidad fought within itself and the PLN refused to cooperate, Carazo was forced to govern by presidential decree. By the end of his term, the nation's foreign debt climbed to a staggering US$3 billion, up from US$800 million, and foreign reserves were depleted. Its per capita indebtedness was calculated to be the world's highest and unemployment rose to 14%. In September 1981, the government officially suspended payments on its external debt and, in November, it halted bond repayments and requested debt payment rescheduling. This move, along with other violations of a pact reached earlier in the year with the IMF, caused the fund to suspend the release of scheduled loan funds and to close down its Costa Rican office.

MONGE'S TENURE: Distancing itself from the now battered and beleaguered Carazo, Unidad nominated 33-year-old Rafael Angel Calderón Fournier, son of a former president. In February 1982, the PLN's Monge won 53% of the vote against Calderón Fournier's 33%. The remaining 10% was distributed among the other candidates, including former president Echandi Jiménez. The PLN increased its seats to 33 in the Assembly, a comfortable majority.

Doctors went on strike in April 1982 for 42 days after the government refused them a US$40 increase in their base pay. At Del Monte's Banana Development Company, 3,000 workers struck, demanding an increase; their wages averaged 67¢ per hour! Six strikers were wounded after Rural Guards fired at them. Monge had run on a *"Volvamos a la Tierra"* or a "Return to the Land" slate; he continued and even increased agricultural subsidies. Monge also announced a "100-Day Plan" designed to deal with the weakening *colón*, enormous public deficit, rising inflation, and a decline in confidence by foreign investors. Under his administration, although the economy's decline was stabilized, with marked reductions in inflation and unemployment, economic problems remained severe. In 1983, teachers, telephone workers, and petroleum workers struck. In September 1983 thousands marched through the streets of San José in reaffirmation of the nation's neutrality. On September 28, the CIA instigated a confrontation at the Peñas Blancas border crossing, using anti-Sandinista guerillas belonging to ARDE, Eden Pastora's Democratic Revolutionary Alliance.

The foreign debt climbed to US$3.8 billion by 1984, exceeding the US$3.1 billion GDP, and a more than threefold increase since 1981. Between 1979 and 1984, the GNP per capita declined 13%, the official unemployment rate increased 69.5%, the *colón* was devalued dramatically and both imports and exports declined. With intraregional commerce cut off and depressed agricultural export prices, the economy was in trouble. Monge also brought back the army in the camouflaged form of the paramilitary Organizacion Para Emergencias Nacionales (OPEN). In May 1984, 20-30,000 people marched through San José,

History

demanding that Monge uphold the nation's policy of neutrality after the nation received US$4.6 million in military aid that year. In an attempt to counteract this drift to the right, fostered by the nation's dependence upon the US, Monge left for Europe on a "Truth Mission" in June and July; although promises of US$375 million in aid from Europe were announced, only a trickle of that amount ever came in, and US aid continued to exercise a dominant influence. Also that year a new labor law replaced the nation's trade union movement with a system of worker-employer cooperatives.

THE 1986 ELECTIONS: In a break with two traditions – one in which parties customarily alternate terms and the other of not electing a candidate on his first try – PLN candidate Oscar Arias Sanchez won over PUSC candidate Rafael Angel Calderón Fournier. Holder of a doctorate in economics from the University of Essex, Arias came from a wealthy family. The PLN also retained a slim legislative majority, with 29 of the 57 seats.

After the US Army Corp of Engineers arrived to begin public works projects involving bridge construction on the Pacific Highway, President-elect Arias, while supporting the plan, made this controversial statement: "If I were President Reagan I would give the US$100 million (in Contra aid) to aid the economies of Costa Rica, El Salvador, and Honduras instead." Just before the election he dedicated the last of the 80,000 homes promised under his National Housing Program.

THE 1990 ELECTIONS: Successful at last after three tries at the presidency, lawyer Rafael Angel Calderón defeated by a 51.3% to 47.2% margin economist and conservative PLN leader Dr. Carlos Manuel Castillo. Castillo's party was plagued by political infighting during the campaign. As there were few substantive differences between the two candidates – both lived in glass houses which the other had the stones to break – the campaign was a ho-hum affair. The issue of corruption lay dormant. Castillo triumphed over the younger Rolando Araya in the Liberation primary after $750,000 in alleged drug money was found wrapped with Araya campaign stickers and after top Araya aide Ricardo Alem was charged with attempting to launder money. (Araya was later cleared of the charges, and – amid much hoopla – Alem was apprehended in Miami in 1995.) The resignation of Liberation deputy Leonel Villalobos was also demanded after he allegedly per formed improper favors for naturalized Costa Rican Fernando Melo, who was accused of links to drug traffickers. After denying it at first, Castillo was forced to admit that he had received a $2,364 donation from Melo in 1985, thus throwing his credibility and morality into doubt. To top this all off, his close friend and former boss, ex-President Daniel Oduber admitted receiving a one million *colón* contribution from US citizen James Lionel Casey, who is wanted for drug charges in the States. On the other hand, Calderón denied an accusation that he had received cash donations of $500,000 in 1985 from Panama's General Noriega.

CALDERON DAYS: With a background that includes a two-year stint as head of the Costa Rican Association for the Defense of Democracy and Liberty (an organization closely linked to the US Republican Party) and a personal friendship with George Bush, whose consultant Roger Ailes contributed to his campaign, there is no mistaking Calderón's right wing orientation. Despite his father's reputation and his nickname of "Junior," he is definitely no friend of the left. Calderón, called by his detractors a *caballo con ropa* (a "horse with clothes"), swiftly moved to raise prices on clothing, housing, fuels, power, water, and telephones. Calderón's administration was marred by an incident in which a drug raid by the Green Beret-trained section of the elite Immediate Action Unit led to the accidental death of a 12-year-old. Despite the trauma it caused, the unit was not dissolved and the boy's killer was dealt with more leniently than the average petty thief. Calderón had promised to cut the fiscal deficit from 30 million *colones* to 20 million; the deficit rose. He promised to cut public sector spending, increase employment, jail all pickpockets, provide small farmers with credit, construct thousands of new homes, repair the roads, and cut taxes! Some houses have been built, but spending has grown, and the other goals remain unaccomplished.

1992 and 1993 EVENTS: On February 21, members of the Commando Cobra, a 12-member Guardia Rural patrol, brutally murdered two unarmed men carrying sacks of marijuana. They are also charged with raping two young Indian women. One of the most noteworthy incidents of 1992 was the two-week takeover of the Nicaraguan Embassy by José Manuel Urbina, a former Contra and nationalized Costa Rican. Seizing the embassy, his group took 21 hostages and demanded both money and political change in Nicaragua. They settled for $250,000 in ransom money and tickets to the Dominican Republic. In 1993, a group calling itself the "Death Commando" took over the Supreme Court. Among the 23 taken hostage were 18 Supreme Court justices. They demanded the release of four prisoners held in Costa Rica on drug trafficking charges, passage to an unspecified country, and $20 million in ransom. Although the terrorists were initially thought to be Columbian, it turned out that the ringleaders were Gilberto and Guillermo Fallas, a pair of Tico brothers who had worked for the Judicial Police and the Ministry of Public Security. Their motivation was Guillermo's perceived need for a liver transplant. The ransom was reduced to $8 million and then to a comparatively paltry $150,000, and the promised passage to Guatemala. They disarmed before boarding the airplane and were apprehended.

THE 1994 CAMPAIGN: The Liberación primary focussed on three contenders. The most controversial is José María Figueres, the son of the former President. A 1976 *Washington Post* article, which resurfaced during the campaign, quotes CIA reports naming "a relative of President Figueres" as a member of a death squad that "executed at least one narcotics trafficker in early 1973 and has sworn to kill more." Although the case – involving the murder of a Mexican drug dealer – was declared closed by a judge in 1976, the 1991 book, *El Caso Chemise*, has revived the controversy, alleging that Figueres, who was working for the narcotics police at the time, murdered the alleged marijuana dealer while he was in his custody. To get the nomination, Figueres defeated Margarita Penón de Arias, wife of former president Arias, who had never held political office. Although Figueres was also linked to a gold mining investment fraud led by US white collar criminals, he still triumphed over the PUSC's Miguel Angel Rodriguez.

THE FIGUERES PRESIDENCY: Figueres has proven unpopular and his policies have evoked controversy because they have been so far afield of what is expected from a Liberación President. Government-owned utility rate hikes during 1994 hit the poor hard, and prices were raised on other essentials as well. In May 1994 riot police fired M-16 rifles at a crowd of some 200 striking banana workers at the Geest plantation complex in the Sarapiquí area. The workers had been blocking road access to protest a wage cut and the dismissal of workers who had joined the union. On September 14, 1994, the President asked the Congress to shut down operations of the bankrupt Banco Anglo Costarricense. Founded in 1863, the bank was the nation's oldest, but had suffered losses of $102 million in previous months as a result of an unauthorized venture in Venezuelan foreign debt bonds along with illegal overdrafts and uncollectible loans. Massive fraud was uncovered at the INS, the national insurance company, and the national public deficit climbed to 267 billion *colones* (around $1.5 billion). In October, the Anti-Drug Police arrested a US citizen with six kilos of heroin in her baggage; this was the largest bust (worth $2 million on the street) in Costa Rican history.

Tropical storm Gordon ravaged the Pacific coast and the Meseta Central in November 1994; the storm forced 1,500 to evacuate and left 600 homeless, causing some $15 million in damages. In June 1995, Figueres announced plans to plant 3.2 million trees before his term runs out in 1998. That May, he forged a pact with opponent Calderón and his Unity Party. In order to relieve the public debt, Figueres had to pass an increase in the sales tax (from 10% to 15%) as well as other taxes, and government sector jobs had to be cut back. A teachers' strike began on July 17. On July 26, tens of thousands of teachers and employees of government agencies slated for closing marched on the Casa Presidencial in Zapote and called for curtailment of the reform plans as well as the overhaul of teachers' pension plans. Violence erupted that evening when 50 out of some 50,000 demonstrators started hurling rocks. Teachers agreed to return to work on August 21 in return for a fresh evaluation of their case before Congress. To relieve the public debt, in late 1995 Figueres had to pass an increase in the sales tax (from 10% to 15%) along with other taxes, and government sector jobs had to be cut back.

Important Dates in Recent History

1948: Nationwide strike, Huelga de Brazos Caidos. Civil War leads to victory for Figueres forces and flight of Calderón and Picado.

1949: Ulate becomes President. Catholicism declared official religion.

1952: Figueres forms Partido Liberación Nacional (PLN).

1954: Election of Figueres.

1955: *Calderonistas* invade and are dispersed.

1958: Conservative Mario Echandi Jiménez elected.

1962: Francisco Orlich Bolmarich elected President.

1963: Costa Rica joins Central American Common Market.

1966: José Trejos is elected President.

1970: José Figueres elected to a second presidential term.

1974: Daniel Oduber Quiros elected President.

1978: Unity party candidate Rodrigo Carazo Odio is elected.

1979: Costa Rica supports Sandinistas.

1982: PLN's Luis Alberto Monge Alvarez is elected. Debt repayment halted.

1983: Presence of Contras on Costa Rican soil raises problems with Nicaragua. IMF agrees to reschedule external debt.

1984: La Penca terrorist bombing. Monge reaffirms neutrality but US opposition to this move results in resignation of Foreign Minister.

1985: United Brands sells its banana plantations.

1986: PLN candidate Oscar Arias Sanchez triumphs over PUSC candidate Rafael Angel Calderón.

1989: President Arias receives Nobel Peace Prize.

1990: PUSC candidate Rafael Angel Calderón elected President.

1994: Figueres elected President. Bankrupt Banco Anglo Costarricense shuts down.

History

Government

With of the strongest democratic traditions in Central America, Costa Rica is one of the most politically stable nations in the hemisphere. The nation has had only two violent interludes in its history, during the periods of 1917-19 and 1948-49. Of the more than 50 presidents, only six have been considered dictators and only three have come from the military. The nation's relatively homogeneous population, its large middle class, traditional respect for the rule of law, geographical isolation, and lack of a large military establishment have all contributed to its political stability.

Political Structure

Despite having declared itself a sovereign republic in 1848, Costa Rica has gone through a number of changes in its constitutional format. Established as a democratic and unitary republic by the 1949 constitution, the Costa Rican government is divided into executive, judicial, and legislative branches. The executive branch consists of the President, two Vice Presidents, and the *Consejo de Gobierno* (Council of Government). Although there is a carefully designed system of checks and balances and presidential power is (by Latin American standards) limited, the President commands the central position of power. His control is restricted by the legislature's right to override his veto, the Supreme Court's ability to establish the constitutionality of administrative acts and legislation, and the one-term, four-year limit.

There is no official army, and the large police force reverts to the control of the Tribunal Supremo de Eleciones (TSE), which supervises the elections (the so-called *Fiesta Política*) during campaigns. A fourth branch of government are the state's 200 autonomous institutions, including the Pacific Electric Railroad, the Social Security Institute, the Electric Institute, the University of Costa Rica, and all banks, including the Central Bank. A unicameral body elected for a four-year term, the National Assembly has 57 members, distributed proportionately, with one for every 30,000 Costa Ricans. It may override a presidential veto with a two-thirds majority. No rubber stamp, its exclusive powers include the right to declare war and peace, determine the national budget, impeach the President, and – disturbingly – suspend civil rights for up to 30 days.

LOCAL GOVERNMENT: Ruled by appointed governors, the nation's seven provinces all have capitals of the same name, with the exception of Guanacaste, whose capital is Liberia. While Alajuela, Heredia, San José, and Cartago lie entirely inland, Guanacaste, Puntarenas, and Limón border the coasts. Provinces are divided into a grand total of 81 *cantones* (counties); these, in turn, are divided into 344 *distritos* (districts). The *municipalidad* (municipal council) of each *canton* controls services ranging from trash collection to road maintenance.

POLITICAL PARTIES: Largest and most influential of these is the Partido de Liberación Nacional (PLN, National Liberation Party), founded by the nation's elder statesmen José "Don Pepe" Figueres. Opposition comes from the currently ruling, more conservative Partido Unidad Social Cristiana (PUSC, Social Christian Unity), a loose confederation of four different parties known from 1978-1983 as the Coalicion Unidad. Other, much smaller and less influential parties include the Partido del Progreso (Progressive Party), the religious and conservative Partido Alianza Nacional Cristiana, the Trotskyite Partido Revolucionario de los Trabajores en Lucha (Revolutionary Party of Workers in Struggle) and the Pueblo Unido, a coalition of two left-wing parties. In recent elections, their combined share of the vote has dropped from eight to around one or two percent. Some voters, disheartened and disillusioned with the two major parties, turn in blank ballots. In the 1990 polls one witty soul plastered pictures of cattle (including one wearing a suit and tie) and of two pigs (one of them feeding) on his ballot, scrawling the word "no" prominently in three places.

ELECTIONS: Costa Rica has universal suffrage for all citizens over the age of 18, and voting is compulsory for all citizens under 70. Turnout has been about 80% in the past few elections. Voting is by secret ballot, with the voter indicating his choice by placing a thumbprint in a box set under the party's name, a full color flag, and the candidate's photo; there is also a separate ballot for the congressional and municipal races. Here one votes for the party, with its full slate of candi dates, rather than picking individual candidates. After voting, each citizen has his or her right index finger dipped in a jar of purple indelible ink. Citizens are automatically registered to vote on their 18th birthdays if they receive a *cedula de identidad*, a numbered identity card, complete with name, address, fingerprints, and photo. The autonomous Tribunal Supremo de Elecíones supervises the electoral process. Composed of three magistrates and three alternates, all selected by the Supreme Court and serving staggered six-year terms, the TSE exerts complete control, even reserving the right to ban an established party. Even though additional advertising is affordable only by the two major parties, all registered parties are granted equal TV and radio airtime. The

Government

government also contributes funds for campaign expenses and 5% of the national budget is distributed to parties in proportion to the votes they received in the previous elections. (The catch is that a party must have received a minimum of 5% to qualify.) National Assemblies (party conventions) choose candidates. Every four years elections are held on the first Sunday in February. The weeks previous to the election are marked by *plazas publicas* (demonstrations featuring sound systems, speakers, and bands), car honking, and flag waving. If the President and two Vice presidents fail to receive 40% of the vote, a special runoff election pits the two top contenders against each other. In the unlikely event that the top two contenders receive the exact same percentage, the oldest will be selected. Of special significance is the fact that the President cannot be reelected and is banned from running for the office again. This may be one reason why Costa Rica's history differs from nations such as the Dominican Republic, where a demagogue like Balaguer may steal elections over and over again.

Economy

To understand Costa Rica's economy you must consider a number of factors. First of all, the nation's small size and relatively small population have hampered industrial development. And the incessant regional instability, along with socio-cultural and political differences, has prevented development of a truly unified regional economic block. Secondly, the nation has always been a plantation economy, with agricultural exports commanding chief importance. Third, the same lack of industrial development that has hampered the economy in other ways has also made it necessary to import a large number of items from the "developed" world (the US in particular), running up a substantial deficit in the process. The last factor is the government's role as employer: about 20% of the population works directly or indirectly for the public sector.

Recent Events

THE 1970s and 1980s: Between the 1960s and the late 70s the GDP grew 6% in real terms annually, with low inflation except during the period surrounding the oil crisis. Per capita income rose from US$838 (1960) to US$1,630 (1979) – a level well above that of any other Central American nation. The economy hit its peak in 1976-77, slowing down thereafter as agricultural expansion ceased and new markets shrank.

The 1980s were turbulent times. President Carazo (1978-82) floated the *colón* in 1980, and the *colón* dropped from 8.54 to the US$ in 1981 to 52 in May of 1982. The national debt reached US$1.3 billion in 1982, nearly 85% of the GNP. The inflation rate hit 100% that year. After Monge took over, the situation improved as he reschedul the nation's $4 billion foreign debt twice. By early 1983, average industrial wages had dropped to a point where they were, at less than 20¢ US per hour, on a par with Haiti. During 1983 aid rose to $350 million, and the trade balance had improved to negative $30 million by the end of the year. The 1988 inflation rate hit 25.3%. Although the administration had agreed with the IMF directive to limit the 1989 deficit to seven billion *colones* (about $81 million), the true figure has been estimated at 14 billion *colones*, an all time high.

THE 1990s: Inflation topped 20% in 1990. In May 1990, Costa Rica re-purchased two-thirds ($1.2 billion) of its outstanding $1.8 billion foreign debt from international banks for the bargain price of $253 million, a deal that was the final achievment of the Arias administration. Under Calderón, the current President, the currency has continued to lose its value. Although devaluation adds to the wealth in local currency of the wealthy agroexporters, it hurts the poor, who must cope with the resulting inflation, and the gap between rich and poor widens still further. It also makes domestic assets cheaper, expediting their passage to foreign control. According to official estimates, some 40,000 Costa Rican families live in extreme poverty, with each household averaging at least seven members. In Los Cuadros, an urban slum (*tugurio*) located a few km from San José, households have an income of only 10-15,000 *colones* per month. Single mothers, who constitute 25% of the population here, have incomes of only 3-5,000 a month! Countrywide, the average income is about $175 per month, and the cost for a basic basket of 69 staple items (reduced from 158 items in 1994 in order to camouflage decay of buying power) is $165!

In March 1995 the World Bank announced it was witholding its share of funds (amounting $100 million) required to implement PAE III, the Third Structural Adjustment Program. It cited policies it viewed as economically unstable, as well as the fiscal deficit (8% of GDP and the highest in Latin America) and high interest rates. The announcement came a day after the government reached an emergency standby agreement with the International Monetary Fund (IMF), which it had hoped would persuade the World Bank to release the needed funds. In order to appease the World Bank, Figueres hopes to put through tax increases and cut government spending.

US AID: Foreign assistance in the years 1981-84 totalled US$3 billion, without which the economy would have collapsed. The economy's small size (with a 1985 GDP of just over $4 billion) meant that these donations were of overwhelming importance. Much of the money was kept out of government hands; AID (The Agency for International Development) set up institutions resembling a "parallel state" to parcel out the funds. In 1984 Costa Rica received US$180 million from US AID, making it the highest per capita recipient (after Israel) for such contributions. The next year the total rose to $231.2 million, including $11.2 million in military aid. The figure dropped off during the Arias years, after he refused to make the nation a center for Contra resistance and the Bush administration reduced aid from $90.4 million in 1990 to $65 million in 1991. But all of this money does not come without some advantage to the US. In 1989, 43% of the nation's imports came from the US. In 1992, the World Bank and the IDB promised to grant $370 million in aid. The Finance Council warned that the new loans constituted a "time bomb." The external debt reached $3.6 billion by the end of 1992, constituting 64% of GDP and 150% of imports. The internal government debt had grown to $967.2 million by the end of 1992, an increase of over 100% since May 1990.

FOREIGN INVESTMENT: One recent element in the economic pie is Japanese investment. Businessmen, who have invested $52 million in the country, are expected to bring in another $100 million for the development of a large tourism complex on Nicoya's Playa Carrillo. To date, they have invested in luxury hotels and other tourist projects, and have purchased a share in LACSA, the national airline.

Investment Scams

Con men are everywhere in the world, and Costa Rica is no exception. Recent examples have included a teak "reforestation" project (cutting down trees and replanting with teak) that promised great returns, but could not deliver. Then there was an unregistered "Rain Forest for Kids Foundation" that launched an aborted attempt to market "Rain Forest Seeds" packets using artwork stolen from a Costa Rican artist. A third scheme – developed in cooperation with the Dutch branch of the World Wildlife Fund – promises exhorbitant profits for investors who put money into its teak farm. One American who operated an investment firm in San José was exposed as a charlatan in late 1994. Such carpetbaggers span all nationalities, from Swiss to Canadian, so let the investor beware!

SOLIDARISMO: Any discussion of the economic situation would be incomplete without mention of *Solidarismo*. Created in 1948 by Alberto

Marten as an alternative to the communist-run labor unions, the over 1,300 *Solidarismo* associations operating nationwide are savings associations that work hand in hand with management. The workers invest a fixed percentage of their wage (generally 5%) into a savings fund, an amount which the company then matches with money from a severance pay fund. (Companies are legally obliged to deposit 8.33% of their payroll in a fund to cover payoffs for dismissals.) While some find the system works well for them, there have been complaints of abuses from members as well as from unions, who claim the *Solidarismo* philosophy is designed to destroy their collective bargaining groups. It is also alleged that many *Solidarismo* groups are run by patsies for management who do not have the best interests of workers in mind. In 1993, the AFL-CIO spoke out against what it felt were clear violations of workers' rights and is striving to have Costa Rica excluded from the Caribbean Basin Initiative (CBI), membership in which gives Costa Rican goods preferential tariff treatment. The labor union believes that such an exclusion would strengthen workers' bargaining position.

LIGHT INDUSTRY: The nation's manufacturing industry dates from the early 20th C., when factories to produce such consumables as textiles, cigarettes, and beer were established. The government later adopted the policy of *desarrolo hacia adentro* (internally oriented development). However, its impact has proved disappointing, and the nation is still heavily dependent upon exports.

Since WWII, the government has nationalized many industries. At first this was confined to banking, power companies, and telecommunications. In the 1970s, agriculture and industry started to become nationalized as well. The government set up corporations to manage projects that were either too expensive for or not of interest to private firms. Along with the enactment of the 1959 Industrial Development Law, establishment of the CACM (Central American Common Market) in 1960 accelerated expansion of manufacturing. The CACM established intra-regional free trade along with protective barriers against outside competition.

The nation's open attitude towards foreign investment, combined with its relatively high educational level, has spurred the economy. The wide variety of goods produced today includes bricks, cement, fertilizers, paints, plastics, solar energy collectors, petroleum products, textiles, cosmetics, adhesives, tires, yachts, and motor vehicle spare parts. The textile industry, in particular, has really bloomed during the past decade or so following the establishment of the USAID's CINDE (Coalition for Development Initiatives), a private agency designed to attract foreign investment. New US laws permitting corporations such as Levi Strauss to shut down US operations and import Costa Rican-sewn

Economy

garments duty-free to the US encouraged this development. There are several hundred or more of these *maquilas*, employing over 50,000 workers, mostly young women. Violations in working conditions are said to be common, and numerous instances of abuse have been uncovered. The companies operate *Solidarista* associations in lieu of unions. The government is in a Catch-22 situation; if it forces companies to comply with regulations, they may move to El Salvador or Guatemala. Costa Rica is second only to the Dominican Republic in total exports. Company profits are sheltered under a 1992 Costa Rican law, and you won't find these goods (as they rationally should be) for sale here. Most of the manufacturing is concentrated in the Meseta Central. Unfortunately, the nation's relatively small population, the vast majority living at or near subsistence level, limits the market for locally produced goods, and the wages are horribly low (around 90¢ an hour in the textile industry).

FREE TRADE AGREEMENTS: In April 1994 President Calderón and Mexican President Carlos Salinas signed a free trade agreement that took effect on January 1, 1995. The treaty provides for a graded transition in which exports from the two countries will be available duty-free in each other's markets. A duty-free trade agreement is hoped for with the US (which purchases some 42% of Costa Rica's exports) in the next few years. However, the fallout over NAFTA and the Mexican "bailout" in late 1994 leaves some doubt as to whether such an agreement will ever be enacted.

TOURISM: This "industry" has grown dramatically. Some 400,600 foreign tourists spent US$164 million in 1988; of these, 123,600 came from the US and Canada. In 1992 more than half a million foreigners visited Costa Rica, spent an estimated $200 million and created 15,000 jobs during the first six months of the year alone. Future growth is expected: an estimated 1.2 million visitors are projected to arrive during 1998. The industry now employs half a million Costa Ricans (17% of the population). Now in second place, after ba nanas, tourism has become a major economic priority and a large number of new hotels are under construction. Unfortunately, many of the hotels (especially on the Nicoya Peninsula) are being built with only short-term profit in mind, and without considering the effect such development will have on the local ecosystem. Some believe it is unwise for any local economy to place too much emphasis on tourism. Instability in the region, a major earthquake, civil disturbances, hyperinflation, even the whims of tourists could depress tourism – sending the economy into a tailspin.

ECOTOURISM OR EGOTOURISM? Sadly, many so-called "eco-tourism" projects are mostly hyperbole. The government lacks any plan or direction, and there is no control over development. Former Costa Rican Tourism Minister Luis Manuel Chacon was presented an "Environmental Devil" award by Robin Wood and Pro Reginwald, two German environmental groups, at the '93 International Tourism Fair in Berlin. Chacon retaliated in the pages of *Condé Nast Traveler* that "those new greens, if you scratch them a little bit, the red will come out." There is considerable debate on what constitutes "ecotourism" in Costa Rica. One travel agency owner actually copyrighted the word "ecotourism" in 1983 and claims all those using it are in violation of his copyright!

OTHER SECTORS: Much of the mining is of nonmetals – sand, lime-stone, and clay. Small amounts of gold, silver, and dolomite are also mined. Various projects have been instituted by Citizens Energy Corporation, a nonprofit organization founded by Rep. Joseph Kennedy III. Much of the potential for hydroelectric power remains untapped. In 1986 the DEA estimated that 20% of the cocaine arriving in the US was funneled through Costa Rica. The largest seizure in history occurred in 1989 when 568 kg were confiscated at Limón airport, along with $13,500 in cash and the plane belonging to the two Colombian pilots. The fact that no arrests were made of Costa Ricans hinted to many of high-level governmental links with drug trafficking. In August 1995, Spanish police apprehended four Italians, allegedly members of the Calabrian mafia, who are believed to have laundered money by investing in Costa Rican hotels. They are alleged to have smuggled some 250 tons of cocaine into the US. They were picked up trying to cash a $21 million check in Luxembourg. The money was reportedly destined for Costa Rica.

Economy

Agriculture

The economy has traditionally around agriculture and animal husbandry – exporting coffee, bananas and, more recently, livestock. Despite a surge in growth, the manufacturing industry's structural emphasis on imports has limited its overall contribution. As there are no mineral deposits of note, the most valuable natural resources are the nation's superior pastures and nutrient-rich fields.

As elsewhere in Central America, the land distribution here is unequal, with a small minority (11,500) of the larger farms monopolizing the largest portion (over two million hectares) of the farmland. Less than one percent of the nation's farms are larger than 1,200 acres (500 ha), but these extend over 27% of the country. Estates with more than 500 acres (200 ha) account for only three percent, but occupy more than half of the land area. According to the 1983 census, 71% of the "agricultural" population are landless agricultural laborers. Owing to the topogra phy and the small size of the average farm, mechanization has had little effect on agriculture. It has been estimated that, if the land were used in an ecologically optimal fashion, agriculture could supply employment for nearly half of the nation's labor force, which would relieve the pressure on urban areas.

In the history of agricultural development, government support and regulation has been crucial: The Consejo de Nacional Producción (CNP) buys basic grains from farmers above purchase price and distributes them through its *expendios*. A problem for small farmers has been that loans have been available mainly for export-oriented production. Traditional export crops include bananas, sugarcane, coffee, and cacao.

ENVIRONMENTAL PROBLEMS: Sadly, the Hispanic-American farmers learned little about agricultural methods and techniques from the Native Americans. The indigenous peoples lived in harmony with the environment, using the forests as a resource, rotating small crops in order to stave off soil depletion. But the new arrivals radically transformed the natural environment, using monoculture to the point where deforestation, soil erosion, and changes in river ecology have reached crisis levels. Forests on steep slopes and in areas of heavy precipitation, which protected the soil from erosion and regulated water supply to the drainage system, were indiscriminately cut down, setting off a chain reaction. Today, ecologists estimate that 30% of the nation faces serious water and wind erosion.

PESTICIDES: An estimated 500 Costa Ricans are hospitalized each year because of pesticide poisoning, and 445 died during the years 1980-89. Such export-oriented crops as cotton, fruit, vegetables, and cut flowers – temperate products being produced in the tropics – must be deluged with pesticides. Pesticide bombardment of the mining fly, which plagues the potato fields, has been so heavy that the fly has developed resistance. Costa Rica spends an estimated $40 million per year on imported pesticides. Pesticide use can lead to tragic results. One recent example was DBCP, a pesticide (marketed as Nemagón) used in Standard Fruit's Río Frio banana plantations to control nematodes. After the chemical was found to cause sterility in humans, the US suspended its use in 1977. In Costa Rica, however, it was not banned until 1988. Some 1,000 banana workers were sterilized by the pesticide. In 1992, they accepted an out-of-court settlement from Standard Fruit, Shell Oil, Dow Chemical, and Occidental Chemical. However, children in the area have died of leukemia, while local women have developed cancer, suffer from mysterious pains, give birth to deformed children, and experience miscarriages. All of this may be linked to the chemical.

Paraquat was reported to be the number one cause of pesticide poisonings between 1986 and 1992 in Costa Rica. The herbicide is banned in Sweden and restricted in the US.

NONTRADITIONAL AGRICULTURE: Called the *cambio*, nontraditional agriculture is growing in importance. Since the early 1980s the government has stressed the export-oriented production of crops such as coconuts, ornamental plants, flowers, pineapples, macadamia nuts, and melons. Income from these nontraditionals soared from $336 million in 1984 to $729 million by 1989. In the near future, the greatly increased acreage planted in macadamias will make Costa Rica the third largest producer of macadamia nuts. However, because of the capital requirements and the high interest rates, it is difficult for the small farmer to switch to crops like strawberries, miniature vegetables, mangoes, and flowers. Support for nontraditional farmers has taken the form of CATS or tax certificate bonds worth up to 15% of the value of the nontraditional crops. These can be claimed as discounts on taxes or can be sold to investors for immediate cash. Unfortunately, the small farmer often sells to an exporter who then cashes in, in effect, on the small farmer's benefits. The farmer loses out because the economy forces him to sell at discount.

COFFEE: Coffee (*café*) production began in 1779 in the Meseta Central, an area with near-perfect soil and climate conditions. A native of Ethiopia, the introduced Arabica blend had been first cultivated in Saudi Arabia. Coffee growing soon surpassed cacao, tobacco, and sugar in importance. By 1829 it had become the major source of foreign revenue. As a nonperishable commodity in an age of slow and costly transport, coffee proved an ideal product and shortly thereafter became the nation's major export, a position it has maintained until recent years. Exports to neighboring Panama began in the late 1820s. After a load was sent directly to Britain in 1843, the British began investing heavily in the industry, becoming the principal purchaser of Costa Rican coffee until after WWII.

The largest growing areas are the San José, Alajuela, Heredia, Puntarenas, and Cartago provinces. Costa Rican coffee is high in both quality and caffeine content; it is often blended with inferior varieties. Local coffee, set at a much lower government-controlled local price, is tinted to prevent diversion to the export market. Coffee production depends upon cheap, seasonal labor. Workers receive only around US60¢ to $1.50 per *cajuela* (basket) picked. Each *cajuela* weighs around 15 lbs. and a good worker can fill as many as 12 per day.

A major blight struck in 1983. As with any plantation crop, one of the major drawbacks is that income is subject to price fluctuations. When world coffee prices plunged 40% after the collapse of the world quota cartel system, Costa Rica joined Honduras, Guatemala, Nicaragua, and El Salvador in 1989 to create a coffee retention plan. Under the plan, their coffee is sold in installments so as to ensure price stability. The export tax on coffee, first initiated in 1955, was abolished in 1994.

BANANAS: Thought to be a native of tropical Asia, the banana (*plátano, banano*) was introduced into the Caribbean and then to Central America sometime after the Spanish invasion. The fruit (which is actually a grain) became well known in the US only after the mid-1860s, and the production of the popular Gros Michael variety was begun by the American, Minor Cooper Keith. He shipped the first 360 stems to New Orleans in 1870. Keith took over the nation's debt to cutthroat British bankers in 1883. In exchange, he was offered control of the completed railway and 800,000 acres or 7% of the national territory. Although much of this land was returned, the remainder became the basis for his company's Costa Rican empire, and Keith's influence seeped into every sector of the economy. A century later, exports surpassed 50 million 40-pound boxes. Financial difficulties in the 1890s drove Keith to merge with the United Fruit Company, who monopolized the nation's banana exports until the late 1950s.

The Standard Fruit Co. began production in 1956, with exports beginning in 1959. A third major transnational company, the Del Monte subsidiary, BANDECO (the Banana Development Corporation), began operating plantations. United Brands subsidiary, Compañía Bananera, closed down operations in 1985 following rising costs and a 72-day strike in 1984 that cost the company $12 million in lost production.

In addition to domination of exports by transnationals, another problem connected with banana cultivation has been the crop's susceptibility to disease, namely Panama disease and Sigatoka (leaf spot). Epidemic diseases in the first quarter of the century led to the temporary abandonment of the Caribbean coastal area and to the establishment of plantations on the Pacific side. With the formation of the Asociación de Bananeros S.A. (ASBANA), a government-subsidized private association, the Atlantic coast banana plantations took off once more, producing an estimated 75 million boxes of bananas and generating $440.9 million for the local economy in 1991. In 1994, 450 million boxes were produced. Costa Rica is now the largest banana producer in the world after Ecuador. Still, outbreaks of black Sigatoka and moka disease reduced production by as much as 30% on some farms.

The European Union quotas have been a center of controversy in recent years. The quotas have been designed to ensure that the EU member states' former (as well as current) colonies won't have their banana industries hurt by competition (read price undercutting) from the huge agroindustrial banana plantations run in Central America by multinational corporations. During 1995, the European Union quotas forced Costa Rica to divert eight million boxes from the EU nations to other markets, resulting in a drop in prices. In 1994 Chiquita cancelled its contract with Difrusa S.A, supposedly because Costa Rica had accepted the controversial quotas mandated by the European Union. Costa Rica accepted the quotas and agreed to accept a 23% market share (none of which Chiquita is privy too). The nation had won two appeals to GATT, but the EU refused to lift the quotas. The US multinationals' opposition to the quotas appears hypocritical in light of the US quotas placed on textiles, sugar, and beef imports from Costa Rica.

Growth has come with a stiff price. Much of the new acreage came through destruction of thousands of acres of virgin jungle near Guapiles. In 1990, Limón's bishop Alfonso Coto denounced the conditions under which workers labor, contending that they are treated unfairly, the wealth is concentrated in too few hands, the industry aggravates deforestation and contamination of rivers, and that the labor organizations (*Solidarismos*, which have replaced the unions) provide neither job security nor adequate working conditions. In 1992, the Holland-based Second International Tribunal on Water condemned Standard Fruit Company for "severely polluting the eastern region of the country." That same year, the Labor Ministry accused 10 banana companies of violating national labor laws by paying substandard wages and refusing to pay overtime. The previous month the banana unions had accused multinationals of hiring some 12,000 illegal workers who are paid less than the minimum wage and denied benefits. In 1994, riot police fired M-16 rifles at a crowd of some 200 striking banana workers at the Geest plantation complex in the Sarapiquí area. The workers had been blocking road access to protest a wage cut and the dismissal of workers who had joined the union. Private guards also fired on workers who attacked administrative offices. Shortly thereafter, the nine-day strike was halted after Geest agreed to recognize the right of SIGTAGA (Agricultural and Ranch Worker Union of Heredia) to organize. On the surface, such an agreement would seem inconsequential as it merely affirms willingness to respect the nation's labor laws. However, with the banana companies having trampled on workers' rights over the previous decade, this was seen by the workers as a major step forward.

Today, most bananas are shipped to the US and Europe. The developed countries have come to expect that their bananas will have no spots. Originally, banana stems were covered with paper for protection. Today, pesticide-imbued light blue plastic bags are used, along with polypropylene cord used to tie up the top-heavy plants. An estimated 6,300 tons of bags are used annually. Unfortunately, most of these end up in rivers or buried in shallow landfills.

To their credit, Bandeco (Del Monte) and Standard Fruit Company (Dole), subsidiaries which export some two-thirds of all bananas, have constructed the nation's largest plastic recycling facility near Siquirres. In the first stage, the plant is processing some 2,150 tons of plastic into pallets for banana shipping, building materials, and fence posts. If this first plant (which opened in 1994) proves profitable, the plan is to expand it to handle the industry's entire plastic bag supply. In return, Chiquita will receive the "Eco-OK" seal from the Rainforest Alliance. No cure has been proposed for the pesticide problem. The banana industry uses a third of the nation's pesticide imports annually, and the National Insurance Institute maintains that 75% of the labor accidents involving pesticides occur in banana-producing areas.

However, banana production continues to grow unabated. Plans are to expand land under cultivation to 123,500 acres (50,000 ha). Current production is around 90 million boxes per year. One possible compromise solution is promised by the Banano Amiga project, which proposes to issue management guidelines. Companies following the recommendations will be issued a seal of approval. No endorsement will be given to any firm that is cutting down forests to expand production. If you wish to protest the activities of the banana plantations in Costa Rica, you can write to Chiquita Brands International, Apdo. 10036, 1000 San José.

Foro Emaus

An umbrella organization working to promoting the rights of workers on banana plantations and against unregulated plantation expansion, Foro Emaus was founded in 1990 in Limón. Members include Catholic clergy, labor union members, and representatives of various environmental groups. The organization's demands include terminating use of short-term banana workers and illegal aliens so as to prevent union organizing, ending use of dangerous pesticides, and stopping deforestation. The organization is also working to change government policy, which currently favors the pro-management solidarity unions, so as to encourage non-solidarity unions. It has received support only from the Limón diocese. In Costa Rica, as elsewhere in the world, the Catholic Church heirarchy remains devoted to maintaining the status quo. Opposition also comes from the government and the banana multinationals.

SUGARCANE: *Caña (Saccharum officianarum)* probably originated in New Guinea; it has become a major crop only since the late 1950s. While it is grown all over the country, the largest areas for sugarcane growing and processing are concentrated in the Meseta Central, in Guanacaste province, northern Puntarenas province, and in northern Alajuela province. An estimated 113,700 acres (46,014 ha) are under cultivation. Except in labor-scarce Guanacaste, almost all the cane is cut by hand. The land is burned before harvesting (January to May) to expedite cutting. Large sugar mills *(ingenios)* dominate, although oxen-powered mills *(trapiches)* can still be found. During the pre-Castro 1950s, little cane was grown, and sugar was imported until the middle of the decade. Stimulated by the Cuban embargo, exports to the US climbed to 60,000 tons by the mid-1960s. In 1989, 45,300 tons were produced.

CACAO: *Theobroma cacao*, the "food of the gods," has been cultivated for upwards of 2,000 years. It is thought to have originated in the Amazon basin on the E equatorial slopes of the Andes. After the Spanish conquest, cacao (known as chocolate or cocoa in its refined form) became the most important crop, and it was used as currency until the 19th C. Then it was replaced by coffee. It only re-emerged as an export crop in 1944. Today, cacao is the only export crop grown under adverse conditions. The vast majority is produced in the Caribbean coastal lowlands, an area which is really too wet to grow cacao properly. While the NE lowlands are superior, cultivation in the region is hindered by the lack of coastal transport; most of the current crop grown there goes to Nicaragua. Quality of the processed cacao is low, owing to the lack of controlled fermentation. Devastated by the fungus monilia since 1979 and plagued by plummeting prices on the world markets, cacao seems to be on its way out. The Ministry of Agriculture has even recommended that farmers substitute other crops.

PALM OIL: The African oil palm *(palma de aceite)*, native to W Africa, was transported to this hemisphere along with the slave trade. The primary oil in use during the Industrial Revolution, it helped to cement the colonial linkage between Europe and Africa. It was introduced to Costa Rica in the 1940s to fill the domestic need for cooking oil. After the pullout by United Brands in the 1980s, it replaced bananas on the W coast. It is cultivated by the Chiquita-owned, government-controlled trans-national monopoly, Cia. Palma Tica (formerly Compañía Bananera), whose subsidiary (Grupo Numar) in San José processes the unrefined oil into cooking fat. The oil is also blended with imported soybean oil to make cooking oil and margarine. Because of its high saturated fat level, palm oil, palm kernel oil and coconut oil (the "tropical" oils) have become a source of worldwide

Economy

controversy. Still, the oil and its various food products are of major economic importance. Costa Rica exports some 12,000 metric tons of oil annually, with a market value of over $4.6 million.

OTHER CROPS: Maize, beans, potatoes, plantains, rice, onions, and sorghum are the main crops cultivated for domestic consumption. Corn, the most important cereal grain in Costa Rica, is used as a staple food (in forms ranging from *tamales* to *tortillas*), as a raw material for industrial products, and as animal feed. Most of the corn is grown on small to medium-sized farms and is usually planted using a digging stick, with two or three seeds inserted in each hole. Approximately 90% of the rice crop (*Oryza sativa*) is grown without irrigation. Unlike maize, it is grown by large-scale farmers using modern methods. Although Guanacaste has been the traditional stronghold for rice cultivation, irregular rainfall has spurred the development of new areas near Puntarenas. Less important crops include cassava, tobacco, and cotton. Quantities of maize, beans, and sorghum must still be imported.

ANIMAL HUSBANDRY: Cattle, first brought here in the 1500s, are the most important component of the livestock industry. Up until the end of WWII, beef, the favorite meat of Costa Ricans, still had to be imported. Export of live cattle (*ganado*) to the US began in 1954, but exports switched to beef so that hides and offal could be used locally. It continues to be the third largest export after bananas and coffee. Local consumption, however, has actually declined as escalating prices have made beef more and more of an unaffordable luxury. Graded low because the cattle is grass-fed and therefore lean, most of the exported beef is made into pet food, TV dinners, and fast food hamburgers.

Although cattle ranching has been hailed because of its magnetic ability to attract greenbacks, it has had devastating ecological consequences, as the clearcutting of forests has produced severe erosion. The massive deforestation of the 1960s through the early '80s was largely the result of a boom in cattle ranching. While beef exports tripled between 1960 and 1978, the ratio of pasture to agricultural land grew to more than 50%, and an estimated 80% of trees felled were either burned or left to rot on the ground. In a pattern that has become alarmingly typical, small farmers cut down the primary forest, farm the land for a few years until it is depleted, resell the land to a rancher, and then move on to the next virgin tract. Although cattle ranches consume vast areas of land, they provide little employment. At their height, beef exports never surpassed 8.6% of total exports. During the 1980s, the price of beef began to drop, and a 1988 boycott led by the San Francisco-based Rainforest Action Network led Burger King to stop purchasing Costa Rican beef. The largest cattle raising areas are in the

Alajuela province's Llandura de San Carlos region, Guanacaste and the northern Puntarenas provinces.

Only a few farms raise pigs commercially. Horses far outnumber mules, sheep, and goats. Although all three birds were introduced by the Spaniards, chickens win out numerically over ducks and geese. There are also turkeys and even quail, used to produce eggs for export.

FORESTRY: Much of the forest has been sold without directly benefitting the economy. Although the Arias administration claimed to have cut the deforestation rate to 30,000 hectares annually while increasing reforestation tenfold, some experts believe the deforestation rate to be much higher. It is now a felony to cut or transport wood illegally, but violators are consistently fined rather than jailed. Contraband wood is often transported at times when forestry officials are off work. The lumber industry accounted for less than 4% of the nation's agricultural earnings in 1985, but thousands are employed in the process of milling and transporting logs. As wood grows scarcer, the price of timber has risen and the number of mills has dropped from 220 in 1984 to around 150 in 1990. Many of the bankrupt mills were the least efficient wood processors.

At the current rate, the nation's productive forests will be depleted in this decade, and that could cost the government up to $150 million a year in wood imports. Even though annual reforestation is planned to equal the area cut, there is still a 15-20 year gap between cutting and the time when the reforested trees are ready for harvest. Export of logs and unprocessed timber is prohibited, but the nation does export around $22 million worth of wood products annually.

FISHING: The fishing industry accounts for only a small part of agricultural production. Lobsters are caught in the Caribbean, while tuna, herring, sardines, and shrimp are fished in the Pacific waters.

The People

(Los Costarricenses)

As is true all over Latin America, Spain and its influence on the culture has been paramount. Barely more than a few thousand Spaniards immigrated between 1502 and 1821, but their impact upon the society was tremendous. Costa Ricans call themselves "Ticos" from the special diminutives they add to their words. Throughout Latin America, diminutives are commonly added in speech. For example *momento* be-

Economy

comes *momentito* – "in a little while." But Costa Ricans change this into *momentico*, using their own unique diminutive form.

Despite the Euro-American "white" Costa Rican image, there has been a great deal of racial mixing over the centuries. Still, Costa Rica is unquestionably the most homogeneous – both linguisitically and ethnically – of any Central American nation. Although there is a definite infusion of African and Native American blood, Ticos share the same language and consider themselves to be Caucasians. Because Ticos have traditionally viewed themselves as egalitarian yeoman farmers, they sometimes refer to their society as classless, despite glaring differences in income and power distribution. In fact, the independent farmer is a dying breed, but other social classes remain strong. In addition to the Spanish stock, French, British, Germans, and Italians have arrived over the centuries and been absorbed into the mainstream.

POPULATION: At the time of Independence, there were approximately 65,000 Costa Ricans. Their numbers grew to around 100,000 by 1850, 250,000 by the early 1900s, to nearly 500,000 by 1927, 2,655,000 in 1985, and an estimated 3.2 million today. An average of 13.8 deaths occur for every 1,000 births. With a current annual growth rate of 2.6%, the population is projected to reach 3.4-3.7 million by the end of the century and 4.9 million by 2025. Some 20% of households are headed by single mothers. Of the 80,000 births recorded annually, teenage pregnancies account for over 14,000, and more than half of all births are out of wedlock. The average life expectancy is 75.2 years, and the infant mortality rate is 16.65 per 1,000 live births, which compares favorably with infant mortality in Guatemala (48.5), Honduras (50.7), and Nicaragua (49.8). Costa Rica ranks 39th out of the 173 nations listed on the Index of Human Development.

Population distribution is inequitable. Average density is 162.2 inhabitants per sq mile (62.6 per sq km), as compared with 83.6 in Nicaragua, 83.9 in Panama, 22 in Belize, and 677 in El Salvador. Over half of all Costa Ricans live in the Valle Central, which comprises portions of four provinces: San José, Alajuela, Heredia, and Cartago, with the largest portion living in the San José metropolitan area. This area encompasses only 5% of the land surface, but the population has actually been even more concentrated in the past, with many outlying areas becoming significantly populated only in the 20th century. Most emigrants go to the US, and that nation receives a higher percentage of immigrants relative to Costa Rica's total population than from any other Latin American nation.

Society

CLASS STRUCTURE: In the earliest times, there was a sharp division between the minority *hidalgos* (gentry) and the *plebeyos* (commoners). The former had servants and owned all of the slaves. Although these differences had largely dissolved by the beginning of the 1800s, a small elite still dominated the nation. In fact, 21 out of the 28 who signed the act declaring the nation's independence were closely related. These *cafétaleros* (coffee barons) came to control the best coffee growing lands along with the *beneficios* (coffee processing plants). Their political power reached its apex between 1821 and 1915. Now known as *la sociedad* (the society), the descendents of the coffee barons – no longer as economically and politically dominant as in the past – still reside in San José. This elite has been joined by other immigrants who made their fortunes in the 20th C., and these days wealth is more likely to impress than family status.

Having expanding substantially during the 20th C., the upper and lower-middle classes also reside in the capital. The middle class tends to believe manual labor is degrading and has a strong belief in the power of education; conspicuous consumption is their badge of success, even though it may be financed by steep debts. Below the middle class is the working class, traditionally referred to as the *clase obrero* or *el pueblo*. Then come the "marginals" – many of whom are employed in illegal occupations.

One social class that has become virtually extinct is the *gamonal*, well-off peasants with a traditional, non-cosmopolitan Tico lifestyle. Usually the wealthiest member of his community, the *gamonal* was highly respected by the villagers and, because they would follow his advice, he was often courted by sharp politicians. If you ask an affluent Tico about poverty in his country, you'll hear about the illiterate, barefoot peasant "who may look as if he has nothing but is very rich." He's referring, of course, to the *gamonal*.

MALE AND FEMALE RELATIONSHIPS: Despite the idealized official version of family life that originates with the Catholic Church, "free unions" are extremely common and 40-50% of all births are illegitimate. In some 20% of these the father is listed as "unknown." Today, to be a *hijo naturale* (illegitimate) is not necessarily shameful. In the upper classes, because patrimony and purity of blood lineage are viewed as being of paramount importance, chastity is vital for women, although men are free to play around. The twin pillars of male-female relations are *machismo* and *marianismo*. The myth of *machismo* rests on belief in the innate superiority of men, whether in work, in politics, or in the arts and sciences. *Marianismo*, which holds women to be morally and spiritually superior, allows women to feel virtuous through their suffering at the hands of men. The supreme compliment paid to a wife and mother is to call her *abnegada*, self-sacrificing. Traditionally, marriage for women is a cross to bear, which gains her brownie points both with society and with God. But it can be quite a painful cross to bear. A 1993 report by the Ministry of Health disclosed that some 40% of all women in relationships are physically abused by their spouses. Beatings are the leading cause of injury to women after illegal abortions, but only some 5% of the perpetrators are ever convicted. A conviction results in a $7 fine. Most rape cases never make it to trial, and a full third of the defendants charged with rape are acquitted.

In a society where men hold the privileges and dominate, females are defined in terms of their relationship with men. Unmarried women are called *señoritas* or *muchachas buenas* (a "good girl," therefore a virgin); single, unmarried females are *mujeres* (women); loose women are *zorras*; prostitutes are *putas*; and *señoras*, married or not, are housewives. Women in consensual unions are legally referred to as *compañeras*, and they have all the legal rights of wives except that they may be forced to testify against their live-in companions in criminal cases. Common among the poor are so-called "Queen Bee" families in which a grandmother runs the house and looks after the children while the daughters go out to work and bring home the bacon.

While many middle and upper class young women tend to have an idealized view of marriage, with some even believing their match to be predestined, their poorer cousins tend to be more pragmatic, viewing a relationship with a man as a way to weasel out of their parents' clutches. While lower class housewives still find themselves housebound, these days things are changing for upper class women. But many of these women still view themselves as extensions of their husbands' occupations; as is the case with their lower class counterparts, many also have little interest in political or cultural affairs and are preoccupied almost totally with their children.

NAMES: Descent is traced through both male and female lines. Children receive both a paternal or first surname and a maternal or second surname, which is often abbreviated. If your father is "unknown," you have only your mother's surname.

Minority Groups

As black slaves were few in number and the Indians were mostly assimilated or dispersed, Costa Rica retains few minority groups. Blacks, Indians, and Chinese constitute only 3-5% of the population.

But few though they are, these groups continue to influence the nation's future as they have its past. All still suffer the sting of prejudice. Many Ticos still believe white to be superior, resulting in condescending attitudes not only toward national minorities but also toward citizens of neighboring countries.

MESTIZOS: Said to compose 15% of the population in the 1950s, *mestizos* had shrunk to 7% by the 1970s. Since it seems unlikely they were captured by visiting alien anthropologists for transport to a research lab on a distant planet, the only explanation for the shrinkage is that "*mestizos*" had been classified as such on cultural, not racial, grounds. Once acculturated, they were accepted and no longer considered separate. Most *mestizos*, descendants of unions between Spanish and Chorotega Native Americans, reside in Guanacaste Province, where they are also known as Guanacasteans. They retain some Indian customs and they have a distinct dialect.

JAMAICANS: The first African-Americans came to Costa Rica as early as 1825 to farm and hunt turtles, but most are the descendants of Jamaicans who were brought in to help build the railroad. After its construction, they stayed on. Finding work on banana plantations, as railway men, or as longshoremen, the newcomers had no desire to assimilate, nor did they have much in common with the Hispanic-Americans. Although they retain their Jamaican patois and their Anglican religious affiliation, the younger generation can speak fluent Spanish.

During the 30s, the depression, banana disease and falling demand put the Caribbean coast plantations out of business. United Fruit's 1934 contract with the government for the Pacific coast plantations prohibited "colored people" from being employed. Many emigrated to the Canal Zone or the US, and most of the remainder became full-time farmers. A 1948 decree, sponsored by consummate patriarchal politician Figueres, awarded them citizenship. Discrimination and prejudice, however, remain strong and have prevented their full assimilation. Today, there are about 30,000 Costa Ricans of Jamaican descent who are noted not only for their domination of basketball and soccer teams but also, increasingly, for their social and political contributions to the society. Many of them have left farming to enter the professions.

INDIGENOUS PEOPLES: Of the estimated 300,000 Indians in Costa Rica, 65-75% live in Talamanca, the mountainous area in the south, where they were either brought or ran for shelter. Although actually quite similar, the Bribri and the Cabecare who inhabit this area view themselves as culturally distinct. The Native Americans are widely

The People

scattered on both the Caribbean and Pacific sides, but those settled on the Pacific slope tend to be more acculturated. The Chorotegas of Guanacaste have been almost totally assimilated, as have the Huetares who reside on the Pacific slope of the Meseta Central and the Malekus who live near the San Carlos region close to the Nicaraguan border. Living in three villages in the SW, the 1,500-2,000 Boruca are the only other remaining Native American tribe of note. They are almost totally assimilated, but they retain community ownership of the land and some still practice traditional weaving. A 1939 governmental declaration granted the Indians certain lands, and the Council for the Protection of the Native Races was established in 1945. But Indians have lost much of their land through deception or violence. During the 1960s, a congressional investigation revealed that most of them live in extreme proverty and many have succumbed to demon alcohol. In 1976 President Oduber declared a state of emergency within the Indian areas and established five zones in which non-Indians were prohibited from renting or buying land. Today, although these laws remain on the books, they are unenforced, and the state of the nation's indigenous peoples remains unchanged. Most have made the transition from tribal to peasant culture, and only an estimated 5-6,000 still preserve their heritage, including their language. Hunting has been replaced by husbandry and the Cabaceres, for example, raise pigs for sale. The indigenous cultures appear destined for extinction through acculturation and assimilation.

In 1990 Guayami tribespeople came to San José to protest their inablility to secure *cedulas* (identification cards). Many of them emigrated from Panama 50 years ago. The process is now underway to pass a law granting them cards; these cards are of vital importance, as without a *cedula* you cannot vote, borrow money, or use the benefits of the government health system.

An encouraging development has been the institution of a Council for Indigenous Rights, which has been set up under the office of Ombudsman Rodrigo Carazo. The council will attend to complaints concerning the violation of laws by the nation's officials and bureaucrats.

THE CHINESE: Once a separate, socially segregated community, the nation's Chinese (*Chinos*) are becoming more and more acculturated. While the oldsters still speak Chinese and believe in the old ways, the Spanish-speaking young are intermarrying and converting to Roman Catholicism. Traditionally, Chinese have either stayed out of politics or supported the most conservative candidate. As is true elsewhere in the world, the small, close-knit Chinese communities exercise considerable economic power relative to their numbers, and this gives rise to resentment on occasion. The Chinese emigrated to Costa Rica beginning in 1873 to work on the railway or on farms. They were harshly exploited. Never confined to the Caribbean lowlands, they soon spread and established shops, inns, and restaurants.

OTHER GROUPS: Sephardic Jews have been in Costa Rica since the beginning of colonization and have been fully assimilated. Before and after WWII, a small number of Polish Jews arrived. They earned their living by selling door to door and were dubbed *polequeandos*. There are also many Panamanian, Nicaraguan, Honduran, and Chilean refugees. Although they are subject to a considerable amount of resentment and prejudice, the estimated 200,000 Nicaraguan refugees provide badly needed cheap labor, especially in the coffee fields. The vast majority lack legal status, so they are readily exploited – performing low-paying, low-prestige, and backbreaking work shunned by Ticos. Resident Americans include multinational corporate employees and pensioners. There's also a small but valiant band of Quakers who have set up a cheese factory near Monteverde in Puntarenas Province, and a colony of Italians in the town of San Vito in the S part of the same province.

Religion

As in every other Latin American nation, the Roman Catholic Church reigns supreme here. Although 95% of *Costarricenses* claim to be practicing Roman Catholics, and most of these attend church, the strength of religious belief and practice varies widely. With the ratio of one priest for every 4,000 Costa Ricans, there are more clergy per capita than in any other Central American nation and Costa Rica is touted as the most staunchly Catholic country in the isthmus.

Surprisingly, the government has frequently shown itself to be anticlerical. This attitude, combined with 19th-C. liberal values, culminated in the Liberal Laws, which permitted divorce, ended religious instruction in public schools, secularized cemeteries, and drove a firm wedge between Church and State. These laws were repealed in the 1940s by President Rafael Angel Calderón Garcia, a staunch Catholic, who reintroduced religion to the public schools.

Today, Catholicism remains the state religion and the only church marriages that have civil validity are those performed by Roman Catholic priests. Although the official Church teaching is that God is all-powerful and the saints are only intercessors on behalf of the petitioner, in practice Ticos act as if the saints are all-powerful and have the ability directly to grant their requests.

Religion

Undoubtedly a reaction to the popularity of evangelical Protestantism, a new movement has emerged in recent years. Known as Catholic Pentacostalism or Spiritual Renovation, this intensified Catholicism involves speaking in tongues, uttering prophesies, and other such activities. The Church leadership initially looked askance at such practices, but they are now accepted. Another innovation is the *Cursillos de Cristianidad*, three-day intensive study courses that have attracted tens of thousands of participants over the past 25 years.

PROTESTANTISM: When the Central American Mission arrived in 1891, they encountered vehement hostility. They were stoned and beaten and the Catholic Church attacked them. The missionaries responded to these attacks by calling the Church "utterly debased and idolatrous." Although the government refused to expel them, in 1901 it forbade them to preach in public, advertise their meetings, or establish schools. Despite this, the Protestants perservered, and other sects arrived. When Billy Graham arrived in 1958, the Catholic Church not only suppressed any announcement, but blacked out all media coverage, including a service attended by 8,000 people. Similarly, the Church was able to block a 1961 parade of various sects commemorating the 70th anniversary of Catholicism. Today, it is common to see the declaration "*Somos Catolicos*" posted by the door – not as an affirmation of faith but to deter annoying door-to-door religious peddlers. Over the decades, however, the prejudice has abated. Ironically, as Catholic-Protestant relations have improved, the sects have grown apart from each other. Today, there are an estimated 40,000 Protestants. With Costa Rica the headquarters for the Latin American missionary movement, there are many bible colleges and publishing houses. Evangelical Protestant sects include Methodists, Baptists, and Pentecostals. They make up a growing percentage of the population. Most Anglicans are Jamaican emigrants and their descendants.

Holidays

Official Holidays

January 1	New Year's Day
March	Festival in Puntarenas
March 19	St. Joseph
April	Easter (three days or more)
April 11	Anniversary of Battle of Rivas
May 1	Labor Day

June 29	Day of St. Peter and St. Paul
July 25	Anniversary of the Annexation of Guanacaste Province
August 2	Virgin of Los Angeles
August 15	Mother's Day
September 15	Independence Day
October 12	*Día de las Culturas.*
December 8	Conception of the Virgin
December 25	Christmas Day

On each of the 17 official holidays (*feriados*), most government and professional offices, some banks, and many stores are closed. During Easter and Christmas weeks, the entire country shuts down almost completely.

Festivals & Events

January

FIESTA PATRONALES DE ALAJUELITA: Held in honor of the Black Christ of Esquipulas, this festival features a colorful oxcart parade, a pilgrimage to the large iron cross overlooking the town, and plentiful consumption of *chinchivi*, a homemade corn beer.

FIESTAS DE SANTA CRUZ: Also held in honor of the Black Christ of Esquipulas, this celebration, held in Guanacaste's cultural capital, includes folk dancing, bullfights, and marimba music.

COPA DEL CAFE: This week-long tennis tournament draws an international collection of talented players, all less than 18 years of age.

February

SAN ISIDRO DE GENERAL: This town's *fiestas civicas* are held from the end of Jan. to the beginning of February. Activities include a cattle show, agricultural and industrial fair, bullfights, and an orchid exhibition.

FIESTA DE LOS DIABLOS: The sole remaining native American festival, this takes place in the village of Rey Curre in SW Talamancas. In an allegorical recreation of the struggle between the Diablitos (the local Borucas) and a bull (representing the Spaniards), masked Diablitos pursue the bull, which is made of burlap topped with a carved

Holidays

wooden head. Local crafts, corn liquor (*chicha*), and tamales are for sale.

March

CARRERA DE LA PAZ: In this footrace, about a thousand people run from San José's National Gymnasium to the campus of the University for Peace in Villa Colón.

NATIONAL ORCHID SHOW: Featuring 500-plus species, this week-end-long festival takes place in the Colegio de Medicos y Cirujanos headquarters in Sabana Sur.

NATIONAL OXCART DAY: Taking place on the second Sunday in March, this celebrates the *boyero* (oxcart driver) and the *carreta* (the wooden-wheeled painted cart); the locus for the celebration is in San Antonio de Escazú near San José.

FARMER'S DAY: Held March 15, this nationwide celebration is headquartered in Tierra Blanca near Poás (whose farmers celebrate deliverance from a plague of locusts in 1877). It is the day devoted to the farmer's patron saint, San Isidro, a humble 12th-C. Spanish farmer.

UJARRAS PILGRIMAGE: Held mid-month, this Orosi Valley procession from Paraiso to the ruined church in Ujarras commemorates the rescue from floods of Ujarras by the Virgin. Her graven image returns with the crowd for the occasion.

BONANZA CATTLE SHOW: The nation's cattlemen assemble at the Bonanza Fairgrounds, on the airport highway in San José, for this event. Featured are prize bulls, bullfights, rodeos, horseraces, and mechanical bulls.

SAN JOSÉ DAY: On this day (Mar. 19), local families traditionally visit Volcan Poás for a hike and picnic.

CRAFTS FAIR: Taking place on the Plaza de la Cultura in San José, 150-200 local artisans exhibit their wares.

FERIA NACIONAL DEL AGUA: This "National Water Festival," a one-week event, takes place at the Parque de la Paz in San José and chiefly features concerts by groups such as Adrián Goizueta and Pura Vida, puppet shows, and mariachi.

INTERNATIONAL FESTIVAL OF ARTS: One of the best festivals of its kind in the Americas, this festival draws together groups from Costa Rica, Nicaragua, Panama, Cuba, Russia, the US, Ecuador, Chile, and other nations for about 11 days. Inexpensive tickets are sold to events at the Teatro Nacional and other venues. Free performances are held nightly at the Plaza de la Cultura as well as in Moravia and elsewhere around the nation.

April

DIA DE JUAN SANTAMARIA: Held in Alajeula, this day's events – a parade with marching bands and majorettes – commemorate Juan Santamaría, Costa Rica's only national hero and the town's pride and joy.

EARTH DAY: In San José's Plaza de la Democracía, an annual three-day Festival of Native American handicrafts is followed by the celebration of Earth Day.

SEMANA SANTA: Much of the country shuts down during Easter Holy Week from Wednesday noon through Sunday. The observances begin on Palm Sunday, when a small procession bearing the "Lord of the Triumph" wends its way through town via streets festooned with flowers and palm fronds in symbolism of Jesus' march into Jerusalem. Thursday night devotees pray and chant in church until dawn.

processions: The week's highlight is a series of processions, the most famous of which are held in Cartago, Santo Domingo de Heredia, San Antonio de Escazú, San José, San Isidro de Heredia, and in San Joaquín de Flores – where all the procession's characters are people instead of sculpted images. The Procession of Silence takes place at around 8 PM Thursday night. The Encuentro procession takes place at mid-morning on Good Friday, and the Procession of the Holy Burial (in which Christ is slowly marched to the cross, accompanied by a grieving Mary, the Apostles, and a band of mourners clad in black) occurs later on between 4 and 5. Holy Saturday ("Judas Day") is marked by firecrackers and, in some villages, an effigy of Judas is hanged to the accompaniment of speeches and petitions. Featuring shepherds and pint-sized angels, the joyous procession of the Resurrection takes place mid-morning on Sunday. If you have a car, you can catch the beginning of a procession in one town and then move on to another town and catch its finale. Procession schedules are available at each Casa Cural.

Holidays

May

MAY DAY: On the first, workers march and the president gives the annual "State of the Nation Address." The Limón area celebrates with cricket matches, picnics, quadrille dances, and domino games.

UNIVERSITY WEEK: This takes place around the beginning of the month. University of Costa Rica students crown a queen, and participate in sports events and a parade. Many local bands also perform on campus.

DIA DEL BOYERO: May 15 is traditionally the start of the rainy season and San Isidro Labrador is honored on this day, the "Day of the Oxcart Driver." The celebration takes place in all of the San Isidros and in San Antonio de Escazú near San José. Activities include parades featuring brighly colored oxcarts, the blessing of animals (extending right down to Puss and Fido) and crops by the local priest. The oxen, in turn, show their piety by carrying paper money to the church on their horns.

CARRERA DE SAN JUAN: On San Juan Day, May 17, around 1,500 run the 22½ km from El Alto de Ochomongo (near Cartago) to San Juan de Tibás, N of San José.

June

ST. PETER/ST. PAUL: The *fiestas patronales* of these two saints is commemorated in towns of the same name nationwide on the 29th.

July

MANGO FESTIVAL: The highlight of Alajuela's year, this celebration offers nine days of parades, music, outdoor food markets, and arts and crafts fairs.

PUNTARENAS CARNIVAL: Beginning on the Saturday nearest July 16 in this port town, the Fiesta of the Virgin of the Sea is celebrated with a regatta featuring beautifully decorated fishing boats and yachts. The carnival that follows has parades, concerts, dances, sports events, fireworks, and the crowning of the queen. Similar events take place in Nicoya's Playas del Coco.

ANNEXATION OF GUANACASTE: Held every July 25, the Anniversary of the Annexation of Guanacaste Province commemorates the province's secession from Nicaragua. Fiestas in Liberia and in Santa Cruz feature folk dancing, marimba bands, horse parades, bullfights, rodeos, cattle shows, and local culinary specialties.

THE VIRGIN OF LOS ANGELES: This festival is Cartago's largest. Every August 1, thousands assemble around Av. Central near Plaza de la Cultura and march towards Cartago. In contrast with the awe that one might expect during such a momentous religious event, the atmosphere is lively, and the devotees display an intimate, convivial relationship with the Virgen. *Fiestas patronales* continue the celebrations on into the month.

DIA DE SAN RAMON: In this colorful tradition, nearly 30 saints from a neighboring town are taken on August 31 for a visit to San Ramon, who resides in the town named after him. His image is taken for a spin around town with the others. The celebration continues as the saint's guests reside in the church for over a week.

SEMANA AFRO-COSTARRICENSE: This cultural week's highlights, celebrating International Black People's Day and taking place in San José, are lectures, panel discussions, and displays.

September

FESTIVAL MARINO: This Guanacaste affair, held in Playa Hermosa, features sandcastle making, water ski and jet ski contests.

DIA INDEPENDENCIA: Held on September 15, the nation's Independence Day (shared by all of Central America) has country-wide parades featuring uniformed schoolkids, majorettes, bands, and the like. At 6 PM the Freedom Torch, relayed by a chain of student runners stretching all the way from Guatemala, arrives in San José, and Ticos join in singing the national anthem. That evening, schoolchildren march in *farole* (lantern) parades, carrying handmade lanterns along the route.

October

LIMON CARNIVAL: Commemorating the nation's cultural diversity, the former Columbus Day (October 12) is now known as the *Día de las Culturas*, and this port city's annual festival is the nation's most famous. Incorporating the Caribbean coast's African-American traditions, it's a miniature version of similar festivals found in Río or Trinidad. There are floats and dance groups.

Holidays

FIESTA DE MAIZ: Honoring corn, this festival is held at Upala in the uppermost portion of Alajuela Province. Corn Queen contestants don costumes made entirely of corn husks, grains, and silk.

COSTA RICA YACHT CLUB REGATTA: Held annually in October and November, this international regatta is open to sailboats of 20 ft (6 m) and over.

November

ALL SOULS DAY: Special church ceremonies are held nationwide on November 2 and families visit cemeteries to pay homage to the deceased.

INTERNATIONAL DOG SHOW: This show, sponsored by the Asociación Canófila Costarricense, features a splendid assortment of dogs.

COFFEE PICKING TOURNAMENT: Held during coffee picking season in the Meseta Central (November-December). *Campesinos* compete to pick berries with maximum speed. This televised event includes typical songs, legends, and poems.

INTERNATIONAL THEATER FESTIVAL: In San José, a variety of theater groups perform plays, puppet shows, and street theater.

December

FIESTA DE LOS NEGRITOS: With wildly costumed dancers in blackface, this festival is on December 8 in the village of Boruca. It is held in honor of its patron saint, the Virgin of the Immaculate Conception, and participants dance to flute and drum accompaniment in time to the *sarocla*, a frame with a horse's head.

DÍA DE LA POLVORA: Honoring the Virgin of the Immaculate Conception on December 8, this nationwide festival includes fireworks, the best of which take place in Jesús Maria de San Mateo (Alajuela Province) and in La Rivera de Belén (Heredia).

FIESTA DE LA YEGUITA: Held in Nicoya in Guanacaste on December 12. Solemn-faced villagers carry the image of the Virgin of Guadalupe through the streets. To the accompaniment of flute and drums, two dancers, one of whom carries a doll, pass through La Yeguita, "the little mare," a hoop with a horse's face. Other festivities include bullfights, fireworks, band concerts, and traditional foods made from corn.

VUELTA CICLISTA: An international cycling tournament which starts in mid-Dec. and lasts until the New Year. Contestants cycle across the country.

CHRISTMAS CELEBRATIONS: Beginning December 15, in a traditional practice known as *los posadas*, children go from house to house asking for a place to stay – just as Mary and Joseph supposedly did in Bethlehem. Accompanied by musicians and carolers, they are given refreshments at each house and they sing carols in exchange. Confetti battles take place along Av. Central on Christmas Eve. Creches of the nativity scene are very popular and a competition is held in San José. Before they are taken down on Candelaria in February, families gather to pray, sing, drink corn liquor and eat traditional sweets.

YEAR'S END FIESTAS: Most events take place in and around San José. These begin during the last week of December and extend through the beginning of January. Bullfights are held at the Zapote ring daily; the *tope*, a procession of horses, departs from Paseo Colón, proceeds along Av. Central and ends at Plaza Viquez. Finally, a dance in Parque Central welcomes the New Year. While the Christmas season is a time of partying and all the bars stay open, people turn solemn at New Year's Eve. Some Ticos believe that if God sees them in church on the first day of the year, he'll make allowances if they are absent during the remainder.

Food

No one would ever credit Costa Rica with great cuisine. All too frequently overcooked and greasy fried foods dominate in small local restaurants. It is a simple and unvarying fare, the product of a nation of farmers struggling to eke out a living on small plots. Despite the spicy reputation of Latin food, Tico chefs appear unfamiliar with the use of spices. During your stay, however, you will find that the cuisine has its own charms and, back at home, you may find yourself pining for a breakfast of *gallo pinto*.

Typical Fare

Campesino food has historical roots. The maize and beans grown by Native Americans, have become staples which, along with rice, have become the principal source of protein in the average Tico's diet. The standard diet consists of tortillas (thin corn pancakes), rice, beans, salad, and bread. *Agua dulce* (water sweetened with raw sugarcane) is the national beverage. In a typical restaurant, there's one surefire bet: the *casado*. A plate of rice served with salad, beans, and meat, chicken, or fish, this dish – as ubiquitous as the hamburger in the US – will probably be your staple meal. *Arroz con pollo* (chicken with rice and vegetables) is one of the most popular local dishes.

DESAYUNOS: "Breakfast" appears on the menu throughout the day. *Gallo pinto* ("spotted rooster"), rice and beans fried together, is the staple breakfast food which varies little from place to place except in price. It comes *con* (with) *huevos* (eggs), *jamon* (ham), etc.

Organic Produce

Although small, the organic movement is growing. It is made up of farmers who believe they must wean themselves from the dependency brought on by imported agrochemicals. The high cost of those chemicals, in a vicious cycle, requires high productivity. An organic market is held every Saturday from 5 am to noon in front of the Escuela San Jerónimo de Desamparados. This is 300 m S and 500 m W of the Cemeterio Desamparados. For information call Patricia Blanco at ☎ 234-9333. In addition, you'll find the Más X Menos supermarket chain has a selection of organic vegetables. The vegetables are grown at Tapezco in Alajuela and are the result of a farsighted member of the Japanese Peace Corps who persuaded an initial eight farmers to try organic farming. Today, the coop has 35 members and grows vegetables ranging from zucchini to broccoli on a total of 20 acres. Organic brown rice is sold at La Mazorca in San Pedro, and Shakti (Av. 8, C. 11) sells organic sugar. Spices and herbs may be found at La Botánica in Quepos on the Pacific Coast. Organic mini-bananas (difficult to cultivate owing to the Sigatoka virus) are grown in the Talamanca region but are reserved for export to the US.

SEAFOOD: *Camarones*, usually very small shrimp, are served with fried rice. Prawns and lobster are available, but expensive. Fish dishes served *en escabeche* have been pickled Spanish-style. Canned locally, Costa Rican tuna may or may not be tainted with dolphin blood.

Other Food

JAMAICAN CUISINE: It is largely confined to the Caribbean coast, and little has survived the voyage. The most common dish you'll find is rice and beans cooked with coconut milk and spices, a version infinitely more appetizing than the Tico rice and beans. Two specialties to watch out for are johnny cakes (originally "journey") and *pan bon*, a sweet, dark bread with designs etched in the batter on top. In some *sodas* (serving snacks and non-alcoholic drinks), you'll also find *agua de sapo*; this "toad water" is iced lemon and raw brown sugar. If you're fortunate, you may be able to find delicacies such as fritters, fry-bread, roasted breadfruit, ackee, and herbal teas.

CHINESE FOOD: You know you're really in a small town when there is no Chinese restaurant! The quality varies from gourmet to grease galore. You may want to ask them to leave out the *ajinomoto* (monosodium glutamate, MSG), a Japanese flavoring derived from soy sauce that, along with cornstarch, ruins the quality and flavor of traditional Chinese cuisine. Curiously, Chinese food is generally accompanied by twin slices of styrofoam-like bread. Some of the most common Chinese dishes have become an integral part of the Costa Rican diet. One example is *arroz con camarones* (fried rice with shrimp) which may be accompanied by greasy *papas francesas* (French fries).

FAST FOODS: Fast food franchises, whose prices and "cuisine" replicate the US originals along with the US prices (although their workers are paid a pittance by comparison) include McDonald's, Pizza Hut, Burger King, and Colonel Sanders. Terms you should be familiar with when ordering pizza include *hongos* (mushrooms), *aceitunas* (olives), and *cebollas* (onions).

SNACKS: *Huevos de tortuga* are sea turtle eggs, thought to have aphrodisiacal properties. They can be found in bars. Eating these eggs, like eating the sea turtle meat served in restaurants, supports further killing of an endangered species.

DESSERTS AND TOPPINGS: The best ice cream is served at the Pops chain which is owned by a consortium, including the right wing publisher of *La Nación*. They meticulously weigh each cone on a scale. Competing chains are Mönpik and Baloons. *Capuchino* is a cone dipped in chocolate. *Cajeta de coco*, made with coconut, *tapa dulce*, and orange peel, is a delicious variety of *cajeta*. *Tres leches* is a cake with filling and frosting. *Tapitas* and *milanes* are foil-wrapped chocolates. Popcorn is known as *palomitas de maíz* or "little corn doves." *Tapa dulce* is strong-tasting unrefined sugar sold in brown hunks. *Dulce de leche* is a thick syrup made with milk and sugar. *Natilla*, cream left out overnight, is a popular topping on many dishes. A common dessert, fruit salad (*ensalada de frutas*) often comes with jello and whipped cream.

FRUITS: Papaya is available much of the year. The two varieties are the round, yellow-orange *amarilla* and the elongated red-orange *cacho*. Watermelon (*sandia*) are also plentiful in season. Don't mistake them for the *chiverre*, a gourd that is candied during Easter. You'll find the pineapple (*piña*) to be sweeter than those you know from home. The core is packed with papain, an enzyme used in making meat tenderizers and best avoided. For similar reasons, avoid eating green papayas. Citrus fruits, originally introduced from Asia, include grapefruit (*toronja*), four types of lemons (*lemones*), mandarins (*mandarinas*), and oranges (*naranjas*). Mangoes come in several varieties and are excellent. *Guayabas* (guavas) have a pink, very seedy pulp commonly used in jam or paste. *Cas* is a similar but smaller and rounder green or yellow fruit. These sour-tasting fruits are used in drinks and ices. *Chan*, a relative of mint, resembles nothing so much as an extraterrestrial beverage. Its furry purple seeds feel like gelatin as they go down. *Maracúya* is an acid-sweet fruit that makes an exotic drink. Introduced from Brazil, its taste is like passion fruit. *Marañón* is the fruit of the cashew nut. It looks like a cross between a prune and a dried fig. *Zapotes* are brown and similar to avocadoes, but with a sweet, bright orange pulp. An unusual delicacy is *palmito*, the tender and delicious heart of the pejibaye palm, which may be boiled or eaten raw. It is considered a delicacy and was once a major source of protein for the Indians. Fibrous in texture, these bright orange fruits are usually boiled in salted water, peeled, halved, and eaten. Other fruits include *granadillas* (passion fruit), *mamones* (lychees), *mamón china* (rambutan), *carambola* (starfruit), *aguacate* (avocado), *melocoton* (peach), and *níspero*.

TOBACCO: Nicotine junkies can choose their poison from at least half a dozen local brands. Males here smoke like chimneys, as do many *joven, señoras, y señoritas*. If you wish to cut down or quit, Costa Rica is an excellent place: single cigarettes are priced at about five cents each and are commonly sold on the street or in small shops.

Food

Costa Rican Food: A to Z

Agua dulce – water sweetened with raw sugarcane.
Almuerzo ejecutivo – a specially priced "executive" lunch.
Arreglados – sandwiches that contain meat and vegetables.
Arroz con camarones – fried rice with shrimp.
Arroz con pollo – chicken with rice and vegetables.
Café con leche – coffee with milk.
Café negro – black coffee.
Cajeta – a traditional fudge-like treat.
Camarones – very small shrimp, usually served with fried rice.
Carne – beef.
Casado – a plate of rice served with salad, beans, and meat,
    chicken, or fish.
Ceviche – a chilled fish cocktail made using *corvina* (sea bass)
    pickled in lemon juice and mixed with cilantro and onion.
Chilasquiles – meat stuffed tortillas.
Chorreados – corn pancakes often sold by street
    vendors in San José.
Corvina – sea bass.
Desayunos – breakfast.
Elote asado – roasted corn on the cob.
Elote cocinado – boiled corn.
Empanadas – corn turnovers filled with cheese, beans, or
    meat and potatoes.
En escabeche – foods that have been pickled Spanish-style.
Enyucados – *empanadas* made with yucca.
Flan – a sweet custard.
Gallo pinto – rice and beans fried together, the staple breakfast food.
Gallos – tortillas filled with cheese, beans, meat, etc.
Guaro – a firewater popular among *campesinos*.
Guiso de máiz – fresh corn stew.
Langostinos – prawns.
Langosta – lobster.
Masamorra – corn pudding.
Melcochas – candies made from raw sugar.
Mondongo en salsa – ox in tomato sauce.
Natilla – sour cream.
Olla de carne – a beef stew.
Pan de máiz – a thick and sweet cornbread.
Pañuelos – a type of pastry.
Papas francesas – French fries.
Patacones – mashed and fried plantains served like French fries.

Patí – snacks made of *empanadas* filled with fruit or spicy meat.
Pescado ahumado – smoked fish made from marlin. It resembles salmon.
Plátanos – plantains, large banana-like grains that must be fried or baked. They are often sliced and fried like potato chips.
Pozol – corn soup.
Pupusas – two *tortillas* fried with cheese inside.
Queque seco – pound cake.
Refrescos – tropical fruit shakes made with milk or water.
Sodas – small alcohol-free restaurants.
Sopa negra – black bean soup which sometimes includes a poached egg.
Tamal asado – a sweet cornbread cake.
Tamales – ground corn and pork wrapped in plantain leaves; traditionally served at Christmas.
Torta chilena – a multi-layered cake filled with *dulce de leche*.
Tortas – a type of bread filled with meat and vegetables.
Tortilla – refers either to an omelette or a small thin *tortilla* (thin corn pancake).
Tortilla de queso – a *tortilla* with cheese mixed in the dough.
Vigorones – a combination of cabbage, cassava, tomato, and onion topped with pork rinds. Invented in Nicaragua.

Drinks

FRUIT DRINKS: *Refrescos* are tropical fruit shakes made with milk or water. They are made from *tamarindo* (the seed pod of the tamarind tree), *moras* (blackberries), *cas*, and other fruits. Some of the most popular items are *pipas*, green or gold drinking coconuts. The vendor opens these with a machete. He hacks off a piece from the edge which, after you're finished eating, serves to scoop out the white, creamy jelly inside. If you want more water than jelly or lots of jelly, just tell the vendor, and he'll hand pick for you.

ALCOHOL: Drinking is a very popular activity, and establishments selling liquor outnumber schools almost three to one. Excellent, locally brewed beers are available in 350 ml bottles in supermarkets, restaurants, *cantinas*, and bars. Brands are the ultra-popular Imperial, the locally brewed Heineken, Bavaria and Bavaria Light and Pilsen. Another brew, Tropical, is a type of ale. In case you missed the news, Miller will be produced in Costa Rica sometime in 1996. *Cerveza cruda* (draft beer) is also available in some local bars. Local bars sell beers for around 50-70¢, and you are expected to drink it there, unless you ask for a cup. Stores sell beers in two types of bottles, nonreturnable and returnable – so identified in raised letters on the glass. You have to get a receipt written out if you want to return them in the supermarkets, but shops generally just rely upon appearance (i.e., if it has a price tag it's not ours!). Costa Rica also produces a few inexpensive varieties of rum as well as sugarcane-distilled *guaro*, a firewater that is the hands-down popular favorite among *campesinos*. Often drinks are accompanied by *bocas*, small dishes of fried fish, *ceviche*, or other snacks. Sometimes you have to pay extra for these.

CAFE: Aside from alcohol, the most popular drink in Costa Rica must be coffee – the nation's only other legal drug. It is served either as *café negro* or *café con leche* (coffee with milk) and is customarily combined with generous quantities of sugar. The traditional way to serve coffee is in a small pitcher, along with a pitcher of heated milk. You mix the two according to taste. Sadly, this custom has largely fallen by the wayside. Coffee can be had *en taza* or, somehow more delicious, *en vaso* (in a glass). It comes in two sizes: *pequeno* (small) and *grande* (large). Despite claims to the contrary, the coffee generally served in Costa Rica is not all that good, unless you compare it with the watered-down truckstop brew found in the States. Most of the ordinary *sodas* sell coffee made from pre-ground powder, which has been either made in a large metal percolator and left to sit, or filtered through a *chorreador*, a cloth filter mounted on a wooden stand. A cup sells for around 40¢.

SOFT DRINKS: Colored sugar water is very much in vogue here and imbibers will find a choice selection practically everywhere. Brands include Coke, Canada Dry Ginger Ale, Squirt, and most of the others. While there is no mineral water, you can ask for *soda blanca*. Soft drinks come in 500 ml plastic disposables, but you might wish to set an example for the locals and send a message to the multinationals by sticking to glass. Milk costs about 50¢ per liter, and long life milk is also available at a higher price. Both are 2% fat.

Dining

TAXES AND TIPS: One thing very confusing for foreign visitors is the system of taxes and tipping. At the better quality restaurants, a 10% service charge is levied on all meals above 10 *colones*, and a 15% sales tax is added on top of this. At the cheaper restaurants, the 15% tax is incorporated in the cost of the meal. The least expensive places, such as *sodas*, incorporate taxes and service in their prices. Costa Ricans almost never leave an additional tip; you can do as you like.

DINING OUT: Most of the nation's finest restaurants – representing cuisines ranging from Swiss to Chinese to Italian – are found in the San José area. While shrimp and lobster are available, they are not cheap. Usual hours for gourmet dining are 11:30-2:30 for lunch, and from 6 or 6:30 to 10 or 10:30 for dinner. While some restaurants are open only for dinner, the ones open for lunch usually feature an *almuerzo ejecutivo*, a specially priced "executive" lunch. To find gourmet restaurants, check the pages of this guide, the yellow pages, *Guide* magazine, or the "On the Town" column in the *Tico Times*. Out in the country, high quality restaurants are fewer and are usually connected to a hotel.

BUDGET DINING: You'll find no lack of of places to eat. There are a small number of local restaurants in every town. Alcohol free *sodas*, which serve everything from *casados* to hamburgers to sandwiches, are your best bet. In a typical *soda*, the menu (which usually includes a *plato del día*, special of the day) is written on a blackboard or painted on a wall. A glass cabinet at the counter contains baked goods and other snacks. Expect to spend about $1-5 per meal. Restaurants offering counter service are generally less expensive. It's always best to ask the price of food before consuming. Although Ticos are not price gougers like the Mexicans, there are unscrupulous people who don't hesitate to jack up the price when the opportunity beckons. In addition, there are the ubiquitous fast-food joints and a proliferation of pizzerias.

TIPS FOR VEGETARIANS: This is most definitely a carnivorous society, so the more you are able to bend or compromise your principles, the easier time you'll have. If you're a vegan (non-dairy product user), unless you're cooking all of your own food, you will find it even more difficult, but the quantity and variety of fruits readily available may be your salvation. Locally grown fruits such as papayas and mangoes tend to be much more reasonable when purchased from vendors, and prices go down at the end of the day. Fruit salads are often drowning in gelatin (an animal product) and ice cream. Ask to have it *sin helados* and *sin gelatina*. If you do eat fish, you should be aware that locals eat it fried and that it may have been fried in lard or in the same oil as chicken or pork. At the very least, it will have been fried in *manteca*, a type of shortening made from hydrogenated palm oil. Be aware that the word *carne* refers only to beef; a dish may still have pork, chicken, or fish in it. Cheese sandwiches will serve you well in a pinch. If you eat a lot of nuts, plan on bringing your own because those available locally are expensive. The same goes for dried fruits such as raisins. Finally, bear in mind that – outside of tourist restaurants – fish may be in short supply at times. Places serving vegetarian food are frequently listed in the text.

Sports & Recreation

BEACHES AND SWIMMING: In addition to the innumerable ocean beaches and rivers, most major hotels and "aparthotels" have their own pools. Olympic-size pools are found at the Cariari Country Club and in Parque de Sabana, where swim meets are sometimes held. The pools fed by Ojo de Agua springs, located S of the international airport, are cold and fresh. Ironically sponsored by McDonald's, the high-fat food purveyor, the International Swimming Tournament is held at the outdoor club in the E part of San José in July or August.

beaches to avoid: According to the National Water and Sewage Service, currently contaminated beaches are Playa Taracoles, Playa Azul, Playa Guacalillo, Playa Quepos, Playa Limon, and Playa Limoncito.

SCUBA AND SNORKELING: Although the former is still an emerging sport here, Costa Rica is an exceedingly fine place to do either. The Caribbean coast's only coral reef is at Cahuita, S of Limón. One excellent area on Guanacaste's Nicoya Penninsula is Playas Hermosa, and the nearby Islas Murciélagos are also among the best locations. El Jardín – an area just off of Bahía Herradura – is famous for its sea fan and soft coral formations. A visit here must be arranged by special charter from Quepos or Puntarenas. The waters surrounding Isla Uvita, just offshore from Limón, have a wide variety of fish, sea fans, and coral as well as the wreck of the *Fenix*, a cargo ship. This is recommended for experienced divers only. Other sites include the Isla de Caño off Osa Peninsula in the NW and the distant Isla de Cocos.

SURFING: To buy or sell your surfboard, try the **Mango Surf Shop**, 75 feet W of the Banco Popular in San Pedro, or the **Tsunami** in Los Yoses. Rental shops are in Limón, Cahuita, Puntarenas, Jacó, and Manuel Antonio. Although there is also surf to be found along the Caribbean, the Pacific coast is famous for its waves.

☞ **Travelers Tip.** The Surf Report (☎ 220-2026) is a tape-recorded English and Spanish surf forecast. It costs 100 colones per minute to call.

Guanacaste locations: The season in Guanacaste runs from late November to early April. Surfing spots are numerous, but hard to reach. To get to Potrero Grande in Parque Nacional Santa Rosa, which features a fast and hollow right point break, rent a boat at Playas de Coco. On the N side of the same park, Playa Naranjo has one of the country's best breaks. Points at Playa Tamarindo are found at Pico Pequeño, El Estero, and at Henry's Point in front of the Third World Bar. Featuring a right and left point break that curls in front of a small rivermouth, Langosta is a km to the S. Avellanas (which has the beach break, "Guanacasteco") lies 10 km S, and Playa Grande is a 20-minute walk (or a shorter drive) to the N. Farther S along the coast are Playa Negra and Nosara. Coyote Manzanillo, and Mal País can be reached by four-wheel-drive during the dry season, but there are no hotels.

Puntarenas and S: To the S from Puntarenas are Boca Barranca, Puerto Caldera, Playa Tivites (and Valor, a rocky point), and Playa Escondito – for which you should rent a boat at Jacó. Near famous Playa Jacó are Roca Loca, 1½ km S, Playa Hermosa (best in front of the almond tree), and other points to the S like Esterillos Este, Esterillo Oeste, Bejuco, and Boca Damas. There's good surfing (but polluted water) in the town of Quepos and, to a lesser extent, up at Manuel Antonio. Set 11 km to the right of Ronacador off the road to Dominical, Playa El Rey features right and left waves. Father S are Playa Dominical and (accessible only by boat) Drake's Bay, as well as Boca del Río Sierpe in Peninsula de Osa. Reachable either by road or by rented boat from Golfito, the left point at Pavones is considered to be one of the world's finest. The southernmost Pacific surfing spot is Punta Burica, which can only be reached by boat; there's no accommodation.

the Caribbean coast: On the Caribbean side, to the N of Limón, are Playas Bonita and Portete; conditions at the former are dangerous. To the S, a long beach break called Westfalia extends S from Limón to Punta Cahuita. Other places are Cahuita's Black Beach, "Salsa" at Puerto Viejo and Manzanillo to its S, and beaches near Herradura.

WINDSURFING: Conditions for windsurfing are said to be among the best in the world. Chilly Lake Arenal features 35-knot gusts every afternoon. (For more details see Parque Nacional Arenal and Environs below.) Other spots include Puerto Soley (a half-hour from Cuajinquil), Playas del Coco, Playa Tamarindo, polluted Playa Puntarenas and the nearby Boca Barranca.

windsurfing packages: Contact **Surf Costa Rica** (☎ 800-771-7873), **Destination Costa Rica** (☎ 223-0656, fax 222-9747; Apdo. 590, San José), or the Ecoadventure Lodge's **Tikal Tours** (☎ 223-2811; fax 223-1916; Apdo. 6398, San José).

WHITE WATER RAFTING: Some of the world's best is found here and is finest during the rainy season. Beginners will want to try the Reventazón, which also has Class V on its upper end. (See description in "Meseta Central" section.) Endangered by a proposed hydroelectric project, the Pacuare flows from the Talamancas to the Caribbean; it is ideal for two- or three-day trips through the tropical jungles. Larger, wider, and more powerful than the Pacuare, the Chirripó is less difficult. A newcomer on the scene, the Río Savegre is a Class II-III run with attractive scenery. For a relaxing trip, Guanacaste's gentle Corobicí is ideal, but don't let the soft current lull you into letting your guard down: drownings have occurred here.

companies: Most offer a series of one-day tours – ranging from Class I to V in difficulty – on the Reventazón, Pacuare, Sarapiquí, and Corobicí. Two-day tours on the Reventazón-Pascua (Class IV), two- and three-day trips on the Pacuare (Class III-IV), and three-, four-, and five-day trips on the Chirripó (Class III-IV) are also available. Special rates for residents and Ticos are offered by some companies. The most established company is **Costa Rica Expeditions** (☎ 257-0776, 222-0333, fax 257-1665; Dept. 235, 1601 NW 97th Av. Unit C-101, Miami FL 33172). Another well known firm is **Ríos Tropicales** (☎ 233-6455, fax 255-4354). Write Apdo. 472, 1200 San José. **Pioneer Tours** is a comparative newcomer on the scene. In Costa Rica, ☎ 253-9132, 225-8117. 225-4735, or fax 253-4687. In the US, ☎ 800-288-2107 or 408-626-1815, fax 408-626-9013. Or write Box 22063, Carmel CA 93922.

US Companies Offering White Water Rafting

California Native	800-926-1140
Mariah Wilderness Expeditions	800-4-MARIAH
Mountain Travel/SOBEK	800-227-2384
Pioneer Raft	800-288-2107
Wildland Adventures	800-345-4453

KAYAKING: Interest in kayaking has grown dramatically in recent years. The Reventazón, with its Class IV and V rapids, has become world renowned as a winter kayaking training ground. The Sarapiquí, flowing N from Volcán Poás through the province of Heredia, has moderate rapids. Others include the Pacuare, General, and the Corobicí. An alternative is sea kayaking. In the US, **Costa Rica Kayaking Adventure** (☎ 415-281-5906; 54 Clairview Ct., San Francisco CA 94131) runs kayaking tours of four days and four nights or five days and four nights. **Ríos Tropicales** (☎ 233-6455, fax 255-4354; apdo. 472, Pavas) has sea kayaking at Curú off the Nicoya Peninsula and from Manuel Antonio. Costa Rica Expeditions has river trips and rents canoes. Gulf Island Kayaking (☎ 661-2392, John Aspinall) also offers trips. Alternatively, ☎ 604-539-2442 or write R.R. #1, Galiana Island, B.C., Canada VON 1PO.

CANOEING: A variety of lodges rent canoes or allow their guests to use them. Some of the best places to canoe are in Tortuguero National Park and Barra Del Colorado Reserve. **Battenkill Canoe** (☎ 802-362-2800; Box 65, Arlington, VT 05250) offers canoeing tour packages.

River Fish

Costa Rica is famous for its deep-sea fishing, but it also has freshwater fish that will delight many anglers. "Most handsome" in Spanish, the guapote (rainbow bass) is a relative of South America's peacock bass. Although found in warmer rivers, coastal lagoons, and lakes, it is most abundant in Lake Arenal, where a tourney is held in May. It fights like the devil once hooked. The high-jumping machaca, related to the piranha, is said to eat anything that hits the water. Unfortunately, they're hard to hook and make bony eating. The mojarra resembles a blue gill and is often found near the shore, concealed beneath shrubbery and logs. They swim right up to the lure, but their small mouths make them difficult to hook. Other river fish include bobo – a semi-vegetarian mullet which may be caught with lettuce, tomato, or bits of banana – as well as snook, vieja, guavine, giant bull sharks, sawfish, and alligator gar.

☞ **Traveler's Tip.** Fishing doesn't have to be super-expensive. While you can't go after sailfish or marlin, you can find a local who will take you out for tarpon or snook. During the snook season (September and October), fish may be caught around the shore area or river mouths. If you obtain a license, you can fish inland. Spanish speakers can get information on fishing at **Deportes Keko** (Av. 20, C. 4/6) in San José.

ANGLING AND DEEP-SEA FISHING: Some of the planet's best sport fishing is to be had here. You can expect sailfish, red and culbera snapper, roosterfish, wahoo, crevalle, snook, tarpon, blue and black marlin, corvina (sea bass) and yellowtail. For the competitively minded, fishing lodges hold tournaments. A fishing license (US$10) can be obtained through your lodge, tackle stores in San José, or from the Ministerio de Agricultura, C. 1, Av. 1, San José, ☎ 223-0829. You will need your passport, tourist card, and two passport-sized photos. Freshwater fishing permits (around $10) are available from the Banco Nacional de Costa Rica's Information Department, open weekdays 9-3 and located behind the Central PO at Av 1, C. 2/4 in San José. It's probably best to bring your own gear for freshwater fishing; note that guapote require a medium rod and a 10-lb line.

areas and seasons: Lake Arenal's guapote season stretches from January 1 through September 30. Although they peak in size from August through mid-October, snook may be caught – near river mouths and along beaches – all year round. Tarpons are caught off the Caribbean coast from January through mid-May, although they may be caught in other months. Sailfish and dorado (dolphinfish) are best caught from July through September, roosterfish in May and June, yellowfin tuna in July and August, and wahoo from June through September.

chartering: Along the Pacific coast, charters are centered at hotel resorts. In the Gulf of Papagayo (Nicoya Peninsula), modern craft can be found at Ocotal, Pez Vela, Flamingo Marina, and at Tamarindo. From Puntarenas, charters operate out of The Yacht Club and the Pacific Marina. Other locations include Playa Naranjo's Oasis del Pacifico, and fishing camps near Golfito and on the Osa Peninsula.

going after trout: The most accessible rivers for fishing are the Tapantí, Copey, and Providencia. Most trout average around 1 lb (454 g), although larger ones have been caught. Chacón farm at San Geraldo is one of the locations stocked for trout.

note: Unfortunately, Costa Rica has failed to ban longline sailfishing; the fish are harvested cheaply by a Florida firm that reportedly grinds them into cat food. Although sailfish export was banned by presidential decree in June 1995, the president rolled back the ban a month later after commercial fishermen from Puntarenas sealed the gulf off to all vessels and also blocked a bridge near Quepos. If you feel strongly that the sailfish stocks should be protected for the sport of future fishermen (who throw the fish back after the struggle), fax President José Maria Figueres, c/o Rick Wallace, Hotel Ocotal at 011-506-670-0083.

Selected Fishing Lodges
Atlantic/Caribbean Coast

Casa Mar Fishing Lodge: In Barra del Colorado. Write PO Drawer 787, Islamorada FL 33036, ☎ 800-327-2880 or 305-664-4615. In Costa Rica ☎ 433-8834 or fax 433-9237.

Isla de Pesca: With housing in A-frames, this is another major fishing lodge. Write Apdo. 8-4390, 1000 San José. ☎ 223-4560 or 221-6673 in San José; fax 255-2533. In the US, ☎ 800-245-8420 or 305-539-1630/1631; fax 305-539-1123. Or write Costa Sol International, 1717 N Bayshore Dr., Ste. 3333, Miami FL 33132.

Parismina Fishing Lodge: This lodge features rooms in wooden cottages. Write Apdo. 7127, 1000 San José, ☎ 222-6055, or fax 222-1760.

Río Colorado Lodge: Located in Barra del Colorado, it offers simple cabins. Write Hotel Corobicí, PO Box 5094, 1000 San José. ☎ 232-8610 in San José. In the US, write 12301 North Oregon Ave., Tampa FL 33612 or ☎ 800-243-9777. From outside the US, ☎ 813-931-4849.

Silver King Lodge: Opened in 1993 and offering facilities that are a bit upscale compared to the others in the area. In Costa Rica ☎ 288-0849 or phone or fax 288-1403. In the US, ☎ 800-VIP-FISH or write Aerocasillas, Dept. 1597, Box 025216, Miami FL 33102.

Tortuga Lodge: A comfortable lodge in Tortuguero run by Costa Rica Expeditions. In San José, ☎ 222-0333 or 257-0766; fax 257-1665. Write Apdo. 6941, 1000 San José or, from the US, ☎ 800-225-2272.

Pacific Coast

Golfito Sailfish Rancho: About a 15-minute boat ride from Golfito, this is the area's oldest established fishing lodge. Write PO Box 290190, San Antonio TX 78280 or ☎ 800-531-7332 or 512-492-5517.

Río Sierpe Lodge: A deep sea and tidal basin fishing lodge located in the NE section of the Osa Peninsula. Scuba and snorkeling day trips to Isla de Caño can be arranged, as can two-day RT cruises to Isla de Coco. Write Apdo. 818, 1200 Pavas; ☎ 220-1712/2121 or fax 232-3321.

Aguilar de Osa: Intimate and high quality, this lodge (☎ 296-2190, fax 232-7722 Apdo. 10486-1000, San José) has 14 thatched-roof cabins with verandas. Perched on a hillside, its garden setting includes a gourmet restaurant and a pool. It offers sportfishing (four boats), scuba, birding, and kayaking. In the US, write Cuenta # 250, 7500 NW 25 St., Miami FL 33122.

SEA EXCURSIONS: Many boat trips are available. The best known is the cruise to Tortuga Island. (See the "offshore islands" section under "Puntarenas to Panama.") Another is the trip to Isla del Coco.

HOT-AIR BALLOONING: Serendipity Adventures (☎ 225-6055; Apdo. 6-4200, Naranjo, Alajuela) offers sunrise air tours from Naranjo, Turrialba, and Arenal; there is a maximum of five passengers per balloon; tours are combined with optional activities such as whitewater rafting. While the Naranjo and Arenal options include pickup at your hotel in San José, the Turrialba flight involves an overnight at Casa Turire before the flight. In the US, ☎ 800-635-2325, fax 313-426-5026, or write Box 2325, Ann Arbor MI 48106. (They can also arrange a number of other excursions.)

Competitive Sports

BASKETBALL: One of the national avocations. Hoops may be had at many a village court, and national games are played at San José's La Sabana.

BOWLING: There are a number of alleys in San José. The Tournament of Nations, considered to be the most prestigious bowling contest in Latin America, is held on Columbus Day, October 12.

GOLF: Cariari Country Club, set W of San José enroute to Alajuela, has the nation's only 18-hole golf course. There is an annual international tournament here. Nine-hole courses are at **Los Reyes Country Club** near Alajuela, **El Castillo Country Club** above Heredia, Escazú's **Costa Rican Country Club**, and **Tango Mar** near Playa Tambor on the S coast of Nicoya Peninsula. A six-hole course is at the **Casa Turire** near Turrialba.

RUNNING: The best place to jog in San José is in the park. Attracting competitors from around the world, there's also a **Hash House Harri-**

ers Club (☎ 228-0769) that runs on Mondays and drinks beer afterwards.

CYCLING: Despite the dangers from diesel exhaust, cycling is a rewarding experience. The major annual event is the **Vuelta a Costa Rica**, a 12-day marathon held in December. The **Recreational Cycling Association** offers family excursions on Sundays. For mountain biking excursions contact the companies listed in the chart below.

Mountain Bike Rentals & Excursions

Company	Tel.	Rentals	Tours
COSTA RICAN OPERATORS			
Bike N'Hike	289-8191	X	X
Centro Commerical, Escazú			
C. R. Mountain Biking	222-4380	X	
Apdo. 3979, San José 1000			
Costaricabike	225-3939	X	
Apdo. 812, 2050 San Pedro			
Geoventuras	221-2053		X
Horizontes	222-2022		X
Apdo. 1780, San José 1002			
Mountain Biking Costa Rica	255-0914	X	X
Rios Tropicales	233-6455	X	X
Apdo. 472, Pavas			
Safaris Corobici	669-0544	X	
Tikal Tour Operators	223-2811	X	X
Apdo. 6398, San José 1000			
OVERSEAS OPERATORS			
Backroads	800-245-3874		
Canadian BackRoutes	416-588-6139		
Journeys	800-255-8735		
Mariah Wilderness Expeditions	800-462-7424		

SQUASH: Courts include **Monte Real** in Sabana Sur and **Top Squash** (right behind McDonalds in the Sabana area).

TENNIS: In addition to courts at various hotels, public hard and grass courts are maintained at **Sabana Park** and the nearby **Costa Rica Tennis Club**, the **Costa Rica Country Club**, and the **Los Reyes Country Club**. The **Cariari Country Club** also hosts the annual World Friendship Tournament in March and April and a tournament for the younger set, the Copa del Café, every January.

Other Sports

HORSEBACK RIDING: Horses are a national pastime. Costa Rica is known for its Paso Fino and Andalusian breeds. Instruction is available at the **Porton del Tajo** (☎ 239-2248) at Cariari Country Club and the **Hipico La Caraña** (☎ 228-6106, 228-6754), about 20 km W of San José in Río Oro de Santa Ana, where international competitions are held annually. Santa Ana's **Club Paso Fino** (☎ 249-1466) specializes in these purebreeds; it gives lessons and offers accommodation and meals. Horse lovers won't want to miss the Horse Parade, held in San José during Christmas week. A large number of lodges have horses and riding is available in places as diverse as Manuel Antonio, Rincón de la Vieja, Cahuita, and Puerto Viejo de Talamanca. Specifics are given in the chapters below, with a special section under "Vicinity of San José."

BULLFIGHTS AND RODEOS: Guanacaste Province, the cattle capital of Costa Rica, holds rodeos and bullfights from November to April in the towns of Santa Cruz, Nicoya, and Liberia. The Cariari Country Club also has rodeos, and rodeos and bullfights are held in San José during the Christmas holiday season.

Practicalities

WHEN TO COME: When you should come depends upon your motives for coming. The best time is generally off-season (April to December), when rates for hotels plummet and there are few visitors to be found in the more popular spots. While it does rain quite a bit during this period, whitewater rafting improves, the Guanacaste region greens over, and showers (largely confined to the afternoon) cool things down. The rain is heaviest in the region surrounding San José. In other regions, such as the Caribbean coast and around Golfito, there is no clearly defined rainy season: it simply rains much of the time year round. If you check an issue of the *Tico Times* after arrival, you can window shop rainfall levels and decide which locations to visit. *La Nación* has a daily report. If you arrive during the rainy season (the Costa Rican "winter"), you may find it is actually cooler in Costa Rica than at home. If camping and hiking are important items on your itinerary, it would definitely be preferable to come in the dry season. If you go to the more inaccessible or untouristed towns, parks, and reserves, crowds shouldn't be a problem, whatever the season.

during Holy Week: Most *josefinos* flee the capital at this time and the streets are deserted. Since this is the only time when you can cross the streets safely, it is the perfect time to visit San José. The drawback is that almost everything is closed. This is not the week to visit the beaches because that is where everyone goes. If you need to hide away, the best bets are the smaller inland towns. You can generally find places to eat, but there won't be much to do other than to watch the festivities. No alcohol is sold on Thursday or Friday, so all bars, *cantinas*, and restaurants that usually sell alcohol are shut tight with *guardia* seals plastered across the door to ensure that no violations occur. Even cases of liquor in the supermarket are sealed up. Be certain to stock up beforehand. Also note that most buses stop running from noon on Thursday through Friday.

WHO SHOULD COME: Costa Rica is definitely not for everyone. If the least little sandfly bite, mosquito sting, or insect sighting takes you aback, this isn't the place for you, unless you confine yourself to the most luxurious resorts along Guanacaste's coast. Much of Costa Rica is for adventurous people, who don't mind being a bit uncomfortable if that's what it takes to experience the country. Unlike Hawaii or even the Americanized Cancún, Costa Rica will definitely require some adjustment on your part. Posh resorts, although available, are *not* what Costa Rica is about, nor is great nightlife. You absolutely must have an interest in nature. A willingness to speak even a bit of broken Spanish will take you a long way. You'll find that the rewards are worth every bit of the discomfort you may endure.

Basics

MEASUREMENTS: The metric system is used; gasoline and milk are both sold by the liter. While road distances are given in kilometers, road speed signs and car speedometers use miles per hour. Land elevations are expressed in meters. In addition to metric, traditional units are in use. Traditional measurements include the *libra* (0.46 kg, 1.014 lbs), *arroba* (10.59 kg, 25.35 lbs), *quintal* (46 kg, 101.40 lbs), *fanega* (4 hectoliters, 11.35 bushels), *quartillo* (3.71 kg, 7 lbs), *carga* (816.4 kg, 1,800 lbs), *manzana* (2.82 hectares, 7 acres), and the *caballeria* (42.5 hectares, 111.68 acres). The *vara* (33 inches) is frequently used to describe distances.

Although Costa Rica operates on Central Standard Time, one can accurately say that time here is measured in *ahoritas*, the uncertain and uncharted time it will take for an official to return to his office or a bus to leave.

electric current: 110 volts AC.

conversions: A meter is equal to three feet and three inches. A kilometer equals .62 miles (about 5/9 of a mile), a square km is equal to about 3/8 of a square mile.

TRAVELING WITH CHILDREN: Costa Ricans love children, and the high health standards are a positive consideration. If you want to bring an infant with you, you should note that disposable diapers are very expensive and not readily available. The environmentally conscious, however, will wish to use cloth. Although many restaurants have high chairs and booster seats, car seats are unavailable when renting a vehicle. If your children are under 18 and stay more than 90 days, they'll require permission from the Patronato Office (C. 19, Av. 6) to leave with you! Both parents must be present in order to secure the permit. If you're a single parent traveling alone, you must have the permission of the other notarized by the nearest Costa Rican consul prior to your arrival. The Parque Nacional de Diversiones, described later in the text, is one way to please fickle children. Other places to visit in the Costa Rica area might include the Butterfly Farm, Acua Mania, and the Children's Museum. Also, check the Friday edition of *La Nación*'s "Viva" section, which lists children's activities. Another way to entertain them is with *Let's Discover Costa Rica*, a coloring and activity book which is widely available.

BRINGING YOUR PET: It's much simpler to leave Fido at home! If you want to persist, you should write far in advance of your visit to Jefe del Departamento de Zoonosis, Ministerio de Salud, 1000 San José, and ask for an importation form.

DISABLED TRAVELERS: Costa Rica has yet to make many concessions to the handicapped. Very few hotels have handicapped-friendly bathrooms and only some are wheelchair accessible. It's best to contact your hotel ahead of time and ask. As buses have no special equipment, getting around by taxi is easiest. Keep in mind it's best to call in advance for one.

PHOTOGRAPHY: Film is expensive here so you might want to bring your own. Kodachrome KR 36, ASA 64, is the best all around slide film. For prints 100 or 200 ASA is preferred, while 1000 ASA is just the thing underwater. For underwater shots, use a polarizing filter to cut down on glare; a flash should be used in deep water. Avoid photographs on land between 10 and 2 when there are harsh shadows. Photograph landscapes while keeping the sun to your rear. Set your camera a stop or a stop and a half down when photographing beaches in order to prevent overexposure from glare. A sunshade is a useful addition. Keep your camera and film out of the heat and protected from rain; silica gel packets are useful for staving off mildew. Replace your batteries before a trip or bring a spare set. Manual SLR (single lens reflex) cameras are preferable to automatics because they will still function without batteries and are not as subject to breakdowns. However, they are increasingly difficult to find. Inexpensive lenses may be more likely to develop mold than their otherwise nearly identical brand name equivalents. Because local developing is very expensive and of generally poor quality, it's better to take your film home for developing. Likewise, avoid having camera equipment repaired here.

rainforest photography: Generally speaking, the bright tropical sun makes Costa Rica a photographer's paradise. However, the dark rainforest is a much more difficult environment. While high speed films can be used without a tripod, your shots will lack the sharpness of detail you get with lower exposure film. Tripods are too bulky to carry; one alternative is to set your camera on a tree stump or rock. If you do this, check your film packaging for information on any adjustments you must make. Amateur flash units are suitable only for close up photography. Whatever you do, don't wait for a sunny day. An overcast day is best for shooting because cameras are incapable of capturing the extreme contrasts between shadow and highlights. Animal photography is a chancy proposition owing to distances and dense vegetation. You can't hesitate or the animal may be gone! If you're intending to shoot animals in their environment, the ideal would be to bring two camera bodies (loaded with ASA 64 and ASA 1000 film) along with 300 mm zoom and regular lenses. After a trip, you'll really appreciate the fine animal photography you see.

Visas

VISAS: American citizens may enter with a passport, driver's license, or voter's registration card and stay for 90 days, but they may not extend that visa without a passport. Canadians must have a passport if traveling by a charter flight. All visitors will be expected to show sufficient funds and a return ticket. Citizens of the following nations do not require visas for stays of up to 90 days: Great Britain, West Germany, Spain, Argentina, Austria, Columbia, Denmark, South Korea, Japan, Netherlands, Finland, France, Italy, Israel, Norway, Romania, and Luxembourg. Citizens of the following nations do not require visas for stays of up to 30 days: Honduras, Guatemala, Liechtenstein, Iceland, Sweden, Republic of Ireland, Switzerland, New Zealand, Brazil, Ecuador, Australia, Venezuela, Mexico, Monaco, and Belgium. All others must have visas. **note:** Costa Rican law requires that you carry identification at all times. The best procedure is to have a copy of your passport's photo page laminated.

EXTENDING YOUR VISA: If you wish to avoid the lines, language difficulties, and the general hassle, you can go to a travel agent and receive an exit permit, which will permit you to stay an extra 30 days. This must be done prior to your tourist card's expiration date, and you must bring along your passport, tourist card, three passport photos, and airline ticket. You should make a copy of the first few pages of your passport for use while the agent is obtaining the permit. You'll be charged a fee, but this will save you two trips to Immigration and a half-day or so of standing in line. At the permit's expiration, you will be required to leave the country for at least 72 hours. In order to extend it more than a month, you must do so at Immigration, although you may go through a travel agent to receive your exit permit before you leave. If you stay more than 92 days, a statement is required from the Ministerio de Hacienda showing that you owe no taxes. The travel agent may be able to get one of these as well. In any case, you'll be expected to show at least US$200 for each month you plan to extend.

You should arrive at Immigration (located in the outlying suburbs of La Uruca) by 7:15 AM in the earlier part of the week. Go to the window labeled "Prorogas de Turismo," where you'll receive a form. Inquire as to the amount of revenue stamps you'll need and purchase those before going to the third (and hopefully final!) line. You'll be given a receipt for your passport, which you'll have to come back for after several days. **overstaying:** A July 1995 crackdown on overstayers resulted in the issuance of deportation orders for 180 foreigners. While it was once possible for you to overstay practically forever, by simply paying a fine at the airport, the government has toughened restrictions and now deports offenders, who may not re-enter the country for 10 years.

Services & Information

☞ **Traveler's Tip.** In the US ☎ 800-343-6332 for information courtesy of the Costa Rican Tourism Institute. It's available from 8-5 Costa Rican time. Inside Costa Rica itself you can ☎ 800-012-3456.

TOURIST CENTERS: Tourist information centers are at the airport and in San José at the Plaza de la Cultura (☎ 222-1090). These are said to be the biggest "white elephant" the government has, and service in the offices can range from excellent to execrable, depending upon who is in charge and whether they feel like abandoning their newspapers or not. Generally, they only give you what you ask for, so be sure to ask for all three maps, which they may or may not have, and for a look at the heavily edited and poorly photocopied sheets giving the low-down on bus transport. You may borrow these and photocopy them in the film shop across the street. Although better maps are available, the giveaway maps (also on sale at bookshops) should be sufficient for ordinary use. The best map available is put out by ITMB in Vancouver and is sold at select bookstores in Costa Rica nationwide.

Tourist Bureau Offices

Costa Rica	**USA**
Plaza de la Cultura	1101 Brickell Ave
Avenidas Central/2, Calle 5	BIV Tower, Suite 801
San José, Costa Rica	Miami FL 33131
☎ 222-1090, 223-1733, ext. 277	☎ 305-358-2150
442-1820 (airport office)	800-327-7033

LAUNDRY: Although laundromats are scarce and incredibly expensive, your hotel can usually arrange to do laundry or hook you up with a launderer. Cheaper hotels have sinks (*pilas*), where you can do your laundry yourself. Located next to Spoon in Los Yoses to the E of downtown San José, **Lava Más** is one of the few self-service joints found in the country. Another is at Pavas near the US Embassy; take a bus from Coca Cola.

What to Take

Clothing	**Toiletries**
socks and shoes	soap and shampoo
underwear	towel, washcloth
sandals/thongs	toothpaste/toothbrush
T-shirts, shirts (or blouses)	comb/brush, nail clippers
skirts/pants	prescription medicines
shorts	Chapstick, hand lotion
swimsuit	insect repellent
hat	suntan lotion/sunscreen
light jacket	shaving kit and mirror
sweater	toilet paper

Other Items

passport/identification	snorkeling equipment
driver's license	earplugs
travelers checks	compass
moneybelt	extra glasses
address book	umbrella/poncho
notebook	rubber boots
Spanish-English dictionary	laundry bag
pens/pencils	laundry soap/detergent
books/maps	matches/lighter
watch	needle/thread
camera/film	frisbee/sports equipment
flashlight/batteries	cooking supplies, if needed

Bring as little as possible, i.e., bring what you need. It's easy just to wash clothes in the sink and thus save lugging around a week's laundry. Remember, simple is best. Set your priorities according to your needs. With a light pack or bag, you can breeze through from one region to another easily. Confining yourself to carry-on luggage also saves waiting at the airport. And, if a second bag of luggage gets lost, you at least have the essentials you need until it turns up. Loose clothing will be more comfortable in this hot country. If you're going to wear shorts, they should be long and loose.

PROTECTIVES: Avon's Skin-So-Soft bath oil, when diluted 50% with water, serves as an excellent sand flea repellent. Sunscreen should have an 8-15 protection level or greater. A flashlight is essential, and you might want to bring two, a larger one and one to fit in your handbag or daypack. Feminine hygiene items are rarely found outside of San José; bring a good supply. Likewise, all prescription medicines, contraceptives, creams and ointments, and other such items should be brought with you.

OTHERS: Subject to a 13% import tax as well as shipping and handling charges, books are often twice US prices, so you'll also probably want to stock up before arrival. It's a good idea to have toilet paper with you, as the least expensive hotels and park restrooms may not supply it. Binoculars are invaluable for watching wildlife. The best models feature internal-focus roof prism designs and are waterproof; high light transmission and high magnification are desirable. Plastic trash bags and an assortment of different-sized baggies will also come in handy. High-topped rubber boots (*botas de hule*) are a good investment (around $8) after your arrival. If you have unusually large feet, though, it is a good idea to bring your own. Batteries manufactured locally are not of the highest quality so you should bring some along.

BUDGET TRAVELERS: If you're a low-budget traveler, you'll want to bring earplugs, some rope for a clothesline, towel and washcloth, toilet paper, cup, small mirror, a universal plug for the sink, and a cotton sheet. A smaller pack is preferable because a large one will not fit on the overhead rack above the bus seats and storage is available only on a few buses.

HIKERS AND BACKPACKERS: If nature is your focus, you'll want to bring a rain parka, walking shoes or hiking boots, a day pack, canteen, hat, binoculars, and insect repellent as well as a bird book or two. Loose cotton trousers are recommended; jeans take a long time to dry. Expect your clothing to get dirty, and there's not much sense in washing your rainforest gear until you get back to "civilization."

There's no perfect protection against rain. Parkas and raincoats are too hot. An unlined Goretex jacket is superior, but still hot. And a poncho can restrict your movement. Umbrellas are useful in open areas, and you can still take pictures. One solution to eyeglass fogging is to use skin divers' anti-fog solution, which you can buy at a dive shop. Standard hiking boots are fine for mountains and arid areas, but army surplus jungle boots are best; buy the kind with light canvas uppers and a heavy-duty sole. You can purchase rubber boots at home or in Costa Rica (see above).

CAMPERS: Perhaps the ideal setup for camping in the forest is to sleep in a jungle hammock with a blanket, which is protected from bugs by a mosquito net and from rain by a fly. If you go this route, you might need to practice sleeping in a hammock – which takes a bit of adjustment – and you'll want to choose the trees where you hang your hammock with care. Smaller ones may be preferable, and try to find one without many ants. As a precaution, soak the cords with repellent. The problem with tents is that they rest on the ground, which tends to be muddy. The most practical tent is likely to be one with plenty of screening, covered by a waterproof fly. Choose high ground and dig a trench. Backpacking stoves are the way to go for meals; buy one that can burn gasoline or kerosene. Camping Gaz-type containers, while available, are hard to find, and it is illegal to carry them on planes. If you have a headlamp-style flashlight, you can free your hands up while you cook or take a night hike. Don't forget to bring water purification tablets or boil your water. There is no safe water in the rainforest.

ANGLERS: Necessities include sleeved shirts and pants, a wide-brimmed hat, and effective sun protection. For the Caribbean coast-bound angler, raingear is necessary, even during the dry season. Although lodges can generally arrange rentals, it's better to bring your own equipment. Bring a 20 lb or stronger line for saltwater fishing.

SNORKELERS: You may be able to rent it on location, but you might be well advised to bring your own equipment. Those afflicted with nearsightedness, but without a strong astigmatism, can have a mask fitted with prescription lenses at some dive shops for around $80. It's not cheap, but it's an invaluable investment if you're a serious snorkeler. You may be able to get by without fins, but you should at least have windsurfing sandals to protect your feet against injury. Remember to avoid damaging the reef at all times!

Phone, Mail & Media

TELEPHONE SERVICE: Unlike some nations, Costa Rica has a fairly reliable phone system, including a good supply of pay phones – although, as Costa Ricans love to telephone, there's almost always a line. Pay telephones take either the new or antiquated varieties of coins, so it's best to carry a supply of both varieties. Always in short supply, the two *colones* coins are being replaced by the five *colones* coins, leading one to suppose that the government has chosen to rectify the shortage by raising the price. Many pay phones also use 10 and 20 *colones* coins, but seem to prefer five *colones* coins. To use a pay phone, wait for a dial tone *before* inserting your coins. Call times are limited and at the end of your time you'll need to pay again. Although one species of machine has you place your coins on a rack to be digested as required, others will give you a signal. Be quick in depositing additional coins or you will be cut off! If you dial and hear nothing or get a busy signal, be sure to redial: it may be a problem with the central exchange. No calls within the country require a prefix. Some villages (Cahuita, for example) have an exchange and operate largely by extensions. In areas where there are no regular public phones, shops, bars, and restaurants rent out their phones. It's best to ask the price before dialing to make sure that it is fair and not a *gringo* rate. The cost can add up and there can also be a wait. If you have a large number of calls to make, you may want to wait until you are in a place with a regular pay phone. Some hotels tack on a surcharge to the bill, allowing you unlimited dialing within the country. If your hotel has a phone in the room, ask about their policy when you check in.

☞ **Traveler's Tip.** When using the pay phones you should obtain a good supply of five *colón* coins and keep them handy. Redial several times if you get a busy signal. In Spanish query "Aló" and follow this with "Se encuentra (name of person you want) por favor?" You will be asked "de parte?", so give your name.

The number for local information is 113. For an English-speaking operator, dial 116. **calling to and from abroad:** When dialing the US or Canada direct, call 001, 116, and the number. Other useful numbers are 112, time of day; 117, San José police; 118, fire department; 127, local police. For an AT&T overseas operater, dial 114. At the Radiográficia (c. 1, Av. 5) in San José, you can phone or wire abroad; either are very expensive. To make a credit card or collect call, contact AT&T operators directly from USADirect phones at the airport, Radiográfica, and at the Holiday Inn, Av. 4, C. 5. **The area code is 011-506,** a prefix which should be applied to all numbers listed in this book when dialing from abroad. Offering the prospect of greatly improved service, phone card phones may be introduced in quantity before the century's end. Cards will be available in denominations of C 200, 500, and 1,000.

POSTAL SERVICE: Window service at the main post office (Correos y Telegráphicos or Coretel, C. 2, Av. 1/3) runs from 7-6 weekdays and 7-2 on Saturday. Other offices are located nationwide. The philatelic department is upstairs. Rates are inexpensive; your color postcard is likely to cost you more than the stamp. Mail generally takes about five days to the US, Canada, or Europe. Sea mail (*marítimo*) usually runs four to six weeks to North America. To ensure prompt delivery, send mail from your hotel desk or a main post office and avoid enclosing anything other than a letter. **receiving mail:** You can have mail sent to you at your hotel or to Lista de Correos (General Delivery); the latter is at window 17 in the main post office. Have your correspondents send it in your name (have the last name written in capital letters), c/o Lista de Correos, Correo Central, San José.

Currently, letters (up to 20 g) cost C 20 locally, C 35 to Central America, C 45 to S and N America, and C 55 to Europe. Postal codes are placed *before* the city or town. In order to bypass the convoluted bureaucracy and the absolutely outrageous customs duties, avoid having anything sent to you other than letters and perhaps a few snapshots. If you do receive a package, you may have to make two trips to the office way out in Zapote and pay a customs fee, which could be more than the value of the package. Have your friends underline both "Costa Rica" and "Central America" to ensure that your letters don't languish in Puerto Rico! If you have American Express traveler's

checks or a credit card, you can have mail sent c/o Tan Travel Agency
(☎ 233-0044) Apdo. 1864, San José. They're at Av. Central, C.1.

note: Mail theft is endemic. In 1993, following a two-year investigation, eight postal workers were fired for allegedly stealing thousands of checks, credit cards, and other valuables sent through the mail. The workers remained on the job during the investigation because Costa Rica's Civil Service laws require such an investigation before workers can be fired.

fax: If your hotel has a machine, they will generally send and receive faxes for you at a fee. The cheapest place to use is a Coretel office. In San José, the main office is at C. 2, Av. 1/3. Go to the Coretel fax window, fill out the form, and head to the telex office upstairs (follow the arrow). Faxes can also be sent via Radiográfica (☎ 223-1609, 323-7932); their offices are at C. 1, Av. 5, open 7 AM-11 PM. If your correspondent includes your hotel's phone number, they will notify you. ☎ 287-0513 or 287-0511. If you send a fax to a post office with the address clearly on it, the post office will deliver the fax to the recipient.

BROADCASTING AND MEDIA: A media censorship board is in operation; its effect is most directly apparent in movies. In the past, all journalists had to be registered with the Colegio de Periodistas, which was a clear violation of the nation's obligations under the Human Rights Convention to which it is a signatory. In May 1995, the Supreme Court ruled the licensing unconstitutional. There are four daily papers. The daily *La Nación* is a horrifically propagandistic right-wing tabloid said to be manipulated by US interests. Its vice-director is vice-president of the Free Costa Rica Movement (MRCL), a right-wing civic organization with an armed militia. The paper also published *Nicaragua Hoy*, a weekly *Contra* newspaper produced by Pedro Joaquin Chamorro. The others are *La Prensa Libre* and *La República* (originally founded by Figueres and his supporters in 1950). They aren't much better and there have been allegations by former *Contra* leader Edgar Chamorro and others that the CIA pays off reporters. There are four weekly newspapers, including *Esta Semana* (the best Spanish language source for news) and the equally fine *Universidad*, published by the University of Costa Rica. Muckraking journalist Martha Honey has called the English-language *Tico Times*, "definitely the best newspaper in Central America." It has a fine staff of investigative reporters. Subscriptions are available and on-line subscriptions are also to be had with the weekly, accessible free on the Internet's World Wide Web (WWW) at http://www.magi.com/crica/ttimes.html. E-mail enquiries may be directed to ttimes@sol.racsa.co.cr. The *Tico Times'* major competitor is *Costa Rica Today*, a relentlessly upbeat weekly tabloid that focuses on the cheery side of Costa Rican life. It also formerly carried full-page ads for Bosque Puerto Carrillo, a teak "reforestation" project whose backers – Terry Ennis and Ralf Stefan Jaeckal – financed the journal (Ennis and Jacekel were ousted from the company in May 1995 by irate stockholders, and the paper carries ads only for the company's parquet floor tiles now. The company had sold some millions of dollars worth of unregistered stock by promising exorbitant profits. Another new entry on the scene is *Costa Rica Aktuell*, a German-language newspaper. *Mesoamerica*, essential for anyone concerned about Central American politics and economics, is published in San José's suburb of San Pedro. The library at the Friend's Peace Center sells copies. For a subscription in the US ☎ 800-633-4931 or write Apdo. 300, 1002 San José. *Costa Rica Outlook*, a valuable bimonthly newsletter geared to travelers, is available only through subscription ($19 in the US, $23 foreign). Write Box 5573, Chula Vista CA 91912-5573; tel./fax 619-421-6002 or 800-365-2342. Topics include scuba diving, wildlife, restaurants and hotels, horseback riding, and other activities. Discount coupons for hotels, language schools, and the like are included. The publishers also operate a full-service travel agency called **Vagabond Tours** (☎ 800-365-2342, 619-421-6002).

RADIO STATIONS: All radio stations are privately owned, either by commercial interests or by religious broadcasters. Most stations play an amalgam of salsa and American rock and schlock. For those missing the concrete jungles of LA, you can tune in for Dick Barkley's "American Gold" from 10 to noon on Saturday and Sunday at 99.5 FM. From 6-9 weekdays, you can hear Dick Barkely's "Good Morning, San José" program. Radio for Peace International transmits on shortwave and broadcasts in English, Spanish, German, and French Creole.

Radio Stations by Frequency

Frequency	Station Name	Programming
500.9 AM	Radio Nacional	Popular (mixed)
670 AM	Radio Monumental	Romantic
700.3 AM	Radio Reloj	Latin pop
760 AM	Radio Columbia	Talk radio
780 AM	Radio America	Latin pop
850 AM	Radio Viva	US/Latin pop
870 AM	Radio Universidad	Classical/ educational
900 AM	Radio Nacional	Popular (mixed)
1080 AM	Radio Alajuela	Latin dance
1440 AM	Radio Puntarenas	Latin pop
1420 AM	Radio Pompa	Popular
88.7 FM	Radio Lira	Popular

91.1 FM	Colorín Radio	Children's
91.9 FM	Radio Puntarenas	Latin pop
93.5 FM	Radio Monumental	Romantic
94.3 FM	Radio Reloj	Latin pop
94.7 FM	Radio Joven	Rock
95.1 FM	Radio Fabulosa	US/Latin romantic
96.7 FM	Radio Universidad	Classical/ educational
96.9 FM	Radio 96	Classical
97.5 FM	Radio Musical	Romantic
97.9 FM	Radio Titania	US/Spanish pop
98.3 FM	Radio Alajuela	Latin dance
98.7 FM	Radio Columbia	Talk radio
99 FM	Radio Azul	Jazz and "new age"
99.1	Radio Sabrosa	Latin dance
99.5 FM	Radio 2	1960-90s hits
101.5 FM	Radio Ultra-Sonic	Popular
101.9 FM	Radio Universidad	Classical/ educational
102.3 FM	Super Radio	1960s/70s US rock
102.7 FM	Radio Uno	US/Latin rock & pop
104.3 FM	Radio Sensación	Spanish popular
105.1 FM	Radio Omega	New popular
106.3 FM	Radio Stereo 106	Muzac

TELEVISION: TV was introduced in 1960; there are now six TV stations. They serve up a combination of the worst American programming rendered into Spanish and bad local imitations of the worst American programming. It is rather dismaying to see MTV in Spanish, featuring videos by heavy metal bands from El Salvador! Cable News Network (CNN) and other cable service in English is available. An interview program in English, Costa Rica Update appears every Thursday at 7 PM on Channel 19; it's rebroadcast at 1 PM.

Costa Rica on the Internet

Costa Rica is on the Internet! The Costa Rica Information Center is at http://www.cool.co.cr. You will find the *Tico Times* at http://www.magi.com/crica/ttimes.html. You can E-mail them at ttimes@sol.racsa.co.cr. *La Nación* can be found at http://www.nacion.co.cr. The Netalog (a catalog of tour and other information run by Zarpe Travel) can be reached at http://www.costarica.org. The tour operator Costa Rica Expeditions can be found at http://www.cool.co.cr.80/usr/cre/crexped.html. A travel and tour agency, Calypso runs a TravelNet which also has a WWW presence.

For information, contact TravelNet at calypso@cosri.com or ☎ 233-3617 in Costa Rica. Brochures can be obtained by mail through http://www.mmink/infosystems/tre.html. Nature lodge and reserve Rara Avis (raraavis@sol.racsa.co.cr.org) may be found on the Web at http://www.cool.co.cr/usr/raraavis/ing/raraavis.html. Check the latest information on Costa Rica from the author of this book at http://www.catch22.com/~vudu.

BBS (bulletin board service) is provided by a number of companies. *La Nación*'s Quorum provides free Internet access. Expresso (☎ 222-4553) offers bilingual service for $15 per minute. Tico Net (☎ 228-6879) offers service from $20 per minute. Read about current developments by perusing Charles Stratford's highly informative articles in the *Tico Times*. BBS (bulletin board service) is provided by **Costa Rica Online** (☎ 226-5427) at ☎ 226-5438 and set your modem to 8-N-1.

Health

Costa Rica is perhaps the most sanitary of the Central American nations. Although tap water in San José is safe to drink, you may wish to exercise caution elsewhere. If you are hiking and camping, either drink boiled water or have iodine tablets on hand. If the taste bothers you, add a little powdered drink mix or squeeze lemon or lime into your water bottle. Take basic precautions such as washing both your hands and pocketknife before peeling fruit. No immunizations are required. You may wish to get a gamma globulin shot to stave off hepatitis A, but the incidence of the disease is low here. Diarrhea (easily remedied by over-the-counter medicines) is much more common than dysentery, the symptoms of which include fever and blood in the stools. Malaria is nonexistent except near Panama on the Caribbean coast and in the Sarapiquí and Limón areas – an effect of poor health practices on the banana plantations. If you plan to spend a long time in these areas, prevent an occurrence with a dose of chloroquine (marketed in Costa Rica as Aralen) and begin two weeks before your arrival. Keep in mind that these mosquitoes bite mainly at night. Outbreaks of dengue fever were also reported in 1994, but this mosquito-borne viral disease should not affect short-term visitors. Leptospirosis, a disease caused by a microorganism, is transmitted to humans from animals through contaminated water. Again, cases have been reported, but it should not be a problem with visitors.

There are plenty of *farmacias* around should you require medicine, but most medications are imported (largely from Europe and the US) and expensive. Costa Rica's health system is reputed to be among the world's best; hospitals and related information are detailed in the San José section of this book.

INSURANCE: An insurance policy has been developed for visitors by the Costa Rica Social Security office and the International Organization of Cultural Interchanges (OICI). Emergency medical insurance ($45 per month, $35 for students) entitles the bearer to hospitalization and surgery at any Social Security clinic or hospital. Although emergency dental care is provided, pre-existing illness will not be treated. The insurance card may be purchased at any ICT-authorized travel agency or tourism business office. Cards valid for longer than one month are available from the OICI (☎ 257-0680, fax 222-7867; Apdo. 687-1011, Y Griega, San José) on the 4th fl. of the Mendioda building on Av. Central.

ILLNESS PREVENTION: While San José water is safe to drink, visitors should exercise caution with water in other locales. If you believe you might have amoebic dysentery, go to **Clinica Biblica** (☎ 223-6422) or **Clinica Americana** (☎ 222-1010) and have a urine test. Medicine can be purchased at any pharmacy. Be sure to wash with soap and water after swimming in a pool or river.

SNAKEBITE: In the *extremely* unlikely event that you should be bitten by a snake, don't panic! Stay still and try to take note of the snake's characteristics (size, color, pattern, and head shape). Non-poisonous snakebites show two rows of teeth marks, but fang marks are lacking. Suck venom from the wound or push it out with your fingers and apply a loose tourniquet. Walk back to the field station. You still have several hours before the venom takes effect. The best way to prevent snakebite is to keep to trails, wear rubber boots, and avoid reaching into holes or under fallen logs. Never chase a retreating snake. Birders should have friends who occasionally focus their eyes on the ground. Keep in mind that snakes may be hanging from low-lying branches. In general, leave snakes alone and they'll do likewise.

INSECTS: Although scarce at higher altitudes, **mosquitoes** are prevalent in the lowlands. Buy insect repellent containing DEET (diethylmetatoluamide) at a 90% concentration or higher prior to your arrival; Seattle-based REI has a comparatively inexpensive brand. A mosquito net is a handy appurtenance, as are mosquito coils (*spirales*); they keep the numbers down. *Pulperías* will sell you one or two if that's all you need, but make sure you get a stand (*suporte*). Avoid inhaling the smoke.

Tiny **mites** barely visible to the naked eye, chiggers are some of the worst pests around. They wait on vegetation, then leap aboard and seek out a nice warm place – generally between your clothing and skin – and burrow in. Their itches can last for weeks. If afflicted, try running hot water over them, which will kill them. Dust your clothes and lower body with sulfur powder to stave them off. Or dissolve locally available *azufre sublimado* under your tongue; it gives your sweat an odor noxious to chiggers. Avoid grassy areas whenever possible. Try antihistamine cream, Euthrax, or Caladryl to help soothe bites.

Watch for **ticks** when you undress because they may not be evident otherwise. If you pull them straight off, you risk leaving their pincers in your skin. Hold a lighted match or cigarette to the bite and squeeze the area to extract the tick. Gasoline, kerosene, or alcohol will encourage the tick to come out.

Repellents are ineffective against **sand gnats**; use antibiotic ointment and, as with all bites, avoid scratching or risk infection.

Should you be stung by a **wasp**, scrape the detached stinger out carefully with your fingernail. If you pull or squeeze it out, you'll pump more venom in!

Unless you're an amateur or professional entomologist, give other insects space to be themselves. Touching seemingly adorable fuzzy or spiny caterpillars may cause painful rashes. Colorful stinkbugs may spray cyanide. Take the precautions listed here, and wear adequate clothing. Except for those that feed upon us directly, most insects harbor no animosity and would prefer a live-and-let-live peace accord.

RIPTIDES: Especially because of the dearth of lifeguards, these are a major environmental hazard. If you are caught in one, yelling and waving your hands is the surest way to drown. Conserve your energy and try to swim in a parallel direction over to where the waves are breaking and ride them to shore. Avoid swimming at dangerous beaches. Some dangerous beaches are Puntarenas's Playa Barranca and Playa Doña Ana, sections of Jaco's beach, the beach outside Manuel Antonio National Park, Playa Espadilla Sur inside the same park, Limon's Playa Bonita, and the section of the beach near the entrance to Cahuita National Park. A good rule of thumb is the larger the wave, the stronger the rip.

Money

The monetary unit is the *colón*, which is divided into 100 *centimos*. Notes are issued in denominations of 100, 500, and 1,000 and coins are minted in amounts of 1, 5, 10, 20, 50, and 100 *colones*. Coins of 25 and 50 *centimos* and five and 10 *colones* notes are still in circulation, anachronistic holdovers from an era when a single *colón* was of tremendous value. The current floating exchange rate is US$1=C 200. Owing to the continuing devaluation of the currency, prices in this book are listed in US dollars. Depending upon the correlation between the exchange rate and inflation (currently around 20%), things may cost more than listed here. In compliance with IMF demands, Costa Rica's currency exchange was liberalized in 1992, and dollars may now be exchanged anywhere.

Changing Money

Most banks impose a service charge for cashing travelers checks. Currency other than US$ can be exchanged only with difficulty. Canadian dollars and British Sterling can be exchanged at Banco Lyon, C. 2, Av. Central. Canadian dollars can also be exchaged at Banex, C. Central, Av. 1. German marks can be exchanged at the Banco Nacional in San José.

Banks are generally open Monday to Friday, 9-3 or 9-4; a few in San José are open later. It's desirable to carry at least some cash with you. Be sure to carry small bills (less than 1,000 *colones*) and coins when visiting villages where change may not be readily available for larger denominations. Unlimited exchange of *colones* is permitted. Major credit cards are accepted by banks, established shops, and large restaurants. Black marketeers operate openly on Av. Central between Calles 2 and 4 and at many other locations. Changing on the black market brings only a slightly better rate. Once trustworthy, the black market has become increasingly infiltrated by con men who will steal your money or give you counterfeit $50 and $100 bills printed in Colombia. The best alternative is the moneychangers who operate in shops around the PO in San José.

CREDIT CARDS: Although there are a large number of establish ments (mostly high-priced) accepting credit cards, don't make them your chief source of cash. At the American Express office in San José (C. 1, Av. Central/1), you may write a personal check to purchase traveler's checks in dollars if you have one of their credit cards. If you are a guest at some select hotels, Visa and MasterCard can secure you cash advances in *colones*, but not dollars. (Visitors should note that Visa traveler's checks have a bad reputation with regard to refunds.) Located in the same building as Paprika restaurant (Av. Central, C. 29/33), Credomatic accepts both Visa and MasterCard. To get here, take the San Pedro bus and get off at Col. Sanders. Located near the cathedral at Av. 4, C. 2, Banco Credito Agrícola de Cartago accepts only Visa for obtaining cash. **note:** Be sure you investigate all of the charges before going this route.

☞ **Traveler's Tip**. In recent years counterfeit bills have proliferated. Most are of the 5,000 *colón* denomination. The bills are generally brighter blue than the regular issue and are likely to feel thinner. Check to see if the watermark (which shows up in regular light) is visible. Also check for the fine-line grid on the blue part of the bill, which is missing from the counterfeits.

PLANNING EXPENSES: There are facilities available to match every pocketbook. Doing your own chartering and/or using local transportation takes more time, requiring schedule flexibility and initiative. If you're seeking comfortable accommodation or taking a tour, you may not find prices much different from those in the US, Canada, or Britain. Compromises are one option – staying in an inexpensive hotel and then splurging on a Tortuguero river trip, for example.

on a budget: Expect to spend from US$20 per person per day at a minimum for food and accommodation. (Information on budget places to stay is given under "Accommodation" below.) Generally, you'll find yourself spending at least US$25 and probably more. The best way to cut down on expenses is to stay in one relatively inexpensive location for a time and to prepare some of your own food. Renting a car is an expensive proposition, but the buses are reasonably priced and service is extensive.

A decade ago, Costa Rica could truly be considered a low-budget destination, but its rise in popularity has pushed prices up dramatically. Consequently, despite a sharp decline in the value of the *colón*, Costa Rica, while cheaper overall than Belize and the US, no longer compares with places like Honduras. Many of the parks – such as Tortuguero and Manuel Antonio – are becoming too expensive for all but the well-heeled and the average Tico has been priced out as well. You may prefer to focus on some of the places that are not as well known. You'll not only cut costs, but also get more out of your trip. **note:** Be aware that anything calling itself a "youth hostel" here has no official status as such and may be more expensive than other, comparable accommodation.

Shopping

Hours vary but stores are generally open 8-6 from Monday through Friday, with some stores closing from 12-2:30 in the afternoon. Most close down Saturday afternoons and are closed on Sundays. Aside from local handicrafts, there isn't much to buy that can't be found cheaper (or at the same price) somewhere else. Many of the handicrafts are imported and then sold at inflated prices. Recently, some interesting souvenirs have been produced, such as Ecopapier, the gorgeous handmade 100% recycled paper made at Upala. It is colored with organic dyes and is pulped with agricultural by-products. Locals, initally funded by a USAID grant, produce it in a small factory. Another recent product is the Rainforest Chocolate Bar, which is made with macadamia nuts and other local ingredients. Craft shops are listed under San José. Also, you can buy a selection of handicrafts in Moravia (take a bus from Av. 3, C. 3/5) and get off before the gas station.

SOUVENIRS: Unique and inexpensive souvenirs include vanilla beans, vanilla extract, Café Rica (the national equivalent of Kahlua), and bags of coffee beans. Buy beans marked "*puro*," indicating that no fillers or sugar has been added during the roasting process. Kábata makes a line of herbal teas and cosmetics; Manza-te also offers a line of tea. *Palmito* (heart of palm) preserves and preserved *pejibaye* (a scrumptious palm fruit that tastes like a cross between a chestnut and a pumpkin) are good for your jaded and worldly friends. High-priced local woodwork and other crafts make good souvenirs. One souvenir that is functional during your visit is the shopping bag fashioned from a rice sack; another is the traditional *campesino* sun hat made from cotton canvas. Souvenirs you won't want to bring out are things made from margay, jaguar, or alligator skins – endangered species all. Should you come across it, black coral jewelery is another product to avoid buying.

BARGAINING: It's customary to bargain in nearly every country of the developing world, and Costa Rica is no exception. Although most of the stores have fixed prices, you can bargain in market stalls, and you should definitely do so with meterless taxi drivers and on boat charters. Hotel room prices are generally fixed, but you can try. Discounts may be given for longer stays or when hotels are empty. In general, no matter how much you can afford to pay, don't agree on the first price. The next person may be a student on a meagre budget. And there is another reason to get the most for your money. With the onslaught of well-heeled tourists, Costa Rica is becoming more and more expensive for the Ticos themselves, who are finding it difficult to vacation or even get by day to day. Don't act as if you are here with your dollars ready to buy the country.

Customs

AMERICAN CUSTOMS: Returning American citizens, under existing customs regulations, can lug back up to US$400 worth of duty-free goods, provided the stay abroad exceeds 48 hours and that no part of the allowance has been used during the past 30 days. Items sent by post may be included in this tally, thus allowing shoppers to ship or have shipped goods like glass and china. Over that amount, purchases are dutied at a flat 10% on the next $1,000. Above $1,400, duty applied will vary. Joint declarations are permissable for families traveling together. Thus, a couple traveling with two children will be allowed up to $3,200 in duty-free goods. Undeclared gifts (one per day of up to $50 in value) may be sent to as many friends and relatives as you like. One fifth of liquor may be brought back, as well as one carton of cigarettes. Plants in soil may not be brought to the US. If you're considering importing a large number of items or are simply bringing back a quantity of souvenirs, you'll want to consult *GSP and the Traveler*, a booklet that outlines the goods admitted duty-free to the US from Costa Rica. It's obtainable from the Department of the Treasury, US Customs Service, Washington, DC 20229.

CANADIAN CUSTOMS: Canadian citizens may make an oral declaration four times per year to claim C$100 worth of exemptions, which may include 200 cigarettes, 50 cigars, two pounds of tobacco, 40 fl oz of alcohol, and 24 12-oz cans/bottles of beer. In order to claim this exemption, Canadians must have been out of the country for at least 48 hours. A Canadian who's been away for at least seven days may make a written declaration once a year and claim C$300 worth of exemptions. After a trip of 48 hours or longer, Canadians receive a special duty rate of 20% on the value of goods up to C$300 in excess of the C$100 or C$300 exemption they claim. This excess cannot be applied to liquor or cigarettes. Goods claimed under the C$300 exemption may follow, but merchandise claimed under all other exemptions must be accompanied.

BRITISH CUSTOMS: Each person over the age of 17 may bring in one liter of alcohol or two of champagne, port, sherry or vermouth plus two liters of table wine; 200 cigarettes or 50 cigars or 250 grams of tobacco; 250 cc of toilet water; 50 g (two fluid ounces) of perfume; and up to £28 of other goods.

GERMAN CUSTOMS: Residents may bring back 200 cigarettes, 50 cigars, 100 cigarillos, or 250 grams of tobacco; two liters of alcoholic beverages not exceeding 44 proof or one liter of 44-proof-plus alcohol; and two liters of wine; and up to DM300 of other items.

Getting Here

Arrival

The best way to get a deal on airfares here is by shopping around. A good travel agent should scan for you to find the lowest fare; if he or she doesn't, find another agent or try doing it yourself. If there are no representative offices in your area, check the phone book – most airlines have toll-free numbers (see chart). The more flexible you can be about when you wish to depart and return, the easier it will be to find a bargain. Whether dealing with a travel agent or directly with the airlines, make sure that you let them know clearly what it is you want. Don't forget to check both the direct fare and the separate fare to the gateway city and then on to San José; there can be a big price difference. Although you should reserve several months in advance, recheck fares before paying for your ticket. Allow a minimum of two hours connecting time when scheduling.

A reliable major carrier serving Costa Rica is **Continental**. They fly nonstop from Houston to San José daily. Connections are available through Houston to most US cities; there are also nonstop flights from Houston to Paris and London. Free trips can be earned through the OnePass system. Call ☎ 800-525-0780 for information and reservations. **Mexicana** flies to San José from Los Angeles and San Francisco via Mexico City. **LACSA**, the national airline of Costa Rica, flies nonstop from Miami, NY (via Guatemala and San Pedro Sula), New Orleans (via Cancún and San Pedro Sula, Honduras), Los Angeles, and San Juan, Puerto Rico. It also flies from San Francisco. **American Airlines** flies from Dallas out of its Miami hub. **TACA** flies from Los Angeles, Houston, Miami, New Orleans, New York, San Francisco, and Washington. Established in 1992, **Aero Costa Rica** flies daily from Miami direct to San José. United Airlines flies daily from Los Angeles, Sam Francisco, and Miami to San José. You may wish to consider stopovers enroute. These are available with American, LACSA, TACA, and TAN-SAHSA; find out if it will cost extra and, if so, how much.

from Canada: While there are few charter flights from the US, many charters operate from here during the winter months for around

C$600. Contact **Go Travel** (☎ 514-735-4526) in Montreal, **Fiesta Way-farer** (☎ 416-498-5566) in Toronto, and **Fiesta West** (☎ 604-688-1102) in Vancouver. Charter flights may also run into Liberia's airport.

from Europe: Iberia, KLM, LTU, Avianca/SAM all fly. **Continental** flies from Paris and London via Houston. **British Airways** flies to Miami. If you are coming from this direction, be aware that many of the flights stop in the Caribbean enroute, so they may be heavily booked. Ask about stopovers.

Costa Rica may also be reached by air from everywhere in the Central and South American region. If you wish to arrange a trip out of Costa Rica by air, you'll do well to purchase your ticket in advance. All tickets purchased in the country are subject to a 10% sales tax.

> ☞ **Traveler's Tip.** When making reservations for your flight to Costa Rica, make sure you receive a ticket issued on a carrier with an office in San José in the event that the ticket needs to be reissued.

BY BUS: Unless you have a damned hard ass and a hell of a lot of patience or plan on taking a month or so to complete the trip, this isn't really a viable alternative. It will cost you less than US$100 for the total fare from Texas or San Diego.

Airlines serving Costa Rica from the US

Aero Costa Rica	800-237-6274
American	800-433-7300
Continental	800-537-3444
LACSA	800-225-2272
Mexicana	800-531-7921
(in Canada)	800-531-7923
TACA	800-535-8780
United	800-241-6522

BY CAR: If you are intent upon driving, you may wish to purchase *Drive the Interamerican Highway to Mexico and Central America*, which was published in 1992. To obtain a copy, send $12.50, plus $2.50 shipping/handling, to **Interlink 209**, PO Box 526 770, Miami FL 33152.

FROM NICARAGUA: When you enter Costa Rica through the border post at Peñas Blancas, you may be asked if you've been taking malaria pills and, if so, to produce them. In the past, there have been reports of travelers judged to be pro-Sandinista being refused entry. At the border, you'll find a branch of the tourist bureau, moneychangers (poor rate for *cordobas*, the Nicaraguan currency; change these before leaving) and a restaurant. If you travel by *Ticabus*, make sure that you get the correct passport back from the driver after he receives them from the immigration officer.

BY SEA: Unless you are willing to take one of the cruise ships – which occasionally dock at the port of Caldera near Puntarenas and near Limón for brief stopovers – there is no regularly scheduled alternative from N America or from other Central American nations. However, a **vehicular ferry service** runs three times a week between Cristóbal in Panamá and Cartagena, Colombia. This eliminates the need to ship your vehicle to S America. For more information, call Rodrigo Gómez or Harry Evetts in Panamá at ☎ 507-64-5564 or 64-5699.

Tours

SUGGESTED ITINERARY: There is no set of "must see" attractions. Everything depends upon your priorities, finances, time, and interests. In a two-week trip, you might sample some of the museums of San José, visit one or more parks or reserves, and swim at a beach on either coast. Another possibility is to stay longer and become a volunteer or study Spanish. Whatever you do, don't try to see the whole country in a week or so. Spend some time in a single area and really get to know it! You can always come back for another visit. In general, it's better to avoid such over-touristed areas as Manuel Antonio, Monteverde, or Jaco, not to mention the overpriced resorts and mega-hotels.

One option for visitors without a great deal of time, or with an urge to savor different experiences, is a tour or excursion. Most of these include hotel pickup, meals, and dropoff in their pricing. The advantage is that you avoid crowded buses, cover a lot of territory, and your driver will not only speak English (or whatever your native tongue) but is likely to be very informative. Disadvantages are the added expense, isolation from the locals, and loss of flexibility. They do provide an easy way to visit many of the national parks, reserves, and wildlife refuges. Although most tours operate out of San José, an increasing number are starting up in other areas. In addition to those listed here, large hotels may offer their own tours for guests.

Getting Here

Package Tours

As they say, all that glitters is not gold. And this cliché remains pertinent when it comes to package tours! If you want to have everything taken care of, then package tours are the way to go. However, they do have at least two distinct disadvantages: Most decisions have already been made for you, which takes much of the thrill out of traveling, and you are more likely to be put up in a large characterless hotel (where the tour operators can get quantity discounts), rather than in a small inn (where you can get quality treatment). So think twice before you sign up. Also, if you do sign up, read the fine print and see what's really included and what's not. Don't be taken in by useless freebies that gloss over the lack of more important features such as paid meals.

Humanitarian Tours

Are you tired of the same old touristic sights? The Educational Resource Center in Santa Ana has put together a group of tours that brings you face to face with Costa Rican realities. The Center helps collect donations for a number of local enterprises working for social change, and the tours are a way of helping fund the projects. Trips run from one to eight days and begin either with a walking tour of Santa Ana or a visit to Guayabo National Monument. In the afternoon, you visit one of eight centers: a State-run orphanage, a Catholic nun-run home for abused or neglected girls, a day care center, an indigenous reserve, a project that employs street children, or others. Rates are $60 pp, pd. Call the **Educational Resource Center** (☎ 282-7368) or **Via Nova America Tours** (☎ 255-1825, fax 255-0061) for more information and bookings.

OPERATORS: One of the best nature tours is operated by **International Expeditions**. They offer 10-day, all-inclusive tours departing from Miami. These explore the Monteverde, Puntarenas, and Tortuguero areas. A special three-day additional visit to Manuel Antonio is also available. ☎ 800-633-4734 or write 1776 Independence Court, Birmingham AL 35216. **Wildland Adventures** (☎ 800-345-4453; 206-365-0686; or fax 206-363-6615) acts as an agent for many Costa Rican firms and offers a tremendous variety of trips; call for their brochure. You may also write 3516 NE 155th St., Seattle WA 98255. **Baja Expeditions** (☎ 800-843-6967) is the US representative for **Ríos Tropicales**. Other companies include **Biological Journeys** (☎ 800-548-7555; in CA, 707-839-0178; 1696 Ocean Drive, McKinleyville, CA 95521), **The Cali-

fornia Native (☎ 800-642-1140; 310-642-1140; 6701 W 87th Place, Los Angeles CA 90045), **Costa Rica Connection** (☎ 805-543-8823; 958 Higuera St., San Luis Obispo, CA 93401), **Geo Expeditions** (☎ 800-351-5041, 209-532-0152; Box 3656, Sonora CA 95370), **Geostar** (☎ 800-633-6633, 707-584-9552; 6050 Commerce Blvd., Ste. 110, Rohnert Park CA 94928), **Journeys** (☎ 800-345-4453, 206-365-0686; 3526 NE 155, Seattle WA 98155), **Miller and Associates** (☎ 509-996-3148; Box 819, Winthrop WA 98862), and **Osprey Tours** (☎ 508-645-9049; Box 23, West Tisbury, Martha's Vineyard MA 02575).

PICKING A TOUR: Find out who your tour leader is. The best tours combine local guides with well-known scientists, and these are generally the most expensive. To really experience the rainforest environment, choose a tour that doesn't move around too much. Otherwise, you'll end up paying for transport and spending time on buses when you could be out in the wild. Be sure that non-park and reserve excursions are optional. If luxury lodging isn't important to you, choose a tour that stays at less expensive hotels. Although small group tours are more expensive than larger ones, they may not be superior. Ten people marching through the rainforest will not necessarily see more than 30 or 40. And, if you don't get along with the others on your small tour, it can be unpleasant. The best tour is one that also allows you time to explore on your own. Keep in mind that you can't follow your normal three-meal schedule and expect to see much wildlife. You should be in the forest before sun-up. You can sleep during the hot afternoon – when the animals do.

Ornithology tour leaders can sometimes be preoccupied with trying to spot as many species as possible, so you can miss other things. It can actually be better to stay in one spot if you want to birdwatch. It's also important to experience the jungle in the night as well as the day, and tours featuring a night hike are desirable. If you're not a birder, a general natural history tour may be better. The real value of this type of tour is in the learning experience and for that you need people who know what they are doing.

TEMPTRESS **CRUISE PACKAGES:** Billed as a "Back Door to Costa Rica," Temptress Cruises runs a variety of superbly organized cruises down the Pacific coast. Whereas they once catered to singles and couples, the stress is now on "family adventures." Three routes run year round from the port in Puntarenas. The *Pacific Voyage* (seven days, six nights) visits Curú, Manuel Antonio, Corcovado and Isla del Caño; the *Curú Voyage* (four days, three nights) visits Curú, Manuel Antonio, and Corcovado; the *Caño Voyage* (four days, three nights) calls at Manuel Antonio, Corcovado, and Isla del Caño. At each day's anchorage, you can choose between a natural history tour conducted by a professional biologist, or a recreational/cultural tour, which might include horseback riding or sunbathing.

A 174-ft a/c diesel-powered vessel, the *M/V Temptress* is equipped with sun deck, swimming platform, small store, and wet bar. Its 33 rooms hold up to 62 guests. The rooms are adequately comfortable, with stall shower, two single beds or one double bed, and a dresser. Complimentary laundry service is provided, as are drinks (domestic brands only). Your shoes are even cleaned for you and set out to dry after hiking! Informative slide presentations are given by guides nightly, and the bar is open until midnight, with music and dancing. On deck there is a telescope that provides a great view of the moon. Books, games, and videos are also available. Snorkeling gear, kayaks, and hydro slides are also part of the package. Water skiing, scuba (if you are certified), and fishing charters (in the two 17-ft Boston Whalers) are available as well.

From the office in San José, you are given a guided bus tour to Puntarenas. A welcome cocktail is followed by introduction of the crew members – all done up in spiffy white uniforms. Imaginatively prepared gourmet meals are served and bread is baked fresh daily. Dietary preferences can be catered to.

These tours are for those who want to experience the range of what Costa Rica has to offer without sacrificing comfort or spending the time required to reach the various ports of call by road. Taking the sea route, you are generally within minutes of your destination each morning. The more energy you have, the more you'll get out of the cruise. With swimming, snorkelling, diving, kayaking, nature tours, and other activities, there is more than enough to keep anyone busy. Contact **Temptress Cruises** at 1600 NW Lejeune Rd., Ste 301, Miami FL 33126. In the US, ☎ 800-336-8423, 305-871-1663, or fax 305-871-1657. In Costa Rica, ☎ 220-1679. Buses to Puntarenas (and the boat) depart from Sabana Norte, Frente Al Colegio Los Angeles (Por ICE de la Sabana), Centro Comercial La Torees, Local #11.

CLIPPER **CRUISES:** Larger and more like a conventional cruise ship, they take passengers to San José, Carara, Manuel Antonio, and Marenco, before going on to Panama aboard a138-passenger *Yorktown Clipper*. Prices range from $3,150 on up for the 10-day cruise, plus three nights on land (☎ 800-325-0010. In MO, ☎ 314-727-2929 collect).

SENIOR CITIZEN TOURS: Elderhostel, a sponsor of inexpensive tours, has a Costa Rica trip. ☎ 617-426-8058 or write 80 Boylston St., Ste 400, Boston MA 02116. **Grand Circle** (☎ 800-321-2835, 617-350-7500, fax 617-728-8840) gears itself towards tourists 50 and over. For those who want to explore the possibility of retiring in Costa Rica, write **Lifestyle Explorations** (☎ 209-577-4081), PO Box 6487, Modesto CA 95355.

NATURE AND ADVENTURE TOURS: It's in to be green these days among tour operators. So many people have jumped into the business of "ecotourism" so fast that they are unable to deliver on their promises. You must choose carefully. The tours offered by the organizations described above generally use one or more of the following Costa-Rica-based operators to handle their logistics. **Costa Rica Expeditions** (☎ 257-0776, 222-0333, fax 257-1665) offers tours to all the major wildlife sanctuaries in the country and operates Monteverde Lodge, Tortuga Lodge, and Corcovado. With a large staff, there's someone in the office from 5:30 AM to 9 PM in case you have a problem or want to make a booking. Write Apdo. 6941, San José. Dealing with groups as well as individuals, **Horizontes** (☎ 222-2022, fax 255-4513) retails a large number of tours, including mountain biking. Seminars and conventions can also be arranged. They're located off Paseo de Colón on C. 28, Av. 2/3. Write Apdo. 1780, 1002 P.E. San José. **Ecotreks Adventure Company** (☎ 228-4029, fax 289-8191; 800-328-2288) arranges diving, sea kayaking, all-terrain vehicle tours and rentals, and other activities. In the US, write Dept. 262, PO Box 025216, Miami FL 33102. They offer two full-service centers: one in Escazú and another in Flamingo Beach. **Geotur** (☎ 234-1867, fax 253-6338), run by former National Park ranger and naturalist Serge Volio, offers naturalist-led one-day tours of Carara Biological Reserve and Braulio Carrillo National Park. Write Apdo. 469 Y Griega, 1011 San José. **Costa Rica Sun Tours** (☎ 255-3518, 255-3418, fax 255-4410) specializes in Arenal and the Tiskita Lodge, S of Golfito. Bicycle tours of Orosi Valley are also offered. Write Apdo. 1195, 1250 Escazú.

Tours by **Río Tropicales** (☎ 233-6455) include white water rafting. Specializing in rafting and kayaking, **Adventuras Naturales** (☎ 233-6455) has packages that include trekking. Caminos de la Selva or **Jungle Trails** (☎ 255-3486) has an unusual variety of hiking and camping trips. Write Apdo. 5941, San José. **Adventure Tours** (☎ 232-8610, 231-5371), headquartered at the Corobicí Hotel, offers a variety of tours and a special trip up the Río Sarapiquí. Private tours are also available. **Interviajes** (tel./fax 238-1212) in Heredia offers a number of inexpensive tours. Write Apdo. 296, 3000 Heredia. **Caribbean Treks and Expeditions** (☎ 223-2125, 233-3993, fax 223-5785) runs a gamut of tours from surfing to rafting and biking. Write Apdo. 363, San José. Based at Playa Tamarindo, **Papagayo Excursions** (☎ 680-0859, 680-0652, 232-6854) operates cruises through mangrove swamps and past turtle nesting sites. Liberia's own **Guanacaste Tours** (☎ 666-0306, fax 666-0307), one of the nation's best tour companies, runs tours to Santa Rosa, Palo Verde, Arenal, and other destinations. Write Apdo. 55, 5000 Liberia.

other tours: Farming out their day tours through other agents, **Cielo Azul** (☎ 232-7066) is one of the most prominent companies. They feature tours of the highlands, Irazú, Poás, Orosi, Lankester Gardens, Arenal, and Sarchí. Costs range from $22 to $69 per person. **Swiss Travel** (☎ 231-4055) also has tours. Other agencies to contact, which have both nature and general tours, include **Cosmos Tours** (☎ 233-3466), **Tikal** (☎ 223-2811, Apdo. 6398, 1000 San José), **TAM** (☎ 223-5111), and **SANSA** (☎ 233-5330), which also offers some package tours.

personalized tours: If you're looking for something a bit more personal and informative, **Personalized Tours** (☎ 257-0507: 24 hours) are a father-and-son operation that can provide everything from trips to Manuel Antonio to quetzal tours or excursions to Curú Wildlife Refuge. Even if they aren't going with you, they can still hook you up with trips and book hotels. This is an ideal place to go for small family groups. It is a great chance for you to meet with Ticos as friends instead of as servants.

Getting Around

Owing to its compact size and well developed transportation system, Costa Rica is one of the easiest Latin American nations to get around. If there's no bus going directly to a place, it's generally possible to take a bus to the nearest dropoff point and hire a taxi from there. Another option, especially for those who have more money than time, is flying.

By Air

Government owned and subsidized, **SANSA** flies daily or several times weekly between San José and Tamarindo, Nosara, Samara, Quepos, Golfito, and Coto 47, near the border with Panama. Since fares are government-subsidized, rates are very reasonable. During the tourist season, flights (which seat only 25-30 passengers) should be booked well in advance. If you don't have a booking, keep in mind that you can always try to fly standby. SANSA has a bad track record for reliability, and it is not uncommon to find your flight cancelled without prior notice. Their office (☎ 221-9414) is just off Paseo de Colón on C. 24. Remember that SANSA considers confirmed reservations only those for which a cash payment has been received, and you must pay for your ticket the day before you leave! SANSA operates shuttle buses to and from the airport. Another, newer airline is the more expensive **Travelair** (☎ 220-3054, 232-7883 fax 220-0413), which flies from San José to Barra del Colorado, Tortuguero, Quepos, Golfito, Palmar Sur, Limón, Nosara, Tamarindo, Punta Islita, Puerto Jiménez, Tambor and Carrillo. Like SANSA, it leaves from Pavas.

SEAPLANE: Anfibias (☎ 296-4244) has a seaplane available for charter for around $300 ph.

HELICOPTERS: HELISA (☎ 222-9219, 255-4138, fax 222-3875) charges around $900 ph for its Eurocopter A-Star 350B, which holds up to six passengers and runs at 150 mph. **Helicopteros de Costa Rica** (☎ 231-6564, fax 232-5265) can carry up to four and is based at the Pavas airport. It rents for $560 ph and can run at 100 mph.

It's also possible to fly with **Costa Rica Expeditions** (☎ 257-0776; fax 257-1665) into Tortuguero. If you want to charter a plane ($100 and up), call **Aeronaves de Costa Rica** (☎ 231-2541), **VEASA** (☎ 232-1010), **Trans Costa Rica** (☎ 232-0808), or **Taxi Aereo** (☎ 232-1579). These planes depart from the smaller Aeropuerto Tobías Bolaños near Pavas, to the W of San José.

On Land

BY TRAIN: Alas, the famous train to Limón runs no more, nor does the one to Puntarenas. There are two short runs from Heredia to San Pedro, a suburb of San José, and from Limón to the Ley River. Bring along toilet paper for either run.

BY BUS: Buses run practically everywhere, although less frequently to more remote destinations. There are comfortable and inexpensive runs on main highways to Puerto Limón, Puerto Viejo de la Talamanca, Golfito, Puntarenas, Liberia, and other major towns. Travel times anywhere within the country are reasonable. It takes about eight hours from San José to Golfito for example.

It's essential to know a bit of Spanish, but only a bit will go a long way. Remember not to flash money around and to keep a close watch on your things while in transit. Baggage can be a problem. Although some buses may have storage below, many do not – including the local buses. Overhead racks inside won't hold large backpacks or suitcases; it's preferable to carry as little as possible. Try to store excess baggage in San José. If there's no buzzer on your bus, yell out "*La parada por favor.*"

reservations: If you're planning to travel on weekends or during three-day holidays, it's advisable to obtain tickets in advance, particu-

Getting Around

larly to and from places such as Puntarenas, Manuel Antonio, the Caribbean coast, and beaches on the Nicoya Peninsula. In any event, if you know exactly how long you're staying, it's always good practice to buy a return ticket upon arrival.

routes: There are over 700 bus routes covering virtually every hamlet, village, and town. Local buses link towns to each other, and long distance bus services link them to San José. They generally leave on the button, and the fare is collected on board. The quality of the bus employed ranges from the huge white buses used on the San José-Puntarenas route to the geriatric Bluebirds found frequently in the countryside. On board, decorations near the driver may include painted murals of seascapes and pictures of Jesus. On the better roads, particularly along the smooth Interamerican Highway, travel is inexpensive and fast. But, on the rougher rural roads, fares and travel times escalate. You'll need patience! One problem is that buses to more remote areas may leave only once or a few times per day. Your hotel, the ICT, and a bar or restaurant near the bus stop are all good sources for information on departures. **note:** Because schedules seldom change, the times in this book should be accurate. But, if you're on a tight schedule or have an early departure, you would do well to double-check.

Pura Natura

Just starting out in 1995, Pura Natura is a service designed to transport tourists around the country in large vans – two 15-passenger buses and a 22-passenger coaster. There are a number of different routes. No. 1 circles around the hotels in San José and travels to Escazú, San Pedro, Heredia, Alajuela, and other locations. No. 2 heads up to the Sarapiquí and San Carlos/La Fortuna areas. No. 3 goes to Manuel Antonio via Atenas, Punta Leona, and Jacó. No. 4 travels from San José to Puntarenas and then on to Liberia and the range of beaches down to Tamarindo. No. 5 goes out to Guápiles and Limón before heading down to Cahuita. No. 6 goes to La Fortuna, Lake Arenal, Tilarán, Cañas, and Liberia. An open pass for a week is $72. In order to ask for a pickup, you'll have to call the office by 6 PM the previous day. In San José ☎ 233-9709/9496 or fax 223-9200. Their offices are in Edificio Cristal, 2 F # 207, at Av. 1, C. 1/3.

HITCHING: Hitchhiking is slow but very possible and a good way to pass the time while waiting for buses in the boonies. Where there are no buses, it could save a taxi fare. In the rural areas, the few Costa Ricans with cars are generally conscious of the transport situation and will stop for you.

BY TAXI: Although reasonably priced, cabs are meterless – except in San José where the meters (*marías*) generally aren't used anyway. They are easily identified by their red color. The fare depends largely upon your ability to bargain in Spanish. But be sure to agree on the price before getting into a cab. But you should negotiate as well as ask around. **determining a fare:** Fares change like the weather. Factors include your apparent affluence, the driver's current psychological state, your own psychological state, your dress, and your pickup point or destination. If you are going to an expensive hotel, it's better just to give the nearest intersection. If you're unsure or the fare appears too high, an effective technique is to ask several drivers. If a San José driver refuses to use his meter, take his permit number and car license (*numero de placa*); the ICT office has the Ministry of Public Transport complaint forms. The meter only goes up to 15 km, so it's necessary to bargain for a further trip. Buses run until 10 or 11 in San José, but stop earlier in the smaller towns, after which you'll be dependent upon taxis. In the outback, many cabs are four-wheel-drive. Finally, remember that the drivers are not tipped. **chartering:** If you are in a group, you might consider chartering a taxi as a less expensive alternative to tours or as a method of getting to and from national parks. Be sure to bargain and set the fare beforehand.

Taxi Rates

Taxis charge 100 *colones* for the first km and 45 *colones* for each additional km. Outside of San José, the charge is 50 *colones* per additional km. Each hour of waiting time is 365 *colones*. These fares apply to trips of up to 12 km; fares must be negotiated for longer distances. After 10 PM, a surcharge of 20% is applied.

Driving

Renting a car is an option, but you should know exactly what you're getting into. With one of the world's highest per capita accident rates, Costa Rica is not an easy place to drive. Macho is often the rule here, and passing on narrow two-lane highways can be dangerous. Even on steep and winding grades, buses and trucks pass in both directions. In San José itself, the streets are narrow and one way; few parking lots or spaces are available. Once you leave the San José area, the accident rate drops. With lower population and income levels, there are fewer cars. And there are over 18,000 miles (29,000 km) of roads to explore. You can use a valid US or International driver's license here for up to three months. A permit is necessary to drive a motorbike of up to 90

Getting Around

cc. Cars may be rented at the airport. Expect to pay around $190/wk for a subcompact plus gas. Unless you have a credit card, you'll have to fork over a whopping deposit. The most useful vehicle, a four-wheel-drive jeep, is the most expensive at around $50/day. Don't rent a four-wheel-drive unless you really need it. Gas costs a bit more than in the US. A state-run monopoly, mandatory car insurance (a steep $8.50-$12 per day with $250 deductible) will be supplied by the rental company. As you should do everywhere, read the contract thoroughly – especially the fine print. Ask about unlimited mileage, free gas, late return penalties, and drop-off fees. Check the car over for dents and scratches and make sure that the agent notes any damage so you won't be charged later. A problem surfacing in recent years has been attempts by rental companies to charge for nonexistent damages. It's preferable to bring your car back in plenty of time for your flight. If you have a video camera, you may want to film your vehicle (inserting a view of a digital watch which shows the date and time).

If you are intent upon driving, you may wish to purchase *Drive the Interamerican Highway to Mexico and Central America*, published in 1992. To obtain a copy, send $12.50 plus $2.50 shipping and handling to **Interlink 209**, PO Box 526 770, Miami FL 33152.

☞ **Traveler's Tip**. You might get a better rate by reserving a rental car in the US. Call the 800 numbers for the major agencies and shop around.

CAMPING VANS: Siesta Campers (☎ 441-2670, fax 438-0416) rents VW camping vehicles complete with cooking equipment, bedding, towels, icebox and sink, portable stove, beach chairs, maps, and hammocks. Rates are around $350-450 pw. Write PO Box 025216, Miami FL 33102-5216.

DRIVING TIPS: Road hazards at night include pedestrians, holes, and livestock. Signs you should know the meaning of include *siga con precaution* (proceed with caution), *ceda el paso* (yield), *peligro* (danger), and *despacio* (slowly). Be sure to fill up at the main towns before heading out to the sticks, where there may be no service stations. Also, while you'll find stations that are open 24 hours in San José, many in the countryside run only from dawn to dusk. Bring a rag to wipe the inside windows in the rain. Unless otherwise posted, speed limits are usually 80 kph (50 mph) on toll roads and highways. Speeders are subject to stiff fines, and you must also remember to use your seatbelt in the front or face a ticket. Avoid driving in congested San José; you may even consider beginning your car rental elsewhere. (Hotels in

Jacó Beach, Manuel Antonio, and in Guanacaste as well as elsewhere have car rental agencies.)

corrupt cops: If a policeman stops you for speeding, don't pay the fine on the spot because this will go straight into his pocket (and it's illegal). Insist on a citation (*"deme un parte"* = "give me a citation"), which you will then have to pay in court. If he appears to have stopped you just to hassel you, pretend to speak no Spanish even if you are fluent. Maintain your politeness. If you are maltreated, get his ID number and report it to the Dirección de Tránsito. Be sure to have your passport (or a photocoy of it) on you at all times. Expect to rent a four-wheel-drive if you intend to travel on the back roads; they can be extremely muddy. Drive defensively.

parking: Never park illegally. Yellow curbs mean no stopping, even if you are in the car. Getting towed is no picnic. If possible, park in a *parqueo*, which will also be safer than on the street. In San José, you will need tokens for the meters; these are sold in *sodas* and in shopping centers.

FINDING PLACES: One way to find things is by using your odometer; another is to look out for the blaring ads for Delta cigarettes which have the names and pointers for major destinations on them. There are also signs denoting the entrance to various *playas* (beaches) along both coasts; your car gives you the advantage of driving in and actually exploring.

Never, no matter how fluent your Spanish is, believe all the directions you are given. Sometimes, in a misguided attempt to please, local people will tell you what they think you want to hear. It's better to ask a few people and get a consensus.

Highway Tolls

Gen. Cañas Highway (to the airport) – 60 *colones*
Próspero Fernández Highway (to Ciudad Colón) – 60 *colones*
Florencio del Castillo Highway (to Cartago) – 60 *colones*
Bernado Soto Hwy (to San Ramón & the Pacific coast) – 120 *colones*
Braulio Carrillo Highway (to Guapiles and Limón) – 200 *colones*

CAR TROUBLE: Costa Rican law mandates that you must have flourescent triangles to place on the road in front and to the rear of your car in case of a breakdown. Call **Coopetaxi** (☎ 235-9966) if you do break down. **If you have an accident,** ☎ 227-7150 or 227-8030 for a traffic cop. Wait for their approval before moving your car, and be sure to get the names and ID numbers of any witnesses. Sketch the area, with the positions of the vehicles before and after the accident shown. Give no statements. Take your set of reflective triangles and put them in front of and behind your vehicle. It is mandatory that you report the accident to the local municipality or Tribunal de Tránsito within eight days. Take a copy of their report – along with your driver's license, police report, insurance policy, and any other relevant information – to the INS (☎ 223-5800, 223-3446) at Av. 7 between C. 9/11.

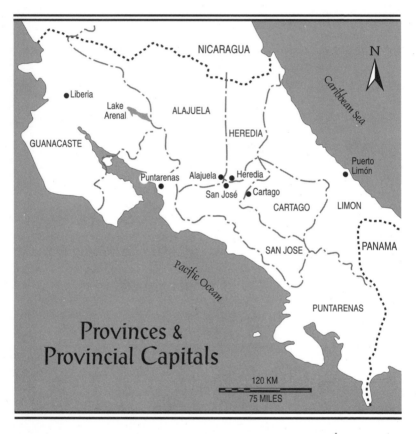

Provinces & Provincial Capitals

RENTAL AGENCIES: For a full list, check the yellow pages under "Alquiler de Automóviles." Some of the more prominent are **ADA Rent-a-Car** (☎ 233-6957), **Budget** (☎ 223-3284), **Dollar** (☎ 233-3339), **Poás** (☎ 221-2331), **Viva** (☎ 231-3341, 232-4333), **Toyota** (☎ 222-2250, 223-8979), **Hertz** (☎ 221-1818, 223-5959), **Global** (☎ 223-5325, 223-4056), **Tropical** (☎ 232-2111), **Elegante** (☎ 221-0136, 221-0284, 233-8605), **Avis** (☎ 232-9922, 442-1321). Many have branches at the airport. In Liberia to the N, there is **Adventura Rent A Car** (☎ 666-2349) in El

Bramadero. Tropical also has a branch in the Hotel Karahé in Manuel Antonio. Most beach resort hotels can also arrange rentals.

Distances matrix (cities with elevation in meters in parentheses):

From \ To	ALAJUELA (952)	ATENAS (698)	CARTAGO (1435)	CIUDAD QUESADA (656)	HEREDIA (1190)	LIBERIA (144)	LIMON (3)	NICOYA (123)	PARAISO (1405)	PASO CANOAS (S.border) (128)	PENAS BLANCAS (N.border) (43)	PUERTO VIEJO (37)	PUNTARENAS (4)	QUEPOS (8)	SAN IGNACIO ACOSTA (109)	SAN ISIDRO DE EL GENERAL (702)	SAN JOSE (1161)	SAN MARCOS TARRAZU (1429)	SAN RAMON (1057)	SANTA CRUZ (49)	SANTIAGO PURISCAL (1105)	TILARAN (564)	TURRIALBA (646)	IRAZU VOLCANO (3432)
ATENAS	23																							
CARTAGO	45	64																						
CIUDAD QUESADA	80	82	117																					
HEREDIA	12	35	33	87																				
LIBERIA	201	169	238	221	209																			
LIMON	179	201	159	254	170	376																		
NICOYA	304	262	345	314	288	77	455																	
PARAISO	50	72	7	125	41	247	140	326																
PASO CANOAS	370	393	325	450	358	581	469	658	333															
PENAS BLANCAS	280	246	318	300	207	78	451	157	322	641														
PUERTO VIEJO	98	120	120	173	86	295	256	374	127	446	370													
PUNTARENAS	95	63	133	115	103	137	269	216	140	446	182	177												
QUEPOS	140	124	163	176	145	198	299	277	170	428	243	233	61											
SAN IGNACIO ACOSTA	49	71	46	124	40	246	188	325	53	378	321	126	139	169										
SAN ISIDRO DE EL GENERAL	154	176	114	229	145	351	262	430	122	215	426	232	245	79	140									
SAN JOSE	20	42	23	95	11	217	159	296	30	349	292	47	110	140	29	134								
SAN MARCOS TARRAZU	91	113	51	166	82	288	194	367	59	270	364	169	183	181	64	103	72							
SAN RAMON	44	22	82	64	52	160	218	239	89	408	238	127	53	114	88	193	59	130						
SANTA CRUZ	257	224	296	278	265	56	431	23	303	621	134	177	193	254	302	407	272	334	216					
SANTIAGO PURISCAL	42	64	65	117	48	239	201	318	72	391	334	135	133	98	71	176	42	113	81	295				
TILARAN	176	142	214	196	183	71	350	150	221	540	149	258	111	172	220	325	191	262	134	56	212			
TURRIALBA	84	107	42	159	75	282	106	361	34	368	357	162	175	205	88	156	65	93	124	337	107	256		
IRAZU VOLCANO	71	93	31	146	62	268	179	347	38	357	323	148	162	192	81	145	52	102	111	323	93	242	73	
POAS VOLCANO	40	63	77	119	46	227	226	320	90	406	303	72	134	180	89	193	56	117	84	297	82	216	120	108

Costa Rica distances in km by road & (in parentheses) elevation above sea level in meters.

By Sea

BY YACHT: The 53-ft *Pegasus* sails from Playa Herradura (S of Jacó on the Pacific coast) to Playa Tambor (on the Nicoya Peninsula) at 1 PM during the tourist season for about $40 OW and $60 RT. Sailboats may also be chartered on an all-inclusive basis for around $850 pd; up to 15 passengers can be accommodated in style on day sails. Call **Veleros del Sur** (☎ 661-1320/3880, fax 661-1119) for information and reservations.

Accommodations

The nation has hundreds of hotels – everything from luxury resorts to simple hostelries. It all depends on what you want, and what you want you can find. *Típico* hotels can be found for a few dollars or less, and nearly every village has basic hotel rooms. If your Spanish is limited, it will be easier to make reservations on the E coast, where nearly all the African-Americans speak English. A 13.4% tax is added. Keep in mind that listing of a hotel in this guide does not necessarily constitute a recommendation.

Making a Reservation

Reservations should be made a month in advance during the dry season and three months in advance for Christmas and Easter. Be sure to reconfirm three days before. During the rest of the year, reservations are a good idea, but you generally can have your pick of rooms. Couples should state whether they prefer twin or double beds. Rooms with a shared bath down the hall are the least expensive. Remember that most tourist-oriented hotels give a 20-30% discount during the low season. The major resorts and hotels have three or four sets of rates: winter, summer, shoulder, and (sometimes) Christmas.

If you arrive without a reservation, the ICT has offices to help you in the airport (which may not be open if you arrive late). However, they will not be much help if you're on a budget. It may not be necessary to book ahead for the large hotels except during the season, but it would be prudent to call for a room and send a deposit to the smaller establishments that do accept reservations. Note that many of the coastal hotels have a San José number. It will be difficult to make reservations for the lower-priced hotels unless you can speak Spanish. (The cheapest of these often do not take advance bookings anyway.) Fax numbers (when available) are listed throughout the text.

TERMINOLOGY: You will frequently encounter the "apartotel." This is an apartment hotel, which has rooms with kitchen facilities. These are often suites and, in addition to daily, usually have weekly and monthly rates. *Cabinas* – literally cabins – are sometimes similar to motels and sometimes identical with apartment hotels. "Villas" and "chalets" are fancier *cabinas*. Found on the outskirts of San José, motels cater to the tryst trade. *Pensións* and *hospedajes* are other names for inexpensive hotels.

Pricing

For the reader's convenience, prices (generally inclusive of 13.4% tax) are listed in US dollars. They are subject to fluctuation and should be used only as a guideline. *Cabinas* are generally cheaper per person for two or more. Local hotels either charge double the single price for a couple or reduce the price only slightly. Wherever you go, there are likely to be one or more newer places not listed in this guide.

Establishments for which no prices are listed are classified as follows: **low budget** (less than $20 d), **inexpensive** ($20-30 d), **moderate** ($31-50 d), **expensive** ($51-90 d), **luxury** ($90-120), and **ultra-luxury** (over $120 d). It's a good idea to get the current rates from the tourist board; they can print them out if you request it at the Plaza de la Cultura office. If they don't list the rates, it's just that the rates haven't been supplied to the board, so use the address or phone number listed to contact the hotel. There are also rental agents on the island.

ON A BUDGET: Among the difficulties you might encounter are blaring TVs, clucking chickens, mosquitoes, spiders, and cockroaches. Some of the rooms are dimly lit. In spite of these drawbacks, the smaller hotels offer a genuine Tico experience, one which often brings you closer to the local people and their lives. Your neighbors will be ordinary, hardworking Costa Ricans, and not wealthy tourists on holiday. And your money goes directly to the local people who really need it. You'll find that you can survive quite well without a/c – a fan, or sometimes nothing, will suffice. And, after you make the adjustment, everything else just falls into place.

TWO-TIER PRICING: In the old days, Ticos and visitors suffered alike and paid alike. These days, with a growing number of hotels affordable only to the wealthiest of the nation's elite, a two-tier pricing system has been instituted across the country (with tacit ICT approval). It is generally found in the tourist spots and the more expensive hotels. Ticos and foreign residents – including American Embassy employees and banana plantation execs – get a secret discount of as much as 40% at many hotels and lodges. Ticos argue that the lower prices help support hotels which suffer in the off-season and that they cannot afford to pay more. These are, however, often the same Costa Ricans who can afford to pay premium prices in Hawaii and Europe. Costa Rica is not the only "tropical paradise" to practice this system. It is common in Mexico and in Jamaica, but is unknown in Europe, North America, Japan, or anywhere workers are paid a wage in line with costs. A better approach would be to charge everyone the same, but with off-season discounts.

Accommodations

A further outrage came in 1994 with the institution of a special $15 per visit rate for the national parks. Despite numerous calls for a change in policy by visitors who felt ripped off, the government was slow to implement any changes. This shortsighted policy has done irreparable harm to the nation's image. Although the park service has made adjustments, the unjust $15 levy has not been repealed. Instead, rates have been lowered at some parks, and a new "Green Pass" has been introduced. Advance entrance rates for Braulio Carrillo, Rincón de la Vieja, Palo Verde Tortuguero, Corcovado, Guayabo, Tapantí, Arenal, Cahuita, and Cabo Blanco are now $7. Advance entrance tickets for Barra Honda and Hitoy-Cerere now cost $5. All of the other parks remain at $10 for advance tickets, and a $15 charge remains in effect for all parks if you pay at the gate. Advance tickets are valid for 90 days after purchase. The "Green Pass" ($29) is valid for 30 days after first used. It is good for admission to multiple parks. A pass may be shared among more than one person at an entry point.

If you're outraged about the steep new park entrance fees (see page 175), send a comment to the **Costa Rica Tour Operators Association** (☎/fax 250-5878); they are soliciting comments from visitors on the increase in fees to present to the Ministry of Natural Resources and Mines. Write them at ACOT, Apdo. 1628, 2050 San Pedro Montes de Oca.

Choosing the Right Place

Every dollar, pound or DM you spend in Costa Rica constitutes a vote. By staying near the parks and reserves in Costa Rican-owned accommodation, you emphasize the importance of conservation and economic potential to locals. Residents who can see the benefits of preserving the forest are less likely to destroy it. You don't necessarily need to sacrifice comfort to stay outside of San José: rainforest lodges are getting more deluxe. They are all listed in the pages that follow.

☞ **Traveler's Tip.** It's always a good idea to consider your eating habits when booking accommodation. For example, if you eat breakfast, you should think about what you may need or want to eat and when. Many hotels serve a complimentary continental breakfast. Consider whether this will satisfy you. Find out what other meals are available and how far it is to other restaurants. Vegetarians or those who simply shun meat and dead fowl will want to know if the restaurant will have anything for them to eat. Remember, it always pays to inquire beforehand, rather than after you have checked in.

FACILITIES: In Costa Rica, you don't necessarily get what you pay for. Some owners have gotten greedy and boosted prices higher than inflation (and their services) should allow. Also, things may not quite be what they seem in the ads. A scarlet macaw in the brochure may simply be a pet and a volcano may be an hour or more away. In some of the less expensive establishments, "hot" water may mean an electrical device attached to the showerhead to warm the water. It's clever, and it does the trick, but it's not as hot as a gas-heated shower.

Handicapped Accessibility

While Costa Rica has made some progress toward accommodating the disabled, it still has a long way to go. No curbs downtown (save those near the Gran Hotel Costa Rica) can be mounted by wheelchairs, buses can not be boarded, and hotels, restaurants, and tour companies alike are ill equipped to cope with the needs of the disabled. The only national park that can deal with wheelchairs is Póas. An organization working to improve the situation is Kosta Roda, a foundation run by French Canadian, Monique Chabot. For more information call her at ☎ 236-5185 or write Apdo. 1312-1100, San José.

BED AND BREAKFASTS: A recent addition to the Costa Rican landscape, B&Bs fill a niche. Generally staffed by expats (although a few have Tico owners), they provide hospitality and information. You can't expect the services you find at a high-priced hotel, but the homey atmosphere more than makes up for it. For information on the newly formed Established Inns and Bed & Breakfasts, contact organization president Pat Bliss (tel./fax 506-228-9200 or E-mail corpfaxi@sol.racsa.co.cr. In the US, write Interlink 358, PO Box 025635, Miami FL 33152. Owners must have been in business four or more years to join. (Pat also has info on the other B & B organizations.)

PRIVATE NATURE RESERVES: These present one of the best opportunities you'll have to gain a deeper understanding of the ecology while simultaneously meeting residents. You can usually expect spartan but functional accommodations, although some are fairly luxurious. Most are out of the way, but many provide transport either included in the rate or for an additional fee. Most are relatively expensive, although some (such as Rara Avis) do give a discount for IYHF card holders. All are described in the text below.

SELECTING A RAINFOREST LODGE: With tourism's growth in Costa Rica, the number of private reserves has grown apace. As any

Accommodations

reader of this book will notice, it has become increasingly difficult to catalog the accommodations available, let alone evaluate them all. Practically everyone who has a patch of forest (or even a denuded cattle farm) wants to jump on the "eco-tourism" bandwagon, some without really understanding what's involved.

As parks (such as Manuel Antonio and Tortuguero) are becoming more clogged with tourists, raising entrance fees for foreigners to extortionate levels, private reserves are playing a more important role. But they are generally not for people on a budget. Costs usually run around $50 per person per day for room and board, not including transportation, a guide, horses, or other extras. If you can't afford this, you're better off hiking and camping in a less frequented park or reserve.

On the other hand, these lodges are not for those who are especially demanding about their accommodations. While most are well constructed and fairly new, the occasional bug is going to get into your room and, if there *is* a generator, it will probably not run all night. You almost certainly won't be near a shopping mall or a boutique – at best, there may be a small store in the lodge or a *pulpería* nearby.

The best way to select a lodge is by asking the right questions. Is there electricity? Hot water? What kind of food is served? How close is the lodge to the main road? What is the fastest way to get there? How much does the transportation cost? What's the least expensive way to get there? Do they have horseback trips? Do they have night hikes? Do the prices include taxes and service charges? Do they have a biologist/naturalist on the premises? What is his or her nationality and qualifications? Are guided hikes included in the price or are they additional? What other tours and excursions are available?

These are some of the questions you may want to ask. Depending on your situation, you may come up with others. Some answers are found in this book; others are not. Keep in mind that some details will have changed from the time this book was written. Allow plenty of time for correspondence with the lodges. Many do not have direct telephones. Whenever possible, deal directly with the lodges and avoid travel agencies. They will save 15-20%, and you'll get the details from the horse's mouth.

Another alternative is to talk to any friends who have recently returned from Costa Rica or to travellers you meet there. But make sure that, in weighing their recommendations, you take stock of any differences in their experience and outlook. A lodge that may seem wild to a Sunday stroller could be too civilized for an avid backpacker. In any event, do write us and let us know *your* recommendations.

CAMPING: Camping is not only a practical alternative to hotels; it may well be that you have no choice. When you're visiting one of the national parks, the nearest place to stay may be many kilometers away. For camping at high elevations, a good bag and tent are required. Avoid staying in pastures, which have ticks and chiggers. Although there are few organized camping areas, more are being added – in places such as Jacó and along the Caribbean coast. If you decide to camp, be sure that your things will be safe. Finally, don't forget about the possibility of renting a car camper (see page 152).

Make Your Opinion Known!

Don't ever think that as a visitor you are not important. Write:

Ing. José María Figueres, President of Costa Rica, Apdo. 520 Zapote, San José, Costa Rica. ☎ 506-253-9676; fax 506-253-7589.

Ing. Carlos Roesch, Minister of Tourism, Apdo. 777-1000, San José, Costa Rica ☎ 506-222-6152; fax 506-223-5107.

Entertainment

Outside of San José, you may have to invent your own nightlife. At worst you might have to watch the stars overhead. Inside the city, there's generally plenty to do. Good sources are the *Tico Times*, Friday's issue of *La Nación*, and posters in front of the National Theater. Suggestions are also noted in the San José chapter as well as under specific listings for other towns.

☞ **Traveler's Tip.** Check the "Weekend" supplement to the *Tico Times* for entertainment, events, and other information.

MUSIC AND DANCE: The Punta Guanacasteco, the national dance, is performed to the accompaniment of the marimba and guitar. The national folk music is played on the *quijongo, ocarina,* and *chirimía* – wind instruments dating back to the pre-Columbian era. These are from Guanacaste Province and are not commonly seen. Modern dance performances take place at the Teatro Nacional, as well as other venues from time to time. Discos abound everywhere, as do juke box-equipped bars. Many discos play song after song of *musica romantica*, mushy rock songs translated into Spanish. Watch as the couples cling to each other, tune after tune. With the distinct exception of San José, where they are basement-class prostitute pickup bars, a bar marked "Centro Social" means a community center with live music.

MOVIES: Most are dominated by the three themes of Kung fu, sex, and violence. Generally, the worst of American movies are shown, with some finer films playing in San José at such theaters as the Sala Garbo and at some of the cultural centers. Out in the boonies, theaters are generally very basic, with entrance fees of less than $1. You can learn a lot about cultural attitudes by going to the movies and noting the audience reaction.

CONCERTS: There are a number of venues. Major groups seldom visit, but the National Symphony performs at Teatro Nacional, as do some other local bands, including the "new song" band, Adrián Goizueta and Grupo Experimental.

GAMBLING: Black jack and other games are found just about everywhere in and around San José. Specific listings are given below under each town. Some casinos also offer craps. This is called *Domino Chino* (Chinese Dominos) here, and you'll find workers shuffling tiles instead of rolling dice; two dominos are turned over at each turn. Bingo is popular out in the provinces. The biggest and most widespread scam is the National Lottery.

Life, Language & Study

Living Here

Many Americans have opted to retire in Costa Rica. There are three categories which will allow you permanent residency: *inversionistas* (investors), *rentistas*, and *pensionados*. To qualify for the first, you need substantial funds to invest. The latter two categories, explained below, require that you show evidence of an adequate fixed income.

Applying for residency is a three-ring circus of red tape. You'll require a statement from your local police headquarters certifying that you have no criminal record, plus naturalization and/or birth certificates for you and any dependents, along with any and all marriage and divorce certificates. You'll also need two copies of your passport, one copy of the passport for each dependent, and 12 passport-size photos (six profile and six front) for each individual involved. Blood tests (VD and AIDS) and a TB chest X-ray are also required. In addition, all signatures on foreign documents must be notarized, and the notarized signature must in turn be authenticated by the county commissioner or secretary of state. The signature must be authenticated by the nearest Costa Rica consul, who will charge $40 per document for this service. And all documents must be translated into Spanish – not by just any translator, but by one that carries the Costa Rica Ministry of Foreign Relations' stamp of approval. Finally, you must swear on paper that you will live in Costa Rica for a minimum of four months each year.

The most popular category is that of *pensionado*. *Pensionados* are required to show evidence of $600/month income from Social Security or a qualified pension fund. To be "qualified" means the company must be at least 20 years old. It must supply a CPA-certified statement of incorporation and financial solvency, which must in turn be certified by a Costa Rican consul. Reference letters from two banks affiliated with the pension plan are required. You will need to present a letter, either from Social Security or from your pension fund, stating that your pension is for life and will be paid to you in Costa Rica. Finally, before receiving your residency permit, you must hand over additional photos and be fingerprinted so that Interpol can check to be sure your documents are not falsified and that you are not a criminal.

Pensionados have rights identical with citizenship, except for the right to work and to vote.

Rentistas differ from *pensionados* in that they must have investments that will guarantee them a monthly income of $1,000. Both *rentistas* and *pensionados* can start their own businesses. They cannot, however, be employed in the country.

Life is not a bed of roses here; *pensionados* complain of the bureaucracy and the frequent switches in government policy towards them. If you do want to relocate, it would be better to stage a dry run of six months to a year. Living in Costa Rica can open new horizons, learning a new language and becoming immersed in a foreign culture by volunteering one's skills. For information contact the **Departo de Jubilados, Instituto Costarricense de Turismo**, Apto. 777, (Av. 4, C. 5) San José, ☎ 223-1733, ext. 264.

Located next to the Jubilados office on the ground floor of the ICT building is the **Foreign Residents Association** (☎ 233-8068, fax 222-7862; write Apdo. 700-1011, San José). For around $900, they will speed your application through in two to four months. Going through a lawyer will cost more and take longer; doing it on your own is only for the most persevering souls among us. **note:** This association encountered financial difficulties after uncovering bookeeping irregularities in 1994, so check about its current reputation.

GETTING A JOB: Foreigners are discouraged from working in Costa Rica, but there are positions that cannot be filled by Ticos and that will help you establish *residencia temporal*. For example, teachers are needed at schools for expatriate children (French, English, German, and Japanese) in the San José area. Language schools require native speakers, the *Tico Times* needs reporters, and the symphony can use musicians. None of these pays a great deal, but they will allow you to stay longer.

Buying Land

If you decide during your stay that you'd like to buy some land, don't expect to do so during five minutes of your vacation. Land titles are a problem here: you must check with a lawyer to make sure that they are correct. Be sure you understand what's written in Spanish. Some of the land has been sold two or three times over. Expect to spend around $100,000 or up for an attractive home with around 250 sq m of land in the Meseta Central. Keep in mind that the sight of a foreigner frequently sends prices rapidly skyward so it might be advisable to send a Tico to scout for you! Find one who's bilingual and pay him or her. Don't depend upon the land values assessed by the National Registry. One approach is to find out the sale price of similar properties in the area during the recent past. Don't rely upon advertisements; word of mouth is more reliable. The local *pulpería* is a good source of information on who wants to sell what. The more information you can obtain the better, so don't hesitate to talk to everyone you meet! Take your time and bargain hard; don't be in a rush. Always use *colones* when drawing up a contract. Find a lawyer who is a real estate specialist to put the contract together. Finally, think everything through and make a considered choice.

GETTING MARRIED: The only officially sanctioned religious ceremony permitted is a Catholic wedding. If you have any other type of wedding, you'll also need to have a civil ceremony, which can be performed by a local priest, notary, attorney, or provincial Governor. A Catholic wedding requires documents from the church(es) where you were baptized and confirmed. You must also take a course in marriage from a local church. Contact the San José diocese at ☎ 233-0198 for further information.Be sure to bring your birth certificates, as well as an affidavit from a US notary attesting to your single status. All of these must be authenticated by the nearest Costa Rican Consulate or Embassy. Likewise, if either partner has been divorced, you'll need a copy of the final judgment, which must also be authenticated.

Volunteering

This may be the best way to experience the country. Opportunities range from sea turtle banding to journalism. For those with an interest in regional politics, an excellent opportunity is a six-month internship for qualified Spanish-speaking college students and graduates at the Institute for Contemporary Studies' *Mesoamerica*, an outstanding monthly that covers regional politics. Participants gain valuable experience in professional journalism. It's possible to support yourself by teaching English (about $3/hr) but you must be available at least half-time. Send a resume, along with recommendations and the months you could be available, to **ICAS** (☎ 233-7112, fax 233-7221), Apdo. 300, 1002 San José, Costa Rica. Another great opportunity if you can speak basic Spanish is to volunteer in a national park. Lodging is free but you must contribute to food and transport costs and a minimum 2½-month commitment is required. For further information, contact Stanley Arguedas, ☎ 257-0922, fax 223-6963. Write **Asociación de Voluntarias de Parques Nacionales**, Servicio de Parques Nacionales, Apdo. 10104, 1000 San José. Begin planning at least three months in advance. The Association of Volunteers for Service in Protected Areas, **ASVO** (☎ 222-5085) is a governmental organization that will hook you up with park guards searching for poachers; or you may write newsletters for the organization. You must volunteer for a two-month minimum and you pay for lodging and meals.

Rara Avis (see description in "Meseta Central" chapter) also needs qualified volunteer guides on occasion. Contact Amos Bien (☎ 253-0844) at Apdo. 8105, 1000 San José, Costa Rica. If you have six months and some skills to offer in a relevant field (agriculture, aquaculture, forestry, ecology, photography, etc.) and want to live in the Talamancan sticks, then **ANAI** might have a volunteer position. A sometimes controversial organization, ANAI is involved with the concept and practice of "Earth Stewardship" in the lowland tropics, resolving the conflict between conservation and development in rural communities. Volunteers are expected to have reasonable conversational experience in Spanish, have their own insurance, and provide their own transportation. ANAI can provide housing and limited assistance with food. A three-to six-month commitment is required on their experimental farm, and volunteers are needed to monitor the beaches in the area during the turtle egg-laying season (May-July). ☎ 224-5090/3570, fax 253-7524, or write Apdo. 902, Puerto Limón 7300, Costa Rica. Or, from May to December, write Dr. William O. McLarney, 1176 Bryson City Road, Franklin NC 28734, ☎ 704-524-8369. If the sea and sea turtles interest you, a fantastic opportunity is to volunteer at the Caribbean Conservation Corporation's **Green Turtle Research Center** at Tortuguero National Park. One- and two-week packages are available. The fee is high because you are helping fund the program, and a substantial portion of the amount may be tax deductible. A limited number of positions are also available for research assistants who receive no salary but are granted room and board. Programs involve both green and leatherback turtles. For more information, contact the Caribbean Conservation Corps (☎ 800-678-7853, 904-373-6441), PO Box 2866, Gainesville FL 32602. You may also fax them at 904-375-2449 or E-mail cccorp@nervm.nerdc.ufl.edu. A worthy organization sending volunteers into the field is **Earth Island Institute's Sea Turtle** Restoration **Project** (☎ 415-488-0370; E-mail: seaturtles@earthisland.org), which features trips to Ostional and Playa Nancite, as well as to Nicaragua's Playa La Flor, a beach near the border. **The University of California at Berkeley** (☎ 415-642-6586) also sends volunteers in the company of researchers to locations that include Lomas Barbudal. Write UREP, University of California, Berkeley CA 94720. **APREFLORAS** (☎ 240-6087; Apdo. 917, 2150 Moravia), the Association for the Preservation of Wild Flora and Fauna, accepts volunteers who will work as guards for the parks (some risk involved) or act as environmental educators in schools. The **Asociación de Amigos de Aves** (tel./fax 441-2658; Apdo. 32-4001, Rio Segundo de Alajuela) works to re-introduce macaws to the wild through breeding, and volunteers are needed to help care for the birds. Aspiring organic farmers can volunteer to work for Erich Orlich (lodging amd meals provided) of the National Association of Organic Farming (**ANAO;** ☎ 223-3030).

The **Monteverde Conservation League** (fax 645-5104) accepts donations at Apdo. 10165, 1000 San José. Researching laws relevant to topics such as forestry, land use and tenure, urban air pollution, and marine and coastal resources, the Centro de Derecho Ambiental y de los Recursos Naturales (**CEDARENA,** ☎ 225-1019, fax 225-5111; Apdo. 134, 2050, San Pedro) is compiling an information bank, which they hope will be used to make the environmentally optimal developmental decisions. If you are a Spanish-speaking person with knowledge of environmental law and research, CEDARENA needs volunteers. A three-month stay is requested. The **Monteverde Institute** coordinates a limited number of international volunteer service projects, which usually center around farming or building, with added courses such as Spanish, biology, or workshops on regional issues. They can also hook you up with a volunteer teaching position in a local school. ☎ 661-1253 or write Tomas Guidon or Polly Morrison, MVI, Apdo. 10165, 1000 San José. Volunteers are also always needed at the reserve itself. Lodging is provided, but not food. Write **Monteverde Cloud Forest Reserve**, Apdo. 8-3870, 1000 San José. **Earthwatch** (☎ 617-926-8200) sends paying volunteers out to assist researchers working in the field. Recent projects include work at the Wilson Botanical Gardens with birds, studying the courtship practices of long-tail manakins in Monteverde, and research into olive Ridley egglaying on Tamarindo beach. Costs are tax-deductible except for airfare. Write 680 Mt. Auburn St., Box 430-P, Watertown MA 02272 or ☎ 800-776-0188. The Volunteer Coordinator for the **School for Field Studies** (☎ 508-927-7777) offers volunteer opportunities in Costa Rica. Write 16 Broadway, Beverly MA 0195-2096. One of the best-established organizations, the Costa Rica Association for the Protection of Nature (**ASCONA**, ☎ 222-2288/2296) works on sustainable development and needs volunteers with scientific or technical backgrounds. Write Apdo. 8-3790, 1000 San José. Retired businessmen and technical advisors might join the **International Executive Service Corps**, a nonprofit partially sponsored by US AID and based in Stamford CT. For more information, write Box 1005, Stamford CT 06904-2005 or Apdo. 70, Centro Colón, San José, or ☎ 233-9855.

The **Free University of Costa Rica** requires volunteers to teach English two hours for one night per week in San José, Heredia Rohrmoser, or Alajuela. Students are not charged tuition, and there is no need for you to be a professional. ☎ 232-5601 between 8 and 6 from Monday to Friday. The **Ministerio de Educacíon** now accepts volunteers to teach English; write Departamento de Inglés, San José 1000. **Barú Adventures** (☎ 800-297-2278) has environmental adventure tours for high school teachers. If you have a minimum of six weeks to commit, **Finca Brian y Milena** is looking for volunteers willing to work on their fruit farm near Dominical; you will be expected to contribute $30 pw towards your food. Write Finca Brian y Milena, Apdo. 2-8000, San Isidro de El General.

Studying Spanish

The more Spanish you speak the better! If you want to travel by bus around the country, negotiate meals in local (*comida típica*) restaurants, and stay in lower-priced accommodations you will need a basic command of Spanish. Even if you don't speak more than a few words, be sure to use them. The more you speak, the more you'll learn, and you won't learn unless you speak. If you regard the country as an intensive language laboratory, your Spanish will improve remarkably within a short time. But if you're going in without any language ability at all don't despair. Sign language is an effective means of communication when the situation arises; another possibility is a writing pad for numbers and prices. **note:** While Costa Rican Spanish is more in accord

Volunteering

with that found in Spain than elsewhere in Latin America, its pronunciation most resembles Guatemalan Spanish.

LANGUAGE SCHOOLS: There are a number of language schools, but study here is much more expensive than in countries such as Guatemala. If you do plan to study here, you'll need at least a few months to make any significant progress. Costs run from $2-5 ph, and $7 ph for private lessons. Most schools are in and around San José. Featuring "Survival Spanish," a one-day, six-hour class, **Mesomamerica Language Institute** (MLI) is run by the Institute for Central American Studies (ICAS, ☎ 224-8910). The cost is $50. It also offers private study and private lessons. For 20 hours a week of study in a small class, they charge $110; you can stay and eat with a family for $85 additional. Write to them at Apdo. 300, San José. The **Costa Rica Language Academy and Latin Dance School** (☎ 233-8938/8914, fax 233-8670; Apdo. 336-2070, San José) offers homestays and private and group lessons; dance, cooking, and musical instrument lessons are also given. Running a Spanish program geared towards those concerned with social and environmental issues, **ICADS** (☎ 225-0508) discusses issues such as agriculture, social justice, and refugees. Write PO Box 145450 Coral Gables FL 33114 or Apdo. 3, 2070 Sabanilla, San José. The **Centro Cultural Costarricense Norteamericano** (☎ 225-9433., ext. 56; Apdo. 1489, 1000 San José) is headquartered in Los Yoses to the E, with a branch in the center part of the city. They charge US$130 for classes lasting two months, two hours per day. Also running a study farm in Santa Ana to the W of San José, **Centro Linguistica Conversa** (☎ 228-6922, 221-7649) offers six to 15 hours of instruction per week. Write Apdo 17, Centro Colón, San José.

INTENSA (☎ 224-6309) holds courses of four to six hours pd, spanning two to four weeks. They can be reached at Apdo. 8110, 1000 San José. **ILISA** (Latin American Institute of Languages) offers two-to-four-week intensive classes. Write Apdo. 1001, 2050 San José; ☎ 225-2495, 225-6713; or toll free in the US, 800-344-MEGA. In the US, you may also write Box 491036, Los Angeles CA 90049; fax 310-476-3123, or ☎ 310-476-8132. In Escazú, **ILERI** (Language and International Relations Institute; tel./fax 228-1687; Apdo. 191, Escazú) has small classes and immersion courses; it's 300 m W of the *correo*. It also has a branch in Panama. Based in San Pedro, **The Costa Rica Spanish Institute** (COSI), has a maximum of four students per class. **Forester Institute Internacional** (☎ 225-3155, 225-0135) has classes ranging from a week to a month. Write Apdo. 6945, 1000 San José, or ☎ 619-792-5693. **Instituto de Lengua Espanol** (☎ 227-7366) has five-week courses beginning in January, June, and September. Write Apdo 100, 2350 San José. **Instituto Universal de Idiomas** (☎ 257-0441, 223-9662) has two- to four-week programs along with a three-day mini-survival course ($75). They are at Apdo. 219, 2120 San Francisco de Guadalupe. With special language learning packages out at Cariari Country Club, **Lisatec** (☎ 239-2225) is at Apdo. 228, San Antonio de Belen. **Communicacion Transcontinental** (☎ 221-3364) is at Apdo. 8501, 1000 San José. They prefer students who can commit for four months. **IALC** (☎ 225-4313) offers both group and individual lessons, with a one-week minimum. Write Apdo. 200, 1001 San José. **"Learning Spanish"** has three branches: one each in San José (☎ 236-8113), in Alajuela (☎ 441-9202), and in Heredia (☎ 237-2792). Based in San José, the **ICAI** (Central American Institute for International Affairs (☎ 233-8571, fax 714-826-8752) limits its groups to six. In the US, ☎ 714-527-2918, fax 714-826-8752, E-mail ICAI@EXPRESSO.COM. Or write Box 5095, Anaheim CA 92814. **Instituto Británico** (☎ 234-9187, 236-7036, ext. 500, and 234-9054, fax 253-1894; Apdo. 8184-1000, San José) holds classes in San José and Liberia. In Dominical, the **La Escuelita de Dominical** (☎/fax 771-1903) provides Spanish classes and arranges homestays. **note:** It can be cheaper to fly to Guatemala ($250 RT), study Spanish there, and return than to take a course in Costa Rica; both living and lesson costs are considerably lower.

> ☞ **Traveler's Tip.** The **ISLS** (Institute for Spanish Language Studies) is a broker that will help you find the school to suit your needs. Placement is free. It also offers a number of other services. In the US, ☎ 800-765-0025 or write 1011 E Washington Blvd., Los Angeles CA 90021.

STUDY SEMINARS: In order to give English-speaking persons first-hand experience with and a better understanding of the people and issues of Central America, the **Institute for Central American Studies** (ICAS, ☎ 227-9928) offers 12-day seminars, providing background on each of the Central American nations and visits to political and other institutions in Costa Rica and Nicaragua. For RT airfare from Miami, hostel or rooming house accommodations, meals, local transport, and the program itself, the cost is $1,150 ($1,000 for students). Airport taxes are not included. Write PO Box 145450, Coral Gables FL 33114 or Apdo. 3, 2070 Sabanilla, San José. The **Monteverde Institute** hosts groups of university students during its summer programs in tropical biology. ☎ 661-1253 or write Tomás Guidon or Polly Morrison, MVI, Apdo. 10165, 1000 San José. The **Central American Institute for International Affairs** (ICAI, ☎ 255-0859) offers the opportunity to meet policymakers from all sides of the political spectrum during its course on Central America. It also has courses in Spanish, art, and Costa Rican education and society. Write Apdo. 3316, San José. The **Organization for Tropical Studies** (OTS, ☎ 236-6696) conducts two-month courses at their research stations, as well as logistical support for doc-toral disserations. Write PO Box DM, Duke Station, Durham NC 27706, ☎ 919-684-5774. The **Institute for Central American Develop-ment Studies** (ICADS, ☎ 225-0508) has structured internships in Costa Rica or Nicaragua, dealing with issues such as agriculture, so-cial justice, and refugees. Work is also a form of study, and the **Council on International Exchange** (CIEE) sponsors a work-travel program. ☎ 212-661-1414 or write 205 E. 42nd St., NY NY 10017.

Colloquialisms

Adios! – In the rural outback only used as "farewell" when leaving for a long time.

Bomba – Gas station.

Buena nota – OK, fine, great.

Hay campo? – Do you have space (on a bus or shared taxi)?

Cien metros – One block.

Maje – Close friend (used by young males).

Mi amor – My love (used by friends of both sexes as a form of address).

Porta mi! – I don't care!

Pura vida – Far out, super; can be used as a greeting.

Salado – Tough luck, that's a shame.

Upe! – Is anyone home? Used in countryside in lieu of knocking.

Vos – The equivalent of "tu" in French, the intimate "you."

UNIVERSITY STUDY: For longer term study, the **University for Peace** (☎ 249-1072/1511, fax 249-1929) has two-year Masters in Com-munications for Peace, Ecology and Natural Resources, and Human Rights degrees. Write Apdo. 199, 1250 San José. One innovative pro-gram is offered through Friends World College's **Latin American Re-gional Center** (☎ 240-7057; Apdo. 8946, 1000 San José). Working on their own, students are awarded credit for their journals. In the US, ☎ 516-283-4000 or write Friends World Program, Long Island University, Southampton NY 11968.

The **State University of New York at Albany** offers one- and two-semester courses at the University of Costa Rica; you must have a minimum of two years college-level Spanish. Write Office of Interna-tional Programs, L1-84, University at Albany, State University of New York, Albany NY 12222. Any student may apply to enter the **Associ-ated Colleges of the Midwest** (ACM) program, although it is primar-ily geared to students attending several Midwestern colleges. The fall semester focuses on language study and the social sciences, while the spring deals with field research in the physical or social sciences. Write 18 S Michigan Ave., Ste. 1010, Chicago IL 60603. In Costa Rica, ☎ 225-0725 or fax 253-5790. Offering one- to three-semester courses, the **University of Kansas** welcomes students of sophomore level or higher at any US college or university. Write Office of Studies Abroad, 204 Lippincot Hall, Lawrence KS 66045. The **University of Costa Rica** (☎ 224-3660, fax 225-5822) gives "special student" status for foreigners, who pay double the local rates. Auditors (*oyente*) are also welcome. Semesters run from March to the end of June and from July to September. During the winter break (December to March) a number of *cursos libres* are given for the price of a small registration fee. Contact **Oficina de Asuntos Internacionales**, Ciudad Universitaria Rodrigo Facio, San José. With two-year masters programs in Ecology and Peace and in International Relations, the **University for Peace** (☎ 249-1072/1511, fax 249-1929) is set in Villa Colón to the SW of San José. Write Apdo. 199, 1250 Escazú. **Note:** for other types of "study," see the listing under "volunteering" above.

> ☞ **Traveler's Tip.** If you'd like to work with a company or NGO and need help connecting, **Ecole Travel** (☎ 223-2240, fax 223-4120) has an "Ecole Experience" that will try to place you with a firm. They also offer a number of low-budget tours. A percentage of your trip fee will be donated to worthy environmental causes such as the Santa Elena Reserve near Monteverde.

Conduct

Currently, despite the straitened circumstances the average Tico lives with (low wages, high interest rates, high inflation), the nation is a comfortable place for visitors. Unlike countries such as Mexico, where open season has been declared upon *turistas*, here you will find yourself treated as a welcome guest. Help keep it that way by showing respect and courtesy in your dealings with locals. As Costa Ricans also consider themselves to be "Americans," it would be polite to refer to yourself as a *norteamericano* if you are a US citizen. Remember that every visitor has an impact, and your behavior will make a difference. It's a sad fact, but you'll see the worst American influences everywhere. Poor people will squander precious funds on overpriced, unhealthy meals at McDonalds, a sporty pair of Reebocks, or Levis – all in lieu of more moderate Costa Rican products. If you have the chance to steer them right, do it!

Sadly, you will meet many foreigners here – real estate salesmen, other budding entrepreneurs, *pensionados* turned into alcoholics – who have no real affinity with the country and might well be happier residing somewhere else. Keep in mind that Latin cultural mores prevail here. Men and women alike tend to dress conservatively. Although shorts are now widespread, skirts are appropriate attire for women in small, conservative villages. Bathing suits are unsuitable on main streets, as is revealing female attire. Unlike other Central American nations, Costa Rica *does* accept skimpy bathing suits on the beaches. And, despite the general conservatism, it is definitely acceptable to kiss and cuddle in public, as any visitor to San José will note immediately. Finally, if you want to be loved and respected by the police, you should carry your passport. In this "democracy," carrying of passports and ID cards is mandatory, and the police may stop you at any time and ask to see identification. But if you don't have it on you, unless you look like you might be a wetback from the N or S, they probably won't bother you.

DRUGS: With the exception of alcohol, coffee, and tobacco, all drugs – from marijuana to cocaine – are treated as narcotics. Sentences of eight years or longer are not unusual.

Theft

Although Costa Rica is being marketed as a "peaceful paradise," any glance around at the painted steel bars, barbed wire, and the signs warning of attack dogs show that thievery is endemic. There's been a dramatic increase in violent crime and mugging. Although the Ticos will blame Nicaraguans or Panamanians for all of the thievery, this, of course, is nonsense. Still, such crime has yet to reach the desperate level of Peru, where a camera, grabbed from around the neck of a tourist, represents a year's income. Take precautions and you should not have any problems. The very best prevention is being aware that you might be a victim. Avoid the slum areas of San José, don't flash money or possessions around and, in general, keep a low profile. Avoid looking affluent. Keep track of your possessions. Things like expensive sunglasses are very popular. Don't leave anything unattended on the beach, and keep off the deserted beaches at night. Avoid carrying anything in your back pockets. Women should carry purses that can be secured under an upper arm. Avoid contact with drug dealers, getting drunk in public, or walking in a secluded area at night. Never, never leave anything in an unoccupied vehicle, not even in a trunk; there are reports of thieves cleaning out vehicles in broad daylight! Locations like the front of major hotels and the area around the Museo Nacional are notorious for automotive break-ins. It's useful to photocopy your passport and keep it separately along with the numbers of your travelers' checks and any credit cards. A wise precaution is to secure any unnecessary valuables in the hotel safe; a more effective precaution is to leave them at home.

☞ **Traveler's Tip**. If you need information about safety in Costa Rica, ☎ 800-012-3456 from within the country. Complaints may also be left at this number.

MODUS OPERANDI: Holy Week, which the *ladrones* do not regard as sacrosanct, is the most dangerous time for thievery. Gangs have special tricks. One is to create a distraction and steal your bag. Another is to spill a bit of ice cream on your back and solicitously wipe it up while fleecing you at the same time. Refuse politely if offered candy or a soft drink on a bus tourists have been drugged and woken up hours later without their possessions. Even if they see a theft or mugging happen, Costa Ricans are reluctant to get involved because of the complications that might result in a trial. Overly friendly Ticos (and foreigners as well) who hang out in tourist areas often may have an ulterior motive. Remember that locals who form sexual liaisons with foreigners often do so with pecuniary gain in mind. And, if you give one of them access to your hotel room, it can be a bit awkward if you later have to go to the police and make a charge! note: Tourists claimed in 1992 that they had been robbed by the police in San José. A new development on the crime scene are the *chapulines* ("grasshoppers"), gangs of youth who jump on unsuspecting pedestrians. They generally gather in the Parque Central, Parque Merced, and Plaza de la Cultura and operate in groups of four. One puts a stranglehold on the victim's neck while others pillage and plunder. Solo tourists are likely targets. Be careful and leave all valuables at your hotel!

Women Traveling Alone

Costa Rican men are not quite as chauvinist as their neighbors. But, perhaps because of their Spanish pedigree, the males are much more verbally aggressive and persistent than in, say, Guatemala. Some women maintain that they appear to be "always in heat." Their favorite activity in life is apparently to *piropear* (compliment) females, hopefully making a *conquista* of a *gringa*. Expect to be called *mi amor* (my love), *guapa* (cute), and other, sometimes less endearing, epithets. Eclipsing even politics and soccer in popularity, flirting is the national sport. If you see a man staring at you intently, don't be alarmed. He's just practicing *dando cuerdo* (making eyes). Married or not, a Tico male will profess to love you with the greatest passion in history. Don't buy it! "Remember," one Tica advises, "the best attitude is one of confidence." On the Caribbean coast, there are a number of "beach boys" available for rent should you be in the mood. But be warned that places like Cahuita, with one woman being replaced by another – over and over – are superb breeding grounds for AIDS.

Men Traveling Alone

Costa Rican women have been mythologized for their great beauty and their good standing as *chineadoras,* women who will take care of men as if they were babies. Of course, this is nonsense. But if you don't think that a number of *gringos* buy the myth, check the classified section of the *Tico Times*. Prostitution is legal in Costa Rica. Although it will not guarantee that a hooker does not have AIDS or some other disease, your chances of safety might be better if you insist on seeing their *carnet de salud*, a health card issued by the government, which must be updated regularly. Avoid being robbed in set-up situations, many of which take place around Parque Morazán, perhaps better called Hooker Central. A favorite technique is for a tart to come up to you and give you a big bear hug while her accomplice grabs your wallet from your back pocket. If you see a young femme disrobing in the moonlight, be aware that she may have two burly accomplices hidden in the bushes. Many other hookers have been known to roll their Johns while they sleep, or have an accomplice steal a wallet or anything else handy. So be careful during the *timo del amor*. In addition, be advised that the government, despite the legal status of prostitution, is adamant that it is not promoting sex tourism. In September 1994, Tourism Minister Carlos Roesch commented that "under no circumstances will Costa Rica accept tourism based on explotiation of women or on totally unnatural acts such as homosexuality."

Environmental Conduct

Respect the natural environment. Take nothing and remember that corals are easily broken. Exercise caution while snorkeling, scuba diving, or anchoring a boat. Dispose of plastics properly. Remember that six pack rings, plastic bags, and fishing lines can cause injury or prove fatal to sea turtles, fish, and birds. Unable to regurgitate anything they swallow, turtles may mistake plastic bags for jellyfish or choke on fishing lines. Birds may starve to death after becoming entangled in lines, nets, and plastic rings. Remember that the national parks were created to preserve the environment and refrain from carrying off plants, rocks, animals, or other materials. Those interested in preserving the environment or in gaining a further appreciation would do well to contact the environmental organizations listed in this book. Finally, remember to treat nature with respect. Riptides, which cause 80% of all drownings, are a danger.

Visitor Do's and Don'ts

☐ Do visit the national parks. Don't litter, disturb habitats unduly, or act as if the parks are a party zone. Do buy soft drinks and other beverages in returnable, not disposable, containers.

☐ Do purchase the work of local artisans. Don't buy alligator-skin or turtle-shell products. These species are endangered and internationally protected. Don't buy archaeological artifacts. Chances are they are fakes. If not, they are stolen goods and amount to pillaging the national heritage. Also, any item removed from an archaeological site deprives researchers of valuable information that might add to our knowledge.

☐ Don't give out gifts to children. This will help turn them into dependent beggars, with regrettable consequences for those who follow in your footsteps. Do take their pictures, play with them, and use them as Spanish language teachers.

☐ If riding mountain bikes, do be considerate of hikers and others on foot. Slow down and don't tear by at top speed. Don't cause erosion by riding on trails obviously unsuited to bikes. Do bike on the roads and hike in the wilderness. Nature is not something to be conquered, but to be experienced.

☐ Do patronize *sodas* and other local businesses whenever possible.

☐ Do practice your Spanish in every encounter you have. Don't isolate yourself from the local culture.

☐ Don't try to do too much in too short a time. Despite what you might think, Costa Rica is a *large* nation. It can take quite a bit of time to get from point A to point B, and there's no advantage to spending most of your time getting there and burning a lot of fossil fuel in transit. If you only have a week, spend time in one area. If you stay in Dominical, for example, try to get to know that area and feel comfortable there. Don't race down to Golfito or over to Cahuita. Do try to enjoy where you are as opposed to where you are going next.

Visiting the Parks & Refuges

The Park Land Dilemma

Although you will see park boundaries defined on maps and Costa Rica is constantly referred to as a country that is saving its forests for posterity, 20% of the land in the parks remains unpurchased and faces harvest. And the land is legally exempt from governmental control as long as it remains unpurchased. In 1995 trees were cut on as-yet-unpurchased land at Manuel Antonio (see "Manuel Antonio National Park" below). The Supreme Court's Sala IV (which makes constitutional rulings) decreed in 1991 that land may be considered part of a protected area only after it has been paid for. And the Expropriation Law, passed in April 1995, states that land must be paid for before being expropriated. Larger parks such as Braulio Carrillo, Tapantí, and Corcovado are under pressure to cut trees. A 1992 National Parks Service estimate put the cost of purchasing the remaining land at around three billion *colones* ($17.3 million), but it is likely to be more than that. Regrettably, the revenue pulled in from park admissions does not go back to the parks for maintenance and land purchase but, instead, 25% goes to the local municipality and the remainder goes to the National Parks Fund. The park service budgeted 245 million *colones* ($1.4 million) for land purchase in 1995, but this was reduced to 60 million *colones* ($347,000). An additional 200 million *colones* ($1.2 million) was used from the National Parks Fund to pay for land. One of the most promising efforts to remedy this structural defect has been the Rainforest for the Austrians project in Las Esquinas (see "Esquinas Rainforest Lodge" on page 449), which has made possible preservation of a large portion of the forest.

National Parks

Many consider these treasures to be the nation's greatest attraction. A total of 11% of the land is with the National Park System, and nearly all volcanic summits are set within biological reserves or the 15 national parks. Although the Park Service should be the best-equipped government agency, it is actually the worst off. Some 350 employees must manage many hundreds of thousands of visitors on a budget that has been increased only minimally from year to year. No permission is now required to visit the parks and biological reserves unless you are planning to conduct research. Opening hours are generally 8-4 daily. If you do need a pass or advance tickets, you should stop in at Park Service headquarters, Av. 9, Calle 17/19, San José, ☎ 223-2398. Otherwise, if you need more information, you must go to the information office at the rear of Parque Bolivar. Office hours are Mon. to Fri. from 8-11:30 and 12:15-3. Radio communication with the other parks, reserves and refuges is available 24 hours a day, so you can contact them with regard to overnight space. ☎ 233-4070. Bilingual staff here can get you the latest scoop on road conditions, etc. At the parks themselves, personnel may only speak Spanish. As staff and space is limited, it is essential that they know when to expect visitors and what their needs will be in terms of meals, camping spaces, bunkrooms – some of which may or may not be available. The Park Service guide is in Spanish. For many of the parks, you'll have to bring your own food, and it may be difficult to get to others without a car. If you take a bus, you may be let off 10-15 km from a park entrance. (The most accurate current transportation information is included in each park description.) Wildlife checklists and maps are sold at the CIDA office at San José's national zoo. Another alternative may be to visit the parks with a tour. (See "Adventure Tours" and the "Getting There" sections of individual national parks for listings). To read up on the origin of the parks, check out David Rains Wallace's fine history of the parks, *The Quetzal and the Macaw* (see Booklist).

PARK FEES: Gate admission to Costa Rica's national parks remains at the discriminatory and rapacious rate of $15 per person, per entry for non-resident foreigners. (Ticos pay 200 *colones*.) However, advance tickets may be purchased at many tour agencies, rental car companies and hotels. Alternatively, you may also purchase tickets and passes from the National Parks Foundation office (☎ 257-2239). It's at C. 23/Av. 15, 300 m N and 150 m E of the Iglesia Santa Teresita.

Advance ticket prices are as follows: **$10** - Póas, Irazú, Manuel Antonio, Santa Rosa, Chirripó: **$7** - Braulio Carrillo, Rincón de la Vieja, Palo Verde Tortuguero, Corcovado, Guayabo, Tapantí, Arenal, Cahuita, and Cabo Blanco; **$5** -Barra Honda and Hitoy-Cerere.

    ☞ **Traveler's Tip.** Passes are valid for 30 days; children under six are free of charge. A family pass is being considered.

WILDLIFE REFUGES: For info on the *refugios*, call the Vida Silvestre at ☎ 233-8112 or 221-9533 or see the individual entries in this book.

SEEING WILDLIFE: Costa Rica's wildlife depend upon camouflage for survival, meaning that they are small and difficult to see. If you're visiting the reserve on your own, with a group or on a group tour, the quieter you are, the more you will see. Early morning and late afternoon are the best times. If you are really serious, camp. During the dry season, the animals come down to drink at waterholes in the early morning and late afternoon. When you return, don't forget to tell every Tico you meet how much you think of the park system. The parks will only survive as long as Costa Ricans value them.

Hiking Tips

☐ Plan your route ahead of time. Make sure that your physical condition is adequate for what you are attempting.

☐ If possible, hire a local guide (*baquiano*).

☐ Let someone know your routing and your expected return time.

☐ Stay on the trail. Heading through the bush can be risky.

☐ Only hike during daylight hours. Should you get lost, find an area where you can be seen from the air or follow a river downstream (as long as it is not swelling). Relax and stay put. Don't waste your remaining resources.

Conservation

Foundations

If you would like to help conservation in Costa Rica, there are a number of organizations that welcome donations. When sent directly to Costa Rica, donations are not tax deductible. The **Fundación de Parques Nacionales** (Apdo. 1008, 1002 San José) works on management, development, and protection of parks and reserves. Working with communities near the parks, the **Fundación Neotrópica** (Neotropical Foundation), ☎ 253-0033, fax 253-4210, is at Apdo. 236, 1002 San José. Boza's *Costa Rica National Parks* ($45 postpaid) and other items are available through them or at their Nature Store at Póas National Park. Membership ($50) brings a subscription to their magazine and a 10% discount at their store. Contact them by E-mail at neotropica@apc.org. One of the best environmental organizations in Central America, the **Caribbean Conservation Corporation** (☎ 224-9215/2053, fax 234-1061) protects the turtles in Tortuguero and is helping develop the Paseo Pantera (Path of the Panther) project, which works to link parks and protected areas within Central America. Write Apdo. 246-2050, San Pedro. Publishers of the environmental monthly, *El Ecologista*, AECO, **The Costa Rican Ecology Association** (☎ 233-3013, fax 223-3925; Apdo. 11812-1000 San José) works with Indians and does research and projects on sustainable development. Donations may be made to Acct. # 0150343-2 at the Banco Nacional. **The** National Association of Organic Farming (ANAO; ☎ 441-2439) is a networking organization for those interested in organic farming. ANAPAO (☎ 224-1770; the Güilombé Foundation) is **The Association of Small Organic Farmers** and is attempting to organize such farmers. Working to protect the nation's aquatic resources such as dolphins endangered by tuna fishermen, APROCA (**Asociación pro Conservación Ambiental**; ☎ 255-3365) can be contacted at Apdo. 1863-1002.

The **Asociación de Amigos de Aves** (tel./fax 441-2658) is working to re-introduce macaws to the wild through breeding. Send donations to Apdo. 32-4001, Rio Segundo de Alajuela or send a tax-deductible contribution (indicate the "Asociación de Amigos de Aves") to the International Wildlife Learning Center, 408 S 10th Av., Hattiesburg MS 39401. **The Pro Fundación Mono Tití**, an organization helping to save the endangered squirrel monkey, which resides in Parque Nacional Manuel Antonio, can be sent donations c/o Dario Castelfranco, Banco Nacional Acct. #22-001849-3, Quepos. The **Green Iguana Foundation** (☎ 240-6712, fax 235-2007), started by German biologist Dagmar Werner, is involved with helping small farmers raise iguanas for food in an effort to ensure their survival while promoting reforestation. Write Apdo. 692-1007, San José. The **Irria Tsochok Foundation in Defense of the Earth** (☎ 225-5091, fax 534-9063) lobbies on behalf of La Amistad Biosphere Reserve. Write Apdo. 1-108-1002, San José. WSPA (☎ 239-7158), the Costa Rican chapter of the **World Society for the Protection of Animals**, runs one of the few animal shelters found in the region and conducts an anti-cruelty program in local schools. Write Apdo. 526-3000, Heredia. Working to expand the Monteverde Biological Preserve, help implement Arenal National Park, and provide community education among other projects, The **Monteverde Conservation League** (fax 645-5104) accepts donations at Apdo. 10165, 1000 San José. You can also direct donations to them for the Children's Rainforest, or to The **Children's Rainforest**, PO Box 936, Lewiston MA 04240. In Britain, write Children's Tropical Forests, UK, The Old Rectory, Market Deeping, Peterborough PE6 8DA, England, UK. The **Costa Rica Association for the Protection of Nature** (ASCONA, ☎ 222-2288/2296) is at Apdo. 8-3790, 1000 San José. One of the best-established organizations, they promote sustainable development. Tax-deductible donations may be made through the World Wildlife Fund. An invaluable watchdog group, its members patrol protected areas on weekends in search of illegal logging. APREFLORAS (☎ 240-6087), the **Association for the Preservation of Wild Flora and Fauna,** is at Apdo. 917, 2150 Moravia. Working to protect Lomas Barbudal, the **Amigos de Lomas Barbudal** (☎ 415-526-4115) is at 691 Colusa Av., Berkeley CA 94707.

ARBOLFILIA (Apdo. 512, 1100 Tibas; ☎ 240-7145) , the Association of Tree Protection, accepts a few volunteers for their work with tree planting. If you wish to see their work, Jungle Trails (☎ 255-3486) offers tours. The **Tsuli Tsuli, Audubon Society of Costa Rica** (Apdo. 4910, San José; ☎ 240-8775) works on migratory bird habitat preservation, river restoration, and espouses environmentally friendly banana production. Another worthy organization to support is the **Nature Conservancy,** which buys land and sets it aside in debt-for-nature swaps. Send tax-deductible contributions to Costa Rica Program, The Nature Conservancy, 1785 Mass. Ave. NW, Washington DC 20036. An organization supporting the Carara reserve is **Fundación Gran Carara** (Apdo. 469, 1011 San José; ☎ 234-1867, fax 253-6338). Researching laws relevant to topics such as forestry, land use and tenure, urban air pollution, and marine and coastal resources, the **Centro de Derecho Ambiental y de los Recursos Naturales** (CEDARENA, ☎ 225-1019, fax 225-5111; Apdo. 134, 2050, San Pedro) is compiling an information bank which they hope will be used to make environmentally optimal developmental decisions.

SEJETKO (☎ 234-7115; Apdo. 1293-2150, Moravia) is an organization that protects indigenous reserves. They need volunteers for work with rural developement and other projects; a one-year minimum commitment is requested. **YISKI** (☎ 297-0970; Apdo. 1038-2150 Moravia) sponsors groups of youth volunteers. If you believe that elevating the quality of social and economic life is a positive step towards ensuring the continued protection of the rainforest, then you may wish to support **KuKula** (☎ 758-4058, 758-3085), a volunteer organization based in Limón, which attends to the needs of street kids with projects including environmental educational camping excursions, medical and dental referrals, attention to individual needs, and more. Write Apdo. 463, 7300 Limón. One other ecologically worthy project is Earth Island Institute's **Sea Turtle Restoration Project**. Send checks c/o Earth Island Institute, 300 Broadway, Ste. 28, San Francisco CA 94133 or join their turtle brigades in Costa Rica.

Adopt An Acre is an innovative program coordinated by the San Francisco Zoo, which purchases rainforest land; donors receive an "Honorary Deed" certificate. Twenty-five dollars purchases a tenth-acre parcel; $32.50 buys a quarter-acre, $65 purchases a half-acre, and $130 buys an acre. This is an ideal gift for someone who has absolutely everything else. Write and make checks payable to Ecosystem Survival

Plan, San Francisco Zoo, Adopt an Acre, 1 Zoo Road, San Francisco CA 94132. Enclose $1.50 additional for postage and handling. **ARCA** (☎ 445-5490; Apdo. 172, San Ramón de Alajuela) is the San Ramón Association for the Conservation of the Environment, which organizes volunteers to fight against illegal logging, river pollution, and hunting. If your interests run toward supporting local highbrow culture, you might wish to donate funds to the financially strapped Youth Symphony and other worthy projects. Write **Ars Musica** (☎ 233-9890), Apdo. 1035, San José.

Selected Ecotourism Projects

A loosely defined term, to say the least, "ecotourism" brings visitors to a community so that the community benefits financially, learning takes place, and the environment is preserved for the future. Here are a few organizations that attempt to do just that.

ATEC. This cooperative has an office in the village of Puerto Viejo on the Caribbean coast. They offer a number of trips, and your fees go to your guide directly. Call or fax ☎ 798-4244; the best times to call are around noon or after 9 PM. *See page 517.*

Coopeunioro (☎ 233-3333). This 13-family cooperative is operated by former goldminers near Corcovado National Park. *See page 470.*

Esquinas Rainforest Lodge (☎/fax 775-0849/0131). The profits from this Austrian-financed lodge are returned to the local community. It's set at the edge of Esquinas National Park, near Golfito. *See page 449.*

Las Delicias Ecotourism Project. Near Barra Honda on the Nicoya Peninsula. It has three inexpensive *cabinas*, a campsite, gift shop, and restaurant. Guides to the caves in the national park are also available through them. To reserve, leave a message in Spanish at ☎ 685-5580. *See page 383.*

San José

Costa Rica's capital city of San José, once a sleepy backwater, is today a mixture of boldly intruding billboards advertising Kentucky Fried and Coke, shanty houses on hillside *tugurios*, and 10-speed bicyclists in spandex, who roam the streets in the company of BMWs and Volvos. Within a single generation San José has been transformed from a quiet town into a crowded, bustling metropolis. It has already engulfed neighboring suburbs and threatens to swallow the nearby cities of Cartago, Alajuela, and Heredia in the process creating one giant megalopolis.

Forecasts are that the greater San José metropolitan area will have over two million inhabitants by the end of this century. With some 660-700,000 people, 30% of the nation lives here. Compared to the slow-paced provincial towns, San José's traffic-clogged streets appear overpoweringly tumultuous. Noisy and polluted, San José has few parks, and its traditional character has been lost in the new, nondescript North American-style architecture. Fast food emporiums – such as Archi's Fried Chicken and Billy Boy Hamburgers – dot the mishmash architectural landscape. Schizophrenia is the name of the game in big cities these days, and San José is no exception. This is a surprisingly eclectic city, where you can expect the unexpected: drive-through ice cream parlors, wild after-hours dancing, or *merengue* at the Pizza Hut downtown.

Despite its size, San José does have its saving graces. It retains some of the characteristics of its birth from a collection of villages. Pastoral surroundings created by agriculture rather than industry are still visible from many areas of this city. It still has a small town core at its heart. Believe it or not, many Joséfinos, as residents of the capital are known, still shop at the neighborhood *pulpería*, hang out at *sodas* and bars, and greet each other by name. And it *is* a cool city: the daily temperature averages around 70°F (22°-25°C). There are a variety of cinemas, theaters, clubs, restaurants, bars, museums, and a whole gamut of services.

HISTORY: Expanding from the initial settlement of Cartago, a group of farmers founded Villa Nueva del la Boca del Monte in 1737. Some time afterward, locals got tired of dealing with such a lengthy nomenclature, and the name was changed to San José, after the town's patron saint. The original settlement was founded largely by Spaniards and creole smugglers, the latter having been expelled from Cartago as punishment for dealing in contraband.

Central San José

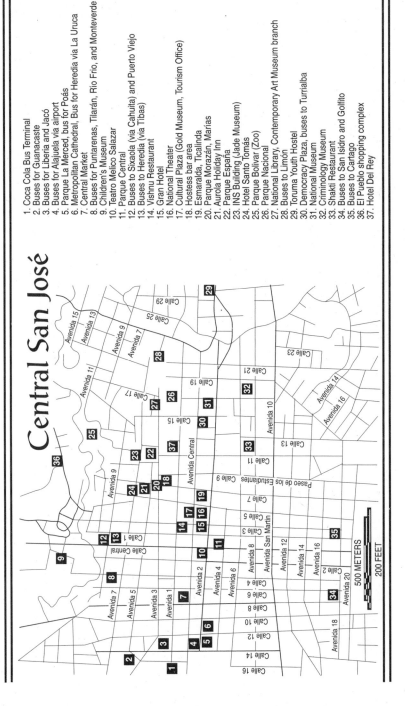

1. Coca Cola Bus Terminal
2. Buses for Guanacaste
3. Buses for Liberia and Jacó
4. Buses for Alajuela via airport
5. Parque La Merced, bus for Poás
6. Metropolitan Cathedral, Bus for Heredia via La Uruca
7. Central Market
8. Buses for Puntarenas, Tilarán, Río Frío, and Monteverde
9. Children's Museum
10. Teatro Melico Salazar
11. Parque Central
12. Buses to Sixaola (via Cahuita) and Puerto Viejo
13. Buses to Heredia (via Tibas)
14. Vishnu Restaurant
15. Gran Hotel
16. National Theater
17. Cultural Plaza (Gold Museum, Tourism Office)
18. Hostess bar area
19. Esmaralda, Ticalinda
20. Parque Morazán, Marias
21. Aurola Holiday Inn
22. Parque España
23. INS Building (Jade Museum)
24. Hotel Santo Tomás
25. Parque Bolívar (Zoo)
26. Parque Nacional
27. National Library, Contemporary Art Museum branch
28. Buses to Limón
29. Toruma Youth Hostel
30. Democracy Plaza, buses to Turrialba
31. National Museum
32. Criminology Museum
33. Shakti Restaurant
34. Buses to San Isidro and Golfito
35. Buses to Cartago
36. El Pueblo shopping complex
37. Hotel Del Rey

San José Transport

ARRIVING BY AIR: All flights enter the country through Juan Santamaría International Airport, 17 km W of San José. You may bring up to US$100 in goods for friends. When you present your voter registration card or birth certificate, your passport will be stamped. If you intend to stay more than 90 days, you should have a passport, which is a prerequisite to apply for an extension.

The tourist information counter is just beyond Customs. Although airport employees may not go out of their way to help you, you should be able to find a number of brochures, a map, and perhaps a complimentary newspaper. There are banking facilities and, should the banks be closed, there are also trustworthy moneychangers. A small shop sells powdered *café puro* as well as the current *Tico Times*, *The New York Times*, and various local papers. Other facilities include a post office and a duty-free shop. No baggage storage facilities are available.

If you have limited luggage, the San José-Alajuela bus stop is just across from the entrance. It costs about 50¢ (change given on the bus) to travel to the terminal at Av. 2 and C. 12 via Paseo Colón. Not all buses go to San José; be sure to ask. A cab to the city will cost you about US$10 – twice as much as you might normally pay for a similar distance to and from a different location. A *colectivo* (shared taxi), if you can locate one, will run you about $2.

FOR ESCAZU: If you're driving to Escazú, take the highway SE towards San José. At the fourth traffic light, you come to (where the National Gymnasium, a round structure, should be on your right and McDonalds on your L), take a right onto the highway. exit right to Escazú and head downhill (with the McDonalds on your left and the Shell station to your R). From "El Cruce" head into Escazú and continue on to your hotel.

LAYOUT: Avenida Central divides the downtown area. This is a place to promenade and window shop. The wide variety of expensive, high-quality imported goods in its stores astonishes visitors from other Central American nations. A continuation of Avenida Central, broad, bustling, and busy Paseo de Colón is another area of interest. What one might call the "Champs Elysées" of San José, this area has seen a number of its elegant houses disappear, to be replaced with fast food emporiums and car dealerships. One traditional-style home, the Casa de Leones, vanished within a three-day period. Trees have also been mysteriously poisoned by an injection of herbicide along this stretch. The street terminates at La Sabana, the former site of the national airport. It has evolved into the nation's largest urban park and hosts the modern art museum. Surrounding the city farther out are the *barrios* (neighborhoods) such as Bellavista, Sabana Norte, Sabana Sur; still farther out are the *Areas Metropolitanas* (municipalities), which are extensions of the city.

GETTING AROUND: It's easy enough to do with a little practice. City buses, costing about 10¢, are slow moving, but run frequently. The fare is marked near the door, and they are identified in the front windshield both by number and destination; the driver will make change. Many either depart from or pass by the vicinity of Parque Central. Smaller (and therefore speedier) microbuses also run. Buses can be very crowded during peak hours (7-9 AM and 5-7 PM). Plan your travel for other times.

  routing: There are innumerable bus routes within the city. Two of the most convenient routes are the *Sabana Cemetario* and the *Cemetario Sabana* buses, which travel parallel ellipses in opposite directions on different streets around the Sabana and then into town. Because of their circuitous and often confusing routing, however, it may be faster to walk. The *Estadio Sabana* runs from the stadium to the Parque Central and back. All three of these provide an inexpensive city tour, but expect to spend about 40 minutes to get back to your starting point. Heading to San Pedro via Los Yoses (departs Av. 2, C. 5/7), the *San Pedro* bus can drop you off near the church and park in the center of the university area. The C. *Blanco* bus runs to the commercial shopping center of El Pueblo. The *El Carmen (Parque de La Paz)* and *San Cayetano* (the baseball stadium) buses run nearly overlapping routes from C. 8 at Av. 4 up along Av. 2 and then down C. 1. The return to the N is along C. Central. Also running to Parque de la Paz and passing by Plaza Viquez (where buses to S suburbs depart) on C. 11, the *Barrio La Cruz* bus runs along C. 7, along Av. 3, down C. 10, and back via C. 2. If you wish to take a bus late at night (from Los Yoses to Parque Central for example), it's best to take the first bus that comes along, even if it is a suburban bus and you have to pay more. (Fares are determined by the length of the route). It's tough to find many buses before 6 AM or after 10 PM.

  getting farther out: Once the site of a now-vanished Coca Cola bottling facility, "Coca Cola," as this rough neighborhood is still known, is the starting point for buses to the suburbs and outlying towns. It's always preferable to board here rather than at the later stops, when it may be difficult or impossible to get a seat. Buses from Coca Cola run to outlying towns like Ciudad Colón, Santa Ana, Escazú, Sarchí, and Naranjo, as well as Orotina and Quepos. Buses for most destinations to the W (including Guanacaste) are nearby.

San José

Suburban Bus Destinations & Stops

Airport (domestic, Pavas), C. 20. Av.1
Coronado, C. 3/Av. 5/7
Curridabat, C. 3, Av. 2/4
Escazú, Av. 6, C. 12/14 (minibus), C. 16, Av. 1/3 (reg.)
Guadalupe, Av. 3, C. Central/1
La Uruca, Av. 3, C. 6/8
Moravia, Av. 3, C 3/5
Pavas, Av. 1, C. 16/18
Sabanilla, Av. 2, C. 5/7
San Ramón de Tres Ríos, Av. 2, C. 5/7
Santa Ana, Coca Cola terminal
Villa Colón, Coca Cola terminal

on foot: Looking at the map, one might expect San José to be a large city. In actuality, it is more like a metropolis compressed into Lilliputian format. It's easy to walk around the central part of the city. The blocks are small and you can cover a considerable distance in 20 minutes on foot. However, be extremely cautious when crossing streets. Drivers appear to regard their fellow humans as squishy things to be run over; they actually seem to speed up when they see you coming! Watch the cars, not the stoplights. As far as the drivers are concerned, traffic lights might as well be permanent Christmas decorations.

finding locations: Laid out in a grid, *calles* run E to W and *avenidas* run N to S. Numbering begins in all directions from Avenida Central. Even-numbered *calles* run to the W; odd-numbered *calles* run to the E. Odd-numbered *avenidas* run to the N of Avenida Central; even-numbered ones run to the S. San José's central downtown area extends approximately .75 miles (1.3 km) from N to S and 1¼ miles (2. 1 km) from E to W. It can be roughly defined as being bounded by C. 20 on its W, Av. 9 on its N, C. 21 on its E, and Av. 20 on its S. You can usually find street numbers on the corners of buildings, but a new set of street signs (containing advertising) is being put into place in the tourist areas. Many streets are still poorly marked. Buildings themselves are not numbered and addresses are expressed in terms of 100 *varas* (slightly less than 100 yards) or, more frequently, in units of 100 meters (*cien meters*); either is the approximate equivalent of a block (an average block is actually shorter). An address given as "Av. 7, C. 9/11" indicates that the building faces either side of Avenida 7 on the block between Calles 9 and 11. Directions may be given from known landmarks, which can make things harder to find: businesses, restaurants, etc. are often advertised in terms of meters from a famous landmark.

by taxi: An average trip costs $2 or less. Although the taxis theoretically have meters (called *"marías"*), they are often either broken, or drivers maintain they are, so price negotiations may be required! Be aware that taxi drivers normally attempt to charge tourists from five to 10 times the correct fare. One way to approximate your fare is to estimate it in terms of nine blocks per km and count the first km as around 60¢, with 25¢ per km thereafter. You should note that there is a 20% surcharge after 10 PM. The fare for trips of 12 km or more must be negotiated. The bright red cabs are equipped with roof lights. It's difficult to find a taxi on weekend evenings so plan accordingly.

☞ **Traveler's Tip**. It's better to avoid taxis that lurk in front of hotels. They may try to tell you that they are legally entitled to charge more because they are providing an additional service. This is a complete and utter fabrication. It's better to walk down the street and find another cab! Make sure you ask the driver to *"prenda la maría por favor"* (please turn on the meter). Have the receptionist at your hotel write down the address for you before you depart. If you speak Spanish, you can save a bit by negotiating with a *pirata* (a "pirate" cab) if you can find one. Call ahead (**Coopetico** at ☎ 224-6969 or **Coopeirazu** at 254-3211) if it is rush hour or should it be raining. Register all complaints with the Ministry of Public Works and Transit (☎ 255-4188).

Downtown Sights

While there is not a great deal of spectacular interest here, the visitor will find it rewarding to spend at least half a day walking around town. The place to begin is in the Parque Central, bounded by C. Central and 2 and Av. 2 and 4. This small park is the perfect place to escape from the surrounding hustle and bustle during the day. It's also an important bus terminal. A gift from Nicaraguan dictator Anastasio Somoza in the 1940s, the giant concrete kiosk in its center was scheduled to be razed as part of a 1993 renovation, but protests have saved it. A new fountain commemorates Costa Rica's first aqueduct. San José has a large number of museums, and most are worth visiting. Admission is free or minimal. The best place to begin seeing these is in the Plaza de la Cultura (see below).

CATEDRAL METROPOLITANA: Colored off-white and not particularly spectacular, the cathedral is most notable for the structure attached to its rear. The administration building represents a merger between 19th-C. San José style and that of Europe; its stone-cased win-

San José

dows and pediments draw from the traditions of Renaissance Italy. At the corner of C. Central on the N side of the square, the **Teatro Melico Salazar** has fluted Corinthian columns, balconies, and pediments with stuccoed relief sculptures. It is a superb place to see theater or attend a concert.

TEATRO NACIONAL: One of the few buildings constructed before the beginning of this century, the Belgian-designed National Theater was financed by *cafetaleros* (coffee barons) and finished in 1897. Often billed as a miniature version of either the Paris or Milan opera house, it replicates neither. Its rust-colored tin roof is typically Costa Rican. The impetus for its construction came after a European opera company, featuring the famed singer Angela Pelati, played in Guatemala in 1890 but turned down a San José date due to lack of a suitable venue. Planned by Belgian architects, its metal framework was the work of Belgian craftsmen. Ornate with baroque decorations and gilded with 22.5 karat gold, its Great Hall of Spectacles seats 1,040. The refreshment area has changing exhibits by local artists. The main lobby, decorated in pink marble, has two sculptures by Pietro Capurrore presenting comedy and tragedy. "Heroes of Misery," the sculpture in the atrium, is the work of Costa Rican artist, Juan Ramón Bonilla. The Carrara marble grand staircase leads up to the foyer, which has paintings and a mural showing the nation's major exports. The ceiling fresco, painted by Italian Arturo Fontana and illuminated by an 85-light chandelier, depicts unclad celestial deities. Another of Fontana's paintings, in the Presidential Box, which is set dead center in the balcony directly over the entrance, depicts Justice and the Nation. In the theater's foyer, a three-part fresco by Vespasiano Bignami represents Dawn, Day, and Night. Replicas of the originals, the furniture in the room to the rear is fashioned from mahogany and has been gold leafed. The floor, originally European pine, was replaced in 1940 with a selection of the 10 varieties of local hardwoods.

One of the theater's unique features was the manual winch which once raised the floor to stage level – an operation performed by 12 men in just under an hour – allowing the stage to be used as a ballroom. Its Renaissance-style facade has statuary representing Music, Fame, and Dance. Statues of Beethoven and Calderón de la Barca, a 17th-C. playright and poet, sit in niches on either side of the entrance. Restored after the 1991 earthquake and reinaugurated in 1993, the building can be visited on your own, day or night (around $1 admission). If you have the chance, see one of the performances held here on a near-daily basis. It may be one of the highlights of your trip. Outside the theater, the drama of the street goes on as vendors flog their wares and an evangelical preacher thumps a Bible against his head as he warns of the nasty events to come.

Paseo Colón Area

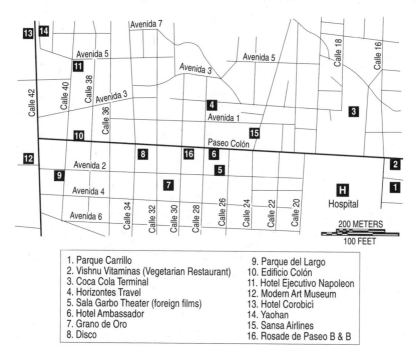

1. Parque Carrillo
2. Vishnu Vitaminas (Vegetarian Restaurant)
3. Coca Cola Terminal
4. Horizontes Travel
5. Sala Garbo Theater (foreign films)
6. Hotel Ambassador
7. Grano de Oro
8. Disco
9. Parque del Largo
10. Edificio Colón
11. Hotel Ejecutivo Napoleon
12. Modern Art Museum
13. Hotel Corobicí
14. Yaohan
15. Sansa Airlines
16. Rosade de Paseo B & B

PLAZA DE LA CULTURA: Situated along Av. Central between C. 3 and C. 5 beside the Teatro Nacional, this multi-level outdoor cultural plaza has underground exhibit halls. The plaza has been largely over-run with vendors who look as if they should be selling at a Grateful Dead concert. A riot of colors, they sell all kinds of things, from Guatemalan clothing and bags to tee shirts and windsurfing sandals. While the government has sought to expel them (and many have been removed), they have justifiably asserted that they are a tourist attrac-tion in and of themselves! You might also see passionately entranced Hare Krishnas here dueling it out to the beat of marimbas. Be sure to head down the stairs and stop by the underground Instituto Costar-ricense de Turismo (ICT), the tourist information center near the corner of Av. Central and C. 5. In front of the National Theater, you'll find the Plaza Juan Mora Fernández, which was re-inaguarated in June 1995. Painters, who had formerly sold their work in the square, were banned after its reopening.

MUSEUMS: Next door to the Plaza de la Cultura is the entrance to the two museums. First, go into the **Museo Numismatica**. It has Native American artifacts, old coins, banknotes, and a 1,000-*colón* gold piece issued in 1970 – which gives you an idea of how far and how fast the currency has fallen. (Open Tues. to Sun., 10-5.) Next door, a small exhibit hall displays works from the Central Bank's art collection. The **Museo de Oro**, entered through thick vault doors set at the base of a beautiful winding marble staircase, has one of the world's finest collections of gold-crafted art – over 1,600 pieces in all, weighing in at 24,000 troy ounces – making it the hemisphere's second largest collection. It's almost surrealistically spooky and quiet, with beautiful displays and immaculately polished parquet floors. Gold pieces featuring animals, people, iguanas, quetzals, frogs, plus jewelry and bells are displayed inside plexiglass cases. As you leave through the vault door at the end, you come upon what might well be a hydroponic garden used in an interstellar craft. Given the spiraling marble staircase, the roof high overhead composed of triangular concrete blocks, the mechanical whir of the a/c, and the occasional "bing" of the elevator, you could be on the set of a science fiction movie. Laser-gun-toting androids might come trotting down the stairs at any moment. If you need a quick escape from San José for whatever reason, this otherworldly environment is the place! It's open weekdays from 10-5. Admission is charged.

MUSEO DE JADE: Misleadingly named, this small jewel of a museum is really a full-fledged introduction to the cultures of Costa Rica's indigenous peoples. There are musical instruments, bows and arrows, an aerial photo of the Guayabo archaeological site, ceramic ocarinas, flints, anthropomorphic *metales* (grinding stones) and others with elaborately carved undersides, a disk with Maya inscriptions, fantastic female ceramic figurines (from AD 700-1100), and a large two-piece incense burner with a marvelous *lagarto* (lizard) carved on the lid. The quality of both the imagery and the technique puts most contemporary art to shame. After some finely crafted carved jade pieces showing South American influences, there's a sitting room with a great view to the north. Give your feet, brain, and eyes a brief rest here, because you'll need it for what's to come. Next is a room displaying ceramic and gold objects. Then the displays change, with room after room of anthropomorphically shaped jade scrapers and other objects from the Pacific coast, many of which show a Mayan influence. Works from the central and Atlantic areas are also on display. These jade pieces did not come from archaeological sites, but rather were purchased from private collectors who bought them from looters. The last room shows some enormous clay phalluses along with phallic ocarinas, masturbating clay men, ceramic hermaphrodite and female fertility figures, and a group of wild-eyed, frantically clutching, copulating clay couples. Finally, out in the hall there's a replica of a 14th-C. Tang Dynasty ceramic horse, a gift from the Chinese Embassy. The museum (☎ 223-5800) is on the 11th floor of the INS (Instituto Nacional de Seguros; Institute for National Security), C. 11, Av. 7. It's open Mon.-Fri., 8-5. Admission is free. And be sure to check out the views before you leave; to the S is the Edificio Metálico (Metal Building), an incongrous green prefab building designed by French architect Victor Balatard. After visiting the museum, head for the intimate **Café Mundo** at Av. 9, C. 11/13 nearby to dine or get caffeinated.

vicinity of Museo de Jade: Also known as the Parque de la Expresión, the atmosphere of the **Parque España** (next to the INS, between Av. 5 and 7 at C. 11) is accentuated by the transplanted tropical trees. Artists sell here on Sun. Across C. 11 is the Spanish-style **Casa Amarilla**, home of the nation's foreign ministry. Stroll through the traditional neighborhoods to the N, where you'll find old tin-roofed homes of brick and wood.

> ☞ **Traveler's Tip.** The **Hotel del Rey** (☎ 221-7272, 257-3130, fax 221-0096) offers free morning tours of the city to all comers. The hotel is near Park Morazán at Av. 1 and C. 9. It's a great way to orient yourself, garner a bit of historical background, and get some good photos.

PARQUE ZOOLOGICO SIMON BOLIVAR: Set at the N edge of the downtown area, off Av. 11, this rather run-down, dank, and delapidated animal prison appears to have been deliberately designed to torture its inmates. The only animals that seem content are the monkeys who swing about joyfully in their concrete enclosure. The cats and many of the other animals seem to be crying "Ay Bendido!" Sights like this make one question whether the nation's much-touted concern for nature and preservation comes from its heart or if this is a national image cultivated to capture ecodollars. Improvement and/or relocation of the zoo has been talked about for years, and this may actually happen some day. If you do come, be sure to stop by the park information office in the rear, although they generally have minimal info in English. (Open Tues. to Fri., 8:30-3:30; Sat., Sun., and holidays, 9-4:30.)

note: Conditions at the zoo have been improving, but it *still* leaves a lot to be desired. There's a new restaurant, habitats for the animals are slowly being upgraded, plants are now identified, and the zoo has a new entranceway. If you walk along C. 11 you can reach a park by climbing the steps next to the *guardia civil* post and the RR tracks, continuing along through Barrio Aranjuez, and taking a left two blocks after the tracks. There are basketball courts and a soccer field here.

San José

MUSEO NACIONAL: Housed in the Bellavista Fortress, the National Museum of Costa Rica was once an army headquarters and barracks. Displays of pre-Columbian artifacts, period religious garb and dress, and other items from the colonial era can be seen. Visible bullet marks on the building's exterior from the 1948 civil war make it a living monument to recent history. The entrance has a small gift shop, a courtyard containing prehistoric basalt balls, and a cannon. The Sala Doris Stone's exhibits include a mastadon tooth, displays of Mesoamerican and South American, anthropomorphic *metates*, and other beautiful artwork. The Sala Arqueologia exhibits miniature brass and gold artifacts, including jewelry. Other rooms show colonial furniture, presidential portraits and statuary, historical photos, and a collection of gigantic stick figures representing cultural groups that have added to the nation's ethnic fabric. There's also a fine collection of folk art, most of which was imported in colonial times from Mexico and Guatemala, as Costa Rica has always had a minimal number of artisans. The most engaging of these is a brightly colored cabinet creche from Guatemala, with a crowned Virgin in its center and the devil – whose face indicates that he may vomit at any instant – lying in the bottom level. (C. 17, Av. 2/Central; ☎ 222-1229, 221-0295.) Open Tues. to Sun. from 9-5. Students with ID free.

vicinity of the Museo Nacional: While you're in the area, you may wish to check out the **Plaza de la Democracia** (Plaza of Democracy), which cost US$1.5 billion to construct, and the Moorish-style, cream-colored legislature building. Set to the N is the **Parque Nacional**, which centers around an allegorical statue representing the five Latin American nations driving out William Walker in 1856 (see page 56). The five females represent each of the five Central American nations, and the two men are Walker (who has a rifle) and one of his cohorts (who lies prostate on the ground). Costa Rica is represented by the flag-waving woman embracing a veiled Nicaragua. The bas reliefs on its base depict the Battle of Santa Rosa, the Battle of Rivas, the seizing of boats in the San Juan del Norte, and Walker's surrender. The statue was cast in bronze and erected in 1895. Scale the viewing platform to have a closer look.

In 1995, construction workers installing underground cables discovered a tunnel running under the park which appeared to connect the former Casa Presidencial with the National Museum (formerly a fort). Apparently, it was intended to allow top officials to commute between the two in the event of a crisis.

Across from the park, the imposing **Biblioteca Nacional** (National Library) has a mural of the sun on the outside. **Galeria Nacional de Arte Contemporáneo** (GANAC), a branch of the modern art museum with rotating exhibits on the W side, is open Mon. to Fri. 10-5, closed 1-1:45 for lunch.

MUSEO DE LA CRIMINOLOGIA: Set inside the Hall of Justice at Av. 6, C. 17, this combination crime museum and museum of judicial history (open from 1-4 on Mon., Wed., and Fri.) displays weapons used in violent crimes, counterfeit lottery tickets and money (including US$), pictures of magic mushrooms, drug paraphernalia, photos of severed hands, and jars containing items like an embalmed hand severed with a machete, an illegally aborted fetus, and severed feet.

OTHER SMALL MUSEUMS: A must for reptile (and particularly snake) fans, the **Serpentario** (☎ 255-4210) hosts a wide variety of species, including poison dart frogs. It's at C. 9/11 on Av. 1, above the El Gran Chaparral restaurant. Admission (around $1.50) is charged; it's open Mon. to Sat. from 10-7. Another imposing relic, a steam engine belonging to the now defunct Northern Railway, stands on a spur in front of the closed Ferrocarril Pacifica station on Av. 20 at C. 2. The station has been converted into the **Costa Rican Railway Museum**, which contains a display of railway memorabilia. It's open 9-4, Mon. through Thurs., and on Fri. from 9-3:30. Artifacts from the life of the former president **Rafael Angel Calderón Guardia** are on display at the museum of the same name in Barrio Escalante at Av. 11, C. 25/27. (It's open Mon. to Fri., 10-4; $1 admission; ☎ 255-1218.) You might also wish to visit the **Museum of Printing**, in the Imprenta Nacional in suburban La Uruca. (Open Mon. to Fri. from 9-3:30.)

The **Children's Museum** (☎ 233-2734, 223-7003) is in the old Central Penitentiary (*Penitenciaria*) to the N of downtown San José on C. 4, N of Av. 9. The building dates from 1848, and it held as many as 4,000 prisoners as recently as 1989. Viewed from outside, it resembles a castle. Inside, you find 34 rooms, each with a different theme. Interactive educational exhibits are on the second level. Temporary exhibition spaces display paintings. A row of cells (*sans* prisoners) remain so you may imagine what the place was once like. It's open Wed. to Sun. 9-noon and 2-5. Ticos pay $3; children of all nationalities under 12 and accompanied by an adult are free, but foreign adults are fleeced for $6. The **Museo de Fotos** (☎ 222-4941), C. 7, Av. Central/1, displays photos from the 18th C. Presenting a portion of the 30,000 negatives taken by Manuel Gómez Miralles, the 175 prints cover Costa Rican history from 1910 to 1930 and include a shot of Irazú erupting in 1917. The **Asociación Cultural Sejekto de Costa Rica (Voz del Indio)** in Sabanilla displays indigenous items and sells crafts. Items include traditional Bribri clothes, baskets, woven bags, flutes, drums, and even a violin. ☎ 234-7115 to make an appointment.

San José

OTHER SIGHTS: Divided by C. 7 and Av. 3 into four individual gardens, compact **Parque Morazán** has a pseudo-Japanese section in the NE. The "Temple of Music," which once hosted concerts, stands in the park's center. The entirety of this small park is now overshadowed by the immense Aurora Holiday Inn, with its reflecting glass panes. On C. 2 and Av. 2/4, the **Post Office Museum** is open Mon. to Fri, 8-5. The former National Liquor Factory has been converted into the **Museum of Contemporary Art and Design,** which serves as a cultural center, museum, and performance space. Here the National Dance Company performs and the National Theater Company puts on plays. Entrance is around $2.50 for *gringos*, but no fee is charged on Sun. and Thurs. from 6-9. Guided tours are conducted in English, Spanish, and French free of charge, and special events take place on the last Thurs. of every month. It's on the NW side of the Parque Nacional at Av. 7, C. 9/11. (note: Lack of funds caused the museum to close in 1995; check with the ICT, the Tourism Institute, to see if it has reopened). Delineated by Av. 2 and 4 and Calles 12 and 14, **Parque Braulio Carrillo** has a four-ft (1.3-m) pre-Columbian stone sphere from Palmar Sur, as well as a statue of the former president. The city's newest plaza, the **Plaza de la Libertad** (C. 13, Av. 7/9) was dedicated in 1994. It features a chunk of the Berlin wall donated by the German government. A plaque commemorates the date when the wall came tumbling down. In the outlying suburb of **San Francisco de Dos Ríos**, there's a footbridge resembling the Golden Gate Bridge in San Francisco.

Outlying Sights

PARQUE METROPOLITANO (LA SABANA): Set at the opposite end of the wealthy Paseo de Colón district is La Sabana, the city's largest park, formerly the site of the national airport. The lake here was drained for the airport and then restored later. Sports facilities include a gym, pool, and stadium.

MUSEO DE ARTE COSTARRICENSE: Housed in what was formerly the airport control tower, the Costa Rican Museum of Art stands on C. 42, at the E side of La Sabana. This Spanish-style building has everything from pre-Columbian to modern art. Included in its collection are portraits, woodcuts, antique sculptured busts, and antique ink drawings of the Gulf of Nicoya and of a festival in Guanacaste. There's also the wooden sculpture, "Los Amantes" by Juan Manuel Sanchez, a giant agricultural mural by Francisco Amighetti, the feminist portraits of Max Jiménez, and a sculptured wooden chair by Juan Luis Rodriguez. The museum is divided into sections, such as *abstraccíon y figuracíon* and *nuevas tendencias*. The latter has works like Rafael Ottón Solis's

"Homenaje a Monseñor Romero" and a batik print on paper by Anabel Martén. Although the area is small, the robust collection is incredibly diverse, and the quality of its varied sculptures is outstanding. Postcards and tee shirts are for sale by the entrance. (Open Tues. through Sun., 10-5.) Take any *Sabana* bus from Av. 3, C. Central/2, or from the Parque Central.

MUSEO DE CIENCIAS NATURALES: Opened in 1959, the Natural Sciences Museum (☎ 232-6427) is located in Collegio La Salle, a school set at the SW extremity of Sabana Park. You can either walk from the art museum or take the *Estadio Sabana* bus from near Parque Central. Stuffed animals are what you'll find here, with over 1,000 birds, as well as monkeys and other forest dwellers. Ring the buzzer at the right and the curator will come to the door, collect the small admission fee, and switch on all the lights for you. The first room to the right has a small archaeological collection. A pleasant place to sit and read, the courtyard has a whale skeleton. One room displays various bottles containing sea urchins, octopi, human fetuses, and bats. There are shells, shells, and more shells; rocks, rocks, and more rocks. Other rooms have dioramas, which are so poorly done as to be almost comedic. Check out the chimp holding the plastic pineapple, and the spaced-out orangutang clutching his plastic pear. Then, there's the fierce-looking mama opposum with the kiddies riding shotgun on top, and the Janus-faced, two-headed baby ox mutation. Finally, the domestic rabbit has such a wild expression and tensely poised posture that he appears to have hopped straight from the pages of Richard Adams' novel, *Watership Down*. If you do come, you'll undoubtedly have fun trying to pick the most obscenely stuffed animal! (Open Tues. to Fri., 8-3, Sat. 8-12.)

MUSEO DE ENTOMOLOGIA: Downstairs in the Facultade de Artes Musicales (music department) of the Universitas de Costa Rica in Sabanilla Montes de Oca, a suburb E of San José, Central America's sole collection of insects features a wonderful display of butterflies, including the turquoise-winged *morpho amathonte*. There are also some dioramas, hercules and elephant beetles, and the totally cute *megaloblatta rufiles*, a four-inch (10-cm) cockroach. To get here, take the *San Pedro* bus near the Teatro Nacional on Av. 2 between Calles 5 and 7; exit when you see the park with the church on your L. (Open Wed.-Thurs., 1-6; researchers welcome anytime, ☎ 225-5555.) Admission is 100 *colones* for Ticos and 200 *colones* for those not among the chosen people. While you're in the area you might want to visit the small, somewhat funky campus and the surrounding area, which has a number of restaurants, including vegetarian-macrobiotic **La Mazorca**, with its own bakery and health food store.

San José

Acua Manía

Central America's largest water park, Acua Manía (☎ 293-2033) opened in Jan. 1995 in the suburb of Cariari to the W of San José. In addition to the extensive aquatic portion, it also has a go-kart course (with 20 karts), an 18-hole miniature golf course, a video arcade, and a fast food restaurant. A wave pool, a "lazy" river, soccer fields, and a tube slide weaving through the trees add to the attraction. Presently, a large pool has a volleyball net over one side and underwater caves with seats and piped-in music in the other; two short slides are behind the caverns. A smaller pool is calmer, and there is a children's pool with water guns, water slides, and sprinklers. There are more than a dozen lifeguards so your children will be safe here. Admission to the park is around $8 adults, $6 children; the go-kart course and miniature golf course are $4 additional apiece. It's open from 10-5:30 on Tues., Wed., Thurs., and Sun. and from 10-10 on Fri. and Sat. Pool use is free after 4 PM.

San José Accommodations

You can find any type of hotel in this area – from fleabags to luxury suites. In general, you may get what you pay for, although this does not always apply. You have the option of staying downtown or basing yourself farther out and commuting. Downtown can be noisy, but it is decidedly more convenient. If you are sensitive to street noise, you'll want to have a quiet room. The least desirable places to stay are around the Coca-Cola terminal, but this is where many of the low-budget hotels are located. If you're looking for intimacy, the **Established Bed and Breakfast Group** may be able to recommend the accommodations best suited to you. However, they are a volunteer organization and will not make reservations for you. They also have a directory ($2) Contact Pat Bliss (☎/fax 506-228-9200) or E-mail corpfaxi@sol.racsa.co.cr. **Bell's Home Hospitality** (☎ 225-4752, fax 224-5884) will connect you with a homestay for $45 d with shared bath and $50 private bath; breakfast is included. Another alternative is Steve Beaudreau's **Costa Rica Homestays** (☎ 240-6829), which offers two accommodation classes in and around San José. The "A" class is in upper middle class homes offering private bath; the "B" class is in more modest homes with shared baths. They're $28 and $24 per day respectively, with discounts for longer stays. Breakfast, laundry, and airport pickup are included. **TurCasa** (☎ 221-6161, 223-1165) is a group of Tico households that offer homestays; rooms are about the same as

Bell's. While *aparthotels* are convenient for longer stays, they tend to lack atmosphere.

LUXURY AND ULTRA-LUXURY ACCOMMODATION: These are defined as being over $91 or over $121 respectively for a single or double, including tax and services. Overlooking Parque Bolívar at C. 13, Av. 9/11, the service-oriented **Hotel L'Ambiance**'s rates include continental breakfast. This six-room and one-suite hotel, filled with antiques and set in a Spanish-style home, has a gourmet restaurant, a/c, and private TV. ☎ 222-6702, 223-1598; fax 223-0481; or write Apdo. 1040, 2050 San Pedro. Rates run from around $90 d plus tax. In the US, write c/o Interlink, PO Box 526770, Miami FL 33152. The five-star 120-room **Amstel Amón** (☎ 222-0655, fax 221-2442; Apdo. 5834-1000, San José) opened in 1993 in Barrio Amón, to the N of Parque Morazón at Av. 7, C. 3 bis. Rooms have phones, cable TV, and a/c. There's a gourmet restaurant, casino, and meeting rooms. Rates start at around $105 s or d, not including tax and gratuities. In the US ☎ 800-575-1253.

The **Britannia Hotel** (C. 3, Av. 11) is another Barrio Amón option. The conveniently located and recently renovated four-star, 50-room **Nuevo Hotel Talamanca** (☎ 233-5033, Av. 2, C. 8/10) has an attached restaurant, casino, and disco. Rooms have a/c or fans, phone, and cable TV. Write Apdo. 449, 10023 San José. Located across from Parque Morazán at Av. 5, C. 5, the 17-storey **Aurola Holiday Inn** (☎ 233-7233/7036, fax 255-1036) is the city's most imposing hotel. Its features include restaurant, pool, a/c, casino, cable TV, parking, and spa. Write Apdo. 7802, 1000 San José or call 800-Holiday in the US. **D'Raya Vida Bed & Breakfast Villa** (☎ 223-4168, fax 223-4147; C. 15, Av. 11/13) is one of the most popular luxury B&Bs. Run by affable Debbie McMurray-Long and her husband Michael, their home has four rooms, each impeccably decorated in a different style. Most unusual is the mask room, which has masks from all of the world. Rates run around $65 s, $85 d plus tax and include transport to and from the airport, travel consulting, and a full breakfast.

Paseo de Colón luxury accommodations: This quiet area has blossomed with restaurants, night spots, and small hotels in the past few years. At C. 30, Av. 2/4, No. 251, the 34-room **Grano de Oro** (☎ 255-3322, fax 221-2782) is a well-located hotel set in a restored mansion. Rooms (smoking prohibited) have phones and satellite TV, brass fixtures with colonial tiles in baths, and hand-crafted wood furniture. Hundreds of tropical plants adorn the premises. On the premises are an acclaimed gourmet French restaurant in a courtyard (breakfast, light meals, and desserts served), a tropical sundeck terrace with two hot tubs, fax, photocopy, laundry/drycleaning and mail service, as well as secure parking. Prices are around $70 for standard rooms, $90 for deluxe, and $120 for garden suites (plus tax). Winter rates are higher. Write Apdo. 1157-1007 Centro Colón, San José or, in the US, Box 025216, Miami FL 33102-5216. Also on Paseo de Colón, the **Rosa del Paseo** (☎ 257-3258, fax 223-2776; Apdo. 287, 1007 San José) is a beautifully restored old home that now operates as a small hotel. Rates are around $100 d, which includes a continental breakfast. If you have problems with noise, be sure to get one of the original rooms to the rear of the house. The **Parque del Lago** (☎ 222-1577, fax 223-1617; Apdo. 624-1007, San Jose; Av. 2, C. 40/42) caters to business travelers. Rooms come equipped with coffee maker, desk, table, cable TV, and hair dryer. Studios with kitchenettes are also available. Facilities include coin laundry and conference room. Rates include breakfast. In the US and Canada ☎ 800-663-8889. Right on the main drag, the 126-room **Hotel Centro Colón** (☎ 257-2580, fax 257-2582) is a Quality Hotel franchise. It charges around $70 d and up. The **Corobicí** (☎ 232-8122, fax 231-5834) has a/c, restaurant, pool, casino, and spa; it's located at the end of Paseo Colón right at the beginning of La Sabana. In the US, ☎ 800-CARIARI or (exc. FL) 800-325-1337; after second tone dial 221. Or write Apdo. 2443, 1000 San José. Another possibility is the **Hotel Ejecutivo Napoleon** (☎ 223-3252/2278, fax 222-9487) which is off of C. 40 at Av. 5, two blocks from Centro Colón. It offers phone, cable TV, secure parking, and a poolside bar. Buffet breakfast is included. Write Apdo. 8, 6340 San José.

in San Pedro: The restored home of the co-owner's grandfather, the **Hotel Milvia** (☎ 225-4543, fax 225-7801; Apdo. 1660-2050 San Pedro) is one of the best places to stay in its price range in the San José area. Its attractively decorated rooms are personalized with individual names and each has phone, TV, fan, and bath. Continental breakfasts (served as early as you need) and dinners (Italian, by request) are served in the small dining room. From the upstairs balcony you can see as far as Irazú on a clear morning. Coffee and tea are complimentary and always available; accompanying desserts are on sale. Named after Milvia, who manages the hotel along with Tico husband Mauricio, the hotel exemplifies what one might expect from a small establishment offering personal service. Originally from Italy, Milvia sells her painted ceramic ware in the gift shop. To reach the hotel, walk 150 ft E from "Del Higueron," then 150 ft N, then 600 ft E again.

outlying luxury accommodations: The two best-known luxury hotels are the Herradura and the Cariari. Located five minutes from the airport and 20 minutes from downtown, the **Sheraton Herradura**'s facilities include a/c, satellite TV, three restaurants (including one Japanese), tennis, golf, and a small orchid garden. ☎ 239-0033, fax 239-2292, or write Apdo. 7-1880, 1000 San José. ☎ 800-325-3535, USA; 800-268-9330, E Canada; or 800-268-9393, W Canada. The framed photos on walls of the **Cariari Hotel** (☎ 239-0022, fax 239-2083) attest to visits by luminaries such as Colonel Harlan Sanders, Ronald Reagan, Warren Beatty, George Shultz, Jimmy Carter, and Henry Kissinger. This resort and country club complex has a/c, TV, pool, sauna, Jacuzzi, shops, and casino. For an additional fee, you may use the golf course, pool, tennis and basketball courts, and gym. In the US, ☎ 800-CARIARI or (exc. FL) 800-325-1337; after second tone dial 221. Or write Apdo. 737, Centro Colón, San José..

Near the Cariari and 1,250 m E of the country club, **Hotel Vista de Golf** (☎ 239-4348, fax 239-4371) offers rooms ranging from standard doubles to suites. Write Apdo. 379, 4005 San Antonio de Belén. In the US, ☎ 800-662-1656. Pool, spa, cable TV, fax are among the services. Set W of downtown on the way to the airport, the 330-room **Hotel Irazú** (☎ 232-4811, fax 232-4549) has a pool, casino, restaurant, spa, and cable TV. Write Apdo. 962, 1000 San José or ☎ 800-223-0888, US; 800-268-7041 E Canada; 800-663-9582 in W Canada. Out on the Carretara Cañas between La Sabana and La Uruca, the Barcelo-owned **San José Palacio** (☎ 220-2034, fax 220-2036) has sauna, steam room, and a gym. Regrettably, they used endangered indigenous hardwoods in its construction and the owners are responsible for the monstrous development at Playa Tambor (see the "Peninsula de Nicoya" section). A $33 million **Marriott** hotel on 30 acres is scheduled to open at Asunción near the airport. Check with the ICT (Tourism Institute) or the Marriott chain regarding its progress.

EXPENSIVE ACCOMMODATIONS DOWNTOWN ($51-90): Many new places have opened downtown, largely to the N of Parque Morazán. Due to inflation, some of the more expensive of these may have moved into the luxury category by the time of your arrival. The 104-room **Hotel del Rey** (☎ 221-7272, 257-3130, fax 221-0096; Apdo. 6241, 1000 San José) is one of the most attractive and reasonably priced in this price range. Rates start at $55 s, $68 d plus tax, and range as high as $125 for master suites; tax is added. It has a restaurant, casino, popular bar, travel agency, fishing, gift shop/newsstand, and offers room service. It's located right near Park Morazán at Av. 1 and C. 9. The hotel was restored in 1994. The original building dates from the 1940s and is now painted pink and white. It also offers free tours of the city (to guest and non-guest alike) and a complimentary airport shuttle.

A bed and breakfast set in a restored coffee plantation home constructed in 1910, the 20-room **Hotel Santo Tomás** (☎ 255-0448/3946, fax 222-3950) is behind the Aurora Holiday Inn on Av. 7, C 3/5. It has French Provincial furniture produced in Costa Rica, Persian rugs, and 14-ft vaulted ceilings. The floors are either handmade tile or pochote (a

San José

native hardwood). English, German, French, Spanish, and Italian are spoken. Each room has its own individual character and unique design. The breakfast (buffet-style coffee, pastries, and tropical fruit) served in an open-air courtyard is another plus; complimentary coffee is available daily until 5. Rates run from around $55/day on up. An 11-room bed and breakfast, the **Casa Morazán** (☎ 257-4187, fax 257-4175) was designed by a famous Costa Rican architect during the 1930s; it offers rooms with cable TV and a/c; some have their own inside patio. Rates are around $65 d. **Fleur de Lys** (☎ 222-4391, 223-1206, fax 257-3637) is a renovated old home with artwork in its bedrooms; a gourmet restaurant is attached, and the owners run Aventuras Naturales, a rafting company. It's at C. 13, Av. 2/4. The intimate bed and breakfast, **Ara Macao** (☎/fax 233-2742), set 50 m S of the Pizza Hut in Barrio California near the National Museum, offers free airport pickup. **La Casa Verde de Amón** (☎/fax 223-0969) is an old home in Barrio Amón (C. 7, Av. 9) that has been made into a bed and breakfast. It has three suites and five rooms, plus a sauna. More expensive suites with cable TV are also available. It received the restoration award from the Costa Rican branch of UNESCO in 1994. Write Dept. 1701, Box 025216, Miami FL 33102-5216. Still another choice in Barrio Amón (Av. 11/C. 3), **Taylor's Inn** (☎ 257-4333, fax 221-1475; Apdo. 531-1000) is a "bed & breakfast hotel," which has 10 rooms with baths and cable TVs. The red-brick building dates from 1910. Rates are around $60 d, not including tax. On Av. Central, C. 1/3, **La Gran Via** (☎ 222-7737, fax 222-7205) is another small hotel. Formerly the Hotel Bougainvillea, the 80-room **Villa Tournón** (☎ 233-6622, fax 222-5211) has a restaurant, a/c, pool, Jacuzzi, and parking. Write Apdo. 6606, 1000 San José.

The **Gran Hotel Costa Rica** (☎ 221-4000, fax 221-3501) is centrally located on the Plaza de la Cultura. There is cable TV, casino, restaurant, a/c, and parking. Write Apdo. 527, 1000 San José. The same owners operate the **Hotel Costa Rica Morazán** (☎ 222-4622, fax 233-3329; C. 7, Av. 1/3), which was formerly the Hotel Amstel. It has a good restaurant. An attractive bed and breakfast set 150 m S of the National Theater (C. 3, Av. 4/6), **Casa 429 El Paso** (☎ 222-1708, fax 233-5785) has a Jacuzzi; rooms with private bath are more expensive. A full Western breakfast is offered. Rooms (tax included) with shared bath are around $50, private bath is $60, suite with patio is $75, and two-bedrooms with shared bath are $60-80 for two to four people. You may encounter difficulties in leaving your luggage here while traveling around the country. **Hotel Europa** (☎ 222-1222, fax 221-3976), on C. Central between Av. 3/5, has cable TV, pool and restaurant. Write Apdo. 72, San José or call 800-223-6764 in the US. Its cousin, the 150-room **Europa Zurqui** (☎ 257-3257, fax 221-4609) in Barrio Tournón is higher priced. The 120-room **Hotel Presidente** (☎ 222-3022, fax 221-1205) on Av.

Central between C. 7/9, has restaurant, cable TV, a/c, casino, disco, and some kitchen-equipped suites. Write Apdo. 2922, 1000 San José. With a/c, cable TV, casino, and sauna, the businessman-oriented **Balmoral** (☎ 221-1919/5022, fax 221-7826) is at Av. Central, C. 7/9. Write Apdo. 3344, 1000 San José. **Gran Hotel Doña Inez** (☎ 222-7443, fax 223-5426), at C. 11, Av. 2/6 across from the Mercado Nacional Artesania, is intimate and upscale; it's near the National Museum. Rooms come with phone, radio, and TV. Prices are around $58 s, $70 d.

La Sabana/Paseo Colón: Located in a quiet neighborhood near La Sabana (C. 40, Av. 5 bis), **Hotel Torremolinos** (☎ 222-9129/5266, fax 255-3167) has suites or full suites with cable TV, pool, sauna, massage, and a/c (full suites only). The **Tennis Club** (☎ 232-1266, fax 232-3867) on the SW side of la Sabana, has a pool, tennis, sauna, gym, and skating rink. Write Apdo. 4964, San José. On Paseo Colón between C. 26/28, the **Ambassador** (☎ 221-8155, fax 255-3396) offers free accommodation for children under 12. The **Napoleón** (☎ 222-2278, 223-3282, fax 222-9487) is at C. 40, Av. 5 near La Sabana. It has a small restaurant, pool, and your choice of fans or a/c.

Los Yoses: The 20-room villa-style **Hotel Don Fadrique** (☎ 225-8186, 224-7583/7947, fax 224-9746; Apdo. 1654-2050, San Pedro) out in Los Yoses and quite popular with visitors, is at C. 37 and Av. 8. Rooms have cable TV, phone, and fan; some rooms have private gardens. Rates are around $55 s, $65 d plus tax for spacious and attractively furnished rooms; breakfast is included. Also here is the 18-room **Hotel Le Bergerac** (☎ 234-7850, fax 225-9103; Apdo. 1107-1002, San José), at Av. 8, C. 35. Rooms in the two converted houses are attractive, spacious executive suites with gardens or balconies, fans, cable TV (in English, French, Spanish, German), and phones. Gourmet French dinners are served evenings in the hotel's restaurant. Rates run upward from $58 s, $68 d plus tax. It's operated by French Canadians as a French inn and has a relaxed, yet elegant atmosphere. The hotel's **El Mango** restaurant serves continental cuisine and is open for breakfast and dinner.

MODERATE ACCOMMODATION ($30-50): In Barrio Amón, 14-room **Kekoldi** (☎ 223-3244, fax 257-5476; Apdo.12150-1000, San José) is a colorful hotel whose name is taken from the Bribri word meaning "holy tree of water." It's at Av. 9, C. 3 bis. The hotel has a restaurant and each room has a Bribri name. Prices range from $15-45. At C. 9 and Av. 9, the 17-room **Hemingway Inn** (☎/fax 221-1804; Apdo. 1711-1002, San José) offers cable TV and continental breakfast. High season rates are around $30 s, $40 d, and $50 t plus tax; subtract $10 for low season rates. The former home of President-Dictator Tomás Guardia (1870-82), **Hotel Don Carlos** (☎ 221-6707, fax 255-0828) is on C. 9, Av. 7/9. It has a restaurant, gym, sun deck, cable TV, and complimentary breakfast. Write Dept. 1686, PO Box 025216, Miami FL 33102. On C. 19, Av. 11/13, the family-run 23-room Caribbean-style **Hotel Aranjuez** (☎ 223-3559, fax 223-3528; Apdo. 457-2070, San José) has a garden, hammocks, courtyards and is actually two connected buildings. Rooms are spacious and have hardwood floors. It serves a complimentary continental breakfast. Prices start at around $25 s with a shared bath. Next to Parque Morázan and directly across from the gargantuan Aurola (C. 5, Av. 3), Tico-owned and run **Diana's Inn** (☎/fax 223-6542) is a pleasure to stay at simply for its affable, helpful staff and relaxed atmosphere. Each room has a TV and some have a/c. A continental breakfast is served. Prices are around $46 s and $50 d. At Av. 7, C. 6/8, the relatively new **San José Garden Court** (☎ 222-3674; fax 255-4613) has a/c, cable TV, breakfast, pool, sauna, and gym. One of the newer hotels, **La Gema** (☎/fax 222-1074) is on Av. 12, C. 9/11; breakfast is served, and it has its own restaurant and bar. Set 700 m N of *pulpería* La Luz at C. 33, Av. 9/11, the **Hotel Don Paco** (☎ 234-9088, fax 234-9588, 10 rooms) is an intimate colonial-style hotel with cable TV; a full breakfast is served. In the US, write Box 22063, Carmel CA 93922 or ☎ 800-288-2107. The **Hotel Mansion Blanca Inn** (☎/fax 222-0423), centrally located at C. 9, Av. 10, is an 11-room bed and breakfast in an old mansion, run by an affable Tico couple in their 50s. It has been recommended by a reader. Write Apdo. 85570, 1000 San José. At C. 5 and Av. 11, the **Dunn Inn** (☎ 222-3232/3246, fax 221-4596) includes continental breakfast in its rates. It is located in a refurbished century-old mansion and has one luxury suite with a Jacuzzi and other features. Write Apdo. 1584, 1000 San José. With some a/c rooms, the **Gran Via** (☎ 222-7737, fax 222-7205; Apdo. 1433, San José) is at Av. Central and C. 13.

The well-designed **Hotel Plaza** (☎ 222-5533, fax 222-2641), featuring a restaurant and TVs, is at Av. Central, C. 2/4. Write Apdo. 2019, 1000 San José. One of the nicest apartment hotels, the **Llama del Bosque** (☎ 225-5350, fax 224-0681) is 100 m S and 50 m W of the Plaza del Sol, a shopping center in San Pedro. It has a pool, offers breakfast, and has kitchenettes. The centrally located (C. Central/Av. Central) Chinese-influenced **Hotel Royal Gardens** (☎ 257-0022/0023, fax 257-1517) can be contacted at Apdo. 3493, 1000 San José. The 25-room **Belmondo Hotel Bed & Breakfast** (☎ 222-9624) has a pool, bar, and restaurant. It's at C. 20, Av. 9 in Barrio Mexico. It also has dorm rooms. Also on C. 20 and 250 m N of the Children's Hospital, the **Mesón del Angel** (☎ 223-7747, fax 223-2781) is a serene 10-bedroom hotel with a phone and cable TV in each room; rates range from around $35 s to $65 quad plus tax. At Av. 7, C. 9, the **Rey Amón** (☎ 233-3819, fax 233-1769; Apdo. 7145-1000 San José) is a small, 13-room hotel set in a restored house. The high-ceilinged rooms have cable TV. Rates include breakfast; with advance notification, complimentary airport pickup is available.

German-run 22-room **La Amistad** (☎ 221-1597) is a comfy bed and breakfast in Barrio Otoya at Av. 11/C. 15. Rooms have cable TV. At Av. 6, C. 11/13 (50 m W of the Veterinaria Drs. Echandi), the **Villa Bonita Inn** (☎ 222-7075) is an apartotel that charges around $50 s or d. **Cacts** (☎ 221-2928, fax 221-8616; Av. 3 bis, No. 2845, C. 28/30; Apdo. 379, 1005, San José) has 36 rooms in a converted house. Rates are around $50 d. Featuring comfortable one- and two-bedroom units, moderate **Apartotel Castilla** (☎ 222-2113, fax 221-2080) is on C. 24, Av. 2/4, a location convenient to the Paseo Colón shopping area. Write Apdo. 944, 1006 San José. The **Cristina** (☎ 231-1618, 220-0453, fax 220-2096) is an attractive apartotel with sunny rooms and a garden. At C. 29 and Av. Central/8, the **Apartotel Don Carlos** (☎ 221-6707, fax 255-0828) rents rooms on a weekly basis only. On the Sabana, two-storey, colonial-style **Apartotel La Sabana** (☎ 220-2422, fax 231-7386) has a/c, cable TV, pool, and an arrangement with a nearby health club. In Los Yoses, **Apartotel El Conquistador** (☎ 225-3022) can be contacted at Apdo. 303, 2050 San Pedro, and **Apartotel Lamm** (☎ 221-4290, fax 221-4720; C. 15, Av. 1) can be reached at Apdo. 2729, 1000 San José. At Av. 4, C. 8, the **Doral** (☎ 233-0665/5069, fax 233-4827) has clean and sunny rooms with phone. Others include **Los Yoses** (☎ 225-0033, fax 225-5595; Apdo. 1597, 1000 San José; rate includes breakfast), **Ramgo** (☎ 232-3823, fax 232-3111, Apdo. 1441, 1000 San José) 100 m S of the Tennis Club at La Sabana, and the Amstel-run **Apartotel San José** (☎ 222-0455, fax 221-6684; Av. 2, C. 17/19; Apdo. 4192-1000, San José), which has 12 one- and two-bedroom suites with TV and kitchenette. In the US, ☎ 800-575-1253. The **Apartotel El Sesteo** (☎ 296-1805, fax 296-1865) is 200 m S of La Sabana's McDonald's. It has 20 one- and two-bedroom units and has a pool and Jacuzzi. Rates are around $40 d.

INEXPENSIVE ACCOMMODATION ($30-40): Set to the W of the Parque Nacional on Av. 1 at C. 11/15, **Pensión de la Cuesta** (☎ 255-2896, fax 257-2272) is a bed and breakfast run by artists. Baths are shared, as is the refrigerator. In the vicinity of Parque Morazán on C. 9 between Av. 1/3, **Pensión Costa Rica Inn** (☎ 222-5203, fax 23-8385) has dark rooms with baths for around $16 s, $20 d; there's a 10% reduction for weekly rental. You can make reservations at ☎ 800-637-0899 in the US. In Canada, ☎ 318-263-2059, or write Box 59, Arcadia LA 7100, or Apdo. 10282, 1000 San José.

The **Hotel Diplomat** (☎ 221-8133, 221-8744, fax 233-7474) is on C. 6 between Av. Central/2. Write Apdo. 6606, 1000 San José. It is popular, has a restaurant, and each floor has a sitting area. Located on C. 24, Paseo Colón/Av. 2, the **Petit Hotel** (☎ 233-0766, fax 233-1938) has

San José

rooms with both private and shared baths. Facilities include free coffee, communal TV, and kitchen privileges. (Note: one reader has written to complain about the cleanliness and size of the rooms here.) At C. 24, Av. 2 across from the Sala Garbo, the **Petit Victoria** (☎ 233-1812/1813, fax 233-1938) offers use of its kitchen as well as cable TV. Write Apdo. 357, 1007 Centro Colón. A block away from the Mercado Central at C. 10, Av. 1/3, the 44-room **Bienvenido** (☎/fax 221-1872; Apdo. 389-2200, San José) is one of the better hotels in this range and is around $20 d.

A cross between a bed and breakfast and a standard hotel, **La Amistad** (☎ 221-1597, fax 221-1409) is set in Barrio Otoya (Av. 11, C. 15), as is the attractively furnished 11-room **Hotel Edelweiss** (☎ 221-9702, fax 222-1241; Av. 9, C. 13/15) and the 20-room **Hotel Vesuvio** (☎ 221-7586/8325, Apdo. 477-1000, San José; Av. 11, C. 13-15). Vesuvio has a restaurant. In the Coca Cola area, **Hotel Alameda** (☎ 221-3045/6333, fax 222-9673; Av. Central, C. 12/14; Apdo. 680, San José) is another formerly grand old hotel. **The Musoc** (☎ 222-9437), next to the Coca Cola terminal (at C. 16, Av. 1/30), is noisy but very popular. There have been reports of left luggage disappearing here. The **Pensión and Hotel Ritz** (☎ 222-4103, fax 222-8849; C. Central, Av. 8/10) has a variety of rooms from single through quad. The **Hotel Fortuna** (☎ 223-5344, fax 223-2743; Av. 6, C. 2/4; Apdo. 7-1570, San José) has 30 rooms of varying quality. You can also try the **Galilea** (☎ 233-6925, fax 223-1689; Av. Central, C. 11/13; around $18 s, $22 d), the **Pensión Centro Continental** (☎ 233-1731, fax 222-8849; Av. 8 y 10 and C. Central), and the **Astoria** (☎ 221-2174; Av. 7, C. 7/9; weekly discounts available). The least expensive aparthotel, at around $175/week and $425/month, is the **Scotland** (☎ 223-0833) in Barrio La California, an old residential area.

in San Pedro: Located on the N side of the University of Costa Rica in San Pedro, **D'Galah Hotel** (☎ 234-1743, 253-7539) has a coffee shop, sauna, and some rooms with kitchenettes. Write Apdo. 208, 2350 San José. Also in San Pedro, the **Maripaz** (☎ 253-8456) is a bed and breakfast with both shared and private baths.

LOW-BUDGET ACCOMMODATION (UNDER $30): It may be hard to stay cheaply at the beaches these days, but there's no dearth of cheap places to stay in town. The very cheapest can be well under $10 a day.

basic places: A very basic but hospitable place with lots of guests from the *gringo* trail, **Ticalinda** (☎ 255-0425, fax 255-0444) is at Av. 2, C. 5, #553; look carefully for the door right next to Esmeralda's. In the same area, **Pensión Palma** (☎ 233-3877) is at Av. 6, C 11/13. The **Principe** (☎ 222-7983, fax 223-1589; Av. 6, C. Central/2) is both cheap and very popular with travelers. Another good place is **Pensión Americana** (☎ 221-4171/9799), C. 2, Av. Central/Av. 2. The 11-room

Hotel América (☎ 221-4116; Av. 7, C. 2/4) charges around $6, but also caters to short timers. Popular with Ticos and backpackers alike (the entrance can resemble a Grateful Dead concert), the **Gran Hotel Imperial** (☎ 222-7899), at C. 8, Av. Central/1, up the street from the Hotel Johnson, is one of the best values around. They will hold your luggage for a fee, provide a pay phone, and have a restaurant. If this is too downscale for your tastes, the **Johnson** (☎ 223-7633, fax 222-3683; Apdo. 6638, 1000 San José), C. 8 and Av. Central/Av. 2 bis, is popular with Tico businessmen, the Lonely Planet travel guide author, and family groups. In a safer area of town, the **Galilea** (☎ 233-6925, fax 223-1689) is at C. 13 and Av. Central. A good place to base yourself if the bus to Limón is on your itinerary is the **Bellavista** (☎ 223-0095/5477, fax 223-8385; Av. Central, C. 19/21). It's within 20 minutes of the Plaza de la Cultura on foot. Also try the **Boruca** (☎ 223-0016, fax 232-0077; C. 14, Av. 1/3), the **Capital** (☎/fax 221-8497, C. 4, Av. 3/5; around $20 d), **Central** (☎ 221-2767, Av. 3, C. 4/6), the **Cocorí** (☎ 233-0081, C. 16 Av. 3 near Hospital San Juan de Dios), **Marlyn** (☎ 233-3212, C. 4, Av. 7/9), the **Morazán** (☎ 221-9083; Av. 3, C. 11/15), the **Otoya** (☎ 221-3925; C. Central, Av. 5/7), the **Roma** (☎ 223-2179; C. 14, Av. 1), **Hotel Colón** (C. 4, Av. 1, #150 N), **Gran Centro Americo** (☎ 221-3362, Av. 2, C. 8), and **Hotel Rialto**, C. 2, Av. 5.

OTHERS: A quiet and secluded oasis attractive to those who want access to the peace movement, **Casa Ridgeway** (☎ 233-6168, fax 224-8910; Apdo. 1507, 1000 San José), in the Quaker-established Centro Por La Paz, offers accommodation: $8 pp in a small dorm room, $10 s, and $16 d. There's an excellent lending library, kitchen privileges, hot water, and the central location (Av. 6 bis, C. 15) can't be beat. Although budget travelers can find better values price-wise elsewhere, it is highly recommended. **La Granja** (☎ 225-1073, 234-8835, fax 234-1676) is a Tico home with shared kitchen. Expect to pay around $15 pp; discounts available for youth hostel card holders. It's 50 m S of the Antiguo Higuerón in San Pedro.

    Toruma Youth Hostel (☎/fax 224-4085) stands on the N side of Av. Central in the eastern suburb of Los Yoses. Tell a taxi driver to let you off at "Albergue Juvenil Toruma cerca de Pollos Fritos Kentucky," or you can take any of the various San Pedro-bound buses that pass by. Its high-ceilinged dorms hold 6-20 guests. It's open 24 hours, and you may stay as long as you wish. However, at around $9 pp with breakfast (and youth hostel card) and $12 pp (without card), it's definitely overpriced and quite a bit more than staying in a low-budget hotel on your own. You also have a shower schedule to contend with on top of the lack of privacy. One distinct advantage of staying here, however, is that you do get to meet a lot of people.

for women: Casa Yemayá (☎ 223-3652, fax 225-3636) provides short-and long-term digs for feminists. It's a sizeable house in Guadelupe. Or women may wish to stay at **Casa de la Mujer** (☎ 225-3784) in Sabanilla, where Ticas and foreigners alike may discuss topics ranging from spirituality to violence against women. Charges are around $10 pn. It's 250 m N and 100 m E of the Mercado La Cosecha on the main street in the suburb of Sabanilla; look for the fifth house on the R.

gay accommodation: Colours (☎ 296-1880, 232-3504, fax 296-1597) is a male-oriented homosexual guesthouse in Rohrmoser. They have fans, pool, and a restaurant and are owned by a Florida travel agency (☎ 800-934-5622, 305-9342, fax 305-534-0362).

renting a room: If you wish to economize and plan on spending a great deal of time in the city, this is the way to go! However, you will need a command of Spanish to find a room. The best approach is to check the classified sections of the newspapers. You can also look for signs at the university campus. You can find either lodging alone or lodging that includes food and laundry. Two specialists that connect you with rooms are **Soledad Zamora** (☎ 224-7937) and her sister Virginia (☎ 225-7344). Another alternative is to stay at **Casas Agua Buena** or **Coopebuena**, which are in San Pedro. These boarding houses provide a total of 18 furnished rooms with rents ranging from $150-250 depending upon size of the room. Shared facilities include phone, kitchen, cable TV, paperback library, washing machine, and living and dining areas. The place is geared toward those without substance dependency problems who want a quiet, friendly place to stay. Researchers and students are welcome. For more information call Richard Stern at ☎ 234-2411.

☞ **Traveler's Tip. Bells' Home Hospitality** (☎ 225-4752, fax 224-5834; Apdo. 185, 1000 San José) will provide you with the opportunity to stay with a Costa Rican family and get more of an inside view of the society and culture. Vernon Bell has a few rooms at home, and he also arranges accommodations with others. Charges are $30 s, $45 d; airport pickups ($10 pp) and dinners ($5 pp) are also available. Vernon will meet you at the airport and give you one of his famous tours. (He's also the author of a pocket-sized guide to San José). In the US, write Dept. 1432, PO Box 02516, Miami FL 33102-5216.

OTHER ACCOMMODATIONS NEAR SAN JOSÉ: If you wish to avoid the hustle of the urban areas you might stay at any of the outlying lodgings suggested under the towns in the "Meseta Central" section. The single most popular location is Escazú, a hilly suburb of San José, which is actually a collection of mountain villages; it has its own section below. Here are some other suggestions. The **Bougainvillea Santo Domingo** (☎ 240-8822, fax 240-8484), is set on a 10-acre estate in Santo Domingo de Heredia, about nine km (15 minutes by car) from San José. Its facilities include restaurant, satellite TV, tennis, pool, jogging trail, and shuttle bus. Pavas has the **Hotel Miravalles** (☎ 231-6186, fax 231-4319), which is near the US Embassy, shops, and restaurants. It has babysitting service and a complimentary shuttle service to downtown. Rates are around $35-50 plus tax, but include a full breakfast.

In the suburb of Tibás, **Roxana's** (☎/fax 235-4440; Apdo. 1086-1100, Tibás) is an inexpensive bed and breakfast that welcomes neither smokers nor children. Rates are $25-35 d including full breakfast and tax. In Rohrmoser, a W suburb of San José, the French country-style **Majestic Inn** (☎/fax 232-9028) is an attractive bed and breakfast with an expresso bar. Also here is **Carrie's** (☎ 232-9028), a bed and breakfast in a four-storey home that charges from $35 d and up. In San Antonio de Belén, the **Villa Belén** (☎ 239-0740, fax 239-2040) is an elegant Spanish colonial estate with gardens, pool, sauna, TV lounge/library. Rates are $70-80 d plus tax and include a continental breakfast. It offers weekly and monthly rates as well.

MORAVIA: In Moravia, moderate-to-expensive bed and breakfast **El Verolis** (☎ 236-0662) has rooms with both private and shared bath. Write Apdo. 597, 2150 San José. You can also try **Casa Margarita** (☎ 285-0525, around $35 d with breakfast) and **Chalet Costa Rica Vista** (☎ 285-0512, about $60 d with breakfast), an attractive mountain home with gardens, waterfalls, and a fireplace.

IN SANTA ANA: The 12-room **Hotel Posada Canal Grande** (☎ 282-4089/4101/4103, fax 282-5733; Apdo. 84-6150, Santa Ana) has a sauna, pool, and restaurant; breakfast is included. The bus comes here. Rates run around $60 s, $70 d, not including taxes; off-season discounts are available. Near Santa Ana in Pozos de Santa Ana, **Paraiso Canadiense** (☎/fax 282-5870; Apdo. 68-6151, Santa Ana 2000) offers one- and two-bedroom apartments with pool and laundry for around $50 pn, $225 pw, and $550 pm and up.

Set on the old road between San José and Tres Ríos enroute to Cartago, the **Casa de Finca 1926** (☎ 225-6169) is a German-owned restored art deco mansion that offers 11 attractive rooms for around $75 d. The home has antiques, plants, and a fountain. In the town of San Ramón de Trés Ríos, a half-hour by bus to the E of San José, the **Bello Monte** (☎/fax 234-3879) is a moderately priced bed and breakfast. The luxurious **Ponderosa Lodge** (☎/fax 273-3818; Apdo. 1151, Y Griega 1011, San José) is set amidst 12 wooded acres and is just across from La

Campina Country Club. The lodge offers "Texas-style hospitality" dispensed by a former real estate investor and banker. It has several miles of trails and its six rooms range from $65 s to $150 d; rates include a full breakfast. They also operate the "All America Limousine Service." In the US, write to Jet Box Miami, Box 25312, #SJO 572, Miami FL 33102-5312. In the same area is the expensive **Casa de Finca 1926** (☎/fax 225-6169). It offers access to public transport and has a garden.

Inexpensive **Apartotel La Perla** (☎ 232-6153, fax 220-0103) is in La Uruca. Near Rancho Redondo, expensive 19-room **Hotel Hacienda San Miguel** (☎ 229-1094, fax 221-3871) is a dairy farm and reforestation project. It offers a cloud forest tour on horseback, heated swimming pool, Jacuzzi, steambath, game rooms, and live music. Rates run from around $60 d (with breakfast) and up. Write Apdo. 6897, 1000 San José. To get here, you need to take a 12:20 or 6:20 PM bus from San José.

IN ATENAS: El Cafetal Inn (☎ 446-5785, fax 446-5140; Apdo. 105, Atenas) is a 10-bedroom bed and breakfast in a modern building on a coffee plantation. Atenas itself is famous for its climate, and the facilities allow you to take full advantage of this. You may lounge in a hammock, bathe in the pool, or walk down to the river. Dinner is served upon request. Rates run from around $40 on up; monthly rates are available.

LA GARITA/ATENAS AREA: The former ox-cart checkpoint is now a center for tourist attractions, and a number of hotels have sprung up in La Garita. Accommodation in the quiet town of Atenas – said to have the nation's best climate – has been slower in coming. **Villa Tranquilidad** (☎ 460-5460) is two km from the attractive fruit-growing town of Atenas along a country road (turn right at the phone booth before the town). Part of an organic coffee farm, this is a bed and breakfast with a pool and a nearby waterfall. Weekly rates here are around $200; monthly, $700. Write Apdo. 28, 4013 Alajuela. You can also stay at seven-room **Ana's Place** (☎ 460-5019) in town for around $55 d including breakfast. Rooms with shared bath are cheaper. Meals other than breakfast are available by request. One km to the left of La Fiesta de Maíz in La Garita, **Chatelle** (☎ 487-7781/7271, fax 487-7095) is a group of nine *cabinas*. Each is named after a volcano and contains furniture from Sarchí and a kitchenette. Rates are expensive. There is a restaurant (different menu daily), pool, cable TV, jogging paths, and other services. Write Apdo. 755, Centro Colón. Just to the W of Alajuela near Parque San José, the expensive 12-room **Villa Raquel** (☎/fax 433-8926) offers complimentary breakfast, tennis courts, and pool. Its kitchen is also available for use. **Carter's Inn** (☎ 487-7007, fax 223-8178) is an open-air home with an indoor fountain. Rates run around $40-65, including a full breakfast, but not tax. Run by Texans, expensive **La Piña Dorada** (☎/fax 487-7220) includes breakfast in its rates. It's on the road heading left (S) around three km from La Garita's school. Nearby, expensive **Río Real** (☎/fax 487-7022) has a/c, phone, pool, and restaurant, as well as a conference room.

Near Orotina at Cascajal de Orotina is **Hacienda Doña Marta** (☎ 234-0853, 253-6514, fax 234-0958), a cattle farm which has horseback riding and a pool. *Cabinas* rent for around $60 d; meals and tours are additional. Also in this area is the luxury **Dundee Ranch Hotel** (☎ 428-8776, 267-7371, fax 267-7050), which is a working ranch with secondary forest reserve. There are two pools on the property, as well as a restaurant with Tico and international fare. Horseback riding, boat tours of the estuary, and tractor-tram rides are available. Rates are around $80 d with breakfast. It's related to the **Chalet Tirol**. Finally, don't overlook the hotels near Alajuela, Heredia, Póas, and Cartago, which are listed later on.

ESCAZU ACCOMMODATION: A mountainous set of small villages popular with both Ticos and wealthy foreigners, Escazú has expanded its range of accommodation in recent years.

in San Rafael: Close and convenient, the **Tapezco Inn** (☎ 228-1084, fax 289-7026) is 50 m S of the church. A blue-and-white colonial-style structure, it has 15 rooms (with TVs and fans), a Tico-style restaurant commanding great views, and pool, Jacuzzi, and sauna. Service is personalized and rates run around $50 s (with breakfast) and $50 d (without breakfast). In San Rafael de Escazú, the 30-room, attractive and distinctive **Hotel Sangildar** (☎ 289-8843, 228-6451/2, fax 228-6454) is 250 m W of the NE corner of the Costa Rica Country Club. Its restaurant, **La Terraza del Sol**, offers a champagne brunch on Sunday. Rooms run around $100 d, including breakfast. In the US, ☎ 800-778-7324. Set on the S side of the Costa Rica Country Club, the **Apartotel Villas del Río** (☎ 289-8833, fax 289-8627; Apdo. 2027-1000, San José, Costa Rica) offers one- , two- , and three-bedroom apartments, suites, and penthouses. All have a/c, cable TV/VCR, kitchen, and other amenities. On the grounds are a sauna, pool, and guarded parking as well. Write Apdo. 1459, Escazú 1250. **Casa de las Tías** (☎/fax 228-5517, fax 289-7353) is a popular, but quiet, five-room bed and breakfast run by foreign service retirees. Rooms each represent a different Latin American nation, and there are spacious gardens as well as a TV/lounge area. Airport pickup can be arranged. Rates are around $65 d. The attractively designed 16-room **Amstel Escazú Country Inn** (☎ 228-1764; fax 228-0620; Apdo. 4192-1000, San José) is right on the main road. It has 16 rooms (with a/c and cable TV), pool, and restaurant. Use of the kitchen is permitted. Rates start at around $50 s or d plus tax. In the US ☎ 800-575-1253. **Apartotel María Alexander** (☎ 228-1507, fax 228-5192; Apdo. 3756, 1000 San José) comes complete with washing machine, cable TV, a/c, pool, sauna, and restaurant. Also in San Rafael are the **Fat Cat** (☎/fax 289-6059), the **Bonaire Inn** (☎ 228-0866/0764, fax 289-8107), and the **Pine Tree Inn** (☎ 289-7405, fax 228-2180).

   in San Antonio: On the way to San Antonio, 1½ km above the church in Escazú, **Park Place** (☎/fax 228-9200) is one of the nation's most hospitable and comfortable bed and breakfasts. If you're looking for a home away from home, then Pat Bliss's bed and breakfast is the place for you. It's like living in your own home, with the other guests part of an instant family. Always extremely helpful, Pat lives across the road and comes over to visit. The spacious alpine-style house has two rooms downstairs and two up, with large baths on each level. There is a comfortable kitchen and sitting area downstairs. A continental breakfast awaits you here each morning, and you are free to use the kitchen at other times. There's also a phone which you can use to make and receive Costa Rican calls. Pat will also quite happily hook you up with locals who will take you for tours at reasonable rates. A washing machine is available for a fee. She charges around US$35 d. In the US, write Interlink 358, PO Box 025635, Miami FL 33152. E-mail her at corpfaxi@sol.racsa.co.cr.

   The **Tara** (☎ 228-6992, fax 228-9651) is modeled after a US Civil War-era mansion and billed as the ultimate in luxury. It is surrounded by 38,000 sq ft (12,000 sq m) of grounds. There is swimming pool, tennis court, and health club. A curving wooden staircase leads up to the 12 rooms, each with a name like "Scarlett" that reflects the theme. The inexpensive-moderate 55-room **Pico Blanco** (☎ 228-3197, 289-6197, fax 289-5189; Apdo. 900, Escazú) is a mountain getaway. An attractive, white colonial-style structure with brick archways and stone patios, it is run by an English expatriate and his Tico family. It has a pool, a couple of *cabinas* (around $60), and an outdoor pavilion where occasional performances are given. Rooms have balconies and some come equipped with refrigerators. In the US ☎ 816-862-1170 or fax 916-862-1187. There are a number of different treatments and packages are available. The "jet lag" ($69) consists of a workout or aerobics class, a steam bath or sauna, a massage, and a Jacuzzi bath with seaweed extracts. A facial ($50 or $75) will clean and revitalizes your pores. A wide variety of other packages ($65-$219) may also include such treatments as reflexology ($30), mud cacooning ($50), and aromatherapy deluxe massage ($75). Room rates are around $90 d and up plus tax. A wide variety of packages are also available. In the US, write Interlink 345, PO Box 02-5635, Miami FL 33152.

   Offering splendid views of the Meseta Central, **Parvati Mountain Inn** (☎/fax 228-4011) has attractive grounds, facilities for meditation and yoga, an art gallery, and vegetarian food. Rates are around $35 d plus tax and with continental breakfast. The **Linda Vista Lodge** (☎ 289-5854, fax 289-8010; Apdo. 785-1250 Escazú), two km NW from central Escazú, rents rooms by the week and month, as well as daily (around $25 s, $30 d with full breakfast). Some rooms have kitchenettes and refrigerators. The Bebedero bus (C. 14/Av. 6; 35 minutes) runs by here. In the US write SJO 998, PO Box 025216, Miami FL 33102-5216. Also in this area is the **White Horse Inn** (☎/fax 289-8659).

in Escazú west: Featuring an outdoor Jacuzzi, gardens, and tennis courts, the **Costa Verde Country Inn** (☎ 228-4080, fax 289-8591) is a moderate bed and breakfast (weekly rates available) with airport pickup for $10 extra. Write Apdo. 89, Escazú or SJO 1313, PO Box 025216, Miami FL 33102-5216. An unforgettable places to stay is the **Hotel California** (☎ 289-7486). Owned by Philadelphian Bruce Cohen, this small hotel provides reasonable but spartan digs. Bruce is a real character and the hotel is great for active, single guys who like to go out and party (as does Bruce). It's 700 m W of the Banco Nacional and 150 m N of the Escuela Corazón de Jesús. Geriatrics, yuppies, and fundamentalist Christians would find it an uncomfortable experience to stay here. Bruce may be hanging around the airport when you arrive. Rates are $15 pp on up, and it should be possible to strike some sort of bargain if you'll be staying around for a while. Near the Escazú Country Club, the **Villa Escazú** (☎/fax 228-9566), a bed and breakfast set in an alpine-style home, charges around $60 d. Its porch is perfect for birdwatching or gazing at the lovely panorama presented.

IN BELLO HORIZONTE: Many of these listed can hook you up with the pool and tennis courts at the Bello Horizonte Country Club. Formerly the house of a German ambassador, **Puesta del Sol** (☎ 289-6581/8775/9043, fax 289-8766) resembles an old ranch house. However, it's really only around 15 years old and has been remodeled to make the transformation from home to hotel. The property's helpful manager Harvey Haber is a sometime ghostwriter as well as the author of the *Insight Guide to Costa Rica*. He also buys farmland and sells it to people interested in preserving it for the future. Second in charge is Xiomara Rivera López, who graduated from college in the States with a degree in anthropology. Rooms are large, attractive, and quite comfortable. Grounds are attractively landscaped and include a pool and Jacuzzi. A lounge area has a stereo system and an adjoining dining room where a full breakfast of your choice is served each morning. The property lies 100 m E and 75 m S of the old Intex factory. Rates are around $69 s, $79 d, $89 t, $99 suite, $110 grand suite – all including full breakfast but not taxes. In the US, write Dept. 305, PO Box 025216, Miami FL 33102.

San José

Escazú

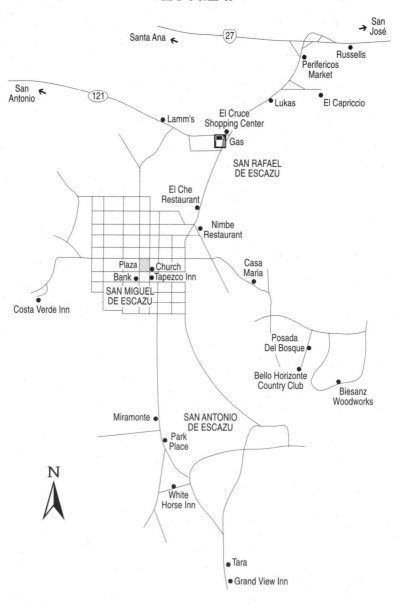

NOT TO SCALE

Spanish colonial-style **Posada Don Quijote** (☎ 289-8401, fax 289-8729) is set high in the hills. It offers spacious rooms with cable TV, phones, and large baths. Personalized service is offered by owners Gordon and Lucy Finwall. It has a full library and artwork by the likes of Chagall, Picasso, and Lichtenstein. Rates are around $55 s, $65 d including breakfast. The homey bed and breakfast **La Posada del Bosque** (☎ 228-1164, fax 228-2006; Apdo. 669, 1250 Escazú) is surrounded by gardens; it charges from $40-55 plus tax and includes a full breakfast. La Posada offers Tico-style hospitality and cooking (including a *típico* breakfast and homecooked dinners). It's also right near Bello Horizonte Country Club. Rates are around $35-45 d plus tax. Airport pickup is $12 extra. An "American-operated" moderate-to-expensive bed and breakfast, **Casa María** (☎ 228-2270, fax 228-0015) is 250 yards (250 m) E of the Palacio Municipal in Escazú and one km E of the church. You can use the kitchen here. A bed and breakfast run by a French couple, **La Evasión** (☎ 228-1141, fax 221-9466) offers hammocks, a hot tub, and sauna for your relaxation. Charges here range from inexpensive to expensive. The 10-room **Hacienda Las Robles** (☎ 289-8775, fax 289-8766) combines modern amenities with colonial-style construction. It's run by a Tico family and each bedroom or suite is named after a volcano or river. There is a restaurant and pool. Rates run from around $65. For low-budget travelers, the **Forest B&B Hostel-Hotel** (☎/fax 228-0132) has rates from $15 on up. Also in Bello Horizonte are the **Rios de Guacamayas** (☎ 228-9074, fax 289-5776), the **Palacio** (☎ 228-1141), and the **Blue Escazú Inn** (☎ 228-6817, fax 228-6557).

others: Opened in 1994 at a cost of $32 million, the 270-room **Camino Real** (☎ 289-7000) is also in Escazú. It adjoins a shopping plaza; a golf course and spa are planned. There is a conference room, restaurant, and other facilities. Rates range from around $150 d on up. The **Hotel Montesol** (☎ 289-5330, fax 289-5345) is an inexpensive hotel two km N of Multi-Plaza, Guachipelin. **Las Golondrinas** (☎ 228-6448, fax 228-6381) has a secluded cabin in an orchard overlooking the valley and surrounding mountains. It's around $50 d plus tax and including continental breakfast.

Set near the Cerros de Escazú, **Albergue de Montaña Hacienda Cerro Panda** (☎ 253-2726, fax 253-3795) is a 2,000-acre cloud forest reserve which has a few cabins priced at around $60 each. Horseback riding and a restaurant are available.

San José Dining & Food

HOTEL DINING: Most hotels have good restaurants. One of the most popular places to dine is the **Hotel Del Rey** (☎ 221-7272, 257-3130).

San José

The Hotel Balmoral's **Restaurante Altamira** serves Spanish cuisine. **Hotel L'Ambiance** (☎ 222-6702) offers gourmet dining in an elegant atmosphere. Reservations are required. The Hotel Britannia offers acclaimed gourmet dishes in **The Cellar** (☎ 233-6667), which is handicapped-accessible. Out in the Paseo de Colón area, the **Grano de Oro** (☎ 255-3322, fax 221-2782) serves gourmet dishes and is quite popular. The **Hotel Cariari** has a Sunday brunch from 11:30 to 3.

BUDGET DINING: San José can be quite a cheap place to eat if you stick to where the poorer locals dine. **Churrería Manolo Chocolateria** (Av. Central, C. 2) is good for breakfast; **Bella Vista** (Av. Central, C. 19/21) specializes in Limón-style fare. Vegetarian restaurants (given their own listing below) are generally competitive price-wise with the cheaper establishments. *Sodas* are the way to go both for price and local color. One of the best is **Soda Palace** (C. 2, Av. 2), where money changers are found; there's good coffee and an entertaining milieu to boot. **Costa del Sol** (☎ 223-1335) is run by friendly Italians and serves reasonably priced pizza and pasta dishes; it's at Av. Central, C. 9/11 and across from the Cine Capri. **Fu Su Ku** (C. 2, Av. 2) serves Korean food; **Chicharronera Nacional** is at Av. 1, C. 3/5. For attractive outoor cafeteria-syle dining, try **Recesos** (Av. 2 and 4 on C. 21), just near the Museo Nacional. **Soda Tico** near Parque Morazán has a cheap breakfast along with a $2 lunch.

Near the Parque Central at Av. 2 and C. Central, **La Perla** offers paella, *huevos ranchera*, and a variety of *refrescos*. If you just want a sandwich, **La Casa de Sanwich** (Av. 2, C. 11) is open 24 hours and has an amazing variety. Specializing in wood-roasted chicken, **Restaurante Campesino** (C. 7, Av. 2/4) also has *palmito* salad. Another reasonably priced place is **Soda Amón**, near the Hotel Aurora in Barrio Amón. Featuring a good variety of *refrescos* and a *casado* at lunch, **Soda La Casita** is at Av. 1, C. Central/1. Known for its mariachi music late at night, centrally located **La Esmeralda** (Av. 2, C. 5/7) has a range of Tico food. Also try **El Escorial** (Av. 1, C. 5/7), **Finistere Food World** (Av. Central/C. 7), and **Soda Central** (Av. 1, C. 3/5), which have a good selection at reasonable prices. Set at the E corner of the Supreme Court Bldg. (Av. 6, C. 21), **La Cocina de Bordolino** specializes in beef and chicken *empanadas* prepared as they are in Tierra del Fuego, Argentina. **Bar/Restaurante La Foresita**, located on Sabana Sur, serves *típico* food. Large **Soda Tapia**, across from the E side of La Sabana, serves reasonably priced local food on tables both inside and out on the street. For real low-budget dining try the **Mercado Central**, the market, an excellent place to sample low-cost traditional Tico food, especially *ceviche*.

IN-TOWN GOURMET EUROPEAN CUISINE: For French food, expensive **L'Ile de France** (☎ 222-4241, C. 7, Av. Central/2) has high quality food and service. A longstanding popular restaurant, **El Balcon de Europa** (☎ 221-4841; C. 9, Av. Central/1) has Italian and international cuisine. **Fleur de Lys** (☎ 223-1206) is a gourmet restaurant offering seafood and other entrées; it's at C. 13, Av. 2/6. **La Bastille** (☎ 255-4994; Paseo Colón, C. 20/22) serves gourmet-quality continental cuisine. **Mezzanotte** is an Italian restaurant in a restored old house in Barrio Amón across from the Hotel Britannia. **Mondial** (☎ 223-7962; Av. 11, C. 15/17) is an Italian restaurant and pizzeria serving dishes prepared over a wood-burning stove. One of the less expensive Italian restaurants, **Casa Italia** is inside the Cultural Center; it's at C. 29, Av. 8. On Paseo de Colón near Kentucky Fried, **Emilio Romagna Ristorante and Jazz Club** serves both Italian and French gourmet food.

For Italian food, try **Miro's Bistro** (☎ 253-4242), which is in Barrio Escalante, a short walk from downtown. **Ana** (Paseo Colón, C. 24/26) has unpretentious Italian food. Also try **Piccolo Roma** (Av. 2, C. 24). **Zermatt** (C. 23, Av. 11 bis; near the Iglesia Santa Teresita) offers Swiss specialties including fondue. **Chalet Suizo** (Av. 1, C 5/7) has a pan-European menu but a definite Swiss atmosphere and the menu includes fondues. A self-styled "Celluloid Restaurant," **Fellini** (☎ 222-3520) is at Av. 4 and C. 36, 200 m S of the Toyota dealership on Paseo Colón. It serves gourmet Italian specialties and *flambé* dishes. Between the hotels Cariari and Herradura, the **Oceanos** (☎ 293-0622) is another gourmet restaurant.

La Mallorquína (☎ 223-7624) in Paseo Colón (C 28/30) specializes in Spanish and French cuisine. **Taska Al Andalus** (☎ 257-6556) offers a wide variety of gourmet Spanish dishes in an attractive atmosphere. It's at C. 3, Av. 7/9 in Barrio Amón, 275 m N of the Automercado. With an elegantly expensive colonial-style atmosphere, **La Masía de Triquell** (☎ 221-5073, C. 40, Av. 2) also serves Spanish food, as does Casino Español (C. 7, Av. Central/1), **El Escorial** (Av. 1, C5/7), and the less-expensive **Casa España** (6 F, Banco de San José, C. Central/Av. 3/5). Hungarian dishes are served at the **Rincón Europeo** (☎ 235-8678) in Moravia.

MIDDLE EASTERN: Las Pirámides (☎ 223-1551) is at C. 32, Paseo Colón/Av. 2. It serves dishes such as falafel, tabouleh, and shish kebab. Across from the Mercedes Benz dealership, **Lubnan** (☎ 257-6071) is at Paseo Colón, C. 22/24.

San José

Selected Gourmet Restaurants in the San José Area

Bijahua, nouvelle Costa Rican
  Near Centro Commercial Calle Real, ☎ 225-0613
Bougainvillea Santo Domingo, European
  Santo Domingo de Heredia, ☎ 240-8822
Chalet Tirol, French
  Near Heredia, ☎ 267-7371
El Balcon de Europa, Italian and International
  C. 9, Av. Central/1, ☎ 221-4841
Grano de Oro, French
  Paseo Colón area (C. 30, Av. 2/4, No. 251), ☎ 255-3322
L'Ile de France, French
  C. 7, Av. Central/2, ☎ 222-4241
La Galería, European
  San Pedro, ☎ 234-0850
Le Chandelier, French
  San Pedro, ☎ 225-3980.
Machu Pichu, Peruvian
  C. 32, Av. 1/3, ☎ 222-7384
Oceanos, International
  Between Cariari and Herradura hotels, ☎ 293-0622

CHINESE AND ASIAN FOOD: There are too many to list all of them here. However, they include San Pedro's **Nueva China** (across from Banco Popular), **Tin-Jo** (C. 11, Av. 6/8), and **Ave Fénix** (200 m W of the San Pedro Church) – all of which serve Mandarin (Tin-Jo also offers Thai dishes and Indonesian *gado-gado*). Neighboring **Don Wang** (☎ 233-6484), C. 11, Av. 6/8, serves Cantonese dishes, including delectable dim sum ("touch the heart" appetizer-sized) dishes. The **Royal Garden Hotel**'s restaurant serves Cantonese fare. Located on the E side of the ICE building in the N of La Sabana, **Flor del Loto** serves up spicey Hunan and Szechuan Chinese specialties. Near the Outdoor Club in Curridabat, moderately priced **Lai Yuin** (☎ 253-5055) specializes in Chinese seafood. **Mariscos del Oriente**, located N of La Sabana, also has Chinese-style seafood. **El Exotico Oriente** (☎ 234-4444), set 50 m N and 25 m W of the Canal 7 Bldg., serves both Thai and Indonesian dishes; it has lunchtime specials. **Restaurante La Nube** (☎ 220-2419) is out in Pavas and 200 m E of the US Embassy. Opened in 1995, the Cantonese-style **Palacio Imperial** (☎ 231-1050, 232-9066) is set in an impressive pagoda-like structure also near the

US Embassy in Pavas. Specializing in Hunan and Szechuan cuisine, **Beijing City** (☎ 228-6939) is in Escazú.

JAPANESE FOOD: The cheapest place with something resembling Japanese food is the lunch counter inside the Yaohan supermarket across from the Sabana and near the Corobicí. Downscale but delicious, **Goyi** (☎ 233-6419) is at Cinco Esquinas, which is off Hwy. 5 enroute to Tibás. It's across from the Lubicentro "El Amigo." Definitely for those with weighty wallets, the **Sakura** out at the Sheraton Herradura specializes in Japanese cooking, as does **Fuji**, housed in the Hotel Corobicí at the NE corner of La Sabana. The medium-priced **Arirang** in Edifico Colón (☎ 223-2838; Paseo Colón, C. 24/26) is a popular Korean restaurant which also serves Japanese dishes, including a sushi platter.

SEAFOOD: The medium-priced **Fuente de los Mariscos** is well known and has branches near Hotel Irazú in the San José 2000 shopping center and at Plaza del Sol shopping center. Another famous seafood restaurant is **Rias Bajas** in El Pueblo. **Lobster's Inn** (Paseo Colón/C. 24) serves up guess what? With a blue-and-white marquee and plenty of parking, **Marisqueria La Princesa Marina** (open 10:30 am-11:30 pm daily on the W side of the Sabana) offers reasonably priced seafood. A number of other restaurants also serve seafood dishes.

PERUVIAN SEAFOOD: Bar Peru Tico, just around the corner from the Hotel Bellavista, has excellent seafood at moderate prices. Another one to try is the **Machu Pichu** (C. 32, Av. 1/3), an extremely popular Peruvian restaurant, often packed at lunch; a variety of spicey appetizers and main dishes are available. It's behind Kentucky Fried Chicken. A third Peruvian restaurant is **El Ceviche del Rey** (☎ 257-1808) on C. 32 at Av. 1, which is 100 m N of the Kentucky Fried Chicken on Av. Colón.

VEGETARIAN DINING: There are a growing number of vegetarian restaurants. Most feature simple but good fare with brown rice used as a base. They usually offer soyburgers, fruit and vegetable salads, and set meals (around $2-$2.50), which are good value. All are singularly disappointing in their lack of seasonings, as is typical in Costa Rica. Ask for tabasco to spice things up a bit. The author's favorite for the food, atmosphere, and price is **Shakti** (☎ 222-9096, open 11-6:30) on C. 13 at Av. 8. Besides the daily specials (around $2.50), it has a wide variety of dishes, including salad, *bistec vegetariano*, herbal teas, granola, and five kinds of spaghetti. **Soda Vegetariana** (☎ 221-5885) is on C. 5 next to the Hotel Europa. Centrally located, attractive **Tangara** (☎

221-3115) is on Av. 1, C 1/3. **Naturama** is at Av. 1, C. 3/5. Although not exclusively vegetarian, **Pipo's** (Av. Central, C. 9/11) offers soyburgers and a vegetarian plate for less than $2. Open Mon. to Fri. from 8-4, **Don Sol** is 50 m E of the Casa Amarilla, the Foreign Ministry, on Av. 7. This is a convenient place to eat either before or after visiting the Jade Museum in the INS building, which, in turn, is 50 m W of the Casa Amarilla. Right near the Plaza de Cultura at C. 3, Av. Central/1, **Soda Vishnu** serves vaguely Indian-style vegetarian food and great fruit salads with ice cream. A clone is around the corner on Av. 1. Try their sandwiches and soyburgers. Another (and often tastier) branch is **Vishnu Vitaminas** (☎ 223-0294) at C. 14, Av. Central/2. Open Mon. to Sat., 8-8; 9-6 on Sun. Specializing in raw food, **La Nutrisoda** (☎ 255-3959) is in the bottom of Los Arcadas. Joe, a dour Hungarian emigrant, offers daily raw food specials, tabouli salad, avocado and humus sandwiches, and handmade sugarless fruit ices. He'll be happy to give you a lecture on the negative effects tourism has had on Costa Rica. Open Mon. to Fri. from 11-7. For other restaurants, check under "San Pedro" below.

OTHER SAN JOSE DINING: One of the best places to try classic Tico food, **La Cocina de Leña** at El Pueblo, has local specialties such as mondongo, *olla de carne*, and banana and *palmito ceviche*. In Sabana Norte and 500 m to the W of ICE, **Las Tunas** (☎ 231-1802) serves lunch and dinner with Mexican and other fare, including seafood. **Louisiana** (☎ 231-5164), set 200 m W of La Sabana on the road to Escazú, serves Cajun dishes.

    fast food: Expensive compared to the healthier meals you can find in any *soda*, fast food appears to be the city's specialty. In San José representations of Ronald McDonald are so omnipresent that you might think he, not Calderón, were president! You will find a veritable who's who of American fast food. There are **McDonald's** (at Av. Central. C. 5/7, across from the Cultural Plaza, and at C. 4, Av. Central/1); **Pollo Kentucky** (Av. 2, C. 6 and Av. Central, C. 2); **Pizza Hut** (Av. 1, C. 3/5, C. 4 Av. Central/2, and at Paseo Colón). Burger King is reportedly on the way and Wendy's can't be far behind. There are innumerable clones such as Archi's and Woopy's about. Don't find them; they'll find you.

    cafés and baked goods: A popular outdoor café for people watching, **Parisien Café** is on the ground floor of the Gran Hotel Costa Rica (C. 3, Av. 2). It also serves reasonably priced meals. The National Theater's **Café Ruiseñor del Teatro** across the way has artwork, marble tabletops, and classical chamber music. This is undoubtedly the plushest place in the country to sip coffee. Intimate and set to the N of the Parque Morazán, **La Esquina del Café** is at Av. 9/C. 3B. Great espressos, cakes, and unique souvenirs are on sale. Another great place to go is intimate **Café Mundo** at Av. 9, C. 11/13; they have excellent pastries and tasty lunches (salads, sandwiches, soups). Other good small coffee shops include **Las Cuartetas** (C. 2, Av. 3/5), **Manolo's** (Av. Central, C. Central/1 and Av. Central, C. 9/11), and **Spoon** (Av. Central, C. 5/7). One of the best bakeries is **Giacomín** on C. 2. **Repositería Fina Coppelia** along Paseo de Colón offers hamburgers, fruit salad, and baked goods. Set off of C. 40 just down the corner from the Iberia office, **Bar/Restaurante Bembec** has outside tables and serves high quality pastries. Fast-food style **Grandma's Canelita Rolls** is on C. 9 near Av. 6; it also offers affordable cappuccino and expresso. On Sabana Sur, the **Oasis Deli** (☎ 296-2813, fax 296-2732) offers a variety of salads, desserts and sandwiches. Out in San Pedro, **Café Maga** is about the hippest place you'll find to imbibe some java (ask for a "Picasso") or have a salad with tuna and heart of palm (ask for a "Borges"). Located on the second floor of a building along the main road though San Pedro, it doubles as a cultural center and art space. **note:** The **Pereficós** supermarket chain also has a bakery in each of its stores.

> ☞ **Travelers' Tip.** Resembling nothing so much as a 1950s-style diner, La Meseta Coffee Shop is open from 9 to 6, Mon. to Sat., and offers coffee ($1.25 per cup) which is brewed according to your selection of a variety of grades. It is on C. Blancos, across from the Motorola factory and near the entrance to its parent firm, the Tostadora La Meseta, which is one of the nation's largest coffee companies.

LOS YOSES FOOD: Good coffee shops here include **Azafrán**, **Spoon**, **Giacomín**, and **Café Ruiseñor**, which also offers quiche, soups, and a salad bar. **Choices** (☎ 225-5230), set 175 m E of the Automercado on the right hand side as one heads to San Pedro, has a great salad bar, crêpes, and luscious desserts. It's not open for dinner. On Av. Central, **Le Café des Artistes** is perfect for hanging out. Dine at **Restaurant La Galería** (☎ 234-0850) or **Paprika** (☎ 225-8971, Av. Central, C. 29/33). In the shopping center next to Cancún, reasonably priced **Valerio's** (☎ 225-0838) has pizza, lasagna, and desserts. **Río** (Av. 2/C. 39) is popular with *los plasticos* and serves typical food, including good *casados*. **Che Pato,** open weekdays, is an inexpensive health-food restaurant with lunch specials. It's in the lobby of the Teatro Carpo, which is next to KFC in Los Yoses. In Los Yoses, 100 m N of the Iglesia de Fatima, **Café 1900** (☎ 225-0819) offers Peruvian as well as international dishes.

SAN PEDRO DINING AND FOOD: This lively student-oriented area offers a wide range of reasonable restaurants. A favorite of college students, **El Pomodoro** pizza is next to the church at the university. Also specializing in pizza, **La Mazorca** (☎ 224-8069) is perhaps the nation's best known vegetarian restaurant; its cosy café atmosphere makes you feel as if you could be in Cambridge MA or Berkeley CA. It's 100 m N and 200 m E of the church. It has its own food market across the street. **Vegetarian Restaurant San Pedro** is a competitor 200 m N of the church. A third is **Ditso**, a macrobiotic joint set 200 m N of the church and near the RR tracks. Located in Centro Comercial de la C. Real, **Ambrosia** serves a mixture of vegetarian and non-vegetarian cuisine. **La Villa** has a swinging bamboo curtain and great atmosphere. **El Jardín del Pulpo** serves Mexican food and **Chily's**, in the Centro Comercial de la C. Real, 75 m E of Banco Popular, serves Tex-Mex. **Omar Khayam** has Arab and other dishes. **El Jorongo** serves Mexican food in an unpretentious environment. **Barabarella** is another Italian restaurant. Set 75 m to the S of the Banco Popular, **El Corrocio Verde** serves French crêpes and has a salad bar.

San Pedro gourmet/continental: For high-class dining, try expensive **La Petite Provence** (☎ 255-1559; Av. Central, C. 27). The nation's classiest French restaurant is the very expensive **Le Chandelier** (☎ 225-3980). It's one block to the left of the ICE building and 100 m to the S. **Il Ponte Vecchio** (☎ 225-9339), 200 m W and 25 m N of the Iglesia San Pedro, offers good Italian food prepared by a chef from NYC at moderate rates. Also in San Pedro (75 m E of Banco Popular, Centro Comercial de la C. Real), **Restaurant Marbella** (☎ 224-9452) specializes in Paella Valencia; it has a flamenco show on weekend evenings. In Guadalupe, **Le Bistro** (☎ 221-1754) also serves French food. **La Galería**, set 125 m W of the ICE building in San Pedro, serves European food accompanied by classical music. The **Villa Franken**, nearby, offers German food. Opened in 1995, the attractive **Bijahua** (☎ 225-0613) offers *nouvelle* Costa Rican cuisine, including dishes such as *lomito* on eggplant toast with shrimp and zucchini *fricasée* and red snapper stuffed with green plantains. To get here turn right at the Centro Comercial C. Real just before the Mas X Menos and head one block farther; it's two blocks S on C. 13, which is fronted by the Galería Miró.

IN CURRIDABAT: Located across from the Outdoor Club in Curridabat, **Via Veneto** (☎ 234-2898) serves Italian food in an elegant atmosphere. Also in Curridabat and near the Pops outlet, **Marcois** has French food.

IN SANTA ANA: Set in a 130-year-old adobe house, **Casa Quitirrisí** (☎ 282-5441) offers a 20-item buffet on Sun. afternoons for around $10. It serves traditional carnivore-geared Tico dishes in the evenings and has live music on Fri. and Sat. nights.

ESCAZU DINING AND FOOD: For cheap eats, try **Restaurante Pollos Yakky** (or other *sodas*) near the main square. Bookstore **Rincón de la Calle Real** (☎ 289-5112) offers lunch in a garden setting. It's near the Pomodoro Restaurant (50 m W and 100 m S of the US Ambassador's residence on the old Santa Ana Road). **Nimbé** (☎ 228-1173) offers Pakistani and other cuisines. It's near the Puesta del Sol. The **Café del Sol** (☎ 228-1645) is 275 m E of the church. **Abacus** (☎ 228-9616) features light dining, including more than 30 varieties of crêpes and over 20 different desserts, as well as *nachos* and *fajitas*; it's next to Tega at San Rafael on the road to Escazú. **Añoranzas** (☎ 267-7406), four km above San Rafael, offers *típico* food and has play equipment for children. On the old road to Escazú – approximately halfway between Los Anaonos Bridge and Parque la Sabana, **Peperoni** (☎ 232-5119) offers Italian food including a salad bar, smoked fish, and desserts. The atmosphere is informal. Another Italian restaurant is **Sale e Pepe**, which serves pizza, pasta, and has a salad bar as well as low-budget lunchtime specials. It's on the Escazú main road, in the Centro Comercial del Valle just to the rear of Pops. Yet another Italian restaurant is **Capriccio Italiano** (☎ 228-9332) in San Rafael Escazú 100 m E and 150 m S from McDonalds. **Vivaldi** (☎ 228-6045) bases its cuisine on items made with pastry dough (such as quiche) and also sells sandwiches and delicious desserts. It's 150 m S of Centro Comercial Blvd. in Santa Rosa de Escazú. Mexican food is served at **Oralé** (☎ 228-6437) in Centro Comercial Trejos Montealegre. Quite popular, **Muy** (☎ 254-6281) is open for dinner daily and for lunch on weekends. It specializes in Tex-Mex BBQ supplemented by Tico entrées and is just above the Pico Blanco Hotel in San Antonio de Escazú.

gourmet: Offering personalized gourmet dining in a classy, private-home-style atmosphere, **Il Tulá** (☎ 228-0053) offers five antipasto dishes and more than a dozen entrées; it's 200 m and 50 m S of the Los Anonos Periférico market in San Rafael. The **Tara** (☎ 228-6992) offers the "Atlanta Dining Gallery." Quite popular with affluent Ticos who come for the view as well as the food, it offers a variety of gourmet dishes, including seafood and vegetarian entrées. **María Alexandra**, in the apartotel of the same name 100 m N of Tega in San Rafael de Escazú, is another gourmet bistro. **Finale** serves low-calorie, no-cholesterol ice cream; it's at the Plaza Colonial. **Rancho Macho** in the hills offers mariachi entertainment in the evenings.

OTHER OUTLYING DINING: Restaurant Villa Bonita (☎ 232-9855), specializing in Schezuan cuisine, is 25 m W of Pavas Shopping Center. **Restaurant Típico Los Americas** (☎ 259-0773) is to the S in San Miguel de Desamparados, alongside Iglesia San Miguel. Its menu includes *chicharronnes*, *mondongo*, and *tamales*.

San José

☞ **Traveler's Tip**. Visitors should keep in mind that San José can be a dangerous as well as friendly place. Make sure to park your rental car in a safe place, and never leave anything of value in it. Likewise, take only minimal possessions when you venture out on the streets and keep away from the areas specified under "theft" in the "Practicalities" section.

San José Entertainment

There's always something to do here! If you get a chance, check out **Cantoamérica**. Led by Manuel Monestel, this band plays a fusion of salsa with calypso, reggae, and even rumba. Their first CD (but fifth recorded release) is called *Por las calles de la vida*. Another band to watch for is **La Oveja Negra**. Others include La Banda, Grupo K-lor, Los Brillanticos, Marifil, and Gene Chambers. Jazz artists to watch for include Editut Trio, Afrocosmos, Manuel Obregón, and Geo jazz. Rock bands include Café Con Leche, Liverpool, and Grupo Cuartel.

Note: San José is becoming increasingly dangerous at night. Visitors should be aware that the red light district begins to the W of C. 8. Also avoid the area around Cine Libano, Av. 7, C. 10-14, and the three-to-four-block area S of Av. 4 at C. 4. On May 1, 1995, a Florida tourist was stabbed to death near C. 6 and Av. 7 after he resisted during a robbery attempt.

CLASSICAL MUSIC: The **National Symphony Orchestra** performs most weekends from April to November at the National Theater. The "Una Hora de Musica" performances, featuring chamber music, are also held here once or twice a month during the same time period. **Chavetas Tavern**, near the Villa Tournón, has a classical music variety program every Mon. night. Many of the cultural centers also feature concerts.

DANCE: The **Compañía Nacional de Danza** holds between two and four performances per year. College troupes of renown are the **Danza Una** of the National University and the UCR's **Danza Universitaria**. The **Instituto Technical** also has a folkloric dance troupe. Other groups include **Cedanza, Codanza, Danza Contemporanea, Danza Libre**, and **Diquis Tiquis**. Composed of teenagers, **San Luis Gonzaga Amateur Troupe** is one of the oldest performing companies. **Danacart** is in neighboring Cartago.

THEATER: In addition to the papers, check the listings on the board in front of the Teatro Nacional. Don't miss a performance at the **National**

Theater if you can help it. Most plays are, of course, in Spanish – with the exception of those presented by the Little Theater Group at the American Cultural Center. No language ability is necessary to enjoy performances by the opera, symphony, and dance (Compania Nacional de Danza) companies. Another outstanding venue is **Teatro Melico Salazar** (Av. 2, C. Central/2). You can see just fine from the cheapest seats here; they allow you to peer right into the orchestra pit and watch the players. The National Theater Company often takes a satirical view in their performances. Performances are listed in *La Nación*. Here are the addresses: **Teatro de la Aduana** (C. 25, Av. 3/5); **Teatro del Angel** (Av. Central, C13/15); **Teatro Bellas Artes** (E side of the UCR campus at San Pedro); **Teatro La Comedia** (next to Mas X Menos supermarket on Av. Central across from the Plaza de la Democracia); **Teatro Carpa** (Av. Central, C. 29; next to Kentucky Fried in San Pedro); **Sala de la Calle 15** (Av. 2, C. 15); **Teatro Chaplin** (Av. 9, C 1/3); **Teatro Laurence Olivier** (Av. 2, C. 28); **Teatro La Mascara** (C. 13, Av. 2/4); **Teatro Arlequin** (C. 13, Av. Central/2); and **Teatro J. J. Vargas Calvo** (C. 3/5, Av. 2).

AROUND EL PUEBLO: Popular with *"los plasticos,"* the area around this imitation Spanish-style shopping center is one of the nation's liveliest. **Cocoloco** has two dance floors, one small *salsa* disco and a darker one, playing more intimate music. Live bands play here mid-week. More conventional **La Plaza** is an attractive disco and *salsa/merengue* club. Dark and steamy **Infinito** has three different discos (rock, Latin, and *salsa*). Other bars include **Amaretta** and **Bar Boquitas**, which has an intimate atmosphere. **Jerry Morgan's Piano Bar** has a glittery interior. **Salón Musical de Lety** has cabaret entertainment. **Momentos** is romantic. **Taina's** has an Argentinian vocalist singing ballads on Fri. and Sat. nights.

OTHER VENUES: Located in the Letras Building, a new open-air theater in the **University of Costa Rica in San Pedro** offers a variety of performances. For information, ☎ 225-5711 and 253-5323, ext. 5433. More regular entertainment is found at **Café Maga** on the second floor of a building along the main road though San Pedro. It functions as a cultural center (films, dance workshops, and graffiti art shows) and art exhibition space.

DISCOS: Located around the middle of Paseo Colón, **Club Copacabana** is a large disco. Hot and sweaty **Disco Salsa 54** (C. 3. Av. 1/3) plays a lot of romantic music; couples cuddle as they dance. **El Tunel de Tiempo** (Av. Central, C. 11/13) comes with a head-spinning, light-spiralling entrance. **O Key** is another disco at C. 4, Av. 6/8. **Members**

San José

is in Centro Colón on Paseo Colón. One of the best around, **Dynasty Discoteque**, located at Centro Comercial del Sur, which is about 10 blocks S of the Teatro Nacional, plays a lot of reggae, calypso, rap, funk, and soul. Featuring disco and *salsa*, **Partenon** is also here. Take the *Desamparados* bus from the N side of the Parque Central. **Disco Las Tunas** (☎ 231-1802) is in Sabana Norte, in outlying Sabanilla.

GAY AND LESBIAN CLUBS: Although the nation's gays attempt to keep things low key, there are a few hangouts. **La Avispa** (C. 1, Av. 8/10) is a popular lesbian bar featuring salsa and merengue music. On C. 7 off Av. 1, **La Torre Tonite** is a mostly gay, high-energy disco, as is **Deja-Vu** at C. 2, Av. 14/16 (which was subject to a shocking raid executed by the homophobic police in July 1994).

BARS: The **Blue Marlin Bar** in the Hotel del Rey is the place to go for fishing yarns. The **Charleston** (C. 9, Av. 2/4) is a video bar that attempts to create a Charleston-like atmosphere. American-owned yuppie bar, **Risa's**, is at C. 1, Av. Central. **Los Murales** (Gran Hotel) and **Las Palmas** (Aurola Holiday Inn) are other alternatives. Open 24 hours a day on a daily basis, **Chelles** (Av. Central, C. 9) is a landmark – a great spot for people watching. A version of the same with booths, **Chelles Taberna** is around the corner. **Bar Peru Tico** is around the corner from the Hotel Bellavista. **Shipwreck Kelly's Marine Bar** (at C. 1/Av.1) proclaims that "it's never too late to waste your life." In the W part of town, **Los Arcos** is a dark and intimate makeout bar. Out in the Paseo de Colón area at C. 28 and Av. 2 next to the Sala Garbo, the **Shakespeare Bar** provides a classy atmosphere. The **Beatle Bar** (☎ 257-7230) is just S of the Hotel del Rey (Av. 1, C. 9) near Parque Morazán.

OUTLYING: In Pavas, **Cocktail's** is popular with a wide variety of expats; it's across from the Super Triangulo. Out in Los Yoses, **Río** (Av. 2/C. 39) is popular with *los plasticos* in their 20s. Also in Los Yoses, **Benigan's** is another trendy bar that caters to a youthful crowd. Decor ranges from a world map to a milk churn to a TV spewing out MTV. In San Pedro, **Rocoles** has a jukebox playing oldies but goodies from the 1960s, and **TX** is a yuppie bar. Also here, **La Villa** (☎ 225-9612), 125 m N of the Banco Anglo, is a well known hangout for academic leftists. In Escazú, **Mac's American Bar** is the place to go for TV sports and boisterous *gringo* jocks.

CLUBS: **Soda Blues** (☎ 221-8368) features live blues and Caribbean music. It's on C. 11, Av. 10/12 and is 200 m S of Cine Real. The **Villa Borghese** (☎ 233-3838; C. 11/13, Av. 9) behind the Casa Amarilla in

Barrio Amón, is a piano bar that presents "the best jazz and blues performed live in a '50s atmosphere." Across from Kentucky Fried Chicken on Av. Central, **El Tablado** has jazz on Mon. and Latin and *Nueva Canción* (progressive folk music). For conservative jazz, try **Emilia Romagna Jazz Club** on Paseo de Colón, which has no cover charge but does maintain a two-drink minimum. On C. 21, Av. 4/6, **Akelarre** is a large house with a variety of rooms; live bands perform here on weekends. It has DJ music on Wed. (no cover). Near the Cine Magaly, which is near the Toruma YH, **El Cuartel de la Boca del Monte**, with white walls and prints, is attractive and one of the classiest places around; it also has live music.

A large mansion, **Akellare** (C. 21, Av. 26) has bands on weekend evenings. **Casa Matute** books similar bands. This historical landmark in French style was built in 1930 for a famous doctor, Ricardo Moreno Cañas. Many Ticos believe he had spiritual powers and still visits patients on their sickbeds. He resided here for eight years, to be followed by Venezuelan Colonel Matute Gómez. He had been forced to flee after his brother, the nation's despot, had been ousted in a coup. He continued to live here until 1958 after his pedophilic taste in little girls stirred judicial ire. Casa Matute also has a restaurant supplementing its several bar rooms.

in San Pedro: **Contravía** (☎ 253-6989) has good live music. You might see La Ovejo Negra or Cantoámerica here. **Bar Rock** showcases heavy metal. On C. Central across from the Banco Anglo, **Club Crocodilio** – complete with large video and a crocodile hanging over the bar – is popular with university students. If you are Chinese or speak Cantonese or Mandarin, the place to go is right next to Salsa 54, where you'll find a doorway marked "Recuerdos de Oro." This leads upstairs to a Chinese bar featuring a giant "Karaoke OK!"

MARIACHI: This has become such a national institution that many Ticos believe they invented it! Centrally located **La Esmeralda** (Av. 2, C. 5/7) is lively and open 24 hours except on Sun. Next to the Barrio México church, **Bar México** also features mariachis. It's in a bad neighborhood; take a bus (C. 6, Av. Central) or hop a cab.

LOWLIFE: Located in a century-old converted sea captain's house that has also served as a conservatory of music, **Key Largo**, the city's most notorious bar ($2.25 admission; C. 9, Av. 3), teems with suggestively winking hookers (first price $100, $200 with no condom!) who aspire to being high class. There's a live band, caged toucans, and a back-room restaurant. Similar but less classy bars like **Happy Days**, **New York** and **Nashville South** are nearby. It's always amusing, if somewhat pathetic, to walk through and watch the grey-haired, paunch-bellied *gringos* having a whirl with wispy, seductive teenage hookers. If you aren't into the scene, the best place to relax and have a drink in the area is probably **Marley's** on Av. Central.

you can leave your hat on: One of many classy-wannabe stripper joints is **Theatre Josephine** (Av. 9, C. 2/4, ☎ 257-2269), which invites you to "envision a scenery traveling through different place through time and space under the most diverse special effects and the most beautiful women in Costa Rica." Several others – almost equally pretentious, overpriced, and uninteresting – are in the vicinity. Some of the city's strip joints are located in the area centering around C. 2, Av. 8. Be careful around here! For those upright souls righteously incensed by the local scene, Club 700, the local branch of the fundamentalist 700 Club, is on C. 1.

San José Cinemas

Bellavista
Av. Central, C. 17/19
221-0909

California
C. 23, Av. 1
221-4738

Capri
Av. Central, C. 9/11
223-0264

Colón
Paseo de Colón/C. 38
221-4517

Laurence Olivier
Av. 2, C. 28
223-1960

Magaly
Barrio La California
223-0085

Metropolitan
C. 28, Av. Central/1
222-1249

Omni
C. 3, Av. Central/1
221-7903

Rex
Av. 4, C. Central/Av. 2
221-0041

Sala Garbo
Av. 2, C. 28
222-1034

Universal
Paseo de Colón, C. 26/28
221-5241

Variedades
Av. Central/C. 5
222-6108

CINEMA: First-run films cost around $1.50 in mostly comfortable theaters. These include the **Magaly** (Av. Central, C. 23), the **Colón 1 and**

2 (Centro Colón on Paseo de Colón), **California** (C. 23, Av. 1), **Capri 1 and 2** (Av. Central, C. 9), **Cine Omni** (C. 3, Av. Central and 1), and **Cinema Real** (C. 11, Av. 6 and 8). Art films are shown at the **Sala Garbo**, an elegant and highly recommended cinema next to **Teatro Laurence Olivier**, Av. 2, C. 28, near Paseo Colón. In case you arrive early, it has a pleasant, if pricey, coffee shop adjoining, or have dinner in a nearby restaurant. To get here, walk 25 minutes from downtown or take the *Sabana Cementerio* bus (C. 7, Av. Central/2), get off by the Pizza Hut and walk a block to the S. Check the ads in *La Nación* for times.

slide/video: Several times per week Dr. Humberto Jiménez offers a presentation on the national parks at **Cine Variedades** ($3, ☎ 231-1236, 255-3518). A question and answer session follows.

GAMBLING: Casino locations include the Del Rey, Cariari, Corobicí, Aurola Holiday Inn, Irazú, Amstel Amón, and Balmoral Hotels. Another popular spot is Club Colónial, on Av. 1 at C. 9.

If the word "gambling" brings to mind row upon row of slot machines in cavernous casinos, you'll be disappointed with Costa Rica's gaming scene. Most casinos only open their doors in late afternoon or early evening. And terminology and practices are both a bit different. Ticos call blackjack *"rommy."* The difference here is that the ace and 10 card combo pays even money. If you receive three of a kind in your first three cards, however, you'll win three-to-one! Although a straight flush pays the same, it will pay out at four-to-one if it adds up to more than 21. Three sevens pay five-to-one. Craps is *domino China* here, and dice are replaced with domino-lookalike tiles. You turn over two tiles at every turn. *Tute* resembles poker. You receive one card up and four down. Pairs pay even, and there are no draws. Two pairs pay two-to-one, three pairs three-to-one, and so on. A royal flush will pay 100-to-one! *Canasta* is the Costa Rican version of roulette, in which a basket filled with red and black balls replaces the roulette wheel.

EVENTS AND FESTIVALS: The **Copa del Café**, a week-long tennis tournament, draws an international collection of talented teenagers. The **Carrera de la Paz** is a footrace held in March. Around a thousand people run from San José's National Gymnasium to the campus of the University for Peace in Villa Colón.

March: The **National Orchid Show**, featuring 500-plus species, a weekend-long festival, takes place in the Colegio de Medicos y Cirujanos headquarters in Sabana Sur. **National Oxcart Day,** on the second Sunday in March, celebrates the *boyero* (oxcart driver) and the *carreta* (the wooden-wheeled painted cart); the locus for the celebration is in San Antonio de Escazú outside of San José. The nation's cattlemen assemble at the Bonanza Fairgrounds, on the airport highway, for the

Bonanza Cattle Show. Featured are prize bulls, bullfights, rodeos, horseraces, and mechanical bulls. Taking place the same month, the **Crafts Fair** on the Plaza de la Cultura has 150-200 local artisans exhibiting their wares.

April: In San Jose's Plaza de la Democracia, an annual three-day **Festival of Native American Handicrafts** is followed by the celebration of Earth Day. Many events are held in and around San José during **Easter Holy Week** (*Semana Santa*) from Wed. noon through Sun.

May: During **University Week**, around the beginning of May, University of Costa Rica students crown a queen, and participate in sports events and a parade. Many local bands also perform on campus. This is a great time to investigate what college life is like here. On May 15, the **Día del Boyero** ("Day of the Oxcart Driver") is held in San Antonio de Escazú near San José. Activities include parades featuring brightly colored oxcarts, as well as blessing by the local priest of animals and crops . On San Juan Day, May 17, some 1,500 participants run the **Carrera de San Juan**, 22½ km from El Alto de Ochomongo (near Cartago) to San Juan de Tibás, N of San José.

August: The cultural week, **Semana Afro-Costarricense**, celebrates International Black People's Day and takes place in San José. Highlights are lectures, panel discussions, and displays.

September: At 6 PM on September 15, the nation's **Independence Day** (which is also that of all of Central America), the Freedom Torch, relayed by a chain of student runners stretching all the way from Guatemala, arrives in San José, and Ticos join in singing the national anthem. That evening, schoolchildren march in *farole* (lantern) parades, carrying handmade lanterns along the route.

November: Sponsored by the Asociación Canófila Costarricense every November, the **International Dog Show** has a splendid assortment of dogs. In San José during the **International Theater Festival**, a variety of theater groups perform plays, puppet shows, and street theater. A **women's march against violence** takes place on November 25, the "No Violence Against Women Day." It departs from the Plaza de la Cultura at 4 PM and winds up at the Plaza de la Democracia. The day is held in honor of the Miraval sisters, resistance leaders who were murdered on November 25, 1960. They were protesting against US-backed despot Trujillo in the Dominican Republic.

year's end fiestas: Commencing with the distribution of the *aguinaldo*, the annual bonus given to salaried workers, the city's liveliest time is during the month of December, when the sidewalks are crowded with *chinamos* stalls selling toys, nativity creche paraphernalia, and fruit such as apples and grapes. Merchants are open for extended hours and the streets get increasingly wilder as the month progresses. During the last week of December and extending through the beginning of January, bullfights are held at the Zapote ring daily;

the *topé*, a procession of horses, departs from Paseo Colón, proceeds along Av. Central and ends at Plaza Viquez. Finally, a dance in Parque Central welcomes the New Year.

> ☞ **Traveler's Tip.** If you have a specific interest or activity, you might want to use it as a way to get a feeling for Costa Rican life and perhaps meet people you might not come across otherwise. For example, you can practice **Tai Chi** every Saturday from 10 AM at the University of Costa Rica's Fine Art School. There's no fee. Or you might wish to bone up on **ultimate frisbee**. This enthusiast's version of the game is practiced every Sun. at 10:30 AM at the University of Costa Rica (call Orlando Leiva, ☎ 225-4075, for info). The **Vegetarian Society** (☎ 231-6582, 232-7230) meets on the first Thurs. of every month. The **Orchid Association** (Apdo. 6351, 1000 San José) meets on the first Sun. of every month. **Scrabble** enthusiasts get together for contests every Tues. at 1 PM at the Dunn Inn. These are but a few examples. You'll find yet others in the *Tico Times*.

Other San José Practicalities

HEALTH SPAS: If you're missing your workout, **Spa Corobicí** (☎ 232-8122), next to the hotel of the same name at La Sabana, has Nautilus, aerobics, and massages; it offers temporary memberships. Affiliated with the Corobicí, **Los Cipreses** (☎ 253-0530) is a "sports medicine" center in Curridabat with three basketball courts, three swimming pools, a half-sized soccer field, and a gym. The **San José Indoor Club** (☎ 225-9344) in Curridabat also offers complete facilities. Near the Indoor Club, **Fisicultura de Oriente** (☎ 253-9014) specializes in massages. Facilities here include pool, sauna, Jacuzzi, and weight room. Out in Moravia, the **Gimnasio y Spa Atélico** (☎ 236-8550) offers physical evaluation and personalized training. Less expensive are the **Gimnasio Exclusivo** (☎ 231-5645) in Sabana Norte and the **G.Y.M. Victoria** (☎ 224-3963) in San Pedro. For a low-calorie, diet-oriented vacation, contact Lisa Ohlenbusch (☎ 239-2225) at **La Estopa**. A licensed massage therapist, **Cheena Sofge** (☎ 232-7532, 228-2395) gives therapeutic massages.

ORGANIZATIONS AND CLUBS: There are innumerable clubs in San José. The US citizens in **Costa Rica for Peace** (☎ 233-6168), off C. 15 on Av. 6B, meet Mon. evenings. **Hash House Harriers** (☎ 228-0769) run on Mon. at 5 PM. Promoting partnership between Costa Rica and Oregon, **Partners of the Americas** (☎ 259-4326) is at Apdo. 219, 2400 San José. The **Krishnamurti Information Center** (☎ 484-4172, 224-

San José

3360), 400 m N and 100 m W of the Parque Morazán's pavilion, holds meetings every other week on Wed.

ASSOCIATIONS: The **American Chamber of Commerce of Costa Rica** (☎ 233-2133, fax 223-2349) can be contacted at Apdo. 4946, 1000 San José. The **Asociación de Pensionados y Rentistas de Costa Rica** is next to the Jubilados office on the ground floor of the ICT building (☎ 233-8068, fax 222-7862; write Apdo. 700-1011, San José).

EMBASSIES: The **US Embassy** (☎ 222-5566) is out in the W suburb of Pavas. The **Canadian High Commission** (☎ 296-4149, fax 296-4270; Apdo. 351-1007, Centro Colón) is on the third floor of Bldg. 5 at the Oficentro Ejecutivo La Sabana, which is behind the Comptroller General's Office on the S side of La Sabana. The **U. K.**'s address is Edificio Centro Colón 110, ☎ 221-5566. The **German Embassy** (☎ 221-5811) is at C. 36, Av. 3A. The **Swiss Consulate** (☎ 221-4829) is at 4th F, Centro Colón, Paseo Colón. For others consult the telephone directory's yellow pages under "Embajadas y Consulados."

Useful Phone Numbers in San José

Aero-Costa Rica (☎ 234-6013)
American Airlines
  (☎ 257-1266)
American Express
  (☎ 223-3644)
Aviateca (☎ 255-4949)
Clínica Americana
  (☎ 222-1010)
Clínica Bíblica (☎ 257-0466)
Clínica Católica (☎ 225-5055)
Clínica Jerusalem
  (☎ 285-0202)
Continental Airlines
  (☎ 223-0266)
Coopetaxi Garage - car trouble
  (☎ 235-9966)
Copa (☎ 223-7033, 221-5596)
Costa Rica Expeditions
  (☎ 257-0776, 222-0333)

Emergencies - ambulance, fire,
  police (☎ 911)
Geotour (☎ 234-1867)
Horizontes (☎ 222-2022)
Hospital San Juan de Díos
  (☎ 222-0166)
LACSA (☎ 232-3555/6/7)
Parques Nacionales
  (☎ 257-0922)
Personalized Travel
  (☎ 257-0507)
SANSA (☎ 221-9414)
SIRCA bus - Nicaragua
  (☎ 222-5541)
TACA (☎ 222-1790)
TICA bus (☎ 221-8954)
TRACOPA bus
  (☎ 221-4214, 223-7685)
US Embassy (☎ 220-3939)

HEALTH: English-speaking doctors and 24-hour service can be found at **Clínica Americana** (☎ 222-1010), Av. 14, Calles Central/1, at the **Clínica Bíblica** (☎ 257-0466), C. 1, Av. 14/16, at **Clínica Católica** (☎ 225-5055) in San Antonio de Guadalupe, and at **Clínica Jerusalem** (☎ 285-0202) in El Alto de Guadalupe. Since charges are uniform if you are not covered by the social security system and the care at these is superior, it's better to go to these private hospitals. While US insurance coverage isn't accepted, credit cards are, and you can have your company reimburse you later. In case of an emergency, go to any public hospital; the nearest one to downtown is **Hospital San Juan de Díos** (☎ 222-0166), Av. Central and C. 16. To call a Red Cross ambulance, ☎ 221-5818.

SHOPPING: Apropox (C. 3, Av. Centes) sells quality clothing. What they don't have in stock, they will make to order. **Arte Libros Regalos**, next to Dankha Boutique (Av. 5, C. 3), sells second-hand goods plus inexpensive used English books. Centrally located, **Galerías Plaza de Cultura** is a general department store at Av. Central, C. 5/7. Others are to the W along Av. Central. A good place for high-quality leatherwork is at the **Artesanías Melety** chain. The most centrally located branch is at Av. 1, C. 1/3. Other depots for leather include **Galería del Cuero**, Av. 1, C. 5, and **Del Río**, C. 9. Lower quality but more affordable goods are found at **Industrias Pesapop**, C. 3, Av. 1/3. For silver ornaments try **La Casa del Indio**, Av. 2, C. 5/7.

CRAFTS AND SOUVENIRS: Local artisans sell daily at C.5, Av. 4, where you may find goods sold by indigenous people from the Bribri, Chorotega, and Guaymi tribes, as well as items from Africa and Russia. The goods are sold directly from the artisans who made them; no middlemen or merchants are permitted. Selling finely crafted but steeply priced wooden bowls, among other items, **La Galeria** is at C. 1, Av Central/1. Other stores in the same price range are **Suraska** (C. 5, Av. 3) and **Atmósfera** (C. 5, Av. 1). **Mercado Nacional de Artesanías**, the National Handicraft Market (C. 11, Av. 2/4), offers souvenirs similar to those found in hotel stores, as does **CANAPI**, an artisans' guild at C. 11, Av. 2b. **ANDA** specializes in crafts such as pottery and gourds carved by Indians. It is on Av. Central between C. 5/7. **Arterica** is next to the Melico Salazar Theater on Av. 2 between C. Central/2. It has an unusual assortment of craft items. On C. 9 at Av. 9, the **Hotel Don Carlos** also has a gift shop with a good selection. **Magia** is at C. 5 between Av. 1/3, and **La Casona** (which has a selection of Central American handicrafts) is on C. Central between Av. Central/1.

    Sol Maya (across from the Hospital San Juan de Dios on Paseo Colón) also sells handicrafts; Guatemalan textiles are sold at C. 3, Av.

3/5. Located behind Iglesia La Soledad, **Casa del Artesano** (C. 11, Av. 4/6) is another craft center. **Costa Rica Expeditions** has a small souvenir shop that also sells books; it's at C. Central, Av. 3. For gourmet coffee beans from all over the Meseta Central, which are roasted on the premises, try **La Esquina del Café** at Av. 9/C. 3B. A unique range of souvenirs are also on sale. A second branch is at Centro Comercial El Cruce in Escazú. Escazú's **Sabor Tico** is set on the Santa Ana side of Plaza Colonial. It sells handicrafts, including coffee, ceramic plates, and batiks. The **Aracne** (☎ 224-0862), located in San Antonio de Guadalupe, 200 m N and 25 m E from the Clínica Católica, is a studio-gallery for indigenous and fine-art textiles and fiber arts. A set of stalls grouped under a single roof, the **International Arts and Crafts Market** sells Costa Rican crafts exclusively. It has restaurants, craft demonstrations, and music and dance performances. It's in Curridabat, a suburb to the E of San José, and is open Tues. to Thurs. and Sun. from 9-6 and on Fri. and Sat. from 9-9. It's closed on Mon. Furniture makers include the talented **Barry Biesanz** (☎ 228-1811) in Escazú and **Jay Morrison** (☎ 228-6697) in Santa Ana. Moravia, a NE suburb, is well known for its leather crafts, including belts, wallets, briefcases, and purses. Sarchí is famous for its *carretas*, painted ox carts, and other souvenirs.

SHOPPING CENTERS: Centro Comercial El Pueblo is a shopping center set up as an imitation colonial village. It's complete with tile roofs, walls of stucco and whitewashed brick, wrought iron lamps, and narrow streets. The nighttime is the right time for boogeying here. Take the *C. Blancos bus* (Av. 5, C. 1/3), a cab, or walk. Less tasteful, another **Centro Comercial** is a few km S of Av. Central. The **National Museum's shop** sometimes has examples of indigenous weaving. Another outdoor vending area is at the stalls on the E side of C. Central, just N of Av. Central. A shop along the S side of the Sabana sells baskets, ornate mats, and ceramics.

> ☞ **Traveler's Tip**. An unusual souvenir for that special friend might be a handmade guitar by one of San José's luthiers, eight of whom reside in a three-block area near central San José's Iglesia La Dolorosa. Emmanuel Mora Torres is at Av. 2, C. 2/Central. Aristides Guzmán has his shop in Cinco Esquinas de Tibás. On C. 2 are the studios of Edgar and Rodrigo Garro; Olman Arguedas is in the other direction, on the same side of the street and in the same block. Martin Prada is one block farther in the same direction and across the street. Omar Corrales Guzmán has his atelier 400 m S of the Instituto de Aprendizaje, Paso Anjo.

San José Malls

Mall San Pedro
San Pedro near the Los Yoses roundabout.
260 stores and 35 restaurants. Opened in 1995.

Metrocentro
Near Cartago's central market.
40 stores, supermarket, and a restaurant.

Multiplaza
Across from the Camino Real Hotel in Escazú.
100 stores, 10 restaurants, and a supermarket.

Novacentro
In Guadalupe at the intersection for Moravia.
30 stores and a supermarket.

Plaza del Sol
E side of town on the way to Curridabat.
50 stores, supermarket, and restaurants.

Plaza Mayor
In suburb of Rohrmoser.
20 stores, bookstore, and supermarket.

CAMPING SUPPLIES: The major store is **Centro de Aventuras** (☎ 255-0618) on Paseo Colón (C. 22/24), which also rents snorkeling, kayaking, or camping equipment. Another store, **Aro Ltd.** (Av. 8, C. 11/13), sells camping gaz refillable cartridges. **Ferretería El Clavo** (C. 6, Av. 8) has *gasolina blanca* (kerosene). Other stores with outdoor gear include **Carlos Luis** (Av. Central, C. 2/4) and **Palacio del Deporte** (C. 2, Av. 2/4).

FISHING EQUIPMENT: The two major outlets are **La Casa del Pescador** (C. 2, Av. 18/20) and **Deportes Keko** (C. 20, Av. 4/6). Tide tables are also available here.

SURFING SUPPLIES: Set 80 ft (75 m) W of the Banco Popular in San Pedro, the **Mango Surf Shop** is one of two alternatives here. The other is the **Keola Surf and Ding Shop** (☎ 225-6280, Apdo. 6280, San José), which is 100 m E and S of the Banco Popular. The latter provides board repair, information, and guides. Also try the **Tsunami** in Los Yoses.

MARKETS: The **Mercado Central** is at C. 6., Av. 1. Here you can buy fresh spices (sold in 10 and 25 gm bags), and fruits and vegetables. There's also a stall selling honey and natural herbs. Herbs are available in bulk at **La Avena Hierba**, Paseo de los Estudiantes (C. 9). A block N, at C. 8 between Av. 3 and 5, is the **Borbón,** which specializes in vegetables. Another market is in the Coca Cola bus terminal at C. 16, between Av. 1 and 3. Held to the W of Plaza Viquez (C., 7/9, Av. 16/20) on Sat. AM, a *feria del agricultor* (farmer's market) offers goods ranging from homemade wholewheat bread to pastries and fruits. Fresh organic produce is sold by **Club Vida Natural,** 100 m S of San Pedro's Restaurant La Nueva China. ☎ 224-8713 or 536-6079 for information. For hardware items try **Ferretería Glazman,** Av. 5, C. 6/8.

FOOD SHOPPING: In addition to the above-mentioned markets, there are a number of places to buy food. King of the supermarkets is the **Mas x Menos** chain. There's a branch on Paseo Colón across from the Ambassador Hotel between C. 24/28; others are across from the Plaza de la Demoocracia (C. 3/5) and in the suburbs. Its chief competitor is the **Automercado** chain (closed Sundays), which is on C. 3/5 at Av. 3, in Barrio Mexico and Los Yoses, and in Plaza del Sol and Plaza Mayor. Set at the end of Paseo Colón on C. 42, **Yaohan** offers a wide selection, but prices are also high. The place is huge and has commando-mentality security guards patrolling with walkie talkies. In case you have an interest in the nation that controls this supermarket as well as the Corobicí, Herradura, and Irazú hotels, SANSA airlines, and a lot of other properties, the Centro Información Japones is on the level above. You can also try out inexpensive Japanese food at **Hinode,** the lunch room downstairs. Out in San Pedro, **Muñoz y Nanne** is renowned for its produce. **Café Moka** sells coffee beans and peanuts at Av. Central near C. 10; many other such shops are in the vicinity.

DRUGSTORES: Located at Av. 4 between C. Central and 1, **Clinica Biblica**'s dispensary is open 24 hours a day. The **Farmacía Cartin** is located on the east side of the Central Market. The **Farmacía del Este** is across from Banco Popular in San Pedro. The **Farmacía del Oeste** is across from the US Embassy.

INFORMATION AND SERVICES: The **ICT** (Tourism Institute) has its information offices in the underground portion of the Cultural Plaza at C. 5 (☎ 222-1090) and at the airport. From any touchtone phone, information is available at 257-4667. In addition to the *Tico Times* and the weekend section of *La Nación,* another useful source for entertainment and events is *Info-Spectacles,* a free flyer.

MAIL: Also known as **Coretel** (Correos y Telégrafos), the main post office (Correo Central) is on C. 2, Av. 1/3. Window service runs from 7 to 6 weekdays, and from 7 to 2 on Sat. You can have mail sent via *Lista de Correos* (Post Restante) here. **American Express** accepts mail addressed to its card and traveler's check holders. They are at 4 F, TAM Travel, C. 1, Av. Central/1.

BANKING: Banks are open from 9 to 3. Certain branches may be open until six. Most banks will also sell you *colones* if you have a major credit card. A money changing operation run by Banco Mercantil is on Av. 2 (C. Central/2). It's open 9-noon and 1-5:45 weekdays. For banking on Sat. AM try the bank across from the Amstel Hotel on Av. 1, C. 7. Canadian dollars can be changed at Banco San José (C. Central, Av. 3/5), Banex (C. Central, Av. 1), BCT (C. Central, Av. 1/3), and Lyon (C. 2. Av. Central/1). You can also change money in larger hotels.

MONEYCHANGERS: At all costs avoid moneychangers on the street. However, there are a number of trustworthy moneychangers who operate from kiosks or markets. These are preferable to the banks because you cut out the red tape. One good place to change money is at the **Villalobos Brothers** (☎ 233-0090/3127), No. 204 on the second floor of the Schyfter Bldg., which is on C. 2, Av. Central/1 near the GPO. Another place to try is **International State** (tel. 233-9892) on the third floor at C. 7, Av. Central/1.

PHONES: Although it may not be hard to find a pay phone in the city, it can be exasperating to try and find one that both works and for which you have the correct coinage. Try hotel lobbies or outside the ICE building at C. 1, Av. 2.

LAUNDRY AND DRY CLEANING: There is a service on Paseo de Colón near Restaurante Bastille (to the W of downtown); **Lavantia Doña Ana** (closed Sun.) is 400 ft (125 m) to the E of Plaza Gonzales near the Ministry of Public Transport to the SE. Another is in the Centro Comercial on the N side of the San Pedro road to the E of Los Yoses. To get here take the San Pedro bus on Av. 2 and ask the driver to let you off.

BABYSITTING: Ask at your hotel or contact **Viajes Colón** (☎ 221-3778, 225-2500).

BEAUTY PARLORS: Jardinera Professional de Belleza Myrtha (☎ 221-0887) is a beauty school offering cheap cuts and other treatments to both sexes. No English is spoken. It's in back of the now-bankrupt and shut Banco Anglo and around the corner from Casa 329 El Paso.

AIRLINES: Continental (☎ 233-0266, fax 233-7146) has its offices at C. 19/Av. 2. You can also reach them at the airport at ☎ 442-1904. **Ameri-**

San José

can Airlines (☎ 255-1607, 255-1911) is in the Centro Cars Building, Sabana Este, which is the enormous reflecting glass VW car sales building next to Yaohan. **LACSA** (☎ 231-0093) is at Av. 5, C. 1/3. **United** (☎ 220-4844) is behind the Contraloria Bldg. in Sabana Sur. **Aero Costa Rica** (☎ 296-1111, fax 253-8098) has its offices in La Uruca. **Aviateca** (☎ 233-8390, 255-4949) is 100 m N of the Banco de Costa Rica in Paseo Colón.

LIBRARIES AND CULTURAL CENTERS: Best for periodicals and books in English is the US-sponsored **Centro Cultural Costarricense Norteamericano** (Costa Rican-American Cultural Center, ☎ 225-9433, ext. 223, 214, 252; 253-5783, fax 224-1480), located in eastern San José on C. Negritos. You'll have to pay a membership fee if you want to borrow books. You can also watch CNN here. Its Mark Twain Information Center and Library has access to data bases including CD-ROM, card catalog, US Congress "Legislate," and "Phonefiche." It's open Mon. to Fri., 8:30-6:30 and Sat. from 8 to noon. On C. 21 just off Av. Central on the E side of the Parque Nacional, the **Centro Cultural de Mexico** (open Mon. to Fri., 3-5) has a small library. Another library is at the **Biblioteca Nacional** (Av. 3 at C. 15). It has a newspaper room featuring foreign journals such as *The People's Korea*. Another is the one at the **University of Costa Rica** in San Pedro. **Alianza Franco Costarricense**, Av. 7, C. 5, has French newspapers and shows films every Thurs. evening. The **Instituto Goethe** highlights German culture and also has a reading room; the *San Pedro* bus passes right by.

MAPS AND BOOKSTORES: Most of the bookstores mentioned here carry the *Tico Times* as well as imported newspapers. **Librería Internacional** (☎ 296-1290), run by Austrian Hans Venier, sells an extensive selection of Spanish, German, and English books. Most of the US titles are priced 10-20% above their US cover price. A specially designed youth section, equipped with floor cushions and a low reading table, has a good variety of children's books. It's in Barrio Dent, 400 m W of Taco Bell, near Mall San Pedro. **Chispas Books** (☎ 223-2240) offers a wide variety of books at reasonable prices. It's on C. 7, Av. Central/C. 1. **Librería Lehmann**, Av. Central, C. 1/3 and **Librería Universal**, Av. Central, C. Central/1, have good map sections (topographics) as well as a fine selection of books. **Librería Quijote**, in the Arcadas Mall at Av. 1, Calles Central/2, has a smaller selection of English books, including some used books. **Shakespeare and Co.** (☎ 233-4995) is 350 m to the N of the Gran Hotel Costa Rica. **The Bookshop** (Av. 11, C. 3/3 bis near the Amstel Amón) has an excellent supply of maps and travel guides. Their prices are higher than elsewhere, but they have a friendly English-speaking staff. It is a combination café, coffee shop, and art gallery. At Av. 3, C. 19/21, **The Bookstop** (☎ 223-5300) is a small bookstore with new and used books; it's in the Centro Comercial de Estación, which is next to the Limón bus station. Advertising itself as the "largest used bookstore in Central America," **Book Traders** has two locations: Av. 1, C. 5/7 atop the Pizza Hut, and in San Rafael de Escazú at Centro Comercial Guachapelin. Another place to buy is at **Gambit,** which is across from the bowling alley, down the way from the Centro Cultural Costarricense Norteamericano in Barrio Dent. Near the center of Escazú and the Pomodoro Restaurant (50 m W and 100 m S of the US Ambassador's residence on the old Santa Ana Road), **Rincón de la Calle Real** (☎ 289-5112) is the nation's most unusual bookstore. In addition to a fine selection of books, it offers lunch in a garden setting, poetry readings, and jazz and classical music concerts.

maps: The **National Geographic Institute** of the Ministry of Public Works, Av. 20, C. 9/11, sells maps and a variety of geographic publications. It is open Mon.-Fri. from 8:30-3:30; the *Barrio La Cruz* bus from Parque Central comes here. The **Ministry of Transport** (Av. 18, C. 9) has street maps of towns and topographic maps. French and Italian magazines are available at **Librería Francesa/Librería Italiana,** C. 3, Av. 1/Central.

NEW AGE INFORMATION: Focusing on "healing arts, ecological consciousness, and world peace," the **Costa Rica Rainbow Connection** (☎ 240-7335, ask for Janine, alias Nalini) is a "holistic network, counseling, and travel service." *Tico Times* regulars and hundredth monkey propagators, **Via Holistica** (☎/fax 282-6107) serve as a free clearinghouse for New Age Services. Whether you're seeking your inner child or need some chakra cleansing, they'll help you to find the appropriate resource. Hare Krishnas can seek out their brethren at the **Hare Krishna Farm** (☎ 551-6752, 227-4505) on the road to Paraiso de Cartago.

DANCE LESSONS: There are a large number of inexpensive dance schools in San José. If you're going to be staying awhile, it's well worth checking them out. With two schools (one on the E side of the US Embassy in Rohrmoser and another 50 m W and 100 m S of the Banco Popular in San Pedro), the **Centro de Enseñanza y Investigación del Baile Popular** (Merecumbé Research and Training Center of Popular Dance) offers training in a variety of steps ranging from *bolero* to *merengue.* They have a special program for tourists (☎ 224-3531/1548). **Danza Viva,** 75 m S of the "Antiguo Higueron" in San Pedro, teaches everything from modern dance to tango and *soca.* **Academia de Baile Popular Malecón** (☎ 222-3214) is 175 m E of the Plaza de la Democracia next to Apartotel San José. It teaches everything from *danzon* to reg-

San José

gae and *mambo*. On Av. Central between C. 25B and 27 on the way to San Pedro, the **Academy de Bailes Latinos** (Academy of Latin Dances; ☎ 221-1624, 233-8938) teaches techniques in calypso, *cumbia, salsa*, and the like. They also have Spanish classes (free dance lessons for students), intensive courses, and private lessons. An added advantage is that there is no enrollment fee.

Planning Your Itinerary

If you've arrived without an itinerary and are confused, there are a number of places in San José where you can get help. **Horizontes** (☎ 222-2022; Apdo. 1780, San José 1002) is a local agency that offers good planning and is popular with many visitors. **Costa Rica Expeditions** (☎ 257-0776, 222-0333, fax 257-1665) will help you plan visits to their lodges as well as a number of reputable hotels. If you're looking for something a bit more personal and informative, **Personalized Tours** (☎ 257-0507: 24 hours) is definitely recommended. This father-and-son operation can provide everything from trips to Manuel Antonio to quetzal tours or trips to Curú Wildlife Refuge. This is a great chance for you to meet with Ticos as friends instead of as servants and to ask them questions. Even if they aren't going with you, they can still hook you up with trips and book hotels. This is an ideal place for small family groups. **Adventureland** (☎ 222-3866, fax 222-3724; Av. 1, C. 1/3), a branch of TAM Travel, offers a variety of tours, lodging, and other adventures. The **Ecotreks Adventure Company** (☎ 228-4029, fax 289-8191) has a branch in Escazú. They arrange diving, sea kayaking, all-terrain-vehicle tours and rentals, and other activities.

From San José

Using the city as a base, many different day excursions are possible. Good day trips include visits to Volcán Poás, Orosi Valley, San Antonio de Escazú, Alajuela, Volcán Irazú, Cartago, Lankester Gardens, Heredia, the Reventazón River for white water rafting, and many others. If you're on a budget, but still want to go on a tour, you should note that the Museo Nacional (☎ 257-1433) offers a number of low-priced tours (around $4 plus transportation), such as educational trips to watch turtles and birds, see volcanoes, and comb beaches for marine fossils.

Selected Car Rental Companies in San José

NAME	LOCATION	PHONE
Accion Rent a Car	Sabana Norte	232-9637
Avis Rent a Car	Calle 36, Ave. 7	222-6066
Budget Rent a Car	Calle 30, Paseo Colón	232-3284
Dollar Rent a Car	Calle Ctl., Ave.	933-3339
El Indio Rent a Car	Calle 40/42, Ave. ctl.	233-2157
Prego		257-1158
		221-8680
	airport	443-2336
	fax	255-4492

BY RAIL: The train lines to Limón and Puntarenas are no longer in operation and there is no remaining train service worth mentioning.

BY BUS: Especially during weekends and holidays, it's preferable to buy your ticket the day before and arrive an hour before departure. Check the times in this guide and recheck them if possible. If there are only a few departures per day, you don't want to miss one! The following buses run from or stop near "Coca Cola": *Ciudad Quesada* and *Fortuna*, C. 16, Av. 1/3 (hourly; 3 hours); *Jacó* and *Carara* from C. 16, Av. 1/3; *Liberia*, Av. 2, C. 14; *Nicoya*, C. 14, Av. 5; *Puntarenas* (☎ 233-2610) on C. 16, Av. 10/12; *Puerto Viejo de Sarapiquí* (in the La Selva area), C. 12, Av. 7/9; *Santa Cruz*, C. 16, Av. 1/3; and *Zarcero*, C. 16, Av. 3. The bus for *Alajuela* leaves from Av. 2, C. 14; *Cañas* from C. 16, Av. 3/5; *Turrialba* from C. 13, Av. Central/2; *Cartago* from C. 5, Av. 18; *Golfito* from near the former Pacific RR at Av. 18, C. 4; *Guápiles* at C. 12, Av. 7/9; *Limón* from near the former Atlantic RR at Av. 3, C. 19/21; *Monteverde* from C. 14, Av. 9/11; *Palmar Norte* from C. 2/4, Av. 18; *San Isidro de El General* (from 5:30 AM-5 PM) at C. 16, Av. 1/3; *Sarchí* (express) from C. 16, Av. 1/3 (twice daily at 12:15 and 5:30); *Santa Cruz* from C. 20, Av. 1/3; *Sixaola* and *Cahuita* and (separate bus) *Puerto Viejo de Limón* at C. Central/Av. 11; *Tilarán* at C. 12, Av. 9/11; and *Zona Sur* from Av. 11, C. 4. Innumerable other buses run. For other destinations, see the "Getting There" section under the specific area where you will be traveling.

note: A four billion *colón* project is underway to construct three large bus terminals in the metropolitan area. Check upon arrival to see if it has been completed. If so, although the departure times are unlikely to change, you will have to contact the ICT (Tourism Institute) for the new departure points for selected lines. In any event, although most of the stops have remained the same for years, locations do shift, so beware!

San José

Destinations by Bus: A to Z

Departure is from San José unless otherwise noted. Times and departure points are subject to change.

Destination	Location/Times	Name/phone
Airport	Av. 2, C. 12/14. every 10 min. (5:30 AM-10 PM) Av. 2, C. 12/14. every 5 min. (4:20 AM-10 PM) every 10 min. (10 PM-midnight) Av. 2, C. 2, midnight-4:30	TUASA 222-5325 222-4650 222-4650
Alajuela	Av. 2, C. 12/14. every 10 min. (5:30 AM-10 PM) Av. 2, C. 12/14. every 5 min. (4:20 AM-10 PM) every 10 min. (10 PM-midnight) Av. 2, C. 2, midnight-4:30	TUASA 222-5325 222-4650 222-4650
Arenal	C. 16, Av. 1/3, 8:40 AM and 11:30 AM	Garage Barquero 232-5660
Brasilito	C. 20, Av. 1/3. Daily: 8, 10:30	Tralapa 221-7202
Braulio Carrillo	C. 12, Av. 7/9. Daily: every 30 min., 5:30 AM-7 PM	Coopetragua 223-1276
Butterfly Farm	C. 20/22, Av. (11, 2) (Guacima Abaja station in Alajuela) Tues.-Fri. (6:20, 9 11, 1)	
Cahuita	C. Central/1, Av. 11. Daily: 6 AM, 1:30 PM, 3:30 PM	Transportes Mepe 221-0524
Cañas	C. 16, Av. 3/5. Daily: 8:30, 10:30, 1:30, 2:15, 4:30	Transportes la Cañera 222-3006, 669-0145
Carara	C. 16, Av. Av. 1/3. Daily: 7:30, 10:30, 3:30	Transportes Morales 223-1109, 232-1829
Cartago	C. 5, Av. 18. Daily every 10 min.	Sacsa 233-5350
Ciudad Quesada (San Carlos)	C. 16, Av. 1/3. Hourly 5AM-7:30 PM	Auto Transportes Ciudad Quesada 255-4318
Coco	C. 14, Av. 1/3. Daily: 10 AM	Pulmitan 222-1650

Fortuna	C. 16, Av. 1/3, 8:40 AM and 11:30 AM	Garage Barquero 232-5660
Guápiles	C. 19/21, Av. 3. Daily, hourly: 5 AM-7 PM (to Limón) C. 12, Av. 7/9. Daily: every 30 min., 5:30 AM-7 PM	Coopelimon 223-7811 Coopetragua 223-1276
Golfito	Av. 18, C. 2/4. Daily: 7, 11, 3	Tracopa 221-4214, 223-7685
Guayabo	Turrialba C. 13, Av. 6/8. Sun., 9 AM; main terminal	556-0583
Heredia	C. 1, Av. 7/9. Daily 5AM-10 PM Av. 2, C. 10/12. Minibuses every 15 min. Midnight-6: every half-hour	Microbuses Rapidos 233-8392
Hermosa (beach) Esquivel	C. 12., Av. 5/7 . (front of Los Rodriguez) Daily: 11:30, 7	666-1249
Irazú Volcano	C. 1/3, Av. 2. (front of Gran Hotel Costa Rica). Sat., Sun., holidays	272-0651
Jacó Beach	C. 16, Av. Av. 1/3. Weekends (express): 7:15, 3:30. Daily: 7:30, 10:30, 3:30	Transportes Morales 223-1109, 232-1829
Junquillal (beach)	C. 20, Av. 3. Daily: 2 PM	Tralapa 221-7202
La Cruz	C. 14, Av. 3/5. Daily: 5, 7:45, 4:15	Carsol 224-1968
Laguna de Fraijanes (Alajuela)	3 bl. W of Central Market. Tues.-Fri. (9, noon, 4:15, 6:15) Sat., Sun. (hourly, 9-5)	COOPETRANSASI 449-5141
Lankester Gardens (Cartago)	Paraiso bus; S side of park. Daily	Coopepar 574-6127
Liberia	C. 14, Av. 1/3. Daily: 7, 9, 11:30, 1, 3, 4, 6	Pulmitan 222-1650, 666-0458
Limón	C. 19/21, Av. 3. Daily, hourly: 5 AM-7 PM	Coopelimon 223-7811
Los Chiles (Caño Negro)	C. 16, Av. 1/3. Daily: 5:30 AM, 3:30 PM	460-1301

San José

Manuel Antonio	C. 16, Av. 1/3. 6 AM, noon, 6 PM	Transportes Morales 223-5567, 777-0318
Matapalo	C. 20, Av. 1/3. Daily: 7:30, 10:30, 2, 4, 6	Tralapa 221-7202
Monteverde	C. 14, Av. 9/11. Mon.-Fri. 2:30 PM, Sat. 6:30 AM	Transportes Tilarán 222-3854
Nicoya	Av. 3/5, C. 14. Daily: 6, 8, 10 AM	Empresa Alfaro 222-2750
Nosara	C. 14, Av. 3/5. Daily: 6:15 AM	Empresa Alfaro 222-2750
Orosi Valley	(Cartago), 100 m S, 300 m W of ruins, Mon.-Fri.: 30 min. Sat., Sun.: hourly	Auto Transportes Mata 551-6810
Palmar Norte	C. 2/4, Av. 18. Daily: 5, 6:30, 8:30, 10, 2:30, 6	Tracopa 221-4214, 223-7685
Panama (beach) Esquivel	C. 12., Av. 5/7 (front of Los Rodriguez) Daily: 11:30, 7	666-1249
Paso Canoas	Av. 18, C. 2/4. Daily: 5, 7:30, 1, 4:30	Tracopa 221-4214, 223-7685
Peñas Blancasz	C. 14, Av. 3/5. Daily: 5, 7:45, 4:15	Carsol 224-1968
Potrero	C. 20, Av. 1/3. Daily: 7:30, 10:30, 2, 4, 6	Tralapa 221-7202
Puerto Jimenéz	C. 12, Av. 7/9. Daily: 6, noon	Transportes Blanco 771-2550
Puerto Viejo (Sarapiqui)	Av. 11, C. Central/1. Daily: 7, 9, 10, 1 PM, 3 PM 4, PM	
Puntarenas	C. 12, Av. 9. Daily: every 30 min., 4-9 PM	Transportes Unidas de Puntarenas 222-0064
Quepos	C. 16, Av. 1/3. 6 AM, 7AM, 10 AM, noon, 2 PM, 6 PM	Transportes Morales 223-5567, 777-0318
Río Frio	Av. 11, C. Central/1. Daily: 7, 9, 10, 1 PM, 3 PM 4, PM	
Samara	C. 14, Av. 3/5. Daily: noon	Empresa Alfaro 222-2750

San Ignacio de Acosta	C. 8, Av. 12. Every 1½ hrs. daily	
Santa Ana	Av. 2, C. 16/18. Every 15 min. until 9 PM	
Santa Elena	C. 14, Av. 9/11. Mon.-Fri. 2:30 PM, Sat. 6:30 AM	Transportes Tilarán 222-3854
San Isidro de El General	C. 16, Av. 1/3. Daily, hourly: 5:30 AM-5 PM	Musoc 222-2422
Santa María de Dota (Los Santos)	Av. 16, C. 19-21, daily 6, 9, 12:30, 3	Empresa Los Santos 223-1002
Siquirres	C. 19/21, Av. 3. Daily, hourly (to Limón): 5 AM-7 PM	Coopelimon 223-7811
Sixaola	C. Central/1, Av. 11. Daily: 6 AM, 1:30 PM, 3:30 PM	Transportes Mepe 221-0524
San Isidro de El General	C. 16, Av. 1/3. Daily, hourly: 5:30-5	Musoc 233-4160
San Vito	C. 14, Av. 3/5. Daily: 5:45, 8:15, 11:30, 2:45	Tracopa 221-4214, 223-7685
Santa Cruz	C. 20, Av. 1/3. Daily: 7:30, 10:30, 2, 4, 6	Tralapa 221-7202
Santa Rosa (entrance)	C. 14, Av. 3/5. Daily: 5, 7:45, 4:15	Carsol 224-1968
Sarchí	C. 16, Av. 1/3. 12:15, 5:30 Daily Express. (Alajuela) C. 8, Av. Central/1. Daily every 25 min.	Tuan 441-3781
Tamarindo	C. 20, Av. 3/5. Daily: 3:30	Alfaro 222-2750, 223-8229
Turrialba	C. 13, Av. 6/8. Daily, hourly	Transtusa 556-0073
Volcán Poás	C. 12, Av. 2/4. 8:30 (Sun., holidays)	223-4481
Zarcero	C. 16, Av. 1/3. Hourly: 5AM-7:30 PM	Auto Transportes Ciudad Quesada 255-4318

San José

BY AIR: Government-owned and subsidized **SANSA** (☎ 221-9414, 233-0397, 233-3258, fax 255-2176) flies daily or several times weekly between San José and Tamarindo, Nosara, Samara, Quepos, Golfito, and Coto 47 near the border with Panama. Their office is just off Paseo de Colón on C. 24. SANSA operates shuttle buses to and from the airport. (For more information on SANSA, see the "Introduction.") Another, newer airline is privately owned **Travelair** (☎ 220-3054, 232-7883 fax 220-0413), which flies from San José to Barra del Colorado, Quepos, Golfito, Puerto Jiménez, Tambor, Palmar Sur, Limón, Nosara, Tamarindo, Punta Islita, and Carrillo. Like SANSA, it leaves from Pavas. While its flights are two or three times as expensive as SANSA's, they are markedly more reliable. In addition, they fly on Sun. to and from Tamarindo, Carrillo, Palmar Sur, Quepos, and Golfito. To get a copy of their latest schedule, check with a travel agent or fax them at 220-0413.

> ☞ **Traveler's Tip**. Costa Rica may also be used as a staging point for a trip to Cuba. LACSA has three weekly flights, and the cost (including airfare) is around $350-500 for four to seven nights, including meals. US citizens will not have their passport stamped and can pay for everything in Cuba using greenbacks – the preferred currency! Contact a travel agent or Cubatur Travel Agency. Also, when departing by air, be sure to keep $15 handy for the airport tax.

Vicinity of San José

HORSEBACK RIDING: Many excursions are available from San José. Average cost runs around $60-$80. All provide transport both ways. At Rancho Redondo, 30 minutes E of the city, **Hotel-Hacienda San Miguel** (☎ 229-1094, fax 221-3871) gives a cloud forest tour. Breakfast and lunch are included. Offering a trip through pasture and along the beach, **L.A. Tours** (☎ 221-4501) visits a farm near Orotina. Breakfast and lunch are included. **Magic Trails** (☎ 253-8146/8160) has a trip to Hacienda Reyes with two routes – along the pasture or through steep Prusia reserve and up to Irazú. Lunch and a snack are included. With rides to Jacó or into the forest, **Rainbow Tours** (☎ 233-8228) has a trip to Rancho Nuevo that includes breakfast, lunch, and refreshments. **Robles Tours** (☎ 237-2116, fax 237-1976), on a farm at Sacramento bordering Parque Nacional Braulio Carrillo, takes you on a ride with panoramic vistas. An oxcart trip is also available. **Tipical Tours** (☎ 233-8466) offers a quetzal search (sightings not guaranteed) up Cerro de la Muerte through cloud forest terrain.

BUNGEE JUMPING: This rather unusual pastime appeals to those who wish to get their adrenalin up and roaring. After being strapped into a harness, you dive 280 ft (86 m) off the top of a bridge (the Puente Negro) into a tropical jungle canyon. You fly until you hit the end of the cord, then rebound, and fall again and again. After the rebounds stop, you find yourself hanging suspended over the canyon. Depending upon the company, either a line is lowered and you hook yourself on to it to be hauled up or you are lowered to the river, unharnessed, and then climb up a rocky slope to return. There are two systems: European and US. Under the US system, the line consists of three to four elastic cords, originally designed by the US military to parachute tanks or jeeps from planes. The European system consists of a specially made elastic cord attached to a thick rope. The harnesses differ in design as well. Contact **Saragundí Specialty Tours** (☎ 255-0011/2055) at Av. 7, C. Central/1a; their Bungy-Bus leaves from the front of the Hotel Costa Rica at 9 AM. Also try **Tropical Bungee** (☎ 233-6455), or **ASP** (☎ 222-4547). Depending upon the company, residents pay about $30-$40 for a jump; tourists pay $40-$55. Spectators pay $4-$5 RT. If you are pregnant and/or have back or neck problems, avoid bungee jumping.

Parque Nacional de Diversiones/Pueblo Antiguo

Ideal either for children or the child in you, this amusement park has a variety of rides. Food here is mostly fast (i.e., greasy), so bring your own nibbles. Pueblo Antiguo, the recreated village in the park, offers a chance to visit a sugar mill, a country store, and a coffee factory, as well as ride through a replica of the famous canals leading to Tortuguero. Its three areas are labeled "the City," "the Country," and "The Coast." Each attempts to recreate the atmosphere of the years 1880-1930. It also has a recreated indigenous settlement, a fish aquarium housed in a Spanish galleon, and a cocoa plant that shows the steps in processing. Professional actors provide ambience. It is a few km W of Hospital Mexico. You should exit the main highway there and take an access road running parallel to the main highway. Catch a bus from Av. 6, C. 10/12 to get here. Admission for foreigners is around $7, and admission to all shows and rides is $30. For more information ☎ 296-2212.

Parque del Este

Situated in the hills above San Pedro in San Rafael de Montes de Oca, this park has a jogging and exercise trail, pool, soccer field, basketball courts, playgrounds, picnic tables, a nature trail, and great views. It's open daily, except Mon., until 4. Admission is around 50¢. Take the *San Ramón de Tres Ríos* bus from Av. 2, C. 5/7.

San José

San José & Surrounding Area

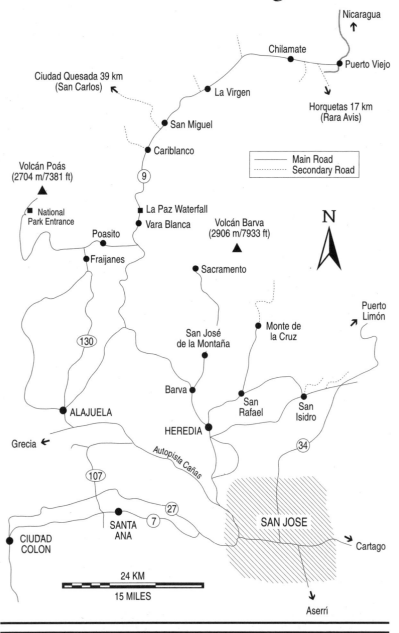

Nicaragua

Chilamate

Puerto Viejo

Ciudad Quesada 39 km
(San Carlos)

La Virgen

Horquetas 17 km
(Rara Avis)

San Miguel

Cariblanco

	Main Road
	Secondary Road

Volcán Poás
(2704 m/7381 ft)

9

National
Park Entrance

La Paz Waterfall

Vara Blanca

Volcán Barva
(2906 m/7933 ft)

Poasito

N

Fraijanes

Sacramento

Puerto
Limón

130

San José
de la Montaña

Monte de
la Cruz

ALAJUELA

Barva

San
Rafael

San
Isidro

Grecia

HEREDIA

Autopista Cañas

34

107

27

SAN JOSE

SANTA
ANA

7

CIUDAD
COLON

Cartago

24 KM

15 MILES

Aserrí

Moravia

Named after Juan Rafael Mora and located seven km NE of San José, the shops in this slow-paced small town feature everything from furniture to leather work. Its most famous shop is **Caballo Blanco**, set on one corner of the plaza. Others include **La Rueda** and **El Potro**. Eat at **Soda San Martín**. **Rincón Europeo** (☎ 235-8678) is for the gourmet set and offers Hungarian food. Hotels here are listed under "outlying accommodation" in the San José accommodation section.

getting here: Take the bus from Av. 3, C. 3/5 or the microbus from Av. 7, C. 6 and disembark at the main stop, two blocks before the main square. From the town, it's 10 km to San Jerónimo de Moravia, another 10 km from the boundaries of Parque Nacional Braulio Carrillo.

Coronado

Actually a collection of three villages – San Antonio, Dulce Nombre, and San Isidro – this country town has a Gothic-style church and good views of San José. **Club Mediterráneo** (☎ 229-0661) is the local gourmet restaurant. They celebrate their *fiestas patronales* on February 15. If you're coming by car, you can head seven km E to Las Nubes, where you will find **Cronopios** (☎ 229-6283; call for times), a restaurant with an attractive atmosphere serving soups, salads, and apple pie.

Snake Milking!

Undoubtedly one of the most unusual places to visit in the Americas, the **Instituto Clodomiro Picando** (☎ 229-0344/0335, fax 292-0485) is situated one km before the town of Dulce Nombre de Coronado on the right side. It is named for its antivenin researcher, Dr. Clodomiro Picado Twight (1887-1944), and was opened in 1972. The institute researches snakes and processes venom into antivenin serum. Held every Fri. afternoon from 1:30 to 3:30, the "milking" demonstration is something no serpent lover will want to miss. A *terciopelo* is pinned down with a hook, then picked up firmly but gingerly. With its jaws pried open, the snake's fangs are pressed against the netting of the venom collection cannister. A pale milk is expelled and the process is repeated again and again. As part of the show, a small *terciopelo* is fed to a *zopilota*, which is immune to its venom. The *zopilata* slowly crushes and then eats it.

One of the smallest, but certainly the most frightening snake, is the *culebra del mar*, found on the Pacific coast from California to Chile, for which there is no serum available. Fortunately, only 10 people have been bitten by it during the past decade. The *biblo la diablo* and the *lora* are small, green, poisonous snakes. Found in Guanacaste, the cascabel rattler is less aggressive than the *terciopelo*. Then there's the coral snake, with its distinctive red, yellow, and black coloring; the false coral, which alternates red, black, and yellow; a boa constrictor that hisses and snaps; and the aggressive bushmaster or *matabuey*. The afternoon's apex comes with the display of the two Asiatic cobras. Mice are crushed to death with giant tweezers and fed to the snakes. Then, in case you came late, there's another display of milking. The booklet, *Aspetos Básicos sobre las Serpientes de Costa Rica,* offers a thorough (albeit Spanish-only) introduction to the nation's snakes. It's open 8-noon, and 1-4, Mon. to Fri. To get here, take a bus from Moravia or from Av. 5, C. 3/5. On the way back, it's a pleasant stroll down to Moravia, less than an hour away.

Aserrí

Situated 10 km past the working-class suburbs of Desamparados and San Rafael, Aserrí, with its clean country atmosphere and whitewashed church, provides a welcome break from the polluted urban environment. Take a bus here from C. 2, Av. 6/8. Check out the large religious statuary by the church altar. **La Piedra de Aserrí** (Rock of Aserrí), SW of town, is a precariously balanced, 90-ft (30-m) boulder with a cave at its base. According to local legend, the witch Na Zárate lived here and would walk the slopes to guard her hidden treasure. **Chicharronera Cacique Acserí** (sic) offers menus carved on pieces of wood shaped like a smiling pig. Bands play on weekends (☎ 230-3088).

El Rodeo

The largest expanse of rainforest still extant on the Meseta Central, this area is just outside of Ciudad Colón, a 30-minute bus ride (from Coca Cola) to the W of San José. Disembark in Ciudad Colón, 300 m before the Plaza Central, and walk three km N (heading to the R). Watch out for the *cementerio,* which is some 500 m from the main road; ask any local for assistance. Take the road to the right from the cemetery, which will head E about one km before starting the descent to El Rodeo. On the way, you'll pass Finca Obla-Di-Obla-Da on the right before reaching the basin, where you cross a stream. Of the well-trodden trails here, one leads up to the **University of Peace**. This unusual university offers a four-month study program in "international indigenous studies," bringing together indigenous people from all over the Americas. Tours of **Radio For Peace International** (☎ 249-1821 for times) are also offered. There are restaurants in Ciudad Colón.

Reserva Guayabo

To get to this Indian reserve, take the *Santiago Puriscal* bus from Coca Cola, C. 16, Av. 1/3. Leaving approximately every 45 minutes and taking about an hour, the trip proceeds through rolling countryside, climbing with hairpin turns and spectacular drops. This chilly reserve, located at Km 30, is home of the Quitirrsí Native Americans, who are noted for their basketweaving ability. Puriscal, at the end of the line, is mainly of note for its seismic activity. This was the epicenter for thousands of tremors during 1990. Its name derives from *purisco*, the time that the beans begin to blossom. If driving in the dry season, an attractive return route is via Acosta (San Ignacio), an unpaved road.

Arbofilia

Operating in the Puriscal area, Arbofilia (☎/fax 240-7145; Apdo. 312, Tibas) is involved with "ecological regeneration" – replanting formerly forested land with native species in an attempt to mimic natural patterns. This type of "analog forest" grows on a two-acre tract where farmers have created a pesticide-free field that includes cacao, citrus trees, pejibaye palms, and other species. The idea is to create a complimentary community which will result in increased yield. Biologists work together with *campesinos*. The latter donate labor while the former provide seeds and training in grafting, greenhouse use, and in tree planting techniques. **Jungle Trails** (☎ 255-3486) offers tours. To contact Arbofilia, ☎ 235-5470 or write Apdo. 312, Tibas.

San Antonio de Escazú

Brightly painted oxcarts ply the streets of this Mediterranean-flavored mountain town, which has a church, colorful adobe houses with outdoor ovens, and views of Volcán Barva and San José. Eat at **Hotel Mirador**, **Pico Blanco** or **Tiquicía**, all with legendary views. Take a bus from C. 16, Av. Central/1. If you only want to go to the preceding town of Escazú, noted for its expatriate community, board a bus at Av. 1, C. 16/18.

San José

Pico Blanco

This reserve protects the surrounding water supply of Escazú. From San Antonio (above), walk uphill from the Parque Central; all roads converge on the reserve. After passing a goat farm and continuing on for several hundred meters, the road winds around the mountain and you lose sight of San José. To the right, you'll see the rainforest. Either head straight up through the large expanse of pasture or continue along the road that wends its way up the mountain. You'll eventually regain sight of the city. Pico Alajuelita can be recognized by the cross that adorns its top. The trails are not clearly marked. Avoid the side trails, which go nowhere. Watch for mythical creatures believed to inhabit the area and go early to avoid the afternoon fog.

Lomas de Ayarco

This affluent neighborhood on the way to Cartago has some of the nation's most opulent dwellings. Robert Vesco's former mansion has room for up to 25 cars in its enclosed driveway. The incredible extravagance of these houses contrasts dramatically with the rural poverty so evident elsewhere. It's as though the rich were spitting in the face of the nation's poor, who struggle to eke out a living.

Los Juncos

This cloud forest reserve is less than an hour from San José. Tours will take you to the reserve's farmhouse for breakfast, around a trail, back for lunch, around another trail, and back to San José. It's also possible to overnight here. Call **Senderos de Iberoamérica** (also known as Green Tropical Tours; ☎/fax 255-2859; Apdo. 675-2200, Coronado). E-mail: greentp@sol.racsa.co.cr. Write Dept. 252, PO Box 025216, Miami FL 33102.

Grecia

This pineapple cultivation and sugar processing center has a church roofed in dark red painted metal. Be sure to visit the workshop of **Paul Smith** (☎ 444-6990), an instrument maker who was one of Monteverde's first settlers.

ACCOMMODATION: You may stay at **Cabaña Los Cipreses, Cabinas Los Trapiches**, or low-budget **Pensión Quirós. La Posada de**

Grecia (☎ 494-2000, fax 494-4660) is a bed and breakfast in the town center across from the park. Rates are around $30, including tax and a continental breakfast. The **Healthy Day Inn** (☎/fax 444-5903) is an apartotel with pool, Jacuzzi, tennis, massage, horseback riding, and restaurant. It's on the road to Sarchí and charges around $30 pp, including breakfast. The **Posada Mimosa** (☎/fax 444-5156) is a new bed and breakfast offering massage therapy, hebal treatments, a pool, and trails. In Canada, ☎ 905-842-4598 or fax 905-842-6458.

near Grecia: **Posada Las Palomas** (☎/fax 661-2401) is an attractive bed and breakfast set on a coffee plantation and fruit farm. It has a small nature reserve with a trail. Rooms and cabins are available; rates are in the luxury range. It's in the hamlet of Rosario, between the Grecia and Naranjo exits on the Interamerican Highway.

Sarchí

This is the nation's most famous crafts center, where family-run workshops make painted oxcarts using traditional designs that have been passed on for generations. The compulsion to paint controls the residents here to the point that even the bus stops and garbage cans are decorated! Souvenirs – including napkin holders, salad bowls, and jewelry – are also made for the tourist market. Visit the **Joaquín Chaverri** factory and sales outlet. Before leaving town, be sure to note the bi-towered, multi-windowed **church**.

OX CART HISTORY: Popularized during the late 1800s, thousands of ox carts (*carretas*) once traversed a muddy road between the Central Valley and Puntarenas, hauling the nation's coffee bean harvest to port for export. Today, the ones produced for tourists bear little resemblance to the comparatively crude originals. The cart wheels came to be decorated with flowers and geometric designs and each cart was designed to produce its own individual sound by a metal ring striking the wheel's hubnut; this was intended to allow the owner to keep track of his workers. Ox carts are displayed in the **Ox Cart Museum**, an old adobe-style house in Salitral de Desamparados, open 10-4. **The Butterfly Valley** (☎ 454-4050) offers tours daily from 8:30-4; US$6 entrance.

GETTING HERE: To get here take the hourly Grecia bus from Coca Cola and connect there with the Alajuela-Sarchí bus. In terms of time, this is better than going to Alajuela and then changing. By car, take the Grecia exit and then turn left behind the church, circle it to the left, and then go three blocks to the right, where a road branches off diagonally for Sarchí. If heading for Naranjo from Sarchí, follow old and scenic Carr. 1. The one place to stay here is in Sarchí Norte. The eight-room

San José

Villas Sarchí Albergue (☎ 454-4644, fax 454-4006;Apdo 34, Sarchí Norte) charges around $30 s, $40 d, including breakfast. It has a pool and offers tours of the area. Transport from the airport is complimentary.

Los Trapiches

If you would like to see how *tapa dulce* (hardened brown sugar) is made, this is the place. The antique cane press (of Scottish vintage) is water-wheel-driven. The runoff cane juice is collected and heated before being poured into molds. There's also a restaurant (☎ 444-6656), pools, and a small lake with rental boats. It's popular on weekends with Ticos and closed on Wed. Make sure the press is operating before you go (☎ 444-6656). From Grecia, drive three blocks past the church, turn left onto Carr. 13, and then follow the signs. Admission is under $1.

Los Chorros

A rough but short trail leads from the road to these falls, which are popular on weekends. From Tacáres, to the W of Alajuela, turn right at the church and head left for two km until the road ends. Ignore the sign prohibiting entrance and follow the path downhill. When you reach the quarry, turn left and then follow the path to the left.

Ojo de Agua

The name means literally "Eye of Water." Here, 200 liters of water per second (6,000 gallons per minute) gush out from underground springs, filling three big swimming pools. Bordering are tennis courts and a lake with rowboats. A mini-gymnasium, five new picnic shelters, and multi-purpose playing courts were added in 1993, and an ampitheater and natural garden of waterfalls is planned. You'll have plenty of chances to meet locals here on weekends. Entrance is around $1. A few km S of Alajuela and to the SE of the airport, Ojo de Agua can be reached by bus from Alajuela, Heredia, or from near Coca Cola at Av. 1, C. 20/22 in San José. Buses run about every half-hour on weekdays and every 15 minutes on weekends.

Butterfly Farm

This farm – one of the largest of its kind in the world and one of the more recent attractions on San José's outskirts – exports butterflies to

Europe. You will witness all stages of the butterfly lifecycle from egg-laying to chrysalis-forming. A highlight of the tour is a ride in a specially designed nine-passenger ox cart, pulled by oxen named Precious and Darling. A 1½-hour bee tour has been added. It illustrates the lives of European and indigenous stingless bees, explaining their role in the environment. The entire farm is now open to visitors. Admission is around $12 for adults and $2 for children (a 1½-hr. guided tour is included). Locals and residents pay considerably less. A restaurant serves Tico and US-style fare.

getting here: Unless you have a car, this can be difficult. It is SW of the airport in La Guácima; you have to take a bus at 11 from Av. 1, C. 20/22 (marked as "San Antonio/Ojo de Agua") and get off at the terminal. From that point follow signs to the farm, which is about 1,000 ft (300 m) away. The trip takes one hour and the return bus leaves at 3:15. A direct bus is now running on Mon., Tues., and Thurs., with three trips daily from the major hotels. For info about buses from Alajuela or Santa Ana, ☎ 438-0115.

La Garita & Environs

This area is becoming increasingly popular as its attractions continue to grow. For La Garita, proceed to Alajuela and then take the La Garita bus. If you're driving, get off at the Atenas turnoff on the Cañas Highway. Accommodation in this area is listed under the "San José Accommodation" section. Just 20 minutes from San José, you'll find the nation's closest approximation of Disneyland. Set 1.5 km to the left of the Fiesta de Maíz (see below), **Bosque Encantado** (Enchanted Forest, ☎ 487-7050) consists of a castle set by a lake, with storybook characters wandering the grounds. It's open on Sat. and Sun. from 8:30-4:30. As the playground and other facilities have not been maintained, it's now visited chiefly for the pool, which is generally crowded. About 3½ km to the right after the Atenas turnoff, follow the billboards to the **Zoo Ave** (☎ 433-8989, fax 433-9140), an exotic bird collection with about 60 species. They also have deer, monkeys and other wildlife on hand. (Open daily 9-4:30; $5 admission; $1.50 for nationals; $1.50 for children.) They are attempting to breed and reintroduce a variety of native species (such as the endangered macaw and the great currasow) to the wild. The zoo is not for profit and the money is put back into wildlife protection.

FOOD: The La Garita area has a number of dining alternatives. **Las Delicias de Maíz** offers the entire range of native maize dishes from corn stew to cheese *tortillas*. Free samples are offered. It's open Fri. to Sun. and is about 2½ km on the left after the Atenas turnoff. Also in the area is **La Llorita/The Green Parrot** (☎ 487-7846) – an attractively decorated restaurant that offers wood-roasted meat dishes (no parrots) as well as salads, sandwiches, and fruit drinks. Take the hourly Atenas bus from Coca Cola to get here. **Chatelle Country Resort (☎ 487-7781)** serves dishes from a different nation daily. Finally, the **Mi Quinta** is a restaurant that also has two pools, dance floor, basketball and volleyball courts, and TVs. A modest admission is charged.

The Meseta Central

This is the nation's principal area, analogous to the Boston-Washington corridor in North America. Although it is also densely populated and contains the nation's capital, the area's size, industrialization, and level of pollution are on a much smaller scale.

This 20-by-50-mile (32-by-80-km) "plateau" – really more a series of valleys intersected by rolling hills – still retains a primarily agricultural base. Much of the land has been shaped by the numerous volcanic eruptions which, over the eons, have also given the soil its fertility. In addition to San José, this region also includes the towns of Heredia, Alajuela, Cartago, and Turrialba, along with many smaller villages.

Although it is sometimes referred to as the "Switzerland of Central America," the area is Swiss only in its orderliness. There is nothing Swiss about either its poverty or its climate. Verdant and shimmering fields of sugarcane grow in the E. Elsewhere, the ever-present coffee colors the landscape in shades that vary from shiny green to red according to the season. Acres of plastic-covered houseplants and flowers being grown for export are another feature on the landscape. Factories are interspersed with pastures and hills covered by coffee plants. You'll see the occasional sugar processing plant, macadamia plantations, a man hacking sugar cane, and teams of men and women picking coffee. However, not all is pastoral paradise. During the rainy season dark grey clouds loom menacingly over hills, and deforestation is always appallingly evident, with treeless plots edging up to the tops of hills. **note:** For organizational convenience, areas on the periphery of the Meseta Central are also included in this section.

EXPLORING: As local wags have it, outside of San José there is a nation called Costa Rica. The Meseta Central is one of the best places to begin exploring that nation. There are three charming provincial capitals (Alajuela, Cartago, and Heredia), dramatic volcanoes, winding roads and rivers, hot springs, old churches, and much more. If you have only time to do a few things, you'll have to choose carefully. Buses are generally plentiful, and the area is perfect for day or overnight trips. The more adventurous you are here, the more substantive your experience will be, and the more memories you'll have to take back home with you.

Suggestions for Exploring the Central Valley

Here are just a few things you might choose to do in this area. All are detailed (along with others) in the text.
- ☐ Go swimming at Acúa Mania (page 194)
- ☐ Visit Irazú (page 281) or Poás volcanes (page 258)
- ☐ Take the Café Britt tour (page 264)
- ☐ Visit Cartago with its cathedral (page 274)
- ☐ Take a stroll around Alajuela (page 253) or Heredia (page 261)
- ☐ Visit the Orosi Valley (page 282), Lankester Gardens (page 276), and/or Tapanti National Park (page 284)
- ☐ See the snake milking at the Instituto Clormido Picando (page 245)
- ☐ Visit the Jewels of the Humid Tropics collection (page 262)
- ☐ Climb Turrialba volcano (page 288)
- ☐ Go white water rafting (page 293)

Alajuela

This pleasant town (pop. 35,000) is located near the airport, just 17 miles (23 km, a 20-minute ride) W of the capital. Founded in 1790, Alajuela is a center for sugar processing, cattle marketing, and small industry. As in other towns, every part is accessible on foot.

GETTING HERE: Take a microbus from San José's Av. 2, C. 12/14; they leave every 15 minutes until midnight and then on the hour. To get here by car, take "la pista" (the Cañas Highway) and exit at the turnoff near the airport.

HISTORY: Originally named La Lajuela in 1657, the town's name was changed to Villa Hermosa, then to San Juan de Nepomucena, before becoming Alajuela (pronounced ah-lah-HWEL-lah) in 1825. Today, it is the capital of the province of the same name.

SIGHTS: A number of three-toed sloths reside in the trees of its charming bandstand-equipped **plaza**. The park's nickname is *"El Parque de los Palomas Muertas"* (The Park of the Dead Doves) and it resembles a cross between a garden and a forest. *Paloma* also refers to the male sexual organ in Panamanian slang, and some contend the name derives from the nature of the park's occupants – retirees who come to stare at lovely young things as they pass by. On its borders are a number of solidly constructed buildings from the era when coffee dominated the local economy. One of these is the teacher's training college. It shares the building with the **Museo de Juan Santamaría** (open Tues.-Sun. 10-6; free admission) which has displays on the war against William Walker.

A remodeled colonial-style *carcel* (jail) dating from 1874, the museum is a pleasant place to sit, more of interest for its ambience than its content. With a dome-shaped roof covered with bright red corrugated metal, the white-columned **cathedral** stands in front of the park. Its interior is more ornate and spacious than those in other towns, and it has large religious statuary – including a very realistic Jesus bleeding and nailed to the cross. This is to the L of the altar in the center of the cupola. There's also an image of the Black Virgin, along with a small, wall-mounted cabinet filled with arms, legs, and other body parts, in case you missed the displays in the cathedral in Cartago. Although it doesn't show now, the cupola, its false balconies and curtains rendered in paint, cracked in half during the March 1990 quake. Some of the town's other buildings suffered fissures. To get to **Iglesia La Agonia**, walk along the edge of the square. You will pass the cupola of the church. Its facade contrasts sharply with the ultra-modern reflective glass bank directly across the street. Continue until you see the immense structure on the R. If it's closed, ask at the shop to get in. Inside, there's a Renaissance-like portrait of Our Mother of Perpetual Sorrow, a brown Christ suspended above the altar, and a number of large murals. One statue depicts a priest holding a cross with a miniature Jesus on it, a skull and flowers resting at his feet. Another town park, a block to the N at C. 2, Av. 3, is named after Juan Santamaría, and his statue is across the way.

FESTIVALS AND EVENTS: Held in Alajeula in April, the **Día de Juan Santamaría** commemorates Juan Santamaría, Costa Rica's only national hero and the town's pride and joy. There is a parade, complete with marching bands and majorettes. The **Mango Festival**, held in July, is the highlight of Alajuela's year, offering nine days of parades, music, outdoor food markets, and arts and crafts fairs.

ACCOMMODATIONS: From a town with only one respectable hotel just a few years ago, Alajuela has attracted a hotel boom. Near the plaza, **Hotel Alajuela** (☎ 441-1241, fax 441-7912) is inexpensively priced and very popular; it also has a few furnished apartments. The rooms in the old portion of the building are the least expensive. The eight-room **Islands Inn** (☎ 442-0573) is set five blocks E of the main square. Rates are around $25 s, $40 d, and breakfast is included. The owner, David Quesada, is a young US-educated Tico who enjoys collecting frogs and raising orchids. An inexpensive bed and breakfast with weekly and monthly rates, **Hospedaje La Posada** is 100 m N and 75 m E from the Red Cross (Cruz Roja), which is three blocks E from the park. **Hotel Villa Real** (☎ 441-4856; call after 4 PM) is an old home which has inexpensive rooms; it's 100 m N and 100 m E of the Parque Central.

Miraflores Apartments (☎/fax 442-6527) are 150 m E, then 50 S, and then 50 E again from McDonalds. Set 700 m N of Parque Central on the way to Tuetal, **Paraíso Tropical Hotel** (☎/fax 441-4882) offers rooms (around $40 d) and apartments ($65) in a garden setting. Less expensive low-class hotels include **El Real** (C. 8, Av. 1/Central), **Moderno** (down the street across the RR tracks), and **El Tucano** (☎ 487-7192) at Turrucales.

outlying accommodations: Situated on eight acres of land three km N of Alajuela, Canadian-run **Tuetal Lodge** (☎ 442-1804) is in Tuetal Norte, two km from Alajuela, and has cabins, treehouses, and camping. Water is solar heated and organic fruits and vegetables are grown in the garden. Camping costs around $5 s, $7 d; treehouses rent for about $9 s, $12 d, and cabins start from $30 s, $35 d; more expensive ones have kitchenettes. Tents are also available for rent. Outside of town and enroute to the town of Poás, attractive **Orquideas Inn** (☎ 433-9346 or fax 433-9740), set in a converted *hacienda* house, offers expensive rooms ($70 d), which include breakfast. Geodesic dome bungalows are planned, and there is a good gift shop. It also has a pool and offers excursions. Write Apdo. 394, Alajuela, or ☎ 800-525-0280 in the US or 800-231-0856 internationally. Set two km from the airport, the relatively new and expensive **Apartotel El Erizo** (☎/fax 441-2840) offers cable TV, one- or two-bedroom apartments, and babysitters. Write Apdo. 61-4050 Alajuela. Just a couple of minutes from the airport, **Hampton Inn** (☎ 443-0043) has rooms with continental breakfast and pool. Rates are around $59 s, $60 d plus tax. In the US, ☎ 800-426-7866. The luxury-priced **El Colibrí** (☎/fax 441-4228) is a set of houses near the Zeta free trade zone, which is W of the airport. Facilities include pool, tennis, and basketball courts. In the Plias de San Isidro area, the luxury-priced **Hotel Buena Vista** (☎/fax 443-2214) is set amidst a coffee plantation. Rooms have cable TV sets and balconies. It has a gourmet restaurant and offers tremendous views. Also don't overlook the nearby Cariari and Herradura ultra-luxury hotels, reviewed under the "San José Accommodations" section.

Meseta Central

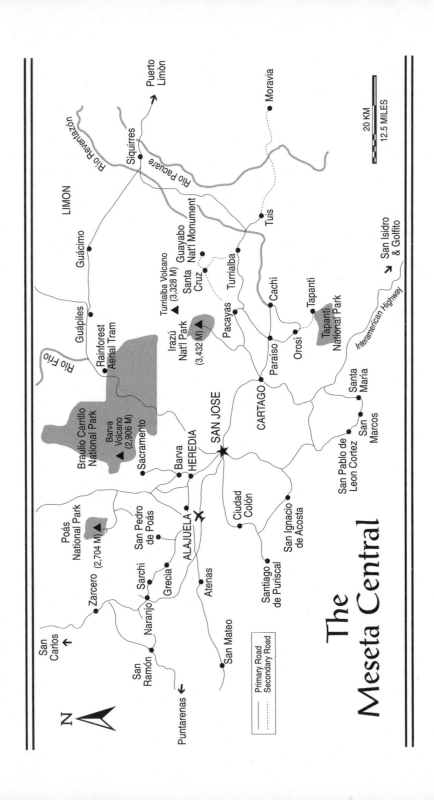

The Meseta Central

FOOD AND SHOPPING: One of the best restaurants is the **Cencerro,** upstairs on Av. Central across from the plaza. **Restaurant El Primer Sabor** serves international and Chinese dishes in an attractive atmosphere. **La Jarra,** at C. 2 and Av. 2, upstairs and a block S from the square, is less expensive and has salads, fish, and shrimp. With country and rock music, **Joey's** serves *norteamericano* and Tico dishes. It's on the S side of the park. **La Cocina de Leña** has traditional Tico dishes with a good selection of seafood. You can also try **Bar Marisquería Evelyn,** to the right of the *museo* and down towards the square. **La Troja,** across the street and just down from the *museo,* has a sophisticated art and jazz atmosphere; a good place to bring a hot date. Live music is also featured here. Right at the park, **Las Américas** (☎ 441-5691) is an "American Bar & Restaurant" boasting no fewer than six TVs plus video projection. They hold an annual Superbowl party. **Asami** (☎ 442-7646) is an authentic Japanese restaurant serving *sashimi, sushi,* and combination platters. It's 75 m N of Pops, near the old church.

Plaza Garibaldi offers open-air Mexican dining with traditional dishes. Specializing in seafood, **La Esquina de los Mariscos** is also open-air and has goodies such as octopus and paella. The specialty of **Marisqueria La Sirenita** is its seafood soup. Just outside of town on the road to Grecia, **Rancho Las Tinajitas** is a good restaurant, serving meat and seafood dishes at a reasonable price. Open daily, the **Mercado Central** (central market) is a fascinating place to eat and to explore. There's also a giant outdoor market every Sat. AM. Although considered a farmer's market, it's actually run by the ubiquitous middlemen, the bane of Costa Rica's marketplace economy. Every type of vegetable and fruit imaginable is for sale. Huge trucks at the rear unload and sell bananas, enormous Japanese-style pumpkins are sawed up, and young boys sell bundles of garlic with all of the enthusiasm of country preachers. Most of the produce is sold in one long row of stalls, each of which is topped with multicolored, beach ball-like umbrellas. A block and a half W of the plaza on Av. Central, **ItalPan** is one of many bakeries. There's not much to buy in town (save for some remarkably tacky souvenirs), but if you're in the market for a casket, there's a great place just 100 ft (30 m) to the left of the *museo.* The **Russian Tea Terrace** (☎/fax 433-9257), located in Tambor on the way to Poás, is a gourmet restaurant opened in 1995. It features dishes such as spicy eggplant, hot borscht, and Russian strudel.

EVENTS AND FESTIVALS: Soccer games are held most Sundays at the stadium. **La Guácima** (☎ 233-3166) has car and motorcycle races every weekend.

Meseta Central

SERVICES: The **Welcome Center** (☎/fax 441-1141; Av. 2, C. 2/4) provides information; it is twinned with the Alajuela Travel Agency next door. It also contains **Central Valley Services**, which offers property management, financial services, and sells real estate. The **ICT** (Tourism Institute; ☎ 233-1733) has a branch office at Av. 4, C. 1/3. **Farmacía Unica** is at the NW corner of the Mercado Central. A former country club, **Campestre del Sol** (☎ 442-0077) has swimming pools, gymnasium, dance hall; open Tues. through Sun., 8-4.

FROM ALAJUELA: Alajuela makes an excellent base for exploring the Meseta Central. A special bus leaves for Poás at 8 AM on Sun. from the S side of the church. Attractions at **La Garita** are described under "Vicinity of San José."

Poás Volcano

(Parque Nacional Volcán Poás)

The world's largest geyser-type crater, Poás is protected in a national park. Its name derives from the thorny bush that grows on its upper slopes. Along with Irazú, Poás is one of the world's most popular volcanoes. Over 500,000 visitors are expected by 1996. Located 23 miles (37 km) from Alajuela and 37 miles (59 km) from San José, it last erupted in 1978, but its crater still boils and steams. As you progress toward its 8,871-ft (2,704-m) summit, the weather becomes cloudier and cooler and coffee plantations give way to pastures filled with dairy cattle and terraced potato patches.

GETTING HERE: A bus runs from the SE corner of Parque Braulio Carrillo (formerly known as Parque Merced) in San José at 8:30 on Sun. and holidays; be there by 7:30 to assure a seat. The ride, in an exquisitely funky "Bluebird" brand bus, takes 2½ hours (including a 20-minute rest stop, where you can breakfast briefly). The bus arrives at 11 and returns at 2:30. Another bus leaves at 9 AM from the SE corner of the plaza in Alajuela. An alternative is to take an hourly bus from Alajuela's Parque de Cemetario to San Pedro de Poás, and then take a taxi (about $20 RT) from there; or go by bus to Poasito, 10 km (six miles) from the crater. Bring along some snacks or a box lunch, a sweater or jacket, and rain gear all year round. If you're driving, take the expressway to Alajuela and then proceed via San Pedro de Poás and Poasito. Another route is to go through Heredia, Barva, Los Cartagos, and Poasito. Admission is charged at the going rate for *gringos*; no more than 1,800 people are permitted in the park at any one time.

ORIENTATION: The first thing you find at the crater is the visitor's center – newly overhauled in 1993 following damage caused by acid rain. It has a slide show in Spanish about the National Parks at 11 and 1, as well as **Cafetería Botos**, a Café Britt concession. There's also the Neotropical Foundation's **Nature Store**, which sells books and crafts. A road leads up to the two lookout points over the volcano. If you've never seen an active volcano before, you're in for an amazing sight. It's approximately 2.4 miles (3.8 km) wide and 1,000 ft (300 m) deep; the lake on the bottom has somewhat muddy waters that change colors depending upon the degree of volcanic activity. If you're lucky, you might see a small eruption of sulphur dioxide and mud, and you might spot bubbling pools of molten sulphur if the water level is low enough.

From the road leading to the crater there's a short trail to Botos Lake, highlighted by a number of *sombrilla de pobre* (poor people's umbrella) plants and dwarf trees. Once believed to have a whirlpool that would suck unwary swimmers through a passage into the active crater, this lake is fed entirely by rainwater, and hosts algae, shrimp, and various species of frogs and toads. Its greenish color is due to the presence of sulfur in colloidal suspension. There is no access down to the lake, and there is only one other trail: the *Sendero Escalonia* runs from the picnic tables past wooden trail markers inscribed with poetic paeans to the environs.

HISTORY: Out of a total of five craters formed, Lake Botos was number three in the line; the present active crater was number five. Although the first European, Mata Guevara, reached the crater at an unknown date, its first mention in a written document was in 1783 and a priest named Arias, arriving in 1815 from Alajuela, baptized it with the name Juan de Dios. The other names, Poás and Votos or Botos, by which the crater has been known, are thought to be the names of indigenous tribes that lived in the area. Curiously, a tourist hotel was built one km from the crater in 1915; it closed in 1924, and no trace remains today. Eruptions have occurred 20 times since 1834 – notably in 1888, 1904, 1905, 1910 (when it shot a fountain of water four km into the air) and from 1952 to 1954. After things settled down, a cone of ash and debris had formed at the site of the lake, which had refilled with water by 1967 and hasn't changed much since. Comprising 13,138 acres (5,317 ha), the Parque Nacional Volcán Poás was established on January 30, 1971. Since 1989, the crater has again become increasingly active, and the sulfur gas and steam ejected have caused acid rain, resulting in the destruction of 75% of Grecia's 1989 coffee crop and causing skin and respiratory problems. Problems accelerated during 1994 when 400 tourists had to be evacuated one day, and many farmers in the area had from 80-100% of their crops destroyed. In addition, some 173 head of cattle suffered from diarrhea and appeared to be intoxicated.

FESTIVALS AND EVENTS: Held March 15, the nationwide celebration of **Farmer's Day** is headquartered in Tierra Blanca (whose farmers celebrate deliverance from a plague of locusts in 1877). It is a day devoted to the farmer's patron saint, San Isidro, a humble 12th-C. Spanish farmer. On March 19, **San José Day**, local families traditionally visit Volcán Poás for a hike and picnic.

ACCOMMODATIONS: Closest to the crater at five km from the entrance, low-budget **Lo Que Tú Quieras** (☎ 448-5213) comprises *cabinas* and a restaurant. **Restaurant Las Fresas** has two two-bedroom *cabinas* for rent for about $40 pn. Billed as a "bed and breakfast" and accommodating up to 15 people, expensive **Poás Volcano Lodge** (☎/fax 441-9102; Apdo. 5723-1000, San José) was originally built by an English family and incorporates elements of Welsh farmhouses, English cottages, and American architecture into its design. You'll find brick and stone walls as well as fireplaces. There are areas of protected forest within the farm. It's set next to the farm called El Cortijo at Vara Blanca in the hills at 6,000 ft (1,900 m). Rates are around $70 d. The **Albergue Ecológico La Providencia** (☎ 232-2498, fax 231-2204) offers a three-hour tour terminating at a waterfall, as well as a restaurant and rooms to stay. Its entrance is marked by a dirt two-km road leading off to the left of the green entrance gate to the park. Day visitors can go on the tour for $25. Rates are around $65 d. Alajuela's Orquídeas is near the village of Poás. See "Outlying Accommodation" under Alajuela for details.

FOOD: It's best to bring your own as there's usually little or nothing for sale at the crater. About 10 miles (16 km) above Alajuela, **Chubascos** has tables set in an outdoor garden. Specialties include strawberry and blackberry shakes, and cheesecake. Other eateries in the Poás vicinity include Italian **Las Fresas** (☎ 448-5567; call ahead for pizza baked in a wood-fired oven), which has an Italian chef, but a German owner. Then there is the bamboo-trimmed **Churrascos Steak House** (in Poasito), **Los Jualares** (three km from Fraijanes; frequently with live music on Fri. and Sat. nights), **El Recreo**, and **Restaurant Volcán Poás. Restaurant Vara Blanca** is at, you guessed it, Vara Blanca, which you will find at the intersection of the eastern road leading to Póas and the Heredia Sarapiquí road; it's also near Poás Volcano Lodge. Another restaurant, mentioned under "Accommodations," is **Lo Que Tú Quieras**, which offers great views and mediocre traditional food.

VICINITY OF POÁS: Open 9-3:30, Tues. to Sun., the **Fraijanes Lake Recreation Park,** about a half-hour down the road from the summit, has paths through cypress and pine groves. A lagoon, an exercise course, basketball courts, a soccer field, trails, and horses for rent (around $1.50/hour) can all be found in the park. Admission is inexpensive. Famous **Cascada de La Paz** (Peace Falls) are five km past Vara Blanca just after Poás turnoff. A charming wooden bridge runs right by it, and a caged Jesus is to one side. The "La Angel" food processing plant, which makes jelly, is farther on. Well off in the distance to the right is the **Caida del Angel,** a magnificent waterfall; a path leads down to it. Another few km to the right is the entrance to **Colonia Virgen del Socorro,** reached by a rough dirt road that runs for several km further. The surrounding area is a fine birding spot. The toll booth collects a voluntary contribution which is used for the protection of this beautiful area. The contributions go into a lottery; there's a monthly drawing.

Heredia

Another in the line of provincial capitals, this university town and coffee growing center of 65,000 sits at the foot of extinct Volcán Barva, seven miles (11 km) from San José. Founded in 1706 and nicknamed "La Ciudad de las Flores," Heredia is one of the most peaceful and relaxing towns in the nation.

GETTING HERE: Take one of the frequent buses from C. 1, Av. 7/9 (via Tibás), from Av. 2, C. 10/12 (via La Uruca), or from the terminal in Alajuela.

SIGHTS: Dating from 1797, the squat, solid, and imposing **church** appears to ruminate about days of yore from its spot on the plaza; its low contours were designed to resist earthquake damage. The bells in this old church were brought from Cuzco, Peru in the colonial era. Supplicants gather in the morning to pray. Inside, there are numerous large statues, including one to the left of the altar which has the Virgin Mary standing on a white neon crescent moon and surrounded by white neon stars. There's also a full length statue of Jesus who's brown-skinned, dreadlocked, clothed in a velvet gown, and fenced-in (presumably) for protection. In addition to several other old colonial-style buildings, **El Fortín,** a Spanish-style fort tower that has become the town's emblem, borders the central plaza to its left. On the N side of the park is the **Casa de la Cultura,** which has art exhibits.

Meseta Central

Tropical Insects Galore!

The **Joyas del Tropico Húmedo** (Jewels of the Humid Tropics, ☎/fax 236-4521) is outside of Heredia in Santo Domingo de Heredia. Here you'll find the Whitten Arthropod collection, containing more than 50,000 insect species. Half-domes in the center of each room closely replicate butterfly and arthropod habitats. Other exhibits detail bio-diversity, parasitism, mimicry, and camouflage. The collection was brought to Costa Rica in 1992 by biologist Richard Whitten. Elder-hostel groups also visit here. It is 100 m E of the cemetery in front of the MOPT building and is open daily from 9-5.

ACCOMMODATIONS: In town stay at low-budget **Hotel Verano** (☎ 237-1616, C. 4, Av. 6), the even cheaper **El Parqueo** (☎ 238-2882) nearby, or the **Colonial** (Av. 4, C. 4/6). More expensive **Hotel Heredia** (☎ 237-1324) is at Av. 3/5. C. 6. Expensive and recently constructed eight-unit **Apartotel Vargas** (☎ 237-8526, fax 238-4698) is some 750 m N of the Colegio Santa Cecilia. It charges around $65 d. **Hotel Val-ladolid** (☎ 260-2905, fax 260-2912; Apdo. 93, 3000 Heredia) is at C. 7/Av. 7. It has a sun deck with a Jacuzzi on its roof, a restaurant, and a travel agency. Rates are in the luxury range and rooms include ameni-ties such as hair dryer, cable TV, and phone. Camping is permitted at **Bosque de la Hoja**, three miles (five km) from San Rafael de Heredia.

outside town: A Canadian-run bed and breakfast in a housing development in Santa Lucia de Heredia, moderate **Los Jardines** (☎ 260-1904) can be reached easily by bus from Heredia. Airport pickup is around $6 extra. **Debbie King's Country Inn** (☎/fax 268-8284) is on a three-acre fruit and coffee plantation. A pink two-storey house, it has three bedrooms and two *cabinas* with kitchenettes. Rates run from $30 s to $50 d (for the *cabinas*) with breakfast. Write SFO 381, PO Box 025216, Miami FL 33102-5216.

Set 1.3 km N from the bridge at San Isidro de Heredia, moderate-expensive **La Posada de la Montaña** (☎/fax 268-8096; Box 5712, Springfield MO 65801; Apdo. 1-3017 San Isidro de Heredia) provides lodging in its main house as well as in the more expensive cabins, which have private bath, kitchen, and fireplace. Rates (including full breakfast) start at $35 s, $40 d plus tax for rooms in the main house with shared bath; packages are available, and there's a 20% discount from May-December. In the US, ☎ 800-632-3892 or E-mail at watzo@aol.com. It's a good place for birders. Also here is coffee plantation **Finca Wa Da Da** (☎/fax 265-8284; Apdo. 465, 3000 Heredia), which has "cozy cab-ins." In the US, ☎ 800-367-9854.

A full 12 miles (20 km) N of San José, the village of San José de la Montaña offers accommodation in the cool hills. **Hotel Cypresal** (☎ 237-4466, 223-1717, fax 221-6244) offers volleyball, conference rooms, pool, fireplace-equipped lounge, horseback riding, and other facilities. Its restaurant has an international menu. Its functional cabins (around $60) have TVs, phones, balconies, and fireplaces. Nearby are the ivy-covered, fireplace-equipped, and moderately priced **Cabinas Las Ardillas** (☎ 221-4294, 222-8134). Inexpensive and tasteful **El Pórtico** (☎ 237-6022, fax 260-6002), up the road, has heated rooms along with pool, Jacuzzi, and restaurant. Located in Parque Residencial del Monte, Monte de la Cruz, Heredia, **Hotel Chalet Tirol** (☎ 267-7371, fax 267-7050; Apdo. 7812, 1000 San José) has 10 two-story Swiss-style chalets with hot water, trout fishing, conference rooms, French cuisine, and a surrounding cloud forest with waterfalls. Airport pickup is available. Rates are around $85 with breakfast.

Located 800 m off the road from Barva to Alajuela and a total of 1.4 km from the town of Santa Barbara de Heredia, ultra-luxury **La Rosa Blanca/Finca Rosa Country Inn** (☎ 269-9392, fax 269-9555) is set at 4,265 ft (1,300 m). The main building's interior features murals and a collection of indigenous art. It has four suites and one master suite, each with its own design theme, as well as two two-bedroom villas (sleep 6-8) with murals, living rooms, and decks. The hotel offers a complete range of services – supplemented by a pool, nature trails, and organic gardens with fruit trees. Gourmet meals are prepared using herbs grown on the property. In the US, ☎ 800-327-9854 or write SJO 1201, PO Box 025216, Miami FL 33102-5216.

FOOD AND ENTERTAINMENT: Lying 450 m E of Pop's ice cream on the plaza, **Café Plaza** has cuisine as diverse as lasagna, pastries, espresso coffee, and stuffed croissants. **Mercado Florense** is 300 m S and and 50 m W of the Church; it has an inexpensive restaurant inside. **Fresas** is set one block from the university. Offering vegetarian recipes and pastries, **Natura** is nearby. For vegetarian food, you can also try **Yerba Buena**. Other restaurants are in the vicinity of the Mercado Central. Student bars near the university include **El Bulevar** and **La Choza**. Also near the univerity, **Le Petit Paris** (☎ 238-1721) serves traditional French dishes such as *ratatouille crêpe* as well as sandwiches and salads. **Bar Barucho,** named after the owner's cat, is a throwback to the 1960s scene in the US; it's 300 m W of the Heredia Stadium. Out near Monte de la Cruz (see below), **Le Barbizon** is a gourmet French restaurant. Another French restaurant is in **Hotel Chalet Tirol**. The **Stein Biergarten** (open weekends) is near Bosque del Río de la Hoja. Four km above San Rafael, **Añoranzas** offers Tico food and a playground for your children.

Meseta Central

INFORMATION: There is a branch of the ICT (☎ 223-1733) at Av. 4, C. 5/7.

Vicinity of Heredia

This is an interesting area to explore. The **Attiro coffee mill** on the outskirts of town is one of several *beneficios* nearby. Outside of **San Pedro de Barva**, the **Centro de Investigaciones de Café** (☎ 237-1915) has a small coffee museum with coffee production antiquities including a display of grinders and carved wooden statues of coffee workers in action. It's open weekdays 7-3. Take the *Santa Bárbara por Barrio Jesús* bus from Av. 1, C. 1/3 in Heredia. If you're driving, turn left in front of the square in Barva and head two km onward to San Pedro and keep to the right.

On the street just past El Fortín to the left (C. 1, Av. 1/3) is the stop for **Barva**. Situated a few km to the N, Barva's grassy plaza has low, thick-walled buildings with red tiled roofs and a baroque 19th-C. church; it has been declared the nation's first historic town. From here you can also continue on by bus to San Pedro de Barva and the coffee museum. When you return to Heredia, be sure to note the house shaped like a miniature castle just before town on the right.

Café Britt's Coffee Tour

One of the most popular tours, the **Coffee Tour** (☎ 260-2748, fax 238-1848) takes place three times daily at the Café Britt facility at Barva. It was presented with a 1995 Award for Tourism Excellence by American Sightseeing International, an international network of tour operators. The theatrical portion of the presentation combines music with comedy to relate the history of coffee cultivation in Costa Rica. If you make a suggestion to improve the tour which is then used, you will receive a free bag of coffee. The presentation takes place at 9, 11, and 3. Those attending the 9 AM performance are also shuttled to the Butterfly Farm, while those attending the 3 PM performance are taken to the Santa Lucía coffee mill. Prices run around $19 for foreigners and $12 for Costa Ricans. If you get there on your own, the price is $14 and $7 respectively. An alternative to the Café Britt tour is the **Orosi Coffee Adventure** (☎ 533-3030, fax 533-3212), which takes visitors to the Esquivel family plantation. However, you must have a large group.

MUSEO DE LA CULTURA: The **Museo de La Cultura** (☎ 260-1619), opened in 1994, is near Santa Lucía de Barva. A Barva bus passes by, but you must walk 1½ km up a hill to reach it. This century-old home once belonged to President Alfredo González Flores; it was donated to the project in 1989 by the now-bankrupt Banco Anglo. It presents a portrait of rural life during the era when coffee was king. The home is constructed with a pre-Columbian technique known as *barbareque*, in which layers of wood, wild cane and wild cane sap, stones, bricks, dung, and mud are used to build walls resembling a thin version of adobe. Rooms are furnished with antiques appropriate to the era. Ticos pay 50¢; foreigners, $1.50. Also on the premises is **La Fonda** restaurant. A museum dedicated to Costa Rican peasant culture is in the works.

Monte de la Cruz

This is still one of the most traditional areas in the Meseta Central and it has a number of dining and recreational facilities nearby or on the way. **Pizza La Finca** (☎ 268-8635) is an attractively set mountain-style restaurant serving homemade pizzas, salads, and special meals on Fridays. It's open on Thurs. from 5-11 PM and on Fri., Sat., and Sun. from noon-11. To get here take the road to San Rafael de Heredia (by turning right at the end of Heredia's main street), then pass the church and plaza and swing N until you see a sign for the La Troja Bar, where you turn right. Keep going for another km. **Bar-Restaurant Monte de la Cruz** is at the site of the **Paradero Monte de la Cruz.** Here, you'll find the remains of a small chapel (dismantled following incidents of vandalism during the 1970s) and picnic areas. Five km from San Rafael de Heredia, **Bosque del Río de la Hoja** is two km down a forest road. There's not much here except for the **Bar las Chorreras,** but the hiking trails traverse forests and meadows, and you may camp here. The **Stein Biergarten** (☎ 267-7021) serves German food; it's open Wed. to Fri. for dinner and on Sat. and Sun. for lunch and dinner. Back on the main road, **El Castillo** is a stately country club. The $5 admission entitles you to use the pool, gym, ice-skating rink, BBQ pits, and to ride the go-carts and the miniature train. Look for it on the right, a few hundred m after the sign for Residencia El Castillo. The turn-off for Monte de la Cruz is another km. To the left is **Hotel Chalet Tirol** (gourmet French food; see description above) with great hiking trails in their private cloud forest reserve, including one with a grove of water-falls.

GETTING HERE: A bus runs hourly until 4 PM from Av. 10, C. 2 in Heredia; it stops two km before Monte de la Cruz, except on weekends when it continues on to the top. By car, take the San Isidro exit to the left approximately 14 km down the Guápiles Highway to San Isidro, where you turn right in front of the church; continue two km to Concepción and then on to San Rafael. There you turn right at the church.

Braulio Carrillo National Park
(Parque Nacional Braulio Carrillo)

The only national park near San José, Braulio Carrillo begins seven miles (12 km) from San José en route to Guápiles and encompasses elevations ranging from eastern lowlands (1,500 ft, 500 m) up to the summit of 9,534-ft (2,906-m) Volcán Barva. If you are going to the Atlantic Coast, it is virtually inevitable that you will pass through this park, the only national park divided by a highway. The surrounding greenery is often enveloped in mist, which brings to mind Chinese landscape paintings. The park's most unusual feature must be the sickeningly orange water of the **Río Sucio** (Dirty River). Its coloration is due to sulfuric deposits on Volcán Irazú. Watch for it below the bridge toward the end of the park in the direction of Limón. Rainfall averages 110-115 inches (2,800-3,800 mm) annually, and it rains almost daily between March and October; the park's E slope is generally overcast when it isn't raining.

HISTORY: After the idea of a highway surfaced in 1973, environmentalists, fearing a repeat of the indiscriminate deforestation that followed the opening of other new roads in the past, argued for the establishment of this park. It was inaugurated in 1978, and the Limón highway opened to traffic in 1987. Under the US AID-funded Foresta project, the park has received funds for more trails and viewpoints, as well as a visitor's center.

FLORA AND FAUNA: The park comprises 108,969 acres (44,099 ha). Some 84% is primeval forest, 11% is used for ranching and farming, and 5% is secondary forest. There are over 500 species of birds; the magnificent quetzal and the black-faced solitaire reside on Volcán Barva as well as on other high peaks.

GETTING HERE: Take the hourly *Guápiles*-bound bus from C. 12, Av. 9. An impressive way to enter the park is by Volcán Barva through the road leading to Sacramento de San José de la Montaña. From Mon. to Sat., the bus to *Paso Llano (Volcán Barva)* leaves from Heredia at 6:30, 11, and 4, returning at 7:30, 1, and 5. On Sun. it runs at 11 and 4. It's possible to enter the park near La Virgen off the road to Puerto Viejo de la Sarapiquí, or via the ranger stations at either Zurquí or Quebrada Gonzales if you are using a four-wheel drive.

Braulio Carrillo National Park

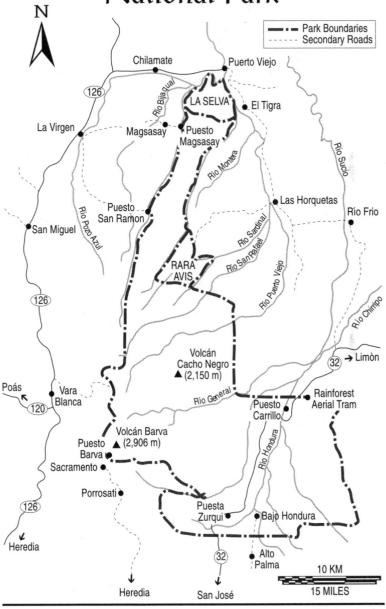

N

Park Boundaries
Secondary Roads

Chilamate

Puerto Viejo

126

Río Bijagual

LA SELVA

El Tigra

La Virgen

Magsasay

Puesto Magsasay

Río Montera

Puesto San Ramon

Las Horquetas

Río Sucio

Río Frio

San Miguel

Río Pozo Azul

Río Sardinal

RARA AVIS

Río San Rafael

Río Puerto Viejo

Río Chirripo

Volcán Cacho Negro
▲ (2,150 m)

32 → Limòn

Poás

120

Vara Blanca

Río General

Puesto Carrillo

Rainforest Aerial Tram

126

Volcán Barva
▲ (2,906 m)

Puesto Barva

Sacramento

Río Hondura

Porrosati

Puesta Zurqui

Bajo Hondura

126

↓ Heredia

32

↓ Heredia

↓ San José

Alto Palma

10 KM

15 MILES

TOURS: If you want to climb Barva in a group, **Geotur**'s tours include a visit to a banana and a cacao plantation en route to Limón, where you lunch and enjoy the beach before returning. ☎ 234-1867. **Jungle Trails** (☎ 255-3486, fax 255-2782) also operates hiking tours here. **note:** It's best to avoid parking near the *miradores* (lookout points) along the main highway. Visitors were robbed by men with guns there in 1992, and break-ins along the roadside are numerous and commonplace. Be cautious before going into the park on your own: one member of a family from Missouri was robbed and beaten by two armed thieves after the group had entered the park in March 1995 to birdwatch. If you are going to visit, you should leave your vehicle by the ranger station or take a bus. Bring little in the way of money or material possessions with you. Let the ranger know where you are going.

HIKING: Inquire at the ranger station (where you pay admission) concerning trails and current conditions. There are two trails accessible from the highway. One, before the tunnel, is sheer and arduous; the other, the *Sendero Botello*, 17 km (11 miles) after the tunnel and 2½ km (1½ miles) before the Quebrada Gonzales station at the park's far end, is less difficult. Both are muddy, and snakes may be a danger. You're likely to spot birds along these trails. There's also a four-day hike from Barva to Puerto Viejo de Sarapiquí with shelters available along the way. En route you descend from 2,900 m (9,514 ft) to 34 m (112 ft).

CLIMBING BARVA: From Heredia, take the 6:30 AM *San José de la Montaña-Paso Llano* bus (Mon. to Sat.) from behind Heredia's Mercado Central. (On Sun., you must first travel to San José de la Montaña and then take a 7:10 *Paso Llano* bus.) Watch for signs at Paso Llano (Porrosati) leading to the entrance, four miles (6.4 km) to the left. Sacramento is four miles (seven km) farther, and from there it is approximately two miles (three km) to the top of Volcán Barva (9,534 ft, 2,906 m). Its main lake is 600 ft (200 m) in diameter. The Danta, another lake, is nearby. Be sure to bring a compass, rubber boots, warm clothing and food – no matter how nice the weather is! Although they were planning only a day hike around the crater, three German hikers were lost in rain and fog for 11 days. Plan to make it back in time for the 5 PM bus (4 PM on Sun.). If traveling by car, you should note that the road after Sacramento is not generally navigable in the rainy season. If you like, you may also purchase cheese and *natilla* (custard) from the dairy farms in the area. Food is available at the **Restaurante Sacramento**. Expect afternoon rains any time of the year and plan accordingly.

Minor Keith built a highway through here in 1881 to connect the capital with the terminal. Fallen into disrepair since completion of the railway line, it now makes a wonderful day hike. Take a bus (Av. 3, C. 3/5) to San Jerónimo de Moravia and then a road to the N. In less than an hour, at the "Alto de Palma" area, you'll come to the old stone pavement, which you can follow for about nine km until you reach the park boundary; entrance is prohibited here.

From Braulio Carrillo to Guapiles

ACCOMMODATION NEAR BRAULIO CARRILLO: Set 3½ km above Paso Llano, **Restaurante La Campesina** serves *comida típica*. A half-km farther up, **Restaurante Sacramento** offers similar food. Both have basic rooms for sleeping and are good bases for exploring Barva. **Los Robles de Sacramento** (☎ 237-2116/2441, fax 237-1976) offers the "finest ecological horseback tour" up Barva. Its lodge is a converted old dairy. Rates run around $50 s, $100 d. Located within 20 minutes by car from both Braulio Carrillo National Park and San José, the **San Jerónimo Lodge** (☎ 292-3612, fax 292-3243) in San Jerónimo de Moravia offers horseback riding and hiking trails. Its nine rooms have private bath, phone, and TV. The spacious, luxurious suites (about $120 s or d) have fireplaces; one has a 360-degree view. Deluxe ($100 s or d) and standard rooms ($80 s or d) are also available. Rates include breakfast. It's 800 m E of the church in San Jerónimo de Moravia.

Another alternative is **Estación Biológica Morpho** (☎ 221-9132, fax 223-1609; Apdo. 3153, 1000 San José) which is off the highway, past the Braulio Carrillo National Park. It has 988 acres (400 ha), with a number of trails. It costs around $10 pp for dorm accommodation, including a guide and use of the kitchen. Entrance is $10, and meals are available for $7 each. A restaurant is 800 m away on the main road. Rooms ($20 s and $30 d) are also available. A number of courses and seminars are offered. These range from "Nature Photography" to "Medicinal Plants of the Rainforest." Make reservations at their office (Edificio Murray, 3 F; C. 7, Av. 1/3). Buses to Guápiles (C. 12, Av. 7/9) go past the stop; ask to be left off at the Río Corinto.

Formerly known as El Tapir, the **Jardin de Mariposas** (☎ 222-5052 in San José) has simple rooms (around $25 s or d), a butterfly farm, a private reserve, and an attractive thatched-roof restaurant. The simple butterfly farm has one room displaying insect specimens, some of which are boxed and for sale, another where you're shown chrysalises and pupae belonging to different species, and a small garden with fluttering blue morphos. The reserve (part of which was allegedly logged to fund the restaurant's construction) might be an excellent place to go for a day's hike and picnic. It's quite beautiful, and wildlife is present. However, the trails are muddy, there are few signs, and you must bring your own water or purify it.

Other alternatives are the **Hotel Villa Zurqui** (☎ 222-3078, fax 257-3242), which has rooms for around $70 d and up, a restaurant, and hiking and horseback riding. The **Río Danta Lodge** (☎ 223-2421, fax 555-4039) is set amidst terraced grounds and features restaurant, hiking trails, freshwater swimming pool, and rooms with balconies. Three-day packages run around $250 pp, including transport, room and board, and guided hiking. Still other places to stay are listed below.

RAINFOREST AERIAL TRAM: Opened in 1994, the long-awaited Teleferico del Bosque Lluvioso brings the rainforest canopy – formerly accessible only to daredevil arbolists – within the reach of the ordinary visitor. If you aren't into strenuous hiking, and have the price of admission, this serves as one of the best introductions to the rainforest around. While visiting the project, note the cables used to secure plants out of harm's way. Admirably, the tramway was designed to minimize environmental impact.

As you glide pleasantly through the treetops, you will have the opportunity to witness primary forest in its natural splendor, the effect that cutting the forest has had, and how primary and secondary forest compare.

history: The tram project was initiated by biologist Don Perry, one of the pioneers of treetop canopy exploration and research. It is a one-of-a-kind-project, not only in its design but also in the way it is attempting to train locals to be guides and bring them into the project. The project was financed by 60 investors who purchased some $2 million worth of shares. The administration first sought out a Russian pilot and his helicopter in Colombia, where they were available for charter. Unfortunately, the helicopter broke down, and the Sandinistas became the second choice after the chief of the Sandinista Air Force granted permission to use a helicopter. Removing the machine guns from its Russian-built M1-17 helicopter, the Sandinista Air Force helped install the tram's towers. At first, the towers swung back and forth, so the tether had to be shortened in order to rectify the problem. It took an entire week, along with a cool $50,000, to finish implanting all 12 towers.

the tour: At the main road you must first register at the guard's booth. A bus (actually a truck with seats) then picks you up and transports you to the first river, where you cross via a bridge and then wait for a second truck-bus to pick you up. Depending upon the numbers of visitors present, you will either take a hike or go on the tram. On the hike, your guide will give you an orientation and then take you around. You might see any of 300 bird species, ranging from a toucan to a woodpecker. Or you might come upon a snake swallowing a frog. The guide provides informative narrative details though both the terrestrial and aerial segments. (If the guide is a local, his English may not be quite up to par; please bear with him).

The tram will transport you in one of its 20 comfortable, smooth-running cars through the canopy via 1.3 km of cableway. It's exceptionately pleasant to pass over the river with its giant tree ferns. Much of the forest is disturbed, but about 60% remains primary. Don't expect to see much in the way of wildlife. Many animals are nocturnal, some are intimidated by the tram, and there has also been hunting in this area in the past. As with rum or wine, the tram should improve with age, as the vegetation grows and the guides gain in experience.

practicalities and accommodation: Be sure to bring binoculars, insect repellant, hat, and rain gear when you come to visit. There's a somewhat pricey restaurant with a limited menu; the soda on the road is cheaper, or you might want to bring your own bag lunch. Note that you can take the tram more than once if things aren't busy. Cabins have been constructed so you can stay here or at the Casa Río Blanco (see next entry), which offers a discount on the tram (otherwise around $50 pp). Keep in mind that, as already noted above, you probably won't see many animals: be aware that the best possible time for sightings runs from 6:30-9 AM and plan your visit accordingly. For current information, ☎ 257-5961 or fax 257-6053.

CASA RIO BLANCO RAINFOREST LODGE: Set on 24 acres (10 ha), Casa Río Blanco Rainforest Lodge (☎ 382-0957, fax 710-6161; Apdo. 241, 7210 Guápiles) is a delightful oasis and one of the closest places to San José to learn firsthand about the wonders of the rainforest. The lodge was founded after US citizens Thea Gaudette and Ron Deletsky arrived a few years back on a trip to Costa Rica, the first edition of this book in hand. When it came time to board the plane at the airport to return, Thea broke down in tears. She felt as though she was leaving home rather than going home, and it was then that they determined to return. After an extensive search, they purchased land set by the bank of a river in a region where both banana plantations and illegal logging have wreaked environmental devastation, and began building their cabins. They act as a collection agency for Zoo Ave and accept unwanted or injured birds. They are also starting a fund for the local school, and donations are welcome.

visiting: A former nurse who majored in biology as an undergrad, Thea is a self-trained and enthusiastic naturalist. She knows her stuff and is one of the nation's best guides. You may reach the trails by heading down into a canyon, an area termed a "riparian corner." There are several small waterfalls and, of course, the Río Blanco. On a night hike with Thea, you'll see bats (who come out at night to pig out on the sugar dispensed by the hummingbird feeders) as well as a poison dart frog or two. A day hike may uncover wonders ranging from a poisonous coiled eyelash viper to a group of copulating millipedes or a moth carcass colonized by wasp larvae.

Don Perry Adventures operates a canopy platform here. Arrangements can be made to volunteer at the lodge; activities include reforestation and counting birds, animals, and plants.

practicalities: A breakfast (generally a *tamale*, fruit and coffee) is included in the rate. Simple meals are served; more abundant (and reasonably priced) Tico repasts are to be found at the restaurant on the main road. Rooms or attractive, simple cabins are available. Rooms (in the main building) have fans and private baths. The lodge is 12 km E of the Aerial Tram; discounts are given and transport can be arranged. Cabins are compact but comfortable. Rates are around $35 s, $50 d, and $65 t plus tax. Guiding as well as dropoffs and pickups are additional; trips off the property (including a horseback ride to a waterfall) are also available.

BOSQUE LLUVIOSO: This private forest reserve (☎ 224-0819/3820, fax 225-5646), a few km off of Km 56 on the main highway, caters to affluent visitors. It will supply an excellent introduction to the rainforest for those with limited time and stamina, covering some 420 acres (170 ha) with paths leading through 49 acres (20 ha). You can easily spend a day here or just an hour or so. All trails branch off of the oval *sendero de los ríos*, so it's easy to try several if time permits. Allow about three hours to tour all of the trails. Included are primary and secondary forests, ferns, tropical fruit plantations, and other sights. There is a restaurant on the premises. Bosque Lluvioso is on the Rancho Redondo Rd. at Km 56 along the highway to Limón. Admission is around $15 with lunch; transport is available. In the US, ☎ 305-384-8503 or fax 305-384-0595.

LAS CUSINGAS BOTANICAL GARDEN: Near the village of Buenos Aires (and accessible by taxi from Buenos Aires or Guápiles), Las Cusingas Botanical Garden (☎ 710-7114 for appointments) covers 25 acres (20 ha). Owners Ulises Blanco and Jane Segleau cultivate medicinal, rare and endangered plants – more than 60 in all. The couple have a cabin that accommodates four; meals are available or you may self-cater on your woodburning stove. They are some 3½ km from the main highway. To get here, look for the large gas station on your L at the third entrance to Guápiles (Soda Buenos Aires will be on your R). Take a R and then continue until you see the gates. A donation is requested.

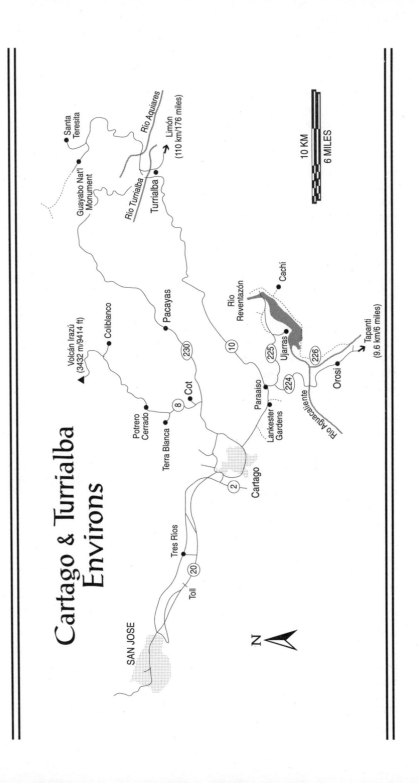

Cartago & Turrialba Environs

SAN JOSE

Toll

20

Tres Ríos

2

Cartago

Terra Blanca

8

Cot

Potrero Cerrado

Coliblanco

Volcán Irazú
▲ (3432 m/9414 ft)

Pacayas

230

Guayabo Nat'l Monument

Santa Teresita

Río Turrialba

Río Aguiares

Turrialba

Limón
(110 km/176 miles)

10

Río Reventazón

Lankester Gardens

Paraiso

224

225

Ujarrás

Cachi

226

Orosi

Río Aguacaliente

Tapantí
(9.6 km/6 miles)

N

10 KM

6 MILES

COSTA FLORES: Spread across 300 acres, this flower plantation (☎ 220-1311, ☎/fax 717-5457) specializes in heliconias. On the farm are waterfalls, fountains, and ponds, as well as some 20 species of birds, including an abundance of hummingbirds. To get here, head left at Guacimo and follow the signs to Costa Flores. Expect to spend around $15 for tours, less if in a group.

GUAPILES: This small town doesn't have a lot to offer, but it is a good place to stock up on supplies. There are a couple of low-budget and other hotels that might be used as a base for exploring the area. The **Cabinas Car** (☎ 710-6523) is clean and inexpensive. The expensive **Hotel Suerre** (☎ 710-7551, fax 710-6376) is in front of the Colegio Tecnico. It is done up in a colonial style with terracotta floors and an entrance marked by pillars. Rooms have a/c and cable TV. Its restaurant offers expensive but tasty dishes. There are a few *sodas* in the town. Taxis leave from the main square.

HOTEL RIO PALMAS/E.A.R.T.H.: E.A.R.T.H. Agricultural School (☎ 255-2000, fax 255-2726 for advance tour reservations) has a forest reserve and also passes on sustainable agricultural techniques. In Pocora, the **Hotel Río Palmas** (☎ 760-0305, fax 760-0296; Apdo. 6944, 1000 San José) has 22 rooms, with a pool and a reserve with trails. Its restaurant serves Costa Rican food. A number of activities (including horseback riding and kayaking) and day trips (Pocora Falls, and other nearby attractions) are offered.

Cartago

Located 14 miles (23 km) E of San José in the Valle de Guarco, this once-impoverished village founded in 1523 is the nation's oldest settlement. Since the 1800s it has also been known as *La Ciudad de las Brumas*, the "city of fog." A former nickname is *La Ciudad del Lodo*, the city of mud. If you arrive on a rainy day, you'll see why. The inhabitants are called *pateros* (potato people), probably because potatoes are such an important crop in this province.

GETTING HERE: Buses run from San José about every 20 minutes. They leave from C. 13, Av. Central/2, near the Plaza de la Democracia. Be sure to get the *directo* bus. If driving, head out to San Pedro via Av. Central and then get on the *autopista*.

SIGHTS: Cartago does not have as many old buildings nor the atmosphere one might expect in a city of its age, largely because earthquakes (in 1841 and 1910), along with raining ash and debris from Volcán Irazú, have destroyed most of its old buildings. If you are coming by bus, you might want to get out at the town's center, where you'll see **Las Ruinas**. Iglesia de Convento, the parish church of La Parroquia, the first parochial church dedicated to St. Santiago, was severely damaged by earthquakes. After the 1910 quake – perhaps owing to the legend that the Creator had cursed the church for its priest's murder of his brother – it was deemed not worth rebuilding. Today, it's a walled park complete with trees, a pond, shrubs, and benches, all of which combine to afford a more attractive park than any found in San José. The plaza built in front has a statue of the opera tenor Manuel Salazar Zuniga. It's a great place to relax and do some birdwatching.

A few blocks away to the E is the town's main attraction: the cathedral. An example of what some call Byzantine style and others call an architectural mishmash, the **Basilica de Nuestra Señora de Los Angeles** (Basilica of Our Lady of the Angels, named after the nation's patron saint) houses a statuette of the Black Virgin holding the infant Christ. Legend has it that on August 2, 1635 a young girl named Juana Periera found a small statuette of the Virgin Mary perched on a rock beside a stream while she was strolling in a forest. Taking the statuette home, she placed it in her collection. Passing the same point the next afternoon, she discovered another identical statuette at the same location. Returning home, she found that the first statuette had vanished, and she placed the new one where it had stood. After this happened three days in a row, she went to the priest who, after having the identical experience, decided to build a shrine at the site.

Today, the rock is found in the church's basement, and thousands credit the stream's water with miraculous powers to heal injuries, handicaps, and even enable supplicants to survive surgery. Arriving supplicants have donated miniature trinkets resembling the body parts requiring healing, and today there are fingers, arms, hearts, stomachs, eyes, legs, livers, lungs, and feet in cases all over the church; many of them are silver medallions. You could spend hours gazing at the collection.

Trophies are the gift of grateful sports teams who allegedly owed their victories to the Virgin's intervention, and there are photos of children next to written testimony extolling the Virgin's healing powers; there's even a geisha doll and a pair of carved wooden oxen being led by a *campesino*. Statuary abounds, and there are also some beautiful confession booths. At the rear to the L of the altar is a collection of life-sized statues, some of which have most unhappy faces. Downstairs, reduced and weathered by years of attention and chiseling, is the original stone, topped with a replica of the Virgin in an elaborate gold case. The original statue, crudely fashioned from a granite-like stone, is rarely removed from its cabinet above the altar. Stolen several times, it has always been returned. Holy water, from the stream that still runs alongside, is available in a shed at the back; you must pay 50 centimes for a container. Across the street in a diagonal from the right of the cathedral's entrance, you'll see a shop ("Venta de Objetos Religiosos"); they sell hands, feet, eyes, and other paraphernalia at reasonable prices.

Open from 9-4, the **Elias Leiva Museum of Ethnography** (Av. 3/5, C. 3/5) houses colonial-era furniture, pre-Colombian artifacts, and other items. Finally, if you have time, you may want to see the art exhibits at the **Casa de la Ciudad** in Edificio Pirie.

PRACTICALITIES: If you're looking for comfortable hotels, there are *none* to be found. If all you want is an inexpensive place to sleep so that you can head up to the top of Irazú the next morning, that can be found near the railway station and the market. Try the **Casa Blanca** in Barrio Asia, the less expensive **Pensión El Brumoso** (☎ 551-4351; Av. 6/8, C. 5) or the **Valencia**. Most of the others rent rooms by the hour for obvious purposes, so if you don't mind creaking springs and frantic gasps coming from the room next door....

FOOD: Bars and restaurants cluster around the basilica. **Pizza y Hamburguesas Maui** is on the N side of the park in front of the Cathedral; a large restaurante is behind it. One of the most attractive places to dine is **Salón París**, which has Venetian and bullfight scenes, and is opposite one corner of the market on the main street. Near the bus station, the large and bustling market, with yet another replica of the Virgin on display, has lunch counters galore. Watch the mother and daughter team in one shop making tortillas. You also might find any type of odd souvenir in its innumerable shops. **Metrocentro** is the town's shopping mall.

FESTIVALS AND EVENTS: The **Virgin of Los Angeles**, held on August 1, is Cartago's largest festival; thousands arrive for this.

Vicinity of Cartago

Cartago's most famous outlying attraction is the Irazú volcano, covered in a separate section below. Five miles (seven km) to the SE of Cartago, **Jardín Lankester**, the Lankester Gardens, named after British expatriate Dr. Charles Lankester who founded them in the 1940s, has one of the nation's finest orchid collections. Although the over 800 species found here bloom throughout the year, the blossoms are at their peak in March. Also featured are fruit trees, groves of bamboo, aloe, hardwoods, bromeliads, and other species. Unfortunately, they're identified only in Latin, so unless you're a botanist it might as well be Greek to you. Guided tours are offered on the half-hour from 8:30 to 3:30 daily. Although you can come through on your own, an employee will tag along behind you to make sure you keep to the route and don't pick anything. To get there, take the *Paraíso* bus from the Cartago terminal and get off at the Ricalit factory and the distinctive, unforgettable dog training school sign, then walk over a quarter-mile (.5 km) down the side road to the S, which leads to the entrance. Admission is around 50¢ for locals and $3 for foreigners. If you want to head outwards and onwards after your visit, take a bus marked "Orosi." (See Valle de Orosi section below). If you're driving, you'll want to check out the spectacular view from the mirador (lookout point) a few km past Paraíso en route to the S. Also near Paraiso is the **Autovivero del Río**, a combined greenhouse and miniature zoo that sells colored volcanic stones, plants, and rabbits. In Paraíso, eat at the **Bar Restaurant Continental**. Finally, on the way back to San José, the **Nuestra Señora de Pilar Religious Art Museum** is on the S side of the Church of Tres Ríos.

Route of the Saints

This road to the S takes one along to semi-remote villages like Santa María de Dota, San Marcos de Tarrazú, San Pablo de León Cortés, and San Cristobal Sur. In the vicinity is also La Lucha, where Don Pepe Figueres had his famous farm. At **Cañon del Guarco**, Km 58 on the Interamerican Highway, a road leads seven km downhill to Copey (stay with Chema here) and then another seven km down to Santa María, where there are some low-budget hotels, including **Hotel Santa María** (☎ 541-1193) and the **Hotel Dota** (☎ 541-1026) . You may eat at **Las Tejas**, open Fri. and Sat. evenings as well as noon-11 on Sundays. From Santa María, buses return at 6, 9, 2, and 4. This makes a great day-trip. Back between Copey and on the way to Providencia, the two-cabin **Finca El Edén** (☎ 541-1299: message only) may be reached by taxi from Santa María or by car from the highway. Each cabin here has a kitchen with wood stove; bring your own food. The owners will sell you cheese and milk. Activities include birding, horseback riding, hiking, and tennis.

Out on the main highway, you can also stay at deceptively named and inexpensive-to-luxury-priced **Albergue de Montaña Tapantí** (☎ 232-0436, 233-0133, fax 233-0778). It offers activities such as trout fishing and hiking, as well as horseback riding and a visit to its namesake. Write Apdo. 26, 1017 San José, 2000. In the US ☎ 800-334-8582. From Santa María, you can also continue on six km to **San Marcos,** which has

Meseta Central

spartan accommodations. From here, a 40-km four-wheel-drive-only road descends to the Pacific highway.

transport: *Los Santos* buses run to Santa María (two hours) from C. 21, Av. 16 bis (☎ 227-3597) in San José at 6, 9, 12:30, 3, and 5. The return from Santa María is at 9, 1, and 4. For Copey, it's best to take a San Isidro bus from C. 16, Av. 1/3, to Cañon del Guarco at Km. 58 and walk or hitch the remaining seven km.

San Gerardo de Dota

At Km 80 on the Interamerican Highway, the entrance to this village is quite a bit farther S. The interior of these cloud forests has been acclaimed as the best place in the nation to see a quetzal. To get here take any San Isidro bus and tell the driver you wish to get off at the "entrada a San Gerardo." Stay at the Chacón family's **Albergue de Montaña Savegre** (☎ 771-1732; Spanish only). It's expensive (around $60 pp), with meals and hot showers included. Efrain, his wife, and 11 children, have 790 acres (320 ha) of peach and apple orchards surrounded by 494 acres (200 ha) of primary forest. A naturalist guide will take you along a trail up to Cerro de Muerte, and a variety of day trips are available upon request. Horseback riding, trout fishing, and other activities are also offered. **Rolando Chacón** (☎ 771-2376), their cousin, has two *cabinas* for around $30 pp, including meals. Luxury **El Trogon** (☎ 222-5463, fax 255-4039) is a set of *cabinas* owned by the same people who run Mawamba Lodge in Tortuguero. Three-day packages are about $250 pp. Horseback riding and trout fishing are also offered. Another alternative is the **Finca Mirador de Quetzales** which is at Km 70.

ACTIVITIES: The nearby **Río Savegre** is filled with introduced rainbow trout. The trail to a dramatic **waterfall** starts near the Bar La Deportiva. **Whitewater rafting** is also popular here; contact **Rios Tropicales** (☎ 777-0674), **Adventuras Naturales** (☎ 224-0889), or any of the numerous other companies for details. Transportation from the junction (nine km on a bad road) is available for around $12 RT if you stay at the Chacón's place. Reservations are advisable for all of these places, and you should prepare for some chilly nights.

Genesis II

Situated at 7,500 ft (2,360 m), just over the ridge of the Talamancas on the nation's Atlantic side, this private reserve lies some 35 miles (58 km) S of San José and near the Dota valley. Some 12 miles (20 km) of trails run through the 95-acre property. Rainfall here averages about 90 inches (2,300 cm). Most mornings are bright and clear, but rain generally falls in the afternoon. The Friedmans are recreating cloud forest on deforested land and have a nursery that is experimenting with alternative methods of propagation.

GETTING HERE: Transportation to and from the airport is included in the rates. If you are coming here on your own, take a San Isidro de El General-bound bus from the Coca Cola depot in San José (C. 16, Av. 1/3). Have the driver let you off at Km 58 across from the Genesis II sign. From there it's four km to the lodge. If driving, you can take a four-wheel drive all the way to their gate; otherwise park at the third sign (not including the one at the bus stop), where your vehicle will be safe.

FLORA AND FAUNA: There are some 20 species of trees here, including palmettos and tree ferns. The 200 species of birds include 50 endemic ones such as resplendent quetzals, emerald toucanets, tropical warblers, collared trogons, and a wide variety of hummingbirds. Sloths and armadillos may also be seen.

PRACTICALITIES: There's no set program here. Visitors generally rise at dawn, drink coffee and have a snack, then leave the house to find birds, returning in time for breakfast. Most of the meals feature garden-fresh food, and any dietary regimen can be catered to. In the main house, there are four bedrooms with two single beds in each; there are two other cabins. All guests share toilet and hot water shower facilities in the main house's two bathrooms. Electricity is available. Rates vary, depending upon the length of stay and number in your party and they include all meals (except alcohol), laundry (for guests staying five days or more), and guides. Tips, phone calls, and transport are not included. Rates are around $75 pp, pn. There are also special rates ($35 pn) for students and academics. Volunteers pay $50 pw for room and board, stay in spartan facilities, and spend five hours per day constructing nature trails. A 19% discount applies for guests staying over a week; a full-day trip to another habitat will also be included. A $200 check deposit (marked "for deposit only") is required. For more information (and current rates and policies), write Steve and Paula Friedman, Apdo. 655, 7050 Cartago. In Costa Rica, ☎ 381-0739, which is a cellular phone.

Meseta Central

Irazú National Park

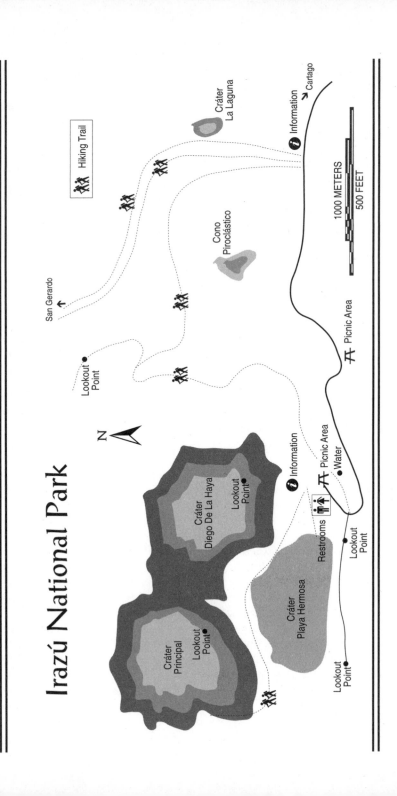

Hiking Trail

Cráter La Laguna

Cono Piroclástico

Information → Cartago

1000 METERS

500 FEET

San Gerardo

Lookout Point

N

Cráter Diego De La Haya

Lookout Point

Cráter Principal

Lookout Point

Information

Picnic Area

Water

Restrooms

Lookout Point

Cráter Playa Hermosa

Lookout Point

Picnic Area

Irazú Volcano

(Parque Nacional Volcán Irazú)

Rising to 11,260 ft (3,432 m), Irazú's prime distinction is that it is one of the world's few volcanoes that can be viewed up close with ease. And, should the day be clear, both the Atlantic and Pacific are visible from its summit. A lumbering menace that has devastated Cartago on more than one occasion, its presence has also had a beneficial effect: the very ash that wreaks devastation is also responsible for the soil's fertility.

ORIENTATION: This mountain is the birthplace of the Chirripó, Reventación, Sarapiquí, and Grande de Tárcoles rivers. It has shot billows of steam up as high as 1,640 ft (500 m) and volcanic debris up to 984 ft (300 m). Diego de la Haya crater is approximately 2,270 ft (690 m) wide and 328 ft (100 m) deep, with a rusty, mineral-colored lake at its bottom; its NW slope has active fumaroles. The principal crater is 820-984 ft (250-300 m) deep, measuring 3,445 ft (1,050 m) in diameter. **note:** Although the crater walls may appear to be safe, a descent to either crater's bottom is dangerous and not recommended.

FLORA AND FAUNA: The vegetation is adapted to high altitude and low temperatures. Wildlife here is scarce but there are forest cats, porcupines, coyotes, and a variety of birds, including the mountain robin and the volcano junco, a chunky sparrow.

HISTORY: Although there are many possible explanations for the volcano's name, the most likely one is that it derives from Iztarú, an Indian word meaning "mountain of tremors and thunder." Although it has held various names, it has been known solely by this alias since 1854. The mountain's first recorded eruption occurred in 1723, and it has erupted some 15 times since. The newly formed crater is now called Diego de la Haya. The next eruption was in 1775, then in 1822, perhaps in celebration of Costa Rica's independence that year. The area was established as a 5,700-acre (2,309-ha) park in 1955. From 1963-65, the eruptions traumatized the region, affecting farming in San José, Alajuela, and Heredia provinces. In 1963, 300 houses were destroyed. The following year, another eruption poured five inches (127 mm) of ash on San José. An estimated 250 million *colones* in agricultural revenues were lost as a consequence. During this period the crater widened from 656 to 1,722 ft (200 to 525 m).

GETTING HERE: On Sat., Sun., and holidays, a bus runs from the front of the Gran Hotel at the Plaza de la Cultura (C. 1/3, Av. 2) in San José. It passes by the Ruinas in Cartago at 8:30 and returns at 12:15. For more information, ☎ 272-0651/2948 or 551-9795. Otherwise, the closest you can get is Tierra Blanca or Linda Vista. From there you must hike, hitch, or grab a taxi. The bus to Linda Vista (8½ miles, 13.7 km, from the crater) leaves Mon. and Thurs. at 5:45 AM from Cartago, arriving at 8. It returns at 12:45, arriving back in Cartago at 2. Ask in Cartago about buses as far as Tierra Blanca. Buses straight to the top of the volcano leave at 8 from Av. 2 across from the Gran Hotel Costa Rica on Wed., Sat., Sun., and holidays; the return trip is at 12:15. Another alternative is to take a taxi from Cartago, about $15 RT after bargaining. It's preferable to visit in the dry season, and it would be a good idea to bring food. Many companies offer half-or full-day tours which stop here. Admission is at the prevailing special *gringo* rate; no more than 950 people are permitted in the park at any one time. **note:** Although there is no guarantee at any time that you will see anything, your chances of finding the mountain not fogged in are much greater if you arrive in the morning. Also, try hanging around for a while because it may clear for a few minutes at any time.

SIGHTS EN ROUTE: On the way from Cartago, you will pass many dairy farms, potato patches, and the immaculate towns of **Potrero Cerrado** and **Tierra Blanca**, "White Land" – so named for the ash or the fecundity of the soil. After the town of Cot, you come next to Potrero Cerrado ("Closed Field"), then you pass a TB sanatorium converted into a juvenile reform school. **Prusia** was destroyed by an eruption, and the surrounding area has been reforested by the Guardia Civil. Now known as **Area Recreativa Jiménez Oreamuno**, it's reached by a short but steep hike; there are picnic tables and trails.

ACCOMMODATIONS: If you have to, you could stay at the inexpensive (but less than wonderful) **Hotel de Montaña Gestoria Irazú** (☎ 253-0827), 12.4 miles (20 km) from Cartago and 7½ miles (12 km) from the crater. Another alternative is to overnight in Cartago. The only place to eat, aside from the none-too-good hotel just mentioned, is at the **Linda Vista**, a somewhat pricey (by local standards) but basic restaurant featuring an incredible display of name cards, *cedulas*, and foreign banknotes.

Valle de Orosi
(Orosi Valley)

This spectacularly scenic area makes a great day-trip from San José, an escape from the urban sprawl into the countryside by car or bus. Among its attractions are scenic outlooks, old churches, a wildlife reserve, and a waterfall. To go by bus, take a Cachí bus to Cartago and then ask to be let off at Ujarrás. You can then walk half an hour to Charrara. (On Sundays, the bus goes all the way at 8, 11, and 12).

TOURS: A number of operators run here, and – if you're on a tight schedule and want to see everything – a tour is advised. Otherwise, you can have fun with the buses.

FESTIVALS AND EVENTS: Held mid-March, the **Ujarras pilgrimage**, a procession from Paraíso to the ruined church in Ujarras, commemorates the rescue of Ujarras by the Virgin from floods. Her graven image returns along with the crowd for the occasion.

MIRADORES: There are two scenic overlooks in the region. Featuring a garden-like setting, **Mirador de Orosi**, a facility constructed by the ICT (Tourism Institute), has some of the most magnificent views in the nation. Take the path to your L; Irazú and Turrialba peaks will be directly in front and, as you continue along, you'll see Orosi on the side with coffee plantations in the foreground. Dammed at its lower end by the Cachí Dam, the Río Reventazón wends its way down the valley.

    nearby practicalities: Near the *mirador* is the **Lost in Paradise Café** (☎ 574-6047), a Canadian-run snack bar with homemade goodies and a gift shop. It's well worth the stop. Also near the *mirador* is relaxed **Hacienda del Río** (☎/fax 533-3308; Apdo. 46, 7100 Paraiso de Cartago), an attractive house once planned as a country club – a plan later abandoned. It is now open for guests, with a restaurant, pool, Jacuzzi, hiking, horseback riding, and numerous hammocks. Tours can be arranged. They will pick you up if you can get to Paraiso and phone them. Rates are around $70 d, including breakfast. In Paraíso, the **Sanchirí Mirador and Lodge** (☎/fax 533-3210) has five spartan *cabinas* (around $30 d) with balconies that command splendid views. There is a restaurant and horseback riding is offered. The **Peña Blanca Bed and Brunch** (☎ 551-9701) has 10 *cabinas* (with stoves and refrigerators), which hold up to four and rent for around $50. Views are great. A bed and breakfast, five-room **Cabinas Los Rápidos** (☎ 225-3506, fax 574-6074) is well to the E of Cachí in the village of Tucurrique right by the Río Reventazón. There is a restaurant and tours can be arranged. Rates are about $25 d.

SIGHTS IN OROSI AND VICINITY: With the nation's oldest active church, Orosi, a village in which Indians were once forcibly resettled, is a pleasant, well-manicured town. It has several *balnearios* (public pools), public baths, and hot springs. Be sure to visit the restored

church next to the soccer field. Built in 1743-86, it has whitewashed walls of sun-dried bricks, paved brick floors, a red tile roof supported by eight square cedar columns set on stone, and religious statuary thought to be the work of Mexican and Guatemalan artists. Next door, the monastery has been converted into a **museum** housing a collection of religious art. There's a Christ in a coffin, elaborate candelabras, clerical robes, and a bleeding wooden Christ, along with other statuary. (Open daily, 1-6, 10¢ admission). Near town, **Beneficiadora Renex** may be visited with Orosi Coffee Adventure Tours (☎ 533-3030, fax 533-3212)

ACCOMMODATIONS: Inexpensive **Albergue Montaña Orosi** (☎ 533-3032, fax 228-1256) is a house transformed into a hotel. The owners run **Restaurant Coto** on the main square. You might also ask about their cabins. Near Tapantí, the **Monte Sky Ecological Mirador** (☎ 220-2337) offers the chance to stay in an old house (around $12 pn with breakfast), a jungle cabin, or camp. Tours (for both individuals and groups) are available. There's a majestic waterfall, and you can see 260 or more species of birds. Owner "Billy" Montero tries to introduce Costa Ricans to the wonders of nature. Also near Tapantí, **Kiri Lodge** (☎ 533-3040) has a restaurant (trout dishes are a specialty), organically-grown fruit groves, and a private reserve. You may hike to here from Orosi or charter a taxi.

WATER FACILITIES: Two thermal pools are in town. **Balneario Termal Orosi** is to the W of town; it's open from 7:30-4 daily and charges around $1 admission. Another is **Los Patios,** which charges a bit more and is open from 8-4, Tues. to Sun. On the lake's N side, another ICT facility offers a swimming pool, picnic area, restaurant, playing fields, boat launching area, and campground.

Parque Nacional Tapantí

The side road to the Río Macho hydroelectric plant, two km after Orosi, leads 12 km to the 12,577-acre (5,090-ha) Tapantí National Park, a reserve now reclassified as a park. It offers nature trails, a good stream for trout fishing (with a permit) and a lookout point. No bus is available; a taxi will cost about $4 OW. It's open from 6-4 so birders should get an early start. Inside, you might see quetzals, olingos, or kinkajous. Jaguars and ocelots are also found here. It rains a tremendous amount in this area, especially between May and October, so you'll want to be well prepared. Approximately 150 streams and rivers run through the park. Fishing is permitted in designated areas.

There's a small exhibit room at the entrance. Nearby trails, including a *mirador*, overlook a waterfall.

To enter the park from its S extremity, known as the **Reserva Forestal Río Macho**, get information from the *pulpería* owner in La Trinidad de Dota, 1½ hrs. S of San José on the Interamerican Highway. There are a number of small waterfalls here, including Salto and Palmitos. The **Sendero Oropendola** leads to a swimming hole and picnic tables. If you leave the reserve and find no taxi available, the best procedure is to walk four km to Río Macho. From here you should be able to get a cab or else hitch a ride with a local. **note:** Accommodations near Tapantí is detailed under Orosi above.

Palomo

This is accessible by a footbridge from Orosi (which exacts a maintenance toll on Sundays) or by a sturdier suspension bridge two km farther on. The chief feature here is inexpensive **Motel Río** (☎ 533-3128, 533-3057) with a swimming pool and restaurant specializing in fresh fish. Some of the units are equipped with kitchenettes. Most buses end their routes here, so if you wish to visit Cachí Dam eight km away, you must either walk, hitch, or backtrack to Cartago, where you catch a bus via Ujarrás.

La Casa del Soñador

Built by the late master woodcarver and retired university professor, Macedonio Quesada Volorin (1925-95), this primitive yet ornate wooden "House of the Dreamer," built late in 1989, rises on boulders by the side of the road right next to the Río Naranjo. The carved female silhouettes gazing out from the windows as you approach represent gossiping women. The shutters pull down to match the outline when the window is closed. His work evokes not only Costa Rica and Latin America but also seems influenced by native American art as well as Dayak and Japanese Buddhist woodcarvings. On one side of the house is a carving of the Last Supper and on the back is a representation of the "Children's Last Supper." The carved door immediately adjacent shows a dog, mother, and child. Inside are carved nativity creches and other woodwork, much of which is made from coffee roots, *tirra*, *cerro royal*, and *pilon* woods. Macedonio was awarded the National Prize for Popular Culture in 1995 and died that same year. His one small bedroom and other workspace is upstairs. He taught disadvantaged locals to carve. His son Hermes continues the work, and his assistants chisel away continuously downstairs.

Meseta Central

Cachí Dam, just down the road, was constructed during the mid-1960s for 182 million *colones*. In the marsh across the road you may be able to spot waterbirds.

Ujarrás

This settlement lies past Cachí Dam 1½ km to the W down a side road. Now a historic shrine, the ruins of **Ujarrás church** are set amidst beautifully maintained grounds with flowers, birds, and a stand of bamboo. Coffee plantations and a reforested pine grove border the grounds. It was built in 1681-93 but was abandoned in 1833 after a flood forced the village to relocate on higher ground. The ruins are currently endangered by the encroaching river. The cross on the grounds was found in a nearby canyon. According to legend, a Huetar Indian found a wooden box in a river and brought it to Ujarrás. From there it could be moved no farther. When opened, it was found to contain a statue of the Virgin, and a church was built right on the spot. This very statue was credited with repelling an invasion by the pirate Henry Morgan and his brigands, who were turned back in 1666 from their attempt to sack Cartago by an outnumbered band of colonial militia. Today she resides in Paraíso, where all of the inhabitants of the time relocated. The statue is now known as Virgen de Candelaria. A fiesta is still held here in mid-March.

PRACTICALITIES: Eat at **Restaurante Típico Ujarrás** or the popular **La Casona del Cafetal** (☎ 533-3280), which has a Sunday buffet and also markets its own labeled brand of coffee. It's one block past the town of Cachí and overlooks the lake. There's dancing on Sat. nights, rental boats and mountain bikes are available, and horseback riding is offered.

NEARBY SIGHTS: The **Lacustre Charrara** recreation area is two km off the main road down a spur from the Ujarrás road. On weekends and holidays the bus goes all the way instead of dropping you at the turnoff. It features a pool, basketball courts, a boat tour of the lake, picnic tables, and a restaurant. It's closed on Mon. The **Ujarrás lookout point** is six km from the Charrara turnoff towards Paraíso. Nearby is the **Veil de la Novio (Bridal Veil) waterfall**. According to legend, a group of family and friends arrived here to celebrate a wedding. The horse went berserk and jumped, taking the bride and her long trailing veil over the cliff.

The Turrialba Area

The name Turrialba (originally "Torrealba") means "white tower" in old Spanish. It has its origins in the enormous columns of white smoke which continuously arose from the then-active volcano. As the number of visitors to Costa Rica continues to grow, this area – because of its great scenic beauty, attractions, and proximity to San José – has come under increased attention.

Turrialba

This agriculturally based town of 30,000 lies 64 km from San José, set at 2,050 ft (625 m) up the slopes of the Turrialba volcano. There's little to pique the interest of a visitor here, but its proximity to the Río Reventazón (whose name means "bursting") has made it a major area for kayaking and white water rafting. Its size and climate make it ideal for relaxation. The town makes a good base for low-budget travelers planning to climb Volcán Turrialba, visit Guayabo Reserve, or check out the surrounding area. Kayakers sometimes come all the way from Canada and rent houses here. Turrialba is also noted for its baseball factory, where workers are paid 6,000 *colones* for a six-day week.

GETTING HERE: A bus runs hourly (7 AM-9 PM) from San José, departing from Av. Central, C. 13. The 65-km trip takes under two hours. A *directo* takes 1½ hours. Buses also run from Siquirres (around every two hours; 1½ hours). En route, the bus traverses a narrow mountain road past villages such as Tres Equis. Overcast hills are off in the distance and coffee plants grow on steep hillsides. You can see CATIE (the agricultural research facility) on the right past Turrialtico and then you descend into the town. If you're coming by car, you can also come via San Isidro de Coronado and Rancho Redondo to Santa Cruz, where you turn for Turrialba.

FACILITIES AND TOURS: Just outside of town, **Balneario Las Américas** (75¢ admission) has two large pools and a restaurant-bar. They sometimes set up a disco and hold dances. **Parque La Dominica** is to the W of town; it has swings and a basketball court. It's next to the Reventazón river which the follies of mankind have rendered fit only for viewing. For those wishing to tour the area, the **COSANA travel agency** (☎ 556-1513) operates tours. **La Calzada** (☎ 551-3677, 556-0465) also offers tours to a local cheese factory, small ponds, and to a sugar cane plant. **Hector Lezama** at the Turrialtico restaurant (☎ 556-

1111) will also arrange tours, including one to the top of Turrialba, but advance notice is required.

WATERFALLS: The **San Antonio waterfalls** are near Santa Rosa and the **Zapote waterfalls** are also nearby. Ask directions in town.

CLIMBING VOLCAN TURRIALBA: From San José or Cartago, you can go by bus to the village of Pacayas. From here you can reach the top of this semi-active 10,995-ft (3,339-m) volcano on horseback or with a four-wheel drive. Another place to start your climb is from the village of Santa Cruz to the N. Although there's a four-wheel-drive road that winds up the mountain, it's too rough to drive more than two-thirds of the 21 km to the top. To hike, proceed from Santa Cruz along the main road for three km, where you'll find the Bar Canada. After turning right here and walking 600-800 ft (200-300 m), you'll see the sign marking the route. Here, you turn right again and ascend. When you come to a fork (about every few km) take the trail that goes up; the other route usually goes to a farm. After about 7½ miles (12 km) of this, you'll come to a group of houses. Ascend via the right fork, and you'll reach a metal gate. In another km or so, you reach a fork where you go right and then through a barbed wire gate (which may be rolled open). Pass by the cow barn and through another wire gate to its L. A few hundred yards (100-200 m) thereafter is the last spot to obtain water en route to the summit. The summit is another km or so up. There's a great camping area on top, and plenty of paths to explore.

ACCOMMODATIONS: Inexpensively-priced **Hotel Wagelia** (☎ 556-1566/1596, fax 556-1596) is the most attractive. Their a/c rooms are in the moderate range (around $65 pp); its **Hotel Wagelia Annex** (☎ 556-1142, fax 556-1596) is a converted old house about a km from town with a pool, restaurant, and basketball court. It charges around $55 d; more expensive rooms have refrigerators and TVs. Also in town are the low-budget **Hotel Central, Hotel Chamanga, Hotel/Pensión Primavera**, and **Interamericano** (☎ 556-0142, low-budget with shared bath). The **Pensión Chelita** (☎ 556-0214) and the **Hotel La Roche** (☎ 556-1627) are other alternatives. About 15 minutes SE of Turrialba by car, luxury 12-room and four-suite **Casa Turire** (☎ 531-1111, fax 531-1075) is set in the middle of a sugarcane, coffee, and macadamia nut plantation. There's a restaurant, five-hole golf course, pool, and gardens. Rooms have refrigerators, satellite TV, and phone. Horseback riding and mountain biking are also available. Rates start at around $100 s or d. If you wish to be near Guayabo, stay at low-budget **Hotel La Calzada** (message ☎ 573-3677, 556-0465, fax 556-0427), named after the indigenous trail that passes through the property. Meals are cooked over a wood-burning stove and geese and ducks reside on the property. Discounts are available here for YH members and students.

To the S of town, seven km along the road to Limón, **Albergue Mirador Turrialtico** (☎ 556-1111; see description below under food) has two inexpensive rooms for rent with private bath; breakfast is included. A few km farther, **Albergue de Montaña Ponchotel** (☎ 556-0111, fax 556-6222) offers two inexpensive two-room *cabinas* with private bath. You can also camp here. Some 19 km from Guayabo, **Guayabo Lodge** (☎/fax 556-0133) is a small home on a dairy farm owned by the Figueres family, of presidential fame. The decor is green and white – the colors of the Liberation Party. Packages (around $70 pp, pd) are available and offer San José pickup.

Naturalists and horse lovers might choose to stay in the expensive 10-room **Albergue de Montaña Rancho Naturalista** (☎ 267-7138), up a dirt road from the village of Tuis to the SE. Laundry service and horse rental are included; there are nature trails and guided birdwatching. They provide an extensive birdlist which describes birds such as the green-backed heron, rufous-tailed hummingbird, tropical kingbird, and the golden-hooded tanager as abundant here. Guided tours to Carara and other areas are offered. Expect to spend about $500/week. Write Apdo. 364, 1002 San José or Dept. 1425, Box 025216, Miami FL 33102-5216 for more information. Also out of town is the 20-unit **Esperanza Reserva** (☎ 223-7074, fax 225-3095), which has cabins, pools, restaurant and, of course, a reserve. Activities include kayaking, fishing, and hiking. Rates are around $110 d plus tax; an all-inclusive package is available. In the US, ☎ 800-213-0051 or fax 401-453-3966.

The eight-room **Albergue Volcán Turrialba** (☎ 273-4335; Apdo. 1632-2050) is an attractive lodge just five km from the crater. It's off a side road between Hacienda la Esperanza and Finca la Central. Meals are cooked on a wooden stove. Facilities include horseback rides (including one to the peak), carriage and ox cart tours, and bicycle tours and rentals. It's accessible only by four-wheel drive. Rates are around $65 pp, including three meals and tax. **note:** Accommodations in the direction of Orosi are found under that section.

FOOD: There are a large number of good places to eat in town. One of the best places in terms of value is **Restaurante El Caribeño**; try their *casado corriente* with fish. A convenient place to hang out, **Soda Valencia** is at one corner of the park. Inexpensive **La Garza** is right by the park and offers seafood. Popular with teenyboppers, **Pizza Julian** is just down the street and also facing the park. **Soda Bar Tico Chino** is one of several Chinese restaurants. There are also a number of supermarkets and a small market. **Café, Mani, Condimentos Turrialba** is across the street from Faro Disco and has health food items. About 10 km E of town, **Ponchotel** offers Tico cuisine. They have a device which will bring your order up to the top of the observation tower. Located just four km from CATIE (the huge agricultural research facility – see below) and two km from Pochotel, **Restaurante Turrialtico** offers spectacular views, coffee-root sculptures by famed primitivists Benjamin Paniagua and Victor Barahona, and traditional-style food cooked over wood stoves. Specializing in Jamaican fare, **Restaurant Kingston** is right outside town. Another good place to eat is at **La Calzada** on the way to Guayabo.

Posada de la Luna is W of the church in Cervantes, halfway between Cartago and Turrialba. This restaurant is nearly as extra-terrestrial as its name implies. Housed in an unassuming red and yellow concrete building and under a corrugated roof with peeling red paint, this restaurant houses one of the nation's most spectacular museums. Among the items on display, some of which are housed in glass cabinets, are a sheathed sword inscribed in Arabic, rusty irons, ancient smashed-up radios, indigenous artifacts, a wooden Buddha, old newspapers (one headline reads "RENDICION TOTAL NAZI"), and a ceramic frog sitting in a brass chair. Packets of *chile jalapeno* are for sale. This is also one of the best places to try *típico* food. The *gallo pinto* and *tortilla de queso* here are legendary.

NIGHTLIFE: There's not much to do. The most exciting place is the frequently packed disco, **El Faro**. There are also three movie theaters; **La America** is in the main square. Bars with unusual ambience include **Bar la Cueva** in Santa Rosa, and (difficult to find) **Bar David** in La Suiza.

SERVICES: Codetel is up one block from a corner of the park.

Guayabo National Monument
(Monument Nacional Guayabo)

Located 12 miles (19 km) NE of Turrialba, this is the nation's most famous archaeological site. It is, however, worth a visit more for its natural surroundings and overall ambience than for its ruins. While similar sites are found in Ciudad Cutris in the San Carlos region and in the Barranca de San Miguel de San Ramón, only Guayabo has been placed under protection. There's a nature trail with two branches, one of which drops down to the river, and there are a variety of mammals and more than 80 varieties of orchids. The archaeological site here is still under exploration, and it is open daily from 8-4. Free and quite informative guided tours are available, but they are in Spanish.

Turrialba

GETTING HERE: Get here from Turrialba by taking the *Santa Teresita* bus (daily at around 10:30 and 1:30); it terminates at the beginning of an uphill gravel road four km away. The bus returns from the cross-roads at 12:45. Another alternative is to take the bus that leaves from Turrialba at 5:15 PM and arrives at around 6:30 PM; it stays overnight and then returns at 5:40 AM. On Mon. and Fri. a bus leaves Turrialba for Guayabo at 11:15 and arrives at 12:45 PM. A bus on Sun. leaves at 9 and returns at 4. You can also take a taxi from Turrialba or hitch.

HISTORY: The settlement here once housed as many as 10,000 and covered an estimated 37 acres (15 ha). It is thought to have originated around 1,000 BC, thrived between 800 and 1300 AD, and declined thereafter. It was abandoned about 1400 AD. The site's stone pedestals were thought to have been built between 800 and 1000 AD. Declared a national monument in 1973, it is the nation's only archaeological park. In order to protect the surrounding premontane rainforest, the Guay-abo River Canyon area was added in 1980; its 539 acres (218 ha) now protect the only extant primary forest in Cartago Province. Begun in August 1989, a five-year restoration plan will increase the excavated area to 50 acres (20 ha).

SIGHTS: The circular mounds (*montículos*) here once supported large buildings. Some of the stones in the walkways (*calzadas*) are decorated with petroglyphs, and there's also a large boulder carved with repre-sentations of the crocodile and the jaguar, both indigenous deities. Al-though the meaning of the petroglyphs found at the site is unknown, it is commonly thought that they were carved to invoke supernatural protection. There's a system of aqueducts, and what may be the na-tion's oldest bridge: a broken black rock which crosses an aqueduct. There are great views from the *mirador*, which has sets of wooden benches placed in rows, making it look like an outdoor theater. At the base of the ruins near the exit is the partial reconstruction of a four-km walkway. Unfortunately, the rest of the land remains in private hands so there is no likelihood of it being restored. The trail to the left leads past the ruins, while the one to the right is a loop trail through secon-dary forest. Across the road from the entrance are the picnic area and toilets. A small exhibition hall with some zoomorphic figures and ce-ramics, as well as another room with an archaeological reconstruction of the site, are nearby.

PRACTICALITIES: Camping is permitted. Nearby accommodations are listed under "Turrialba" above. In addition to the aforementioned **La Calzada**, there are a number of places to eat here. **Soda La Palma** is closest to the reserve's entrance. **Soda La Orquídea** is in the Colonia Guayabo which you pass on the way up.

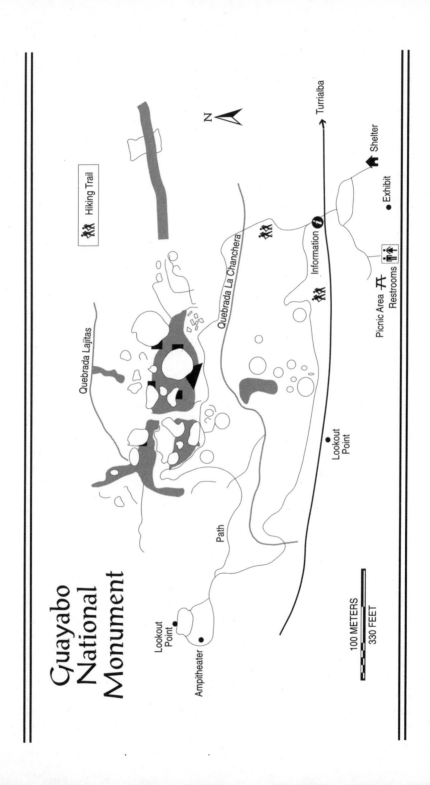

Guayabo National Monument

Quebrada Lajitas

Quebrada La Chanchera

Path

Lookout Point

Ampitheater

Lookout Point

N

Turrialba

Information

Shelter

Exhibit

Picnic Area

Restrooms

Hiking Trail

100 METERS
330 FEET

Other Attractions Near Turrialba

White Water Rafting

One of the most popular activities for visitors to Costa Rica, even those who are not particularly athletic, is rafting on the Río Reventazón, the "foaming" river. The Class II rapids on this river serve as an excellent introduction to rafting for the inexperienced. This is one way to discover that a river has a life and personality all its own. Of the four companies rafting on the river, **Costa Rica Expeditions** (☎ 257-0776, 222-0333, fax 257-1665) is the longest established. Its owner-managers, Michael Kaye and Howard Solomon, first opened the river up for rafting in 1979. After a hotel pickup and a stop for a Costa Rican-style morning feed, you'll be bused through Turrialba to the river, where the rafts and equipment are assembled. You'll be given safety instructions and perform a trial run before departure. Going down the river, you can expect to spin around backwards – one of the thrills! You'll pass oropéndola nests, giant ferns, hanging epiphytes, sloths in the treetops, and perhaps some agricultural workers; you may even spot a crocodile or toucan. There might be a place where you have to disembark and then reboard because of dangerous riptides, and you'll stop briefly for swimming. Lunch (stew, beans, rice, fruit juice, salad) is served in a tent off the river bank. After passing through some more rapids (and traversing a kayak endurance course), you'll come to the end of the run. The rubber rafts are hauled up and, after changing, you're on the way to a hotel where you'll watch the videotape of your trip. Then, it's back to San José. The other companies, such as **Ríos Tropicales** (☎ 233-6455) and **Adventuras Naturales** (☎ 225-3939), differ in small details such as lunch sites. Expect to pay around $65 for the day.

CATIE

Four km E of Turrialba on the road to Limón, the Centro Agronomico Tropical de Investigación y Enseñanza, a 27,500-acre agricultural research station, provides assistance to the small farmer. Established in the 1930s, it is one of the world's five major centers for tropical agricultural research. Supported partly by overseas governments, research here is devoted to producing high-yielding, disease-resistant varieties of bananas, coffee, and *cacao*. Other research projects include studies on improving palms, plantains and on breeding livestock that will thrive on pasture alone without supplemental feed. New species are replicated in a tissue culture lab and packed for shipment worldwide. Tropical agricultural instructors from all over the world gather here for study. The world's largest collection of papers and books on tropical agriculture is here. There's also a collection of hundreds of species of palms. Visiting birdwatchers should be aware that, in addition to a lagoon, there's also a trail behind the administration building to Río Reventazón.

visiting: If you wish to tour the grounds with an English-speaking guide, ☎ 556-1149 three days ahead of time to arrange an appointment. The tour includes a visit to the seed lab and bank, the meat and dairy farm, as well as the orchid, coffee, *cacao*, and other research facilities. Organized groups are preferred. If you want to drop by, you can visit the nature trail on your own, but you will be denied access to the rest. Ask in town concerning buses.

Puerto Viejo de la Sarapiquí Region

This wet but wonderfully scenic area is set on the slopes above the Caribbean coast to the N and NE of Braulio Carrillo Park and also bordering La Selva. Depending on which of the two routes you take getting here, you may pass pejibaye palm plantations, two of the nation's most beautiful waterfalls, banana plantations, lush bamboo thickets, and some superb scenic outlooks.

The Virgin of Sarapiquí

As the start of the next milennium nears, Virgin Mary sightings are on the increase. One such sighting took place in the hills above San Vincente de Miguel, 120 km N of San José, where then 15-year-old Jorge Arturo first spotted her in 1993 near a weathered tree trunk in a pejibaye plantation. Since that date, Arturo has become a celebrity and regularly communicates with the spirit. He says she speaks to him in Spanish and changes her robe each time she appears. A statue has been erected in the "Holy Forest" where she appeared (designed to match Jorge's description), but he claims that the apparition is much more beautiful than the statue. Jorge now plans to become a priest.

Pilgrims still flock to the spot. Visitors collect purified water dispensed from a pump near the statue; cement walkways have been put in along with restrooms and parking spaces. An ambulance stands by on "apparition" days, but a radio campaign has educated attendees about the dangers of staring straight into the sun, so cases of sun-damaged vision that were once a problem have decreased. A booth in the parking area sells transcripts of monthly messages and religious paraphernalia in return for a donation. The money collected will be used to erect a church.

The only hitch is that the Church does not recognize the site and *La Nación* has published an admonition from the Bishop of San José warning Catholics not to visit the sight until the apparitions have been officially recognized. Few people lay claim to having actually seen the Virgin, but some claim to have seen cloud formations resembling Jesus, the sun changing colors, and even attendees surrounded by halos. Meetings – attracting believers from as far away as the US and Italy – are held on the first of every month and are led in devotions by a priest. Jorge stands near the altar at 2 PM: the Virgin transmits her message, and he lets everyone in on it.

getting here: Buses (4½ hours) depart six times daily from Av. 11, C. Central/1. One at 9 follows the Carr. Guápiles via Braulio Carrillo before turning N towards Horquetas and La Selva, then terminates at Puerto Viejo. The bus at 1 runs back through to San José. The one at 4 goes the same way but stops in La Virgen. The buses at 6:30, noon, and 3 take the route above Heredia. A San Carlos-Río Frio bus (two hrs.) leaves at 6, 9, and 3.

Rara Avis

If you only have time to visit one private nature preserve, this is the one to see! January, February, and March are busiest here. Established as a corporation in 1983, Rara Avis S. A., comprising 1,500 acres (600 ha), is the only place of its kind in the world. Biologist-entrepreneur Amos Bien's philosophy is that development and conservation can be compatible and mutually reinforcing. His hope is to set an example that the local people will follow. One way is through tourism: the reserve is already the largest employer in Horquetas. Another is through utilizing the rainforest commercially without destroying it. Future projects planned include the commercial production of tree ferns, wicker, and wood, all to be done in an ecologically sustainable fashion. At present butterflies are being exported in cocoon form to Europe.

Rara Avis (☎/fax 253-0844; Apdo. 8105, 1000 San José) lies 2,000 ft (700 m) above the often-inclement Caribbean coast; you have a 75% chance of being rained on if you come for a short visit. So don't plan your schedule too tightly. May is rainy and is also "horsefly month"; October is a good month to visit. It is constantly booked, so reservations are a must. **note:** You may also contact Rara Avis by E-mail at raraavis@sol.racsa.co.cr or find them on the World Wide Web at http://www.cool.co.cr/usr/raraavis/ing/raraavis.html.

GETTING HERE: This is the fun part! When you reserve, Amos will instruct you when and how to meet the tractor near Las Horquetas; it pulls a green canvas-covered cart with seats. The normal transit point is the "casa de Roberto Villalobos," (☎ 764-4187), where the Rara Avis office is located. A "Jungle Train" truly worthy of the name, this infamous "tractor from Hell" takes you on a bumping and jarring four-hour ride, traversing only nine km in the process. Fording two rivers en route, you pass slowly moving panoramas of local life, past rolling hill after rolling hill of sadly deforested terrain, most of it cut down by local farmers who eke out a living using the land for pasture. As an additional bonus, during the ride you find out how clothes feel while they're in the dryer. Finally you arrive at El Plástico, a former prison colony site. The name relates to the fact that prisoners slept on the ground outside under plastic tarps. The renovated lodge here formerly housed administrators. Surrounded by volcanoes Barva, Turrialba, Irazú, and Cacho Negro, the Caribbean coast is also visible from here. Check out the framed portrait of the Patron Saint of the Jungle upstairs. El Plastico and the surrounding 1,400 acres (572 ha) are owned by Selva Tica (☎ 253-0844). In the dry season, you will have lunch here before proceeding; in the wet season, you'll likely continue on to the waterfall lodge where you'll dine and recuperate. The last stretch of the road has been improved and is now accessible by tractor or on horseback.

SIGHTS: The chief attraction is the spectacular two-tiered **Catarata Rara Avis**, which has a swimming hole at its base. An alarm, installed after three Canadian students drowned in a freak avalanche of water, warns of flash floods coming from above. Another attraction here was a design of the modest and innovative biologist Don Perry. The Automated Web for Canopy Exploration (AWCE) was a motor-driven cable car that took two researchers back and forth and up and down in the forest canopy. Engineered by John Williams, the system used three steel cables strung between two trees on opposite sides of a ravine. To construct it, five men spent over two weeks fighting knee-deep mud. Unfortunately, it was later removed and installed at the site of the present Rainforest Aerial Tram near Braulio Carrillo National Park as a test device. A canopy platform, however, may have been installed by the time you arrive. **other attractions:** A birdwatcher's paradise, Rara Avis has had confirmed sightings of 335 species. Check out the hummingbird feeder as well as the area by the bridge. Other attractions include the spectacular collection of butterflies, the beautiful sunsets, the amazing night noises in the forest, and the lights of the banana plantations in the distance on a clear evening.

PRACTICALITIES: Albergue El Plastico charges around $45 pp ($22.50 for student groups). There are four rooms with a total of 10 lower bunks and nine upper bunks, along with shared hot showers and flush toilets. The eight-room **Waterfall Lodge** ($80 s, $75 pp d) can hold up to 32. Each room is equipped with a double bed, a single, and two fold-down bunks. There are hammocks for lounging outside and a reading area upstairs where a pressure lamp attracts an incredibly diverse flying entomology museum every evening. They have a two-night minimum stay. Although large groups may leave at any time, departures for small groups are scheduled for every Tues., Fri., and Sunday. Aside from the meals, nothing else is available for sale, so anything you might require (including candy or any other snacks) should be brought with you. The beer, soft drink, and phone concessions belong to the cook. While Rara Avis has a large supply of rubber boots, essential for exploring the reserve, there is no guarantee that a pair will fit you, so you might consider bringing your own.

La Selva Biological Reserve

Deservedly or not, La Selva is second only to Monteverde as the nation's most famous private natural reserve. Located near the confluence of the Puerto Viejo and Sarapiquí rivers, this 3,707-acre (1,500-ha) tract is owned and operated by the Organization for Tropical Studies (OTS), and its main function is as a research station for visiting biologists. In the 1950s tropical biologist Dr. Leslie Holdridge began an experimental farm (*cacao, pejibaye*, and laurel) on the present-day site. In 1960, he sold the farm and the surrounding old growth to the OTS. There are a large number of lowland forest nature trails. On a walk, you might see anything from poison dart frogs to sloths to *caimáns*. With over 100 species of mammals, 400 species of birds, thousands of species of insects, and 2,000 plant species, La Selva could never bore a naturalist. The 8.7-acre (3½-ha) Holdridge Arboretum, site of a small field of *cacao* with a rich overstory of shade trees, contains more than 240 species, more than two-thirds of the native tree species at La Selva; its openness makes it easy to view the tree crowns.

PRACTICALITIES: Reservations are essential. A day visit is around $18, which includes lunch. Three meals in the cafeteria and a night in the "rustic" quarters (bunkrooms with shared hot water bathrooms) cost around $90. The hefty fees help support on-going research. Contact OTS (☎ 240-6696, fax 240-6783; Apdo. 676, 2050 San Pedro) about overnight stays. For day visits call La Selva directly at ☎ 710-6897. Ask about their bus that runs three times a week. While in the area ask about **El Bejuco**, a reserve which is free of entry and operated by an ex-manager of La Selva. Also in the area is the family-run **Eco-Lodge** (☎ 766-6122 -mornings, fax 766-6247), which offers rooms with bunk beds for $15 pp. Activities include hiking, birding, volleyball, and eating substantial meals ($4-$6).

Selva Verde River Lodge

Located in Chilamate, five minutes W of Puerto Viejo, the attractively designed lodge (☎ 710-6077, fax 766-6011) has a 600-acre (243-ha) forest reserve across the river. This large establishment is popular with those who want a more comfortable experience than at Rara Avis. Among the tour groups using it are Elderhostel. There's the river lodge trail, a self-guiding 45-minute nature trail right on the premises (with a centuries-old *gavilán* tree numbering among the giants), the river (good birdwatching) is readily accessible, and a butterfly garden is across the road. To visit the reserve you head out to the main road, turn right, then turn right again and cross the bridge. Get a map from the reception and follow any of the trails through the secondary forest, which has patches of old growth. You may see white-faced monkeys.

GETTING HERE: Selva Verde will provide transportation from San José by prearrangement. Otherwise, the bus will drop you by the entrance if you let the driver know. Another option is to take a taxi from Puerto Viejo. If you're driving, it's conveniently located right off the highway.

PRACTICALITIES: The large lodge is divided into two portions, which are on opposite sides of the road. The main portion is a series of attractive structures accessed by a beautiful covered boardwalk. En route to your room, you pass by a stream with turtles basking in the sun. You might see an armadillo dart across a path or a hummingbird flit by. Each room is equipped with hot water shower, fan, and dresser. Hammocks are on the balconies. Across the road and well back along a slope, a set of five bungalows are aligned along a black-painted wooden walkway. There are four beds (two bunk beds) in each room plus a fan, walk-in closet, and bath. Prepared with fresh vegetables, meals are served buffet-style in the spacious dining room above the bar and gift shop. A new library is also here. Activities include nature walks, rafting, bike tours, canoe trips, a river boat tour, guided trail walks, and a butterfly garden tour. The premises are non-smoking, with several special smoking areas provided. Rates start at around $75 pp, single-occupancy, and $65 pp, double-occupancy, including meals but not tax. Bungalows rent for $35 pd and up for student groups and $46 for four and up. Write Costa Rican Lodges, Ltd., 3540 NW 13th St., Gainesville FL 32609 or ☎ 800-451-7118; in FL ☎ 800-345-7111.

La Quinta de Sarapiquí

This Tico-run lodge (☎/fax 761-1052) is set by the side of the Río Sardinal between La Virgen and Puerto Viejo. Each of the 10 rooms (around $50 d) has fans and porches. There is a restaurant, game room, and a 10-acre (four-ha) reforested tract. Activities include hiking, swimming, mountain biking, horseback riding, and birding.

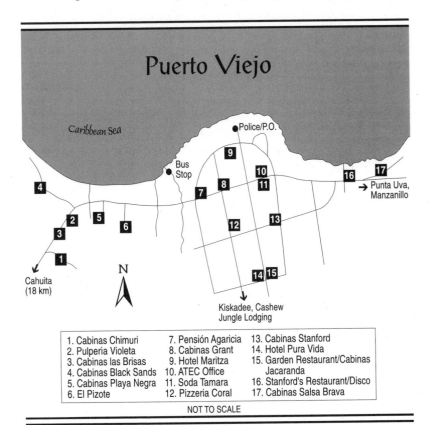

Puerto Viejo

Caribbean Sea

Police/P.O.

Bus Stop

→ Punta Uva, Manzanillo

N

Cahuita (18 km)

Kiskadee, Cashew Jungle Lodging

1. Cabinas Chimuri	7. Pensión Agaricia	13. Cabinas Stanford
2. Pulpería Violeta	8. Cabinas Grant	14. Hotel Pura Vida
3. Cabinas las Brisas	9. Hotel Maritza	15. Garden Restaurant/Cabinas
4. Cabinas Black Sands	10. ATEC Office	Jacaranda
5. Cabinas Playa Negra	11. Soda Tamara	16. Stanford's Restaurant/Disco
6. El Pizote	12. Pizzeria Coral	17. Cabinas Salsa Brava

NOT TO SCALE

Other Puerto Viejo Area Attractions

El Gavilán Lodge

Covering 432 acres (175 ha) and lying 90 km from San José by the Río Sarapiquí in Río Frio, this private reserve opened in 1989.

PRACTICALITIES: One-day to one-week packages (including San José pickup for $20 pp; four-person minimum) are available. There are 12 rooms with private bath, hot water, and fan. German/Spanish cuisine is served. Vegetarians can be catered to. Although there's a BYOB policy in effect with respect to alcohol, delicious tropical fruit drinks are served. One-day excursions from San José, including a boat trip on the Sarapiquí or horseback riding, are also available, as are river trips to Barra Colorado and whitewater kayaking on the Sarapiquí. Write Apdo. 445-Zapote, 2010 San José, fax 253-6556, or ☎ 234-9507.

Oro Verde Station

Nestled between the Sarapiquí and the Sucio rivers, this spartan but expensive lodge is set amidst a large garden and in a former cattle ranch. Three-day packages (around $200 pp) are offered. ☎ 233-7479 or fax 223-7479.

Puerto Viejo Town

Once an important and bustling trade settlement in the long departed days of river travel, the town is chiefly of note for its low-budget hotels: **Cabinas Restaurant Monte Verde** (☎ 766-6236), **Hospedaje Santa Marta, Hotel Gonar** (☎/fax 766-6196), **Hotel Santa María**, and **Restaurant Cabinas La Paz**. More expensive is **Mi Lindo Sarapiquí** (☎ 766-6281), which offers attractive rooms above its restaurant for around $20 d. Hospitable **Hotel Bambú** (☎ 766-6005, fax 766-6132) offers modern rooms with TVs for around $50 d, including breakfast. **Cabinas Manglares** are to the left before town. There are also a number of inexpensive places to eat. The *soda* by the water is a good place to hang out; Don Justo here can help you with transport.

La Virgen

The area in and around this village offers a number of options. At about $4 pp and right in the village, **Cabinas el Río** is one of the only truly low-budget places to stay. It's near a *comedor* and next to a store. Behind it, you can follow a black bridge past attacking geese (the charge of the white brigade) to a really nice covered patio complete with hammocks – a perfect spot to relax. Set at the end of the village on the way to Selva Verde, **Rancho Leona**, a restaurant run by Leona and Ken, has a library and art studio. **Kayak Jungle Tours** (☎/fax 761-1019; La Virgen de Sarapiquí, Heredia) is headquartered here. Seed jewelry and tee shirts are on sale. Trips, from beginning to advanced, run around $75 pp. for a day; longer trips (to Caño Negro and Tortuguero) are more expensive. Kayakers lodge at the Rancho for two nights. Trips ($250 pp) on the Río Bongo in Nicoya are also offered from Sept.-Nov. They serve everything from salads to eggplant parmesan and banana splits. You can also eat at **El Rancho de Doña Rosa** near La Selva. The 34-room **Islas del Río**, a moderate to expensive hotel (☎ 710-6898, 233-0366, fax 233-9671) is six km W of Puerto Viejo. Also set up as a "youth hostel," it's unfortunately not very impressive for the price. **Rancho Turisticos Los Venados** is near La Virgen and has meals, a pool, and hiking; live music is featured nightly; it's open 7AM-11PM daily.

MUSA: On the right in the village of La Tigre as you approach Puerto Viejo from Horquetas, this female-run cooperative sells local herbs. You can tour their farm and learn about natural remedies. Unfortunately, due to petty squabbling, it is not as enchanting as it used to be.

TRAVELING UP THE SARAPIQUI: Many lodges offer trips up here. One of the most unusual is the Río Colorado Lodge's trip up the Río Sarapiquí from Puerto Viejo. (See the "Barra del Colorado" section for details). Heading as far as Río San Juan, a public launch also departs from the pier between 10 and noon, returning at 5 the next morning.

FROM PUERTO VIEJO: There are two routes. The more scenic is toward Chilamate and down. The other is on gravel roads through the heart of the banana plantations and past bamboo groves – an equally fascinating excursion. Watch for the aerial tramways that transport the bananas.

The Monteverde/Arenal Area

Over the past few years, this area has become one of the most popular for visitors. Centrally located, it can easily be visited on the way to Guanacaste. The main attractions in this area include the cloud forest reserve (described in the following section), the other sights near Monteverde, and the active Arenal volcano and its nearby artificial lake of the same name.

EXPLORING: A rental vehicle is the best way to get around here because public transportation tends to be poor. You can take the buses, but you must be patient. March and April are the best times to visit Monteverde because this is when you are most likely to see a quetzal.

Monteverde Biological Reserve

(Reserva Biológica del Bosque Nuboso Monteverde)

If you haven't heard the name Monteverde before your arrival in Costa Rica, you certainly will have before long! Although Costa Rica has any number of cloud forests, Monteverde – despite its dusty, winding road – remains both the most accessible and the most developed. The combination of the Quaker colony, the reserve, and years of hype have transformed the area into a major tourist destination and big business. An incredible 50,000 visitors enter the reserve annually! Don't be under the illusion that Monteverde is a town. It isn't! Monteverde is a community of Quakers who have come here to live apart from American "civilization." It is ironic that, in doing just that and in seeking to preserve the cloud forest, they have attracted unwanted attention and loosed the devil of development upon themselves. Unless you have some particular fascination with Quaker-operated dairy farms, there really isn't much to see or do in Monteverde aside from visiting the reserve or related sights. And you should keep in mind that it rains a lot: have your umbrella in hand at all times! If you're mainly here for the reserve, a day or two is sufficient, unless you're a research biologist. If you want to explore the area, you will want to stay longer. On the other hand, don't rush your visit. You should plan on spending at least one full day (i.e., two nights) in Monteverde to fully appreciate the reserve. Be sure to have warm clothes handy on the way up and be ready to take off your sweater as you descend to sweltering lowland Guanacaste on the return stretch. It's better to have your own rubber boots for rainforest exploration (although the main trails in the reserve are well maintained), but most hotels will rent or lend you a pair.

The Golden Toad

Aside from the quetzal, the nation's most famous creature is the golden toad, so far sighted only in Monteverde's rainforest preserve. In 1983, University of Miami researcher Marc Hayes spotted hundreds; none have been seen since 1987. This is part of a worldwide decline of amphibians (also encompassing glass frogs and rain frogs), and no one knows what the cause is. Some think that acid rain and airborne pesticides may be to blame. Some scientists maintain that amphibians may be a canary in a coalmine, a portent of coming ecological disaster. Others connect this depletion with a concomitant increase in lawyers, politicians, and advertising executives. For the story of the golden toad and its subsequent disappearance, with an informed account of the disappearance of frogs all over the world, see the superb book, *Tracking the Vanishing Frogs* by Kathryn Phillips.

Monteverde/Arenal

Monteverde

FLORA AND FAUNA: Vegetation is profuse and, despite the 300 species of orchids, very green. The 2,500 plant species include 200 types of ferns. Many of the canopy plants take their nutrients directly from the mist and dust suffusing the air. The reserve is not all cloud forest: there are relatively dry areas, swamps, and dwarf trees. There are a wealth of other reptiles and amphibians, around 490 species of butterflies, and some 100 species of mammals.

sighting a quetzal: If you really want to see one, you're likely to be disappointed! One way to ensure a sighting is to visit in the wee morning hours, especially in the nesting months (March-June) when they are most conspicuous. Painted picture signs along the trail demarcate Quetzal Country. (For more information about the quetzal, see the description on page 41.) In addition to the quetzal, other birds to watch out for include the great green macaw, the ornate hawk-eagle, the bare-necked umbrella bird and the three-wattled bellbird, not to mention 50 varieties of hummingbirds.

HISTORY: Founded in 1951 by Quakers from Alabama seeking a better spot to live after some had been imprisoned for refusing the draft, the Monteverde farming community came in, purchased land, and struggled to establish itself. It eventually discovered cheese-making, which now provides its principal income as well as that of the area's numerous Tico dairy farmers. Over the years the colony has grown, and some non-Quakers have settled here as well. The cloud forest reserve was initiated by George and Harriet Powell in March 1972. Originally, 6,200 acres (2,500 ha) of land were set aside as a reserve; another 24,700 (10,000 ha) have been added.

Tourism has grown to become the area's major "industry" during the past decade; as recently as 1974 Monteverde received only about 400 visitors per year. But the financial benefits of "eco-tourism" remain outside of the community; much of the money stays parked in San José or in the States. Intelligently, the area's long-established cooperative loans its funds for what it views as long-term sustainable investments: handicrafts, coffee cultivation, and dairy farming. The local population has now grown to around 3,500 – a 25% increase in the past five years or so.

GETTING HERE: From the *Terminal Tilarán* (☎ 222-3854; C. 12, Av. 9/11) in San José a bus (around $4) leaves at 6 and 2:30 PM daily during the high season. Costa Rica Expeditions also has a bus that runs to its hotel. The Albergue Santa Elena (☎ 224-4085: reservations) offers a bus (around $7) which departs from the Toruma Youth Hostel and makes several stops in San José before heading to Monteverde. Also, most hotels can arrange van transportation from San José. By car, take the Interamerican Highway (Carr. 1), to the junction at Km 149 (look for the iron bridge crossing the Río Lagarto; it's easily missed) and then proceed another 20 miles (32 km) along a steep and dusty dirt road. It may be impassable without a four-wheel drive during portions of the rainy season. The best photos will be from the right-hand side of your vehicle.

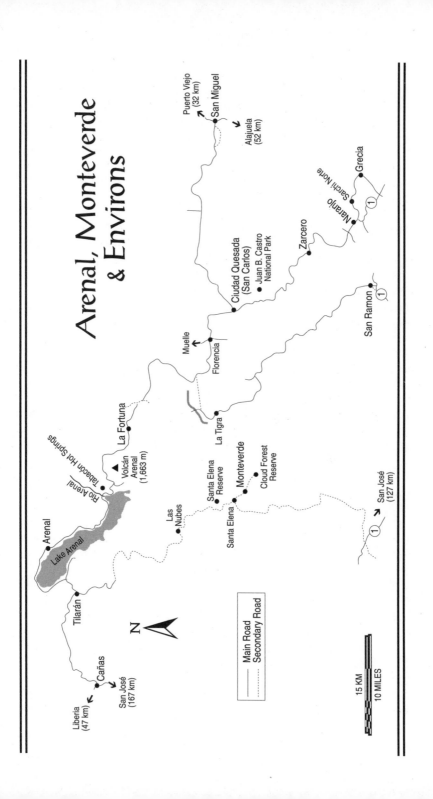

Arenal, Monteverde & Environs

Puerto Viejo (32 km)
San Miguel
Alajuela (52 km)
Grecia
Narango Sarchí Norte
①
Zarcero
Ciudad Quesada (San Carlos)
Juan B. Castro National Park
San Ramon
①
Muelle
Florencia
La Fortuna
Volcán Arenal (1,663 m)
La Tigra
Tabacón Hot Springs
Río Arenal
Santa Elena Reserve
Monteverde
Cloud Forest Reserve
Santa Elena
Las Nubes
San José (127 km)
①
Arenal
Lake Arenal
Tilarán
Cañas
San José (167 km)
Liberia (47 km)

N

Main Road
Secondary Road

15 KM
10 MILES

FROM PUNTARENAS: This route is convenient if you're coming from Montezuma, Manuel Antonio, or if you are unable to take a direct bus from San José. A daily bus runs at 2:15 PM from the bus shelter along the oceanfront and a block away from the Puntarenas-San José bus station. To meet this bus if you are coming from San José, you must leave San José by 11 AM. Or you can take the 12:45 PM San José-Tilarán bus (☎ 222-3854, C. 12, Av. 9/11) and transfer at the Lagarto junction on the Interamerican. Your hotel will send a taxi to meet you in Santa Elena if you have made reservations in advance.

FROM LA FORTUNA/TILARÁN: From La Fortuna (Arenal area) you need to take a bus to Tilarán at 8 AM (three hours). Then take a bus to Santa Elena at 12:30 PM (3½ hours). It may not come all the way in the rainy season so plan on walking for around an hour.

FROM THE NORTH: Take any bus along the Interamerican. Get off at the Lagarto junction and take the first arriving bus up the hill.

BY CAR: The road from the Lagarto junction off of the Interamerican leads to Santa Elena and Monteverde. A shortcut from San José is to take the Sardinal turnoff (look for it some 20 km before Puntarenas), head left from the town central square, and then continue on to Guacimal, where you join with the regular road. A third option is to head from Tilarán to Quebrada Grande and Cabeceras and then go up via Turín (to the left) or Las Nubes (to the right). Allow around three hours, and don't attempt this route during the wet season.

ORIENTATION: From the junction at Lagarto, your bus climbs two hours along a winding, dusty road, passes thoroughly deforested terrain, and then enters the village of Santa Elena. It stops in town and then heads up the hill towards Monteverde. If taking the afternoon bus from San José, you may have to stop and switch into a smaller bus, which appears to have been designed for midgets: woe unto those with long legs! The bus usually also stops at a slightly overpriced basic restaurant which has a deer tied up in the back; your bus driver and conductor will help dish out the food and then retire to the back room to eat.

From the town, two badly rutted roads lead toward the cloud forest reserve and then eventually merge. (A separate road leads out in the direction of the Santa Elena Reserve). The N road passes by the clinic, and the S road passes by Costa Rica Expeditions' Monteverde Lodge. After the merger, the first landmark is El Sapo Dorado to the left. Up the hill, you pass the Heliconia, Monteverde Inn, Manakin, Cabinas Los Piños, and the Monteverde Conservation League. The road veers off to the left, with the gas station and nearby souvenir stand. It leads to Hotel Belmar, the El Bosque, the Co-op, the Lecheria, Pensión Flor Mar, the Friend's Meetinghouse and School, the Fonda Vela, the taxi and telephone service, and then, onward and upward, past Villa Verde, past the estate of legendary nature photographers, the Fogdens, to the reserve entrance.

Monteverde Sights

There are a growing number of things to do here. Suggestions are detailed below and in the Santa Elena section. For an overview of the area, hike up to the TV towers from behind the Hotel Belmar. On a clear day, you can see as far as Nicoya. Aside from visiting the two reserves, one of the butterfly gardens, and/or going horseback riding, you can also hike down (and up!) to the waterfalls in San Luis.

MONTEVERDE CLOUD FOREST PRESERVE: Straddling the low continental divide in the Cordillera de Tilarán at the junction of Alajuela, Guanacaste, and Puntarenas provinces, the reserve (or "preserve" depending on your preference) ranges from 4,000 to 5,800 ft (1,200-1,800 m) in elevation. Here, you are about to enter cloud forest country, one of the most luxurious found in all of the Americas. From May to October it rains almost daily.

visiting the reserve: Stop in the visitor's center (☎ 645-5122, fax 645-5034; open 7-4) where you pay, ask your questions, and receive a detailed trail map of the reserve. Entrance fee is around $8 for adults. There is a discount for students, residents and nationals ($1); children under 15 are free. Weekly passes are available. In addition to the entrance fee, tour groups are now required to pay a user's fee of $10 for each visitor they bring in. (All of this brings in revenues of some $850,000 annually!) Only 100 visitors are now allowed in the reserve at one time, so – if planning an early hike during tourist season (mid-December-April) – you might wish to buy your admission ticket the previous day to avoid disappointment.

There's a restaurant and gift shop. Guided, four-hour nature walks ($24 including admission) are conducted every morning; proceeds go towards an Environmental Education Fund. Night hikes (you might see phosphorescent mushrooms or an olingo) are also offered in season. Inside the reserve, the steps in some areas are fashioned from logs with a covering of netting to prevent slippage. As you go farther, the trails become less "civilized" and, therefore, less traveled. It's safe to refill your canteen at either of the two waterfalls.

suggested routing: This depends on your disposition and time requirements. You might go out on the **Sendero Nubose**, then go down the **Sendero Brillante** to Marker No. 28 where there's a view at the "ventana" (window), with rainforest stretching off into the distance. Then hike back up the **Sendero Pantanoso** and either along the **Sendero Río** (with a stop at the gorgeous, two-tiered waterfall) and then back. Two side trails, the **Sendero Bosque Eterno** and the **Sendero George Powell**, connect the **Sendero Río** with the Chomongo.

MONTEVERDE CONSERVATION LEAGUE: To prevent Monteverde from becoming a green, isolated island in a sea of deforestation, this organization (☎ 645-5003, fax 645-5104) is endeavoring to expand the reserve by the end of the century to 30,000 acres (12,141 ha). Its offices are open weekdays 8:30-12:30. The admission (around $4) includes a printed trail guide. Birds and white-faced capuchin monkeys abound. They also have night tours at 7; call for reservations.

RESERVA SENDERO TRANQUILO: This 200-acre (81-ha) reserve on the family farm of David Lowther (reservations: ☎ 645-5010) is a good place to see wildlife. The tours ($15) take three to four hours and are limited to groups of six. Enroute you are shown virgin and secondary forest, as well as denuded land.

PARQUE DE AVES: This reserve is in the village of Cerro Plano, halfway between Santa Elena and Monteverde. It's open daily until 4 PM and admission is around $5 pp. The property includes banana groves, coffee fields, and secondary forests. Coming here with a guide would be preferable.

BUTTERFLY GARDEN: One of the nation's best, this garden exhibits some 40 species of butterflies in a forest that has been covered with a fine screen. It's open 9:30-4:30 daily; $5 admission. The entrance is marked by a path beginning at the Hotel Heliconia. Follow the butterfly-shaped signs. Other attractions in the area include the **Parque Ecológico** ($5 admission; open 9-5 and for night tours), where wild animals are fed, and the **Serpentario Santa Elena** (☎ 645-5243; $3 admission), which offers guided tours.

SANTA ELENA RAIN FOREST RESERVE (RESERVA SANTA ELENA): Five km NE of Santa Elena, this 900-acre (364 ha) reserve has around 10 km of trails and is open from 7-5. You can see Volcán Arenal from here. You need a four-wheel drive to reach the reserve. It was created by the local high school in cooperation with Youth Challenge International, a Canadian organization. Admission is about $5. Some local guides can show you around. It's quite a bit less developed (and less crowded) than the Monteverde reserve and has mostly secondary growth forest. Many birds seen here are not found in the Monteverde reserve. ☎ or fax 645-5238 to arrange a guided tour.

> ☞ **Traveler's Tip.** Serious birders will want to pick up a copy ($5) of *An Annotated Checklist of the Birds of Monteverde and Peñas Blancas* by Michael Fogden. Published in 1993, it includes a list of 452 species, around 330 of which breed in the area. A great souvenir of the Monteverde area is a package of Café Monteverde, which is grown and processed by a local cooperative.

BEN: Begun in 1988 and already extending over 17,000 acres (7,000 ha), El Bosque Eterno de los Niños (BEN, the Children's Rainforest) is perhaps the world's most singular rainforest conservation project, and it is the product of a single farsighted individual. Teaching in Fagerveig, Sweden, Sharon Kinsman (originally from Maine) was showing slides of the cloud forest to her class when a student volunteered his pocket money to help save rainforest land. The class had soon accumulated funds sufficient to purchase 40 acres; students from the US, the UK, and Germany also pitched in, and the preserve continues to grow. Fifty dollars buys an acre. Send contributions in care of the Monteverde Conservation League, the Nature Conservancy, or the World Wildlife Fund. In return, you'll receive a letter showing how many acres you've saved.

Monteverde Practicalities

MONTEVERDE ACCOMMODATIONS: New hotels are sprouting faster than mushrooms after a spring shower, many of them quite attractive and tasteful. While you probably won't require reservations off-season, they are mandatory during the dry season. Christmas and Easter are booked months in advance. Write Apdo. 10165, 1000 San José to reserve any of these hotels. First out of Santa Elena enroute to the preserve, the **Finca Valverde** (☎/fax 645-5157), a coffee plantation, has five cabins for around $45 d; there are some short trails, a restaurant, and horseback riding. Expensive **Monteverde Lodge** (☎ 645-5057, fax 645-5126) is run by Costa Rica Expeditions. It has private bus service from San José, a Jacuzzi, conference room, gardens, some short trails, and a multimedia slideshow ($5) daily. Rooms are around $90 d. Run by a friendly and informative couple, **El Sapo Dorado** (☎ 645-5010, fax 645-5180), a bar and international restaurant outside of Santa Elena, has 20 attractive cabins for $60-70. There's hiking and occasional live music. Write Apdo. 9-5655, Monteverde.

The attractive and secluded **Pensión Monteverde Inn** (☎ 645-5146) is set at the top of a hill and reached by a road that goes past the Butterfly Farm. It offers eight rooms with private bath and two with shared bath; rates are around $15; packages with food are available; they will cater to vegetarians. It has friendly and helpful owners, a private 28-acre (11 ha) preserve, horseback riding, and other amenities. The moderate, Spanish-style **Hotel Heliconia** (☎ 645-5109, fax 645-5205) is another of the hotels closest to Santa Elena. It has bathtubs, a Jacuzzi, and conference rooms and its international restaurant is reserved for guests. Rates are around $45 d. Next door, moderate **El Establo** (☎/fax 645-5110, fax 645-5041) has carpeted rooms and includes breakfast in its rates. The address is Apdo. 549, 2050 San Pedro. It borders a private reserve, and offers personal service, horseback riding, and a den with a fireplace. Rooms are around $40 d. One of the best values outside of Santa Elena proper, low-budget **Pensión Manakin** (☎ 645-5080) charges around $20 d (for private rooms) or $5 pp (for rooms with shared baths); meals are inexpensive; it's off the road to the right. Low-budget **Pensión El Pino** (☎ 645-5130) is a homestay next door.

With kitchen facilities in some rooms, moderate **Cabinas Los Piños** (☎ 645-5005/5252) range in price from $35-$75. They stand in front of expensive **Hotel de Montaña Monteverde** (☎ 224-3050, fax 222-6148), whose cabins adjoin a farm and woods. It has Jacuzzi, sauna, private reserve, conference room, TV den, gardens, and a restaurant. Rates run from around $70 d to $125 for a "honeymoon suite" with a private Jacuzzi. Write Apdo. 70, San José or ☎ 800-327-4250 in the US. The imaginative, expensive **Belmar** (☎ 645-5201, fax 645-5135; Apdo. 17-5655, Monteverde) rises like an Austrian chalet atop a hill. It has 34 comfortable rooms with fine wood finishing and private baths with showers. Rates are around $50 d. Its international restaurant serves healthy food and there's a pool.

Along a turn-off from the main road, **Soda Manantial** rents out spartan low-budget rooms. Inexpensive **Hotel y Restaurante El Bosque** (☎/fax 645-5129) gives good value; it's priced at around $30 d and guests receive a 10% discount at the restaurant. It may also be possible to camp here.

About one km off the road to the right, inexpensive **Pensión Monteverde Inn** (☎ 645-5156) has good scenery. Low-budget **Pensión el Tucán** (☎ 661-1007) is nearby. It has both rooms and more expensive *cabinas* of recent construction. Attractive, moderate **Hotel Fonda Vela** (☎ 257-1413, fax 257-1416) is second or third nearest to the reserve. Rooms range from $55-$70 d. It offers horseback riding, trails, and an attractive international restaurant with good food. Inexpensive **Cabinas Mariposa** (☎ 645-5053) is just across the road; it has three cabins (about $25 d with Costa Rican breakfast). Inexpensive-moderate **Hotel Villa Verde** (☎ 645-5025, fax 645-5115) has space for 25 guests and is 1,500 ft (500 m) above the Fonda Vela. Charges here run from around $90 d with three meals included and around $35 less without meals; it has very good food at reasonable prices and vegetarians are catered to upon request. More expensive villas ($75) house five. A conference room is on the premises. Students and researchers can also stay right in the reserve field station's dorms on a space-available basis. The cost is $20-30 pp including three meals. ☎ 661-2655 six weeks or more in advance for reservations.

    outlying: Home of the Canopy Tours, the **Cloud Forest Lodge** (☎ 645-5243) is on a former cattle farm, which has cloud forest tracts with trails. There are nine cabins, a small restaurant, and a TV lounge. Rates are $55 d. Eco Lodge San Luis is described below following the Santa Elena section.

MONTEVERDE FOOD: The vast majority of the hotels have restaurants. **El Sapo Dorado** has vegetarian as well as other health-conscious entrées. In addition, the inexpensive **El Bosque** is open from 12-9 daily except Wed. **Hotel Fonda Vela** also has a fine restaurant, as does the **Villa Verde**. Nearest to the preserve and run by a young US expat couple, the **Hira Rosa** has good vegetarian dishes, including tabouli, humus, and salads. **Soda Manantial**, the **Cerro Verde Restaurant** and the **Bar Restaurante La Cascada** (both near the gas station) are other good places to eat. Pricey (by Costa Rican standards) ultra-popular **Stella's Bakery** (☎ 645-5052) has coffee, brownies, German chocolate cake, and pies, as well as lunches (pizza, salads, lasagna, and the like). Birdwatch from the back patio as you imbibe caffeine. If you have wheels, it's much better to buy provisions in Santa Elena. You can visit the **Lechería** or "Cheese Factory" (☎ 645-5029; open Mon. through Sat. from 7:30-12, 1-3:30; Sun. 7:30-12:30), where you watch the manufacturing process and get to sample the nation's tastiest cheese.

Monteverde Music Festival

A series of high-quality concerts are presented at 5 PM daily at the Fonda Vela Hotel during the dry season. Latin American, jazz, and classical concerts are presented. Buses will meet you at your hotel. From the beginning of January to mid-February annually. For information, ☎ 645-5125/5119 or fax 257-1413 or 257-1416.

Monteverde/Arenal

ENTERTAINMENT: There's not much to do here during the evenings. The liveliest place (especially on Sat. nights) is the **Bar Restaurante La Cascada**, which is near the gas station. (Other entertainment is listed in the Santa Elena section.)

MONTEVERDE SERVICES AND SHOPPING: There are no public phones in Monteverde except at the taxi and telephone service up the hill. Check at your hotel to see if the rate is reasonable (one charges as much as 45¢ extra a minute!) and, if not, go up the hill or down to Santa Elena.

Horseback rides can be found at **Meg's Riding Stable** (☎ 645-5052) as well as other places, including **La Estrella** (☎ 645-2751), and **El Establo** (☎ 645-5110); watch for signs or ask your hotel desk. **Establos Santa Elena** rents horses for $8/hour ($6 for children). They also offer a number of tours including one to El Gran Mirador ($30; six hours), where you can see Arenal and another, an overnight trail through the forest to Lake Arenal. Dubbed "The Road Less Traveled," their overnight trip stops at Castillo (spartan digs) for the night; it's six hours on horse each way and costs $70-$85 pp depending upon the group's size. The cheapest horse rental is to be found at the **El Túcan** which charges $5/hour.

Canopy platform access ($40) is offered by **Canopy Tours** (☎ 255-2693, 645-5243, fax 255-0061). You head up a large fig tree, zip across to another platform, and then descend. A natural history tour is also included. **Mount Cycle Adventures** (☎ 645-6042/5061) offers mountain bike tours.

shopping: Open from 8-5 daily except on Sun. (10-4), the **CASEM** (Comité de Artesanías Santa Elena-Monteverde) gift shop (☎ 645-5006) has local crafts and embroidered goods. While the goods may not enchant you, your purchase supports struggling local craftswomen. **Sarah Dowell's Studio** is a short climb above the cheese factory. Open Mon. to Sat., 8-12, 1-5. There's also a watercolor art gallery and the **Hummingbird Gallery** (☎ 645-5030), a photographic gallery dedicated to the work of the famous Fogdens, just before the reserve to the left. It has a wildlife slide show (daily at 4:30), with the fee going toward establishment of a quetzal reserve.

Santa Elena

This small mountain village, situated on a ridge towering over the coastal plain, is the closest town to Monteverde. With its small church and rusting buses, it takes on a special ambience when the fog rolls in. In recent years it has been changing and is becoming more and more touristic, so get here fast. Nevertheless, the town remains a delightfully unpredictable place, where you might see a mother and baby in an all-terrain vehicle, a team of horses, and a milk truck with rattling metal cannisters.

SANTA ELENA ACCOMMODATIONS: Many of the places here have always been low-budget and spartan, which makes it the ideal place for the traveler rich in spirit but poor in pocketbook. However, a few pricier places have been added or remodeled. Popular with backpackers and very central, the **El Túcan** (☎ 645-5067) has rooms ($3 pp) with shared bath as well as more expensive rooms with private bath and cabins (good value!) available. **Hospedaje El Banco**, behind the Banco Nacional, has tiny rooms for around $3. Inexpensive and remodeled in recent years, the **Hotel Arco Iris** (☎ 645-5067, fax 645-5022) is nearby. It has great views and an international restaurant serving dishes flavored with garden-grown herbs; rates run from $10-35 pp. They charge $3 pp for camping. The low-budget **Pensión Colibri** (☎ 645-5067) charges around $4 for basic rooms; meals are available. **Pensión Santa Elena** (☎ 645-5051) charges about $8 for rooms with shared baths. **Pensión El Sueño** is near the church. Rates here include meals, and the more expensive rooms run around $60 d with private bath. The **Bed and Breakfast Marbella** (☎ 645-5153), 10 m E of the Banco Nacional and run by a friendly Tico couple, offers rooms from $20 d (no breakfast; shared bath) up to $54 (four in room with private bath and breakfast). **Cabins Don Taco** (☎ 645-6023) have carpeted rooms. Offering a tie-in with the "youth hostel" chain, the **Albergue Santa Elena** offers low-budget rooms and camping. On the way to the reserve, the **Miramontes Hotel** offers rooms and camping. Farther on after the turnoff is the **Sunset Hotel** (☎ 645-5048/5228), which has a restaurant. (Accommodations farther out of town are listed above under the Monteverde section.) If you wish to stay in this area for a longer period contact **Maximo Ramírez** (☎ 645-2951) concerning homestays at a ranch 11 km away. You have to ride a horse or hike in; food and accommodations run around $5 pd.

FOOD: There are a number of places to eat. Budget travelers swear by the **El Tucán**; it would also be a good place to visit, get a cup of coffee, and sit outside watching the world go by. The **El Daiquiri Restaurant** (☎ 645-5133) is across from the church: they have inexpensive *casados* and they also own one of the local public telephone franchises. Service can be slow, so be prepared for a wait. **Pizzeria de Johnny,** renowned for its pasta and wine, is right before the Heliconia. The town's most versatile place, hospitable **Chunches**, serves expresso and snacks, has a washer and dryer, sells books (including this one), stationery, and other items.

food shopping: In addition to a number of small shops, there's the **Panaderia Jimenez** (which sells granola, bread, muffins, and cookies), the **Supermercado La Esperanza** (which also has a public phone), and (right next door) the **Coopesanta Elena**.

ENTERTAINMENT: The evening mass at the church comes complete with singing and guitar accompaniment. Visit the lively bar at the **Taberna Valverde**. At the entrance you might see a horse tethered up next to a sleek silver four-wheel-drive Suzuki jeep. Inside, cover versions of songs ranging from a Spanish version of "My Tutu" to Joe Cocker's remake of "With a Little Help From My Friends" blare over loudspeakers. If you don't dance yourself, have fun just watching the locals work out. The **Disco Orquideas** is out of town on the way to the Santa Elena Reserve. **El Sapo Dorado** is a bit farther on up the steep hill and a bit upscale as well.

Another, quite unusual, alternative is the ATV and motorbike races held on Sun. out of town near the Disco Orquideas. If you're staying in Santa Elena and want to visit the reserve, you can either walk uphill or take the bus from town early in the morning when it comes up to the top, near to the reserve. If you wish to get to the Santa Elena Reserve from town, you'll either have to walk or charter a vehicle.

FROM MONTEVERDE: The road down is the same one you came up on. With great views of the Gulf of Nicoya and the Nicoya Peninsula, it's a twisting and turning ride down; sit on the left for the best views. Buses to San José run daily at 6:30 AM and at 3 PM. When you want to leave, you can flag down the bus anywhere from the Lechería on down. Be sure of getting a seat, buy a numbered seat ticket from the Hotel El Bosque (☎ 645-5221); it's better to do this as soon as you arrive. The Albergue Santa Elena also has a bus, which is geared to backpackers; its terminus is at the Toruma in San José. A bus runs to Puntarenas at 6 AM daily; change for San José at the Lagarto junction.

other destinations: A gravel road runs from Santa Elena to Tilarán. The same road branches off for the Santa Elena Reserve and again for Los Juncos. The area is beautiful and birds abound, but it is also heavily deforested. During the school year (March-November), a milk truck runs daily to Cabeceras (three hours), where you can connect to Tilarán. Ask at the Restaurant Daiquiri (☎ 645-5133) about current schedules. You can also do this with a four-wheel drive. It's a lovely drive past formerly forested pastureland and definitely the way to go, as opposed to a repeat journey to the Interamerican Highway. A bus also runs from Santa Elena to Tilarán. It departs at 7 AM but does not leave from Santa Elena during the rainy season. From Tilarán, a San Carlos bus (which passes La Fortuna enroute) leaves at 12:30. From the main highway at the Lagarto junction, buses run to the NW; the junction for Nicoya (via a ferry crossing of the Río Tempisque) is at Km 168. Parque Nacional Barra Honda is en route.

by car: See "getting here" above and take the opposite route back to your destination.

Vicinity of Monteverde

Ecolodge San Luis

This beautifully designed lodge-research complex in a gorgeous location at 3,300-4,600 ft (1,000-1,400 m) is near primary cloud forest and other ecosystems. It lies on 162 acres (65.6 ha) at the valley's head. Whereas there are any number of avowedly "ecological" lodges in Costa Rica, there is only *one*, Ecolodge San Luis, a place created with the avowed intention of bringing together researchers to mingle and share their work with visitors. Designed to attract the intelligent, curious, and environmentally concerned, the lodge consists of three complementary, interlocking components: housing and other facilities for students and researchers, a tropical garden and forest reserve, plus a separate lodge. Ongoing projects include an organic garden, coffee harvesting, and reforestation. There's also a fruit grove with 60 different fruit tree species. Tropical biology's trailblazers Drs. Milton and Diana Lieberman are the driving force behind the lodge. The Liebermans live just up the hill in Monteverde and are well known researchers in the forefront of their field.

GETTING HERE: Take the Panamerican to the Sardinal junction and follow the signs for Monteverde until you reach the San Luis turnoff, then follow the San Luis road to the Alto San Luis school, where you turn right. The lodge may also be reached by horse (prior arrangement necessary), car, or sturdy vehicle from the San Luis turnoff near the Hotel Vela in the upper part of Monteverde. If you head down here at night on horseback, the fireflies put on a tremendous strobe light show.

BIRDING: There's tremendous birding in the area, and you may spot toucans right from your hammock. You might see as many as 75 species of birds per day here. Species seen include quetzals, laughing falcons, black hawk-eagles, great black hawks, sunbitterns, spectacled and mottled owls, common potoos, keel billed toucans, emerald toucanets, and a number of hummingbirds. A stay at the lodge includes guided birding, so this is a tremendous opportunity for birders.

PRACTICALITIES: Only one tree had to be felled when the lodge complex was built, and it fits beautifully into its surroundings. Actually a converted cow barn, an attractive wooden building houses a dormitory that sleeps up to 30 in bunk beds. A nearby bath house has powerful hot showers and flush toilets. Its kitchen and lounge serves family-style meals. There's also a library. Electricity is provided by a generator. Each set of secluded cabins contains 12 rooms commanding great views of the distant hills; there are 36 rooms altogether. Simple *campesino*-style meals are served. Vegetarians can be catered to, and the Tica chefs are getting better and better at it. (They found the very idea befuddling at first). Rates are around $45 pp, pn in dorm accommodations; this includes all meals, programs, and guiding. The new lodge cabins are in the luxury range. Special rates for students, researchers, and residents are offered. In Costa Rica ☎ or fax 645-5277 or write Apdo. 36, Santa Elena de Monteverde. In the US, ☎ 206-623-8850 or write Dept. SJO 2280, PO Box 025216, Miami FL 33102-5216.

CATARATA SAN LUIS: To get to these beautiful falls, follow the directions to Ecolodge San Luis as above. Then, follow the river 40 minutes up to the falls; it's a somewhat rigorous trip, so be sure to allow enough time.

CANITAS: Just a few minutes N of Santa Elena on the Tilarán road, this settlement has hotels, restaurants, crafts, horse rentals, and guides. **Los Tornos** has a gold mine containing chalk and crystal deposits. Three hours on horseback from a fork situated before the town, the Quesada family's **El Mirador** (☎ 645-5087 for information) in **San Geraldo Abajo** is a set of spartan cabins and a dorm. Good rainforest hiking and some seven waterfalls are here. Views of both Lake Arenal and the volcano are stupendous. Cars (four-wheel-drive) can get here from February to May; otherwise you'll need to horse it. Very inexpensive packages are available.

El Trapiche

This processing plant (☎ 645-6054) still makes the traditional *tapa dulce* (brown sugar); it's open from 10-7 daily and has a restaurant and souvenir shops. The plant is in the village of **Cañitas**, which has some low-budget hotels, restaurants, horseback riding, and forest guides. **Los Tornos** has an abandoned gold mine.

Parque Nacional Arenal & Environs

This area is just beginning to be explored by overseas visitors; a great part of it has been proclaimed a national park on paper, but not in practice. Afternoon breezes blow across Lake Arenal – an artifical 32-sq-mile (82-sq-km) lake, created by damming a river. The lake is surrounded by rolling pastures and feeding dairy cows. While the river originally flowed E, it has been rechanneled by the dam, and its waters now flow NW.

The town of **Nuevo Arenal** was built by the ICE to resettle the inhabitants after construction of the dam. The same holds true for Nueva Tronadora on the other side of the lake between San Luis and Río Chaquita. Composed of 50-70% pastureland, the San Carlos area to the SE was developed after the 1963 eruption of Irazú left much of the Meseta Central covered with ash and unsuitable for dairying. Today, many of the farms here have been snatched up by expatriates.

GETTING HERE: This is one of the easiest areas to access from either San José or Liberia. You may traverse part of the N central plain, either by driving or taking a bus from Tilarán around Lake Arenal via Fortuna to Ciudad Quesada and returning via Zarcero and Sarchí to San José. Specifics are provided below.

Tilarán

As you approach from a distance, this small, virtually untouristed settlement high above Guanacaste plain appears as a white square amidst rolling green pastureland. The name comes from a combination of the indigenous words *tilawa* (of many waters) and *tlan* (the spot or the place). Tilarán is a government-planned settlement constructed between 1909 and 1912. The town is cool, with a breeze that will really be a welcome relief if you're coming from the stifling Guanacaste plains. If you have the time to spare, it's a nice walk up to the cross on the hill overlooking the town. A rodeo and livestock show is held here during April.

GETTING HERE: Take a bus from C. 12, Av. 7/9 in San José. Another alternative is to approach via Ciudad Quesada, from Monteverde, or from Cañas.

SIGHTS: In addition to the lake and the hotsprings, there's at least one innovative project. Set five km from Nuevo Arenal and 11 km from the dam, **Arenal Botanical Garden** is the wondrous creation of Michael LeMay; it's open 9-4 daily, and admission is $4. In addition to the

Monteverde/Arenal

self-guiding paths that take you past some 3,000 plants, a serpentarium and fish pond may have opened by the time you get there. San Francisco-based Kenentech has begun building a $20 million **wind power plant** near the town. The plant will power 60 turbines and is expected to supply 2.7% of Costa Rica's total energy supply.

Sports at Arenal

Fishing and windsurfing are what's popular here. During the dry season, winds blow across the lake in 20 to 70 knot gusts. **Tico Wind** (fax 695-5387, ☎ 800-678-2252) rents boards for $45 pd or $250 pw, which includes your choice of equipment; lessons are also available. Others to contact include **Villas Alpino** (fax 695-5387), **Tilawa** (☎/fax 695-5050), **Rock River Lodge** (☎/fax 222-5457), and **Adventuras Tilarán** (☎/fax 695-5008). Horseback riding is offered at **The Stable** (☎ 253-3048); it's a good way to explore the area. Owner "Gordo" Murillo offers tours of his 500-acre farm and the area around lakes Arenal and Coter. The farm is at Km 47 outside of Nuevo Arenal.

PRACTICALITIES: Everything is on or very near the main square. The nicest low-budget place to stay is **Cabinas Mary** (☎ 695-5749, around $8); **Hotel Grecia** and **Hotel Central** are other alternatives. Resembling a motel, **Cabinas Naralit** (☎ 695-5393) is inexpensive, charging around $30. **Hotel Yasmine** (☎ 695-5043) has rooms for about $18. **Cabinas Lago Lindo** (☎ 695-5555) has spartan rooms for $15. A final alternative is inexpensive **Cabinas El Sueño** (☎ 695-5347), with rooms for $25. Right by the lake (and the first of many; see below), the **Hotel Bahía Azul** (☎/fax 695-5750) has rooms with TVs and refrigerators for $40 and up. Of the many restaurants, the most deluxe is the **Catalá El Parque**, which has good service and reasonable prices. **Aventuras Tilarán** (☎ 695-5008), which operates the outlying Albergue Arenal, arranges tours.

ENTERTAINMENT: For a drink, **Maleko's Bar** has the best atmosphere. **Films** are shown at the theater. Lots of hearthrobbin' tambourine beating and chanting takes place at **Iglesia Biblical Emanuel.** There are basketball hoops in the main square, but you'll have to bring your own nets.

FROM TILARAN: On the way down to Cañas are immense ranches on green, almost totally deforested slopes filled with cattle munching their way to the slaughterhouse. Buses from San José depart at 5, 6:30,

7:30, 10, 2:30, and 3:30. From Cañas, you may change for Liberia. For San José, buses leave at 7, 7:45, 2, and 4:55; for Tronadora at 11:30 and 4; for Cabecaras at 10 and 4; for Parcelas at 11:30 and 4; for Puntarenas at 6 and 1; for Libano (abandoned gold mines) at 11:30 and 4; for Guatuso at 12:30; for Arenal at 10, 4, and 10; and for San Carlos at 7 and 12:30. If you're driving to Monteverde, you can take a dirt road that goes via Quebrada Grande.

OUTLYING ACCOMMODATIONS: Located at the first corner of the lake you come to after leaving town, headed toward the lake and Tabacón, **Mirador Los Lagos** (☎ 695-5169/5484, fax 695-5387; Apdo. 97-5710, Tilarán) has a restaurant and comfy *cabinas* for around $50 d with hot water. As the name implies, it offers good views, with facials, massages, and yoga classes to boot. Vegetables are harvested from their organic garden, and personalized service is offered.

The 24-room **Hotel Tilawa Viento Surf & High Wind Center** (☎ 695-5050, fax 695-5766; Apdo. 92, Tilarán) is patterned after the Palace of Knossos in Crete. It offers windsurfing rentals and lessons, mountain bikes, canoeing, fishing, tennis, pool, handicap accessibility, and a restaurant (varying reports). Rooms are about $75 d; more expensive ones have kitchenettes. There are great views from the second floor. A number of packages are also offered.

The six attractive rooms ($35 d) at the **Mystica Lake Lodge** (fax 695-5387) have painted animals on their doors. Each has a porch with lakeside views, and breakfast is included in the rates. The hotel's creators, an Italian couple who first arrived on an exchange program, found the area to be magical and mysterious – hence the name. Its Italian restaurant (with pizza-oven) offers great views.

Next to the atmospheric Equus B.B.Q. Restaurant, **Xiloe Lodge** (☎ 259-9806/9192, fax 259-9882) offers simple cabins from $40; they sleep from three to four. It has a pool or you can head down to the river. There is horseback riding on the property, and a "Full Moon Dance" is held monthly. Admission is free, and disco and salsa tunes fill the evening. Informal horseraces also take place on the track nearby.

Near the village of Guadalajara and run by a helpful Tico couple, intimate 10-cabin **Río Piedras** (☎ 695-5247) charges around $15 d. The restaurant is open from 7AM-10PM and serves Tico food including fresh guapote. They also offer horseback riding, fishing, and boating. The Dutch-owned **Villas Alpino** (fax 695-5387) offers five inexpensive, attractively decorated *cabinas* (around $40). Each *cabina* holds up to four and has its own stocked kitchenette as well as parking space. **Rock River Lodge** (☎ 222-4547/7338, fax 221-3011) has cabins priced from $35 d and rooms for $50 d. Its restaurant serves breakfasts and dinners. Offering small rooms in a garden setting, 12-room **Albergue and Club**

Altura de Arenal (☎ 222-6455) charges around $50 d, including breakfast. After passing the Albergue, the rocky gravel road gives way to a paved road.

Eco-Lodge Lago Coter (☎ 221-4209, fax 221-4209), a moderate-expensive "ecotourist"-oriented lodge stands at Lake Coter near the town of Nuevo Arenal. The comfortable facilities include a wooden plank-lined rainforest trail, with mountain biking, windsurfing, sport fishing, sailing, hiking, canoeing, and horseback riding offered. All equipment (right down to binoculars) is provided for its trips. Rooms (lodging only) are around $60 s and $75 d. A number of packages (including lodging, meals, and programmed activities) are available. Tours include excursions to Caño Negro, Palo Verde, Corobicí River rafting, Ocotal (a beach tour), and a trip to Arenal and the Venado Caves.

Chalet Nicholas (fax 695-5387) is a bed and breakfast guarded by Great Danes and set near land being reforested by the owners. It offers three rooms for around $40 d. Videos and books are plentiful, and horseback riding, hiking, shore and boat fishing, or canoeing are all available. **Puerto Las Lajas** (☎ 694-4169, fax 695-5387), a bed and breakfast commanding great views, rents large rooms for $30 d. There's horseback riding, windsurfing, fishing, hiking, and a floating dock set at the bottom of the hill.

in Nuevo Arenal: The town of Nuevo Arenal sprang up when the area's original residents were relocated after the lake was created in 1973. This relatively affluent village, with its gravel streets, now has a number of places to stay – up from zero just a few years back! Least expensive ($15 d) is the six-room **Lajas Restaurant and Hotel** (☎ 694-4169, fax 695-5387). Seven-room and six-*cabina* **Hotel Aurora** (☎ 694-4245, fax 694-4262) charges $40 d including breakfast. Satellite TV is available in the lobby. Outside of town and on the way to Venado, **Toronto Cabins** (☎ 694-4131/4057, fax 694-4058) rent out for $12 d, including breakfast. Recently built **Hotel Joya Sureña**, under the same management, has a restaurant, game room, meeting room, and pool. Five-room **Villa Decary** (fax 694-4086; Nuevo Arenal 5717 Tilarán, Guanacaste), two km E of town, is a converted coffee finca with attractively decorated rooms; each has its own entryway. There's good birding near the villa. Rates are $45 s and $50 d, including full breakfast; a separate bungalow can be rented for $275 pw.

Back in town, the only place to eat (other than Lajas) is the Italian **Ristorante Tramonti**. An intimate bed and breakfast in a 38-acre (16-ha) farm managed by artists, **La Ceiba** (fax 695-5387) charges $20 pp including breakfast. You can hike, birdwatch, milk goats, garden, or sail here. Unsurprisingly, it has an enormous ceiba tree on the premises. Nine km from the dam, **Club Marina Arenal** (☎/fax 239-0040) is housed in a former dairy farm; it has seven attractively decorated pool and cable TV. Horseback riding is available, and a trail leads down to the marina, which has catamarans and windsurfers. Set eight km from the dam on a denuded hilltop, Swiss chalet-style, three-storey **Los Héroes** (☎ 441-4193, 228-1472, fax 233-1772) is like something right out of the alps. You expect to see Heidi come running across the lawn with blond pigtails and a plaid skirt, and a surly St. Bernard arrive with a wooden cask secured under its neck. It charges around $50 d including breakfast for attractive, carpeted rooms. Needless to say, there are some Swiss dishes on its restaurant's menu, and there's a pool. Catering to fishermen (guapote heaven!) and naturalists alike, luxury priced **Arenal Lodge** (☎ 289-6588, fax 289-6798) is almost at the end of the lake, about four km up a gravel road and some 17 km W of La Fortuna. Facilities include Jacuzzi, restaurant, billiard table, and library. Rates run from $75 d. Fishing costs $175 for four hours. One couple wrote us in early 1996 to describe the Lodge as "extremely pleasant, well run, clean, and the staff friendly and helpful."

near the volcano: The closest place to stay near the volcano is **Arenal Vista Lodge** (☎ 220-2121/1712, fax 232-3321). It's near the village of El Cairo, 14 km W of La Fortuna and across the Río Agua Caliente. Attractive Swedish-style cabins are $65 d. Deluxe junior suites are also available ($100 d). There is a glass-enclosed restaurant, and activities include mountain biking, birding, hiking, horseback riding, boat tours, and fishing. The second closest place to stay near the volcano is at the **Arenal Volcano Observatory**. This macadamia plantation, owned by the wealthy Aspinall family, was established as an official research station of the Smithsonian Institution and the University of Costa Rica in 1987. A chasm cut by the Río Agua Caliente separates it from the volcano. Now open to guests, it offers home-cooked meals and five rooms with private bath and hot water. Good excursions from here include the macadamia farm, a hike up adjacent Cerro Chato, with its green crater lake, and across the hardened lava flows. Rates (including three meals) are $55 pp. Packages are available. Write Costa Rica Sun Tours, Apdo. 1195, 1250 Escazú, ☎ 233-8890, 255-2011, or fax 255-4410/3529. Their offices in San José are on Av. 7, C. bis 3/5, which is in back of the Holiday Inn. **note:** Other places to stay are listed under "La Fortuna" below.

Vicinity of Arenal

Parque Nacional Tenorio

This 25,000-acre (10,000-ha) national park was created in 1994. Only 30% of the land is in government hands. There are no facilities as of yet.

Venado Caves (Cavernas de Venado)

These large caves (admission around $3) are hardly your typical tourist spot. To explore them, it is necessary to wade through a river and get down and crawl on your hands and knees at times. The caves were first visited in 1945, explored by a Frenchman in 1962, visited by representatives of the US Atomic Energy Commission in 1969, and additional chambers ware discovered in 1990. Bats number in the thousands, and you may see frogs and insects. Inside, the caves are a white and cream color with numerous stalactites and stalagmites (including one that looks like a papaya). Although each of the 12 chambers is tall enough to stand in, passageways between them are not.

practicalities: Flashlights, helmet and face mask are recommended, as are good shoes. Guides and flashlights are offered by the Finca Don Julio for a two-hour excursion. Be sure to bring extra clothes if you visit. No liability is assumed by the landowners, so you visit at your own risk. You can stay at low-budget **Cabinas Las Brisas** in the town of Venado four km away. A bus runs from San Carlos to Venado at 2, a 2½-hour trip.

Los Lagos

These two small lakes, a few km N of La Fortuna, offer swimming and paddleboating. Admission is less than one dollar. The first lake is three km from the entrance, while the second is a two-km walk further through the forest. A restaurant and campground are on the main road in the direction of Tabacón.

Tabacón Springs Resort & Spa

This is one of the world's great hot springs, named after a large-leaved plant that is a cousin of tobacco. The average water temperature is about 104°F (40°C). Tabacón (☎ 222-1072, 322-0780, fax 221-3075) is about 2½ miles (four km) beyond Lake Arenal. It's across a causeway and past a few km of lush scenery. Expanded and remodeled in recent years, it now has a gourmet restaurant, five pools (two for children and three for adults), tiled waterfalls, massage rooms, changing rooms, lockers, gardens, and a curving water slide. It's open daily 10 AM-10 PM. Admission is steep – around $8 for adults and $4 for children; the fee is reduced significantly after 6. (If you can't afford this, lower-cost bathing opportunities are available nearby.)

getting here: If you take a morning bus (2½ hrs, $1.20) from Arenal, you can return in late afternoon. The road is bad, and there are likely to be encounters with cows and brahmin bulls blocking the road. Try to avoid the area on weekends.

accommodations: A set of 32 luxury rooms (many with their own hot spring Jacuzzi) are planned here and may have been constructed by the time of your arrival. A group of two-room cabins ($40d) with picture windows facing the volcano, **Cabañas de Montaña de Fuego** (fax 479-9106) is one km before the hot springs. Camping ($2) is also available, as are camping equipment rentals. There are hiking trails on the property and horseback riding is available. Another alternative, **La Jungla** is two km from the springs and offers camping and cabins.

Arenal Volcano (Volcán Arenal)

This majestic 5,358-ft (1,633-m) active volcano, with its sheer, symmetrical cone, occasionally rumbles, throwing up ash and rock. It is dangerous and definitely not recommended for climbing. One tourist died and another was severely burned climbing its slopes in 1988. Arenal is best viewed from a distance at night, when the fiery bursts and shooting molten rocks are visible. Its last eruption in 1968 eradicated the town of Pueblo Nuevo, killing 78. During this eruption it shot out huge incandescent blocks. Most of these disintegrated when they landed, but many left impact craters from six to 90 feet wide as far as 10 km from the volcano. **note:** Arenal has been declared a national park, but there is no advantage in paying the full fee, except that this permits you to get a bit closer. Despite the increase in fees, the road continues to be in terrible shape, and there are no facilities.

La Fortuna

The town closest to Volcán Arenal, this somnolent settlement has become a magnet for visitors in recent years.

GETTING HERE: Take a San Carlos bus at 6:15, 8:40, and 11:15 AM daily from Coca Cola (C. 16, Av. 1/3; four hours) in San José or board the bus at San Carlos (1½ hours). There are also buses that continue to Tabacón (13 km farther). **by car:** Drive via Naranjo, Zarcero, San Carlos (Ciudad Quesada), Florencia, and Muelle (three hours plus) or to San Ramón, then La Tigra and on from there (a bit shorter but less scenic).

SIGHTS: To get to **Catarata La Fortuna,** follow the well-marked dirt road leading S from the left side of the church. Go 5½ km to the small parking lot overlooking the falls. From here a trail leads down to the falls' base. This trail becomes unusable during the rainy season, when it is also likely to be necessary to have a four-wheel drive if you drive in. If you would like to get here by horse, contact El Paraiso and Prof. Adrian Lobo in town or Finca de Cito on the road to Lake Arenal. Another attraction is the **Laguna Cerro Chato** – an undeveloped, forested lake eight km from town; the last three km must be traversed on foot. **Los Lagos** (☎ 479-9126), just outside town, is a large finca with lakes, horseback riding, paddleboats and water bikes, and camping. The **Venado Caves**, 45 minutes from town, may only be entered with a guide. It's a muddy, slippery, clammy, oozy, bat-ridden, and quite adventurous experience. Expect to see sights as diverse as a papaya-shaped stalagmite, fossilized seashells, and cave-dwelling fish. Discovered after the finca's owner fell in a hole, the caves have been open only since 1991. Most area hotels will arrange a tour. (For more info see their mention under "Vicinity of Arenal" above).

ACCOMMODATIONS: Fortuna has a range of accommodations, some of which will fit any budget. Facing the park, low-budget **Hotel y Restaurante La Central** (☎ 474-9004, fax 474-9045) is nearing a half-century of operation; rooms are about $4. Its neighbors include **Cabinas Emi** (☎ 479-9076) and low-budget/inexpensive **Cabinas La Amistad** (☎ 479-9035), which charges about $5, as does **Cabinas Grijalba** (☎ 479-9129). **Cabinas La Tejas** (☎ 479-9077) offers attractive rooms with shared bath for $4. The people are friendly and will help with tour planning; ask them to connect you with William, who can take you to the mini-volcano, Chato. **Cabinas Carmela** (☎ 479-9010) charges $10 pp. **Cabinas Rolopz** (☎ 479-9058) has bright rooms for $25 d including breakfast. Eight-room, inexpensive **Burío Inn** (☎/fax 479-9076; $20 pp) includes continental breakfast. It has a garden in its rear. Inexpensive **Cabinas San Bosco** (☎ 479-9050) is 200 m N of the gas station; it has rooms from $20 d; there is a pool and observation area. Inexpensive, three-storeyed **Hotel Las Colinas** (☎ 479-9107) has attractive rooms ($7 pp) with private baths and hot water. Down a quiet side street, **Cabinas Ribera** (☎ 479-9048) charges $10 pp for rooms with fans and baths. **Cabinas Guacamaya** (☎ 479-9087) has two attractive cabins for $35 d. **Cabinas Rosi** (☎/fax 479-9023) offers basic rooms with hot water and fans from $20 d; one more expensive room has a kitchen. Set six km E of La Fortuna, **Las Cabañitas** (☎/fax 479-9091) has *cabinas* for $80 d. Facilities include a restaurant, two pools, and a poolside palenque, a thatched-roof pavilion like those used by the Indians. One km further is **Rancho el Corcovado** (☎/fax 479-9090/9178), which is on a 150-acre (62-ha) farm. Guests may pick their own fruit, fish in the lake, ride horses, or milk cows. Facilities include a restaurant, pool, and tennis, volleyball, and basketabll courts. Rooms are $50 d. Set off the road between La Tigra and Chachagua, **Hotel Bosques de Chachagua**

(☎ 239-1049/0328, fax 293-4206) has 240 acres (100 ha) of primary forest on its 370-acre (154-ha) grounds. There are 15 cabins ($75 d), restaurant, horseback riding, tours, and hiking. Packages are available. The 15-unit **Cabinas Rossi** (☎/fax 479-9023) has one room with kitchen, a coffee shop, and picnic tables.

> ☞ **Traveler's Tip**. Female travelers should avoid a man who may greet you at the bus stop and will try to get you to go to his *pensión*. He takes care of the place for his family, lives there alone, and has a reputation for molesting female guests.

FOOD: In addition to the hotels that have restaurants, you may dine at **El Jardín**, which has a playground and is across the road from the gas station. Open-air **Choza de Laurel** serves Tico-style food on long picnic tables. Thatched-roof **Restaurante Rancho La Cascada** is next to the park. **Restaurant Pizzeria Italian** offers a variety of that nation's dishes. Another good restaurant is **El Lirio y Luna**; also try **El Jinete**, **El Río**, and **Terruño**. **La Vaca Muca** (a pricey tour-bus stop) can be found three km W and on the way to the volcano. **El Coquito** is well out of town on the way to San Carlos. Set nine km from town on the way to Muelle, **El Catalán** offers Spanish dishes, including lobster *maresme* and *tortilla español*. Wash it all down with sangria.

TOURS: Be wary of touts on the street who may claim to be tour guides. The **Burío Inn** provides tours of Caño Negro, Arenal, the Venado Caves, and other destinations. Cost is based upon the number of participants. Also call **Aventuras Arenal** (☎ 479-9133), which has a sunset cruise on Lake Arenal or **Sunset Tours** (☎/fax 479-9099). Contact **Natanael Murrillo** (☎ 479-9087) about fishing trips on Arenal. **Repuestos y Acesorios** rents mountain bikes.

Ciudad Quesada (San Carlos)

Situated 48 km N of Naranjo and 95 km from San José, this town (pop. 27,000) is most commonly known as San Carlos because it's located near the San Carlos Plains, a major agricultural area. To get here, take a *directo* bus (preferably). They run near-hourly (5AM-6PM) from Coca Cola at C. 16, Av. 1/3). Or you can take the Tilarán-San Carlos bus at 12:30.

ACCOMMODATIONS: The inexpensive 50-room **Hotel La Central** (☎ 469-0766, ☎/fax 469-0301; Apdo. 345, 4400 Ciudad Quesada) charges US$25-30 for its rooms with showers; there's also a casino and guarded parking. Down the street, the recently constructed **Hotel Don Goyo** (☎ 460-1780) has sunny rooms with baths and a restaurant. It's similarly priced. Also just off the park, low-budget **Hotel El Retiro** (☎ 460-0275) is one of the cheaper places; others include the **Diana, Lily, París, Los Frenandos, Uglade,** and **La Terminal. El Nido Bed and Breakfast** (☎ 460-1322, fax 460-1145), to the N of town amidst landscaped gardens, charges around $50 d; some rooms have shared bath. **Balneario San Carlos** (☎ 460-0747; Apdo. 345, 4400 Ciudad Quesada) features a pool, two children's pools, restaurant, a small lake for fishing and boating, and a roller skating rink. It has *cabinas* with refrigerator and hot water for US$10. Dances are held on Sundays. To get here, follow the signs five blocks NW of the park.

FOOD: Restaurante Tonjibe, on the square, offers pizza, pasta, seafood, and rice dishes; live music accompanies dinner. Set inside the Centro Comercial on the plaza, the **Casa Loca** offers seafood, sandwiches, and a wide selection for carnivores. Gourmets will appreciate **Los Parados Restaurant and Pizzeria** (☎ 460-5302), which serves jumbo shrimp cocktail, sandwiches, and grilled fish, among other dishes.

INFORMATION: The **Chamber of Tourism** (☎ 460-1672) offers maps and advice; it's generally open from 8:30-11 and 12:30-5 except Wed. afternoon and weekends.

SHOPPING: An *artesanía* cooperative in the park's NW corner sells local arts and crafts.

FROM SAN CARLOS: Beyond San Carlos, a road runs to La Fortuna, near Volcán Arenal, then over the Tilarán range to Arenal Lake and down to the Interamerican Highway at Cañas. From San Carlos, a Río Frio bus leaves at 6, 9, and 3. Buses for Fortuna leave at 6, 9, 1, and 4:30. Buses for Tilarán via Fortuna and Tabacón leave at 6 and 3.

Vicinity of Ciudad Quesada

Juan Castro Blanco National Park

(Parque Nacional Juan Castro Blanco)

Declared a national park in 1993, this area lies just to the S of San Carlos. It covers some 60,000 acres (24,000 ha), protects the sources of several rivers, and serves as a refuge for birds such as the quetzal. Juan

Castro Blanco is named after a local individual who promoted national preservation in the area. European mining interests were denied permits to stripmine sulfur deposits here in 1990.

Complejo Turistico Tilajari & Nearby Hotels

Tilajari (☎ 469-9091, fax 469-9095) – in Muelle de San Carlos, 22 km N of San Carlos – is the area's plushest hotel. It is run by James M. Hamilton, a former Peace Corps volunteer who has lived in the area for more than two decades. His establishment offers luxury-priced a/c rooms and suites with private terraces.

Facilities here include sauna, two pools, racquetball courts, and three lighted tennis courts, amidst 40 acres bordering the Río San Carlos. You can take part in excursions including horseback riding through the 600-acre cattle ranch or go on a guided hike through the 1,000-acre tropical rainforest preserve. Trips to Caño Negro, Fortuna's waterfall, Arenal volcano (30 km away, despite the hotel's deceptive logo), and the Venado Caves are also available. Rates are $75 d for standard rooms and $95 for suites. Write to the hotel at Muelle, San Carlos.

Some nine km N and near Boca de Arenal, **Río San Carlos Lodge** (☎ 469-9179/9194, fax 460-0391) is an old home with five rooms, gardens, pools, and a restaurant; prices are around $60 d with breakfast.

La Quinta Inn Bed and Breakfast (☎/fax 475-5260), overlooking the Río Platanar, is run by Costa Ricans returned from two decades in the US. Facilities include volleyball and basketball courts, pool, hammocks, and a sauna. Bunk beds are $10 pp and rooms in their home are $35 s, d, or t. Group rates with meals are available.

La Garza (☎ 475-5222, fax 475-5015) is a 600-acre (248-ha) cattle farm with a 723-acre (300-ha) private reserve near Muelle on the way to La Fortuna. It has attractively furnished *cabinas* ($68 d), a pool, a restaurant in a converted farmhouse, and a three-km hiking/jogging trail. Horseback riding, guided tours of the reserve, tubing and swimming in the river, and fishing are offered.

Ciudad Cutris

These pre-Columbian city ruins are five km N of Venecia, an hour's bus ride from San Carlos. There is a basic *pensión* where you can stay in Venecia. There are no facilities at the site itself and it is on privately owned land, so ask permission before you trespass.

El Tucáno Country Club

The large white gates of this expensive French Canadian-managed inn (☎ 460-3141, 233-8936, fax 460-1692, 221-9095) open onto immaculate grounds. It is eight km NE of Ciudad Quesada and Aguas Zarcas at Agua Caliente de San Carlos. The premises include saunas, thermal baths, three swimming pools, whirlpools, a small zoo, and a nearby miniature golf course. A first-class spa is in the works and may be available by the time you arrive. Packages are available. The day use fee is around $2 pp. Rates run from $66 d to $175 for the "presidential suites." While here, be sure to visit **El Marina Zoologica** (☎ 460-0946), a nearby nonprofit facility that rehabilitates and then releases injured, confiscated, and abandoned birds, reptiles and mammals, as well as exotic pets. To get to the country club from San Carlos, take a San Miguel, Pital, Aguas Zarcas, Venecia, or Río Frio bus. From here you can drive E 20 miles (32 km) to Hwy. 9. From El Tucáno, you may turn E on Hwy. 9, head toward Puerto Viejo de la Sarapiquí, or turn right where you'll find a lovely stretch of road leading to San José via Heredia.

The Republic of Airrecú

In 1995, a small group of Costa Ricans residing in Nicaragua near the Costa Rician border established the short-lived Republic of Airrecú, a name taken from the Malekú word for "Friendship." They formed the 47-sq-mile (123-sq-km) nation claiming that the area had been ceded mistakenly to Nicaragua. President Agusto Rodríguez presented documentation on behalf of their claim to United Nations representative Hans Krutz at San José in June. The "nation" – comprising some 5,000 souls – centered around the border town of Jomusa. The residents were understandably peeved because they had been settled there by the Costa Rican government under an agrarian project some two decades ago. The mistake was discovered in 1994 when the border was surveyed by satellite. The original demarcation in 1900 was now shown to be incorrect. It was the wish of the insurgents to become a Costa Rican municipality. The rebellion took place despite assurances by the Costa Rican government that residents would be resettled within Costa Rican borders. But the rebels were swiftly crushed by Nicaraguan troops.

Laguna del Lagarto

Founded by Vinzenz Schmack, the Laguna del Lagarto (☎ 231-6006, 232-9816, fax 289-5295, 231-3816; Apdo. 995-1007, Centro Colón) lodge is one of the most remote in the nation. After purchasing 265 acres (110 ha) of virgin rainforest in 1981, Schmack attempted to farm it, then switched to tourism. The lodge has 14 rooms with private baths, six with shared bath, and a restaurant; more cabins are planned. Activities include hiking, canoeing on the lake, and a boat trip up the Río San Juan (usually on Tues.). Rates are $53 pp, including meals. **getting here:** The lodge is past Pital and Boca Tapada. A paved road leads to Pital, then it's 18 miles along a gravel surfaced road to Boca Tapada; the lodge is four km farther along a firm gravel road.

Caño Negro Wildlife Refuge
(Refugio Nacional de Fauna Silvestre Caño Negro)

This swampy 24,633-acre (9,969-ha) tract is one of the most inaccessible of the nation's wildlife refuges and, for that reason, one of the least touristed. It's 77 miles (124 km) N of Ciudad Quesada and 36 km E of Upala. A lake covers some 1,977 acres (800 ha) of the refuge, and you need a boat to explore. Endangered species residing here include *caímans*, crocodiles, ocelots, pumas, cougars, river otters, and tapirs. Among the ample birdlife are Nicaraguan grackles and the nation's largest colony of neotropic olivaceous cormorants. Camping is permitted, and there is also limited, low-cost lodging (see below). Boat and horse rentals are available. Contact the reserve via the San José radio number (☎ 233-4070) or call 460-1301, the area's public phone.

GETTING HERE: A bus runs daily from Upala. Take a direct bus from Av. 5, C. 14 at 2:45. **tours:** The best time to visit is during the rainy season when there's the maximum amount of water. If hiring your own, expect to pay $40-90 depending upon the type of boat and number of passengers. Ask at the **Restaurant El Parque** (by the *muelle*; ☎ 471-1032/1090: ask for Julia Pizarro), where you can also dine.

LOS CHILES ACCOMMODATIONS: Stay at the low budget Tico-style hotels or the **Caño Negro Lagoon Lodge** (☎ 225-1073, fax 234-1676), 15 km to the S, which provides simple rooms for $50 d, a restaurant, and tours (on foot, by boat, or on horseback).

UPALA ACCOMMODATIONS: In Upala you can stay in the inexpensive **Hotel Rigo**, **Pensión Isabela**, or the **Pensión Buena Vista**. Martin

Bernard (☎ 228-4812, 289-8139) of **"No Frills"** offers low-budget accommodation as well as trips on the Río Frio and to Nicaragua. Near Upala, **Los Ceibos Lodge** (☎ 221-7641, 222-4059, fax 233-9393) offers horseback riding and guided walks. Buses run from San José to Upala (☎ 257-0061; C. 16, Av. 3/5). **getting here:** For $60 and up, you can also charter a boat from Los Chiles (stay at low-budget **Río Frio,** ☎ 471-1127) to make your way five hours down the Río Frio and back. Numerous lodges and tour companies also run tours up here. In the dry season, they can't go all of the way.

Caño Negro
National Wildlife Refuge

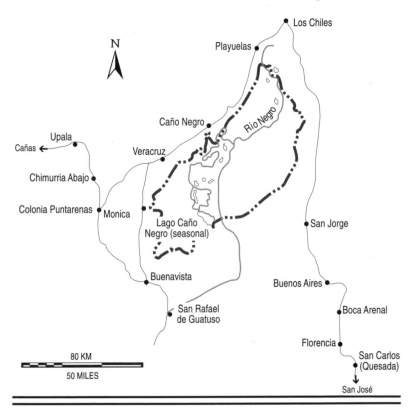

☞ **Traveler's Tip.** If you really want to get away from it all, travel from Los Chiles by boat into Nicaragua. The town of San Carlos is on Lake Nicaragua. Spartan sportfishing **Hotel Mancarrón** is on the Isla Sonentiname on the lake. The lake came to fame when the late Catholic priest and Sandinista Culture Minister Ernesto Cardenal established a commune to propagate a mix of the arts, revolutionary fervor, and liberation theology. The border is closed on weekends. Flights and a river ferry (12 hours) connect the area with Managua. This route is strictly for *true* adventurers.

South from San Carlos

Zarcero

This is famous for the dozens of boxwood hedges that stand in front of its cottage-style church. These are in the shape of animals (bull, rabbit, and an elephant), dancers, oxcarts, even an airplane and a helicopter. **getting here:** The bus (about 2½ hours) leaves from the corner of C. 16 and Av. 3 near Coca Cola daily at 9:15 or you can take any of the hourly San Carlos buses from Coca Cola. Check in the Soda Los Amigos, to the S of the park, for the bus schedules. From Zarcero you can go on to the Arenal area. If you're driving (1½ hours), get off at the Naranjo-Ciudad Quesada exit. **practicalities:** The **Hotel Don Beto** (☎/fax 463-3137) has two rooms with private bath and two rooms with shared bath. Breakfast is available and Tica owner Flora Salazar is knowledgeable about the area. Rates are from around $20 d for a room with shared bath. If you're in the mood for Italian food, try **Restaurant La Montaña** just before the town. Roadside stores in this vicinity sell good jams and excellent cheeses.

San Ramón de Alajuela

This farming town, set on the main highway to Puntarenas SW of Zarcero, boasts an enormous *feria del agricultor* (farmer's market) every Saturday and a small **museum** (Museo San Ramón), open weekday afternoons.

Bosque Nuboso de Los Angeles

This 2,000-acre (810-ha) private reserve, owned by ex-President Rodrigo Carazo, has a two-km walking trail, waterfalls, rivers, and horseback riding. In addition to the virgin cloud forest, there's pasture and farm land. Admission is $14; a guide is $7 additional. Near the entrance, expensive **Hotel Villablanca** (☎ 228-4603, fax 228-4004; Apdo. 247-1250, San José) has 20 small cabins with fireplaces for $100 d and rooms in the main house for $80. Food is $25/day extra, and you must pay a trail fee daily! Lower-priced dorm rooms with cooking facilities are also available. Meals are served buffet-style. To get here, take the road from San Ramón to La Tigra – pick it up 200 m W of the hospital N of town. Follow the signs to Villablanca and the cloud forest. A paved road gives way to gravel. There's no bus transport from San Ramón (20 km away). A taxi costs $10 OW.

Valle Escondido Lodge

This lodge (☎ 231-0906, fax 232-9591; Apdo. 452, 1150 La Uruca) is set in a valley to the N of San Ramón and Los Angeles. It is in San Lorenzo (a town also linked by road with Santa Cruz and Ciudad Quesada), surrounded by 400 acres (162 ha) of pastures and primary forest. The lodge has 19 attractively furnished rooms (around $60 d), an international restaurant, and live music on Saturdays. Horseback riding, mountain biking, river swimming, tours, and hiking are available.

San Rafael de Guatuso

This small town, surrounded by cattle ranches, retains a laid-back cowboy atmosphere. Maleku Indians, who live in three *palenques* (or traditional houses) nearby, practice subsistence farming and sell carved gourds to visitors. Stay at the 10-room **Albergue Tío Henry** (☎ 460-2058) above the veterinary supply store. Rooms with shared bath are $10 and those with private bath and a/c are $20. Tío Henry offers tours, including a horseback trek that passes El Arbol de la Paz (an old tree made into a peace symbol by Oscar Arias). It continues on to a village where you dismount, dine on coffee, *tortillas*, and fruit, then continue on foot to the La Paz waterfall.

Ujuminica

This 1,500-acre (600 ha) crocodile and *caimán* farm lies on the banks of the Río Frio, downriver from San Rafael de Guatuso and near Caño Negro reserve. Its name means "crocodile fell in the trap" in the Maleku language. Meals are served in a thatched-roof restaurant here.

Hotel de Montaña Magil

The Magil Forest Lodge, in the Guatuso hills of Guanacaste, has rooms with bunk beds, writing desks, and private baths. Boat excursions to Caño Negro are also offered. To get here, take the road from Ciudad Quesada heading towards Florencia. Crossing the Río San Carlos, the road heads for Monterey and then on to San Rafael de Guatuso. There, you cross the Río Frio on the rope bridge and head onward to Colonia Río Celeste. There is no public transport and a four-wheel-drive vehicle is recommended – especially for the last three km. Over 250 species of birds and animals, such as sloths, tapirs, ocelots, and jaguars, are found in the surrounding private preserve, but you have to climb a hill to get there. Rates (including food) are expensive. For information, contact **PCI Tours**, 8405 NW 53 St., Ste. A 108, Miami FL 33166, ☎ 305-594-2149. Or contact Hotel de Montaña Magil (☎ 221-2825, 233-5991, fax 233-6837), Apdo. 3404-1000, San José.

The Northwest

Guanacaste

Costa Rica's relatively arid NW is largely contained in the province of Guanacaste, an area quite distinct from the rest of the nation; its culture is largely *mestizo* with some surviving Chorotega customs, such as use of the digging stick in agriculture and traditional forms of pottery. Another survivor is the *punto guanacasteco,* which has become the national dance. Its name comes from the guanacaste (earpod) tree, which offers shade in the pastures. In 1824, Guanacaste's inhabitants seceded from Nicaragua and elected to join Costa Rica.

A sort of late 20th-C Central American version of the Wild West, Guanacaste is indisputably cattle country. *Boyeros*, tenders of oxen, and *sauderos*, the local cowboys with their ornately decorated saddles, are mythologized folklore figures. Bullfights are commonly seen in Santa Cruz, Liberia, and Nicoya. The bull is not injured in these confrontations.

PENINSULA DE NICOYA: The most popular piece of the region is the Nicoya Peninsula. There are literally dozens of beaches, some of which have seen little in the way of commercial exploitation. The downside is that there is also very little in the way of tourist amenities, the nicest beaches are the most difficult to get to, and most of the coastal villages get buses only once a day; if you miss them, that's it. The upside is that you really have the place to yourself once you are there, and there are no hawkers, male prostitutes, or most of the other problems that plague the beaches of Third World nations in the Americas. If you find things a bit rough-going, keep in mind that gradually roads are getting paved. So what may be a bumpy, dusty ride today, could be a nostalgic memory by your next visit. And you may want to thank your lucky stars that you visited when you did, because prices continue to skyrocket.

But the peninsula is not all beaches. There are also sugarcane, teak and *pochote* (rosewood) plantations. Nicoya is a region of villages. You can tell when you're in a truly small town because there are no Chinese restaurants! There are a larger number of thatched-roof dwellings than you might see elsewhere, a reflection both of limited transportation and low income levels.

Ferry Schedules to & from Nicoya Peninsula
Times subject to change

From Puntarenas	From Playa Naranjo
3:15	5:10
7	8:50
10:50	12:50
2:50	5
7	9

From Puntarenas	From Playa Tambor
4:15	6
8:45	10:30
12:30	2:30
5:30	7:15

From Puntarenas	From Paquera
6	8
11	12:30
3	5

CLIMATE: Flat and dry, with ranches occupying large expanses of former rainforest, this province turns green almost overnight after the rainy season commences. If you treasure solitude, May and June are really the months to visit Guanacaste. This is the rainy season, but it is also green and, as the hotels are practically empty, you can stay wherever you choose.

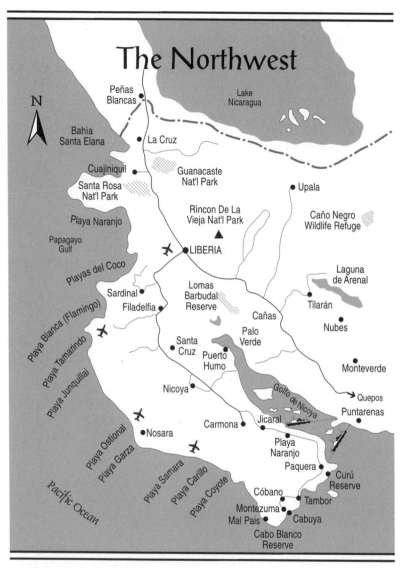

The Northwest

Peñas Blancas

Lake Nicaragua

N

Bahía Santa Elana

La Cruz

Cuajiniquil

Guanacaste Nat'l Park

Upala

Santa Rosa Nat'l Park

Playa Naranjo

Ríncon De La Vieja Nat'l Park

Caño Negro Wildlife Refuge

Papagayo Gulf

LIBERIA

Playas del Coco

Sardinal

Lomas Barbudal Reserve

Laguna de Arenal

Tilarán

Filadelfia

Cañas

Nubes

Playa Blanca (Flamingo)

Santa Cruz

Palo Verde

Puerto Humo

Playa Tamarindo

Monteverde

Playa Junquillai

Nicoya

Golfo de Nicoya

Quepos

Puntarenas

Carmona

Jicaral

Nosara

Playa Ostional

Playa Naranjo

Playa Garza

Paquera

Curú Reserve

Pacific Ocean

Playa Samara

Playa Carillo

Playa Coyote

Cóbano

Tambor

Montezuma

Mal Pais

Cabuya

Cabo Blanco Reserve

The Northwest

EXPLORING: A two-lane road, mostly paved, leads from the Puntarenas ferry terminal through Liberia, and on to Santa Cruz, Nicoya, and Jicaral, and there is plenty of bus transport along this route. This is one area where renting a car would definitely be an asset. You might want to rent one, tour around a few days, staying in different places, then settle down in one spot for awhile. One approach is to do a circle, going up via Liberia and then on to Santa Rosa or Guanacaste park, next heading over and back through Nicoya. If you pick Tamarindo,

Nosara, or Sámara, you may have the added advantage of flying back, thus avoiding a somewhat grueling bus ride. Should you choose to drive, please don't let the seemingly light traffic lure you into speeding. At any time, you may come around a bend and encounter a *campesino*, a steer, bicyclists, or a halted vehicle. Another option would be to take the ferry from Playa Naranjo or (if you can get there) from Paquera. A final option would be a Travelair flight from San José or Liberia to the coastal beaches; or you might fly to Liberia and take a bus from there. Despite the dust and the heat, Nicoya is a cyclist's paradise. There are few cars and the surroundings are beautiful. Other regional activities include rafting down the slow-moving Corobicí, swimming, diving, sailing, horseback riding, and hiking.

Cañas

At Km 188, this hot and somnolent farming center (pop. 21,000) marks the turn-off to Tilarán and Lake Arenal. To get here, take one of five buses daily from C. 16, Av. 1/3, San José or take a Tralapa bus from C. 20, Av. 3. Base yourself here for the Palo Verde National Park or other reserves; otherwise, stay in Liberia or up in cooler Tilarán. **practicalities:** Lowest-price place here is the **Hotel Familiar** at the NE corner of Av. 3 and C. Central. Stay at low-budget **Cabinas Corobicí** (☎ 669-0241, $7), six blocks E from the highway, or the slightly more expensive **Hotel Cañas** (☎ 669-0039, fax 669-1319, $15 d), which has private baths. Other low-budget alternatives here include the **Gran Hotel** at the NW side of the plaza, **El Corral** (☎ 669-0622, $30 d) or **Guillén** at the SE side of the plaza, and **Luz**. In addition to local cuisine, there are a number of Chinese restaurants, including the **Lei Tu**, just off the plaza. Inside the El Corral, **Transporte Palo Verde** (☎ 669-1091) runs trips ($35-50) to Palo Verde in a motor launch via the Río Bebedero. To go directly to Liberia or Tilarán, use the new terminal at C. 1 and Av. 11; for San José or Liberia/La Cruz, stand by the highway and wait.

Centro Ecológico La Pacifica

This moderate Swiss-owned and managed 3,300-acre (1,332-ha) establishment (☎ 669-0050, fax 669-0555; Apdo 8, 5700 Cañas, Guanacaste), is located off the E side of the highway six km (four miles) N of Cañas. Named for the lady who designed the Costa Rican flag, this private reserve has labeled trees, over 225 species of birds, and a pool. All of the hardwood *cabinas* are equipped with fans and private baths; some also have hot water and kitchens. Many of the photos in Dan Jantzen's classic *Costa Rican Natural History* show the captive animals here. Besides the forest reserve, which comprises one third of the area, visitors may tour the farm and the reforestation project. Added features include the nature trail, *Sendero del Chocaco*, and a small museum in a restored Spanish hacienda which details life as it was in Guanacaste 100 years ago. A restaurant, **Rincón Corobicí** is right on the river of the same name, just after the entrance. It operates a small campsite. River rafting tours ($35) down the gentle Corobicí are run by **Safaris Corobicí** (☎/fax 669-1091/0544; Apdo. 99, Cañas) and depart from here. They also rent bikes and operate mountain bike tours. **note:** There have been drownings on this river, so take care.

Las Pumas

Created and managed by Swiss expat Lilly Hagnauer, former owner of La Pacifica, this is one of the world's most unusual zoos. You'll find jaguars, margays, pumas, and ocelots. All of the animals were rescued from the traps of poachers and most are delivered courtesy of MINEM, the Ministry of Natural Resources, Energy and Mines, which is responsible for snaring illegal hunters. Lilly's collection began in 1967 after a friend gave her a margay. The collection has kept on expanding ever since. Cages are nothing fancy, but are functional. Each cat has its own story for Lilly to tell. There is no point in re-releasing most of the animals into the forest as they would find it difficult to reacclimate. In addition, the shrinking wilderness is making their very survival increasingly uncertain. Lily finances the animals' upkeep through the sale of pastel-colored budgerigars and through visitor donations. Admission is free, but contributions are welcome. Las Pumas is near the Rincón Corobicí restaurant (see above). It's open from 8-5 daily.

Las Juntas de Abangares

This was formerly a gold mining center for the region and these mines once attracted an international community of goldseekers. This is reflected in the ethnic diversity of the current inhabitants. **sights:** The **Eco Museo** is an old mine structure. It is four km from the **Caballo Blanco Cantina**, which also exhibits antiques from the gold mining era. The community of **Los Angeles** is nearby and is accessible only by four-wheel drive or on horseback. Boston still has a community of gold panners. **practicalities:** Las Juntas can be reached by bus from San José (C. 12, Av. 8; 11 and 5 PM; ☎ 222-1867), Puntarenas, and from Cañas (30 minutes). *Geoaventuras* (☎ 221-2053, 282-8950, fax 282-3333) offers tours of the mining area. Stay at low-budget **Cabinas Las Juntas** (☎ 662-0069). Eat here or at **Las Gamelas** or **La Familiar**.

Lomas Barbudal
Biological Reserve

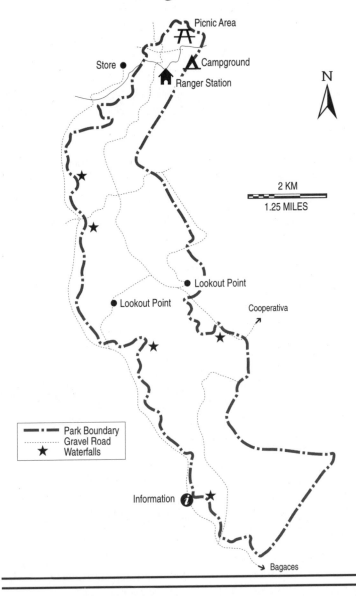

Picnic Area

Store

Campground

Ranger Station

N

2 KM
1.25 MILES

Lookout Point

Lookout Point

Cooperativa

Park Boundary
Gravel Road
★ Waterfalls

Information

Bagaces

La Ensenada Lodge

This small lodge offers the opportunity to participate in the daily activities of a farm. The farm raises cattle and produces papaya, salt, and watermelon. There are great opportunities for birdwatching, photography, and horseback riding. You can also water-ski, windsurf, and play tennis. The lodge is on the coast, 40 km to the S of Cañas. ☎ 228-6653/2655 or fax 228-5281.

Lomas Barbudal Biological Reserve
(Reserva Biológica Lomas Barbudal)

Meaning "bearded hills," the origin of this reserve's name is obscure. This area was put under protection in 1986, partially because of its value as a watershed; as one might expect there are a number of natural springs. It also serves as a refuge for migrating birds, including egrets, herons, and grebes. Some 200 species of birds have been identified thusfar. There are also over 250 species of bees that live alone rather than in hives. The reserve has a number of the extremely rare cannonball trees (*balas de cañón*), whose dangling pungent fruits are hard spherical capsules the size of bowling balls and can number up to 300 per tree. The largest of the 175 species of trees present, the sandbox tree lures scarlet macaws from nearby Palo Verde National Park to feed on its fruit. Camping is permitted and there's a refreshment stand and a swimming hole.

GETTING HERE: About three hours by car from San José, this biological reserve has its station nine miles (15 km) SE of the town of Bagaces, four miles (six km) from the Km 221 marker on the Interamerican Highway; it's just half an hour from Liberia. Four-wheel-drive vehicles are recommended during the rainy season. If you arrive in Bagaces, you can get to the reserve by chartering a taxi (about $20 RT including waiting time). Otherwise, it's about six km each way from Pijijue, which is on the Interamerican Highway halfway between Bagaces and Liberia.

PRACTICALITIES: Admission to the reserve is by voluntary donation. The **Centro Patrimonial de Lomas Barbudal** (☎ 670-1062/1029), a visitor and community center, offers information as well as lodging for volunteers. An interpretive trail guide brochure is available. The best trail runs along the Río Catuyo NE from the Centro Patrimonial 1½ km to a small waterfall. A loop trail is planned. **Bagaces** is an attractive place to base yourself while visiting the reserve. Very basic

The Northwest

cabins are available for rent. The best of the lot may be **Cabinas Eduardo Vargas,** which has no sign but is near the plaza. Also try **Hotel Miravelles. Albergue Las Sillas** is set halfway between Bagaces and the turnoff for the reserve. **note:** In March 1994, the reserve was hit by a fire that raged for eight days, destroying 2,000 of its 2,400 acres. The forest is still recovering.

Liberia

Liberia (23,000 pop.), the provincial capital of Guanacaste, is also its major town. Nicknamed *Ciudad Blanca* (White City) because its quartz-based subsoil was once used along with lime to construct the roads, Liberia was founded in 1769 and is the only city with its own flag. The town is clean and attractive, with flamboyant-shaded streets and more bicycles than cars. There are no street signs, so you pretty much have to ask directions to get around. The separation from Nicaragua, which was announced in 1814 and finally confirmed by an 1820 plebescite, is celebrated on July 25. Most areas can be reached by bus, but you'll want to have a car if you plan on doing day trips.

GETTING HERE: Buses leave from C. 14, A. 1/3 in San José daily at 7, 9, 11:30 and at 1, 4, 6, and 8 for the four-hour trip. Also buses run from Av. 3, C. 18/20.

by air: An important new development, the Aeropuerto Tomás Guardia "opened" in 1992 and has since been "inaugurated" and renamed twice: it's now known as Aeropuerto Daniel Oduber Quirós. The airport is largely intended to service charter flights, but it has yet to receive any. Latest word (late 1995) was that the airport was waiting for fire fighting equipment, which would allow it to comply with US Federal Aviation Agency standards. Flights should start arriving here before the next century. Travelair (☎ 220-3054, 232-7883, fax 220-0413) flies to and from San José and Tamarindo out of here.

SIGHTS: There's not a lot to do in Liberia except walk around. Many of the houses have a colonial flavor. The corner homes often have a door *(puerta del sol)* on each side of the corner. The town square has an avant-garde church that vaguely resembles a Swiss chalet with a large broadcasting antenna. Grackles flock in the trees here at dusk, and a band plays occasionally in the evenings. **La Agonía**, in a verdant and quiet neighborhood, is a white church with a small park in front. It dates from the era when the region was still part of Nicaragua and is the perfect destination for a late afternoon stroll. The **Casa de la Cultura** (open Tues. to Sat., 9-noon, 1-6; Sun. 9-noon), three blocks to the S of the main plaza, has an exhibit about the *sabaneros*, the region's cowboys, as well as an information service. If you're heading up for Santa Rosa, you might want to visit the **ecological museum**, located in the old customs house once used to check incoming cattle. Here volunteers from the UCR are working in conjunction with the NPS to create an ecological museum that will cover the area's life and culture, also including a plant nursery. It's at Agua Buena, near the turnoff from the Interamerican Highway for Santa Cecilia.

ACCOMMODATION: Liberia is a popular place during peak season, so you'd be well advised to make reservations prior to arrival. Moderate ($45 d) 60-room **Hotel Nuevo Boyeros** (☎ 666-0995/0722, fax 666-2529; Apdo. 85, Liberia, Guanacaste) has friendly management, comfortable a/c rooms with double beds and cold water shower, two pools surrounded by palm trees, and an outdoor lounge, as well as a large dining room. Moderate and slightly cheaper 23-room **Hotel El Bramadero** (☎ 666-0371, fax 666-0203), with a/c or fans, pool, and restaurant, is located right at the crossroads across from the Nuevo Boyeros. Write Apdo. 70, Liberia. Luxury priced but well-maintained and comfortable, the 44-room **Hotel Las Espuelas** (☎ 666-0144, fax 225-3987; Apdo. 58-1000, San José) has a/c, pool, restaurant, and gift shop. It's about two km down the road towards Santa Cruz. Nearby 23-room **La Ronda** (☎ 666-0417) is inexpensive and has a pool. Located 2½ blocks to the right from Farmacía Lux in the town's center, inexpensive 24-room **Hotel La Siesta** (☎ 666-0678, fax 666-2532) has a pool and is quiet. Moderate 52-room **Hotel El Sitio** (☎ 666-1211, fax 666-2059; Apdo. 134-5000, Liberia) is on the road towards Nicoya (175 m E of the Gasolinera Emesa) and has rooms with both fan and a/c, phone, and TV. Facilities include restaurant, car rental, three conference rooms, and two pools. You'll need reservations for all of the above during the dry season.

Inexpensive **Hotel Daysita** (☎ 666-0197/0897, fax 666-6927), next to the stadium, has comfy rooms with fans as well as disco, two pools, and restaurant (groups only). Once the best low-budget place to stay during its incarnation as the Hotel Oriental, the 27-room **Hotel Guanacaste Travel Lodge** (☎ 666-2287/0085, fax 666-2287) has now become a "youth hostel" and moved into the inexpensive range. It's just around the corner from the El Bramadero. Prices range from $6 (dorm) on up. Other low-budget places include **Hotel Rivas** on the main square, **Hotel Liberia** (☎ 666-0161; 75 m S from the church), divey **Hotel Cortijo**, and **Pensión Margarita** (☎ 666-0468), which is practically next door to the Cortijo and 250 m E of the park. Other alternatives include **Pensión Golfito** (☎ 666-0963) and **Pensión Central** near the park.

Liberia

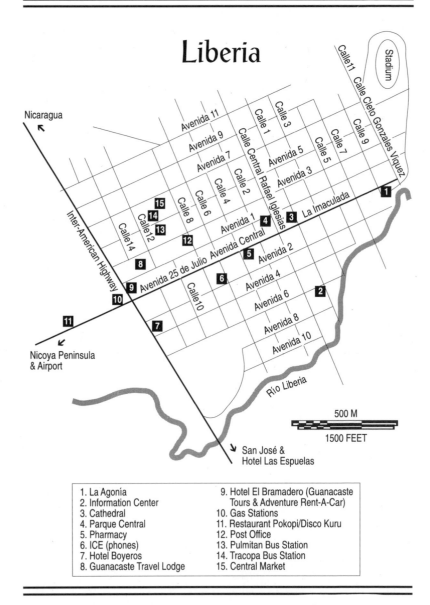

1. La Agonía
2. Information Center
3. Cathedral
4. Parque Central
5. Pharmacy
6. ICE (phones)
7. Hotel Boyeros
8. Guanacaste Travel Lodge
9. Hotel El Bramadero (Guanacaste Tours & Adventure Rent-A-Car)
10. Gas Stations
11. Restaurant Pokopi/Disco Kuru
12. Post Office
13. Pulmitan Bus Station
14. Tracopa Bus Station
15. Central Market

FOOD: Many restaurants are around or near the central plaza and the church. **Panadería Alfa** (5 AM-9 PM) is good for breakfast. **Panadería y Repositería Montevidio** is just down from the church. Also in the vicinity, inexpensive 24-hour **Restaurante Do Las Tinajas** has pizza, fried chicken, and fish. An attractive place to dine is the **Jardín de**

Azúcar, which has a wide selection and counter service. Near the church and the information center, **Pizza Pronto** serves pizza and cocktails in an attractive setting. Some of the numerous Chinese restaurants near the market are **Hit Wa** and the **Chop Suey.** Others are grouped together in back of the church. **Soda La Rueda** and **Rancho Guayami** are pleasant places to eat down the street from the restaurant at the **Nuevo Boyeros,** which has 24-hour service. The expensive but popular **Gran China** is across from the Boyeros, as is **Relax-Comidas Rapidas.** Intimate **Restaurante Pókópí** (meaning "very much" in Chorotega), along the road to Santa Cruz near the fire station, has a wide variety of continental dishes, including pizza, fishburgers, and shrimp.

SERVICES AND ENTERTAINMENT: There's no branch of the ICT here as yet. The best information source is your hotel or The Casa de la Cultura (see above). At Centro Commercial Bambu, **Galería Fulvia** (☎/fax 666-1679) sells the work of local artisans as well as imported newspapers. Run by a native of Ecuador, it is one of the few cultural spots in Guanacaste. Owner Fulvia Cárdenas Forero also produces a literary magazine. With offices in El Bramadero, **Adventura Rent A Car** (☎ 666-2349) offers car rentals. With offices in the same hotel, **Guanacaste Tours** (☎ 666-0306, fax 666-0307; Apdo. 55-5000, Liberia), one of the nation's best tour companies, operates tours to the Playa Grande, Santa Rosa, Palo Verde, rodeos and bullfights, and to three Nicoya beaches. **Turistas Amigo** (☎ 654-4238, fax 654-4039) offers tours ranging from turtle watching to Tamarindo's mangroves. **GuanAventura** (☎/fax 666-2825) is a mountain bike rental and repair shop. **Libreria Arco** has great postcards. **Instituto Británico** (☎ 666-0966; fax 253-1894; Apdo. 8184-1000, San José) offers Spanish courses.

ENTERTAINMENT: There's a movie theater and **Salon Riabeli** has live music on occasion. The trendiest place in town is undoubtedly the **Disco Kurú** (the Chorotega name for the *guanacaste* tree) next to the Restaurante Pókópí along the road to Santa Cruz. One other alternative for entertainment is to check out some of the local characters. You might find Jesus Christ wandering the streets with his staff. Bearded and barefooted and wearing a white tunic, Jesus has now married and is accompanied by his wife and a band of small girls (all in white).

EVENTS: The **Fiestas Civicas de Canton** are held the first or second week in February, except during an election year when they take place in mid-March. Three events – the Annexation of Guanacaste, Día de Santiago, and the Feria Ganadera – are celebrated simultaneously on July 25. The Anniversary of the Annexation of Guanacaste Province commemorates the province's secession from Nicaragua. The fiesta has folk dancing, marimba bands, horse parades, bullfights, rodeos, cattle shows, and local culinary specialties. The **Semana Cultural** takes place during the first week of September. On December 24, the **Pasada del Niño** (children's parade) takes place.

FROM LIBERIA: This is the transport hub of the NW. Buses leave for San José at 4:30, 6, and 7:30 AM, and at 2, 4, and 6 PM. Buses for Playas del Coco beach leave at 5:30, 8:15, 12:30, 2, 4:30, and 6:15. Buses depart for Playa Hermosa and Playa Panamá at 11:30 AM, and 7 PM; for La Cruz and Peñas Blancas (Santa Rosa and the Nicaraguan border) at 9 and noon and, passing through from San José headed to the same destination, at noon and 5. For Filadelfia, Santa Cruz, and Nicoya, buses depart at 5, 6, 7, 8, 8:30, 9, 10, 11, noon, 1, 2, 3, 4, 5, 6, 7:30, and 8:30. The sole Cuajinquil bus leaves at 3:30. Puntarenas buses depart at 5, 8:30, 10, 11:15, and 3:15. For Bagaces (Lomas Barbudal), Cañas (connections for Tilarán), and Monteverde (at the junction), take a San José-bound bus (6, 6:30, 9, 12:15, and 5 from the *Tralapa* terminal; *El Pulmitan* runs more frequently) or take a Bagaces/Cañas bus at 5:45, 1:30, or 4:30. **note:** All times are subject to change; be sure to check beforehand.

Las Imágenes Biological Station

This 2,470-acre (1,000-ha) ranch N of Liberia, between the Interamerican and Rincón de la Vieja, has a working water wheel, batallions of butterflies, birds, and deer. Horseback trips to Rincón de la Vieja and neighboring San Antonio Cattle Ranch are offered. Transportation can be arranged through the Hotel Las Espuelas (☎ 666-0144, 225-3987). Room and board is around $60 pp, pd. Write c/o Hotel las Espuelas, Apdo. 88, Liberia, Guanacaste.

Rincón de la Vieja National Park
(Parque Nacional Rincón de la Vieja)

One of five active volcanoes in the Guanacaste range, Volcán Rincón de la Vieja, NE of Liberia, rises to 6,216 ft (1,895 m). The mother of 32 small rivers and streams and 16 water-collecting gorges, it is surrounded by a national park that preserves 34,799 acres (14,083 ha), including tropical dry forests, bubbling mud pots, steaming vents in the earth, hot springs, and a whole host of wildlife. Still relatively undiscovered, the park is starting to get more visitors. Get here soon!

Rincón de la Vieja
National Park

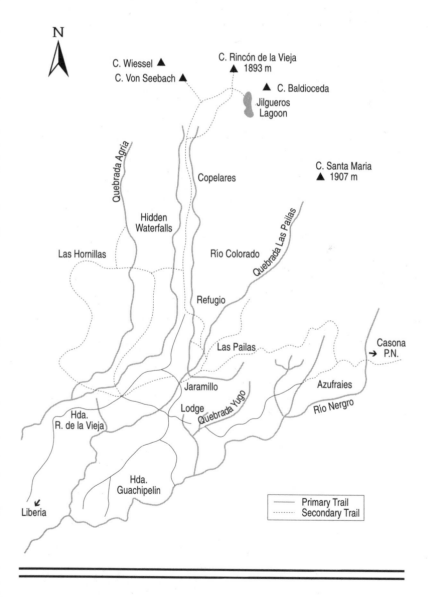

N

C. Wiessel ▲
C. Von Seebach ▲

C. Rincón de la Vieja
▲ 1893 m

▲ C. Baldioceda

Jilgueros
Lagoon

C. Santa Maria
▲ 1907 m

Quebrada Agria

Copelares

Hidden
Waterfalls

Las Hornillas

Río Colorado

Quebrada Las Pailas

Refugio

Las Pailas

Casona
P.N.

Jaramillo

Azufraies

Lodge

Quebrada Yugo

Río Nergro

Hda.
R. de la Vieja

Hda.
Guachipelin

Liberia

Primary Trail
Secondary Trail

FLORA AND FAUNA: Found in groves, twisted and aromatic copel clusias delineate the border between the tropical intermediate forest and the volcano's summit. The national flower, the guaría morada orchid is found in the park's borders. Owing to the presence of four life zones within the park, wildlife is very diverse. There are peccaries, coatis, tapirs, sloths, jaguars, and white-faced, spider, and howler monkeys, as well as over 300 species of birds, including the Montezuma oropendola and the three-wattled bellbird. One of the most eclectic inhabitants is a type of cicada that croaks just like a frog.

HISTORY: Its name probably derives from the old lady who once lived there. The region was first explored by German Karl von Seebach in 1864-65. The main crater's last active period was in 1966, when it erupted violently, inundating grazing land on the S slope. Eruptions continued into the next year. It erupted again in 1966-67 and in July 1970. The second most recent eruption came in May 1991 when the volcano spewed a torrent of ash, rocks, mud, and water, destroying two bridges and leaving 500 nearby residents stranded. The park closed its doors temporarily in November 1995 after tons of volcanic ash, mud, and debris rained down on the peak's N side. The most severely impacted settlement was the Agroindustrial del Sur, a government-sponsored 16-family community that found its creek transformed into a gorge. Unfortunately, the gorge is right by the entrance, which means they must lower themselves down into it and then climb back up again in order to exit. A bridge across the Río Penjamo was also destroyed.

GETTING HERE: There is no public transportation to the park. You must either hitch, hire a taxi, or drive in your own (preferably four-wheel-drive) vehicle. One route to the park (25 km N of town) leaves through Liberia's Barrio Victoria and heads to the Santa María sector. Another route extends off of Guadaloupe, five miles (eight km) N of Liberia on the Interamerican Highway. It passes through Currubandé and the Guachipelín Hacienda, where you can stay at the Albergue or the nearby hotel.

SIGHTS: Volcanic ground activity here is paralleled only by places in the Minhasa area of Sulawesi in Indonesia, Central Java's Bleduk Kuwu, Northern California's Lassen National Park, and in some of Japan's national parks. Situated 7½ miles (12 km) from the park headquarters, **Las Pailas** (the large pans) covers a 123-acre (50-ha) area. In separate sections, semi-enclosed by brush, are boiling mud pots, vent holes leaking sulfurous steam, and mud leaping wildly from pits in the ground. Surrounding vegetation is coated with spots of white mud. At the seven bubbling grey mud holes called **Sala de Belleza**

(Beauty Salon), you may dip in a finger, let the mud cool off a bit, and apply it to your face as a mud pack. Surrounded by wild cherry, **Las Hornillas** (the kitchen stoves), a group of sulfurous fumaroles, are found on the devastated SW slope. The outdoor hot springs of **Los Azufrales**, reaching temperatures of 108°F (42°C), are two miles (three km) from headquarters and are surrounded by groves of *encino* trees. The hidden waterfalls are composed of four falls, three of which are more than 230 ft (70 m) high. They are located on the SW slope of the volcano and have a bathing hole at their base. The whale-shaped, 15-acre (six-ha) **Laguna Jilgueros** (Linnet Bird Lagoon), SE of the active crater, has a small island inside; quetzals, tapirs, and linnet songbirds inhabit the area.

CLIMBING THE VOLCANO: It's about 22 miles (35 km) to the top and back, and the trip can be made in one day on horseback. **Las Espuelas**, the park post beyond the mud pots, is the best place to base yourself for a climb. You may wish to hire a guide, as the routes are not clearly marked and it's easy to become disoriented when fog descends. There are two routes: high and low. The high route goes directly to the summit, while the low one passes by it. From the hot springs a mean-dering cattle path leads to the summit; when in doubt, steer right. This path leads through private property (ask permission) to Las Pailas. From here you climb to Las Espuelas, where you should fill your canteens. Camping places are at the tree line; you might wish to stop for the night if it's overcast. The trip to the crater's edge and back takes a good two hours; be sure to watch the weather because you can easily get lost in the mist. If it's clear, you'll find the trip well worthwhile: the summit commands a view that can stretch as far as Lake Nicaragua, taking in the Nicaraguan peaks of Concepcíon and Madera and the Peninsula de Nicoya to the W. **other trails:** The *Sendero Bosque Encantado* – with a small waterfall, mosses, ferns, and orchids – lives up to its name of "enchanted forest."

ACCOMMODATIONS: The park's adobe headquarters building has only camping sites (around $2.50 pp) and food ($5 per meal) available. Call the park's radio contact number (☎ 695-5598) in advance. Another alternative within the park is to camp, and this is the best way to see wildlife. You can camp by the hot springs or, if you wish to see tapirs and possibly quetzals, camp by the lagoon; the best months for this are March and April. You may also be able to stay in the old administration building: contact the NPS concerning the current situation. Low-budget **Albergue Rincón de la Turista** is in the village of San Jorge near the main park entrance. Its owners, originally from San

José, rent out horses and guides. Also in San Jorge are low-budget **Miravieja** (☎ 666-1045/2004) and **Rinconcito** (☎ 666-0636/2764).

Another alternative is **Albergue Rincón de la Vieja** (☎ 225-1073/8835, fax 234-1676), a small but comfortable lodge and cabin run by born-again environmentalist Alvaro Wiessel Baldioceda on his Hacienda Guachipelín. In the middle of the estate, you'll meet Alvaro's four cats, three dogs, and a toucan. A water-powered turbine provides power. From the lodge, all parts of the park are accessible on horseback or on foot. In addition to the prices listed here (with YH member prices in parentheses), Alvaro has a number of packages available. Horses for 1-10 hours with guide cost $36/day ($15/day); guide alone is $10/pp, pd ($5/pp, pd); beds are $15 ($8) each; meals are $10 ($6); and RT transport from Liberia is available for $8 pp. For more information write Apdo. 114, Liberia.

Yet another place is the seven-room **Hacienda Lodge Guachipelín** (☎ 441-6545/6694/4318, fax 442-1910; Box 636-4050, Alajuela). It charges $50 d; meals are reported to be costly. The inexpensive **Santa María Volcano Lodge** (☎ 666-1948: messages, fax 666-2313) is in Colonia Blanca, which is 18 km from San Jorge. It can be reached via Bagaces. You can also stay at **Buena Vista Lodge**, described directly below.

Buena Vista Lodge

(Albergue Buena Vista)

The relative remoteness of this lodge (☎ 695-5147, fax 695-0090; Apdo. 373, Liberia) is one of its assets. Getting here is an experience in itself. You must travel 12 km N of Liberia along the Interamerican Highway, turn right at the crossroads for Cañas Dulces, and proceed three km farther to Cañas Dulces, then drive another 10 km. You pass through a six-km stretch of the vast 3,840-acre (1,600-ha) Hacienda Buena Vista, owned by Hermanos Ocampo Fernandez. The lodge is at the end of the finca's rough road and next to a large expanse of secondary forest. The views here are spectacular, and the sunsets even more so. Climb up to the plateau on the right to view them.

ACCOMMODATIONS AND FOOD: The lodge has 11 rooms. They face a screened central courtyard with a garden containing flowering plants. Set atop a pastureland, some of which is being reforested, the lodge deserves its name. There are plenty of chairs both inside and out to lounge around in. The food is basic fare (beans, rice, fried plantains, and accompanying fish, fowl, or meat), but it is cooked on a wood fire and is universally popular. The special large, thick tortillas are an added attraction. If you're lucky, you can also sample the *coyol* (palm wine). A palm is cut down, and a square hole chiseled through it. The palm wine (a sweet, clear fluid) flows into the opening and is scooped out. Rooms are around $18 for a bunk bed, $21 for a twin-bed, and $50 for a room with a bath. Meals are about $7 for breakfast and $9 each for lunch and dinner. Special prices are offered for Ticos and residents.

HIKING AND TOURS: There's a combination of secondary forest and brush (96 acres, 40 ha) right behind the lodge. The trails are beautiful; one leads to a small waterfall. You can either ride 25 minutes or go on foot to the hot springs and steambath (a small house built atop a steaming mudpool), which are surrounded by pools of boiling mud. The path to these is through pasture. On the way, you pass by *guanacaste* trees. A guide is suggested if you do go here. One of the most popular rides is to the **Hidden Waterfalls** in Rincón de la Vieja National Park. As you climb on horseback, you face Volcán Orosi and Volcán Rincón de la Vieja off on the horizon. Below, the plains of Guanacaste unfold and Santa Roque, Liberia, and Playas del Coco are spread out before you. The first waterfall you come to is Calingueros, which you can only view from a distance. The next is called Boriñquen. Owing to its smell, the third is known as La Mina de Azufra. The fourth is called Tobagan and is good for swimming. Bamboo groves connect the last two. Other horseback trips (including one to the crater) are available.

Santa Rosa National Park
(Parque Nacional Santa Rosa)

This is the nation's oldest national park, accessed via two entrances off of the Interamerican Highway some 23 miles (37 km) N of Liberia. Ironically, Santa Rosa was originally protected in order to preserve a battlefield. It was here that Costa Ricans battled with William Walker, successfully fending off his attack (see "History" section in the Introduction). In addition to a plethora of wildlife, the park has dry tropical forests and white sand beaches.

GETTING HERE: Although there is no door-to-door service, buses will drop you eight km from the entrance. Take a bus to Peñas Blancas from San José (5 and 7:45, C. 16, Av. 3, ☎ 255-1932) or a La Cruz (not Santa Cruz) bus from Liberia at 5:30, 9:30, or 2 and ask to be dropped at the "entrada a Santa Rosa." As you approach from Liberia, the landscape suddenly opens up to a vast and desolate range on either side – a miniature version of the American West transported to Central

The Northwest

America. You almost expect the Marlboro Man to come charging in on one side of the highway and the Lone Ranger and Tonto to appear in the distance on the other. The sense of desolation so prevalent during the waterless dry season increases as you realize that this was once all tropical dry forest. A sign marking the Guanacaste Regional Conservation Area pops up to your right and – presto! – tropical dry secondary forest appears, along with a sign for the entrance to Santa Rosa on your left. From the entrance, you can either walk or hitch a ride (easy during the dry season) for the remaining 4½ miles (7.2 km). As it can be deathly hot, travel this stretch as early in the day as possible. **tours: Geotur** (☎ 234-1867; fax 253-6338), **Guanacaste Tours** (☎ 666-0306, fax 666-0307; Apdo. 55-5000, Liberia), and **Jungle Trails** (☎ 255-3486) all sponsor tours.

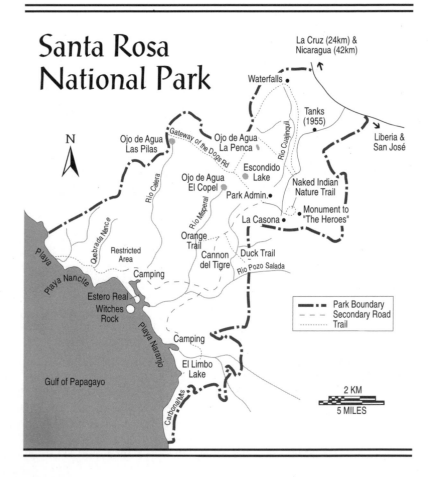

PRACTICALITIES: The official camping facilities are excellent, and the fee is around $2.50 pp. Toilets, showers, and water are provided. As there are fig trees for shade and no mosquitoes, you could sleep outside during the dry season. Tapirs, though seldom seen, are present here. They often both bathe and defecate in the same water, so it's advisable to carry your own. The *comedor* will provide meals if you order in advance. You can also camp at Argelia and at Estero Real. Accommodation ($25 w/meals; $10 pp for room only) is also provided in the **Centro de los Investigaciones Daniel Janzen** (☎ 695-5598), which opened in 1993. Write Apdo. 169, Liberia. For groups, reservations are recommended eight days prior to arrival. Another alternative is to stay in the **Santa Rosa Lodge** (☎ 233-3333: message for José Luis Cabada) which is on private property in the park; it can hold six or more; rooms have fans and shared baths. The nearest lodge outside the park to the S is the inexpensive **Santa Clara Lodge** (☎ 666-0473, fax 666-0475, beeper 257-8585; Apdo. 17, Liberia), which is four km from the small town of Quebada Grande. Pickup in Liberia is available for no extra charge. There are seven rooms, some of which have shared baths. It has a bar, restaurant, small mineral pool, and horses for rent. The lodge also offers an all-day horseback trip up to the top of Cerro Cacao. Six waterfalls and a forest are also on the property. Rates are $20 s and $35 d with breakfast; youth hostel card holders are offered a discount. In **Quebrada Grande**, you may stay at the low-budget **Central Social la Mata de Caña**, which serves hearty lunchtime fare.

  volunteering: Earth Island Institute's Sea Turtle Restoration Project sends volunteers into the field here at Playa Nancite. For more information, see "volunteering" in the introduction. You can also try calling the Centro de los Investigaciones Daniel Janzen at the address given above.

FLORA AND FAUNA: Vegetation varies from pastureland to cactus, from calabash forest to mangrove swamps by the coast. Fauna ranges from green iguanas and ctenosaurs, to sloths, tapirs, and opossums, howler and spider monkeys, white-tailed deer and coyotes, even including 15 species of bats and 253 types of birds (including great currasows). Some 3,410 varieties of butterflies and moths are among the 10,000 or so insect species. Extraordinarily large numbers of crabs live near the coast. The best time and place to see animals is at dawn or dusk during the dry season at the watering holes scattered through the park. Even during the wet season, when the animals have no need to congregate at waterholes, wildlife abounds here. Despite the year's heaviest rainfall, a September visit is a good time to see leatherbacks laying eggs.

SIGHTS AND HIKING: You can stay as close as you like or as far afield as 12.4 miles (20 km); try to plan your walks before 8 or after 4. Note that the roads to the beaches are closed in *invierno*, the rainy season. Historic *hacienda* house **Casa Casona** (open daily, 8-4) contains a reconstruction of the Battle of Rivas. Its contents include period furniture, farm tools, rifles and swords, as well as a natural history exhibit. There are also stone corrals dating back more than 300 years. *Sendero Indio Desnudo* runs in back of the house; animals abound along the trail. In the dry season, wait for their arrival by the water hole near the three rocks with petroglyphs. Over two acres (one ha) in area, **Platanar**, a natural lake, is four km N of the Casa Casona. A number of fossils can be found five km upriver from where the road crosses the Río Nisperal. An indigenous rubbish heap with potsherds galore is near the Casa Argelia. There's a well here, along with toilet facilities, and you can camp. The navigable Argelia estuary's birds range from roseate, white, green, and great blue herons to the Mexican tiger bittern.

THE BEACHES: These are ideally explored over two or three days. You walk along a four-wheel-drive track, ford a stream, and come to a sign marked "La Cuesta," where you descend 2½ km to the sea, passing a viewpoint called the "Cañon del Tigre." At about 66 ft (20 m) in elevation, there is a crossroads: the right hand path, El Estero, leads to a picnic area about four km away, where there are toilets and camping. You must bring your own water. The left hand one, **La Playa**, extends to **Playa Naranjo** via a small river (fill your canteens), a salt marsh abounding with waterfowl, and Casa Argelia, a rangers' home and camping area. Despite a population of sandflies and mosquitoes, this four-mile (six-km) beach, where leatherbacks nest in September, is a splendid place to be. **Laguna el Limbo** at its S end is another area for birdwatching. **Isla Peña Bruja**, a gigantic rocky refuge for seabirds, lies just offshore. This "witch rock" is legendary in the surfing universe as the spot with "the perfect wave." Continuing to the S, the beach changes to rocky bluffs. To the N, there's an estuary. Crossing it, you follow the trail back inland to the Estero Real picnic area. During the dry season, this may be navigable by four-wheel drive; ask the rangers. About four km and two or three hours away, a steep, winding path leads to isolated, two-km **Playa Nancite**, a Pacific ridley turtle nesting beach. October is generally the busiest month. A small stream provides water for camping, but a permit is required. To get here from Argelia, you must follow the beach to the N. It is best to plan this particular leg of the hike to coincide with low tide. You will have to cross a river and wading is not possible at high tide.

HISTORY: The site of the historic battle of Rivas and its surrounding area was declared a national park in 1966. Originally a second and non-contiguous portion of the park, the Murciélago Addition, established in 1979, added 24,700 acres (10,000 ha). This land was expropriated from ousted Nicaraguan dictator Antonio Somoza and was the remainder of the "state within a state" he had built in Guanacaste. In 1987 the Arias administration added the land separating the two parts, making a total of 122,352 acres (49,515 ha). Included in the addition was another historical site: the airstrip used by the CIA to supply the Nicaraguan Contras.

SECTOR MURCIELAGO: This addition to the park, comprising some 24,710 acres (10,000 ha), is spectacularly scenic. **getting here:** One bus daily runs from Liberia at 3 PM, returning at 7 AM; a 12:30 PM bus runs from La Cruz and returns at 6 AM. By car, you must first pass the Santa Rosa road junction and then turn left towards Cuajinquil; from there you can proceed four km N to Playa Junquillal or 12 km SW to Bahía Santa Elena and then another eight to Playa Blanca. All of the roads are bad, and passage is best attempted during the dry season with a four-wheel drive. **sights and practicalities:** Down a dirt road from Cuajinquil is isolated **Playa Junquillal** where you can camp, but you need to bring water. The Murciélago ranger station has swimming holes and a camping area. The alternative is to stay at low-budget **Cabinas Santa Elena** (☎ 679-9112, leave message) near Cuajinquil and some four km from Playa Junquillal. The fishermen here can take you out on trips; negotiate per boatload. Swim at Playa Blanca on the peninsula's tip. A car can make it out here during the dry season. Many of the coves formed by the irregular coastline are excellent for camping.

> ☞ **Traveler's Tip.** For an unusual excursion in this part of Costa Rica, visit **Rancho Avestruz**, an ostrich farm 33 km N of Liberia. It's open for hour-long tours on Sat. and Sun. at 10, 1 PM, and 3 PM. Buy your tickets 15 minutes in advance. Admission is around $4 for adults and $2 for children.

Guanacaste National Park
(Parque Nacional Guanacaste)

The Guanacaste National Park comprises 210,000 acres (84,986 ha), ranging from mangrove swamps at the edge of Santa Elena to cloud forests on the slopes of Volcán Cacao. It was established in 1989 to protect animals and their migratory paths. The 150,000-acre (60,704-ha) central area is where biologist Daniel Janzen hopes to restore the dwindling tropical dry forest.

The Guanacaste Conservation Area is an attempt to bring a large tract of land (423 sq miles) under a single plan and to have it benefit the entire community. This is sensible because animals do not live within a single environment but travel according to season as well as food and water supply. Likewise, locals have to make a living and must accept the parks. The idea is to have the park benefit the community both via tourism and employment. Locals will be trained to help with the search for new seeds, chemicals, and drugs. The park presently employs 87 locals and runs an educational program for elementary school children. The area incorporates rainforest, cloud forest, dry forest, rivers, beaches, coral reefs, and some 325,000 plant and animal species. Sadly, much of the forest has been damaged, with only two areas retaining their pre-Columbian foliage.

Costa Rica's dry forest is different from that of temperate climes in a number of ways. For one thing, there is no lightning, so trees have not developed thick bark for protection. As a result, they are easily destroyed by fire. And the seasonal, heavy rainfall encouraged the trees to develop a closed, highly diverse canopy.

PRACTICALITIES: Cacao Biological Station, located amid cloud forests, has spartan dormitories reserved for researchers. From Potrerillos on the Interamerican, drive seven km on a dirt road to Quebrada Grande and then another 10 km; it's about an hour on foot or horseback from there. Paths from the station lead to the summit of **Volcán Cacao** and to Maritza (three hours on foot). Also accessible by a four-wheel-drive vehicle road, **Maritza** (around $20 pp, pd for room and board) sits at the base of **Volcán Orosí**. Featuring around 80 petroglyphs amidst pasture, **Llano de los Indios** is less than two hours away. To get here, drive 15 km, about an hour, on a dirt road beginning opposite the Cuajinquil turnoff. You'll have to open and close six barbed wire gates on the way. Note, however, that you need to have a guide along or you won't be granted permission to enter. Splendidly scenic **Pitilla Biological Station**, located on the side of the mountain, has spartan dormitories and is reserved for researchers; you must have a four-wheel drive or, better yet, a horse. To get here turn right at a guard station approximately five minutes N of the Cuajinquil turnoff and then go about 25 km (15 miles) on the paved road to Santa Cecelia, then nine km on a dirt road to Esperanza and the station. Pitilla hosts para-taxonomists affiliated with INBio, the Institute for Biodiversity, headquartered in Santo Domingo de Heredia. For information on the park call the **Guanacaste Regional Conservation Area** (☎ 695-5598) in Santa Rosa; it's best to show up there in person first to make arrangements.

Guanacaste National Park

Nicaragua

La Cruz

Santa Cecilia

Upala

Río Sábalo

Río Ánimas

Hacienda Los Inocentes

Río Mena

Río Chon

N

Río Sorioli

Río Sapoa

Volcán Orosi (1,487m)

Cacao Trail

Río Las Haciendas

Río Pizote

Maritza Field Station

Los Indios Trail

Cerro Cacao (1,659m)

Cuajiniquil

Río Tempis Quito

Cacao Field Station

Río San Josecito

	Park Boundaries
	Secondary Road
	Trail

La Casona

SANTA ROSA NATIONAL PARK

4 KM

Liberia

The Northwest

The Jaragua Dilemma

A popular pasture grass introduced from Africa has become the
nemesis of the tropical dry forests. Jaragua follows the path of fire,
and, as fires have been set by accident, arson, and by ranchers intent
on killing tree seedlings coming up in pastures, jaragua has sprung
up in the swaths opened up by fire. Conservationists see the key to
restoring these forests as fighting fires, and to that end the park
service has been specially equipped, built fire roads, and constructed
fire breaks. The idea is that trees will return to the land and that
everything else will follow. The 23 tree species that are wind-dis-
persed will propagate during the dry season, but the remaining

300-plus species must be planted by the park service. These days, after years of protection from fires, some areas are beginning to regain their cover, but it will still take decades for the canopy to reclose. Tropical dry forest once covered Pacific coastal lowlands stretching from Panama to Mexico and covered an area the size of France. Today, they have shrunk to a mere 2% of the total area and only part of this is under protection.

Los Inocentes

Another nature preserve molded from a cattle farm, this *hacienda*, named after Nicaraguan Inocentes Barrios who owned the place, is a frequent stopover for tour groups. In addition to horseback riding and nature watching on the estate, day trips can be arranged to Santa Rosa and other locales. Room and board in the remodeled *hacienda* house (built in 1890) runs about $50 pp, pd. An added attraction is a swimming pool. Many researchers have stayed here, and extensive background information on the area is available. For more information or reservations, ☎ 265-5484 or 679-9190, fax 265-6431, or write Apdo. 1370, 3000 Heredia.

GETTING HERE: Turn right at a security post five minutes N of the Cuajunquil turnoff, where the sign reads "Upala" and "Santa Ana"; follow the road for 14½ km until you see the "Los Inocentes" sign. By bus, disembark at La Cruz and take a taxi; ask if a pickup is possible here when making reservations.

La Cruz

This small border town is the northernmost point you're likely to reach in Guanacaste unless you head for the border at Peñas Blancas. Nearby Playa Jobo is the nearest beach. Playa Pochote and Playa Nubes are also in the vicinity.

PRACTICALITIES: Buses from San José (around five hours) run from C. 16, Av. 3 (☎ 255-1058) at 5 AM, 7:45 AM, and 4:15 PM. The return run is at 5:45, 8, and 11 AM, and 4 PM. Buses also run from Liberia; check "Getting There" below for times. Buses run to Playa Jobo at 5, 10:30, and 1:30. If headed on to Nicaragua, see the section at the end of this book.

Places to stay include low-budget **Cabinas Santa Rita** (☎ 669-9062), the low-budget **Cabinas Maryfel** (☎ 669-9096), and the more basic **Pensión La Tica**. The **Hotel Iguana** (☎ 679-9015) offers simple rooms for $18-36. **Amalia's Inn** (☎/fax 679-9181) has attractive rooms ($50 d) with a pool and views. Low-budget **Hotel El Faro** is between the gas station and La Cruz on the highway. **Colinas del Norte** (☎ 679-9132, fax 679-9064) is a moderate lodge (around $55 d) set on a cattle farm just off the highway; it serves unusual local dishes and offers horseback riding. Inexpensive **Cabinas Las Salinas** (☎ 233-6912, 228-2447/0690; Apdo. 449, 1007 San José) at Bahía Salinas one km to the S, where you can also camp or park your trailer. A restaurant, horseback riding, and boat rental are available. Much more expensive is Los Inocentes (see above).

food: Windblown **Restaurant Ehecatl** (Chorotega for "Wind God") overlooks the Bahía Salinas. Another alternative is the **Soda y Comedor Santa Marta**.

Isla de Boñanos Wildlife Refuge

(Refugio Nacional de Fauna Silvestre Isla de Boñanos)

Sitting three miles (five km) offshore from Puerto Soley, SW of La Cruz, this 37-acre (15-ha) reserve protects nesting seabirds: brown pelicans, American oysterbirds, and magnificent frigate birds. There are no facilities here, and visits are prohibited, but you can watch the avian action from offshore. You may be able to hire a boat in Puerto Soley.

Northern Nicoya Peninsula Beaches

Peninsula Nicoya's sandy coast is a major part of Guanacaste's claim to fame. Because of the higher comparable airfares and poor infrastructure, the coast's beaches are not exactly Acapulco – although the government and developers are pushing them in that direction. In fact, there are still relatively few facilities, most are difficult to reach, and accommodation prices are high (some would say overpriced) for what you get. They are still worth visiting. But get here fast.

Playas del Coco

Although the term "Playas del Coco" is also used to refer to all of the beaches in the area, it's commonly used for this beach in particular – the major Tico tourist center on Nicoya's coast. The place is pleasant enough, but there's not really all that much here. Despite the name, there are not many palm trees. Off-season and on weekdays, it's a very

The Northwest

peaceful place. But on weekends and holidays, it is noisy and overrun. The beach is dramatically situated on an extensive horseshoe-shaped bay dotted with gigantic boulders. Some fishing boats and North American yachts occupy much of the offshore harbor. The only advantage to coming here is the range of accommodations available for low-budget travelers. If you have the money, it's better to go somewhere else.

GETTING HERE: Buses leave Liberia at 5:30, 6:30, 11:30, 12:30, 5:30, and 6:30 for the half-hour trip. On the way you pass by Sardinal, a town where the major industry is beef, not sardines, and where three different styles of commodes (take your pick!) stand in a store window across from the park. One *Pulmitan* (☎ 222-1650) bus per day leaves from C.14, Av. 1/3, San José at 10 AM for the five-hour trip to El Coco.

ACCOMMODATIONS: Most places are fairly basic and inexpensive, in keeping with the budgets of the mostly Tico clientele. Be sure to shop around; some places are overpriced. Low-budget **Cabinas Catarino** (☎ 670-0156) are basic, but have cooking facilities. Inexpensive **Cabinas Las Brisas** (☎ 670-0155, 221-3292) have private baths and fans. Inexpensive 16-room **Cabinas Chale** (☎ 670-0036, fax 670-0303) have refrigerators, basketball courts, and a swimming pool. Rates are $20 and up. The **Hotel Luna Tica** (☎ 670-0127, fax 672-0392) has inexpensive rooms. Similarly priced, the **Hotel Anexo Luna Tica** (☎ 670-0279) is nearby. Low-budget to inexpensive **Cabinas El Coco** (☎ 670-0276, fax 670-0167) are directly on the beach; more expensive rooms have a/c. **Bergeron's B&B** (☎/fax 670-0451) has inexpensive rooms. The **Casino de Playas** has low-budget and inexpensive rooms. The rooms are better than the food. Inexpensive (around $30 d) **Pirate's Cove Hotel** (☎ 670-0367, fax 670-0117) is W of the soccer field. Five-room **La Villa del Sol** (☎/fax 670-0085) is an intimate French Canadian-run bed and breakfast with a garden and pool. Rates are $40-50 d. One km from the village, moderate-luxury **Flor de Itabo** (☎ 670-0292, fax 670-0003; Apdo. 32, Playas del Coco) is one of the classiest joints in the area, with a/c and pool. Moderate **Hotel Palmas de Coco** (☎ 670-0367, fax 670-0117; Apdo. 18, 5019 Playas del Coco) has both a/c and fan rooms, as well as a pool. You can also try **Rancho Armadillo** (☎ 670-0108, 223-3535, fax 267-0441, 670-0441). This is a bed and breakfast with model armadillos scattered about and guarded by two stone armadillos at the front gate. It has a pool and is presumably popular with armadillos. Rates are around $25 s and $50 d. It's just S of the main road into the village; turn right where the road divides and watch for a rock reading "Rancho Armadillo." **Cabinas Costa Alegre** (☎ 257-1039) is on the road way out of town just past the junction for Hermosa. It has an enormous thatched pavillion restaurant with two adjoining pools.

In the opposite direction (heading towards Ocotal), the **Condos del Pacifico** (☎ 228-9439, fax 222-5113) has rooms for $30 d and a pool. About 2½ km to the E of Playa de Coco is luxurious **Hotel El Ocotal** (☎ 670-0321, fax 670-0083), overlooking a great beach with tide pools. Rates run from $80 s, $90 d, not including tax; children under 12 are free. Rooms have a/c, fan, refrigerator, satellite TV, and phone. Facilities include restaurant, Jacuzzi, pools, tennis court, as well as other activities. Diving and dive packages are available and organized by **Diving Safaris** (☎ 670-0321, fax 670-0083; Apdo. 121-5019, Playas del Coco, Guanacaste). Dive packages, certification, trips to Catalina Island (lots of manta rays) and the Bat Islands (cow-nosed rays, bull sharks) are all available. (☎ 800-327-5662 in the US.) Right beyond it, luxury fishing resort **Bahía Pez Vela** (☎ 221-1586, 223-7490, fax 255-4039; Apdo. 7758, San José) has six *cabinas* and a small black sand beach. On the way to Playa Ocotal, moderate **Hotel Villa Casa Blanca** (☎/fax 670-0448; Apdo. 176, 5019 Playa Ocotal) is a Canadian-managed 10-room, two-condo bed and breakfast ($60 d on up), with tennis court and pool. Horseback riding, fishing, diving, and bike rental can be arranged. **Vista Ocotal** (☎ 293-4330, 239-2154, fax 293-4371) has rooms (about $60), villas, and studios, with a pool and Jacuzzi.

FOOD: Some of the least expensive and possibly the best places to eat are **Soda Teresita**, **Soda Paraiso**, **El Jicarito**, and **Jardín Tropical**. Another alternative is **Gaby's On the Beach**. **El Pozo** is an Italian restaurant which is on the right as you enter the village; they offer a good selection for vegetarians. Set 300 m down a dirt road found to the right as you enter town, **Ciao** is another Italian restaurant, as is **Pizzeria Pronto** about three blocks from the main plaza. **Papagayo Restaurant** is by the harbor and serves seafood. **Rosticeria don Humo** is another alternative. Offering dishes such as vegetarian lasagna, baked goods, and even brownie sundaes, **San Francisco Treats** is on the right just before El Pozo. The **Pirate's Cove Hotel** serves an international menu. Across from the malinche-tree-lined soccer field is a **supermarket**.

SURFING: Hire a boat from Tamarindo, Ocotal, or here to take you out to **Potrero Grande**, where a right point break with swift and hollow waves is found. It's also known as "Ollie's Point" after Oliver North.

TOURS AND SERVICES: Tienda Mareas offers souvenirs as well as utilitarian beachgoing items. **Corinsa Stables** (☎/fax 670-0244) has 30 trail horses. They're 450 m past the gas station beyond Sandoval.

The Northwest

Frontera Tours (☎/fax 670-0403, fax 221-6174) offers guides, fishing, snorkeling, and other services.d other services.

Dive Operators in Guanacaste

Diving Safaris de Costa Rica
Apdo. 121-5019,
Playas del Coco
☎ 670-0321,
800-327-5662
fax 670-0083

Mario Vargas Expeditions
Playas del Coco
☎/fax 670-0351

Virgin Diving
Hotel La Costa
Playa Hermosa
☎ 670-0472
fax 670-0403

Costa Rican Diving
Santa Cruz
☎ 654-4021
fax 654-4148

Holiday Scuba
Hotel Aurola
Playa Flamingo
☎ 654-4010, fax 654-4402

Pacific Aquatic Adventures
Nosara, ☎/fax 238-0378

Tropic World
Playa Tambor
☎/fax 220-4402

Fiesta Dive Center
Hotel Fiesta
Puntarenas
☎ 663-0808, ext. 462
fax 663-1516

Rich Coast Diving
Playa del Coco
☎ 670-0176, fax 670-0165

ENTERTAINMENT: There are a number of discos here. Try the **Discoteque Cocomar.**

FROM PLAYAS DEL COCO: Buses return to Liberia at approximately 6:30, 7:30, 12:30, 1:30, 6:30, and 7:30. The San José bus leaves at 9:15 AM. Playas del Coco can be used as a base to explore the surrounding area, but public transportation is scarce.

Playa Hermosa

Several kms long, much quieter, and just N of Playas del Coco, this curved, comely beach lives up to its name. Good swimming and water sports are available here. **getting here:** A direct bus leaves San José (C. 12, Av. 5/7) at 3:20 for here and Playa Panamá. A bus – which continues on to Playa Panamá – runs from Liberia at 11:30 AM and returns at around 4.

ACCOMMODATION: Surrounded by gardens, pleasant **Hotel Playa Hermosa** (☎/fax 670-0136; Apdo. 112, Liberia) is right on the beach. It has rooms for $40 d along with a restaurant. **Rancho Grande Cabins** (☎ 670-0205) caters to surfers; rooms are $50 and are complemented by a Mexican restaurant. **Restaurant/Cabinas Vallejos** (☎ 670-0417) offers simple rooms with private baths for $10 pp; it has a restaurant. **Villa Boni Mar** (☎ 670-0397) has a set of duplexes with kitchens for $40 on up. **Aquasport** (☎ 670-0158) has one *cabina* for rent. Overlooking the beach, ultra-luxury **Hotel la Costa** (☎ 670-0283, fax 670-0211) is the most remote and fully-equipped resort imaginable. Outside visitors are prohibited from entry and, aside from the rich elite, the only Ticos you'll meet here will be your servants. It's the perfect spot for those who are ignorant about Costa Rica and want to remain so. If money is no object and your idea of travel is isolated escape, this is the place. It offers 100 villas and 54 rooms with a/c, phone, and TV; there's a restaurant, conference room, and pool. Scuba and fishing are available. (In the US and Canada, ☎ 800-572-9934). The luxury-priced eight-unit **Hotel Las Corales** (☎ 257-0259, 255-4978, fax 255-4978; Apdo. 50, 2000 San José) – with pool, kitchen, Jacuzzi, a/c, and conference room – is nearby. One reader reported that the hotel was in bad shape in 1995. The 14-room French Canadian-run **Hotel de Playa "El Velero"** (☎ 670-0310/0330, fax 670-0310) charges $75 d on up. Write Apdo. 449-5019, Playa Hermosa. Facilities include tours, sailing ($55 pp for a five-hour sail), pool, equipment rentals, and a gourmet French restaurant. The **Playa Hermosa Inn** (☎/fax 670-0163) is a large house with a pool that rents expensive rooms and an apartment. **Bed and Breakfast El Oasis** (☎ 670-0222) charges around $45. It has a pool and horseback riding. **Villa Boni Mar** (☎ 670-0397, 487-7640) has a pool and offers apartments that hold up to six for $50. Opening sometime in 1996, the 320-room luxury **Sonesta Beach Resort Costa Rica** will have two restaurants, casino, pool, and will incorporate reforested areas. The aim is for the low-rise units to be invisible except for their red tiled roofs.

FOOD: There are several inexpensive seafood restaurants on the beach. **Cabinas Playa Hermosa** has an Italian restaurant. **Aquasport** specializes in *paella*.

SERVICES: At about the middle of the beach, **Aquasport** (☎ 670-0158) rents out a range of equipment: surfboards, windsurfing boards, sailboats, kayaks, and snorkeling gear. They also sell groceries, cash travelers checks, rent their phone, and act as a post office; they also rent out rooms ($20 d) and an apartment.

The Northwest

Playa Panamá

This long, sweeping, deserted beach looks out onto the Gulf of Papagayo. It is named after the Panamá tree, found here in abundance. Get here soon before the planned development of the area materializes. Bars and *pulperías* are at the S end; the best option here is camping to the N. **Playa Nagascola** across the bay is an Indian archaeological site; hire a fishing boat to take you across. The Fiesta de Virgen del Mar is held here July 8.

practicalities: Stay at the recently constructed **Playa Chorotega Resort** (☎ 670-0492), which can be low-budget if there are four or five of you. Campers can stay very inexpensively at **Jardín del Mar** (☎ 231-7629), which also will rent you a tent for around $5.

The Papagayo Project

The only one of its kind in Costa Rica, this highly controversial government-owned project on the Bahía Culebra at the N end of Playas de Coco had its origins under the Oduber administration (1974-78), but has come of age only recently. The government has completed purchase of some 5,000 acres surrounding the bay, which has 17 beaches; the infrastructure (wells for potable water, electricity, telephones, and roads) has been put in place. No environmental impact study has been done because – according to former Tourism Minister Chacón (who served during the Calderón administration) – none was required by law. He criticized environmental groups for "not wanting any tourism" and in 1994 he called officials with the Ombudsman's office "liars." Theoretically, the resorts are to be attractive and not environmentally destructive, but much of the land to be used for hotels is currently covered with tropical dry secondary forest. Altogether four projects have been approved by the ICT and some may have opened by the time you arrive. In mid-1995 Grupo Situr was building the three-star Caribbean Village (also known as Alegro Resort). A temporary order from Sala IV (the Supreme Court) temporarily halted construction while it studied a motion claiming Situr's activities were damaging archaeological sites. In March 1995, former Minister of Tourism Luis Manuel Chacón, 11 former members of the ICT, and the Papagayo Gulf Tourist Board of Directors were indicted on embezzlement and other charges. All have denied any misconduct. They have been accused of approving concessions without approving oversight plans, failure to demarcate the 50-meter beach zone, and permitting the concessionaires to build infrastructure in lieu of taxes rather than allowing public bidding on construction. According to Joyce Zürcher of the Ombudsman's office, the developers "have destroyed mangrove swamps and constructed however they feel like."

Plans call for a total of 15,000 rooms, a marina, two golf courses, and a polo field. A 22-acre project, El Wafou will feature 50 bungalows at first and then a second set of 50. La Esmeralda will have 100 bungalows and then a second set of 100 on 25 acres. The Costa del Rey will offer 150 hotel rooms, 150 condos, 100 homes, and a golf course. The Ecological Country Villas will include 21 condos, and the Fiesta Papagayo will be a 250-room hotel. In 1995, the Holiday Inn chain announced plans for construction of the $14-million, 250-room Crowne Plaza Resort Guanacaste. Finally, the Jardín del Mar will have cabins and campsites. At least three or four other projects are lined up for approval. Some 1,200 rooms here are projected to be available within four years.

The first hotel to open, the luxury **Costa Smeralda** (☎ 670-0044/0032, fax 670-0379) is just over the hill from Condovac La Costa on Playa Buena. At present it has 68 Spanish-style villas; more are planned. It claims to have the finest service of any resort of its class in the nation. Rates are $90 d on up. The second hotel in the area to open, the 100-room a/c **Malinche Beach Resort** (☎ 233-8566, fax 221-0739) offers five-star all-inclusive accommodation in semi-private villas with porches. Each has two bedrooms, refrigerators, marble floors, pine ceilings, and satellite TV. It has two restaurants, a fitness spa, conference facilities, and scuba and other watersports. **note:** This hotel lost its concession in December 1995 after the Comptroller General's Office determined that the company running the resort belonged to the son-in-law of former tourism minister, Luis Manuel Chacón, under whose tenure the concession had been originally granted. However, the hotel will continue to operate as normal while the ICT evaluates the ruling.

The Northwest

Heading South to Flamingo

The next set of beaches are still the peninsula's resort central, although the southern tip is emerging as a competitor. The road network makes this almost a separate region. Buses run as far S as Potrero. To get here by car from Playas del Coco, continue S on 21 to an intersection on the other side of Filadelfia and take the road that heads SW. Or take any bus and get off at Comunidad (also known as Bar Tamarindo) at the intersection of the Liberia-Nicoya road. You can also take any bus and get off at Belén, where buses pass at approximately 10:30 and 2:30 for Playas Brasilito and Potrero. Just after the town plaza, a road leads to Huacas where you go right, then right again after about 200 m to reach Brasilito, Flamingo, Potrero, and Pan de Azúcar. The Hotel Herradura runs a/c buses ($40 RT, five hours) from San José to Potrero on Mon.,

Wed., and Fri. at 9; they return Tues., Thurs. and Sat. at 7 and 2. Tralapa (☎ 221-7202) runs a *directo* from C. 20, Av. 3, daily at 8. Another, slower Tralapa bus departs San José daily at 10:30; it passes through Santa Cruz at around 2:30. Buses return to San Jose at 7 and 2. SANSA (☎ 221-9414, 233-0397, 233-3258, fax 255-2176) flies on Mon., Wed. and Fri. Travelair (☎ 220-3054, 232-7883 fax 220-0413) also flies. **Note:** Information on getting to Playas Grande, Tamarindo, and Junquillal is in the "Parque Nacional Las Baulas" section below.

Matapalo

This village is reached by heading straight on from Huacas rather than taking the Brasilito turnoff. Playa Grande (see description below) is straight on from the town. Overlooking Playa Conchal, the luxury-priced **Condor Club** (☎ 654-4050, fax 654-4044) is five km from Playa Brasilito. Facilities include pool, disco, restaurant, tennis, basketball, volleyball, tours, TV, and a/c. The **Hotelito y Pizzeria La Paz** (☎/fax 654-4259) is an attractive pizza place with picnic tables outdoors. Rooms run from about $30-60. Down the road to Playa Puerto Viejo, **El Encanto** serves Costa Rican dishes.

Brasilito

Set across from the lagoon and river mouth, this settlement has a mediocre grey sand beach, fishermen, small stores, basic *cabinas*, and good camping. Two buses per day from Santa Cruz run here. **Cabinas Brasilito** (☎ 654-4013) are near the soccer field. Dark rooms with fans run around $25. **Hotel Brasilito** (☎/fax 654-4237) has 15 rooms ($30), a restaurant, horseback riding, and boat tours. **El Caracol Cabinas y Restaurant** (☎ 654-4073) offer attractive rooms with fans ($30) as well as a thatched-roof restaurant. Moderate ($30 pp) **Cabinas Conchal** (☎ 654-4257) have fans and offer boat and bicycle rentals as well as horseback riding. Luxurious condominium hotel, **Hacienda Las Palmas** (☎ 231-4343; Apdo. 10, 5150 Santa Cruz, Guanacaste) is up on the hill just outside of town. It offers a/c, pool, restaurant, and cable TV. Inexpensive **Mi Posada** (☎ 680-0953) has basic rooms with private baths. Exclusive, luxurious **Hotel Villas Pacifica** (☎ 654-4137, fax 657-4138; Apdo. 10-5051, Santa Cruz) has five apartments, a rental house, a pool, cable TV, a/c, sportfishing, and a gourmet restaurant. In the US, ☎ 817-738-1636 or fax (817) 738-9240. Go along the beach half an hour to reach **Conchal**, a sheltered white sand beach with a huge shell mound. There are no facilities; if you wish to camp here, get water from the local ranch hands.

Playa Flamingo

Just five min. N of Brasilito, this development's real name is Punta Plata. There's no town here and very little shade.

ACCOMMODATION: Flamingo Tower B&B (☎ 654-4109, fax 644-4275) is the most reasonably priced (around $60). It offers great views, a/c, and refrigerators. The ultra-luxury **Fantasia Flamingo** (☎ 222-4109, fax 654-4024) has rooms and apartments, casino, restaurant, and attractive landscaping. The huge, ultra-luxury **Flamingo Beach Hotel and Presidential Suites** (☎ 233-7233, fax 255-1036) offers 23 two-bedroom condos with maid and laundry service, 30 deluxe rooms, and a 90-room beach hotel, car rental, tennis courts, water equipment rentals, three pools, boutiques, gourmet restaurants, sportfishing, private airstrip and the only full-service marina S of Acapulco. Also ultra-luxury **Flamingo Marina Resort** (☎ 257-1431, 233-8056 fax 221-8093) has a variety of lodging ranging from eight Jacuzzi-equipped suites to four- and five-person apartments, plus 23 standard rooms. It has a restaurant, cable TV, and a/c. Breakfast is included in rates. **Villas Flamingo** (☎/fax 654-4215) has two-storey ultra-luxury villas with two bedrooms, kitchen, terraces, and a pool. Luxury to ultra-luxury **Mariner Inn and Restaurant** (☎ 654-4081, fax 654-4024) offers attractive a/c rooms and suites and has a pool. A bed and breakfast 2½ km from Bahía Flamingo, **Sunset House Inn** (☎ 680-0933) overlooks the coast.

FOOD: Amberes Restaurant has European cuisine as well as a disco and casino. Aside from the gourmet hotspots, you can eat at **Marie's Restaurant** (☎ 654-4136), run by British-born Marie Yates, which has its own swimming pool and a variety of local specialties (marked on a blackboard) at reasonable prices. They include French toast, a Mexican platter, and seafood. Or try **Tio's Bar and Restaurant** (just outside town) or the **Marina Trading Post.**

SERVICES: Marina Trading sells clothing, souvenirs, and snacks. Set outside the town, **Flamingo Beach Sports Center** has tennis courts, softball, and a golf driving range. The **Flamingo Marina** (☎ 654-4203, 222-8303) provides electricity and owners can park boats here while they travel around the country. **Ecotreks Adventure Company** (☎ 228-4029, fax 289-8191) arranges diving, sea kayaking, ATV tours and rentals, and other activities. They have two full-service centers: one in Escazú and another in Flamingo Beach. Car rental is available in the area.

The Northwest

Playa Potrero

Potrero Beach is around the bay from Flamingo and six km from Brasilito. From here, you can walk to deserted, secluded beaches such as Danta, Dantita, and Precita.

ACCOMMODATIONS: There are a wealth of accommodations here. This beach's foremost resort is the expensive **Bahía Flamingo Beach Resort** (☎ 654-4014). It's spacious, with restaurant and pool; rentals include water sports craft, bicycles, and horses. *Norteamericano* video flicks are the rage at night. Write Apdo. 45, Santa Cruz, Guanacaste. At the nearby estuary you can see wildlife, and low-budget camping allows full use of their facilities. The 35-room **Bahía Potrero Beach and Fishing Resort** (☎/fax 654-4183; Apdo. 45-5051, Santa Cruz) has restaurant, pool, scuba, fishing, windsurfing, water skiing, kayaking, and horseback riding. Lushly landscaped, it has a relaxed, low-key atmosphere. Rates are luxury to ultra-luxury.

There are a number of smaller places. Located three km before the village, **Cabinas Cristina** (☎/fax 654-4006) offer three inexpensive units ($35 pn) with cooking facilities and refrigerator. There is also a small pool and a house for rent ($65). **Casa Los Ocho Hijos** (☎/fax 654-4014) has rooms with fans for $12. **Maiyra's** (☎/fax 654-4213) offers cabins for $30 and camping for $2. **Cabinas Costa Azul** (☎ 654-4183) are similarly priced and has a restaurant. **Bar/Restaurant/Cabinas Rancho Azul** (☎ 654-4153) have spartan cabins ($30 for three). **Cabinas Isolina Beach** are quiet and similarly priced; some units have kitchens. **Casa Sunset Cabinas B&B** (☎/fax 654-4265) have a pool and rent for $55. **Casa Salty Pelican B&B** has a room for $50. **Palmiras Royales** (☎/fax 654-4252) offers a/c rooms with kitchenettes; rates run from $30 on up, and weekly and monthly rentals are available. Luxury **Windsong Cabinas** (☎/fax 654-4291) have large rooms with refrigerators. **El Amancer** has rooms for $60 with a/c, kitchenettes, and terraces.

FOOD: Annie and Panchita's **The Bistro** (☎ 654-4014) serves a wide variety of dishes ranging from eggplant parmesan to antipasto. It also doubles as a social center, and performances ranging from opera to drama are often held here. It's not easy to reach. Other places to dine include **La Perla Restaurant**, **Los Palitos Restaurant** (Chinese dishes), and the **Soda y Restaurant Playa Potrero** (which also has a mini mart). The **Surfside Way Liquor/Super** provides alcohol and culinary goods. **Surfside Bakery** sells you-know-what.

SERVICES: Guanacaste Connections (☎/fax 654-4227) makes travel arrangements. **Jalisco Horseback Riding** (☎ 654-4106) provides tours as well as private lessons. **Bongo's Laundromat** will take care of your laundry. You can study Spanish while in Playa Potrero by contacting **Academia Pacifica** (☎ 255-1001).

Playa Pan de Azucar

Located 15 km (nine miles) past the turnoff at Huacas, this beach, claimed by the hoteliers to be the most beautiful in Costa Rica, provides a scenic backdrop for the luxurious 26-room **Hotel Sugar Beach** (☎ 654-4242, fax 654-4239; Apdo. 90, Santa Cruz, Guanacaste). Facilities include a restaurant, pool, and charter boat rental. Rooms are a/c and have ocean views. New units are duplexes facing a central lawn. Expect to pay from $100 d on up with tax. Activities include boogie boarding, snorkeling, kayaking, volleyball, fishing, and horseback riding. In the US ☎ 818-905-5605 or 800-458-4735 in the US and Canada.

    Isla Santa Catalina, a rocky islet about 10 km offshore to the W, is one of the nation's few spots where the bridled tern nests (from late March to September). Rent a boat from one of the resorts. The bus runs only as far as Potrero.

Las Baulas National Park

(Parque Nacional Las Baulas de Guanacaste)

Playa Grande, formerly known as Tamarindo National Wildlife Refuge, is a 230-ft-wide beach that serves as a nesting site for leatherback turtles from November to January. As many as 200 of these bulky *baulas* may nest here then; it's also a popular surfing spot. The first 412 ft (125 m) from the high tide mark, starting at the point to the N of Playa Grande and stretching S to include Tamarindo and Playa Langosta, was formally declared a national park in July 1995. Turtle watching is now permitted only from platforms along the edge of the beach, and the operation is supervised by local guides. Be aware that this area is a reserve. Don't hasten the extinction of the sea turtle. If contributing to this park, be sure that you send money directly to Fundación de Parques Nacionales or other involved organizations. Money placed in collection boxes you see may not go for this purpose.

VISITING: The offshore groves of protected mangroves, which include all five species and occupy the majority of what once was the

1,236-acre (400-ha) Tamarindo reserve, can best be seen by boat. Rent one in Tamarindo. To get here, proceed straight ahead on the road from Huacas rather than turning right for Brasilito. There are no direct buses, but buses to Flamingo from San José (10:30) and Santa Cruz (10 and 2) stop in Matapolo (see above), where you can get a taxi on to Playa Grande.

ACCOMMODATIONS: Set about a half-km before Playa Grande and around two km from the beach itself, inexpensive **Centro Vacacional Playa Grande** (☎ 237-2552) offers large rooms with kitchens for $30. It has a pool and restaurant. Expensive ($80 d) 11-room **Hotel Las Tortugas** (☎/fax 680-0765, 223-2811; Apdo. 164, Santa Cruz de Guanacaste) is ecologically oriented and has a restaurant, turtle-shaped pool, horseback tours, canoes, fishing, scuba, surfing and boogie boarding; they also provide good information here. It is attractively designed to minimize impact on nesting turtles. Some rooms have a/c. Rates are $85 d ($50 d during the low season). **Rancho Las Colinas** (☎/fax 293-4644) has a restaurant, horseback riding, and water sports. Rates run from $60 up to ultra-luxury. **Casa Mirage** (no ☎), near the beach, rents out rooms for $40 on up. Billed as a "conservation project," **Villa Baula** (☎ 228-2263, 289-7666, 680-0869; Apdo. 111-6151, Santa Ana 2000) has a pool, restaurant, and tours. More basic digs are to be found at **Cabinas Las Baulas**, two km from the beach.

> ☞ **Traveler's Tip.** Exercise caution while swimming at either Playa Grande or Playa Tamarindo. Visitors have drowned in these waters and emergency rescues are commonplace.

Playa Tamarindo

This small fishing village is fast developing a resort atmosphere. Once a quiet and peaceful town, it is becoming more and more garish, as the beer and cigarette advertising placards move in and the surfers cruise the beach in their cars. The area is famous for deep-sea fishing – especially for sailfish and marlin. Playa Grande, across the bay, has been transformed into a wildlife refuge (see above). The prosperity exuded by the resorts here contrasts sharply with the impoverishment of the surrounding countryside. While here, be sure to check out Playa Langosta, which is a short drive away. To get to the surrounding beaches, take buses from Villa Real, three km away.

GETTING HERE: This resort is 13 km (eight miles) S of Huacas and is easily reached by public bus (six hours, 320 km) from San José; it's about an hour from Liberia by car. An *Empresa Alfaro* bus (☎ 222-2750) leaves at 3:30 PM from C. 14, Av. 5 and a *Tralapa* bus (☎ 221-7202) leaves at 4 PM from Av. 3, C. 20. Buses depart Santa Cruz for Tamarindo daily at 6:30 AM, 3 PM, and at 8:30 PM daily. By car (one hour from Liberia), the Tamarindo turnoff is 13 km S of Huacas; SANSA (☎ 221-9414, 233-0397, 233-3258, fax 255-2176) flies Mon., Wed., Fri., and Sat. The flight continues on to Playa Sámara. Travelair (☎ 220-3054, 232-7883, fax 220-0413) flies daily, and its Nosara and Carrillo flights also stop here. Most hotels have airport pickup.

ACCOMMODATIONS: A reasonable deal can be had at **Al and June's** place, run by a retired Canadian couple. There's a TV and use of the kitchen is included. Also ask about their rental apartment. Their gate is just S of the beach from Bahía Flamingo. Catering to surfers, the **Rodamar** has camping ($2 pn) and spartan *cabinas* ($20 pn). Inexpensive **Cabinas Pozo Azúl** (☎ 680-0147, 654-4280) have fans, hot plates and refrigerators. **Oleaje Hotel** (fax 654-4223) has five Spanish hacienda-style a/c *cabinas* for $50. Expensive 22-room a/c **Hotel Pueblo Dorado** (☎/fax 222-5741) includes a restaurant and pool. Write Apdo. 1711, 1002 San José. The 34-room luxury **Hotel El Milagro** (☎/fax 654-4042; Apdo. 145, 5150 Santa Cruz) has a disco, scuba diving, horseback riding, a casino, and other activities. On a hill 150 m from the beach, the ultra-luxury, attractively designed **Hotel El Jardín del Eden** (☎ 220-2096, 654-4111, fax 654-4111) offers 18 rooms and two apartments, two pools, and a Jacuzzi. Inexpensive **Pensión Doly** (☎ 680-0174) has spartan but clean accommodations. Inexpensive **Cabinas Marielos** (☎/fax 654-4041) feature a garden environment, a communal kitchen, and bike and boogie board rentals. Ultra-luxury 70-room **Hotel Tamarindo Diría** (☎ 289-8616, fax 289-8727; Apdo. 6762, 1000 San José) has a/c, tennis, pool, satellite TV, conference room, Jacuzzi, and a restaurant. Rates include breakfast. Fan-equipped **Cabinas Zully Mar** (☎ 226-4732) are clean, inexpensive, and centrally located. **Cabinas Alberto** have large rooms with fans for $20. The **Bella Vista Village Resort** (☎/fax 654-4036; Apdo. 143-5150 Santa Cruz), in the hills near town, offers six luxurious thatched-roof *cabinas*; all have fully equipped kitchens. There's a pool, restaurants are nearby, and the hotel provides services ranging from car and sports equipment rental to tour bookings. Rates run around $90 during the winter season and go down to $50 during the "green." More isolated, luxury-priced 57-room **Tamarindo Resort** (☎ 223-4289, fax 255-3785) is set 150 m S and 200 m E of the Diría. It's an American-owned set of *cabinas* with fan or a/c; there's a pool and restaurant. The **Pasa Tiempo Hotel and Restaurant** (fax 654-4223) has its thatched-roof units centered around a pool. It charges $65 d. Across the street are the a/c **Nahua Garden**

Suites (fax 680-0776), a set of attractively designed ultra-modern condos ($80) that also offer weekly and monthly rates. There's a pool, garden, and kitchens. Rainbow-colored in keeping with the name, Cabinas y Restaurante Arco Iris have cabins with imaginative decor ($30) and vegetarian dishes in their restaurant. The Giapama Bungalow Village (☎/fax 654-4036) is a set of luxury two-storey units that can hold up to five. Albergue Mamire is next to the Bar Patchanka. It has six rooms priced from $40 up to the luxury range. Elegantly and innovatively designed, Hotel Capitán Suizo (☎/fax 680-0853) offers split-level rooms. It has an open-air restaurant and a pool. Rates are luxury to ultra-luxury.

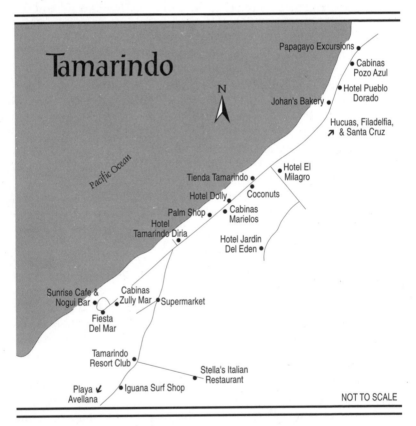

Tamarindo

N

Pacific Ocean

Papagayo Excursions
Cabinas Pozo Azul
Hotel Pueblo Dorado
Johan's Bakery
Hucuas, Filadelfia, & Santa Cruz
Hotel El Milagro
Tienda Tamarindo
Coconuts
Hotel Dolly
Palm Shop
Cabinas Marielos
Hotel Tamarindo Diria
Hotel Jardin Del Eden
Sunrise Cafe & Nogui Bar
Cabinas Zully Mar
Supermarket
Fiesta Del Mar
Tamarindo Resort Club
Stella's Italian Restaurant
Playa Avellana
Iguana Surf Shop
NOT TO SCALE

FOOD: Hotel restaurants are listed under "accommodations" directly above. The Sunrise Café/Nogui's is at the end of the main drag and offers Tico dishes (as well as lobster) at reasonable prices. Fiesta del Mar specializes in seafood. Tercer Mundo also has fresh fish. Bahía Flamingo has fish specials. Coconuts is pricey but good, as is Restaurant **El Milagro**. Others include **Arco Iris Veggie Restaurant, Stella's Italian**, and the **Cordon Bleu**. Another place to try is **Johan's Belgian Bakery**, open 6-5:30. The **Supermercado El Pelícano** is well stocked. You can rent rooms, houses, boogie boards, umbrellas, beach chairs, and other things next door.

ENTERTAINMENT: During the tourist season, the **Resort Club Tamarindo**, a surfer's watering hole, offers weekly live concerts. Music ranges from *merengue* to *reggae* and *salsa*. Ask around about other discos. Another alternative is the **Disco Carpe Diem**.

INFORMATION AND TOURS: Set at the end of the road, the **Tamarindo Information and Welcome Center** offers advice. Check out the locally produced *Tamarindo Newsletter*. Located at the town's entrance, **Papagayo Excursions** (☎ 680-0859/0652, 223-3648, fax 680-0859, 225-3648) offers a range of excursions from scuba to fishing or horseback riding. **Tamarindo Sportsfishing** (☎/fax 654-4090) has two boats. If you've always wanted to ride around in a **horse and buggy**, Charles Boeger operates one as a taxi and tour bus. He's generally found in front of the Hotel El Jardín del Edén during the evening. The **Robert August Surf Shop** is where to buy your surfing gear. The thatched-roof **Iguana Surf** (fax 654-4019) rents surfing equipment, offers surfing lessons, organizes water-based tours, and has a small restaurant. The **Palm Shop** (☎/fax 654-4223) offers services ranging from information to air tickets and film developing.

FROM TAMARINDO: Buses depart for San José at 5:45 (Empress Alfaro) and 8:30 AM (Tralapa). SANSA and Travelair also fly.

Playa Junquillal

Another wide, nearly deserted beach and surfing hotspot. Sea turtles also nest here.

GETTING HERE: *Tralapa* (☎ 221-7202) runs a direct bus daily (six hours) at 2 PM from Av. 3, C. 20, San José. Other buses run from Santa Cruz. You can also take the Tamarindo flight (see above). By car from Tamarindo, head 18 km S to the "27 de Abril" intersection. Then turn right and go 12 km to Paraiso, where you turn left. If coming directly from Liberia, turn to the right before Santa Cruz and proceed to the "27 de Abril" intersection.

ACCOMMODATIONS: El Castillo Divertido (☎ 680-0015) is an attractive hotel which has rooms from $35; breakfast and dinner are served. Similarly priced, the **Guacamaya Lodge** (☎ 223-2300, 210-1000) has rooms with terraces facing the pool and a thatched-roof restaurant. **Hotel Hibiscus** (☎/fax 680-0737) is on the outskirts of town; it has rooms for $40 and a European-style restaurant. An exclusive, nature-oriented resort, luxurious **Hotel Serena** (☎ 680-0573) has fans, pool, sauna, tennis, horseback riding, and an extensive videocassette collection. Luxurious and isolated **Hotel Antumalal** (☎/fax 680-0506), named after the Chilean god of the sun, has a/c, a gourmet international restaurant, disco, tennis courts, two pools, diving, hiking, volleyball, beachside campfires, horses, and fishing with locals. There are 23 cabins ($85) and 11 bungalows (similarly priced); both have fans. Write Apdo. 49, Santa Cruz, Guanacaste. Least expensive is **Hotel Playa Junquillal** (☎ 680-0465); they charge campers $4/night for the use of their facilities. **Junquillal Bar/Restaurant/Cabinas** has basic rooms for $30.

   Expensive-luxury Canadian-owned **Iguanazul** (☎/fax 680-0783, ☎/fax 232-1423; Apdo. 130, 5150 Santa Cruz) has 24 room and is about a km N of the beach. It has a pool, gourmet restaurant, game room, snorkeling, volleyball, surfing, video (extra $10/night), mountain bike rentals, and horseback riding, as well as tours. It has its own bus service ($40 RT) twice a week. An additional two to three hotels are planned, along with some 40 homes, 60 condos, and an organic farm. Rooms run $60 d, $80 quad and up. To get here turn left at the soccer field and follow the signs.

FROM JUNQUILLAL: The direct bus to San José generally departs at 5 AM. It's possible to continue down the coast all the way to Playa Carrillo, but a four-wheel drive is recommended.

Playa Avellanas

This popular surfing beach, which has the reef break "Guanacasteco," is five km S of Tamarindo and 4½ km N of Paraiso. Surfers stay at **Freddy's Surf Camp**, but you should be wary of thieves. Also here and catering to surfers, **Gregorio's** (☎ 226-7914) charges $20 for its cabins; it has a restaurant. Moderate ($45) and attractive **Lagartillo Beach Hotel** (☎ 257-1420, fax 221-5717) has a pool. It's a short walk to Playa Lagartillo. At nearby Playa Negra is the inexpensive **Mono Congo** (Apdo. 177-5150, Santa Cruz), which is owned by a Florida architect; it's popular with surfers such as Robert August (from the "Endless Summer" movies). Rates are around $40. At Playa Punta Pargos, **The Reef** is a set of three cabins, with a restaurant and campground. It also caters to surfers and is a short walk from Playa Negra.

Playa Nosara

The name of this village derives from the river which, in turn, is named after an Indian. The daughter of a chief, Nosara married a young warrior named Curime from another tribe. Despite his outsider status, he was appointed guardian of some gold statues. After another tribe attacked, Nosara slashed her wrists to prevent their capture, and the blood springing from her wrists generated the river. Many retired foreigners live in this area, the peninsula's center of expatriate life. Wildlife abounds – owing both to the nature reserve and a moratorium on hunting that stretches back nearly two decades. However, the reserve is threatened by the construction of a new hotel. The Nosara Civic Center is fighting this development. Surfers flock to the mouth of the Río Nosara and to Playa Guiones; snorkelers will want to explore the reefs off of Playa Guiones. **note:** The town of Nosara is five km from the beach. Things are spread out, so a car is definitely an asset. For a delightful sendup of the development at Nosara, be sure to read the article "The Eden Project" in the April 1995 issue of *Conde Nast Traveler*.

GETTING HERE: In San José, take a bus from Coca Cola at 6 AM daily. There's generally one bus (three hours) per day from Nicoya at 1 PM. It returns at 6. (The road may be impassable during the wet season.) **by car:** A four-wheel drive is mandatory during the wet season and desirable at other times. **by air:** SANSA (☎ 221-9414, 233-0397, 233-3258, fax 255-2176) flies here and has package tours. Travelair (☎ 220-3054, 232-7883 fax 220-0413) also flies daily. Ask your hotel if they will pick you up.

ACCOMMODATIONS: Campers should stay near **Olga's Bar**, a restaurant on Playa Pelada that will supply water. (Be sure to check over your bill carefully). Next to the gas station in the village of Nosara (five km inland from the beach), low-budget eight-room **Cabinas Chorotega** (☎ 680-0836) supply fans; baths are shared. **Cabinas Agnnel** are another, similarly-priced alternative. In the village and open for lunch, **La Lechuza** is popular with resident expats. Luxury-priced 16-room **Hotel Playas de Nosara** (☎/fax 680-0495; Apdo. 4, 5233 Nosara) offers a pool, restaurant, and spectacular views of both beaches. They will meet you at the plane. A moderate bed and breakfast with a good restaurant, **Almost Paradise** (☎/fax 680-0763) has a hillside garden with a fruit orchard. The **Gilded Iguana** (☎/fax 680-0749), serving expensive soups and sandwiches, rents moderately priced furnished efficiency apartments ($50). Bridge is played here on Saturday. The **Condominio de las Flores** (☎ 680-0696) has two-bedroom, two-bath apartments for $500 pw, $1,500 pm. The recently constructed inexpensive-moderate **Rancho Suizo Lodge** (☎ 253-4345, 233-1388/1888, fax 257-0404; Apdo. 14, Bocas de Nosara, 5233 Guanacaste) is near the beach and offers a restaurant, tours, and evening video screenings. Around 3½ km from the beach, **Casa de las Huacas** (fax 680-0856) is an expensive bed and breakfast ($50 d) set on a hill. In the US, ☎ 800-241-6865 or fax 305-289-1195. Set four km out and also Swiss-owned, the hospitable **Hotel Estancia** (☎/fax 680-0378; Apdo. 37, Nosara) has eight units, a restaurant, pool, kitchens, and tennis court. Rates are $60 and up. Horseback riding, tennis, fishing, biking, and snorkeling are offered. Santa Fe-style **Casa Lagarta** (☎/fax 680-0763) has rooms for $55 with breakfast as well as mangrove and horseback tours. **Cabinas and Restaurant Almost Paradise** (☎/fax 680-0856) had its start as an art gallery, metamorphosed into a restaurant, and now has rooms for $50 with breakfast. Coffee is included; dinner reservations for non-guests are available. **Giardino Tropicale Restaurant, Pizzeria, and Cabinas** (message ☎ 680-0378) offers Italian meals and rooms from $15 on up. For information on weekly or monthly **home rentals**, which include maid service and utilities, ☎ 680-0747.

on Playa Guiones: **Playa Guiones Lodge** (☎ 232-3637/2100, fax 231-6346) is a set of thatched-roof cottages at the beach's S end. Facilities include horseback riding and scuba. **Hotel Estrella del Pacifico** (☎/fax 680-0856) is set to the N and is attractively landscaped; facilities include pool, restaurant, and tennis court. It has rooms from $40 and up. **Casa El Tucán** (☎/fax 253-6253, 680-0856) is across the road. Their large rooms (which have kitchenettes) rent for $55. Camping is also available. The **Monkey Trail** (☎/fax 227-0088) is a nice home with amenities such as a washing machine; it offers weekly and monthly rentals, as well as one-night stands.

FOOD: Some restaurants are listed under "accommodations" above. The only Tico-priced restaurant in town is **Restaurant Nosara** right by the soccer field. **Monkey Business** sells sandwiches and whole wheat bread; they also rent boogie boards. **Supermercado La Paloma** and **Supermercado Nosara** provide your food supply needs. One of the most popular eating spots for resident expats is **La Lechuza**, about two km from the beaches towards the village. Set between Nosara and Garza, **La Dolce Vita** offers gourmet food; it specializes in Italian dishes and fresh seafood. **Pascholi Jungle Bar and Restaurant** is on Playa Guiones and serves Continental-style lunches and dinners. Also on Playa Guiones, **La Dolce Vita** is an Italian restaurant with home-grown veggies and herbs.

YOGA: For information about retreats here, ☎ 800-999-6404 in the US or 233-8057 in San José.

FROM NOSARA: A bus returns to San José at 1 PM and to Nicoya at 6 AM. SANSA and Travelair also fly.

Ostional National Wildlife Reserve
(Refugio Nacional de Vida Silvestre Ostional)

Established to protect this vital nesting site for ridley, leatherback, and green turtles, this 9,692-acre (3,923-ha) reserve also contains stretches of forest inhabited by coatis, monkeys, kinkajous, and other wildlife. As many as 120,000 ridleys arrive during four- to eight-day stretches between July and December; these are separated by two- to four-week intervals. In exchange for patrolling the nests, locals here have been granted limited rights to harvest the eggs of the first arrivals. Other attractions here include **India Point**. The beach here has innumerable ghost crabs and other crabs, as well as lizards. There are also many tide pools containing everything from sea anemones to starfish. When you visit, report to the turtle cooperative at the beach's upper end.

GETTING HERE: A bus (four hours) runs here daily from Santa Cruz at noon during the dry season; it can be approached by road either from Santa Cruz through Marbella (dry season through July or later) or you can drive through a river (dry season only) N from Nosara.

VOLUNTEERING: Earth Island Institute's Sea Turtle Restoration Project sends volunteers into the field here. For more information see "volunteering" in the Introduction.

PRACTICALITIES: ☎ 680-0467 for *cabina* reservations, as well as information on turtle activity. Locals will sell you meals and low-budget *cabinas* are available for rent.

Bahía Garza

With thatched huts and cool sea breezes, exclusive and luxurious **Villaggio la Guaria Morada** (☎ 680-0784, 233-2476, fax 222-4073; Apdo. 860, 1007 C. Colón, San José) offers diving, sportfishing, horseback riding, a restaurant, and a disco. Be careful when signing for bills here; mistakes have been reported. **Casa Pacifico B & B** (fax 680-0856) has rooms for $20 pp with breakfast. They also have a restaurant. **Vida**

Ville Super Mercado here has a wide selection of natural foods and also sells fish and lobster.

Playa Sámara

With a long grey beach that widens at low tide, this fishing and farming settlement is popular with windsurfers and swimmers; it has more facilities than the average village. To get to adjacent Playa Cangreja, you can walk through the river or ride around the airstrip.

GETTING HERE: Roads leading here are in bad shape. *Empresa Alfaro* (☎ 222-2750, 223-8227, 223-8361) runs direct, six-hour buses daily at noon from Av. 5, C. 13/14 in San José. The bus schedule to and from Nicoya varies according to the season, but generally leaves around 3 and 5, with one rainy-season departure at noon. They return at 6 AM and 2:30 PM. Call *Empresa Rojas* (☎ 685-5353) in Nicoya to confirm.

by car: If you're driving from Nosara, you'll have to ford two small, shallow rivers. It's about a 1½-hour drive direct from Nicoya.

by air: The airport is at Playa Carrillo, five minutes by car from Samaná. SANSA (☎ 221-9414, 233-0397/3258, fax 255-2176) flies on Mon., Wed., and Fri. Travelair (☎ 220-3054, 232-7883, fax 220-0413) flies daily.

ACCOMMODATIONS: Campers should stay at **El Acuario**, 100 m S of the soccer field; a campsite (shower and toilets) is $1. There are a number of *hospedajes* and *cabinas* here, of which the most attractive is **Hospedaje Yuri**. Others include **Cabinas Milena**, **Caginas Magaly**, and **Cabinas Punta Sámara**. More costly **Cabinas Los Almendros**, featuring a restaurant and disco, still qualifies as inexpensive. **Hotel Discotheque Playa Sámara** offers basic lodging for $20; it has a restaurant. Run by Germans, moderate **Hotel Marbella** (☎/fax 233-9980) has both rooms and apartments. It offers a restaurant as well as bike, car, motorbike, and surfboard rentals. The **Belvedere**, also German-run and across the street, is a bed and breakfast that houses its guests in A-Frame *cabinas*. The **Hotel Giada** (☎/fax 685-5004) has attractive European-style rooms for $35. Luxury to ultra-luxury **Villas Playa Sámara** (☎ 233-0223/7587, fax 221-7222), at the beach's N end around 3½ km from town and a km from Playa Carrillo, promotes itself as an "art and nature" resort. Facilities include pool, windsurfing, fishing, scuba, horseback riding, tennis, casino, and restaurant. All-inclusive packages are available. Expensive-luxury 20-room **Hotel Las Brisas del Pacifico** (☎ 680-0876, 233-9840, fax 233-5503, 661-4040, fax 661-1487; Apdo. 490, 3000 Heredia), set apart from the village and to the S of the beach, has outstanding German cuisine, fans, pool, Jacuzzi, horseback riding, and watersports equipment. German is also spoken. Luxury **Hotel Sámara Beach** (☎ 233-9398, fax 233-9432) offers attractive rooms with a/c or fans. Moderate Quebecquois-run **Casa del Mar** (☎ 232-2241, fax 685-5004) is a refurbished home turned into a bed and breakfast. Rates run from $40 for a room with shared bath. **Cabinas Comedor Arena** (message ☎ 685-0445) offer 12 *cabinas* for $30. **Cabinas Belvedere** are set on a hill and serve breakfast. Italian-run **Isla Chorra** (☎ 253-0182 in San José) is the town's largest development and offers well designed *cabinas* and apartments. They cater to wealthy Ticos as well as foreigners. Rates are $75 pn for one of the 10 *cabinas* (each holds five) and $110 for one of the four apartments (they hold six). It has an Italian ice cream parlor, boutique, and restaurant. On a hilltop overlooking the ocean, **Apartotel Mirador de Sámara** (fax 685-5004) is an elegant and intimate hotel with six apartments and a mirador that has tremendous views. Five km S of Sámara at Esterones/Playa Buena Vista, German-run **Bahía Montereyna** offers low-budget accommodations in geodesic domes. A free shuttle service leaves at 5 PM from the Sámara bus terminal. No reservations are possible; just drop in.

FOOD: In addition to the fare offered by hotel restaurants, **Colochos** serves inexpensive seafood dishes.

Playa Carrillo

Some five minutes by car from Sámara, the waters off this white sand beach are becalmed by the offshore reef. There are spartan, inexpensive *cabinas* here as well as a local restaurant, the **Bar Restaurant El Mirador**. Specializing in fishing, the luxury-class **Guanamar Beach & Sportfishing Resort** (☎ 239-0033, fax 239-2292) offers fans, restaurant, pool, private airstrip, horseback riding, and water excursions, including diving. Its sister resort is Isla de Pesca on the Caribbean coast, and "two-ocean fishing" can be arranged. Write Apdo. 7-1880, 1000 San José. In the US, ☎ 800-245-8420, 305-539-1630, fax 305-539-1123 or write **Costa Sol International**, 1717 N Bayshore Dr., Ste. 3333, Miami FL 33132. From Carrillo, the road to Hojancha is bad, but it's paved from there to Mansión. If you're traveling S towards Playas Coyote and Caletas, you must ford the Río Ora at low tide.

Playa Coyote

This is a beautiful and untouristed beach. The easiest way to get here by road is via Jicaral. A car would be perfect for exploring this area.

Direct buses leave for Coyote at 3:30 from C. 12, Av. 7/9. In the same area are Playa Islita and Playa Jabilla (good surfing). At the former is the 30-room **Hotel Hacienda Punta Islita** (☎ 231-6122, 296-3817, fax 231-0715; Apdo. 6054-1000, San José), which has a private airstrip, Jacuzzi, gym, tennis courts, pool, restaurant, conference room, fishing, horseback riding, and other facilities. Travelair (☎ 220-3054, 232-7883 fax 220-0413) flies here daily from San José. Set halfway between Cabo Blanco and Playa Sámara on the SW coast, **San Francisco de Coyote** offers accommodations and is four km from the beach. Stay and eat at low-budget **Rancho Loma Clara** (☎ 670-1236).

Santa Cruz

Surrounded by hills, this small, somnolent, but very attractive town (pop. 15,000) has the ruins of a bell tower from an old church and more greenery than you'll find in all of San José. Settled around 1760, its original name (*Las Delicias*) was changed in honor of a wooden cross which had been placed on the house of one of the first settlers. The town is a possible base for visiting the Brasilito and Flamingo beaches. The traditional brown Chorotega-style pottery commonly seen here comes from **Guaitil**, a craft center near Santa Bárbara, 10 km to the E. A bus runs there about every two hours between 7 and 5. Here, you may watch artisans knead clay, sand, and water, and form it into coils with which they hand-build pottery. Shop at the Cooperative for items.

GETTING HERE: *Tralapa* buses (☎ 221-7202) leave for Santa Cruz from Av. 3, C. 18/20, at 10:30, noon, 4, and 6. Also try the *Alfaro* Co. on C. 16, Av. 3/5. Most buses to Nicoya (☎ 222-2750; C. 14, Av. 5) also run through Santa Cruz. The town can also be approached from Liberia, Nicoya, and the beaches.

PRACTICALITIES: Stay at either the moderate **Hotel Diriá** (☎ 680-0080/0402, fax 680-0442; Apdo. 58, Santa Cruz, Guanacaste) or the less expensive 40-room **Sharatoga** (☎ 680-0011, Apdo. 345, Santa Cruz, Guanacaste), both of which offer a/c and swimming pools. While the Sharatoga is next to the Tralapa terminal, the Diriá is on the N outskirts. **Hotel La Pampa** (☎ 680-0348) has rooms from around $25 (with fans) and up (for a/c). It has the **Restaurant Las Casuelas. La Estancia** (☎ 680-0476, fax 680-0348) is slightly cheaper. There are some low-budget places, including **Pensión Santa Cruz** next to the Tralapa bus station and **Pensión Isabel** (☎ 680-0173), a block away and more peaceful. You can also try low-budget-inexpensive **Hospedaje Avella-**

nas (☎ 680-0808) near the Banco Anglo. **Coopetortillas,** a former airport hangar converted to a cooperatively run restaurant, stands three blocks S of the church on the main square. Featuring videos every evening, **La Taberna** serves pizza and Chinese grub. For **nightlife,** check out thatched-roof **Salon Palenque Diría** or the Diría or Sharatoga hotels on weekends. The **Malambo Boutique** is the place to go for clothes shopping.

festivals and events: The celebration held every January 15 in honor of the **Black Christ of Esquipulas** includes folk dancing, bullfights, and marimba music. Each day commences with a Catholic mass. Booths sell handicrafts. Held every July 25, the **Anniversary of the Annexation of Guanacaste Province** commemorates the province's secession from Nicaragua. Featured are folk dancing, marimba bands, horse parades, bullfights, rodeos, cattle shows, and local culinary specialties.

FROM SANTA CRUZ: A Tamarindo-bound bus departs at 6:30, 3, and at 8:30. At 10:15 and 3:30 buses leave for Paraíso, four km from Playa Junquillal. Buses for San José run from 4:30, 6:30, 8:30, 11:30, and 1:30. Call *Tralapa* (☎ 221-7202) to confirm schedules. The bus for Tamarindo leaves at 3:30 from the bus stop two blocks W and one block N of the church. For Paraíso (four km from Playa Junquillal) buses leave at 10:15 and 2:30. Another alternative is to hire a taxi to the beaches. Bargain!

Nicoya

Nicoya (pop. 10,000), 48 miles (78 km) from Liberia, is the last stop in a slow-moving but beautiful bus ride. Named after an indigenous chieftain, this pleasant place is the peninsula's major town and makes a good base for exploring the area. Its chief attraction is the recently restored white colonial **Iglesia San Blas,** which also functions as a religious art museum.

GETTING HERE: *Empresa Alfaro* (☎ 222-2750) buses leave San José from C. 14, Av. 3/5 at 6, 8, 10, noon, 1, 2:30, 3, and 5; advance tickets are mandatory. The 296-km trip takes around six hours. While some buses cross by the Tempisque Ferry, others arrive via Liberia.

by car: Allow four hours for the trip. Watch for the ferry signs after you pass the Las Juntas turnoff. Another approach is via Liberia and down past Santa Cruz.

ACCOMMODATIONS: There are a few cheap digs. Down the street and across from Coretel, **Hotel Ali** is low-budget, as is **Hotel Elegante**

(☎ 685-5159). **Hotel Anexo Playa Sámara** (☎ 685-5544) is near the town's entrance; it's also low-budget ($6 pp). Rooms have private baths and fans. **Hotel Chorotega** (☎ 685-5245) is one of the more attractive options. Airy **Pensión Venecia** (☎ 685-5325) next door is slightly more expensive. Slightly upscale, a/c **Hotel Jenny** (☎ 685-5050) is still inexpensive, as is **Los Tinajas** (☎ 685-5081) in the town center. At the edge of town, **Hotel Curimé** (☎ 685-5238, fax 685-5530; Apdo. 51, Nicoya) has 20 noisily a/c cabins with refrigerators, TVs, and separate living areas. Rates are $50 d.

FOOD: A large number of Chinese restaurants, including **Restaurant Jade**, border the square, where fruit drinks are served from stands. Near the park, **Café Daniela** offers Tico food, pizza, and bakery.

Fiesta de la Yeguita: In this event, held on December 12, solemn-faced villagers carry the image of the Virgin of Guadalupe through the streets. To the accompaniment of flute and drums, two dancers, one of whom carries a doll, pass through La Yeguita, "the little mare," a hoop with a horse's face. Other festivities include bullfights, fireworks, and band concerts; traditional foods made from corn are dispensed.

FROM NICOYA: The bus station is at the edge of town. Buses depart for San José at 4:30, 6:30, 8:30, 11:30. Liberia-bound buses depart half-hourly or hourly from 4:30-7; Playa Naranjo buses leave at 5:15 and 1; Mansíon at 9:30, 11:30, 2:30, 4:30; Nosara at 1; Sámara at 3; Quebrada Honda at 10 and 3; Cupal at 10 and 3; Belén at 6:30, 12, and 4; La Virginia at 12 and 4; Quirmán at 6 and 12; Juan Diaz at 10 and 2; Playa Parmona at 9:30, 12, and 1; Hojancha at 11:30 and 4:30; Pozo de Agua, Puerto Humo (Palo Verde), and Rosario at 2; and Moracia and Corralillo at 10:45 and 3. **note:** The above times are subject to change.

Barra Honda National Park
(Parque Nacional Barra Honda)

The 5,671-acre (2,295-ha) Barra Honda park is nine miles (14 km) from E of Nicoya. The series of caverns found here – delving 50-600 ft into the bowels of the earth – are Barra Honda's star attraction. The water and the hiking trails are the only other attractions. You can visit the caverns only in the company of a ranger guide. The abundant animal life in the caves includes bats, rats, birds, and sightless salamanders and fish.

Barra Honda National Park

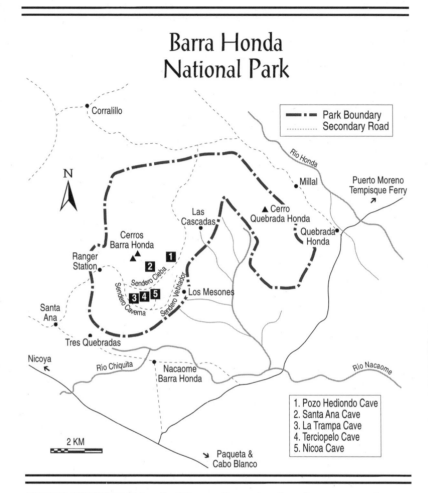

Park Boundary
Secondary Road

N

Corralillo

Río Honda

Millal

Puerto Moreno
Tempisque Ferry

Las
Cascadas

▲ Cerro
Quebrada Honda

Quebrada
Honda

Cerros
Barra Honda

▲

Ranger
Station

1

2

Sendero Ceiba

3 **4** **5**

Sendero Caverna

Sendero Veblador

Los Mesones

Santa
Ana

Tres Quebradas

Nicoya

Río Chiquita

Nacaome
Barra Honda

Río Nacaome

2 KM

Paqueta &
Cabo Blanco

1. Pozo Hediondo Cave
2. Santa Ana Cave
3. La Trampa Cave
4. Terciopelo Cave
5. Nicoa Cave

The Northwest

GETTING HERE: Take the Nicoya-Santa Ana bus (at noon, under two hours) or the Quebrada Honda bus, which passes within one km of the entrance. It's a two-km walk to the park from Santa Ana. From Nicoya, buses also depart for Barra Honda village (six km away) at 10:30 and 3.

by car: If driving from San José, take the Tempisque Ferry (or the bridge, once complete) and then go through Quebrada Honda and Tres Esquinas to get to the park. From Liberia, take Carr. 21 S and turn N just before Mansión.

tours: San José's **Ríos Tropicales** (☎ 233-6455, fax 255-4354) offers tours; they are well equipped for cave exploration. **Turinsa** (☎ 221-9185) also runs tours. **Olman Cubillo** is an independent tour operator

(☎ 685-5580, Spanish-only), and **Luis Alberto Diaz** (☎ 685-5406) in Barra Honda also offers tours.

EXPLORING THE PARK: The nearly flat, white mesa here can be climbed from the NW side. Atop the 1,186-ft (575-m) summit, there are a large number of holes in the rock and reverberating echos as you walk. Bordered by whimsically shaped rock formations, the view from the S edge is extraordinary. To get here, follow the *La Ojoche, la Trampa,* and *la Terciopelo* trails. The six-km *Sendero al Ceibo* leads to a waterfall graced with formations of calcium carbonate.

HISTORY: Because visitors had taken the smell of bat excrement emanating from Pozo Hediondo for sulfur and the whirring of bat wings for volcanic activity, Barra Honda had been mistakenly thought to be a volcano. At the behest of the NPS, the Cave Research Foundation of the US surveyed the caves in December 1973. The results show that these caves date from the Paleocene epoch, some 70 million years ago. Their spectacular formations are the result of dissolution of limestone by calcium carbonate in rainfall over millions of years.

Geothermal Power

A geothermal plant at Volcán Miravalles (☎ 220-7338 for tour reservations) produces 5% of the nation's electricity; capacity will expand to 10% when a second plant opens in 1997 or 1998. The plant is powered by underground vapor which, once the humidity has been removed, drives the turbines. **Miratur** (☎ 673-0260) offers tours here that include a trip through the plant and a dip in the hot springs. The nearest place to stay is at **Parador Las Nubes del Miravalles** (☎ 671-1011, ext. 280), which has a restaurant and camping; they will take you to nearby waterfalls and to **Las Hornillas**, steaming mud pots similar to those found near Rincón de la Vieja.

THE CAVES: One of the most heavily explored caves with the most numerous and striking formations, **La Terciopelo** (Fer-de-Lance) is 180 ft (55 m) deep. One formation in this cave, known as the organ, produces different musical tones when struck. **La Trampa** (The Trap), with a total depth of 590 ft (108 m), has the steepest dropoff, at 171 ft (52 m). Containing the largest caverns, it has one whose interior is composed of eye-dazzling pure white calcite. **El Perico** (The Parakeet) is 69 ft (21 m) deep. Home to millions of buzzing bats, **Pozo Hediondo** (Fetid Pit) sinks to 361 ft (110 m), and the **Sima Ramón Canela** (Ramón Canela Pothole) is 115 ft (35 m) deep. **Los Seis** (The Six) descends to 656 ft (200 m). Human remains have been found in Nicoa cave. Santa Ana has small grottos containing minutely intricate and delicate formations. There also are amazing collections of stalactites and stalagmites. Other unusually shaped formations found in the caves resemble grapes, curtains, fried eggs, pure white chalk flowers and needles.

PRACTICALITIES: If you wish to go into the caves, make arrangements a week in advance; no visits are allowed during the rainy season or during Holy Week. While there's no water on the mesa, there is a designated camping site near Terciopelo which has water and picnic tables. Another good spot, which has streams, can be found in the forest, but it's 1½ hours away and is difficult to locate.

    warning: In March 1993 a German newlywed couple wandered off the trails here and died from dehydration. Let the rangers know where you are going and be sure to carry plenty of water.

    Las Delicias Ecotourism Project, run by locals, has opened three inexpensive *cabinas* ($12 pp), a campsite ($2.50 pp), gift shop, and restaurant. Guides are also available through them. This is a unique project and worthy of your support. A stay here allows you to explore not only Barra Honda but also surrounding national parks such as Palo Verde and Santa Rosa, both of which are 1½ hours by car. To reserve, leave a message in Spanish at ☎ 685-5580. About 20 minutes drive away in the direction of Quebrada Honda, **Observatorio Natural Montaña Vista de Halcón** (☎ 685-5411/5881, 237-6240; Apdo. 985, Heredia) is a traditional ranch house, with camping, and tours to a nearby waterfall and lookout point.

Palo Verde National Park

(Parque Nacional Palo Verde)

At the head of the Gulf of Nicoya, in the "V" formed by the merger of the Río Tempisque with the Bebedero, this park is set amidst limestone hills. Most of the park either floods or turns to swamp during the rainy season, with the exception of the limestone outcrops to the N. There's a nature trail along a dike, but the birds assemble on the riverbanks during the dry season; a boat would be ideal. Named after the famous biologist, **Refugio de Vida Silvestre Dr. Rafael Lucas Rodríguez** makes up the adjoining jigsaw puzzle piece of this reserve. While this park-and-reserve combination may seem an integral whole to the visitor, slightly different rules and regulations apply to the wildlife refuge and to the park (see below).

FLORA AND FAUNA: Hundreds of different species of waterfowl either migrate here or reside permanently; among these are the rare jabiru stork and all manner of ducks, spoonbills, and herons. At park headquarters you can see the scarlet macaw in a tree pining away for his lost mate. One of the reasons that macaws are endangered is that they mate for life. At the waterholes you can observe armadillos, deer, peccaries, howler monkeys, and coatis.

HISTORY: The park was originally the S end of an enormous ranch, extending from the Río Tempisque to the slopes of Volcán Miravalles. It was established by David Russell Stewart in 1923 and was commonly known as Finca Wilson after Stewart's pseudonym. At that time the Organization of Tropical Studies (OTS) chose Palo Verde as the dry forest site for a comparative ecosystem study, a relationship which has continued to this day. The government expropriated the property for an ITCO agricultural project in 1975, and the Palo Verde National Wildlife Refuge was created in 1977.

GETTING THERE AND PRACTICALITIES: For information, ☎ 670-1062, which is the number for the Tempisque Conservation Area Headquarters in Bagaces. From San José take the 7:30 AM bus (C. 14, Av. 1/3) to Cañas, where you transfer to the 11 AM Bebedero bus from the market. From Bebedero you can either hike three hours to the park, passing by nine miles (15 km) of rice plantations on rough roads, or take a taxi. If you've called ahead by radio (☎ 233-5473), rangers might be able to pick you up. Although the ranger's bunkroom is available by reservation, you'll need to bring your own mosquito net; you can also camp at park headquarters. Across the river from the park, **Rancho Humo** (☎ 255-2463, 255-3573; Apdo. 322, 1007 San José) offers inexpensive-moderate accommodation with good food. It contains two properties: the Zapandi Lodge ($40, rooms sleep four) – done in mock indigenous village style – and the more deluxe 24-room Rancho Humo Hotel ($85 d), which has a/c rooms and balconies. It's near the village of Puerto Humo. Horseback riding and trips to Palo Verde are offered. Italian-run **La Ensenada** (☎ 228-6653/6655, fax 289-5281) is S of Palo Verde; it's expensive, but rates include horseback and boat tours. Another alternative instead of staying in the park is to stay in Cañas and drive out daily.

TOURS: Based in Liberia, **Guanacaste Tours** (☎ 666-0306, fax 666-0307; Apdo. 55-5000, Liberia) operates a fine tour here. After hotel pickup early in the morning, you are sped to the dock in an a/c bus, where you board a boat for the park. Along the river, startled birds fly up as you approach, monkeys scamper through the trees, and crocodiles scurry into the water – leaving a muddy groove in their wake. Pizotes and sloths may also be sighted. After a picnic lunch ashore, you walk to the administration building. Along the way you might see birds and families of iguanas. A corral at the center of the administrative area occasionally holds steers. After hiking around the area, you return to the boat and are treated to a spin past the Isla de Pájaros ("Island of Birds"), which is populated by cormorants, cattle egrets, ibis, and herons. Located in the Hotel El Corral in Cañas, **Transporte Palo Verde** (☎ 669-1091, fax 259-0544) runs trips ($35-50) to Palo Verde in a motor launch via the Río Bebedero.

Refugio de Vida Silvestre Palo Verde

This refuge, also known as the Rafael Lucas Rodríguez Caballero Wildlife Reserve, occupies the N portion of the reserve. It contains a variety of habitats, ranging from marsh and lagoons to dry forest, evergreen groves, and pasture. Inhabitants include deer, peccaries, white-faced monkeys, waterfowl, and crocodiles. In addition to wildlife, from its trails you can see the adjacent Río Tempisque, the Isla de Pájaros at its center, and the Tempisque flood plains.

PRACTICALITIES: At Puerto Humo, across the river from the refuge, there's a makeshift dock with a marooned boat and a pig wandering in the mud foraging for food. Nearby are ducks, chickens, longhorn steers, and cud-chewing cattle. Ask around about renting a boat. A bus runs here from Nicoya. Keep in mind that this route is better attempted during the dry season. The other entrance to the refuge is 32 km to the left from the gas station in Bagaces, which is to the N of Cañas. You may be able to stay at the OTS (Organization for Tropical Studies) facility in the reserve if it's not chock-a-block with researchers. They charge $50 pd for a room (you must bring your own food and, possibly, water). Contact them (☎ 240-6696, fax 240-6783; Apdo. 676, 2050 San Pedro) before your arrival. **Guanacaste Tours** (☎ 666-0306, fax 666-0307; Apdo. 55-5000, Liberia) runs tours here for $85 pp. For more information regarding this reserve, contact the **Departamento de Vida Silvestre**, Ministry of Agriculture (☎ 233-8112; C. 19, Av. Central/2).

Tempisque Ferry

This ferry (20 minutes; ☎ 661-1069) crosses at 3:15, 7, 10:50 AM and at 2:50 and 7 PM. It returns at 5:10 and 8:50 AM and at 12:50, 5, and 9 PM. In recent years, there have been problems with this service. The old ferry, badly in need of replacement, stopped operating in 1990. The

The Northwest

new $500,000 ferry, contracted during the regime of His Excellency Oscar Arias, had too much draft for the shallow route and its design was incompatible with either of the ferry piers. Happily, this conflict has been solved. If crossing with your car, expect to spend about a half-hour total. Late afternoon (after 2 PM) and Sundays (after noon) are the worst times to cross. There can be delays of an hour or more. If crossing from E to W, birdwatchers should check out the small estuary about 300 yards (300 m) from the ferry entrance, which teems with life during the winter season. **note:** Plans are underway to build a bridge near the site of this ferry, and it may be done in 1996. However, don't hold your breath!

The Southern Nicoya Peninsula

This area is so difficult to reach from the N that it's really almost a separate region; administratively, it's considered part of Puntarenas, rather than Guanacaste. Infrequent buses run from Nicoya to Naranjo, but from there to Paquera you need your own vehicle. Two ferries, to Naranjo and to Paquera, ply the waters from Puntarenas. Another dead-end route is to take a bus from Jicaral to Playa Coyote, a deserted beach with few facilities. This is true horse and cattle country – an area with many thatched-roof homes, where you can watch the monkeys scamper through the trees lining the roadside. You can walk mile after mile without seeing a passing vehicle, which is just as well considering the dust on the roads. Unfortunately, a large portion of this area has been degraded through development; see "Playa Tambor" below.

GETTING THERE BY BOAT: A ferry (☎ 661-1069; around $1.50 for passengers, $6 for cars; 1½ hours) runs from Puntarenas to Paquera at 6:15, 11 (dry season only), and 3 daily. It's operated by the Barcelos, who developed Hotel Playa Tambor. An a/c section upstairs ($4) offers respite from the heat. If driving, be there as early as two hours beforehand or you may not get on the next boat. The ferry from Puntarenas to Playa Naranjo (☎ 661-1069; around $1.50 for passengers, $6 for cars; 1½ hrs.) runs at 7, 11, and 4.

by yacht: The 53-ft *Pegasus* sails from Playa Herradura (S of Jacó on the Pacific coast) to Playa Tambor at 1 PM during the tourist season. Cost is about $40 OW and $60 RT. Food and drinks are not included and are for sale on board, but you can bring your own if you wish. Call **Veleros del Sur** (☎ 661-1320/3880, fax 661-1119) for information and reservations.

Playa Naranjo

There's no beach and only a small settlement here. But there are a few places to stay in the area. On the edge of town towards Nicoya, the inexpensive-moderate **Hotel de Paso** (☎ 661-2610) has rooms with a/c or fans, pool, and a restaurant. With a shuttle bus that meets the ferry, moderately-priced 36-room **Hotel Oasis del Pacifico** (☎/fax 661-1555; Apdo. 200, 5400 Puntarenas) has fans, restaurants, pool, and some rooms with hot water. It also offers tennis, horseback riding, a gym, and fishing. For around $3, you can use their pool, beach, and shower facilities for the day. Inexpensive-moderate **Rancho Bahía Gigante** (☎/fax 661-2442; Apdo. 1866, San José), seated on the bluff overlooking Bahía Gigante, on the way to Paquera, has a pool, nature trails, pier, fans, restaurant, horseback riding, and fishing. The more expensive condo units have kitchens.

Paquera

Staying in this town might be an alternative to staying overnight in Puntarenas and catching the 6 AM ferry. However, the ferry terminal is five km from town, and you'll have to squeeze yourself on beforehand because it's always packed by the time it passes by. With only two short intersecting streets, there's not much to do, except perhaps shop for a machete or a saddle in the general store or shoot pool. **Cabinas "Ginana"** (☎ 661-1444, ext 119) are down the road to Tambor from the town center. Their garden restaurant has the most pleasant environment. **Cabinas Rosita** are farther on. **Salon Bar Indico**'s posters include Rambo, Bruce Lee, Marilyn Monroe, Judas Priest, Madonna, and a chimpanzee soccer star. There are also two other large salons as well as another bar.

Curú National Wildlife Refuge

(Refugio Vida Silvestre Curú)

With three sand beaches (all of them private) and a wide variety of flora and fauna, this family-run reserve covers 3,000 acres (1,214 ha). Included are a farm of 770 acres (312 ha), a wildlife refuge (84 ha), and an area of *Regimen Forestal* forest land (1,100 ha) under protection. The main ranch house complex is where you first arrive. You'll find a monkey and a number of iguanas residing here. Mangos are also grown, and it's interesting to watch the family and workers bring in the harvest.

HISTORY: Federico Schutt de La Croix established a plantation here in 1933 and made clear to his wife that he wished the surrounding nature to be preserved. In 1974, squatters invaded the area, and much of it was declared by the government to be a *Regimen Forestal*. The wildlife preserve designation came in 1982.

FLORA AND FAUNA: Seven habitats are found here: beach, littoral woodland, mangrove swamp, deciduous forest, semi-deciduous forest, and hill forest. Reforestation is underway, with 10 different native species being planted. White-tailed deer, white-faced capuchin monkeys, and over 222 species of birds can be seen. Leatherback, Pacific ridley, and hawksbill turtles also nest here.

GETTING HERE: Curú is off the main highway between Paquera and Cóbano, and you can also visit by boat, as many guests staying at Playa Tambor do almost daily. It's not necessary to have a reservation; you will need to pay at the gate. The reserve is open daily from 7-4.

PRACTICALITIES: Spartan cabins may be available if they are not occupied by researchers. Food is simple but well prepared. Vegetarians will be catered to. Mangos are served in season. Contact Doña Julieta by phone or fax at ☎ 661-2392 or at 223-1739 in San José. (Note that there is no direct phone to the premises). You may also write to Apdo. 206-5400, Puntarenas.

TOURS: Personalized Tours (☎ 257-0507: 24 hours) will bring you here on a package from San José and will do an outstanding job of guiding you around. If you're in a small group, and would like to visit here with a guide who will become a friend, this is the way to go!

HIKING: There are a number of wonderful hikes here. Most of the land you pass through has been disturbed, but there are birds and monkeys aplenty. One of the easier hikes is the *Finca de Los Monos*. Another trail, the *Colorada*, leads in the opposite direction and passes by a lookout point. If it's been raining, you should take the bottom fire road. Follow the sign at the open pasture to **Punta Quesada**, a small but gorgeous beach with uniquely attractive layered rock formations. Both here and elsewhere along the coast you can see Isla Tortuga offshore. Be sure to keep to the trail, pack out your rubbish, and remember that no alcohol may be brought into the reserve.

Bahía Ballena/Playa Tambor

On the S coast of Nicoya Peninsula, Playa Tambor in Bahía Ballena is a calm, black sand beach. Many *norteamericano* retirees have settled in this area.

getting here: The Cóbano-bound bus goes here from the Paquera ferry terminal. The 53-ft *Pegasus* sails from Playa Herradura (S of Jacó on the Pacific coast) to Tambor at 1 PM. It returns at 8 AM. Call **Veleros del Sur** (☎ 661-1320) for information and reservations.

Cacti

Any visitor to the Nicoya Peninsula will notice the proliferation of cacti and other scrub vegetation. Cacti were classified into a single genus comprising 24 species by Linnaeus in 1737. The name is Greek for "the bristly plant." The oldest fossilized cacti are found in Colorado and Utah and date from the Eocene Era some 50 million years ago. Cacti have evolved to suit a hot, dry climate. Evolution has transformed their leaves into spines and their branches into areoles – localized regions that carry spines and/or bristles. The stems are responsible for photosynthesis. Shade and light diffusion is provided by bumps, warts, ribs, spines, and hairlike structures. These structures also serve to hinder evaporation and hold dew. The thick, leathery flesh stores water effectively, is resistant to withering and can endure up to a 60% water loss without damage. Stomata (apertures) close during the day so as to stave off water loss, but they reopen at night to allow water to enter. Blossoms generally last for only one day, and nearly all secies depend upon animals for pollination.

ACCOMMODATIONS: The **Tambor Tropical** (☎ 288-0491), comprising 10 *cabinas* handcrafted in hardwood, is an adult-only facility with a restaurant and Jacuzzi. Rates range from $125 d (including continental breakfast) on up. In the US, ☎ 503-363-7084. Next door, low-budget/inexpensive **Hotel Dos Logartos** (☎ 661-1122, ext. 236) is named after the two points in the distance that appear to resemble crocodiles. Other alternatives are inexpensive **Cabinas El Bosque** (☎ 661-1122, ext. 246) and **Cabinas Tambor Beach**. Eat at **Tania** (Italian food; 400 m N of the school), **Dos Logartos**, **Soda Carlos**, or at **Cristina's**, across from the school. Cristina's also has low-budget *cabinas*. **Pulpería Los Gitanos** is down the beach from Dos Logartos.

At the village of Pochote to the N, **Zorba's Cabinas** offer attractive cabins for around $25. The **Restaurante El Río** serves local dishes; it's on the Río Panica two km from Tambor.

On the S end of the bay, the **Bahía Ballena Yacht Club** has a **restaurant** with a different culinary theme every night. Everything from scuba to sea taxis can also be arranged here. Past Tambor's, the ultra-luxury 18-room **Tango Mar Surf and Saddle Club** (☎ 223-1864, 661-2798, fax 255-2697; Apdo. 3877, 1000 San José) has a pool, restaurant, satellite TV, tennis, fishing and diving gear, car rentals, and the nation's only seaside golf course. Accommodation includes standard rooms, one- or two-bedroom thatched *cabinas*, two- and three-bedroom villas, and two-bedroom beach villas. (The Hotel La Hacienda has been converted to a dormitory for the Playa Tambor Hotel).

Guanacaste Highlights

This area's popularity has spawned a large number of attractions. Here are some you won't want to miss:

☐ **Cabo Blanco**. A lovely reserve set at the tip of Nicoya Peninsula (page 394).

☐ **Rincón de la Vieja National Park**. A beautiful park with an active volcano, hotsprings, and wildlife (page 345).

☐ **Palo Verde National Park**. One of the best places in the world to see birdlife (page 384).

☐ **Barra Honda National Park**. A set of caves which has a nearby group of locally run places to stay (page 381).

☐ **Santa Rosa National Park**. Beaches, tropical dry forest, and a historical site (page 350).

☐ **Curú National Wildlife Refuge**. This, the nation's only family-run reserve, combines a farm, mangrove jungle, beaches, and trails (page 387).

☐ **Las Pumas**. A refuge for jungle cats (page 337).

☐ **Ostional National Wildlife Reserve**. A turtle nesting area (page 375).

☐ **Las Baulas National Park**. Another nesting area for sea turtles (page 368).

Playa Montezuma

The most popular spot in the region among visitors, this remote area contains some of the nation's finest beaches. While it used to be a backpacker's heaven, with loads of cheap accommodations, prices have skyrocketed as Costa Rica's popularity has increased. And there is now a drug problem in evidence here, along with male prostitutes who impress the women by diving off waterfalls. With one or two exceptions, there's no separate phone exchange, so to call out you must dial ☎ 661-1122 (the operator in Cóbano) and ask for the proper extension.

GETTING HERE: A **ferry** (one hour, $2) leaves from Puntarenas to Paquera at 6 and 3; additional runs on Mon., Thurs., and Sat. at 11. Spend the night in Puntarenas if you want to make the first boat. The return run is at 8 and 5 (additional runs on Mon., Thurs., and Sat. at 1). Buses from Montezuma depart at 5:30 and 2 to meet these boats. A small, packed bus (marked *directo*) leaves from the ferry landing to Cóbano and Montezuma. At times the two-hour journey may seem so sluggishly interminable that you'll think you're on a slow boat to China. The Casa de Huéspedes Alfaro also has a more expensive bus. If it's the rainy season, buses terminate in Cóbano, seven km from Montezuma. There you can take a communal taxi, from $1-5 depending upon the number of passengers.

   direct by boat: The *Simba*, a 54-ft PT boat dating back 45 years, departs from the Bananas Bar in Puntarenas daily at 1 and returns from Montezuma at 7 AM. It holds 30, has a cafeteria on board, and takes three hours. Tickets cost around $15. The journey is well worth it. Enroute, you might pass anything from mating turtles to a beached whale. For more information, contact the Polar Bar in Puntarenas (☎ 661-0723). The boat operates only from December-August.

   by car: There's no real advantage to driving here, but if you do you should be aware that during the rainy season the road is basically impassable unless you are driving a four-wheel-drive vehicle.

ACCOMMODATIONS: During the dry season, it's better to call ahead (☎ 661-1122) to reserve; ask the operator for the ext. listed below. To write the hotels listed, address the envelope to Montezuma de Cóbano.

   low-budget: Just a few years ago you could get a room here for $3. Now prices have risen sharply; you'll be lucky to find one for $10 and will get very little value for that. The two lowest-budget places in town (at around $8 pp, pn) are **Pensión Arenas** and **Hotel Lucy** (ext. 273). **Hotel Montezuma** (ext. 258) is a bit more. **Cabinas La Cascada** (ext. 263) are inexpensive. Low-budget **El Caracol** offers thatched-roof accommodation. Low-budget/inexpensive **Hotel Moctezuma** (ext. 258) is next to Chico's bar.

  inexpensive/moderate: In the moderate range, **Cabinas El Jardín** (ext. 284), at the entrance to town, offers rooms (around $50) with private bath and fan. It has an Italian restaurant. Right across the road is inexpensive and comfortable **Hotel La Aurora** (☎/fax 661-2320) which has a balcony with hammocks as well as a shared refrigerator. It charges around $20. **Cabinas El Tucán** (ext. 284) has rooms for $15. **Hotel Amor de Mar** (ext. 262) provides inexpensive-to-moderate accommodation. They have a good restaurant and a homey atmosphere. **Hotel Montezuma Pacifico** (ext. 200 or ☎ 222-7746; Apdo. 470-2120, San José), next to the church past Parque Infantil, charges in the moderate-to-expensive range depending upon whether rooms have fan or air conditioning and/or a kitchen included. It has a restaurant and offers transport from San José. Set 50 m N of the church and in front of the park, **Albergue El Tajalín** (fax 661-2320) offers 18 rooms ($35) with private bath and fan. Past the waterfall to the L, **Villa Esmeralda** (ext. 262), has inexpensive rooms with shared bath and fans. They also have a more expensive *cabina* that rents for $20/day. **Cabinas Mar y Cielo** (☎ 661-2472) has inexpensive rooms that include a fan and private bath. Nearby are inexpensive **Cabinas El Capitan** (☎ 222-3790). A final place in town to try is **Hotel Chico** (☎ 661-2472). Near Lucy's, **Casa de Huéspedes Alfaro** (ext. 259) provides inexpensive accommodations with private baths.

  outlying accommodations: For a respite from the hectic (in season) village, try the eight-room, Spanish ranch-style **Finca Los Caballos** (fax 642-0025). This "Ranch of the Horses" is set above a river and next to tropical forests. Activities include birding, renting bikes, hiking, and day and overnight horseback rides. Its restaurant serves "gourmet quality healthy food." Rates are $35 s, $45 d plus tax. **Hotel Los Mangos** (ext. 259, fax 661-2320) has 10 expensive bungalows, eight inexpensive rooms, restaurant, pool, mountain bikes, and horseback riding. On the beach about a 15-minute walk from town, enterepreneurial *norteamericano* and Dutch expats **Lenny and Patricia** (☎/fax 642-0272) have a beautifully designed set of hand-crafted cabins overlooking the beach; each has a refrigerator, stove, sink, toilet, miniature fan, and an exterior cold water shower. A similar two-bedroom cabin is nearby, as are a number of concrete domes with similar facilities. They charge $50 pd during the dry season and $20 pd during the wet season. Weekly rentals are about $250 ($150 during the wet).

They also have large dome tents available at a cheaper rate. Contact them at El Saño Banana (ext. 272). Other outlying accommodation is listed under Cabo Blanco.

note: Sadly, Karen Morgensen died in 1994. Her property – once one of the most delightful places for low-budget visitors to stay – has been donated to the park service. Karen was one of the nation's leading environmentalists. Her husband Olaf was responsible for the establishment of Cabo Blanco and (to a large extent because of his brutal murder there) of Corcovado National Park. The land has been titled Reserva Absoluta Olaf Wessberg in his memory. It is closed to the public.

FOOD: Practically every hotel here has its own restaurant. Most popular is **Chico's Bar**. Food in Montezuma is comparatively expensive (around $5 per feed and up), partly because almost everything is brought in, and partly because the locals have found that tourists will pay that much. During the peak season and early in July, a number of small restaurants service Ticos and charge moderate prices. But the rest of the year the least expensive restaurant is the small porch-top place on the right side of the road up the hill and after the waterfall on the way to Cabo Blanco. **El Saño Banana** serves vegetarian food; dinners are around $4 per person, which includes admission ($1 otherwise) to the laserdisc cinema, showing flicks nightly. (Even if you don't see them, you can definitely hear them!) **Marisqueria y Soda La Cascada** is just to the right of the entrance to the waterfall. The **Brothers and Sisters of Mother Earth Restaurant**, up the hill, is well worth a visit. There's no sign. **Soda Momaya** is on the beach. **Pizzeria del Sol** sells slices. A **vegetable truck** arrives once a week. The *pulpería* is legendary for overcharging foreigners. They also have a small restaurant, so ask before you eat.

SERVICES: Centro Internacional de Comunicación (☎/fax 661-2320) is everything from a book exchange to a fax center to a reservations bureau. It's generally open from 8:30-1 and 3-8. **Finca Pura Vida** (marine band 23) rents out motorbikes and conducts horseback tours.

COBANO PRACTICALITIES: If you should need or want to stay here, the **Hotel Caoba** (ext. 219) has rooms for $8 with shared bath, more with private. There is a restaurant. The **Cabinas Gremlar** (☎ 642-2225) are cheaper and also have a restaurant.

SIGHTS: The beaches are the premier attraction of the area. From the village, the main ones are on the right as you face the sea – one after another. Exceptional among the exceptional, **Playa Grande** appears to stretch on forever. There are two waterfalls. The first is reached by a seemingly interminable walk (around 1½ hours) past beach after beach. It falls into a cove that is inaccessible at high tide. The second is to the right after the bridge on the way to Cabo Blanco. After a short path, you reach the river, which you follow as best you can until the falls comes into view. At its base is a swimming hole. Don't climb this waterfall; an American visitor fell to his death in 1990.

FROM MONTEZUMA: It's possible to walk or to ride horses even as far as the Cabo Blanco Biological Reserve, which is undoubtedly the best side excursion. A taxi marked "Cabo Blanco" (around $10 pp, RT) also makes the trip; the driver will wait for you to return. Unless you have your own vehicle, getting out of Montezuma can be every bit as exhausting as getting in. To meet the morning ferry, take a taxi (the price depends upon the number of people) at 4:30 to Cóbano, where you meet the bus at 5 and reach the pier in plenty of time for the 8 AM ferry. (During the dry season, the bus should leave directly from Montezuma.) Another alternative is to charter a group taxi at 6 all the way to the ferry; this allows you to sleep later and to enjoy a more comfortable ride. Yes, this is a "democracy," but you'll still have to produce your passport before you can buy a ticket (around $2). From the dock in Puntarenas, it's a 10-minute walk to the bus stop. Another alternative is to take the *Simba* (see under "getting here" above).

boat charter: Located across from the Hotel Montezuma, the boatmen's cooperative will arrange charters around the Montezuma area and to points as far afield as Nosara, Puntarenas, Jacó, Manuel Antonio, and Dominical.

Cabo Blanco Absolute Nature Preserve

(Reserva Natural Absoluta de Cabo Blanco)

One of the most isolated sections set aside for nature, this 2,896-acre (1,172-ha) peninsula is open to visitors from 8 to 4. You need either a horse, a four-wheel drive, or a taxi to get here. No camping is allowed. Bring your own water. **tours: Seaventures** (☎ 255-3022) runs three-day sailboat excursions here.

FLORA AND FAUNA: In addition to the large variety of trees, there are innumerable animals, ranging from monkeys to anteaters, cougars to jaguars, as well as a great variety of birds. Frogs and toads congregate around a pond in the center of the reserve. A number of small caves also house bats. Tide pools abound at Balsita and Pais beaches: here you can find crabs, starfish, mollusks, and sea cucumbers. Leaving their caves to lay eggs, crabs appear on the beaches *en masse* from March to June.

Cabo Blanco
Absolute Nature Reserve

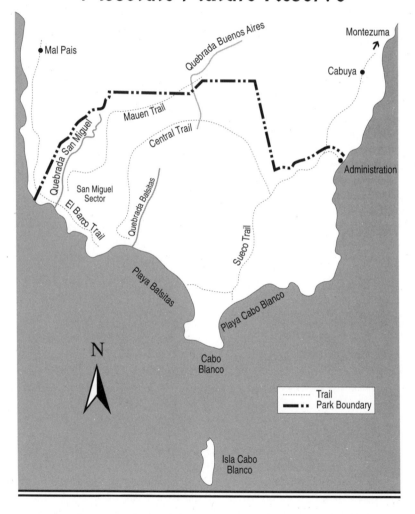

HISTORY: This "white cape" has been known since the days of the *conquistadores*. Although the reserve was established in 1963, it is the only stretch of wilderness in the nation that had already been pre-served intact before the creation of the NPS in 1970. This protection was due to the farsighted vision of Olaf Wessberg, a Swedish expatri-ate, who raised the money to save the area; a plaque near the museum memorializes him.

SIGHTS: Covered with thousands of seabirds, **Isla Cabo Blanco** is about two km from the reserve's S tip. A rocky mound with almost sheer walls, it measures 1,604 by 259 ft (500 by 140 m). If you have a boat, it's possible to land on the island and climb to the top by the abandoned lighthouse. At the reserve's tip, the great mass of rocks which gives the reserve its name dates from 20 million years ago. There are magnificent views of the sea and diving birds from the paths that run along the tip. On the W side, **Playa Balsita** is one of the na-tion's few totally undeveloped beaches. Unfortunately, the sand fleas here make life miserable. **Playa Cabo Blanco** is on the other side and is linked by a trail. Both are about three hours RT from the ranger sta-tion. Ask there if the tide levels will allow you to return via the beach.

ACCOMMODATIONS: Cabinas Las Rocas (fax 661-2320) are an in-expensive homestay near Cabuya. Rooms run around $20. Discounts are given for long-term stays, and Spanish classes are available. **Estu-dio Los Almendros** nearby has camping and offers movement classes. **Hotel Celaje** (fax 661-2320) is also in the area and has moderate cot-tages grouped around a pool and near the beach. Fernando Morales (☎ 661-3234: message) has a variety of inexpensive rooms for rent in his house which is now known as **Cabinas Cabo Blanco**. He's just S of the Río Lajas, some five km from Montezuma. He also offers camping for less than $2 pp, and Spanish lessons are also available. **Restaurante El Ancla de Oro**, nearby and about 1½ km from Cabo Blanco, offers inexpensive thatched-roof *cabinas* plus camping. **Pensión Cabo Blanco** is also here, as are the low-budget **Cabinas Lila**. The **Paniagua Guevara** family have a campground and operate a low-budget homestay; they're about a half-km before the reserve. You can also camp near the river, where you can see herons and pink ibis. **Soda Las Gamelas** is next to the *pulpería*. **El Saloon** is a combination disco, art gallery, Italian restaurant, and tour booking office.

Playa Mal Pais

On the other side of Cabo Blanco (entrance to which is closed from here), this relatively remote area has accommodation in the form of *cabinas* (reservations: ☎ 661-1122, ext. 300) and camping. **Bosque Mar** (☎ 226-0475) also has inexpensive *cabinas*. There are generally around

300 visitors here at any one time; many of them surfers. You can charter a taxi or else hike from Cobano. A **restaurant** serves meals for about $6. **El Sanctuario de la Luz** (☎ 642-0238) was established in 1995 by a group of New Ageists (one of whom saw a vision of the same beach while staying at the New Age town of Sedona, Arizona).

Playa Manzanillo

Set about 14 km NW of Mal Pais, this beach is long and shaded. Eat at the **Atardecer Dorado** ("Golden Twilight") Restaurant.

From the Nicoya Peninsula

If you don't want to drive all the way back N to the Tempisque Ferry crossing or back to Liberia, you can cross on ferries from Playa Naranjo at 9, 1, and 6 and from Paquera at 8 and 5, with additional service at 1 on Mon., Thurs., and Sat. A bus runs from Naranjo back to Nicoya, where you can get a bus for Liberia. Travelair (☎ 220-3054, 232-7883, fax 220-0413) flies from Playa Carrillo to San José.

Puntarenas to Panama

This area was until recent years among the least explored by visitors. Most headed S from Puntarenas to Manuel Antonio and skipped the rest. These days, it is becoming increasingly developed, with both the Golfito area and the Osa Peninsula enjoying a population boom. There are the botanical gardens of San Vito; the national parks of Chirripó, Corcovado, and La Amistad; a number of privately owned and operated lodges and reserves; and the surfing hot spot of Pavones.

EXPLORING: If you use SANSA (☎ 221-9414, 233-0397, 233-3258, fax 255-2176), you can fly to Quepos, Palmar Norte, Coto 47, and Golfito. Travelair (☎ 220-3054, 232-7883 fax 220-0413) also flies to Quepos, Golfito, and Palmar Sur. Planes also fly into the Osa Peninsula, but the only non-charter (also with Travelair) is from Golfito to Puerto Jiménez. Buses run to San Vito and as far S as the Panamanian border. Remote points serviced range from Carate, at the edge of Corcovado National Park, to the up-and-coming but ultra-remote resort beach of Zancudo. The Interamerican is the best road. Scheduled to be paved by sometime in 1996, the 61-km *Costanera Sur* runs from Barranca to Palmar Sur. The $10 million project includes 13 bridges. A second major road under construction, a 38-km four-lane highway, will run from Ciudad Colón near San José to Orotina (near Jacó) on the coast.

Puntarenas

The Pacific coast equivalent of Limón, Puntarenas (pop. 92,000) is a major port town, with little to offer the visitor in terms of sights. It does serve as a transit point to the Gulf of Nicoya and the Nicoya Peninsula. Near the major port of Caldera, which nowadays handles the shipping business, Puntarenas remains the business center of the western region. Placed on the extended sandspit which gives it its name, it has universally been described in disparaging terms. While Limón has a funky kind of charm, Puntarenas has perhaps more funk than charm. But it's not nearly as bad as its detractors make it out to be. Among the pluses are an attractive yacht club and port headquarters, as well as a very friendly populace. And, as it is only four blocks wide for most of its length, you're never far from the sea. It is also on its way to being a beach resort again. Restaurants now line the waterfront, water quality levels have improved dramatically, and spiffy new beach cleaning equipment now operates daily. The construction of the cruise ship port right in town should help the recovery still further.

GETTING HERE: *Empresarios Unidos de Puntarenas* (☎ 233-2610, 232-3961) has non-stop buses leaving from C. 16, Av. 10/12 in San José every 20 minutes daily from 6 to 7 AM for the two-hour, 110-km trip. Local buses (via San Ramón de Alajuela, Esparza) depart 4, 6, 10:30, noon, 3:25, 5, 7:30, and 9. Buses also run from Liberia (8:30 AM) and from Quepos, as well as from other locations. Train service has been discontinued.

HISTORY: Founded during the 18th C., Puntarenas was opened to foreign ships in 1814, but few arrived until 1846 when the completion of the cart road opened the coffee export trade. It was unattractive because it lacked a natural harbor; proper wharves and customs sheds were constructed only in the 1870s. After its linkage to San José by rail in 1910, it became the paramount Pacific lowlands port and commercial center. But since construction of the outlying commercial port of Caldera in the 1980s, Puntarenas retains only its fishing industry. The town suffered considerable damage during the March 1990 quake.

SIGHTS: Except for the church, there's not much to see, only the seaside atmosphere to savor. Take a walk along the **Paseo de los Turistas**, a tree-lined walkway adjoining the beaches. Cruise ships dock at Caldera to the S.

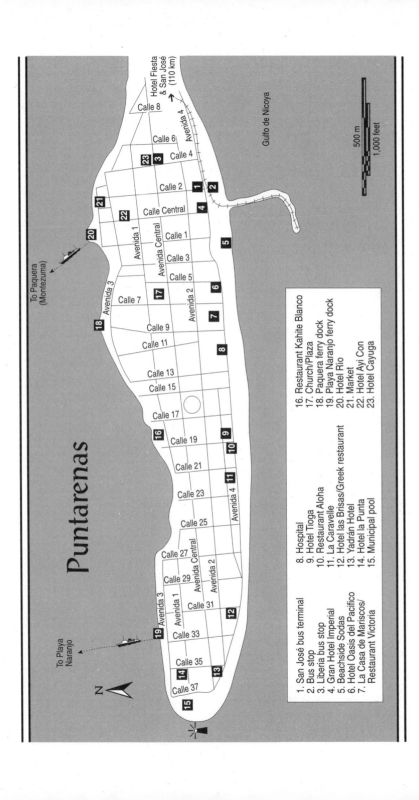

Puntarenas

Gulfo de Nicoya

Hotel Fiesta & San José (110 km)

To Paquera (Montezuma)

To Playa Naranjo

Calle 8
Calle 6
Calle 4
Calle 2
Calle Central
Calle 1
Calle 3
Calle 5
Calle 7
Calle 9
Calle 11
Calle 13
Calle 15
Calle 17
Calle 19
Calle 21
Calle 23
Calle 25
Calle 27
Calle 29
Calle 31
Calle 33
Calle 35
Calle 37

Avenida 4
Avenida 1
Avenida Central
Avenida 2
Avenida 3
Avenida 4

N

500 m
1,000 feet

1. San José bus terminal
2. Bus stop
3. Liberia bus stop
4. Gran Hotel Imperial
5. Beachside Sodas
6. Hotel Oasis del Pacifico
7. La Casa de Mariscos/ Restaurant Victoria
8. Hospital
9. Hotel Tioga
10. Restaurant Aloha
11. La Caravelle
12. Hotel las Brisas/Greek restaurant
13. Yadrán Hotel
14. Hotel la Punta
15. Municipal pool
16. Restaurant Kahite Blanco
17. Church/Plaza
18. Paquera ferry dock
19. Playa Naranjo ferry dock
20. Hotel Rio
21. Market
22. Hotel Ayi Con
23. Hotel Cayuga

swimming: Although outlying areas remain polluted, it's now entirely safe to swim right in town. To reach the best nearby beach, **Playa Doña Ana**, take the Mata Limón bus. The **Marine Historical Museum** is next to the INS building downtown; *gringos* are charged $1, locals 50¢.

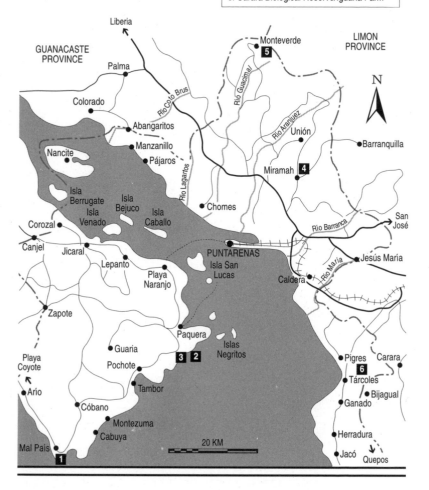

Puntarenas Province

1. Cabo Blanco Absolute Reserve
2. Curú National Wildlife Refuge
3. Tortuga Island (boat trip destination)
4. Peñas Blancas Wildlife Refuge
5. Monteverde Reserve/Santa Elena Reserve
6. Carara Biological Reserve/Iguana Farm

FUTURE PLANS: Cruise ship docks are planned for downtown Puntarenas along with an artisan's plaza, a convention and recreation complex, an aquarium, and a new museum (in the historic port master's office). A park is planned for Barranca, and Isla San Lucas, a former penal colony, will be restored. The renovations are being funded through a $15-million grant from the Taiwan government. Look for some of these changes if you are visiting in 1997 or later.

RESERVA FORESTAL PENAS BLANCAS: This forest reserve, NE of the city off the Interamerican Highway, is the nearest plot of nature. Established to protect valuable watersheds, this 5,930-acre (2,400-ha) reserve has no facilities, but there are a few trails along the Río Jabonal, which cuts through its center. Rising from 1,970 to 4,600 ft (600-1,400 m), it supports tropical dry and moist zone deciduous forest as well as wildlife, including monkeys, racoons, pacas, kinkajous, opossums, and 70 species of birds.

ACCOMMODATIONS: In the event that you need to overnight here, a wide selection of places to stay is available. However, it can be difficult to find a room on weekends. One block N of the microwave tower, inexpensive **Hotel Cayuga** (☎ 661-0344; Apdo. 306, 5400 Puntarenas) is not wildly atmospheric but it has a/c and is clean and modern. Rooms are $15-30. It is near the downtown bus stop. On the Paseo de los Turistas (Av. 4, C. 5/7), inexpensive **El Oasis del Pacifico** (☎ 661-0209, fax 661-0745; Av. 4, C. 3/5) has rooms from around $35, a small pool, and a blaring disco. **Cabinas Central** (☎ 661-1484) are comfy and charge around $15 d. **Hotel Las Hamacas** (☎ 661-0398/1799) is the least enchanting of the centrally located hotels. It has fans or a/c and a pool. Rates run about $20 d. Cheaper is the low-budget **Chorotega** (☎ 661-0998; C. 1/Av. 3); its rooms with private bath are in the inexpensive range (around $25 d). Even cheaper and relatively clean, 44-room **Ayi Con** (☎ 661-0164) provides fans or a/c and is near the market at C. 2, Av. 1/3.

Inexpensive to moderately priced 46-room **Hotel Tioga** (☎ 661-0271, fax 661-0127; Apdo. 96, Puntarenas) is located near downtown facing the beach. The hotel was a crowd pleaser in its heyday and is still a comfortable place to stay. It has a/c, pool, restaurant, and beach umbrellas. Rates run from $25 d and up plus tax. **Casa Alberta** (☎/fax 663-0107) has a special weekly rate that includes food. It has a pool, and fishing is available. **Hotel Colonial** (☎ 255-3234, 661-1833, fax 255-3122) offers large a/c rooms with balconies for $55 d with breakfast. It has a pool, private dock, tennis court, and disco. On C. 25 just in from the sea, **Cabinas El Jorón** (☎ 661-0467) charges $20 d for rooms and $55 for cabins with a/c and refrigerators. The 28-room **Gran Hotel Impe-**

rial (☎ 661-0579), a wooden structure near the bus stations at the corner of Paseo de los Turistas and C. Central, faces the water. One of the best inexpensive hotels, it has a classic Caribbean character. On C. Central/Av. 3 next to the Paquera boat dock, the **Hotel Río** is in the low-budget range. Slightly more expensive are the **Pensión Cabezas** (Av. 1, C. 2/4) and the **Pensión Chinchilla** (C. 1, Av. C /2). A bit cheaper if you get the rooms with shared bath ($25), the **Gran Hotel Chorotega** (☎ 661-0998), is at Av. 3 at C. 1. Near the tip of the peninsula and the ferry dock is **Hotel Las Brisas** (☎ 661-4040, fax 661-2120), a moderate hotel with seaward-facing rooms. It was built by owner Peter, who speaks English, Spanish, Italian, and his native language of Greek; his restaurant also serves Greek specialties (see "Food" below). The a/c rooms are comfortable and priced around $50 d with discounts for longer stays available. In the same area, inexpensive **Hotel la Punta** (☎/fax 661-0696) has a pool and restaurant. It charges $30 d; a/c rooms are higher. Luxury 42-room **Hotel Yadran** (☎ 661-2662, fax 661-1944) has two pools and two restaurants. Its rooms offer a/c, cable TVs, and phone. It also has two conference centers: one holds 30 and the other 100. The **Hotel San Francisco** is run by an old Canadian couple who charge low-budget rates; it's right on the beach and a five-minute drive E of the bus station.

Cocal hotels: In the Cocal area three km E of downtown are three modern hotels. The 35-room **Hotel Portobello** (☎ 661-1322/2122, fax 661-0036; Apdo. 108, 5400 Puntarenas) is on the road from San José. This highly attractive hotel has a/c, pools, and a restaurant. Prices are 60 d. In the same area and somewhat less expensive, 56-room **Club Hotel Colonial** (☎ 661-0271/1833, fax 661-2969; 29-1931 in San José; Apdo. 368, 5400 Puntarenas) has a/c, a restaurant, pools, tennis, marina, and parking. Rates include breakfast. It's popular with vacationing middle class Tico families. Write Apdo. 368, 5400 Puntarenas. Another place to stay in the vicinity, the inexpensive **Costa Rica Yacht Club** (☎ 661-0784) has a pool. It charges $35 and up. **Cabinas Orlando** (☎ 231-5304, 663-0064) charges from $25 d. It has a restaurant and a pool.

San Isidro area: **San Isidro Hotel and Club** (☎ 663-0031, fax 221-6822) has cabins ($50), five pools, restaurant, disco, game rooms, and volleyball and basketball courts. About eight km to the E, **Cabinas San Isidro** has special rates for YH members; reserve through the San José YH (☎ 224-4085). Moderately-priced **Cabinas los Chalets** (☎ 663-0150, fax 225-3520) feature a pool and are perhaps the plushest. Other inexpensive *cabina* compounds are in the vicinity. Many buses run between San Isidro and central Puntarenas.

in El Roble: Designed with upscale foreign group tourism in mind, the 174-room ultra-luxury **Fiesta Hotel** (☎ 663-0185/0808, 223-8051/2, fax 663-1516 or 223-7789) provides a/c, cable TV, pools, casino, conference rooms, restaurants, volleyball, tennis, gym, Jacuzzi, water sports equipment, and fishing. A new set of junior suites has been added. Write Apdo. 171-5400, Puntarenas. In the US, ☎ 800-336-8423 or 305-871-1663; fax 305-871-1657. Or write 1600 NW Le Jeune Rd., Ste. 301, Miami FL 33126. **Casa Canadiense** (☎ 663-0187) in this area has kitchenettes and fans, charging $35 d.

Esparza: About 20 km from Puntarenas, this small town offers an alternative to staying in town. Try the low-budget **Pensión Fanny** (☎ 663-5158), the **Pensión Cordoba**, or the pricier **Hotel Castanuelas** (☎ 663-5105). Buses run here hourly.

FOOD: Open-air diners line the beach, and a row of attractive new *sodas* line the waterfront. Although the area yields a lot of shrimp, most are exported, making them expensive locally. The **Hotel Las Brisas**, near the terminal for Nicoya, serves the only authentic Greek food in the nation. Try their salad with olives and feta cheese or their fish cooked Greek-style (when available); prices are reasonable and the food and service are good. Other good eateries include the waterfront's **La Caravelle** and **Restaurante Miramar**. Sample the **Mandarin** or the **Restaurant Victoria** for Chinese food. The **Hotel Cayuga** has another good restaurant downtown. Others are in the vicinity of C. Central and Av. Central. You may also eat at any of the town's many inexpensive *sodas* or in the central market. The **Restaurant Kahite Blanco**, featuring music and dancing on weekends, is on the N side at Av. 1/C. 19.

TOURS: The catamaran *Calypso* (☎ 661-0585, fax 233-0401) offers day tours, stopping at a secluded beach (see "Islas de Tortuga" below) in the Gulf of Nicoya. It brings passengers from San José and departs from the yacht harbor. Combination tours are also offered. **Taximar**, a charter service, takes individuals or groups out to fish or for a cruise. The *Lohe Lani* (☎ 663-0808, ext. 472), a 60-ft catamaran, has two-hour cruises ($25 adults, $15 children) three times daily out of the Fiesta Hotel.

WATER SKIING: Club Aqua Ski (☎ 634-4056) in Mata de Limón offers water skiing, kneeboards, and banana boating. It's open daily from 6:30-6:30 and ski lessons are around $6 per class; water skiing is approximately $50 ph.

ENTERTAINMENT: Puntarenas has many bars. The **Hotel Yadran** has a disco and a casino.

Puntarenas to Panama

FESTIVALS AND EVENTS: Beginning on the Sat. nearest July 16, **Puntarenas Carnival**, the Fiesta of the Virgin of the Sea, commences with a regatta featuring beautifully decorated fishing boats and yachts. The carnival that follows has parades, concerts, dances, sports events, fireworks, and the crowning of the queen. During the dry season, the **Casa de la Cultura** presents a number of plays and concerts.

MARINAS: The **Hotel Portobello**, **Colonial**, and the **Yacht Club** offer complimentary mooring and use of their facilities for visiting sailboats.

FROM PUNTARENAS: This is the aquatic jumping-off point for Nicoya. For Playa Naranjo, a large vehicular ferryboat (☎ 661-1069) leaves at 7 and 4 daily with additional trips at 11 on Thurs., Sat., and Sun. The launch to Paquera on Nicoya Peninsula leaves from behind the market twice daily at 6 and 3 except Sun. and is met on the other side by a bus to Cóbano. There's also an additional car ferry that departs three times daily for Naranjo; it's met by a bus to Nicoya and Santa Cruz. **by bus:** When returning to San José, even a day or two after a holiday, buses can be crowded, and you may be forced into a lengthy wait in the sun. Buses leave from Av. 4 (C. 2/4) one block E (towards the mainland) of the main square. Other buses leave from the seaside shelter opposite the bus station for San José. These include the *Santa Elena* bus (the village before Monteverde) at 2:15, and the *Quepos* bus at 4 and 2:30; the *Barranca* bus leaves from the market.

Vicinity of Puntarenas

The Costanera, one of the nation's newest roads, runs to the S, passing Playa Doña Ana, Mata Limón, Caldera, Playa Táracoles, Playa Herradura, Carara Biological Reserve, Playa Jacó, Esterillos, Quepos, and down to Playa Dominical, before cutting inland to San Isidro de El General. Between Puntarenas and down the coast to Jacó and beyond, there are a number of good surfing beaches.

Dona Aña Recreation Area

This sheltered beach about two km S of town, along with neighboring Boca Barranca, is popular with surfers. Stay at inexpensive **Hotel Río Mar** (☎ 663-0158) and eat at the **Soda Dona Aña**.

Mata Limón

This is one of the nation's original beach resorts, set on an estuary across from the port of Caldera. Split in half by a river, which is crossed by a wooden footbridge with one plank missing, it has two separate entrances along the highway. The train stop is in the N part where there are two older hotels. The S and main part has several *cabinas* and the **Costa El Sol** restaurant (☎ 670-4008), which offers tour bookings. Check out the wildlife – everything from crocodiles to scarlet macaws – in the mangrove swamps upstream. It may be possible to charter or rent a boat to get around. **Hotel Viña del Mar**, **Villas Fanny**, and **Villas America** offer basic accommodation. More expensive are the **Manglares** (☎ 634-4010) and the **Casablanca** (☎ 222-2921). Also try **Cabinas Las Santas** (☎ 441-0510, 441-0013), which has cooking facilities.

The Offshore Islands

Islas de Tortuga

One of these islands in the Gulf of Nicoya is privately owned and rented out for day use by charter companies. With its own beach and coconut glade, this is a popular destination for excursions. Three or four boats may arrive here almost simultaneously, which tends at times to make this private paradise a bit cramped. Of the tour companies operating excursions out here, **Calypso Island Tours** (☎ 255-3022, 661-0585, fax 233-0401) is the longest and best established. Aboard their catamaran the *Manta Raya*, you cruise past beautifully landscaped islands through the Gulf of Nicoya and on to the Pacific. Food and fruit are served on the way. You are bussed in from San José or you can board in Puntarenas. A gourmet buffet lunch (loads of vegetables, beans, *corvina*, and *tortillas*) is served at tables covered with white table cloths in a shady grove on the beach. But the price is steep at $89 ($84 in Puntarenas). Package tours, including Monteverde and destinations in Guanacaste, are also available. The other lines differ mainly in details. **Bay Island Cruises** (☎ 296-5551, fax 296-5095) has an air-conditioned boat with tinted windows, while the **Fantasy Yacht Tours** (☎ 222-4752, 255-0791, 661-0697) are geared toward those with smaller pocketbooks. Other competitors are **Costa Sol** (☎ 239-0033) and **Sea Ventures** (☎ 255-3022).

Puntarenas to Panama

Isla San Lucas

Once a penal colony, San Lucas has now been closed. The government is planning to do something with it sooner or later.

The Biological Preserves

One of the nation's most beautiful scenic regions, the Gulf of Nicoya is sprinkled with an array of glistening, gem-like islands. Rescued from development, the islands of **Guayabo** and the two **Negritos** were protected in 1973 and **Los Pájaros** followed in 1976. Together, they comprise 363 acres (147 ha), all covered with thorny *huiscoyol* palms and huge populations of birds. Really just an enormous, almost inaccessible 17-acre (6.8-ha) rock, Guayabo has over 200 nesting brown pelicans, the largest such colony found in Costa Rica; frigate birds and brown boobies abound as well. Some 11 miles (16½ km) S from Puntarenas, the twin Negritos (198 acres or 80 ha in total area) are separated by the Montagné Channel. Both are difficult to rach. Set 13 km (eight miles) NW of Puntarenas, nine-acre (3.8-ha) Pájaros shelters a variety of nesting seabird species, including the easily terrorized pelican.

   tours: Contact **Senderos de Iberoamérica** (also known as Green Tropical Tours) at ☎/fax 255-2859; Apdo. 675-2200 Coronado; E-mail: greentp@sol.racsa.co.cr; write Dept. 252, PO Box 025216, Miami FL 33102 in the US.

Isla Gitana

Lying off of Puntarenas near Bahía Gigante, this island – run by US expats Linda Ruegg and Dany Haizman – boasts a full-service marina, four *cabinas* ($50 including meals), pool, laundry service, kayaks and windsurfing equipment for rent, a jungle bar, and a restaurant. Potlucks are held each Sat. at 4:30 PM. The Haizmans will meet arrivals at the Paquera pier ($15 pp) or at Bahía Gigante ($3 pp) by prior arrangement or they can pick you up in Puntarenas or Paquera at other times. ☎ 661-2994 for more information.

Carara Biological Reserve
(Reserva Biológica Carara)

Near the mouth of the Río Grande de Táracoles and by the Río Turrubales, both of which partially form this park's N boundary, beautiful

Carara Biological Reserve protects what remains of the central Pacific coast's once-abundant forests. There are a number of access roads, making for easy hiking, and a trail near the ranger station leads to riverside hot springs. Camping is prohibited. **note:** Admission is charged at the prevailing *gringo* rate. Two of the most popular trails are now limited to 60 at a time.

GETTING HERE: Buses between Jacó and San José pass by the entrance. Ask the driver to let you off. You can also take the Hotel Irazú shuttle which runs to Jacó S of here. The best times to visit are early morning and late afternoon. As Carara is 68 miles (110 km) from San José, you may want to base yourself at more proximate Jacó. If you're driving, don't leave anything of value in your car as thefts in the area are common. One really good way for the novice to go is with **Geotur** (☎ 234-1867). Serge Volio and his group of trained biologists conduct professional tours. You are guided around portions of the reserve in the morning, lunch and relax in Jacó during the hot early afternoon, and then return briefly before going back to San José. The tour leader also packs a scope, which enables you to view the wildlife close up. Another popular tour in the area is to Río Grande de Táracoles, where the **Jungle Crocodile Safari** (☎ 643-3231 in Jacó) offers a tour led by a croc-wrestling Tico. The beasts are fed with large chunks of horseflesh. **Manglares de Carara** (☎ 257-9682/5691) runs tours of the area's mangroves, which are ideal for birdwatching.

The Iguana Mama & Her Iguana Park

The Iguana Park (☎ 240-6712, fax 235-2007), one of the nation's most innovative projects, opened in 1994. This is the pet project of German-expatriate biologist Dagmar Werner and her Fundacíon Pro Iguana Verde. Werner is currently a professor in the Wildlife Management Program at the National Autonomous University in Heredia. For more than a decade, Werner has been popularizing the idea of using iguanas as a substitute for beef. She headed a 1983 Smithsonian-run breeding project in Panama when she first hit upon the idea. Breeding iguanas in captivity increases their survival rate from five to 95%. The park began breeding iguanas in 1989. Now, more than 100,000 iguanas have been released in Panama and Costa Rica. Werner frequently lectures at community centers and youth clubs. Because the iguanas need leaves to feed on, locals are encouraged to plant and conserve trees. If their diet is supplemented with cheap protein ("Iguana Chow"), they will grow faster and may gain up to twice as much weight as they would otherwise. One farmer can raise 100 six-pound iguanas on 2½ acres of land if he follows Werner's instructions.

Werner maintains that 2½ acres of forest transformed into pasture produces only 33 lbs of beef annually, but the same area still forested might yield more than 300 lbs of iguana flesh each year. Although iguanas have been eaten for some 7,000 years (Belizeans know them as "bamboo chicken"), they have fallen out of dietary favor in recent decades. Werner hopes to rectify this by marketing them as an exotic dish. Because iguanas are an endangered species and protected, this takes some fancy footwork. However, her projects are gaining both Costa Rican and Panamanian government support.

The farm contains an information center, trails, a restaurant ("iguana burgers" and the like), and a giftshop/handicraft center. Enter the enclosure, and you may spend as much time as you wish with these green beasts. Most of the iguanas you see will be released at the age of seven months; others will be kept for breeding purposes. Entry fees range from $2.50 for locals and students to $10 for foreigners; trail guides are $10 extra. Profits are earmarked for community development and reforestation. **Canopy Tours** (☎ 226-1315, fax 235-2007) also will take you here for around $30.

getting here: To get to the park, head past the Athenas and Orotina entrances and pass over railway tracks. Rather than driving down the road to Jacó, go under the bridge and continue until you reach a sign reading "Puriscál, San Pablo, and Coopebarro." Take this road to the right toward Coopebarro and stay on it for a couple of minutes until you see the sign for the park.

FLORA AND FAUNA: Most of the area's original forest cover and the surrounding ecosytems remain intact. Carara is in a transition zone between the dry N Pacific and the more humid S. It has 61 plant species, six species of palms, and a number of huge trees, including the *ceiba*. Its small lake is almost entirely covered by water hyacinths and other aquatic plants. Carara, meaning "river of crocodiles" in the Huetar language (presumably after the denizens in the Tarcoles), has a wealth of animal species, many of which fled from the surrounding terrain after their abode had been transformed into oil palm plantations and became laden with toxic waste. Hummingbirds, toucans, and scarlet macaws number among the avian all stars.

At present a controversy rages between Prof. Chris Vaughn (who is in charge of the artificial macaw nests at Punta Leona) and Prof. Dagmar Werner concerning macaw breeding. While Vaughn, who has been studying the macaw population for more than five years, believes the population is sustainable at current levels. Werner holds that macaws must be bred in captivity and reintroduced. This would involve capturing wild birds, an action Vaughn strongly opposes. The government has called the reintroduction plan "unnecessary."

HISTORY: The reserve's land was originally part of La Coyolar, a 44,478-acre (18,000-ha) estate founded by Fernando Castro Cervantes. After his death in 1970, the *hacienda* was controlled by a foreign corporation until it was expropriated by the government in 1977 for the purpose of settling landless farmers. The next year 11,600 acres (4,700 ha) were peeled off to form the reserve. An organization working to support the reserve is **Fundación Gran Carara** (Apdo. 469, 1011 San José; ☎ 234-1867, fax 253-6338).

ACCOMMODATIONS: Lodges are beginning to spring up around the circumference of the reserve as its fame grows. The least expensive places are in Tárcoles (see below). Luxurious **Hacienda Doña Marta** in Cascajal de Orotina offers six *cabinas* surrounding a swimming pool and lounge area. The farm raises mangoes for export, cattle for milk and meat, and grows *pochote* trees for commercial use. For more information, ☎ 253-6514, fax 269-9555 or 234-0958. Another lodge near the reserve's entrance is luxurious **Villa Lapas** (☎ 288-1611, fax 293-4104). It has 47 rooms with either a/c or fans and is set in a canyon near the river. There is a restaurant, conference and game rooms, pool, horseback riding, and hiking trails. Rates run around $75 d. An alternative is **Tárcoles Lodge** (☎/fax 267-7138), run by the same folks who bring you Rancho Naturalista, a nature lodge near Turrialba. The lodge is surrounded on three sides by saltflats on which thousands of birds flit about at low tide. Expect to spend about $400-500/week, including transportation; there is a three-day minimum (including transport) at $70-$80 pd. Various packages/tours (including one of the estuary by boat) are also available. Write Apdo. 364, 1002 San José or Dept. 1425, Box 025216, Miami FL 33102-5216 for more information. Near San Mateo amid four acres of tropical gardens, **El Rancho Oropéndola** (☎/fax 428-8600) has a pool and trails. Rates are $50 for a cabin, and a full "American" breakfast is included.

LA CATARATA: This 200-m-high waterfall (☎ 236-4140) is set off by itself near the town of Bijagual. Open daily 8-3 during the dry season, the property is owned by French Canadian Daniel Bedard who, working with seven other men six days a week and 10 hours per day, took seven months to clear a path. There is a charge of $8 for entry. It's a strenuous 45-minute hike to the falls, and you should bring sufficient water. A bed and breakfast and campsite are planned. To get here by bus, take the 8 AM *Orotina* bus from San José and then take the 11:30 AM *Bijuagual* bus from there.

The Southwest

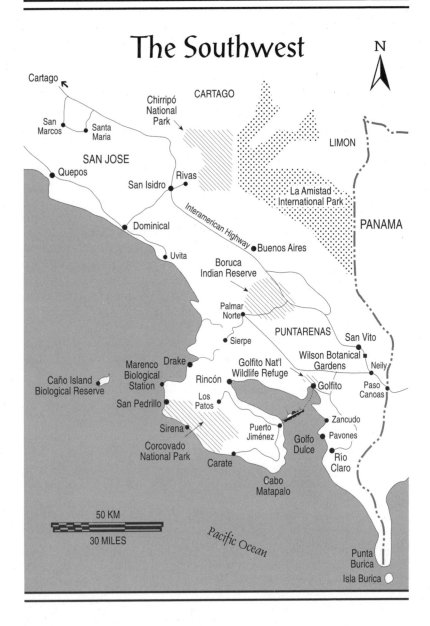

N

Cartago

San Marcos

Santa Maria

CARTAGO

Chirripó National Park

SAN JOSE

Quepos

San Isidro

Rivas

LIMON

La Amistad International Park

Dominical

Interamerican Highway

Buenos Aires

PANAMA

Uvita

Boruca Indian Reserve

Palmar Norte

Sierpe

PUNTARENAS

San Vito

Marenco Biological Station

Drake

Golfito Nat'l Wildlife Refuge

Wilson Botanical Gardens

Neily

Caño Island Biological Reserve

Rincón

Golfito

Paso Canoas

San Pedrillo

Los Patos

Zancudo

Sirena

Puerto Jiménez

Golfo Dulce

Pavones

Corcovado National Park

Carate

Río Claro

Cabo Matapalo

50 KM

30 MILES

Pacific Ocean

Punta Burica

Isla Burica

Pacific Coast Beach Towns

Punta Leona

This area is named after its large rocky point, which is said to resemble a crouching lion. Formerly a private club, expensive/luxury **Hotel Punta Leona** (☎ 231-3131, fax 232-0791) offers a/c, restaurants, disco, soccer, and basketball. Beaches are nearby, and rooms with kitchens are available. Also here is **Leona Mar** (☎ 231-2868), a 24-room set of condos which are for sale and for rent (around $160 pn and up during the high season). Facilities include a/c, cable TV, and full kitchens with microwaves and dishwashers. Surrounded by trails, it overlooks the beach and has a pool. Guests are permitted access to all of Hotel Punta Leona's facilities. Be sure to ask about the radio-tracking devices being installed on macaws hatched here. In October 1994, President José María Figueres strapped himself into a harness and was raised into the treetops to secure the first of 20 nest boxes. The purpose of the six-foot-long boxes – built of plastic and designed to resemble the holes in trees customarily used as nests – is to provide additional nesting sights and protection from poachers.

    J. D. Water Sports (☎ 669-0511, ext. 34) is also located here.

Playa Herradura

Three km down a gravel road from the highway, this sheltered black sand beach is the site of one of the most ambitious development projects in Costa Rican history. Hotel Playa Herradura is planned to have a casino, disco, an elaborate water slide, and convention facilities for 350. The Canadian Department of External Affairs has asked for the extradition of Kenneth Ford, the entrepreneur behind the project, who is wanted there on charges relating to a $1.5 billion fraud. However, there is no extradition treaty between Canada and Costa Rica. The issue is still playing itself out in the courts. Another memento of outsiders, the dock here was constructed for the filming of the movie *Columbus*. Inexpensive **Cabinas Herradura** (☎ 643-3181) can hold up to 10. **Cabañas del Río** (☎ 643-3029) has small, inexpensive two-bedroom houses. A newcomer on the scene, the **Los Sueños Resort** is another hotel alleged to have damaged the environment. The **Faro Escondido** is a condo and home development project at Playa Escondida Finally, **campers** can stay at the campsite.

    from Herradura: The 53-ft *Pegasus* sails from Playa Herradura to Tambor (on the S tip of the Nicoya Peninsula) at 1 PM. It returns at 8

AM. Call **Veleros del Sur** (☎ 661-1320) for information and reservations.

Tárcoles

This is an undeveloped fishing village one km from the highway. To get here, disembark at Invu de Tárcoles and walk for 20 minutes. Lying 600 yards from the center of town, **Hotel El Parque** is in the inexpensive range. The low-budget **Cabinas La Guaria** (☎ 661-0455) and the more expensive **Cabinas Carara** are also here. For scuba, **Centro de Buceo Joaquín** offers 17 different courses as well as international certification.

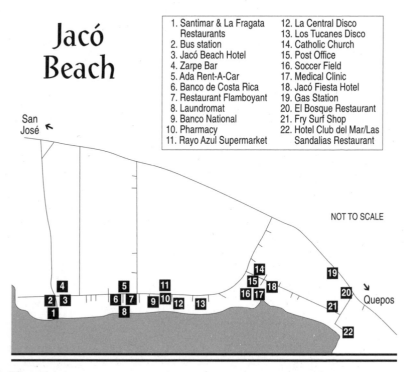

Jacó Beach

1. Santimar & La Fragata
   Restaurants
2. Bus station
3. Jacó Beach Hotel
4. Zarpe Bar
5. Ada Rent-A-Car
6. Banco de Costa Rica
7. Restaurant Flamboyant
8. Laundromat
9. Banco National
10. Pharmacy
11. Rayo Azul Supermarket

12. La Central Disco
13. Los Tucanes Disco
14. Catholic Church
15. Post Office
16. Soccer Field
17. Medical Clinic
18. Jacó Fiesta Hotel
19. Gas Station
20. El Bosque Restaurant
21. Fry Surf Shop
22. Hotel Club del Mar/Las
    Sandalias Restaurant

San José

NOT TO SCALE

Quepos

Playa Jacó

Largely popularized by the efforts of the Hotel Irazú, which opened its Jacó Beach Hotel here, this small settlement has been transformed into a resort village catering to charter tourists. It has one of the nation's famous surfing beaches, one with dangerous rip currents; only capable swimmers should enter its waters. (If you are caught, don't try to fight a rip current: just swim parallel until you are freed from its grip, then return to shore.) If you're not a surfer, you won't find the rock-laden beach to be particularly attractive and you may prefer to hang out by your hotel's pool. Jacó is a place for those who appreciate satellite TV, a pool, and creature comforts. Adventurous travelers who want to explore Costa Rica will not be very happy here. The ICT has built **Núcleo Bri Bri**, a complex near the beach with parking, showers, and lockers. The town is basically one main street with hotels on either side. For information on the area, contact the Jacó Chamber of Commerce (☎ 643-3003).

> ☞ **Traveler's Tip**. The surf along the main part of the beach is for experienced surfers only. Mellower waves are at the end of the beach, which is more sheltered. Surfing is actually at its best here during the rainy season.

GETTING HERE: Buses (☎ 223-1109, 232-1829, 643-3135) leave Coca Cola (C. 16, Av. 1/3) at 7:30, 10:30, and 3:30 for the 3½-hour, 102-km trip; they're packed on weekends (when there are express departures at 7:15 AM and 7:30 PM). All buses to and from Quepos also pass by. Or you can take the much more expensive (around $14) Hotel Irazú shuttle (☎ 232-4811), which saves at least an hour and is more comfortable. It leaves at 9:30 and returns at 2. Advance reservations are required. Buses from Puntarenas depart at 5 AM or 1:30 PM from near the former train station. **driving:** It's about a two-hour drive from San José: take the Atenas turnoff (don't miss it!) on the Puntarenas road. From Puntarenas, it's an hour on a good road.

ACCOMMODATIONS: Ask about discounts from May to December here. Inexpensive **Centro Vacacional Bancosta** (☎/fax 643-3016, ☎ 223-3326) is the first place you come to on the N end; kitchens are included. Inexpensive **Cabinas Gaby** (☎ 442-0354, 643-3080, fax 441-5922) has rooms with kitchenettes ($35 d) as well as a pool. Run by Germans, moderate **Hotel Pochote Grande** (☎ 643-3236, fax 220-4979) has a pool. Next to the main bus stop, low-budget **Cabinas Antonio** (☎ 643-3043) is clean, has fans, and stands next to **Restaurant Fragatas**. The pleasant 23-room **Cabinas Las Palmas** (☎ 643-3005) has gardens, parking, and more expensive rooms with kitchens. **Cabinas Los Ranchos** (☎ 643-3156) offers inexpensive rooms with stove, refrigerator, and private bath. On the beach 100 m (300 ft) from the bus terminal, inexpensive Belgian-run **Hotel El Jardín** (☎ 643-3050) has a fine, expensive restaurant and includes breakfast in its rates. Nearby, low-budget **Cabinas y Restaurante Clarita** (☎ 643-3013) is good value. Cousin of the Irazú, luxury **Hotel Jacó Beach** (☎ 220-1441/1725, 643-3064, fax 232-3159) has a restaurant, swimming pool, and rents surfboards. A discount is offered for surfers with their own boards. It's often packed with Canadian charter tourists. Its sister establishment, the **Jacó Princess**, a set of luxury villas with kitchens, is across the street. In the US ☎ 800-227-2664. Around the corner and down the street, the 30-room expensive-luxury **Copacabana** (☎/fax 643-3131) has wonderful colorful murals on its walls. Facilities include restaurant, live entertainment, kayak and boogie board rentals, and a satellite dish for TV sports reception. Clean, if a bit sterile, **Cabinas Garcia** (☎ 643-3191) is inexpensive. The inexpensive **Hotel Lido** (☎ 643-3171) is nothing special; it does have a pool. Catering to surfers, friendly, low-budget/inexpensive **Cabinas Emily** (☎ 643-3328/3513) will do everything from fixing your surfboard to helping you bring it from San José. If you're in a group of six to eight, inexpensive **Cabinas Las Sirenas** (☎ 643-3193) is good value. Renting three bedrooms by the week, luxurious **Chalets Tangerí** (☎ 442-0977/3001; Apdo. 622, 4050 Alajuela) has kitchens and adult and children's pools.

Expensive **Hotel Tangerí** (☎ 643-3001, 442-0977; fax 643-3636, 433-2819) has a/c or fan and refrigerator. **Cabinas Pacific Sur** (☎ 643-3340) is clean and inexpensive. Run by Texans, inexpensive **Los Ranchos Bungalows** (☎/fax 643-3070) caters to the surfing crowd. It has accommodation for one to eight persons and rates run from $30 d. The **Villa Creole Apartotel** (☎ 643-3298) offers a pool, choice of a/c or fans, and a pool. **Apartotel Flamboyant** (☎/fax 643-3146) has cabins for around $50 and a pool. Simple **Cabinas Cindy** (☎ 643-3485) are low-budget. Inexpensive and good for groups, **Hotel Bohio** (☎ 643-3017) offers seven apartments as well as eight older *cabinas*. **La Cometa** (☎ 643-3615) is an inexpensive hotel run by French-Canadians. Moderately priced and placid Austrian-run **Villas Miramar** (☎ 643-3003) offers pools, gardens, and kitchens. It's next door to the Bohio. Moderate **Paraiso del Sol** (☎ 643-3250, fax 643-3147) is on the beach. Attractive, moderately priced **Apartotel Las Gaviotas** (☎/fax 643-3092) has a pool and rooms (around $650) with kitchenettes and patios. Popular with surfers, moderate **Cabinas Nirvana** (☎ 643-3502) has a small pool and units with kitchens. Expensive **Paraíso del Sol** (☎ 643-3250, fax 643-3137) is a group of modern apartments with pool, a/c and fans, and kitchen. Moderate eight-room **Cabinas Zabamar** (☎ 643-3174) has one adult and two children's pools, as well as refrigerators in its rooms. **Camping El Hicaco** (☎ 643-3004) provides beachside sites; it has a restaurant. On the beach, luxury a/c **Hotel Cocal** (☎ 643-3067, fax 643-3082) has pools, gardens, casino, and a restaurant. Inexpensive, basic **Cabinas Recreo** (☎ 643-3012), next to the Banco Nacional, has a pool.

Inexpensive motel-style **Cabinas Doña Alice** (☎ 643-3061, 237-1412) is near the beach and the Red Cross. Their newer *cabinas* are in the moderate range and are nicely done up. There's a restaurant, and weekly rates are available. Inexpensive **Cabinas Calypso** has some rooms with kitchens. **Cabinas Marea Alta** (☎ 643-3317) are inexpensive units with cement floors and a utensil-less kitchen; it's to the back of a *soda*. Featuring a pool and kitchenettes, **Apartamentos El Mar** (☎ 643-3165, 730-1098) are safe and secure. With kitchens as well as a small pool in front of each unit, moderately-priced *cabinas* **Casas de Playa Mar Sol** (☎ 643-3016, 223-3326) are ideal for families. **Apartamentos y Tienda Nicole** (☎/fax 643-3384/3501) offers rooms with kitchens for around $40. **Sole D'Oro** (☎/fax 643-3172/3247) has rooms with kitchenettes (around $60), Jacuzzi and pool. **Condotel Jacó Tropical** (☎ 643-3511) has a set of two-storey cabins (around $40 d) with kitchens. **Hotel Jacofiesta** (☎ 643-3147, fax 643-3148) has a restaurant, pools, a/c, cable TV, and is one of the best hotels in the area. Inexpensive **Chalets Santa Ana** (☎ 643-3233) is across the street and good value for groups. Kitchens are in the higher-priced units ($35). One- and two-bedroom moderate **Restaurante y Cabinas Naranjal** (☎ 643-3006) is next to the Catholic Church. Moderate **Hotel Club Marparaíso** (☎ 643-3277, 221-6601) has fans, Jacuzzi, pools, and more expensive units with kitchens. Check out their newest rooms. **Cabinas John Paul** (☎ 643-3106) are next door to it. Also offering camping (around $2 pn), low-budget **Cabinas Madrigal** (☎ 643-3230) is somewhat deteriorated. **Los Canciones del Mar** (☎/fax 643-3277) is an expensive oceanfront condominium hotel with a pool. The **Malparaiso Hotel and Club** (☎ 221-6544, 643-3277, fax 221-6601) has both adult and children's pools along with a restaurant. It charges $45. **Beachside Apartotel Catalina** (☎ 643-3217, fax 643-3544) offers suites from $30 d; it has a pool.

Hotel Hacienda Lilipoza (☎ 643-3062, fax 643-3158) has ultra-luxury a/c suites with TVs and phones, two restaurants, pool, tennis courts, and horseback riding. The **Zabamar Resort** (☎/fax 643-3174) has nice rooms for $40 d and up. **Mar de Luz** (☎ 643-3259) has attractive a/c rooms with private terraces ($60); it has a pool. The expensive-luxury **Los Villas Paradise** (☎ 296-2022, fax 296-2023) offers large rooms from $55; it has a restaurant, pool, and Jacuzzi. **Hotel Pochote Grande Jacó** (☎ 643-3236, ☎/fax 220-4979) has a pool, gardens, and rooms ($60 d) with refrigerators and balconies. Popular and friendly **Hotel Club de Mar** (☎/fax 643-3194; Apdo. 107-4023, Jacó) has fully equipped apartments with balconies. It has a library, pool, and restaurant. Horseback riding is available on trails behind the hotel. Surrounded by nature, it's out by itself on the S end. Rates run from $80 d, including tax. Outside of town, the ultra-luxury **Hotel Hacienda Lillipoza** (☎ 643-3062, fax 643-3158) has tennis courts, restaurant, a/c, cable TV, pool, and other features.

FOOD: Good places to eat include **Cabinas Doña Alice, El Jardín,** and **Pollo Asado Borinquen**. In the midst of mango trees near the gas station on the S end of town, **El Bosque** is good for breakfast as well as for seafood. **Java Beanies Coffee House** serves affordable breakfasts. **Capitán** Coco serves fish and chips. **Pizzeria Bri Bri**, next to the ICT facility (Tourist Board), has passable pizza. One of the best places to try is **Restaurant Marisquería Los Manudos**, on the street leading to the airport, which has *ceviche* and a wide variety of seafood ranging from octopus to sautéed whole fish. **El Ceviche del Rey** has Peruvian dishes, and **Jacó Bell** serves Mexican food. The Canadian-owned **La Piraña** serves sandwiches, salads, and other items for lunch; surfers have their own menu. There are also a number of vegetarian dishes, and an international menu is offered at dinner. It's in the Yellow Corner Arcade. Others to try include **Restaurante El Gran Palenque Barcelona** (Spanish cuisine accompanied by live guitar music) and **Restaurant Fragatas**. Expresso is served at a restaurant across from the Bohio. Shop for food at the **Rayo Azul**.

SERVICES: Both a **public phone** and a **coin laundry** are near the Aparthotel Flamboyant. Change money at **Banco Nacional**. The local pharmacy, **Botiquin Garabito**, is near the bank. The PO and a health center are at the **Centro Municipal** at the town's S end. **Car rental** is available at the Hotel Jacó Beach's **Fantasy Rent-a-Car** (☎ 220-1441), from **Elegante** (☎ 643-3224), and from others. Boats for cruising or fishing can be rented next to the bus stop; ☎ 643-3002. Rent bicycles from hotels, the store next to the Hotel El Jardín, or at the **Ferretería Macho e Hijos**. **Fun Rentals** (☎ 643-3242) has everything from snorkeling gear to bikes and scooters. Taxi companies include **Taxi 30-30** (☎ 643-3030) and **Taxi Jacó** (☎ 643-3000).

El Bujo is a unique gift shop that shares space with The Garden Café along the main street. The Yellow Corner Arcade, at the strip's S end, contains the **Heliconia Art Gallery** as well as the **Loro de Plata** jewelers. **Salva la Selva** (☎ 643-3622), at the end of the beach near the Hotel Club de Mar, is the nation's only surf shop. They sell custom designed boards. Boogie board and surf board rentals are also available. **Rafting Safaris** (☎ 643-3151, 221-5371) offers runs down the Río Tulin, along with a BBQ lunch.

ENTERTAINMENT: Jacó has a lively nightlife. Try **Disco La Central** (right on the beach opposite Tienda La Flor), **Foxy's Disco** (on the road to the airport), or the disco at the **Hotel Jacó Beach**. **Papagayo Disco** is next door to Los Ranchos. **Centro Vacacional Bancosta** (☎ 643-3116) has live calypso on Thurs. and Sunday.

FROM JACO: Buses run to San José at 5 AM and 3 PM. Inquire about buses to San José arriving from Quepos and those running to Quepos or Puntarenas.

VICINITY OF JACO: Highly attractive **Villa Caletas** (☎ 257-3653, fax 222-2059) is set between Jacó and Tárcoles. Set atop a steep hill accessed by a gravel road, this resort is done in French Renaissance style and designed for honeymooners and couples seeking a romantic getaway. It has an unusual pool, a gourmet restaurant, and attractively landscaped grounds. The beach can be reached either by hiking or in a four-wheel-drive vehicle. It has eight-rooms, 13 villas, and two jr. suites. Rates are $115 d and up. Stretching some 10 km, **Playa Hermosa** is about five km S of Jacó; surfing contests are held every August. On the outskirts of the beach, 43-room two-storey luxury **Hotel Terraza del Pacifico** (☎ 643-3222, fax 643-3424) is the nicest place to stay. It has an Italian restaurant, which also serves up *típico* fare, a small gambling room, and motorbike rentals. Rooms have cable TV, a/c, and phone. Moderate **Las Olas** (☎ 643-3687) caters to surfers; it has a pool and fans and kitchens in the rooms. Less expensive **Cabinas Vista Hermosa** (☎ 643-3422, fax 224-3687) are next door. Also here are **Villas Ballena** (☎ 643-3373/4) which offer cabins with kitchenettes. You may dine at reasonable **Ola Bonita**. **Esterillos Oeste** is 22 km S. It has heavy surf but is relatively undeveloped. You may stay here at low-budget **Cabinas Las Caletas** (☎ 771-2143), the inexpensive **Famoso** (☎ 779-9184), and **Cabinas Don José** (☎ 238-1876). **Playa Esterillos Este** is 30 km to the S. Stay here at luxury-priced and secluded **Hotel El Delfín** (☎ 771-1640; Apdo. 2260, 1000 San José), which has a pool, library, table tennis, shuffleboard, horse-shoe pitch, and bicycles. Another alternative, opened in 1991, is the 10-room French-speaking **Auberge du Pélican** (fax 777-9108, ☎ 643-3207; Apdo. 47, Parrita 6300), which charges $30 d (shared bath) and $40 d (private bath); taxes are additional. It has a restaurant, pool, and bar. Two rooms are handicapped-accessible. The moderate **Fleur de Lis** (☎ 779-9117, fax 779-9108) is a set of cabins. Less frequently visited, Playa Bejuco and Playa Palma are farther along and inland. **Parrita**, on the Río Parrita and 44 km S from Jacó, has basic accommodations.

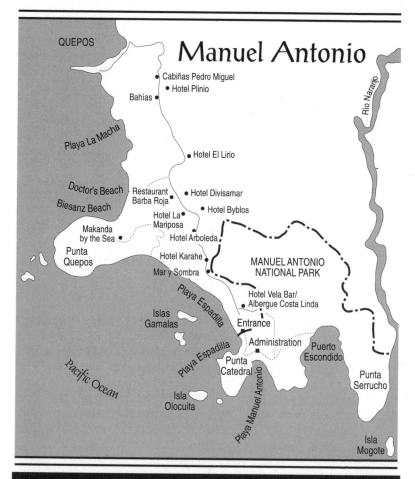

QUEPOS

Manuel Antonio

- Cabiñas Pedro Miguel
- Hotel Plinio

Bahías

Río Naranjo

Playa La Macha

- Hotel El Lirio

Doctor's Beach

Biesanz Beach

Restaurant Barba Roja • • Hotel Divisamar

• Hotel Byblos

Hotel La • Mariposa

Makanda by the Sea •

• Hotel Arboleda

Punta Quepos

Hotel Karahe •

MANUEL ANTONIO NATIONAL PARK

Mar y Sombra •

Playa Espadilla

Islas Gamalas

Hotel Vela Bar/ Albergue Costa Linda

Entrance

Playa Espadilla

Administration

Puerto Escondido

Pacific Ocean

Playa Espadilla

Punta Catedral

Punta Serrucho

Isla Olocuita

Playa Manuel Antonio

Isla Mogote

Quepos & Manuel Antonio

Sometimes you'll hear it called Quepos, at other times Manuel Antonio. While Quepos refers to the town (8,000 pop.) just before the resort area begins, the name Manuel Antonio refers to **Parque Nacional Manuel Antonio**, the national park, as well as the surrounding resort area. There are three major **beaches** which, taken together, extend for 1½ km. Two of these, Espadilla del Sur and Playa Manuel Antonio, are sheltered and offer safe swimming. (Playa Manuel Antonio now has lifeguards). Although the area is strikingly beautiful, it is becoming increasingly expensive – many maintain ridiculously overpriced – and no longer the haven for low-budget travelers that it was years ago. If you're serious about your love of nature and want solitude, you might give this park a miss. The park itself is overcrowded. While its ideal maximum capacity is said to be 300 visitors per day, it currently receives plus or minus 1,000, and it is not unusual for 5,000 to visit during a weekend. One study projects that the park will be receiving 400,000 visitors per year by the end of the century. By contrast, 1991 saw only 30,000 visitors.

> ☞ **Traveler's Tip**. Despite its reputation, Manuel Antonio doesn't have to be expensive. Discount tickets for the park may be purchased at Ríos Tropicales or at Mike Lynch Travel. Off-season, rooms are discounted up to 50%, and there are always a large number of inexpensive *cabinas* available. By eating in the local restaurants in Quepos, you can trim your expenses further. Keep in mind that Feb. and March are both the hottest and driest months. Bring everything you need with you, especially prescriptions, film, and insect repellent. You may or may not be able to buy it here.

HISTORY: This area was first explored by Juan Vásquez de Coronado who found the Quepoa, a subtribe of the Borucas, when he arrived in 1563. These Indians were largely wiped out in succeeding years by disease, intertribal warfare, and theft of their lands by the Spaniards. Built by United Fruit in the 1930s, Quepos, like Golfito, was originally laid out as a company town, established to service nearby plantations. Production of African palm oil supplanted bananas as the local crop during the 1950s, after Panama disease had destroyed the banana crop. As a result, Quepos became the only town in Costa Rica to suffer a population decline during the second half of the 20th C. The name "Manuel Antonio," applied to the area at the S, came from a now-vanished memorial plaque to a Spaniard who died during a skirmish with a group of Quepoa. Like Cahuita and (in part) Tortuguero, Manuel Antonio, the smallest national park, was established to preserve the offshore marine life, which would otherwise have been finished off by the development of tourism facilities. Around a half-century ago, it was public land, before the government gave it away. An American purchased the area in 1968 and erected iron gates to prevent access by outsiders. The townspeople responded by demolishing them. The municipal government ruled that, as the road was public, barriers could not be erected. Tiring of the problem, the owner sold the property to a Frenchman in 1972. He, in turn, erected concrete barriers to prevent cars from passing. After journalist Miguel Salguero suggested that the park be nationalized, the local community enthusiastically rallied around the cause. The fact that the new owner was working on plans for a resort clinched the matter. The land was expropriated from the owner, and the 1,685-acre (682-ha) park was established in November 1972. It was increased by more than 988 acres (400 ha) in 1980. Today, with some 250,000 visitors each year, it is the most popular park after Poás and Irazú. The park was hard hit by a tropical storm in 1993; it will need another decade to recover fully.

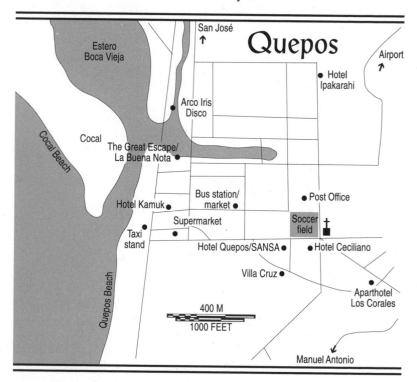

ENVIRONMENTAL PROBLEMS: In February 1992, Park Director José Antonio Salazar announced in the *Tico Times* that "we have a park which is dying." The park has become an "island" because squatter settlements and touristic development have barred animals from access to areas outside of the park. This is a particular problem for the endangered squirrel monkeys because the park's area is too small to sustain a healthy population. Many hotels do not have proper sewage systems, and the waste flows into an estuary that runs through the local streams and lagoons before ending up in the ocean. Salazar charges the owners with a "destructive mentality," maintaining that "they want to earn money as quickly as possible, and they don't care what happens to anything else." In 1995, Salazar revealed that 1.75 ha of land declared to be park territory (but not yet purchased) had been clearcut illegally. "The government has owed them for the land for 22 years. I think the owners have tolerated a lot," Salazar commented. The clearcut land was on property owned by a consortium of US and Costa Rican lawyers. According to Salazar, 175 million *colones* ($1 mil-

lion) are needed to purchase the land and the park brought in an estimated 138 million *colones* in 1995. But 25% goes to the local municipality and the remainder goes to the National Parks Fund. Currently,
none of the money is reserved for purchasing park land, but proposed
legislation may change this.

Certainly, the changes of the past few years have been destructive.
The privately owned path that ran down from the Mariposa to the
beach has been widened so as to allow heavy equipment access to build
a beach resort, and the squirrels and sloths have fled. Hundred-year-
old royal palms were toppled in the process. In 1993, Tourism Minister
Luis Manuel Chacón called for the partial or total razing of 23 businesses near Manuel Antonio that are 50 m or less from the high tide
mark. Although construction in front of this line is prohibited, enforcement is lax or subject to exceptions on any official level, given a little
palm grease. The minister also cited a number of businesses, such as
Restaurant Mar y Sombra and Cabinas Manuel Antonio, that have
failed for years to meet health regulations for proper garbage disposal
and sewage systems. The beaches are now often covered with rubbish,
the lagoon at the park's entrance has been polluted, and water is not
rationed because of increased demand. Still, no regulatory and zoning
plan has been put into place as of yet. Without one, the long-term future
of the park's fragile ecosystem appears bleak.

Tití Monkey Foundation

This foundation has been set up to purchase land for Manuel Antonio
National Park. To donate call Darío Castelfranco (☎ 777-0535) or
write Apdo. 182-6350, Quepos.

GETTING HERE: Indirect buses leave for Quepos from the W end of
Coca Cola at 7, 10, 2, and 4 for the 145-km, five-hour trip; buses go on
to Manuel Antonio from here. Direct buses for Manuel Antonio (four
hours) leave from Coca Cola at 6, 12, and 6. For information call
Transportes Morales at ☎ 223-5567, 777-0318. If you're having luggage
placed in the baggage compartment, keep an eye out; things have been
stolen. Buses from Puntarenas (231 km, 3½ hours) leave at 5 AM and
2:30 PM. Contact **Transportes Blanco**, ☎ 531-1384. Buses run from San
Isidro to the S at 7 and 1:30.

by air: SANSA (☎ 221-9414, 233-0397/3258, fax 255-2176) flies
daily except Sun. for around $25, and **Travelair** (☎ 220-3054, 232-7883,
fax 220-0413) also flies daily.

Puntarenas to Panama

GETTING AROUND: It's a great area to walk around in, but the roads to the park make for a very steep walk back. Buses ply regularly back and forth on the 20-minute, seven-km run between the terminal in Quepos and the park entrance. Many hotels have shuttle services, and the Lynch Tourist Service operates an a/c bus (60¢) from Quepos to the beach in season. The developed portion of the park itself is quite small. Rental cars are available from a number of hotels here, but it's preferable to reserve them while still in San José.

SIGHTS AND HIKING: Next to town is an astonishingly wide beach. At low tide you might see a local practicing his karate moves or some expatriate American jock types hauling surfboards out of their four-wheel-drives. You are advised not to swim at this beach, which has been found to be contaminated. Up the hill is the old banana plantation residence compound; it now services the palm oil trade. A town within a town, this private estate is pretty amazing. It even has its own cliffside swimming pool complex perched above the sea, with surrounding thatched huts. The area's fishing operation is just across the bridge on the way out of town. **trails:** Up the hill in Manuel Antonio, a trail leads down to the beach from the Mariposa; continue along the road, turn left by the house just across from the Biesanz *cabinas*, and then follow the trail down. Another trail goes to the right down to nearly deserted **Playa Biesanz**, which offers good snorkeling. **Gaia Animal Shelter:** On the road between Quepos and Manuel Antonio, this shelter adopts animals captured from the wild and prepares them for reintroduction. Admission is around $4 for foreigners and $1 for Ticos; children under 12 are free. ☎ or fax 777-0535 for an appointment.

VISITING THE PARK: You must walk through an inlet (or wade during the rainy season, when the water may reach waist-level or higher) to get to the entrance (open 7-4), where you pay. Admission is at the current *gringo* rate; the park is closed on Mon. Numbers are restricted to 600 per day Tues. to Fri. and 800 on Sat. and Sun. The first beach, **Espadilla del Sur**, has a number of *manzanillo* (machineel) trees; steer clear of them! This northernmost beach, curved and rather steep, has large, boulder-like islets just offshore. The next path leads to **Cathedral Hill**, a detour offering great views of the surrounding seascape including views of the 12 offshore cays that are part of the park. This enormous rocky promontory separating the two beaches was once an island. Over the course of tens of thousands of years, sand deposits have now connected it to the mainland – a feature known as a *tambalo*. The ancient forest here includes *sura*, *panama*, *guapinol*, royal palm, and other species. Right across the way, **Playa Manuel Antonio** is the best place to stop for a swim. The most beautiful beach, it is calm, with a gentle slope; at low tide it has a shallow pool on its W side filled with hundreds of multicolored fish. From here, a steep path leads to a *mirador* with a great view. If you proceed across another promontory, past the turnoff for the administrative building, you come to the park's third beach, **Puerto Escondido** ("Hidden Harbor") – a beach that practically disappears during low tide. From here a very deteriorated trail leads across Punta Serrucho to **Playita de Boca de Naranjo**. Watch your valuables closely while on these beaches.

FLORA AND FAUNA: There are at least 138 species of trees here, including the *vaco o lechoso* (milk tree) which, when tapped, produces a milky sap that was once an important dietary staple. The nation's only dangerous tree, the *manzanillo* lines the beaches. (See "forbidden fruit" under "Plant Life" in the Introduction.) A small red mangrove swamp lies behind Espadilla Sur. The park also is home to the black *guapinol*, a dark-leaved tree found only here and in a few forests farther S. All told, there are 99 mammals (including 59 bats) and some 353 species of birds. The park is one of the best places around to see agoutis, rodents that appear to be a cross between a rabbit and a guinea pig, with the mannerisms of a squirrel. During the early morning and late afternoon hours, watch out for capuchin, squirrel, or white-faced monkeys, and three-toed sloths.

As you proceed along the paths in the park you'll notice the most ubiquitous wildlife: scores of bright orange-and-black-shelled land crabs (*tahalín*). They duck quickly into their homes on your approach. With their orange eyes and eggplant-purple claws, they look like the creation of a hyper-imaginative toddler turned loose with his first set of Crayolas. If cornered, these crustaceans will raise an open claw in defense.

PARK CONDUCT: It is illegal to anchor a boat closer than 100 m to the shore. Under no circumstances should you feed any animals! Do not contribute to the garbage problem.

QUEPOS ACCOMMODATIONS: Although you'll be closer to the beaches if you stay up the hill in Manuel Antonio, many visitors prefer Quepos and its small town flavor. It's generally less expensive for food, better value for lodging, and has a great disco, the **Arco Iris**. The major drawback is that thievery is becoming increasingly common – even when hotel guests are asleep in their rooms. One of the best places to stay, although no longer the bargain it once was, is inexpensive **Hotel Ceciliano** (☎ 777-0192). It is run by friendly, hospitable, and lively Señora Ceciliano, who lives together with her family in the ultramodern house next door. This hotel has clean rooms with fans and private baths, as well as other rooms with shared bath. Be sure to get a room away from the TV set, and bargain for the large dorm rooms if you come with a group. Nearby, low-budget **Hotel Quepos** (☎ 777-0274), above the SANSA office, is quite alright; it charges around $20. Nearby **Cabinas Helen** (☎ 777-0504) offers rooms for $8. Moderate, attractive **Villas Cruz** (☎ 777-0271, fax 777-0050) has kitchens and porches. The moderate/expensive a/c 28-room **Hotel Kamuk** (☎ 777-0379, fax 777-0258) is one of the priciest places in town. Facilities include a/c, phones, bar/restaurant, casino, coffee shop, and boutique. Write Apdo. 18, 6350 Quepos. **Hotel El Parque** (☎ 777-0063) is low-budget and spartan. **Hotel Sirena** (☎ 777-0528, fax 777-0171) is an expensive-luxury hotel with a/c and pool.

Inexpensive **Hotel El Pueblo** (☎ 777-1003) is right near the bus station and charges $25 on up. Inexpensive **Hotel Mario** (☎ 777-0339) is another option, as is moderate-expensive a/c **Hotel Paraíso** (☎/fax 777-0082), which has kitchens. Low-budget to inexpensive accommodations include **Hotel Majestic, Hotel Mar y Luna** (☎ 777-0394), 12-room **Hotel El Malinche** (☎ 777-0093, mosquito coils mandatory, around $15; more expensive a/c rooms $30), **Hotel Ramus** (☎ 777-0245), and the **Viña del Mar. Apartotel El Coral** is just around the corner from **Hotel Linda Vista**. Inexpensive **Cabinas Ana** (☎ 777-0443, 223-5567) holds up to five and is near the soccer field. Low-budget, hospitable **Cabinas Doña Alicia** (☎ 777-0419) has three rooms in some of its units. Near the church, inexpensive **Hotel Ipakarahi** (☎ 777-0392) is good value. Also here is inexpensive **El Cisne** (☎ 777-0590). Expensive **Hotel Villa Romántica** (☎ 777-0037) is owned by Germans; it has a pool. **El Mirador del Río** (☎ 777-0290), one of the newest places and in front of the bus station, offers *cabinas* and camping. Write Apdo. 88, Quepos. Set 120 m E of the bus station, **Hotel Villas Morsol Inn** (☎ 777-0307) has a/c, refrigerator, laundry service, and hot water. Another alternative is the 12-room **Hotel del Mar** (☎ 777-0543). Write Apdo. 77, Quepos. Low-budget **Villas Verano** (☎ 777-1495) is a set of small cabins; homestyle meals are served in a nearby home. The **El Paraiso Apartotel** (☎ 777-0082) offers expensive suites and apartments; it has a restaurant. (Accommodations further up the road are listed under "Manuel Antonio Accommodations" below.)

out of town: Just down the road from the airport, **Hotel Rancho Casa Grande** (☎ 777-0330/1646, fax 777-1575) is an attractive hotel owned by Quepos natives. It has a restaurant, pool, Jacuzzi, tennis court, hiking, and horseback riding. Rainforest is nearby. Expect to spend $100 d and up. **Dennis and Lucrecia Arnold** (☎ 777-1379, fax 777-1558) have a farm on the Río Naranjo, 14 km inland from Quepos.

They serve a great lunch to visiting birdwatchers and have a cabin for rent.

just before town: Cabinas Los Horcones (☎ 777-0000) has low-budget *cabinas* for less than $20. **Villas del Arenal** (☎/fax 777-0171) has expensive, fully furnished apartments with kitchens, TVs, and a/c. There is also a pool, Jacuzzi, and restaurant.

MANUEL ANTONIO ACCOMMODATIONS: Since this is a major tourist area, things tend to be pretty pricey and are becoming increasingly so. There are more than 100 licensed facilities now operating in the area! Proceeding up the hill from Quepos, **Club Caribe** (☎/fax 777-0134) has rooms from $20; Italian and Tico dishes are prepared upon request. **Cabinas Geylor** (☎ 777-0561) have rooms for $15 with private bath. **Apartotel Los Corales** (☎ 777-0006) has rooms with fans and kitchens that are in the moderate range. **Cabinas Tauro** (☎ 777-0229) have rooms for $15 d (☎/fax 777-0037). **Mil Rios** (☎/fax 777-0595) is in a private reserve; rates start around $30 d and kitchenettes are available. **Condominios El Pájaro Azul** (☎ 777-1046, fax 777-1241) is a set of luxury one- and two-bedroom houses; it's next door to **Restaurante La Arcada**.

Ultra-luxury **Villas El Túcan** consist of one- and two-bedroom houses without kitchens. Inexpensive ($25-35) five-unit **Cabinas Pedro Miguel** (☎ 777-0035, fax 777-0279), one km out, has a pool and a *típico* restaurant that operates in season. Across the road, atmospheric **Hotel Plinio** (☎ 777-0055, fax 777-0558; Apdo. 71, Quepos, Puntarenas) offers three different types of rooms and has hammocks. Moderate rates ($60 and up) include breakfast. The moderate/expensive 20-room **El Mirador del Pacifico** (☎/fax 777-0119) is owned by Germans. It's topped off by a bar/restaurant. Featuring a pool, Jacuzzi, kitchens, private terraces, and a/c or fans, Santa Fe-style **Mimo's Hotel** (☎/fax 777-0054) is in the expensive range; its rates include breakfast. **Bahías Hotel** (☎ 777-0350, fax 777-0279) is expensive, but moderate in the low season. It has a pool, and some units have Jacuzzis. **Sula Bya-ba** (☎ 777-0597, fax 777-0279) is another expensive hotel. Expensive **Bungalows Las Palmas** (☎/fax 777-0051) are thatched-roof condos with a pool. The 22-room **Hotel California** (☎/fax 777-1062) has a pool, Jacuzzi, waterfall, and restaurant. The **Hotel Las Tres Banderas** (☎ 777-1521, fax 777-1478) offers moderate a/c rooms with TV/VCRs, fans, refrigerators, microwaves, and balconies; many command views. Rates are $60 d plus tax. **Hotel Villa Teca** (☎ 777-1117, fax 777-0279; Apdo. 180-6350, Quepos) offers 40 ultra-luxury duplexes with a/c, pool, Jacuzzi, and restaurant. Inexpensive **Cabinas Tropicales** (☎ 777-0455) are reasonably priced (for this area). Up a hill, **La Colina** (☎ 777-0231) offers moderate rooms, which are set below the French Canadian owners' home. Surrounded by a private nature reserve, luxury **Cabinas el Salto** (☎ 777-0130, fax 241-2938; Apdo. 119, Quepos) offers a pool, horseback riding, a bar and restaurant. Breakfast, dinner, and a nature tour are included in rates. Expensive **Hotel El Lirio** (☎/fax 777-0403; Apdo. 123, Quepos) has fans and hot water; breakfast served. **Apartments Flor Blanca** (☎/fax 777-0032) has a/c rooms for $30 with refrigerators. **Villa Escondida Apartments** (☎ 777-1138) has luxury units. Luxury **Hotel las Charruas** (☎/fax 777-0409) is across the road. Moderate/expensive **Hidden Village Cabinas** (☎ 777-1138) has rooms from $55 d; more expensive units have kitchenettes. Expensive **Villas las Amapolas** has a Jacuzzi and gardens. **Villas Oso** (☎/fax 777-0233) have rooms from $60 on up. The appealingly designed **Tulemar Apartotel** (☎ 777-0580/1325, fax 777-1579; Apdo. 225-6350, Manuel Antonio) has a pool, snack bar, trails, and mini mart; its octagonal cabins ($170; hold up to four) have TV/VCR, phones, kitchenettes, hairdriers, and a/c. The **Ylang-Ylang Ocean View Apartments** (☎ 777-0184) has rooms from $65 with kitchenettes. Farther up, luxury **Hotel Divisamar** (☎ 777-0371, fax 777-0525) has 37 rooms with hot water, a/c or fans, restaurant (high season only), and pool. Write Apdo. 82, Quepos. **Cabinas Buena Vista** (☎/fax 777-0345/1002) has two nice homes available for weekly rental ($400-600 pw).

The ultra-luxury **Hotel La Mariposa** (☎ 777-0355/0456, fax 777-0050), perched on a hillside with a classic postcard view of Punta Cathedral off in the distance, is renowned throughout the land for its view and atmosphere. The Spanish-colonial-style hotel centers around its terrace restaurant which has white archways and pink chairs. A lower level holds a swimming pool and bar. Below in a semicircle are five two-storey white houses containing two rooms with two beds each. Taking a bath in your room here is like bathing in a small garden. The hotel strikes a happy medium between elegant politeness and warm informality. It's named after the butterflies that continued to frequent the area even after the structure was completed. Check out the early Quepos weatherstone. Their van offers free shuttle service to and from SANSA or Travelair flights as well as to and from the park. ☎ 800-223-6510, US; 800-268-0424, Canada; or write Apdo. 4, Quepos. The ultra-luxury **Makanda-by-the-Sea** (☎ 777-0442, fax 777-0032; Apdo. 29, Quepos), a series of isolated villas, is nearby. It has hammocks, gardens, and views galore. Down the road from the Mariposa, anthropologists and real estate magnates, the Biesanzes, offer two beautiful *cabinas* with caretaker; a funicular leads up to them. For information, contact agent Robert Benton in Escazú (☎ 228-9373).

Set on Punta Quepos, 55-room **El Parador** (☎ 777-1414, fax 777-1437) is an ultra-luxury hotel with miniature golf course, tennis courts, Jacuzzis, pools, health club, disco, gourmet restaurant, cigar smoker's lounge, and a helicopter pad. It opened in 1995 and is Spanish Mediterranean in style. Luxury and ultra-luxury **Hotel El Dorado Mojado** (☎ 777-0368) is next. A bed and breakfast, inexpensive **Altamira Inn** (☎ 777-0477) follows. The expensive-luxury **Villas Nicholas** (☎ 777-0375, ☎/fax 777-0358; Apdo. 111, Quepos) has a pool and restaurant; **Villas El Parque** (☎ 777-0096, fax 777-0538) is owned by the same people. It has 18 one- and two-bedroom units with balconies and tremendous views. It also has a pool and restaurant. Opened in 1995, **Si Como No** (☎ 777-1250, fax 777-1093) is a new 27-room and five-villa complex designed to harmonize with the environment. There's a pool, Jacuzzi, water slide, nature trails, restaurant, and conference room. Only one tree was removed to build the property. Hotel sewage is converted to fertilizer, and all wood used in construction came from tree farms. Rates are $125 d on up. In the US, ☎ 800-506-4299. Ultra-luxury **Albergue Turístico El Byblos** (☎ 777-0411, fax 777-0009; Apdo. 15, Quepos) has a/c cabins for up to three and pool, restaurant, and hot water. It has received mixed reports.

Ultra-luxury **Hotel Villas las Mogotes** (☎/fax 777-0582) was once the late folksinger-songwriter Jim Croce's summer abode. Facilities include a/c or fan and pool; the villas have kitchens. **El Colibrí** (☎/fax 777-0432; Apdo. 94, Quepos), featuring a garden and rooms with fans, refrigerators, and hot plates, accepts no children under the age of 10. Rates are $75 d. **Casitas Eclipse** (☎ 777-0408) are a set of luxury Mediterranean-style dwellings; some rooms have kitchens. Located off of a dirt road, expensive **La Quinta** (☎ 777-0434; Apdo. 76, Quepos) has rooms with or without kitchenette for $70. The **Villa Nina Hotel** (☎ 777-1628/1554, fax 777-1497) has rooms from $50 and up, including breakfast. Rooms have kitchenettes and balconies. Luxury **Arboleda Beach and Mountain Hotel** (☎ 777-1056, fax 777-0092; Apdo. 55, Quepos) has beachfront cabins with bath, fan, and terrace on its 19-acre (eight-ha) grounds; surfboard and catamaran rentals are available. Luxury to ultra-luxury **Apartamentos Costa Verde** and **Condominios Verde** (☎ 223-7946, 777-0584, fax 777-0560) have kitchens. With a pool and cabins, expensive-luxury **Karahé** (☎ 777-0170, fax 777-1075; Apdo. 100, 6350 Quepos) offers a restaurant, fans, and refrigerators. Restaurant meals are included in luxury-unit rates. They also have some inexpensive *cabinas*. Down at the beach, moderate **Cabinas Piscis** (☎ 777-0046) includes a small restaurant.

The moderate a/c **Hotel Delmar** (☎ 777-0543), to the left of Piscis, has a restaurant and garden with views. Near the Mar y Sombra and right on Playa Espadilla, inexpensive **Cabinas Ramirez** (☎ 777-0003) has dark and noisy fan-equipped *cabinas* that hold up to four. **Cabinas Espadilla** (☎ 777-0416; Apdo. 30, Heredia), with equipped kitchenette and fans, are inexpensive. Also inexpensive, **Cabinas Los Almendros**

(☎ 777-0225) have fans and a restaurant. Billed as a "youth hostel," spartan low-budget to moderate **Costa Linda** (☎ 777-0304) has cooking facilities. **Cabinas Aymara** are also low-budget and nearby. **Vela Bar** (☎ 777-0413; Apdo. 13, Quepos) has inexpensive and moderate *cabinas* to its rear; some have balconies, a/c, and kitchens. The luxury **Hotel Villabosque** (☎ 777-0401, fax 777-0401) has fans or a/c. The **Grano de Oro** (☎ 777-0578) also has low-budget rooms next to its restaurant. Low-budget **Cabinas Irarosa** are next. Moderate **Cabinas Los Almendros** (☎ 777-0225) are on the left at the road's end. Also here are **Cabinas ANEP**, very low-budget cabins that are owned by the public employees' union and rented to the public during slack periods. Back on the main road, inexpensive **Hotel Manuel Antonio** (☎ 777-0212/0255) has fans and a restaurant. Write Apdo. 88, Manuel Antonio, Quepos. Other places to stay in the area include luxury **Hotel Del Valle Pura Vida** (☎ 777-0040), moderate **Cabinas Harold and Carolyn** (☎ 777-0331), and luxury **Hotel Casa Blanca** (☎ 777-0368). Because of sustained environmental damage, camping is no longer permitted inside the park, but you can camp on Playa Espadilla. Don't leave your things unattended.

HOME RENTAL: If you're staying for a while, this is an option you might consider. Many houses are advertised by signs. Anita Myketuk (☎ 777-0345) of the Buena Nota has a house for rent. Also ☎ 777-0292 for other options.

> ☞ **Traveler's Tip.** Highly recommended by readers, the **El Mono Azul Restaurante Natural** (☎ 777-1548; Apdo. 297, Quepos) is off the main road in Manuel Antonio. It serves salads, pizza, fish, and home-made pastries at very reasonable prices by area standards. Movies (with Spanish subtitles) are shown nightly at 7:30. Their eight *cabinas* range from $35 on up.

MANUEL ANTONIO FOOD: Nearly every hotel has its own restaurant. Low-budget travelers will find pickings sparse; most restaurants are designed for those with oodles of moola. The most famed place to eat is the **Mariposa**, where continental breakfast (including coffee, cheese, rolls, and *gallo pinto*) is laid out from 7:30 to 10 daily. The fixed menu dinner, with their unique French-influenced cuisine, is served from 7:30 PM. Call for reservations. They also have à la carte food available during the day. **Hotel Plinio** is renowned for its Italian food and homemade bread. **El Byblos** rivals the Mariposa for French cuisine. **Bahías** offers 46 different varieties of cocktails and seafood dishes. Serving US-style food, the **Barba Roja** bar (opposite the Divisamar) is expensive but popular. For Italian food you might try the

Restaurante La Arcada near the Villas El Túcan. **El Acuario** is nearby; it offers daily specials. **Pizzeria Italian Club** also has Italian dishes. **Asia Restaurant** serves Korean and Japanese food. **Pickles Deli** serves ice cream, salads, and sandwiches; it's in the Centro Si Como No. Set next to the Hotel Villas del Parque, the **Mambo Grill** (☎ 777-1073) is reached by a steep set of stairs. It has a limited but tasty menu which includes Tex-Mex dishes as well as seafood. The Arboleda Beach and Mountain Hotel has the **El Cangrejo** snack bar and the **Mallorca** restaurant. The **Iguana Azul** is near the Arboleda. **Mar y Sombra**, set where the road from Quepos meets the beach, is the most reasonably priced of the beachside restaurants; the **Del Mar Bar** is nearby. **Vela Bar** offers vegetarian and seafood specialties. **El Mono Azul** (☎/fax 777-1954/1548) is 1½ km from Quepos on the right. Tasty meals, served in the restaurant, feature homemade wholewheat bread.

QUEPOS FOOD: The best dining values for low-budget travelers are in and around the bus terminal in Quepos. There are any number of moderately priced places to eat. The most popular with foreign visitors is **El Gran Escape (The Great Escape)**. Try the seafood at the **Quepoa** or eat at the **Pizza Gabriel**. Also try the **Nahomi, Angelus**, the **Arrecife**, and **Margarita Bill's**, which has Tex-Mex food. The **Hotel Kamuk** has some of the most exclusive dining in Quepos. **George's American Bar and Grill** serves... you guessed it. Others include **Soda Ana, Restaurante Isabel, Café Triangular, La Torre de Pizza, El Kiosko**, and there are a number of places across the bridge. Over the bridge heading out of town, **Mirador Bahía Azul** has moderately priced seafood. **Dazies** (☎ 777-1772), outside of town on the way to the Dominical, offers authentic fish and chips and shrimp and chips as well as grilled shrimp and salads.

☞ **Traveler's Tip.** In Quepos, **Café Milagro** (☎/fax 777-1707) offers good coffee (including expresso and cappucino) and tasty sweets and other delights. Beans are also available for sale. It's 150 m N of El Gran Escape and 100 m S of the bridge.

SHOPPING AND SERVICES: Anita Myketuk's **Buena Nota** (☎ 777-0345) is a gift and information center located by the beach and near the bridge marking the entrance to Quepos. There's also a branch in Manuel Antonio. **Galeria Costa Rica** is another store in town. Run by two expats, it offers a wide variety of goods. Another place for info is at the **Quepos Activities Center** (☎ 777-1526), across the street from the bus station. The **Lynch Tourist Service** (☎ 777-1170/0161, fax 777-1571) will hook you up with something suitable for your interest. **La Botánica** (☎ 777-1223) sells organically grown spices as well as natural health and beauty products. **Botíca Quepos**, on the corner of the main drag heading towards Manuel Antonio, is the local pharmacy. A **laundry** is around the corner from the Restaurant Isabel. Dr. Cecilia Quesada, an English-speaking **dentist**, has her office downstairs from the Hotel Quepos. **language study: La Escuela D'Amore** (☎/fax 777-1143), a "Spanish Immersion Center," is next to the Hotel del Mar, which is 200 m from Playa Manuel Antonio. ☎ 414-781-3151 or 213-912-0600 in the US or write Apdo. 67, Quepos. **horseback riding: Marlboro Stables** (☎ 777-1108) and **Equus Stables** (☎ 777-0001) both offer riding.

FISHING AND TOURS: Leodan Godinez, an enthusiastic and youthful environmentally conscious expert on local flora and fauna, conducts walking tours through the park. He'll point out animals you might not otherwise see and show you medicinal herbs, trees, and plants. On the hike – which is tailored to suit your age, physical condition, and interests – you might see sloths, monkeys, and agoutis. You can make reservations through the Mariposa (☎ 777-0355/0456). *La Mamá de Tarzán* (☎ 777-1257/0191), a cruise catamaran, departs from the pier in Quepos at 9 and 2 daily; the 3½-hour tour costs $35 for adults and $20 for children. **Ríos Tropicales** (☎ 777-0574, 233-6655, fax 255-4354) and **Unicorn Adventures** (☎ 777-0489) offer a variety of excursions; the former has kayaking. Sailboat trips are available by calling ☎ 777-0424. For fishing charters, contact **Costa Rican Dreams** (☎ 777-0593, 239-3387, fax 239-3383 in San José; Apdo. 79, 4005 San Antonio de Belén, Heredia). The **Blue Inn** (☎/fax 777-1676) runs fishing trips out of here as well as Drake Bay and Flamingo. Also try **Skip's Sportfishing** (☎ 777-0275). **Amigos del Río** (☎ 777-0082) offer boat trips, rafting, horseback riding, and mountain biking, as well as snorkeling. **Rios Locos** (☎ 777-1170, fax 777-1571) also offers rafting and kayaking tours. The *Temptress* stops at the park during some of its cruises. Their naturalist will lead you on a hike, you'll have lunch at the beach, and there'll be time enough for swimming, kayaking, and diving.

   by boat: *Corcovado Express* runs a $75 tour and trip to Drake Bay. ☎ 233-9135/3892, 777-0505. In the US, ☎ 800-374-4474 or write Apdo. 659, 1150 La Uruca.

EVENTS: The three-day **Fiesta del Mar**, Festival of the Sea, takes place around the end of January.

VICINITY OF QUEPOS: Playa Isla Dama, a beach five km from town, has the *Tortuga*, a floating bar and restaurant. The former catamaran has a turtle-shaped roof. It's open daily from 10-7 and may be reached by a two-minute water taxi ride from Pueblo Real.

FROM QUEPOS: Buses return from Quepos to San José at 5 AM, 8 AM, 2 PM, and 4 PM. Direct buses depart Manuel Antonio at 6, 12, and 5. Buy advance tickets at the bus terminal office, which generally closes for lunch between 11 and 1. The Puntarenas bus departs at 5:30 AM and 2:30 PM. Both the San José and Puntarenas buses pass by Playa Jacó. If you take the San Isidro-bound bus (daily at 5 and 1:30, five hours), you pass through extensive palm oil plantations on the way to Dominical. The ride really gives you a feel for the immense size and range of the industry, the workers and their lifestyle, and the monotonous but fascinating plantation-style architecture that characterizes such developments. Bridges on the way bear the imprint of the US Corps of Engineers.

Heading South from Quepos

Matapalo

This village, set 25 km from Quepos, has surf and a small number of hotels and restaurants. There are no phones. As usual, be wary of rip tides. To get here, take a San Isidro-bound bus from Quepos. **Soda y Cabinas Oasis** is low-budget and serves meals. **El Ranchito** is a similar affair. **Cabinas Matapalo** has two *cabinas*. Inexpensive **La Terraza del Sol** has *cabinas* and a French restaurant. **El Coquito del Pacifico** (☎ 233-1731, fax 222-8849) has rooms from $40; it also has a restaurant and rentals. There are a few other places. Moderate **Coicita** (☎ 777-0161, fax 777-1571) is a spice farm that offers river rafting and horseback riding; packages are available.

Hacienda Barú

Hacienda Barú, a private nature reserve, has an 830-acre (330-ha) hacienda with rainforest, lowland forest, pasture, cacao plantations, fruit orchards, mangroves, a beach, and an estuary. There are over 200 acres of untouched old growth rainforest here as well as another 260 acres with secondary growth. Hunting has been prohibited here since 1976. Part-owner Jack Ewing, along with biologist Jim Zook, has put together a 22-page list of birds, mammals, and amphibians seen here. You might see anything from a puma to an anteater or a chestnut-mandibled toucan here.

GETTING HERE: The estate is one km NW of the Río Barú along the road from Quepos to Dominical. Keep your eyes peeled for the "HDA. BARU" sign or ask at the El Ceibo gas station.

TOURS: A variety of tours are available, and accommodation is in the works. You can hike in the rainforest, watch birds in the lowland swamp area, trek all day, visit petroglyphs, or camp in the jungle and possibly see nocturnal mammals. Horseback tours are also available, including a "horse and hike" special; these start at $10/hour. Hikes range from $12.50 to $60 pp for one person and drop in price as others join. Some of their other tours include trips with Rancho La Merced ($30 pp with lunch) and with the Duarte family (at their Oro Verde Private Biological Reserve), who can provide simple accommodation ($20/day pp for room and board). You can tour their *trapiche*, an oxen-powered sugar mill. The Ewings also rent their inexpensive cabins, which are near their El Ceibo gas station. ☎/fax 771-1903 for information and reservations (24-hour advance notice). Leave your name, the number of people in your group, your approximate time of arrival, and the type of hike that interests you. If inquiring in advance, you can write Jack Ewing at Apdo. 215-8000, San Isidro de El General. "A Night in the Jungle" is a tour involving a combination of horseback riding and hiking. This is Jack's favorite tour. Departing in late afternoon, you cross fields, proceed through bush, cross the road and climb up into the hills. Leaving your horse, you climb for an hour – passing a couple of boulders inscribed with fading petroglyphs and hiking past some examples of mature rainforest canopy trees – before arriving at a wooden, tin-roofed cottage. Your bed is already laid out for you in a screened enclosure. Everything you need for the night or next morning has been brought up for you, including your evening meal (which your guide reheats and serves) and your breakfast. Along the way, your guide will point out local trees, birds, and animals. A scope is set up at the site so you can do more animal spotting. You can take a cold shower if you wish and can read by a camping gaz lantern. Your guide will probably retire early and you'll be on your own to savor the sounds of the night. Early the next morning, after breakfast, you'll hike down to the main road and return.

The newest venture at Barú is a canopy platform. Only three people plus the guide are permitted on the platform at any one time. To get here, you pass through a cacao plantation whose dark, gloomy atmosphere gives it the feeling of being inhabited by demons, then through pochote plantations, and finally up some improvised steps to the platform, where you will find a powered winch at the base of a tree; looking up, you can see another platform 100 ft (33 m) above the ground. You will be strapped in and then hauled up through the bottom of the upper platform. Emerging, you are freed, then tied to another safety leash. The canopy surrounds you on all sides, and the view is spectacular. You may or may not see any signs of life. It all depends upon your luck. After a half-hour at the top, you can rappel yourself down by pulling the cord up. Although you control the pace of your descent, it's still a bit scary at times.

Playa Dominical

Located in a spectacular natural area, this seaside village lies 19 miles (30 km) S of Quepos and 22 miles (36 km) W of San Isidro. The beach here is beautiful, but rip tides can make it deadly. The area has only been settled since the early 1900s when Victor "Chucuyo" Sibaja settled here and planted – along with bananas, rice, and beans – *dominicos*, a variety of plantains. A *dominical* is a plantation that grows *dominicos*. Before the 1930s, there were no roads here. The first public telephone was installed in 1977.

Since the beginning of the 1990s, Dominical has undergone a radical transformation from a somnolent village almost entirely lacking in tourist facilities to a glittering magnet for surfers, aspiring developers, and rainforest conservationists. In some areas, the Ticos have sold out and US expats control all of the property. This has resulted in a real boom in the area, and the completion of the road will spur the boom even more. Although there have been and are bad apples present, the majority of the foreign owners are both anti-development and environmentally conscious. And they seem to be having some success against their more greedy compatriots.

These days the town is developing, the road to Quepos has been asphalted, and tourism is booming, with locals getting involved in tourism as well. Iguana hunting has decreased, and the Friends of Nature are working to stave off turtle poachers by collecting eggs to be placed in a turtle nursery.

GETTING HERE: Other than the buses from Quepos at 5:30 and 1:30 (four hours), you can take a Uvita-bound bus from San Isidro at 7, 1:30 or 3 or a Quepos-bound bus at 5 and 1:30. If driving, you should note that the only paved (albeit potholed) stretch of road is between San Isidro and Dominical. Allow an hour.

ACCOMMODATIONS: Recently constructed expensive/ultra-luxury (depending upon facilities) **Villas Río Mar** (☎ 771-2333, fax 771-2455) are near the Río Baru; the most expensive units have two bedrooms with kitchen. At the entrance to town is inexpensive ($25) **Albergue Willdale** (☎ 771-1903, fax 771-0441), also known as Cabinas

Willy. They rent river kayaks, inner tubes, and a sailboat; there's also a gift shop. The same owner rents **Villa Cabeza de Mono**, which overlooks Uvita and Playa Hermosa. The fully furnished villa rents for $900/week and has a kitchen (food supplied) and pool. It is accessible by four-wheel-drive. In town and near the beach are the inexpensive **Cabinas Nayarit** (☎/fax 771-1878), which also have houses for rent (low-budget if there are six of you). Also inexpensive are **Cabinas San Clemente** next door, and low-budget **Cabinas El Coco** (☎ 771-2555), which have a weekend disco. Inexpensive **Cabinas La Residencia** (☎ 771-2175) are nearby. The **Río Linda Hotel** (☎ 771-2009, fax 771-1725) offers rooms with a/c or fans from $40; it has a Jacuzzi, pool, and the **Maui Restaurant**. Slightly higher-priced but very high quality (hardwood cabins with private bath and fans), **Hotel-Cabinas Punta Dominical** (☎ 225-5328, fax 253-4750; Apdo. 196, 8000 San Isidro de El General) has good food and horse rentals. Trips to Isla del Caño can be arranged here. Low-budget **Cabinas Roca Verde** (☎ 771-1414) are approximately a km S of the village. Rooms with private bath are inexpensive. On a ridge overlooking the ocean, British-run **Pacific Edge** (☎/fax 771-1903) charges $40 per cabin. Attractive cabins are lighted with solar power (12 V). It has a restaurant. The pleasant **Villas Río Mar** (☎ 771-2264, 225-5712) have private thatched-roof bungalows, pool, Jacuzzi, and bar. They charge $100 d; Ticos receive a substantial break.

   outlying accommodations: These can be booked through the **Selva Mar Reservation Service** (☎/fax 771-1903). **Hacienda Barú** (see page 432) has its own cabins. Overlooking the Río Baru, **Mike's Cabins** start at $25. Rates at moderate **Cabinas Escondidas** include breakfast. Other meals ($8 pp) are additional. A beach is nearby. There are three cabins, and guided nature walks, horseback riding, mountain bikes, Tai Chi or Chi Kung classes, and snorkeling equipment are available. Food is vegetarian, and meals are popular with visitors. **Cabinas Río Lindo** (☎ 710-0866), near the town's entrance, have rooms for about $40. Two km from the main road, **Restaurant El Manú** (☎ 235-6895) rents out cabins and villas with pools. A horseback ride and walk away, the **Finca Los Duarte** offers two basic *cabinas* for $20. **Las Casitas de Puertocito** (☎ 710-0866) are six split-level cabins halfway between Dominical and Uvita. Rivers and beaches are nearby, and there is horseback riding and a restaurant.

   Escaleras area accommodations: Running along a mountainous dirt road near the village of Dominicalito, this is becoming an increasingly popular place to stay. Mike and Woody Dyer's **Finca Bella Vista** (☎/fax 771-1903) centers around a traditional red mahogany farmhouse. It commands a tremendous view, best appreciated while lounging on the porch in one of the comfortable hammocks. Rooms are simple and share two showers. There's also a kitchen/dining area. Woody lives in the house nearby with his personable wife Yorlenny and their two children. Food is simple, hearty fare such as scrambled eggs with peppers and homemade *nachos* with cheese, beans, vine-ripened diced tomatoes, and *natilla*. This is a good place if you want to relax and take it easy. Woody has a great horseback tour of the waterfall (see box, next page), along with other excursions, and he also has a small house for rent. Pickup in Dominical is available. Rates are $15 pp, pn.

Nearby, **Finca Brian y Milena** (☎/fax 771-1903; Apdo. 2-8000, San Isidro de El General) offers visitors the chance to explore life on an experimental fruit farm that produces over 100 varieties of fruits, nuts, and spices. Brian will show you around the farm, and you may be lucky enough to sample durian or rambutan in season. (Brian will also show non-guests around for a charge of $22 pp, which includes lunch). Brian and Milena also have a wood-fired riverside hot tub, and their farm commands panoramic views of the area. Milena cooks with vegetables from their garden, and her style is unique. She describes it as "Costa Rican cooking with a healthful twist." Herbal teas are also available. Charges are $36 pp, pd ($38 if you are here on your own), with a discount of $2 pd applied as you stay longer (second day is $34, third day is $32, etc.). Rates include cabin, three hot meals (plus breakfast on the day you leave), hiking tours, and the riverside hot tub. The cabin is spartan and is reached by heading up a small hill; you have complete privacy. Hiking and horseback tours are available. A four-day trek to Salto Diamante (a series of seven waterfalls; see box, next page), stopping at the homes of locals along the way, is also offered. There are five different packages available. If you wish, they will meet you at any one of five locations in Dominical, with a horse for you at an additional charge ranging from $10-20 pp. This is not the place to stay if you want to be waited on and catered to hand and foot; Brian and Milena have their own lives to lead. For the most rewarding experience, hang around for a few days and get to know them and the area. Otherwise, you'd be better off spending the night in town.

Up the hill a few km and *far* up the scale from the previous two, **Escaleras Inn** (☎/fax 771-5247) is run by a couple fleeing from the jungles of Los Angeles. This extremely attractive bed and breakfast is geared toward those who want comfort along with personalized service. Denise, an ex-caterer, cooks gourmet meals, which are also available by reservation ($12-16) to non-guests. Floors are done up in lovely purplewood and colorful art and fabrics decorate the rooms. Views – whether from the pool or the deck – are knockout. There are two bedrooms in the house (around $45 pp, including breakfast and dinner)

Puntarenas to Panama

as well as a separate set of cabins ($60 pp, with breakfast and dinner). In the US, write Ste. 2277 SJO, PO Box 025216, Miami FL 33102-5216.

> ☞ **Traveler's Tip**. If you just show up at a hotel or lodge in the Dominical area you should be able to negotiate a better rate, provided they have space available. It helps if it's off-season, if there are two or more of you, and if you plan on staying more than a night or two. Arriving without a reservation gives you the option of checking out several places and finding the right one for you. If you're going to be arriving late or coming during Christmas, for example, you may wish to use Selva Mar to reserve (☎/fax 771-1903) or contact those places with direct lines in advance.

FOOD: Soda Laura (pancakes, *casados*, or fish and shrimp) or **Soda Nanoya** are recommended. Probably the only gourmet restaurant in the world with broken surfboards hanging suspended from its ceiling, **San Clemente** serves everything from Tex-Mex to Cajun to pizzas. Entrées range from grilled mahi mahi to French toast stuffed with fruit. It's on the left side of the road and just past the soccer field as you enter town. You can also eat at **Roca Verde, Mani Gordo, Mare Nostrum**, the **Maui Restaurant, Punta Dominical** (great views) or at palm-thatched **Salon el Coco**. A new addition is the **Dos Hermanos** market. Up in the hills in Escaleras, **Escaleras Inn** offers gourmet meals by reservation. The **Deli del Río** is a combo pizzeria, deli, and bakery. Enroute to Uvita, the **Casitas del Puertocitas** serves Italian food.

FISHING: Call **Roca Verde** at ☎ 771-2333. They also offer scuba diving and snorkeling. Another possibility is **Río Mar Boat Tours** at the same number.

A "Rainforest Island" for Dominical

Many Dominical area landowners are aware of the problems wrought by deforestation and are trying to do something about them. One proposal is to create a wildlife sanctuary on the other side of the mountain. This area – around Santo Cristo, Esceleras, and Cabeza de Mono – has suffered deforestation and impoverished local farmers are feeling the effects in reduced crop yields. The concept is to create a "rainforest island" on the remaining 120 acres of virgin forest, which is owned by 12 neighbors.

Waterfalls in Dominical

One of the nation's most impressive waterfalls is right near Dominical. **Salto de Santo Cristo** is also known as Catarata Nauyaca. Entrance is on private land, so you must pay a relatively steep 500 *colones* pp to enter. In return, you get the right to rent an inner tube, which you can use in the pool below the falls. There's a sort of improvised shower-curtain structure to one side near the base of the falls where you can change clothes. The two-tiered falls are well worth the effort. One path to the left leads off to a great view of the first tier. Another, to your right, leads down to the pools at the second tier.

Woody (at the Bella Vista) offers one of the best trips here, simply because his horses go by a longer and more scenic route. While others start from the coastal road and cut across, Woody's trip leads up the Esceleras road and through the forest. Enroute, you pass by majestic vistas, and your guide may point out a sloth or a toucan. When you pass through the deforested stretches, you'll know you're in the vicinity. You dismount inside the pochote plantation that surrounds the entrance. Santo Cristo is less scenic during the rainy season when its waters are often dirtied by soil runoff.

A closer alternative, **Catarata Posa Azul** is up the road from the Bella Vista on the Dominicalito Rd. It's a good place to cool off after a beachside excursion.

Finca Brian and Milena sponsors two-night trips to Catarata Santo Cristo and on to **Salto Diamante**, a stellar set of seven falls. Longer stays (of up to five days) can be arranged. You may stay under a rock overhang (if you have a tent) or with a hospitable local *campesino* family. The trip has proved highly popular; stop by and talk to Brian about arrangements.

TOURS: Contact the **Selva Mar Reservation Service** (☎/fax 771-1903; Apdo. 215-8000, San Isidro de el General) for complete information about outlying accommodation, area tours, and other opportunities. These include tours to Rancho La Merced, boat excursions in Uvita, and their visit to the farm of the Duarte family, where you will see traditional sugar making. You can visit their offices in San Isidro. In the US, write c/o AAA Express Mail, 1641 NW 79th Av., Miami FL 33126. The Roca Verde has **"La Primera Tienda,"** a gift shop that also books tours. Also inquire at the post office/information center next to San Clemente Restaurant.

STUDYING SPANISH: The **La Escuelita de Dominical** (☎/fax 771-1903) conducts Spanish classes and arranges homestays. Youth hostel card holders will receive a discount.

FROM DOMINICAL: You have three basic choices: head for Uvita, go back to Quepos, or travel up to San Isidro and proceed from there. One direct bus currently runs from Uvita at 5 AM and Dominical at 6 AM, then continues on to Quepos and San José. The return runs at 4 PM and arrives back in Dominical at 9 PM. From Dominical you can travel to San Isidro at 7 AM and 3:30 PM. **note:** Be sure to confirm these times with local residents because they can change.

Uvita National Marine Park

(Parque Nacional Marina Ballena Uvita)

Located S of Dominical, this is the nation's newest (and only offshore) reserve. It includes the most extensive coral reef on the Pacific coast, as well as the offlying Islas Ballena (nesting grounds for brown boobies, frigatebirds, and ibises), where humpbacked whales tour in the company of their offspring from Dec. to April.

ACCOMMODATIONS: To get here, follow the directions under Dominical above. **Camping** is permitted at Playa Piñuela; get your water from the park service there. Low-budget travelers can stay at the **Cabinas Delgado**, next to a lumberyard. Inexpensive **Cabinas Los Laureles** (☎/fax 771-1903; $10 s, $18 d) are set amidst laurel trees. Meals and horseback riding are available. **Rancho La Merced** (☎/fax 771-1903) is owned by the Tico president of Selva Mar Reservation Service. This working cattle farm includes a forest reserve and offers a day's rounds with the cowboys ($60 pp) if you wish. Its **Cabina El Kurukuzungo** is secluded and rents for $35 d; meals are provided upon request or you can cook for yourself. At the edge of the village, **Cabinas El Coco Tico** (reservations: ☎/fax 771-1903; $20) offer six motel-like units. You can eat in the family's soda nearby. **Soda La Cooperativa** is the place to go for food.

in Bahía: This settlement is near the beach and two km S of the bridge over the Río Uvita. The cheapest place to stay is with **Victoria Marín**, whose home is next to the *telefono publico*. Low-budget **Cabinas Villa Hegalba** have private baths. **Cabinas Bejuco** (☎/fax 771-1903) charge from $35 d.

FOOD: The **Soda La Cooperativa** is on the main highway, the Costanera Sur, before you turn toward the coast. A *pulpería* belonging to the Diaz family is nearby. They'll show you how to get to the waterfalls and accompanying pools on the Río Cortezal.

SEEING THE PARK: Low tide offers many snorkeling spots. Fishermen can take you out to watch birds, fish, snorkel, or scuba dive. **Selva Mar Reservation Service** (☎/fax 771-1903) can arrange tours through here and will provide for boat transport. You can also contact León Victor Gonzales by leaving a message at his *pulpería* in Uvita (☎ 771-2311). Located right before Uvita and just after Playa Hermosa, **Rancho La Merced** (reservations 24 hours in advance: ☎/fax 771-1903) also offers horseback tours covering the beach, river, mangrove, and rainforest. Lunch is included.

   diving: Ballena Divers can take you out to Caño Island ($80-110) or let you dive offshore ($60).

San Isidro de El General

This town (pop. 32,000), lying 85 miles (137 km) from San José and founded in 1897, has grown up since the opening of the Interamerican Highway: the first cars arrived in 1945! It's a pleasant place, with the ambience of the frontier. You will see *campesino* cowboys strutting their stuff down the main street. The town is ridiculously compact. Note the prosperity of the town center: almost every home is nice and shelters a car. San Isidro is a good base; the beaches at Dominical are just 22 miles (35 km) away.

GETTING HERE: If you're going to Golfito by bus either from San José or from Quepos, you'll probably want to break your journey here. It's also the perfect place to base yourself for a trip to Chirripó. On the way, you pass over **Cerro de la Muerte** (Hill of Death), the highest spot on the Interamerican Highway. Watch on the left for the ruins of a shelter; it's possible to see both coasts from here when it's clear. This is *páramo* terrain – highland shrub and tussock fields more common in the Andes than in Costa Rica. It is a dangerous stretch of road to drive through if there's fog. Starting here, during the next 28 miles (45 km), the road drops down from 10,938 ft (3,334 m) to 2,303 ft (702 m). From San José, three companies run buses hourly (☎ 223-3577, 222-2422, 223-6866) along C. 16, Av. 1/3. Get advance tickets on weekends and holidays. From San Vito, buses leave at 6:30 and 1:30.

SIGHTS: For information about the area, contact Chamber of Commerce President Luis Quesada (☎ 771-2525) at the Hotel Chirripó. Its main square has what surely must be one of the nation's least architecturally endearing churches – a pink and white concrete structure whose bells appear to be undergoing an epileptic fit each time they ring! Inside, the church isn't much better. Up by the front to the right of the altar are slots for *caritas* (San Isidro, Jesus Crucificado, etc.), and the small room behind contains a mysterious white box covered by a white veil: it represents the body of the crucified Christ. Inaugurated in 1990, the town's cultural complex has a 400-seat theater, museum, exhibit hall, and workshops for artisans and fine artists. It's next to Café el Teatro. The new market in town is well worth a visit, and the old one has been transformed into the **Southern Regional Museum**, which displays items from the area's indigenous peoples. **Centro Biológico Las Quebradas**, born out of the need to protect the surrounding water supply, is the area's newest project. ☎ 771-0532 for information or write FUDEBIOL at Apdo. 44, 8000 Quebradas, Pérez Zeledón. A beautiful **waterfall** is a few km past Brujo on the right. It's also possible to tour the **Pindeco pineapple processing plant** in Buenos Aires to the S.

ACCOMMODATIONS: The best deal around for low-budget travelers is the **Hotel Astoria**, under the "Derby" Restaurante Pepe Timba neon sign on the square. The rooms with private bath ($4 pp) are the best value. Try to get one of the six rooms to the rear of the reception desk. Similarly priced is the *pensión* behind El Jardín restaurant and down from Cinco Menos. Low-budget **Hotel Chirripó** (☎ 771-0529) is right beside the park and across the way. Inexpensive **Hotel Amaneli** (☎ 771-0352) is also right in town; be sure to get a room which is not facing the Interamerican Highway. Low-budget **Hotel Iguazú** is one block from the square.

    outlying: Inexpensive, clean a/c **Hotel del Sur** (☎ 771-0233; Apdo. 4, 8000 San Isidro de El General), five km (three miles) S of town offers a restaurant, pool, gardens, tennis court and other sports facilities. *Cabinas*, which sleep up to five, are also available. If you have a car, you could also stay near San Gerardo de Rivas at **Finca La Cascada**. It has a simple cabin with electricity and hot water. Rates are $35 (1-3); a guided hike is also available. Also here is **Posada del Descanso** (☎ 771-0433), which is run by a Tico family and has room and board for $10 pp. A third alternative is the eight-room **Talari Albergue de Montaña** (☎/fax 771-0341; Apdo. 517-8000 Costa Rica), a mountain lodge at Rivas. German, Dutch, French, and English are spoken. Facilities include a pool, birdwatching, restaurant with Tico-style food, and trails. Rates run from around $25 s, $35 d. To get here by car, you head S and then take the first left after the Río Jilguero. If you're coming by bus, they can pick you up in San Isidro with advance notice. (Other accommodations near Chirippó are listed under that section.)

FOOD: A good place to eat lunch or dinner is the **Marisqueria Marea Baja** near the main square. Also try the **Restaurante Los Reyes** and **El Tenedor**. The classiest cuisine is at **Hotel del Sur**. Cheap food is found at the **Soda Nevada**, at **El Ranchito** (across from the park), and in the **Mercado Central**. If you have a car, the **Orchard of Good Health** is three km further along the Interamerican to the S and on the right.

ENTERTAINMENT: There isn't much to do in the town itself – unless you catch one of the mobile discos coming through. One place that you will want to check out is the wonderful roller disco on the N side of the park; the best view is upstairs. Also check out the **Non Plus Bar** and **El Prado**. Next to the Bank de Costa Rica, the **South Río** has a live band on Sat. If you're around on a Sat. afternoon, you can visit the *subasta* (stockyard), where **auctions** take place; you might see them selling teams of oxen.

FESTIVALS AND EVENTS: The town's **fiestas civicas** are held from the end of Jan. to the beginning of Feb. Activities include a cattle show, agricultural and industrial fair, bullfights, and orchid exhibition. On May 15, the **Día del Boyero** ("Day of the Oxcart Driver") is celebrated. Parades feature brightly colored oxcarts and animals and crops are blessed by the local priest.

WHITEWATER RAFTING: Largely a Class IV river, the Río General poses a challenge for even the most experienced river runner. **Ríos Tropicales** (☎ 233-6455, fax 255-3454) and **Costa Rica Expeditions** (☎ 257-0766, 222-0333) are among the companies offering river and kayaking trips. Check with them for details.

SERVICES: The best place to change money is at **Bazar Xiomara**, across from El Cinco Menos.

ORGANIZATIONS: The **Comité Conservación** (☎ 233-3333, pager; Helga Wegener, Apdo. 235-8000, San Isidro) is striving to stave off deforestation in this area.

FROM SAN ISIDRO: *Tuasur* and *Musoc* (☎ 222-2422, 710-0414) run direct buses hourly to San José. The 136-km trip takes 3½ hours and costs around 600 *colones*. *Tracopa* (☎ 771-0468) runs indirect buses. Buses for Uvita and Dominical (1½ hours) depart daily at 7:30, 1:30, and 3:30. Buses for Quepos run at 7 and 1:30, passing through Dominical. A bus (five hours, ☎ 773-3010) runs to Puerto Jiménez (on the Osa Peninsula and a gateway to Corcovado) at 5:30 and noon. There are also connections to San Vito (5:30 and 2:30), Palmar Norte, Ciudad Neilly, and Golfito.

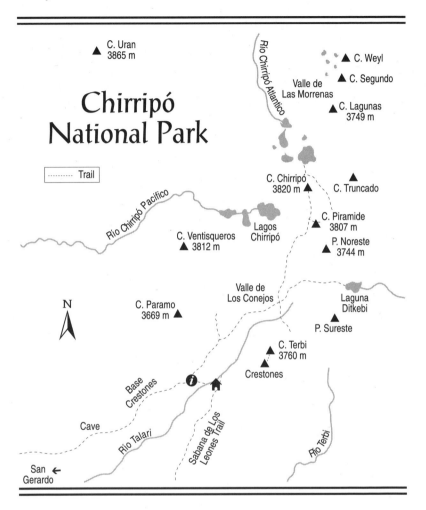

Chirripó National Park

(Parque Nacional Chirripó)

Made into a park in 1975, this 105,000-acre (42,500-ha) area includes 12,530-ft (3,819-m) Cerro Chirripó, the nation's highest point, as well as two other peaks over 12,500 ft (3810 m). The area is famed for its *páramo* – a high, tundra-like zone that often frosts over, though it never snows here. A hiker's paradise, it's best explored during a two- or three-day hike using mountain shelters. **note:** Be aware that there is a limit of 40 visitors pd so be sure and reserve in advance. A fire started by careless hikers lodging in a hut near Monte Sin Fé in 1992 consumed some 5,000 acres. Be very careful with fire!

> ☞ **Traveler's Tip**. During the peak season (January to April), you would be well advised to purchase advance tickets and passes from the National Parks Foundation offices (☎ 257-2239). It's at C. 23/AV. 15, 300 m N and 150 m E of the Iglesia Santa Teresita.

GETTING THERE AND PRACTICALITIES: Take a bus from San Isidro de El General at 5 AM and 2 PM (be sure to take the bus to San Gerardo de Rivas) or charter a taxi (around $15); it's a beautiful two-hour ride up to the San Gerardo entrance. Check in at the ranger station, where it's possible to camp. There's a steep shortcut up to the park from here, which can cut an hour from your time (see below). If you're planning to make it up to the mountain hut in one day – a rough trip with an altitude gain of 6,900 ft (2,100 m) – it's better to stay put here for the day. In town you may rent out a room at **Soda and Cabinas Chirripó, Soda El Decanso, Cabinas Marín, Albergue Turístico Chirripó** (which sits atop a gigantic boulder overlooking the river), or at **Roco Dara**, which has baths with hot water and cheap meals. All are low-budget. **Elimar** is more expensive because the rooms have private baths; it also has a bar/restaurant. To reserve a room at any of the above, ☎ 771-0433, ext. 106, and leave a message. During the rainy season, it rains daily, generally in the afternoon, so you'll have to get an early start. There are three mountain huts where you can stay.

TOURS: Jungle Trails (☎ 255-3486) offers tours, and **Costa Rica Expeditions** (☎ 257-0776, 222-0333, fax 257-1665) can tailor a tour for you. Warm clothes and sleeping bag are necessities, as temperatures often drop to freezing. Bring binoculars, rain gear, a compass, and at least one liter of water pp. Waterproof boots are needed in the rainy season. Fires are prohibited in the park, so you must bring a stove if you intend to cook. Two basic maps are provided at the station; if you plan to go off the beaten track at all, you should have purchased a map in San José. Don't count on the rangers to be well informed about the park, though they may be able to give you an idea of the number of people hiking there and help you rent a pack horse and guide should you want them. The local hotels can also be of help. **porters:** Locals will carry your pack (around $20 per load each way with a limit of 30 lbs); arrange in advance at the ranger station.

Puntarenas to Panama

FLORA, FAUNA, AND TOPOGRAPHY: The lakes at the peak – the only ones of their kind in Central America – were formed by glaciation more than 25,000 years ago during the Pleistocene Era. *Páramo* covers 25 sq miles (65 sq km). The Sabana de los Leones (Savanna of the Lions), situated at 10,170 ft (3,100 m), is so named because "lions" (pumas) and cougars are frequently spotted here. Surrounded by a cloud forest, the "savanna" itself is treeless, covered instead with six different types of *páramo* vegetation, including dwarf bamboo. There are 73 species of birds; variety diminishes as the altitude increases. Quetzals are abundant. Another feature of the higher cloud forest, the *jilguero* (black faced solitaire) cries out from the treetops. The *páramo* extends from 10,826 ft (3,300 m) upward. The often-thick, stunted vegetation rarely tops 12 ft (four m). The most common tree is the evergreen oak.

ENTERING THE PARK: The best way is via the "Thermometre," which was once a shortcut and is now the main route. From the ranger station turn left and walk through the village. Going right at the first fork, descend and cross a bridge, then continue on to another river and bridge; get water here. After a few houses, you'll see a sign marked *"Cerro Chirripo"*; walk through the pasture. Keeping about 300-600 ft (100-200 m) away from the forest on your right, head up until you come to a wired enclosure with a gate to its right. Enter and head right, following a path, which ends suddenly; then follow the ridge on your left up to a wire fence crossed by a set of stone steps. You are now on the main trail, *Fila Cemeterio de Maquina*, which runs along the ridge. The park boundary is about one or two hours farther, and the first camping spot (*Llano Bonita*: a flat, grassy area) is two or three hours after that. Signs are placed about every two km along the way. To get water, follow the trail another 20-30 minutes from Llano Bonito to find a fork on the left marked *"Agua Potable 200 m."* There's a rough shelter here (not a place you would choose to sleep in) and a steep path behind it takes you down to a small stream. Continuing through a steep, once burned-out area *(La Cuesta del Angel)* for another three to four hours, you enter *Monte Sin Fé* and then reach a small stream with a large cave *(refugio natural)* to the left, where you can sleep if necessary. Next you must climb *La Cuesta de los Arrependitos* ("Hill of the Repentants"), where the trail circumnavigates the side of a mountain. The first proper shelters are another hour or so away; you'll pass a *"Valle de Leones"* sign about 20 minutes before it, and the shelters lie in the valley below the sharp, accordion-folded peaks of Los Crestones. The two dorm-style cabins at *Refugios Base Crestones* sleep up to 40 in all. Both have kitchens with potable water and cooking utensils. Flies can be horrific. Depending upon your physical condition, it will have taken you eight to 16 hours to reach the first Crestones hut and ranger station.

NEARBY HIKING: Surrounded by rocky peaks and mountain passes, sandy **Valle de Los Conejos** (Rabbit Valley), from which all the rabbits beat a hasty retreat after the 1976 fire, is covered with dwarf bamboo. Cerro Crestón borders it on the SE, and its pinnacles rise towards the N and W. Lakes are found at the base of the **Valle de los Morrelas** and **Valle de Lagos** (Moraine and Lake Valleys). These cold, crystal-clear lakes, which measure up to an acre and sometimes freeze over, are popular bathing spots for tapirs and the entire animal community – from large cats to brocket deer to rabbits – arrives and drinks its fill on occasion. (Stay in Valle de los Morrelas at the hut; obtain keys from the San Gerardo ranger station.) From the hut, you can climb **Cerro Urán** and head along the *Camino de los Indios*; you should hire a local to show you the way.

    other approaches: You may also begin from **Canaán**, a village a few km further into the valley. This is a bit longer, but avoids the steep beginning. Stay in the low-budget **Cabinas Navarro** (☎ 771-0433, ext. 101) next to the *soda*. An entirely different, only recently opened route commences at **Herradura** and extends over Cerro Urán and Chirripó; it necessitates hiring a guide, which may be arranged through Parques Nacionales. Stay at the low-budget *cabinas* in Herradura

MOUNTAIN CLIMBING: Chirripó is not as difficult to climb as it appears. On a clear day, it's possible to see the Valle de General, parts of the Atlantic and Pacific Coasts, the Turrialba and Irazú volanoes, and several other peaks. Continue on to the second hut and follow the sign. It's about an hour to the base of Chirripó Grande and then another half-hour to the top; the **Lago San Juan** (chilly swimming) is on the way. Start before dawn from the second hut to get the best views. There's also a trail from here to **Cerro Terbí** (12,352 ft, 3,765 m), a peak which, unlike Chirripó, can be seen from the first hut. From the top of this peak, you can see well down into Panama. **Los Crestones**, a series of steep, needle-like rock pinnacles, are nearby; they can also be reached from the first hut in about an hour. From the first hut, there's a rough trail down to **Sabana Chirripó**, a large, light-brown marsh. From the top of Cerro Terbi, you can continue on to Pico Sureste (12,247 ft, 3,733 m), Pico Noreste (12,283 ft, 3,744 m), and Cerro Pirámide (12,490 ft, 3,807 m). Other peaks that may be climbed include Cerro Páramo (12,136 ft, 3,699 m), Cerro Ventisqueros (12,506 ft, 3,812 m), Cerro Uran (10,935 ft, 3,333 m), Loma Larga (12,254 ft, 3,735 m), Cerro Truncado (12,680 ft, 3,865 m), and Cerro Laguna (12,300 ft, 3,749 m).

A Cable Car for Chirripó!

Based in San Isidro, the Interinstitutional Commission on the Cable Car Project, a weighty mouthful of an organization, has been planning to construct a cable car that would run 12-16 km up to the top of Chirripó peak. The $30 million project – to be built by an Austrian or Italian firm – would take a few years to construct; more than a dozen pylons would be needed. It is projected to bring from 500-2,500 visitors into the park daily. This stands in direct conflict with the 40-person daily limit imposed by the park service. Proponents maintain that the project will allow the elderly and disabled access to the park and boost the local economy. Opponents counter that it is legally impermissible, that it might set an uncomfortable precedent for commercial exploitation of the parks, and that it will have adverse effects upon the area. For example, plants on the *páramo* can take years to recover after being stepped on, and animals' migration paths might be interfered with. More visitors might also cause forest fires. Moreover, the high cost of construction would lead to high ticket prices. This could give the project an elitist tone and local tourism entrepreneurs, who are making out OK as things stand, could be squeezed out. In short, the cable car could be a disaster for the park. Please send your comments on the proposed project to the Asociación Ambientalista de Pérez Zeledón, Apdo. 482, 8000 San Isidro de El General.

VICINITY OF CHIRRIPÓ: There are **hot springs** near Herradura. To get here, continue up the road for a km or so until you see a brown house to your left; turn right and go up a steep trail for 15 minutes; you may need to pay a small fee at the house. About three hours on foot from the village of Herradura, three km from San Gerardo de Rivas, is low-budget **Pensíon Quetzal Dorado** (☎ 771-0433, ext. 109). It's another good place from which to explore Chirripó and Cerro Urán. At Rivas-Perez Zeledón, **Talari Mountain Resort** (☎ 771-3102) has eight rooms, pool, restaurant, and horseback riding. Rates are from $35 d plus tax, including continental breakfast.

From San Isidro to Golfito

Finca Anael/Dúrica Biological Reserve

This self-sufficient reserve is operated by a group of back-to-the-landers who farm organically and raise goats. Expect to spend $40 pp for food and lodging; all profits go toward buying more land. To get here, you must drive on a bad road for an hour from Buenos Aires, then hike or horse it in. Arrangements (Apdo. 9, Buenos Aires; fax at the PO 730-0003) must be made a week in advance. Call Annie McCornick (☎ 240-2320, fax 223-0341) or Amancio (☎ 730-0028, Spanish only).

Las Esquinas National Park

(Parque Nacional Las Esquinas)

North of Golfito, Las Esquinas is one of the nation's newest national parks, and it is the only one in Costa Rica directly connected with a lodge. The flora and fauna of Las Esquinas have many of the citizens of the nation of Austria to thank for their preservation.

GETTING HERE: The lodge is accessible by regular cars all year round. From San José, drive 300 km S for five-six hours to Villa Briceño (Km 37) and follow signs four km farther to the lodge. From Golfito, take the dirt road six km to La Gamba, then follow signs. Pickup can be arranged at Villa Briceño if you're coming from San José by bus. (Take a bus bound for San Isidro and change or take a Golfito or San Vito bus and get off at Villa Briceño.)

HISTORY: Originally part of Corcovado National Park, the area was designated Sector Esquinas and later Las Piedras. US-born Austrian classical violinist Michael Schnitzler, a resident of Vienna, is the guiding light behind the creation of the park and its lodge. Michael and his wife first came to Costa Rica in 1989 and fell in love with the country and its people. Returning six months later, they bought a home at Playa Cacao near Golfito. As they became aware of the deforestation problem, Michael found himself uncomfortable enjoying the natural surroundings while trees were tumbling all around. Flying over in a plane, he and his wife noticed that the Esquinas forest was being cleared. Inquiring, they were told that the area had been declared a national park by decree and the government was looking for people to buy the property. There were about 140 landowners at the time, many of whom had logging permits. Under Costa Rican law, even though the area had been designated a national park by the Ministry of Parks, the Ministry of Agriculture could issue logging permits as long as the land was in the possession of private owners. So in 1991 Michael started an Austrian nonprofit organization, Rainforest of the Austrians. Logging has ceased in the areas surrounding the lodge; a little over half of the Esquinas forest has been saved from destruction and has become part of the park. Symbolic certificates are presented to donors. The average donation has been around $40 and more than 20,000 certificates have been sold.

At the 1992 Earth Summit in Rio, Austria pledged to spend $18 million on tropical Third World projects over the next three years. The criterion was that the projects be involved with helping the people and saving the forest at the same time. It took two years, but Michael finally persuaded the Austrian government to back his project. The area's residents have realized that tourism promises more income than logging and hunting, so they are now enthusiastic. All lodges employ locals. The difference is that all of the other lodges are in private hands (mostly owned by foreigners) and much of their profit goes abroad. Esquinas profits, by contrast, are to be channeled toward community ventures such as building a new school, bringing in a doctor and dentist, and agricultural projects. It is estimated that the community will not see real benefits for three to five years. Currently, the foundation is supporting small endeavors, such as buying pencils and schoolbooks. A research station at the entrance to the property is run by the foundation in conjunction with the University of Vienna and this lodge is open to students and biologists from all over the world who are pursuing rainforest research. So far, students from Germany and Austria have been studying everything from climatology to frogs, plants, and butterflies.

The three underlying themes of the project are conservation (supported by the Austrians), sustainable development (supported by the Austrian government), and research. It is the only project of its kind in the world. Monitoring its effects will be a simple process because there is only this small lodge and one community of 70 families. Reports must be submitted to the Austrian government through the end of 1997. The project is financed through Austria's Development Aid Program, and the lodge is owned by the Austro-Costa Rican nonprofit "Asociación Progamba." Its employees are all members of this association.

Land has been purchased by the Park Service via checks given directly to the landowners. The Park Service conducts negotiations with the landowners and decides which tracts to prioritize for purchase and what price to pay. Almost all of the land (except for one small valley with 20 families) is unpopulated. The owners live outside the park so no expropriation has been necessary. Payment, on average, is about $320 per hectare.

HOW TO HELP: Donations to the park may be sent to Regenwald Der Osterreicher, Postfach 500, A-1181, Vienna, Austria. Each $15 donated purchases 500 sq m. You will receive a certificate in return.

The Teribes

Térraba is the main settlement of the Teribe indigenous people of Central America. The Teribe were moved here in 1710 after a team effort on the part of Franciscan missionaries leagued with the Spanish militias. Although those who remained in Panama have managed to retain much of their culture, those in the Costa Rican reserve have lost most of their heritage. Teribes own only some 10% of the reserve's land; the remainder has been sold to outsiders attracted by the expansion of the PINDECO/Del Monte plantation. The Asociación Cultura Teribe is the main activist organization here. Over the course of the past few years, they have completed a number of projects, including a *rancho cultural* (meeting place), tree nurseries, a health clinic, and have offered a number of workhops – ranging from Teribe spiritual teachings to workshops for locals. They have also opened a small museum. The medical clinic will use traditional remedies, and a garden with medicinal plants has been started. Visitors who are genuinely interested in the Teribe culture are welcomed. Contact the Asociación Cultural Indígena Teribe (ACIT) or the Comisión Cultura Teribe, who will show you around and exchange ideas. Visitors are asked not to shoot pictures indiscriminately. Donations may be made in the form of checks and made out to the Asociación Cultural Indígena Teribe and mailed to them at Terrabá, Buenos Aires, Puntarenas.

HIKING: Anyone may visit and hike the trails free of charge. Expect to spend a minimum of several hours if the visit is to be worthwhile. Trails here are steep and sometimes treacherous. Be sure to carry one of the bamboo staffs you'll find by the lodge. *Terciopelos* (pit vipers) are common so stay on the trails. A number of trails begin from behind the lodge. The trails interconnect in a chain and pass by some small waterfalls. There's also an old logging trail that leads past beautiful heliconias to some old growth trees. On the trail you might see blooming heliconias, bromeliads, and birds such as the *pavon*, hear howler monkeys, or have a *terciopelo* cross your path. Most of the trails extend through hilly secondary forest.

ACCOMMODATIONS: The place to stay here is the **Esquinas Rainforest Lodge** (☎/fax 775-0849/0131). The 10-room lodge houses its visitors in five very attractive two-unit cabins that overlook the pool and main lodge. The main building incorporates a living area, library, shop, bar, and dining area. The lodge's Brazilian-born chef prepares a wide variety of culinary delights, including Viennese dishes. A stream

Puntarenas to Panama

feeds the filtered pool. Set near the lodge, the research station accommodates five to eight student researchers. You'll probably see one or more of them during the course of your stay. Rates are $95 s, $130 d, $165 t, including three meals and taxes. Special rates are offered to students, residents, groups, and for long-term stays. Packages (which incorporate stays at Punta Encanto or Villas Playa Cacao) are also available. Excursions include hiking, swimming, kayaking, fishing, horseback riding, excursion flights, and other activities.

Golfito

Hot and humid Golfito was established as a company town to service nearby banana plantations. After disease and strikes led United Fruit to flee from the Limón area in 1938, the company set up shop in Golfito, literally constructing the town from scratch. Approximately 15,000 migrated here and the town bustled with vitality. But prolonged strikes, among other factors, led to the area's abandonment in 1985. The copper sulfide residues from pesticides used in banana cultivation have made the soil unsuitable for anything but African palms, which do not require much labor. Establishment of a duty-free zone here has brought about some improvement, but it threatens to ruin the languid, seedy atmosphere that gives the town its appeal. With new hotels and restaurants springing up like mushroooms, the area may never be the same again. On weekends, the town now is filled with Ticos arriving to shop in the duty-free zone. Topping all of this off, the area is in the midst of a property boom. Still it has a truly majestic backdrop of virgin rainforest, and locals continue to calculate time not in terms of hours but according to low and high tides.

GETTING HERE: It takes seven hours by bus over the Talamanca mountain range on the Interamerican Highway. Buses (☎ 221-4214) leave from San José (C. 2/4, Av. 18) at 7, 11 and at 3 for the eight-hour, 339-km trip. You can also take any *Zona Sur* bus to Río Claro, where one of the frequent buses from Villa Neily can be intercepted. From San Isidro, direct buses depart at 10; otherwise, you will have to change at Río Claro (where you can catch a bus or a *colectivo*). SANSA (☎ 221-9414, 233-0397, 233-3258, fax 255-2176) also flies daily, as does Travelair (☎ 220-3054, 232-7883, fax 220-0413).

GETTING AROUND: Inexpensive buses run from Las Gaviotas through to the duty-free port and airport. Shared taxis are around 75¢ to $1 a ride. Water taxis run to outlying destinations. They are quite expensive and you have to bargain.

SIGHTS: There really isn't much to do around the town of Golfito itself. One yachtie pundit tells the story of two decked-to-the-heels *gringas* who walked into Las Gaviotas at Playa Tortugas and asked where the beach was! The honest truth is the nearest beach is two hours away and named after a mosquito. Getting sloshed is more popular than getting splashed: the main pastime in Golfito is sipping beer and shooting the bull. The town is full of characters, including a number of aging retired military expats, and it's a joy to have a drink here. There's not much for teetotallers to do except take a walk through the Pueblo Civil and on down to the Zona Americana – which has now been retitled the Zona Libre since it became duty-free. The main sight in town is the recently constructed church and brick-lined square which were built by Warner-Enigma Pictures for the film *Chico Mendes*. This was supposed to be filmed in 1993 but ran into difficulties with the rights so was never filmed. You might also want to hike up the hill to the facility-free, wet and very wild **Golfito National Wildlife Reserve**. This 3,235-acre (1,309-ha) reserve safeguards the area's water supply. The more than 125 species of shrubs and trees include four that are nearing extinction: manwood, plomo, butternut, and purple heart. In addition, there are more than a dozen species of fern, 11 of heliconia, and 31 species of orchid. Four types of monkeys reside here, as do margays, jaguarundis, agoutis, pacas, and anteaters. During the wet season, there are more than 70 species of birds in residence. Camping is permitted, but the unmarked trails leading to sites are slippery. The easiest access is via a gravel road running from the beginning of the soccer field near Las Gaviotas; only the first of the eight km is passable except by four-wheel-drive vehicles.

ZONA LIBRE: This last project of the Arias Administration, Costa Rica's answer to the pyramids, opened in 1990 under a cloud of confusion. Created to spur business in economically moribund Golfito, the complex has excited enormous controversy, becoming the subject of innumerable banner headlines in the national press. San José's businesses (mainly the Av. Central crowd) felt the competitive crunch, and pushed unsuccessfully to have the "duty-free" zone's duties knocked upwards from the current 60% of normal duty, a move which would have undoubtedly transformed the complex into another governmental white elephant or, given the size and scale of the project, a white mastadon. The original plan was to have visitors spend a minimum of 72 hours. Since the computerized enforcement mechanisms were not ready, and there were too few hotel rooms to make minimum stays enforceable, the limit was initially waived and will be applied in incremental stages as hotel capacity increases. Currently, Ticos are permitted to purchase $400 worth of merchandise every six months and must stay overnight.

ACCOMMODATIONS: Because there are a limited number of hotel rooms, it is impossible to get a room if you arrive on weekends when the consumers converge here. Next to the airstrip, expensive **Hotel Sierra** (☎ 750-0666, fax 750-0087), at $75, offers a disco, a restaurant, and tours. Nearby are the **Koktsur** (☎ 775-0327, fax 775-0703), which charges $12, and the **Jardín Cervecerio Alamedas** (☎ 775-0126), a seafood restaurant with *cabinas* for $25. Next to Jardín Cervecerio Alamedas and near the airport, **Hotel Costa Sur** (☎ 750-0871, fax 750-0832) is inexpensive (about $25). The comfortable, family-run **Cabinas Casa Blanca** (☎ 750-0124, $10 d) are S of the Zona Libre and in front of the ICT office. **Hotel Golfo Azul** (☎ 775-0871) has rooms for $40 d. Low-budget **Hospedaje Familiar** (☎ 750-0217) is across the street; kitchen access is permitted to guests. Right across from the entrance to the former United Fruit dock, the **Hotel Del Cerro** (☎ 750-0556, fax 750-0551) has a restaurant and inexpensive rooms (about $25 d). The **Centro Turístico Samoa del Sur** has moderate *cabinas*. Opposite it, the relatively new **Cabinas Miramar** have rooms for $10 with private bath. Near the municipal dock, low-budget **El Uno** has windowless rooms. Another low-budget place ($15 d) is **Hotel Golfito** (☎ 750-0047); get one of the two rooms facing the water. The **Delfinia** (☎ 750-0043) falls in the low-budget range and has shared baths; more expensive rooms have a/c. **El Puente** (☎ 750-0034) is higher priced and has a/c. The inexpensive **Costa Rica Surf** (☎ 750-0034; Apdo. 7, Golfito) is a popular hangout. Its rooms are about $16; ask for one of the few with windows. The low-budget **Pensión Familiar** is well down the road towards the pier. One of the best places to stay is moderate **Las Gaviotas** (☎ 750-0062, fax 750-0054; Apdo. 12, Golfito), which doubles as a yacht club/restaurant. The very large, comfortable rooms have a/c and hot water. Stay in the ones called "*cabinas*"; they have separate entrances. New and more expensive two-bedroom apartments are available. There's also a new pool, and a gym with Jacuzzi and sauna is planned. It's outside of the main part of town at the end of the bus line. Nearby, **El Gran Ceibo** (☎ 750-0403) offers eight low-budget ($17) *cabinas* with fan and private bath. Three inexpensive a/c *cabinas* ($30) are also available. Farther out on the road to Río Claro, **La Purruja Lodge** (fax 750-0373) offers low-budget *cabinas* with baths for $17. To the NE of town, inexpensive **Cabinas Palmer** (☎ 750-0357, fax 750-0373) are near Restaurant Siete Mares.

FOOD: There are a number of good places to dine within the compact Pueblo Civil. One of the best is **Louis Brene's Pequeno Restaurant**, which has large portions, long hours, and good prices. A survivor of the jungles of Los Angeles, Louis speaks wonderful English. Another good value is **El Jardín**, serving vegetarian plates, pizza, and other dishes at affordable prices. **Restaurant La Eurekita** is set in the middle of the Pueblo Civil overlooking the water. **El Balcón** is above the Hotel Costa Rica Surf. Others include **Femary Pizza Restaurant** near the former RR station and **Bar and Restaurant Cazuelita**, which is near the airport and serves up Chinese dishes. Outside town (around C 200 by taxi) is the **Río de Janeiro Restaurant**, which offers spaghetti and other food popular with *norteamericanos*. They also rent horses and can take you for a ride, if given advance notice, at $5 per hour. The open-air, thatch-roofed **Rancho Grande** is nearby. In a converted home, **Jardín Cervecerio Alamedas** serves seafood and cold beer. Other places to try include the **Costa Rica Surf** and Chinese **El Uno** near the dock. **Las Gaviotas** has a good seafood restaurant, as does **Restaurant Siete Mares**, outside of town to the NE. For an unusual meal, try dining on the *Fiesta*, a floating restaurant berthed in the Sandbar Marina on the peninsula.

ENTERTAINMENT: This town really gets lively only on weekends. The **Samoa** has a disco with live entertainment; another disco is the **Palanque**, and the **Club Latino** is down the road. In the Pueblo Civil and on the main road, **Gemini's** (a disco) has the **San Golfo Video Bar**.

EVENTS: An annual five-day **Marine Festival** is held every Oct. Activities include surfing competitions, parades, and a songfest.

SERVICES: The ICT (☎ 775-0496) may be able to provide some information. Watersports rentals and information are available at the **El Surfari** (☎/fax 775-0220) across the street from the Hotel Costa Rica Surf. They are also the local reps for Rainbow Adventures and can book the lodge. The **Centro Turístico Samoa del Sur** rents bicycles and boats. The **Hotel Sierra** runs tours. Marinas include **Las Gaviotas** (☎ 750-0062, fax 750-0544) and the **Eagle's Roost Marina**, which is between town and the Sandbar Marina. The **Sandbar Marina** (☎/fax 750-0874/0735) operates a fishing barge tour aboard the *Fiesta* (a floating restaurant berthed in the marina) and provides jet boat rentals and fishing, snorkeling, and scuba diving trips. Their boat, the *Phoenix*, runs luxurious sportfishing charters with gourmet meals. The **Asociación de Boteros** (☎ 750-0712) offers expensive water taxi services. Rates are about $60 to Puerto Jiménez, Playa Cativo, or Pavones, $2.50 to Playa Cacao, and $52 to Casa Orquídeas. The office is across from the ICE (the electricity and phone company).

FISHING: Steve Lino (☎ 775-0268) is one of the most popular local charter operators. The luxurious *War Eagle* (☎ 750-0838) offers fishing trips. In the US ☎ 714-632-5285 or fax 714-632-1027. Write Box 124, Golfito. The owners also operate **Eagle's Roost Marina. Golfito Sport Fishing** operates two boats. Write Apdo. 73, Golfito or ☎ 288-5083, or fax 750-0373. At Sandbar Marina, **Phoenix Charters** has three boats and a barge. ☎ 750-0874, fax 750-0535, or write Apdo. 85, Golfito. In the US, ☎ 800-435-3239. **Hidden Treasures** (☎/fax 750-0373) offers trips on the luxurious *Inzan Tiger*. In the US, write 1101 SW Washington, Ste. 120, Portland OR 97205. To charter the *Venecia* ☎ 233-9355/9567. Outside of town, the foremost fishing camp is the **Sailfish Rancho** (see description in following section). Also try **Leomar** (☎ 750-0230, fax 750-0373), or **Zancudo Pacific Charters** in Zancudo (☎ 750-0268, fax 750-0105).

FROM GOLFITO: San José buses leave from near the ferry terminal at 5 AM and 1 PM. SANSA (☎ 221-9414, 233-0397, 233-3258, 775-0303, fax 255-2176) flies from the airfield, as does Travelair (☎ 220-3054, 232-7883, fax 220-0413), which also stops at Palmar Sur en route. If they tell you the flight is full, it's worthwhile to show up anyway; two seats are always held until the last minute for passengers coming from Puerto Jiménez, and chances are that you'll get on. For Puerto Jiménez, the gateway to Corcovado, you can take the ferry next to El Uno, or fly (with Travelair) for a reasonable sum.

Along the Golfo Dulce

Golfito is growing in touristic terms by leaps and bounds. And much of the expansion has been along the Golfo Dulce ("Sweet Gulf") to the N of town. Unfortunately, this area is only accessible by boat, which can make visiting expensive unless you're on a package tour. All places here are owned and run by expatriates.

Playa Cacao

Playa Cacao is the nearest beach area which is swimmable. To get here, you must take a water taxi (about 20 minutes), or in the dry season brave the "road" that was built in 1968. There are a few places to stay. **Villas Playa Cacao** (☎ 227-7924, fax 226-3957) are luxury cabins that rent for around $300-600 pw. Also here are **Bungalows Las Palmas** (around $35 d, $50 t), which has a number of fruit trees surrounding six white conical bungalows with thatched roofs. Leave a message in Spanish at ☎ 750-0375 or fax 750-0373. **Siete Mares**, a restaurant that serves Tico food, burgers, and sandwiches, is nearby.

Playa San Josecito/Casa Orquideas

About half an hour from Golfito by boat ($20-35 each way), this botanical garden contains some 50 varieties of fruit trees, 50 types of palms, over 100 species of orchids, and 25 different heliconias. Public tours ($5 pp) are offered from 7-10 AM Mon. to Thurs. Ask about tours at the Surfari in Golfito. A cabin is available for $150/week or $500/month, including transport to and from Golfito. You must bring your own food. Solar powered 12-volt electricity, refrigerator, and cooking facilities are provided. For more information, leave a message with Bob Hara at ☎ 775-0353 or write Apdo. 69, Golfito. You can reach them via marine band 68 as well.

Also in the vicinity is **Dolphin Quest** (☎/fax 775-1742; message in Spanish, 775-1481) a project still in its formative stages. Access is by boat ($20-30) to Playa San Josecito (ask Chico at the *muellecita*. the little dock, if Raymondo's boat is in town); be sure to bring a flashlight and other necessitities. Rates are $25 s, $40 d for camping; $35 per person for dorm; or $50 s, $80 d for private room. Rates include meals, use of kayaks, and snorkeling gear. Conditions are *very* basic. Activities include scuba, snorkeling, fishing, kayaking, hiking, and horseback riding. Massage and acupuncture are available. For more information including an informative newsletter, write Apdo. 141, Golfito or Box 107, Duncan Mills CA 95430. In the US, ☎ 707-869-1242 during Sept. and Oct.

Golfito Sailfish Rancho

About a 15-minute ride by boat from Golfito, this is the area's oldest established fishing lodge. Write PO Box 290190, San Antonio TX 78280 or ☎ 800-531-7232 or 512-492-5517.

Punta Encanto

This former fishing camp has been refurbished as a 12-room, two-storey lodge. A generator provides lights and hot water until 9, after which solar cells take over. Waterfalls and trails are on the property. Guided hiking is available, as is volleyball, scuba, fishing, canoeing, and croquet. Boat tours and bay fishing are also possible. Rates are $130 d and $95 s; they include meals and RT transport from the airport (if staying for three nights or more). For information, ☎ 735-5062 or fax 735-5043. In the US, ☎ 800-543-0397.

The Ston Forestal Controversy

In the early 1990s, a new pulp mill was planned by Ston Forestal, a subsidiary of Stone Container Corporation, for construction at the head of the pristine Golfo Dulce. Thousands of acres of farmland and secondary forest were planted with gmelina, a fast-growing Asian softwood. Some farmers were forcibly removed. It was feared that the mill would fill the valley with noise and bring huge tankers up the Golfo Dulce, destroying the mangroves, reefs and marine mammals in the 20-mile bay. Concerns for wildlife were voiced over the effects of more than 180 projected daily tractor-trailers on the wildlife passing through the Reserva Golfo Dulce, which would be split in two by the road leading to the dock. The issue was the site chosen, not the concept itself.

Stone countered that there was no proposed corridor linking the two park areas and the area had already been extensively deforested, with only secondary growth remaining. They also had an environmental impact statement approved by the Costa Rican government. The company further claimed that the patterns of deforestation would change only when new economic options were provided and that their project was one such option. In September 1994, the Comptroller General's Office anulled a 1992 agreement by the Calderón administration permitting construction of the $20-million facility. This move came just before a Greenpeace protest was slated to begin.

In early January 1995, Ston announced that it was moving the mill site from Punta Estrella to Golfito. This was a victory for AECO, the major Costa Rican environmental organization opposing the location. Three of AECO's leaders died in a mysterious fire in December 1994 and did not live to see the victory. (Arson has been ruled out as a cause.) Ston currently has 42,000 acres (12,000 ha) of leased land on the Osa Peninsula that have been planted with forest, and it plans to export wood chips from here to Mexico and the US.

Arco Iris/Rainbow Adventures Lodge

This ultra-luxury lodge (☎/fax 775-0220; Apdo. 63, Golfito) and nature preserve's prices include transport to and from Golfito and all meals, as well as non-alcoholic drinks, snorkel gear, a jungle tour, and taxes. There are two attractive cabins and a main house. Set at Playa Cativo along the Golfo Dulce, they offer swimming, fishing, snorkeling, kayaking (including night tours on moonlit, phosphorescent eve-

nings), and birdwatching, along with tours of the park and other locales. Food is basically vegetarian and seafood, but carnivores will be
catered to as well. There are a a variety of trails near the premises, and
it's easy to see monkeys and other wildlife. The **Buena Vista Beach &
Jungle Lodge** is a sister of the Arco Iris; it's just down the beach and
offers similar services and amenities, but has a better view and a bit
more sea breeze. Rates are in the $85-$100 pp pn range, which includes
tax but not service. All bookings are made from the States. Call Michael Medill at ☎ 503-690-7750, fax 503-690-7735, or write or 5875 NW
Kaiser Rd., Portland, OR 97229.

Cabinas Caña Blanca

These two expensive all-wood cabins (☎ 775-0373, fax 750-0373; Apdo.
34, Golfito) are set to the N of Playa Cativo and have small libraries,
mosquito nets, dining tables, and modern kitchens with small refrigerators. Airport transfers (three-night minimum) are included. Porches
command ocean views. There are hiking trails (look and listen for
howlers), as well as snorkeling off the private beach (bring your own
equipment). Tours and fishing with light tackle are available, and
Peruvian-style meals can be served on request. Rates are from around
$180 pp for three nights (including transportation).

South from Golfito (Punta Burica)

One of the nation's most remote areas lies S of town. The most famous
establishment here is the nature lodge of Tiskita (see below). A road
leads past deforested farmland and then crosses a river via a winch-
driven ferry. After the ferry (an experience in itself), it's more cattle
farms and then a great view off to the right as you near the ramshackle
village of Pavones.

Playa Zancudo

Aptly named after the mosquito, this large beach is becoming increasingly popular during the dry season. It's $50 to get here by water taxi.
A boat also runs here from the municipal dock on Mon., Wed. and Fri.
at around noon or 1 PM (about $2 pp). It departs Zancudo for Golfito
at 6 AM on those same days. A bus (three hours) may still run here
from Golfito during the dry season. Otherwise, you can take the bus to
Ciudad Neily and then a bus at 1 PM on to the beach. It's a two-hour
drive from Golfito in a four-wheel-drive.

Most places to stay here charge about $8 pp. You can try low-budget **Río Mar, Cabinas Zancudo, Susie's, Hotel Pitier** (☎ 773-3027), **Cabinas Tranquilo,** and **El Coquito.** More upscale are inexpensive **Los Almendros** (☎ 775-0515, $30) and inexpensive/moderate **Cabinas Sol y Mar** (☎/fax 750-0353), which has a restaurant with famous fishburgers. The latter is a half-hour walk from the main part of the village. Susan and Andrew Robertson's **Cabinas Los Cocos** (message ☎/fax 775-0353) offers accommodation in refurbished banana company homes ($17 pn, $30 pw) and they also rent a slightly higher priced cabin. **Zancudo Boat Tours** is attached to Los Cocos. In addition to providing bus service to and from Golfito and surfboard, paddle boat, and boogieboard rentals, they will also take you anywhere you want to go, but advance booking is required. Nearby is inexpensive **Restaurant and Cabinas La Vista**, which has a small zoo. **Casa Tranquilidad** (☎/fax 775-0449 or fax 775-0373; Apdo. 136, Playa Zancudo) is a bed and breakfast with fishing and jungle boat tours. Rates are $30 s, $40 d. In Canada, ☎ 604-525-4403 or fax 604-728-3417. The **Estero Mar** (☎ 750-0056) is the local hangout and has the only public telephone. Eat at **Hotel Pitier** or **Los Almendros.** The latter also offers river and ocean sportfishing charters. The **Escuela Ecología** (☎ 414-743-7434) conducts six-day adventure-oriented ecology courses here. **note:** For a unique insight into *gringo* purchases at Zancudo, be sure to read the article "The Eden Project," which appeared in the April 1995 issue of *Condé Nast Traveler.*

Pavones

A legendary surfing spot, and surfing is the only reason to come here. This isolated hamlet has been embroiled in a controversy which – owing to the intervention of US Senator Jesse Helms – may have international implications. The conflict concerns a ranch formerly owned by imprisoned drug dealer Danny Fowlie, a US citizen now serving a 30-year sentence. Middlemen have sold the property, and the new US expat owners have confronted squatters that have been living here for more than a decade. No resolution to the conflict is in sight, but Helms has demanded the US owners' rights be enforced by the Costa Rican government, just as he has with similar cases.

Water taxis to Pavones cost $60 RT or you can take the daily bus at 2 PM; it returns at 5. Driving, you should take the Golfito-Río Claro road 10 km before turning towards Conte and driving another 10 km. There's a short ferry ride from Conte across the Río Coto. Allow two hours for the trip. Very basic to moderate accommodation and food are available. The **Pavón Tico, Doña María Jiménez's** *cabinas,* and the *pulpería***'s rooms** (next to the soccer field) are all possibilites. **Cabinas**

La Ponderosa (☎ 775-0131, fax 775-0631) charges $35 pp, pd including three meals. Cabins have fans and baths. A TV lounge/bar supplements the restaurant. In the US, ☎ 407-783-7184 or write them care of the managers' concerned mother Elena at 5281 NE 19th Av., Ft. Lauderdale FL 33308. Two km to the S, inexpensive **Bahía Pavones Lodge** is another alternative. Prices include breakfast. Reservations should be made in advance through the Tsunami Surf Shop on Av. Central in Los Yoses. To go back to Zancudo, you can either drive (several hours, but only in the dry season) or Walter Jiménez, who can be found near the school, will take passengers on charter.

Tiskita Lodge

Owned by Peter Aspinall, this private 400-acre (162-ha) farm has a 37-acre (15-ha) orchard with over 100 varieties of fruit, from guava and durian to starfruit and guanabana. Guests are given a tour and permitted to sample fruit. The fruit trees insure superb birdwatching in the area and they lure animals from the surrounding primary forest as well. Horseback riding is available, as are excursions to Corcovado and other trips. It's necessary to fly or charter a taxi to get here. The lodge is designed for those who require convenience but can do without luxury; if your primary reason for being in Costa Rica isn't nature, there's no sense in coming here. Rates are $65 s, $75 d, and $85 t and include the services of a guide. Meals are served family-style in the main house. Fare is limited in variety but plentiful. Dishes include your basic meat, rice and beans, vegetables, and salad. Breakfast may feature fruit, such as fresh mangoes from the garden, cereal, and pancakes. Coffee is always available. Breakfast is $7, and lunch and dinner are $11. Packages are offered, some of which provide tie-ins with other lodges in Corcovado and Manuel Antonio. There are discounts for student groups. The nine groups of simple two- to three-unit stone-and-wood cabins have concrete floors, cold water open-air showers, and verandas (some with hammocks), which are visited by charming human-wary iguanas. Electricity is provided by generators, which shut off at 9. There are a wide variety of well maintained trails through primary and secondary forest, a waterfall, lovely bathing pools, and plenty of birds and spider monkeys. Bird cries are ever-present, as is the crash of surf in the distance. Obtain a map and ask about any confusing turns if venturing off on your own. Stairs leads down to the beach with its rough surf. Be sure to bring everything you need; boots are available. Donated materials for the village school would also be appreciated. Write Costa Rica Sun Tours, Apdo. 1195, 1250 Escazú or ☎ 233-8890, 255-2011, or fax 255-4410/3529. Their offices in San José are on Av. 7, C. bis 3/5, in back of the Holiday Inn.

Puntarenas to Panama

Fundación Tiskita

Created in 1992, this foundation aims to purchase and to reforest land in the vicinity of the lodge. Farmers in the area are to be taught new agricultural methods and schoolchildren to be educated about the environment. Send contributions to Apdo. 1195-1250, Escazú, Costa Rica.

Casa Punta Banco

Down the road from Tiskita Lodge, this six-bedroom house (four double beds and six singles) has two baths with hot water showers and a fully equipped kitchen, a generator, and a washer and dryer. An extensive tract of primary rainforest surrounds the lodge. Guests will be met at the airport in San José and be taken to a bed and breakfast in Moravia; from San José you can fly or drive to Golfito. There you'll meet the manager, who will help you reach the lodge. There's a full-time caretaker on the property, who also acts as a guide. Information booklets are available. You will find low-budget accommodation at a number of places in the village; expect to pay $5 pp. Horseback riding is also available. Watch for the enormous roosters! Activities in the area include body surfing (watch for rip tides!), sampling fruits from the orchards, snorkeling, exploring the tide pools, horseback riding, watching nesting sea turtles (in season), and surf fishing. Prices range from $700 pw for one or two, with $50 more for each additional person. In the US, ☎/fax 810-545-8900/0536 or write Continental Associates, 202 W Fifth Av., Royal Oak MI 48067. In Costa Rica, contact Warner (Warren) Gallo at Apdo. 5, Golfito; ☎ 775-0666/0924 or fax 750-0087.

Ciudad Neily/Villa Neily

This banana and oil palm plantation town is seven km NW of the border with Panama. There's no particular reason to visit, but it's a good place to make bus connections. There are a large number of budget-priced hotels, including the **Pensión Familiar** (cheapest), the **Hotel Bulufer**, **Cabinas El Rancho**, **Hotel El Viejero**, **Hotel Nohelia**, **Hotel Central**, and **Hotel Las Vegas**. More expensive are the **Hotel Musuco**, **Cabinas Helga**, **Cabinas Fontana**, and **Cabinas Heyleen**. You can meet Belgian expatriate Lillian at her **Bar Europa** or eat at the **Restaurant La Moderna**, the best in town.

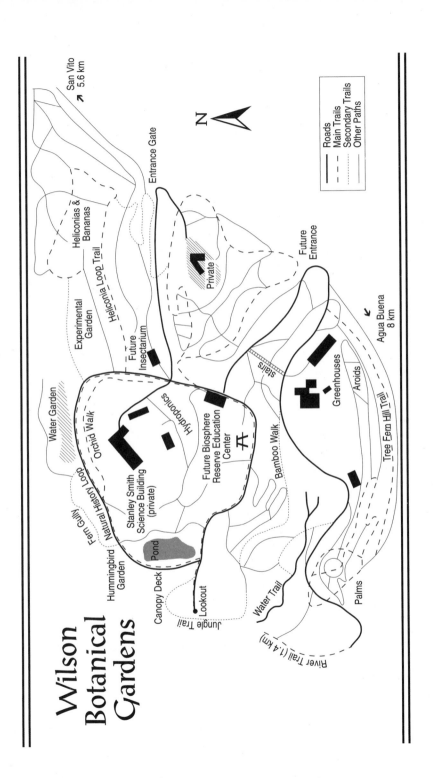

Wilson Botanical Gardens

San Vito 5.6 km

Entrance Gate

N

Roads
Main Trails
Secondary Trails
Other Paths

Heliconias & Bananas

Heliconia Loop Trail

Experimental Garden

Private

Future Entrance

Agua Buena 8 km

Water Garden

Future Insectarium

Orchid Walk

Stanley Smith Science Building (private)

Natural History Loop

Fern Gully

Hummingbird Garden

Pond

Canopy Deck

Lookout

Jungle Trail

Hydroponics

Future Biosphere Reserve Education Center

Bamboo Walk

stairs

Greenhouses

Aroids

Tree Fern Hill Trail

Water Trail

River Trail (1.4 km)

Palms

from Neily: Running buses to San José (around seven hours), the Tracopa terminal here is on the N side of the town's plaza; San Isidro buses also depart from here. For Golfito you can catch buses from the stop at the SE corner of the plaza or at the bus terminal in the town's NE end. Buses leave at 7 and 3 for Puerto Jiménez on the Osa Peninsula. For Paso Canoas (Panama), go to this terminal or take a bus from the plaza. **note:** If you want to be guaranteed a seat, go to the terminal.

Coto 47

Seven km SW of Neily, this is the closest airport to Panama. SANSA (☎ 221-9414, 233-0397, 233-3258, fax 255-2176) flies here. The main reason to fly here would be to save time if you are going on to Panama.

Paso Canoas

The main reason to come here is as a stop on the way to Panama. Many Ticos come through on their way to shopping excursions in Panama and hotels are often full on weekends and holidays. Stay at the **Hotel Miami, Hotel Palace Sur, Cabinas Interamericano, Hospedaje Hortensia,** or the **Cabinas Los Arcos**. If these are full, head back to Ciudad Neily. Tracopa buses run between here and San José. For more on travel to Panama, check "For Panama" at the end of the guide.

Wilson Botanical Gardens

(Jardín Botánico Wilson)

The Gardens were founded by Robert and Catherine Wilson in 1963, with the original intention of establishing a tea plantation. The land is adjacent to a 590-acre (225-ha) mid-elevation forest reserve. It's now the most extensive botanical garden in Central America.

The 25 acres (10 ha) of gardens are beautifully landscaped – some areas cultivated in a more European style, others wild – shaded by palms, oaks, and tree ferns, among many other trees. The preserve is maintained by the Organization for Tropical Studies, which also operates La Selva and the Palo Verde Field Station. The Gardens maintain over 1,000 genera of plants from some 200 families, one of the world's finest collections of bromeliads and other tropical flora, including orchids, ferns, heliconias, marantas, and palms. The palm collection may be the world's largest, with more than 700 species. There are 278 species of birds in the area. In 1983, UNESCO designated the Gardens, along with the forest area (which has six km of trails), as part of the Amistad Biosphere Reserve, which is some 25 km away and borders the national park of the same name.

GETTING HERE: First get to San Vito (see "getting there" under "San Vito" in the following section). Take another bus or taxi for the last six km. By car, take the Interamerican S past Buenos Aires to the San Vito turnoff on your left, crossing the Río Térraba. From Golfito (to which you can fly), you take the Ciudad Neily bus or drive, heading S to Ciudad Neily, turning N on Carr. 16, up the steep road to Agua Buena, the closest town to the Gardens.

PRACTICALITIES: A self-guided nature trail booklet is available. Admission is free on Sun. Half-day visits are $3 and full-day visits $6 ($12 including lunch). Costa Rican citizens and residents receive discounts on entrance. For day visit reservations (reserve by 10 AM the same day), and for information on group tours (two-day reservation required), ☎ 773-3278, fax 773-3278, or write: Robert and Catherine Wilson Botanical Gardens, Apdo. 73, San Vito de Jaba, Coto Brus 8257. For reservations to stay in the dormitory ($55 and up pp, pd, including meals) or the cabins ($75 pp, room and board; rooms have refrigerators), contact the Organization for Tropical Studies (☎ 240-6696, fax 240-6783; write Apdo. 676, 2050 San Pedro). **note:** The Gardens' botanical station was gutted by a fire in 1994 and still has not reopened, though it may have been rebuilt by the time you arrive.

San Vito de Java

This town, at an elevation of 3,150 ft (960 m), was settled by Italian immigrants and was originally dependent on coffee growing. It is located in the fertile Cotos Brus Valley and early settlers hoped that they would be on the Interamerican Highway, thus providing access to plantations in Costa Rica and Panama where there was demand for fresh fruit, vegetables, and dairy products. Now home to 37,000 residents, San Vito makes a good base for visiting La Amistad International Park or the Wilson Botanical Gardens.

GETTING HERE: Take *Tracopa's* San Vito bus from C. 2/4, Av. 18, in San José (six hours, ☎ 221-4214, 773-3410). They depart at 4:45, 8:15, 11:30, and 2:45 PM. Another line, *Sáenz y Ureña* (☎ 223-4975) leaves at 7 and 2 from Av. 16/18, C. 13 near Plaza Víquez in San José. *Empresa Alfaro* (☎ 223-8229) also runs from C. 16, Av. 5 at 6:15, 8:15, 11:30, and 2:45. Get a *directo* bus if possible. The best time to depart is early, so that you can enjoy the mountain scenery. Numerous buses also run from San Isidro (at 5:30 AM and 2 PM) and Golfito (via Ciudad Neily). The very scenic US-built road from Ciudad Neily to San Vito was constructed in 1945 because of its strategic proximity to the Panama Canal.

PRACTICALITIES: Stay in **Hotel Collina Annex, Hotel Tropical, Hotel Pitier** (☎ 773-3006), or in **Cabinas Las Mirlas** (☎ 773-3054) which are next to the offices of the Ministerio de Agricultura. **Hotel El Ceibo** (☎ 773-3025) has a restaurant and is in back of the Municipalidad. Its rooms are sunny and attractive and run $20 d. Low-budget **Albergue Firenze** (☎ 773-3206) can be found down the road to Río Terraba, which begins to the left of the town's entrance. A bit farther on are low-budget, clean **Cabinas Las Huacas** (☎ 773-3115); they operate a weekend disco. Attractive **Paolo's Guest House** (☎ 773-3407) is a two-storey home surrounded by tropical forest. Rates run around $30 and you can use the kitchen. If you wish to stay near, but not in, the botanical gardens, **La Cascadas Cabinas and Restaurant** is about 600 m before the gardens on the left hand side coming from San Vito. For Italian food try the **Mamma Mia Pizzería**, which is in an old house and has low prices, or the **Restaurant Liliana**. Liveliest nightspot is the **Disco Banarara**.

FROM SAN VITO: Buses to San José (*directo* at 5, regular bus at 7:30, 10, and 3) and San Isidro (6:30 AM and 1:30 PM) leave from the Tracopa terminal (☎ 773-3410) at the S end of town. From downtown, buses run to Neily, the La Amistad Park towns of Las Mellizas, Las Tablas, and Cotón, and to other local destinations.

Osa Peninsula & Corcovado National Park
(Peninsula de Osa & Parque Nacional Corcovado)

Owing to its isolation, biological diversity, and its large areas of old growth forest and other undisturbed regions, the Osa Peninsula is one of Costa Rica's most important natural areas. The bulk of it is contained in Corcovado National Park. Located in the heart of the SW's Golfo Dulce region, it has extensive stretches of mangroves to the N, a large forested plateau on its W flank, and a huge lagoon in the center, which is nearly surrounded by mountains. In addition, there are estuaries, wetlands, rocky headlands, rivers, waterfalls, and beaches. Its lowland forest, the area's largest, is the last bastion of indigenous plants and animals in the nation's SW. Surrounded by jolillo palms, 2,471-acre (1,000-ha) Laguna Corcovado, a herbaceous freshwater

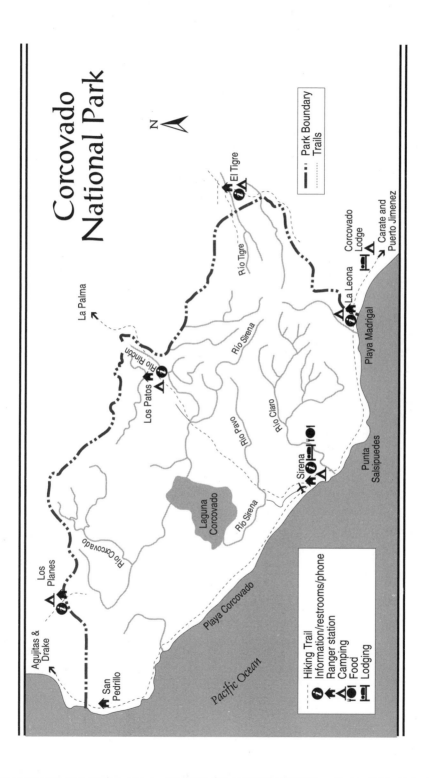

Corcovado
National Park

Park Boundary
Trails

--- Hiking Trail
ℹ️ Information/restrooms/phone
🏠 Ranger station
▲ Camping
Food
Lodging

N

La Palma

Los Patos

Rio Rincón

El Tigre

Rio Tigre

Rio Sirena

Rio Pavo

Rio Claro

Rio Sirena

Laguna
Corcovado

Rio Sirena

Rio Corcovado

Los
Planes

San Pedrillo

Aguijitas &
Drake

Playa Corcovado

Pacific Ocean

Sirena

Punta
Salsipuedes

Playa Madrigal

La Leona

Corcovado
Lodge

Carate and
Puerto Jimenez

marsh in the lowlands' center, provides a home for waterfowl, reptiles, and amphibians. The one drawback to all of this is that there are few trails: for the most part you must walk along the beach.

FLORA AND FAUNA: Eight different habitats have been identified, and the park has the nation's greatest wealth and variety of wildlife; there are 13 major ecosystems here. The forests are prototypical rainforest: a multitude of species, tall trees with spectacular buttresses, large vines and woody lianas. Each of the 13 distinct habitats hosts innumerable species. Areas of high foliage density, such as the Llorana Plateau, contain over 100 tree species per acre. In places, canopy height reaches 180-262 ft (55-80 m). These are the highest trees in the nation! The park's largest tree is a silk cotton about two km from the midpoint of the coast. With a large number of endemic species, the park is also rich in fauna. In an area only half the size of Yosemite National Park, there are 285 species of birds, 139 species of mammals, 16 species of freshwater fish, and 116 reptiles and amphibians. It may be the last remaining Costa Rican habitat of the severely endangered harpy eagle. Corcovado offers a visual feast of wildlife. Among the other endangered species here are squirrel monkeys, jaguars, tapirs, white lipped peccaries, and scarlet macaws.

TWO LEGGERS: Former inhabitants of the park, the *oreros* (gold panners), once resided by the river, eking out a living. After environmentalists protested that silt generated from their panning was filling up the lagoon, they were legislated out of existence, but were promised compensation. When this was not forthcoming, they arrived *en masse* in San José and camped out in the parks until payment was made. Panning continues today on the park's outskirts and, despite the destruction it causes, the government has only infrequently taken action against it. (The last raid was in July 1995.) Another conflict is with squatters, who see the park's lands as the last frontier. **Fundación Neotrópica** (☎ 253-2130) is trying to deal with this threat through its BOSCOSA project, which attempts to find positive, productive, and ecologically sustainable solutions to the dilemma.

HISTORY: The idea of turning Corcovado into a national park was put forward in 1970. But the area's remoteness, the creation of other new parks, and the lack of funds prevented its realization. As the decade wore on, more and more families began to settle in the peninsula, hunters were decimating the wildlife (in one instance shooting an entire herd of peccaries just for amusement) and one lumber company, which owned a major section of the future park at that time, cemented a logging partnership agreement with various Japanese companies.

The brutal 1975 murder of Swedish expatriate Olof Wessberg, who was investigating the park's potential as a national park, helped spur President Oduber to start Corcovado. The original 88,956-acre (36,000-ha) park was created in October 1975; 19,113 acres (7,735 ha) of rugged highlands in the peninsula's center were added in 1980, making a total of 108,069 acres (43,735 ha). The park was closed briefly in 1994 when 90 gold panners were peacefully evicted and in 1995 when 150 were ousted. The forests surrounding Corcovado are being logged at an alarming rate. For a full account of the fascinating story behind the park's creation, read *The Quetzal and the Macaw* by David Rains Wallace.

GETTING HERE: There are a number of ways to enter both the peninsula and the park. The way you choose will depend upon your time, finances, and energy. **from/via Golfito-Rincón-Corcovado:** Only a madman would take this route, but you'll want to know about it. Inquire in Golfito concerning boats to the small settlement of Rincón. If you can get one, it's about a 12-hour hike from there to Rancho Quemado and three additional hours to the Río Drake, where you can swim and relax. From there the next town is Drake, and then it's another 90 minutes to Agujitas. If you can't get a ride from there with a boat to the park station of San Pedrillo (one hour), you must walk another 20 km (12 miles). In all of these towns, only the most basic provisions, along with a small selection of fruits, are available. It takes 2½ hours down the beach to **La Llorona** ("Weeping Woman"), which has a 100-ft (30-m) waterfall cascading onto the beach. Get underneath and experience an intense needle-like shower that varies in intensity from spot to spot. There's a beautiful archlike rock formation along the beach, and you may see hundreds of red fiddler crabs. From the beach there are two indistinct trails: one goes to a waterfall (you must swim across a river and clamber over rocks to get to it); another (two-three hours) goes to a shelter near Laguna Corcovado. Another alternative is to walk along the beach four hours to Sirena. You must wade through three sand flea-infested rivers (Llorona, Corcovado, and Sirena) that can be crossed only at low tide and, as there's no shade, the sun beats down unmercifully. You must put your pack on your head, cross the river naked, all the while scratching sand fleas and watching out for the small sharks that reside at river crossings. Be sure to check tide tables before departing! **via Golfito-Puerto Jiménez-Corcovado:** This route is described under "from Puerto Jiménez" in the "Puerto Jiménez" section that follows. **by plane:** Aeronaves de Costa Rica (☎ 750-0278) offers charter planes that will fly you in to Sirena from Golfito (around $120/planeload). From San José you can fly with SAETA (☎ 232-1474/9514) for about $400/planeload. **other**

routes: Other alternatives are to fly in to Marenco Biological Station on the N side of Osa Peninsula or to Corcovado Tent Lodge next to its S border, then enter via boat and use one of the many lodges at Drake Bay as a base (see "Drake Bay" for specifics). Alternatively, visit aboard the *Temptress.*

PREPARATIONS: It's better if you can bring your own food, as you'll be less of a burden for the park personnel. While a tent is not mandatory, a mosquito net and spray-on insect repellent are. It's too hot and humid for rain gear, but an umbrella is another must, as are rubber boots. Be warned that the chiggers (in the meadows and woods) and sand fleas (on the beaches) are ferocious, so take appropriate precautions! All of the roads become impassable after a rain; four-wheel-drive vehicles here often use snow chains to get through the mud. If you're planning to fly into the park, you must call the ranger station in advance (☎ 735-5036, fax 735-5011). You can also visit them at their headquarters next to the Banco Nacional in Jiménez and inform them of your arrival date and length of stay. All ranger stations can provide accommodation and meals given advance notice – preferably one week.

Puerto Jiménez

This small town is a jumping-off point for Corcovado National Park.

GETTING HERE: From Golfito fly with Aeronaves de Costa Rica (☎ 750-0278) daily at 6 and 2 for under $10 pp. You can also charter a plane (for about $55) or a water taxi ($35). There's a bus from Ciudad Neily at 7 and 3 which you can intercept at Chacaritas, also known as Piedras Blancas, on the Interamerican. You can also connect with this bus by taking a *Zona Sur* bus from San José, in which case you should leave as early as possible. From San Isidro de El General, a bus (five hours) runs here at 5:30 and noon. By car, you should follow the Interamerican to Piedras Blancas. There you turn right towards Puerto Jiménez, which is another 50 km farther.

PRACTICALITIES: Regrettably, the town is on its way to two-tier pricing for accommodations so be sure you don't get gouged! Low-budget **Cabinas Marcelina** (☎ 735-5007, fax 735-5045) has six rooms with bath and fan. **Cabinas Brisas del Mar** (☎ 735-5028, fax 735-5012) has nine low-budget rooms. **Vivero y Jardín Joyosa** (near the Texaco station) and **Pensión Quintero** are also low-budget. **Cabinas Manglares** (☎ 735-5002, fax 735-5121; Apdo. 55-8203, Puerto Jimenez) has raised its prices substantially to $35 d, but not its accommodation standards. You can see scarlet macaws and toucans on the grounds. Opened in 1995, **Cabinas Iguana Iguana** (☎ 735-5158) has seven rooms with private baths in its main building, three more with a shared bath in another building, and six *cabinas*. Rates are $15-25 d during the high season. There is a restaurant on the property. Transportation to Corcovado can be arranged. The **Agua Luna** (☎ 735-5034/5108/5033) is a group of moderate cabins with a bar and good restaurant that offers a/c, bathtubs, TVs, and refrigerators. A variety of tours are hosted. **El Bambú** is a campground about a km N of town, offering meals. They have guides and rent tents, bikes, hammocks, horses, and a single car.

FOOD: The nicest place to eat here is **Agua Luna**, but the local center for services and hanging out is **Soda La Carolina** (fax 735-5073) on the main drag. You can also try **Comidas Típicas la Campesina. El Rancho** is a good place to have a drink during the evenings.

OUTSIDE TOWN: Cabinas Playa Blanca are less than an hour N of town near La Palma, and there is spartan accommodation where the bus stops in La Palma (the nearest town to Los Patos in the park). Also to the N is **Albergue Ecoturistico El Tigre** (☎ 783-3937), which has rooms with baths for $30. Horseback riding and hiking are available. A bit farther N, the **El Tucán Cabinas and Restaurant** (☎ 775-0522/0033) has low-budget rooms.

SERVICES: Coretel's office is at the corner of the soccer field. Next to the Banco Nacional de Costa Rica, the **park office** (☎ 735-5036) is on a street running parallel to the main street. They can give you some information, a permit sheet which you bring with you, and (perhaps) maps. A pay phone is available on the main street. **Tobaga Loaciga** (☎ 735-5092; marine radio ch. 12) offers tours and fishing trips along the Golfo Dulce. **Everyday Adventure Tours** (☎ 233-6378, fax 735-5073) conducts kayaking and hiking trips. **Escondido Trex** (☎/fax 735-5206) offers kayaking and other single- and multi-day trips to the Corcovado and Gulfo Dulce areas. It's located in Soda La Carolina.

FROM PUERTO JIMENEZ: A morning bus (at 5:30), the express bus to San Isidro, and trucks (one hour) run regularly to the small village of La Palma. Be sure to visit the Women's Group of La Palma, **ASOFEP** (fax 735-5116), who operate a cafeteria, library, and tourist information center. You may stay here at low-budget **Cabinas Corcovado** (☎ 774-0433: message). From here it's about 12 km (three to four hours on foot along a gravel road) to the NE entrance at Los Patos – on the way you must traverse the Río Rincón 19 times. Cars make the trip (one hour) during the dry season, and you can lease your own vehicle if you wish. The area around Los Patos tends to be wet and slippery. Accommodation and food can be arranged in advance at the ranger station here (about $8 for lodging; $5 for a meal). Or you can stay with **Coopeunioro** (☎ 233-3333), a 13-family cooperative operated by former goldminers. These farmers have 250 acres of forest and aim to expand this to 2,500 acres in order to form a buffer zone around Corcovado. Food and lodging (for up to 12) cost $15 pp, which includes transport from La Palma. It's then another four to six hours by trail to Sirena. En route there are six km of mountain forest trails and 14 km of hiking through rainforest. You will have to cross a number of streams, which can come up to your thighs in the rainy season. (Watch out for poisonous spiders that spin their webs along the trail.) From Sirena, you can proceed to Playa Madrigal (four hours) and camp at La Leona, where it's an eight-hour hike back down to Puerto Jiménez or four to five hours (15 km) to Sirena, a trail which must be negotiated at low tide. You'll pass a rusting ship at Punta Chancha.

via Carate: Every Mon., Wed. and Fri. pickup trucks (about $4 OW) run from the town S along the coast on a very bad road to Carate near La Leona. Along the way you pass by areas as deforested as Guanacaste, followed by other stretches that are lush and majestic. Contact Cirilo Espinoza at the *pulpería* next to La Carolina. Taxis can also be chartered through the park office. Once in Carate, it's less than an hour's walk to La Leona ranger station. Don't swim here because of the strong current and the danger from sharks. However, camping near the *pulpería* is fine and popular.

LEAVING THE PENINSULA: After visiting majestic and exhilarating Corcovado, the deforested regions surrounding it leave you with a sense of loss and depression. A bus runs all the way to San Isidro; from there you can get a bus to San José. Another bus runs to and from Ciudad Neily. There's also a boat (6 AM) and a flight (with Travelair) to Golfito daily.

Lapa Ríos

One of the nation's most unusual projects, 20-bungalow Lapa Ríos (Apdo. 100, Puerto Jiménez) is the only Costa Rican rainforest resort of its kind. It caters to upscale adventurers, while genuinely preserving the surrounding rainforest. A million dollar-plus project, the ridge-perched hotel has one of the most dramatic overlooks in the Osa Peninsula.

HISTORY: Opening in 1993, the hotel was the result of a long-held dream on the part of owners, John and Karen Lewis, a musician and a lawyer from Minneapolis. The Lewises had served in the Peace Corps in Africa, then hit upon the idea of a reserve that would protect the rainforest, while generating an income for themselves. They decided that Costa Rica was the ideal place to start such a venture. The site of Lapa Ríos fulfilled their list of 25 specifications, and construction began in 1990. The reserve comprises 750 acres of old growth and 250 acres that are being reforested. Other projects such as orchid growing, iguana and butterfly farming, and fruit and vegetable farming are in the planning stages.

PRACTICALITIES: The beautifully designed hotel is constructed of tropical hardwoods, all obtained with permits. The front part, a large thatched pavilion, is the reception and dining area. Its spiral staircase leads up to a catwalk with a 360-degree panorama of the surrounding area. From the patio and swimming pool there's a wonderful view straight across the Gulfo Dulce. The white-walled and thatch-roofed *cabinas*, downhill and spaced out in succession, are next. Inside each of the rooms are two beds with mosquito nets; the windows are covered with netting, which keeps out insects while letting in the breeze. The walls use *caña blanca* wood, the desk is made with *almendro* (almond), the roof is of *mangle* (mangrove), and the floor is of *cristobal*. Food is included and is good. Dishes are largely continental. Service is impeccable and very formal. Prices run $230 d per day. You can contact the office in Puerto Jiménez (☎/fax 735-5130) from Mon. to Fri., 8-5 and Sat. 8-2. The lodge can be reached directly through Coopeserimec, a phone patch service, at ☎ 775-0120.

SERVICES: A beachside *cabaña* is under construction. It's about 15 minutes to the beach, which is largely rocky but beautiful. You may want to stop in at the eclectic, spartan New Age lodge, **Tierra de los Milagros**, whose owner, Edie, asked not to be written up in this guide. The woods are glorious even if the paths are a bit treacherous and steep in parts. It's easy to see animals such as howlers, the tree buttresses and ephiphytes are impressive and, unlike many other "eco-resorts," you really are in primary forest here. Night stays in the jungle are planned. Although a guide is suggested, one isn't necessary if you're a seasoned hiker. The two main trails are the Osa and the Waterfall. You can also hike along the banks of the Río Carbonera. Sportfishing, tours of Corcovado, tree planting in the "Volunteer Rainforest," and other activities should be available by the time you read this.

Bosque del Cabo

This is 20 km from Puerto Jiménez. In the expensive range, this remote 350-acre eco-resort is above Playa Matapolo at Osa's S tip. The entrance is past Lapa Ríos a few km and to the left. Prices range from $65 pp, d to $75 pp, d, depending upon the quality of the digs. Food is included. Horseback riding with a guide is $15 pp, pd. It should cost you $22 to charter a taxi from Puerto Jiménez. If you book directly and don't come through a travel agency, you will receive a discount. There's a waterfall and guided horseback tours are conducted. The owners, Philip and Barbara Spier, an American/Tica couple, are looking for physically fit guests who enjoy exploring the area's beaches and trails; box lunches are available. A goal here is to reintroduce scarlet macaws to the wild, but funding (as well as someone to organize the project) is lacking so far. There's no electricity, but you will find peace and quiet and nature in abundance. ☎ 735-5206 or fax 735-5073.

Other Lodges

Like Drake Bay and Dominical, this once-remote area is developing fast. **Hacienda Bahía Esmeralda** (☎/fax 289-6227) is a luxury-priced five-room guesthouse. It has a pool, horseback riding, kayaking and is near to both rainforest and beach. **Encanta la Vida** (☎ 735-5062, fax 735-5043) offers horseback riding and fishing. Rates are $150 d.

Sirena & Vicinity

Stay either in the attic of the ranger station or pitch a tent down below the station. Expect to pay $3 per meal. And be prepared to meet some of the local inhabitants: giant cockroaches, chiggers, and ferocious, insatiable mosquitos. Horses can be hired here and there are laundry facilities. Although much of the land around the station is secondary growth, there's a path running through old growth to the Río Claro. Since it's ringed by swamps, Laguna Corcovado is accessible only by boat. There's one path, marked *"Quebrada Camaronero,"* that heads toward it. Unless you relish the prospect of being gobbled by sharks, you should avoid swimming in the ocean. The Río Sirena and Río Claro are safe enough, as long as you keep out of the crocodiles' jaws.

GETTING HERE: From La Leona, it is a walk of four to five hours (15 km) along a beach and past Punta Salsipuedes to inland trails and then through the jungle, until you meet the Río Claro. There you cross and head for Sirena. **from Sirena:** It's a 25-km hike (six or seven hours) to

San Pedrillo, the park's NW entrance and ranger station. Fifteen of these km are along the beach, seven are via rainforest, and the last three combine jungle and beach. Be sure to walk the beach at low tide; otherwise you will find it swallowed by the sea. After about a km on this hike you come to the swiftly flowing Río Sirena, which can reach three-four ft in width during the rainy season (a bit over three ft in the dry). After this crossing, it's some two hours to the Río Corcovado, which is around two ft deep at low tide. The Río Llorona is a further two hours. Soon after you come to the Piedra Arco, a huge greenery-covered rock arch, the track veers off into the jungle: keep an eye out. At low tide, you can reach **Catarata La Llorona**, which cascades beachward; it is the larger of two waterfalls you come to. After a few hours on the main trail you reach a beach. From there it's an hour to the Río San Pedrillo, where you can stay and eat. Here, you will find trails and a beautiful waterfall, which you can clamber up to and bathe in. It's reached by a path along the river. From here a trail follows the coast six miles (10 km) to Bahía Drake.

Corcovado Tent Camp

On the beach, about 1½ km W of Carate at the S entrance to Corcovado, this innovative lodge is the brainchild of **Costa Rica Expeditions** (☎ 257-0766, 222-0333, fax 257-1665; Apdo. 6941, 1000 San José), whose founder Michael Kaye has been coming to this area for decades. The lodge is not for those who wish to have their every need attended to. The individual who will enjoy it the most is the person who is entranced, rather than appalled, to find a boa constrictor stretched out near the toilets. It is for those who enjoy simplicity and closeness to nature but want more creature comforts than are found at the ranger station.

ACCOMMODATIONS AND FOOD: The white 10 x 10 ft tents are closely spaced and have two single beds each. Some are on the beach, while others are in a clearing above the kitchen. There are shared baths, electricity (three times daily) for the dining and bar/hammock area, and crystal clear drinking water from the reserve's stream. Served buffet-style on two long tables, the food is quite good, especially considering that it must all be brought in by air or boat. Specialties include macadamia pancakes for breakfast, pitchers of fruit juice with meals, and filling entrées of rice, beans, vegetables, salad, and fish or meat. Dietary needs can be catered to upon request. Prices vary according to the package you have, but you can expect to spend $60 pp, including meals.

Puntarenas to Panama

GETTING HERE: A 15-minute charter flight from Golfito or a 45-minute charter from San José brings you here. It's a 30-45 minute walk from the landing strip; your luggage is loaded on a horse-pulled cart.

EXCURSIONS: Sunset horseback rides are available. The beach is at your front door; the sunsets are magnificent, and dinoflagellates eerily illumine the beach at night. It's fun to hike up Quebrada Leona, a beautiful creek. You'll see plenty of crabs, birds, lizards, and perhaps a snake or other wildlife. One of the resident biologists can take you down to the park (US$20 plus park admission), and you can hike up the Río Madrigal with him or her. The steep reserve behind the lodge, where there's a loop trail, is also well worth visiting. It's easy to see toucans, scarlet macaws, and other birds, and iguanas climb trees and slither across the property. You can do a lot of birdwatching from your hammock or from your deck, if you have one of the tents perched higher up.

THE CANOPY PLATFORM: This is an interesting way to access the rainforest canopy. From the lodge, it's an easy 1½-hour hike up to the beginning of the loop trail, where the platform is. Along the way, you're given a guided natural history tour of the area. The 160-ft ajo ("garlic") tree holding the platform is very sturdy and allows for a superb panoramic view. It took 12 days and eight people to build the platform. Just finding the right tree took a month because it needed to have limbs large enough to support the platform as well as a good view. The fiberglass floor is reinforced with graphite; railings are aluminum. You are attached to a harness and rappelled with a winch up to the 120-ft-high platform (and then down again). At the top, you are fastened into a harness and can have a look around. Monkeys arrive when the tree is fruiting. It's $75 pp for the excursion.

Drake Bay & Vicinity

This placid bay is becoming a site for thriving ecotourism lodges. Sir Francis Drake allegedly set foot here in 1579, thus the name. Regrettably, a road is planned here, which may spoil the area's charm. Deforestation is reportedly taking place now along its planned route. Drake Bay, La Paloma, and Cocalito are all on one side of the river. Aguila de Osa is across the swinging footbridge over the river to the left; the path to the village is on the right. Marenco is about an hour's walk away. **getting here:** Your hotel can arrange transport from San José, or you can take a bus to Palmar from C. 4, Av. 18 in San José at 5 and 7 AM; ☎ 221-4214. Alternatively, SANSA flies to Palmar, as does Travelair (☎ 220-3054, 232-7883, fax 220-0413). From Palmar, you take a bus or charter a taxi to Sierpe, 20 miles farther. From Sierpe, it's a couple of hours downriver and then out to the ocean and Drake Bay. Local dugouts do the route, but they are crowded and occasionally capsize. *Especiales* are faster and available for charter; bargain to get the local rate. Returning, you can generally find a ride with a local. **from Quepos: Corcovado Express** runs a $75 trip to Drake Bay. ☎ 233-9135/3892, 777-0505. In the US, ☎ 800-374-4474 or write Apdo. 659 1150 La Uruca.

Drake Bay Wilderness Camp

This expensive lodge on a peninsula by the Río Agujítas – one of the first in the area – offers a number of guided tours. Accommodation is in attractive cabins and large tents. Rates run from $50 pp (in tents) and $70 pp (in cabins), including meals; children are discounted. Scuba, fishing, and tours are offered. Charter flights and packages (with meals) are available. ☎/fax 771-2436, 284-4107, 285-4367, or write Apdo. 98, 8150 Palmar Norte, Osa.

Aguila de Osa

Intimate and high quality, Aguila de Osa (☎ 296-2190, fax 232-7722; Apdo. 10486-1000, San José) has 14 thatched-roof cabins with verandas. Its garden setting, perched on a hillside, includes a gourmet restaurant and a pool. It offers sportfishing (four boats), scuba, birding, and kayaking. Rates run from $200 d on up. In the US, write Cuenta # 250, 7500 NW 25 St., Miami FL 33122.

La Paloma Lodge

La Paloma (☎/fax 239-0954; radio ☎ 239-2801; Apdo. 97-4005, San Antonio de Belen, Heredia) is perched atop a hill on the same side as Drake Bay Wilderness Camp. This set of luxury-priced digs (five thatched-roof *cabinas* and five rooms) offers tours, horseback rides, scuba, kayaking, canoeing, and complimentary use of snorkeling and fishing gear. There's a pool and all rooms have solar-heated hot water as well as ceiling fans. Packages (four nights including transport $600-700) are available.

Puntarenas to Panama

Cocalito Lodge

This Canadian-run lodge, also on the Drake Bay side, is set on one of the most beautiful spots along the bay – a beach with wonderful sunsets. It has a restaurant downstairs, and spartan but attractive rooms upstairs. There's no electricity, except that provided by solar and hydroelectric power. In addition to the standard tours offered by everyone, they have sportfishing, a mangrove tour, horseback rides, scuba, and a night at a "jungle inn." Expect to pay $50-65 pp, including meals. Packages are also available. For more information ☎ 786-6150, fax 786-6291, or 519-782-4592. Write Apdo. 63, Palmar Norte.

Drake Village Accommodations

Other, lower-priced accommodations are near the village of Drake, which comprises about 250 families. Inexpensive **Albergue Jinetes de Osa** (☎ 253-6909, 284-3743) provides bunk beds, can arrange stays with local families on trips, and has rates that include meals. Less expensive are **Casa Mirador** (☎ 227-6914), set on a hilltop, and **Cabinas Cecilia** (☎ 771-2436), which has two six-bunk bedrooms. The latter offers a variety of trips, including an Isla de Caño excursion. The **Cabinas y Restaurant Jade Mar** (☎ 771-2336) has rooms for $60.

Corcovado Adventures Tent Camp

This basic tent camp at Playa Caletas charges $75 pp, pd with meals. It's about an hour on foot from here to the village. There's a small beach and trails. Sportfishing (through owner Larry Hustler's Sport Fishing Costa Rica) can be arranged. Corcovado Express runs a $75 tour and trip here. Packages are also available. ☎ 233-9135/3892, 777-0505. In the US, ☎ 800-374-4474 or write Apdo. 659 1150 La Uruca.

Aguijas

This small village, down the beach from Drake, has basic accommodations offered by Cecilia Steller for about $18 pp including food. Horses with guides are available for $25 pd including lunch. Leave messages at ☎ 771-3336 or write Apdo. 84, Palmar Norte.

Marenco Biological Station

Remote and roadless, this is one of the nation's foremost privately established reserves, covering 1,250 acres (500 ha). Its bamboo and wood bungalows, originally set up as a base for biological researchers exploring the wonders of the peninsula, are perched on a hill and have a capacity of 40. A "Rainforest Trail" runs behind the dining hall. It leads to the Río Claro and then along the Beach Trail and back to the main facilities. Optional tours include day visits to Corcovado, Isla de Caño, and the Río Claro. The way to get here is by chartered plane or by a combination of boat and overland travel. Packages are available. ☎ 221-1594, fax 255-4513, or write Apdo. 4025, 1000 San José. Their offices are in El Pueblo.

Río Sierpe Lodge

This is an expensive deep-sea and tidal-basin fishing and nature lodge in the NE section of the peninsula. Scuba and snorkeling day trips to Isla de Caño and Isla Violin can be arranged, as can fishing, hiking and horseback riding and two-day RT cruises to Isla de Coco. Facilities include 11 attractive cabins and a library. Write Apdo. 149-2150, Moravia, ☎ 223-9945, 257-3812, or fax 233-2886. Transport is available from Palmar. Special rates are available for independent travelers, naturalists, and student groups. Arrival at the lodge is by boat.

Caño Island Biological Reserve
(Reserva Biológica Isla de Caño)

This 480-acre (200-ha) park, 12 miles (20 km) off the coast, rises 296 ft (90 m) above sea level. Most of the 740-acre (300-ha) island is covered by virgin tropical wet forests. The island was apparently at one time an indigenous cemetery and, later, a pirate hideaway. Some go so far as to claim that it was the inspiration for Robert Louis Stevenson's *Treasure Island*. Although the tombs have been looted, perfectly fashioned stone spheres remind you of their presence. Its central plateau floods during the rainy season. Nearly transparent water surrounds its high cliffs and miniature 100-yard (100-m) beaches. In 1973, the island was rented out to a foreign firm that intended to start a tourist development. The planned wharves and marinas would have devastated the surrounding coral reefs, the largest colony on the Pacific coast. Curiously, however, the disclosure of plans for a nude beach as part of the development were what doomed the plans. Still, much of the old growth forest was leveled. In 1976, this island was declared part of Corcovado National Park, and it gained independent status in 1978. Its name is believed to derive from the Costa Rican Spanish slang for "fresh water gutter," so called because of its many streams.

FLORA AND FAUNA: Compared to mainland Corcovado, there are few species here. There are some 60 varieties of trees, the most prominent of which is the giant milk tree, which provides a drinkable sap. Boa constrictors number among the four species of snakes. A legacy of the pirates, the wild pigs here were exterminated by Sergio Jiménez and his son Tony on behalf of the park service.

GETTING HERE: Unless you have your own boat, a tour or charter is the only way. These can be arranged with virtually any lodge in the vicinity. And on any given day you're more than likely to encounter a group from another lodge sharing the beach. The *Temptress* also visits here. After an optional hike with a naturalist to explore the trails, you'll have lunch on the beach and plenty of time to snorkel and enjoy yourself.

HIKING: This is the only way to see the aboveground portion of the island. Most of the indigenous relics here have been looted, so the park asks that you not carry daypacks or other bags on the trail. After you get up the hill and along the trail, you begin to comprehend what has been lost through looting and deforestation. There are some splendid old growth trees festooned with epiphytes and some old stone spheres, as well as bits of stonework on the ground. It takes about 30 minutes to get up the hill to the first junction. The trip to the lighthouse (40 minutes each way) is wonderful, but it's a precipitous climb, so you need permission in advance. To the left the trail continues for another 20-25 minutes, where a short trail goes up to a *mirador*; another continues on, then turns off, leading to some spheres and Indian relics. If you continue straight, you'll come to a small waterfall.

Isla del Coco National Park

(Parque Nacional Isla del Coco)

This steep and rocky volcanic island, blessed with abundant springs and waterfalls, can be accessed only at Chatham and Wafer Bays. By the small stream at Chatham – named after an 18th-C. expeditionary ship – there are a number of rocks inscribed with the names of arriving mariners. Wafer, larger and a few km to the W, is named after a 17th-C.

actor, physician, and writer who kept company with pirates. The island is about 311 miles (500 km) off the Pacific coast and measures 21 by 13 miles. As one might guess, it was named because of the abundance of its coconuts. But the coconuts are few and far between, with most palms belonging to the species *Rooseveltia franklinia* (named after FDR, who visited the island four times). This tree looks like the coconut palm from a distance. The island gets 276 inches (7,000 mm) of rainfall per year; its highest point is 2,080-ft (634-m) Cerro Iglesias. A tourist mysteriously disappeared from here in 1989.

GETTING HERE: The *Okeanos Aggressor* (☎ 220-1679, 800-348-2628, 504-385-2416, PO Drawer K, Morgan City LA 70381) and **Ríos Tropicales** (☎ 233-6455, fax 255-4354; Apdo. 472, 1200 San José) both have very expensive trips. The former is recommended for dive fanatics: that's about all you do on the trip. Also running dive trips are **Lost World Adventures** (☎ 800-999-0558) and **Escenarios Tropicales** (☎ 224-2555, fax 234-1554). The National Park Service might be able to help with chartering. A visit can be expensive. The government charges for entry, anchoring, and landing a plane. No visit may exceed 12 days.

FLORA AND FAUNA: Although there are not many animals here, those present are not afraid of man, since they have been given no reason to be. To date, over 70 endemic species of plants and 70 types of animals (largely insects) have been identified here. Birds include frigatebirds, white terns, masked and red-footed boobies, green and blue herons, peregrine falcons, and many others. Three of the seven land birds are endemic, including the Coco Island finch, closely related to the species found on the Galapagos. The other two are the Cocos cuckoo and Ridgeway's papamoscas. Reptiles and amphibians are entirely absent, except for two small lizards. Because mammals were not here when the finely-tuned ecosystem evolved, feral pigs and cats wreak havoc. In their search for roots and grubs, pigs dig up the ground, causing trees to topple and soil to erode. The same type of devastation is wrought by goats and deer, though their numbers are smaller. Cats prey on birds and lizards; their only virtue is that they keep down the population of rats, another imported species with no natural enemies. Many cultivated plants have also gone wild here, including coffee and guava – which threatens to supplant some of the native species.

HISTORY: Legendary Portuguese pirate Benito Bonito and Captain James Thomson and his crew, who made off with the Peruvian valuables they had contracted to escort, are among those alleged to have

Puntarenas to Panama

buried treasure on the island. Historical happenstance gave Costa Rica sovereignty over the island after it rescued 13 seamen shipwrecked here when a Chilean frigate capsized in 1832. German treasure hunter Augusto Gissler spent 18 years here from 1889 on, searching for treasure unsuccessfully under the cover of a government "agricultural" contract.

A notable incident in island history occurred in 1992, when ships belonging to the militant environmental group Sea Shepherd attacked six Costa Rican fishing boats with paint-filled bullets. They were responding to a tip from a park guard who alleged that the boats were killing dolphins and using the meat as shark bait. The shark fins are exported to Japan, where they are prized as a delicacy. As a consequence of overfishing, the hammerheads here may be wiped out by the decade's end. Common practice is to slice off the dorsal and pectoral fins, then toss the maimed animals back in the water. Rudderless and unable to swim and therefore to hunt, the sharks starve to death. The boats denied they were fishing inside the protected park waters.

In a 1992 development that disturbed environmentalists, the government approved a high-tech search by a US computer magnate for treasure thought to have been buried by pirate William Thompson. The search was carried out by an ultra-light aircraft equipped with pontoons for sea landing and takeoff. Meanwhile, scuba divers carrying "proton magnetometers" relayed information to a boat stationed offshore. The $5 million search, they hoped, would lead to $800 million worth of booty. However, at the time of the contract's expiration, the entrepreneurs had come up empty handed. The government announced its intentions to ban further ventures.

The first ranger station was established here in 1992, but equipment is still inadequate to patrol the 15 km of offshore reserves. Unfortunately, illegal fishing is still common. The Friends of Coco Island Foundation is intent on conserving the island and its offshore marine life.

La Amistad International Park
(Parque Internacional de la Amistad)

This enormous 479,199-acre (193,929-ha) "friendship" park straddles the upper slopes of the Talamancas and may someday mesh with a promised twin park in adjoining Panama. Both areas protect invaluable watersheds. The nation's newest park, it has more than doubled the size of the park system. No facilities or services are available and there are very few trails. Elevation within the park ranges from 650 to 11,644 ft (200-3,459 m).

FLORA AND FAUNA: The park has rainforest, cloud forest, and *páramo*, with resident populations of jaguars, tapirs, and pumas. The 400 bird species include quetzals and harpy eagles.

GETTING HERE AND GETTING AROUND: Take the bus from San José to San Vito, then on to Las Mellizas. The few trails are all unmarked. Contact the NPS regarding the possibility of hiring a guide and horse. If you have a car, this would be a good day trip from San Vito or San Isidro. Contact **Costa Rica Expeditions** (☎ 257-0766, 222-0333, fax 257-1665) regarding custom-tailored tours. Camping is permitted near entrances at Las Mellizas (easiest to access and best for hiking), Aguas Calientes, and at Helechales. Easiest to access, Las Mellizas is best for hiking. To get here take a San Vito-La Lucha bus (9:30 AM departure) and walk six km, or drive all the way. Trout fishing is possible here with a permit. Horses and guides can also be hired. A group of 40 *cabinas*, **La Amistad Lodge** (☎ 233-8228 or 773-3193 for reservations, fax 255-4636) offers accommodations for around $60 pp, including three meals. They can arrange horses and guides, and you can camp as well. Their travel agency, Rainbow Tours, offers a four-day all-inclusive tour for $500. In the dry season, an ordinary car can make it up to the Río Coton, which is a km from the farm. For current information, check with the Wilson Botanical Gardens. Another alternative is to stay with the **Sandí family** (Miguel Sandí, La Lucha, Sabalito, Coto Brus 8257), who will serve you lunch or dinner if given minimal advance notice. They'll pick you up in San Vito, but it takes five hours RT. You can camp on their property. Again, check with the Wilson Botanical Gardens.

Other Southern Locales

Palmar Norte/Palmar Sur

This small town, straddling the Río Grande de Terraba, lies 125 km S of San Isidro. The only attractions here are its mysterious *esferas de piedra*, stone spheres that can be found in backyards and other locations. The town is a gateway to Osa and Corcovado. (See "Drake's Bay" under "Corcovado and Osa.")

PRACTICALITIES: Drake's Bay Wilderness Camp and other lodges may pick you up here. You can take a bus to Palmar from C. 4, Av. 18 in San José at 5 and 7 AM; ☎ 221-4214. **SANSA** (☎ 221-9414, 233-0397, 233-3258, fax 255-2176) and **Travelair** (☎ 220-3054, 232-7883 fax 220-0413) both fly here. Stay at the low-budget **Hotel Xenia** (☎ 786-6129) or the **Casa Amarilla** (☎ 786-6251), which is better; make reservations. Eat at the **Restaurante Chan Jeng** underneath the disco. The nearest outlying accommodation is at **Estero Azul Lodge** (☎ 233-2578, 221-7681, fax 222-0297; Apdo. 1419, 1000 San José), which offers boat trips, fishing, or diving.

Mystery of the Spheres

Stone spheres are found in only two locations on the planet – Mexico and in Costa Rica. They range from three inches to about four ft in diameter. No one knows how they were formed. Geologists hold that a volcano spat magma into the air: landing in a hot-ash-filled valley, the globs cooled into spheres. Others believe they were made with stone tools. Golfito resident David Bolland believes they were shaped by waterfalls tumbling into a man-made pit.

Sierpe

Buses run here from Palmar. The low-budget **Hotel Margarita** is the cheapie alternative. More upscale is the nine-room Canadian-operated **Hotel Pargo Rojo** (☎/fax 788-4859), which has rooms with fans and private baths for $17 s, $23 d; a/c is $5 additional and refrigerators are available for rent. Two deep-sea fishing boats take guests on tours, fishing, diving, and on island excursions. A catamaran and a canoe are also available, as is horseback riding. They will coordinate reservations and transport to the Drake Bay lodge of your choice. In Canada ☎ or fax 705-286-4859 or write Box 725, Minden, Ontario K0M 2K0. For dining, try **Rosita's** or **Restaurante Las Vegas**. Hotel Pargo Rojo operates a riverside *soda*. From Sierpe, it's a couple of hours downriver and then out to the ocean and Drake Bay. Local dugouts do the route, but they are crowded and occasionally capsize. *Especiales* are faster and available for charter; bargain to get the local rate. Returning, you can generally find a ride with a local.

Rey Curré

At this village in the SW Talamancas between Paso Real and Palmar Norte there's an indigenous craft cooperative. **Fiesta de los Diablos.** This is the sole remaining Native American festival, taking place here every February. In an allegorical recreation of the struggle between the local Boruca Indians and the Spaniards, masked *Diablitos* pursue a bull, representing the Spaniards, which is made of burlap topped with a carved wooden head. Local crafts, corn liquor (*chicha*), and tamales are for sale.

The New Dam

This planned dam, a $2.3 billion privately financed project, would flood an area of 115 square miles (300 sq km) from Buenos Aires to Coto Brus. The dam was first planned in the 1960s and was nearly built in the 1970s to power a proposed ALCOA aluminum refinery, but that was cancelled after a student protest. The village of Curré will be flooded and, not surprisingly, the area's indigenous peoples oppose the loss of their ancestral lands. In addition, some 15 miles (25 km) of the Interamerican would be submerged. That would necessitate rerouting the road through the Cabagra Reserve which, in turn, would leave it open to invasion by squatters. The dam is moving ahead because, for reasons best known to itself, the ICE (the electricity and telecommunications agency) has agreed to provide Mexico with electricity by 2004. Even if this deal disintegrates, ICE (the electricity and phone company) plans to construct a smaller reservoir which will sell energy to other nations in the region.

Boruca

This indigenous village is 11 miles (18 km) off the Interamerican Highway. During the school year, a bus (two hours) leaves for here from Buenos Aires at 1:30. If you walk in, get off at the *entrada* about half an hour by bus after Buenos Aires, and take the two-hour (eight km) path branching off the main road. Lodging can be arranged with a local family if you ask at the *pulpería*, or in advance through **Tur Casa** (☎ 225-1239). The local version of **Fiesta de los Negritos**, on December 8, has wildly costumed dancers in blackface. It is held in honor of Boruca's patron saint, the Virgin of the Immaculate Conception. Participants dance to flute and drum accompaniment, as the *sarocla*, a frame with a horse's head, moves through the streets.

weaving: Boruca women are famous for their weaving. Dyes are produced from leaves, bark, and even a mollusk. Products include placemats, blouses, rugs, bags, and table runners. **museum:** An **Eco Museo** has opened here.

Puntarenas to Panama

The Caribbean Coast

This is the banana frontier, covering almost 20% of the nation's land mass and with over 170,000 inhabitants. Although today less than 25% of the population is of African-American heritage, you'll still hear the distinctive local English dialect all along this coast. A common greeting is "Whoppen" ("What's happening") and "all right" or "OK" is substituted for *adios*. Fortunately for the visitor, the touristic potential remains virtually untapped, with mile after mile of palm-lined beaches lining the coast.

Anytime is a good time to visit this area, but the best time for the southern beaches is Sept. and Oct. There's really only one main road: it runs across to Limón and then down the coast to Sixaola. Bus service is good. The major tourist spots here are Cahuita and Puerto Viejo. In addition to the coral reef offshore at Cahuita, parks on this coast include the internationally renowned Tortuguero, Barra del Colorado Wildlife Refuge, Hitoy-Cerere Reserve to the S and, far to the S, the Gandoca-Manzanillo Wildlife Refuge. Tortuguero, Barra del Colorado, and Caño Negro (to the W of Tortuguero) are set to be linked with similar wildife refuges in Nicaragua under the SI-A-PAZ agreement. However, deforestation by banana plantations and cattle farms is swiftly undermining the probability of the plan's effectiveness.

Barra del Colorado National Wildlife Refuge
(Refugio Nacional Barra del Colorado)

The waterway system terminates at 227,332-acre (92,000-ha) Barra del Colorado. Although Barra del Colorado was once a prosperous lumber center and cargo depot, timber depletion has led to its demise. Much of the W portion of the reserve remains unexplored, but infrared satellite photos show that illegal logging is proceeding in this area at an alarming rate. As with Tortuguero, rainfall here is in excess of 250 inches (6,250 mm) per month. The flora, fauna, and local cultural milieu resemble Tortuguero's. Waterways are lined with raffia and *manicaria* palms, *cativo*, bloodwood, and wild tamarind. There are over 240 species of birds. Hundreds of thousands of bright yellow alemanda butterflies cover the trees during the winter months.

GETTING HERE: It may be possible to get back and forth between Tortuguero and Barra del Colorado via infrequent coconut barges that sometimes take passengers, or you can charter a boat, which is very expensive. From Barra Colorado village (pop. 900), the Río San Juan goes up to the Sarapiquí, which leads in turn to the small town of Puerto Viejo. From there a rough road goes down to San José. You may also drive from Guápiles through Cariari N to Puerto Lindo (or take a bus leaving at 2 PM). From there it is 20 minutes to Barra by boat. **by air: SANSA** (☎ 221-9414, 233-0397/3258, fax 255-2176) flies here on Tues., Thurs., and Sat. **Travelair** (☎ 220-3054, 232-7883, fax 220-0413) also flies daily except Sun.

by the river: Another way to get here is the Río Colorado Lodge's trip up the Río Sarapiquí from Puerto Viejo. One of the most unusual adventures in Costa Rica, this tour features enthusiastic and informative guides. It runs from Puerto Viejo up the Río Sarapiquí to the Río Colorado Lodge and then back to San José. First, you are bussed from your hotel to the dock at Río Frio. Along the way, you stop for breakfast, pass waterfalls, and get to see a lot of beautiful countryside. After boarding the *Colorado Queen*, you cruise up the dark green Sarapiquí; swallows fly low over the water. Blue plastic bags strewn across roots by the bank are discards from the banana plantation, disturbing reminders of the industry's ill effects. You might see birds such as blue herons, dairy cows grazing by the banks, epiphyte-laden trees, riverside homes, women washing clothes, and children bathing. The river widens and becomes shallower, passing by a largely deforested stretch. Sadly, there is no virgin jungle (primary tropical forest) along here. You pass by Oro Verde on your left 10 minutes before the junction of the Sarapiquí with the Río San Juan. Report at Costa Rican customs here. I was processed by a guy wearing dog tags and camouflage pants, while two soldiers kicked a soccer ball back and forth. You then cross over to the Nicaraguan side, where a man in complete camouflage garb collects the sheet with your name and passport number. Formerly, before the Contra insurgency, there were a lot of people living here. Although it has been declared a reserve, some have returned.

You'll next pass the house of the woman with 22 children. Seventeen of them are still alive. The woman's husband died after being bitten by a poisonous snake. Sometimes the widow comes out and waves. The wide river continues as you swing right onto the Río Colorado. The narrow San Juan del Norte continues on to Greytown (San Juan del Norte) but you need a canoe to pass. As I re-entered Costa Rica, the Nicaraguan station was manned by an old man wearing a Mazda cap and unlaced boots. The entrance to the post's building was plastered with conservation posters. No new colonization is allowed along this stretch. Then it's back to Costa Rica. The "Policia Frontier" reside in a thatched hut, with submachine guns mounted on the side. You pass by an enormous ceiba tree as you head up the Caño Bravo, the more jungly of two passages, although still largely secondary forest. Howler monkeys swing through the trees above. The river is dazzlingly green on both sides, with thatched huts and coconut palms dotted here and there. A while later, Barra del Colorado comes into sight, and you pull up at the lodge. The middle of the river contains sandbars, and the other portion of the village lies across the wide river. If you haven't already dined on the boat, you'll have lunch at the lodge. After a relaxing afternoon and evening's stay (during which you will tour the village and possibly join an optional night tour on the river), the *Colorado Queen* then plies the Tortuguero waterways down to Moín the next day. (If you wish, you can stay on and fish in the area, then fly out.)

The next morning after breakfast you head out through a narrow passageway which widens and then you turn to the first canal, flanked on both sides by palms, and pass a family *finca* (established before the reserve was declared).

Stopping at the ranger station, you take a brief walk along the interpretive trail before continuing on to Siquirres. Priced at $200, the tour may be reversed on occasion, in which case the route will vary and during green sea turtle nesting season (July, August, September), a special excursion will be made to see turtles nest. For more information and booking, ☎ 800-243-9777 in the US.

ORIENTATION: Barra is a very small village. An asphalted airstrip cuts down its middle and a soccer field is next to it. While the Río Colorado Lodge has access to the village directly, Silver King is cut off. Tarponland is right near the Río Colorado Lodge. The place to go here is definitely the amazingly long and wild beach. To the right you can see the island of Uvita off the coast of Limón.

ACCOMMODATIONS/FISHING LODGES: This area is famous for the giant tarpon (*sábalo*), which have secured the area its reputation worldwide. All places to stay are very expensive and packages are available. Founded by Archie Fields, **Río Colorado Lodge** (☎ 232-8610/4063 in San José; 800-243-9777 in the US) offers simple cabins with Jacuzzi and satellite TV. The only lodge set right near the Colorado's river mouth, it offers good fishing year round. Comfortable rooms feature private baths, hot showers; three buffet meals are served. In the evening, guitarists from the neighboring village often drop by to strum a few numbers. There's also a small zoo as well as a quiet lagoon perfect for swimming. The **Río Colorado Lodge** (☎ 232-4063/8610, fax 231-5987) is no longer the plushest lodge available, but the others can't compete with its atmosphere. Rooms are comfortable but not lavish, with fan, twin beds, and hot water shower. Dinner features fish and another main course, along with vegetables, corn bread, and desserts such as flan. Breakfast is served on the front patio, and you order à la carte from a selection including omelettes. Packages run from six days, five nights (around $1,300) to eight days, seven nights ($1,950). Write Hotel Corobicí, PO Box 5094, 1000 San José; 12301 North Oregon Av., Tampa FL 33612; ☎ 800-243-9777 or 813-931-4849 outside the US. **Cabinas Tarponland** (☎ 710-6917) is the only place even close to budget-priced. Expect to spend $120 per three-days for simple digs, food, and transport.

Silver King Lodge, opened in 1993, offers very comfortable facilities, which are a bit upscale compared to the others in the area. They have 19-ft Carolina skiffs, canoes and kayaks and other boats, a good restaurant, a giant Jacuzzi, and video/book library. In Costa Rica, ☎ 381-0849 or fax 943-8783. In the US, ☎ 800-847-3474 or 813-942-7959 or write Aerocasillas, Dept. 1597, Box 025216, Miami FL 33102. The other lodges are across the river. With housing in A-frames, **Isla de Pesca** (☎ 223-4560 or 221-6673 in San José, fax 255-2533; Apdo. 8-4390, 1000 San José) is another major fishing lodge. In the US, ☎ 800-245-8420, 305-539-1630/1631, fax 305-539-1123 or write Costa Sol International, 1717 N Bayshore Dr., Ste. 3333, Miami FL 33132. They also have a tropical river safari up the Corobicí. **Casa Mar Fishing Lodge** (☎/fax 221-8661; PO Drawer 787, Islamorada FL 33036) has 12 rooms and offers three-day packages for $1,000. In the US, ☎ 800-327-2880 or 305-664-4615. On the edge of the village of Parismina, **Parismina Fishing Lodge** (☎ 222-6055, 288-2446, 236-0348, fax 222-1760, 236-1718) features rooms in wooden cottages. They also have a "wild monkey nature tour" and tours of the Tortuguero canals. Write Apdo. 10560, 1000 San José or ☎ 800-338-5688 in the US. They have been highly recommended by readers. Expect to spend $1,500 pp for a three-day fishing package. **Parismina Tarpon Rancho** (☎ 257-3553, fax 222-1760, 800-862-1003) offers both fishing and eco-tourist adventures. **Parismina Lodge** (☎ 768-8636) offers spartan rooms as part of a three-day $165 pp package. **Samay Lagoon Lodge** (☎ 240-8245, 236-7145; Apdo. 12767-1000, San José) is a German endeavor, an ecologically designed luxury 16-room hotel. It offers canoe tours, fishing, and evening turtle watching tours. A half-hour boat trip upriver, the **Delta Wildlife Lodge** (☎ 253-7816, fax 233-9357) has hiking, swimming, boat trips, and turtle watching. Three-day packages run $250 pp.

FOOD AND SERVICES: In the village, there are minimal facilities available, aside from those mentioned above. **Soda Naomi**, painted a brilliant raspberry and white, is one of the only places where you can make a phone call, buy food, watch TV, and (sometimes) eat. **Pulpería Ceci** has bread and a few other food items, as does **Pulpería Ricardo Fernandez**. **Soda La Fiesta** has light food and drink; a red and white sleigh-on-snow tapestry graces its wall.

On a Houseboat

One of the most unusual ways to get around Costa Rica's Barra del Colorado area is on the *Rain Goddess* (☎ 231-4299, fax 231-3816; Apdo. 850-1250, Escazú), a houseboat 65 ft long by 18 ft wide. The boat is the creation of Dr. Alfredo Lopez, an MD born in Costa Rica but partially raised in California. Dr. Lopez, a licensed retired physician, also uses the houseboat to provide free medical care for indigent locals on both sides of the border. His belief is that tourism must have local benefits. He hires local hunters to guide tourists who want to photograph animals, in the hope that they will learn the value of preserving wildlife. The boat has six staterooms with baths. Fully carpeted and a/c, it has a gourmet seafood restaurant, cellular phone, and TV/VCR. It is designed for fishermen who want to go where few have fished before, as well as for nature tourists. Each trip takes a minimum of six and a maximum of 12, and a trip is three days or longer. Boarding is at Barra del Colorado; you either fly or boat in. Rates are $600 pp for three days and two nights of a nature tour or $1,600 for five days and three nights, including three days of fishing. In the US, ☎ 800-308-3394.

OTHER ACCOMMODATIONS: Set in Isla Brava within the refuge, **Finca La Cecilia** is a five-bedroom thatched-roof lodge. Set in Caño Zapote on the road to Puerto Lindo, **Panatanal** offers accommodation for up to six. Boat rides, hiking, and horseback riding are offered. Room and board are $25 pp, pd. For more information contact the Asociacíon de Microempresarios Turisticos de Pococí (ASOMEP; ☎ 767-7010/7245).

La Penca

You will probably want to know about this small border town more than you will want to visit it. On May 30, 1984 an explosion here at a press conference, called by ARDE leader Eden Pastora at his jungle camp off the San Juan River, killed three journalists and five Contras, leaving 26 wounded. The incident was alleged by journalists Martha Honey and Tony Avirgan to have been set up by 29 US officials, right-wing US citizens, Costa Rican security forces, and the CIA in an attempt to discredit the Sandinistas and provoke US intervention. Evidence uncovered in 1993 and disclosed by Avirgan and Honey points to Vital Roberto Gaguine, an Argentinian ultra-left terrorist, now dead. It is still not clear who was behind him. They have found evidence that the Sandinistas may have been involved in the bombing. A good way to learn more about this incident, and to get an overview of the Iran-Contra affair, is to see the 1988 movie *Cover Up*, directed by Barbara Trent. Ask your video store about it or order a copy for $34.55 postpaid from The Empowerment Project, 1653 18th St., Ste. #3, Santa Monica CA 90404. Many contradictions remain unresolved. Be sure to read Martha Honey's book, *Hostile Acts*.

Tortuguero National Park
(Parque Nacional Tortuguero)

The area known as Tortuguero, "region of turtles," is on the E side of the country, N of Limón. These flatlands (Las Llanuras de Tortuguero) were formed over millions of years as sediment washed down river systems and was trapped and stabilized by vegetation such as raffia palms. It is one of the nation's most popular parks (around 30,000 visitors per year); its waterways are excellent places to see wildlife. A tropical wet forest life zone, the average annual rainfall here exceeds 197 inches (5,000 mm); while June and July are among the rainiest months, August and September are drier than usual. Altogether, there are 11 habitats here ranging from herbaceous marsh communities to high rainforest. The area's center is the small village of Tortuguero.

FLORA AND FAUNA: Despite the rampant deforestation surrounding it, Tortuguero remains an area that fulfills the Westerner's expectation of a tropical jungle. There are over 2,000 plant species, including 400 species of trees. The coconuts found here are introduced relics of the days when plantations flourished in the area. Seagrapes dominate the coastal dunes.

Of the 16 endangered mammals in Costa Rica, 13 are found in or near the park, including the rarely sighted manatee. Although the area to the W of the park has been ecologically devastated through logging and hunting, jaguars, three-toed sloths, and river otters populate the portion E of the Sierpe hills. The 57 species of amphibians and 11 types of reptiles include three of the four species of sea turtles, crocodiles, *caimáns*, as well as poison dart, transparent glass, and smoky frogs. The more than 300 species of birds include green macaws, violaceous trogons, Montezuma oropendolas, Central American curassows, keel billed toucans, greenback herons, and yellowtailed orioles. The gar (*Attratosteus tropicus*) is considered to be a living fossil because it resembles similar species that lived during the upper Cretaceous 90 million years ago. It has a body covered with bony or plaque-like scales and ranges in length between four and seven ft (1.25 and 2 m). Its long, narrow snout supports strong jaws lined with crocodile-like teeth. Often it lies motionless, as if suspended in the water. Because of its tasty, bone-free flesh and practice of laying its eggs in shallow water, the fish is endangered. There are some 54 other fish species as well.

HISTORY: The Caribbean's largest nesting area for the green sea turtle, Tortuguero originally gained fame as a hunting ground. The first settlers were closely related to the Maya. The area's first Spanish settlement was at San Juan de la Cruz some 25 miles to the N. In the mid-1700s, cacao plantations were established at Matina, 25 miles S. Native Americans and Afro-Caribbeans worked the plantations, but repeated raids by the Zambos-Moskitos forced their abandonment by 1848.

In the 1700s, Tortuguero was famous for turtle meat, oil, and shells. In 1912, an 18-ton vessel, ironically named the *Vanguard*, began running loads of turtles between Limón and Tortuguero. A turtle turner, known as a *velador*, was assigned to each mile of the 22-mile beach. His task was to turn turtles on their backs and tie a log to their flippers; they were then floated out to sea and collected offshore. Beginning in the 1940s, a series of sawmills transformed the local economy before each went out of business. When the last closed in 1972, the village's population declined to around 100.

Tortuguero's rise to prominence in the public eye resulted from Archie Carr's study of sea turtles in the 1950s. In 1959, responding to the threat posed by poachers, logging, and wild dogs, Carr and Costa Rican scientists and conservationists formed the Caribbean Conservation Corps (CCC), the first non-governmental conservation organization to be established in the Caribbean. Although a 1963 executive decree gave protection on paper by establishing a turtle reserve, the creation of the national park (also by executive decree) in 1970, provided the power to deter poaching. Canals were constructed during the early 1970s, and the first public phone was connected in 1972. In 1975 the reserve was expanded to nearly 50,000 acres (19,700 ha), including 15 miles (24 km) of nesting beach. The effort was dealt a setback after the Legislative Assembly voted in 1979 to reduce offshore turtle hunting limits from 12 to three miles. Although the 12-mile limit was maintained in park waters, the reduction meant that the *barricada* of turtles would have to swim through enemy waters to reach safe haven. An international letter-writing campaign resulted in a presidential veto of the bill. In 1982, the first electric generator began running in the village. The area had begun to catch up with the times.

ENVIRONMENTAL PROBLEMS: As with all of the parks, a number of environment-related controversies have emerged. The raising of park fees (to $15 per entry) has spurred guides to take visitors to the four km of beach N of town, an area not included in the park. Thus, you now have as many as 200 people surrounding a single turtle.

Great controversy has been aroused by the plan to build a road to Tortuguero village. The town's Development Council has spearheaded the "No to the Highway" group, which maintains that a road would have a devastating effect on the community. Another danger to the park has been posed by the banana plantations. More than 74,000 acres (30,000 ha) on its borders have been converted to banana plantations, resulting in the loss of some 14 billion rainforest plants and trees. On June 9, 1992, Costa Rican authorities accused the British multinational Geest Caribbean of violating the 1969 Forestry Law. Allegedly, the company cleared 948 acres (400 ha) of primary and secondary forests in the Siquirres and Pococi areas. Millions of dollars have been spent in clearing terrain, including illegally cutting trees along river banks – a practice that contributes to soil erosion and results in waterway sedimentation. Some of the territory involved adjoins the park, and the habitats of sloths, green macaws, and monkeys were destroyed in the process. Company officials claim that they were granted permits by local forestry officials and cleared no forest. There have already been a number of mysterious fish kills in the area in recent years which environmentalists blame on agrochemicals. The fish population has declined, and leatherback turtles have mistaken the blue plastic bags (presumably) for jellyfish and choked to death. In addition, Park Director Eduardo Chamorro has recommended that locals not eat fish from the canals because of the pollution.

Until recently, Tortuguero remained the only one of the larger parks not to have been enlarged since its creation. Although numerous studies since the 1970s had recommended that the park be enlarged from 19,700 to 80,000 ha, no action had been taken. In 1992 the decision to add 10,000 ha to the park (which will be purchased in the future) was announced, with the intention of joining it to Barra del Colorado, forming a megapark. This expansion is critical to increase the survival prospects of the jaguar and white-lipped peccary. Donations are needed to cover the $1,000-per-acre cost. Send them to CCC, Box 2866, Gainesville FL 32602, or you can contribute to the Fundación Neotropica.

The latest affront to the area's integrity came in early 1996 with the unauthorized clearing of a 100-ft-wide (30-m) swath of rainforest (some of which included national park territory) for construction of a road between Tortuguero and the village of Palacios. Although permission has been received to build the road as far as the park entrance (some four km from the village), the move is encountering opposition from the park service.

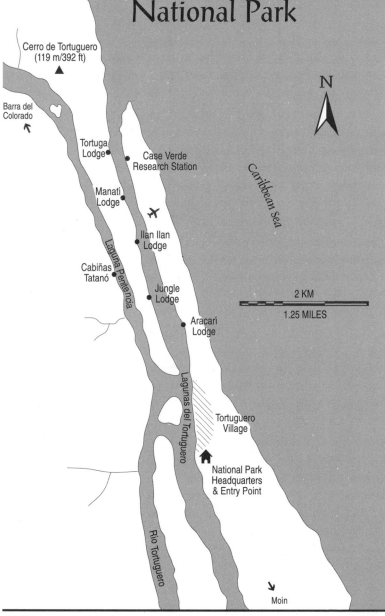

Tortuguero National Park

Cerro de Tortuguero
(119 m/392 ft)

Barra del
Colorado

Tortuga
Lodge

Case Verde
Research Station

Manatí
Lodge

Ilan Ilan
Lodge

Cabiñas
Tatanó

Jungle
Lodge

Aracarí
Lodge

Laguna Penitencia

Lagunas del Tortuguero

Caribbean Sea

N

2 KM
1.25 MILES

Tortuguero
Village

National Park
Headquarters
& Entry Point

Río Tortuguero

Moín

ORIENTATION: Commonly known as Los Canales, 99 miles (160 km) of inland waterways flow up the NE coast to Tortuguero and then on to Barra Colorado where these eight rivers merge into a series of lagoons. Utilizing the already existing natural channels, canals were dug during the 1970s to connect them, thus providing a natural waterway in a region where no highway would be feasible. Extending from the transport center of Moín to the N of Puerto Limón, every type of craft from dugout canoes and fishing boats to tour boats ply these waters. The first village, 32 km upriver, is Parismina. Then, you come to the park office, the village of Tortuguero (spread out on a narrow peninsula), Jungle Lodge and, across the river, the Mawamba Lodge. On the same side of the river are the Ilan-Ilan, the Manatí, then the smaller Aracarí and, farther upriver, the Tortuga Lodge with the research station beyond. The waterway indirectly leads on to Barra del Colorado.

TOURS: Tour boats are the way to go if your schedule is inflexible. They will stop for wildlife photos. With the demise of the government boat, there's no alternative but to charter your own boat, which is a relatively expensive option; unless you have a group, it might be cheaper to fly both ways. Many tour companies travel the canals, and all offer a variety of schedules. Packages run from $155 to $400 depending upon the lodge and length of stay at the lodge. **Costa Rican Expeditions** (☎ 257-0776, 222-0333, fax 257-1665) will either fly or boat you in to their Tortuguero Lodge. (You will receive a banana along with a cartoon.) Limón's **Hotel Matama** (☎ 758-1123) also offers boat trips as far as Parismina where you overnight. *The Mawamba* (☎ 223-2421, fax 222-4932) will take you slowly upriver to their **Mawamba Lodge**, owned by textile magnate Mauricio Dada. A bonus is that you can walk between the village and the lodge. **Agencia Mitur/Tortuguero Jungle Adventures** (☎ 255-2031, 255-2262, fax 255-1946) has trips aboard their *Colorado Prince;* you stay at the Ilan-Ilan Hotel. Their office is on Paseo de Colón, 10 m W of the Hospital de Niños. (There have been some complaints received about their operation.) **"La Jungla"** S. A. (☎ 758-2843, 234-1297) also has launches and tours. One of the least expensive companies, **Cotur** (☎ 233-0155/6579/0133/0226, fax 233-0778) busses you to Moín where you board either the *Miss Caribe* or the *Miss America* to the Jungle Lodge. **Adventure Tours** (☎ 232-4063), affiliated with Río Colorado Lodge in Barra Colorado, offers a number of packages, including a trip up to the Nicaraguan border. (See trip description in the "Puerto Viejo de la Sarapiquí" section.) **Laguna Lodge** (☎ 255-3740) will also take you up. The *Francesca* (☎ 226-0986), piloted by local ecology experts Fran and Modesto Watson, will take you on a trip for $160 pp including meals, accommodation, and services. If you wish to visit the canals and come back the same day, Limón's **Laura Tropical Tours** (☎ 758-2410) will accommodate you. The $65 fee includes lunch.

THE TRIP UP THE RIVER: The first thing you notice is the wide expanse of the greenish-brown water, flanked on both sides by tropical vegetation. You steam upriver, passing yellow highway signs denoting the kilometers to nearby villages at intersections, the wildlife-filled greenery reflected on either side. Along the river, you might see howler or spider monkeys, caymans, turtles, white egrets, great blue herons, night herons, toucans, blue-green kingfishers, a sleeping sloth snuggling on a branch overhead, floating water hyacinths, or mud turtles jumping and splashing in the water. If you stop for a moment you can hear the intense hum of insects contrasting with the surf pounding in the distance. You may want to stop at the **Jalova Ranger Station**, which will involve paying the admission fee ($15 unless you have a pass). There is a new nature trail and a Visitors' Center here. After the ranger station, the canal widens and everything save nature vanishes.

ON YOUR OWN: The *Gran Delta*, the government-run launch, is no longer running. Although you will still have to pay $50 pp RT ($25 OW), doing it on your own has clear cost advantages over going on a tour. However, you have to have time and be flexible in your standards. **Alfred Brown** (☎ 758-0824) and **Modesto and Fran Watson** (☎ 226-0896) both take passengers. Another alternative is to go to the dock at Moín around 8 AM and see what's available. In the village, ask Albert and Dama next to the Pancana Restaurant concerning return trips. Transport (around $8) is also available to the Geest banana plantations near Cariari. From there you can get transport to San José. Priority is given to village residents. Call the *pulpería* at ☎ 710-6716 for information.

GETTING HERE: Travelair (☎ 220-3054, 232-7883 fax 220-0413) flies here. You can also fly into Tortuguero with Costa Rica Expeditions in a smaller plane for $90 OW; they land at the airport near the research station. As you depart from Pavas airport, you pass over the suburbs of San José and across the majestic, generally cloud-shrouded mountainous expanse of Braulio Carrillo National Park – tropical greenery at its most splendid. As if conducting an ecology lesson along its flight route, the plane next passes over huge banana plantations and stretches of deforested land. The canals and beaches of Tortuguero come into view just before the plane touches down.

    coming via Moín: The only hotel here is the Moín Caribe (see "accommodations," under Limón, below). Two *típico* restaurants are here. Ask permission to visit the compound of JAPDEVA, the government agency in charge of the area's economic development, where you can observe river port operations underway. Just N from Moín is the an ICT-run park and farther N, at Playa Barra de Matina, is a refuge for nesting sea turtles.

LODGES: Most of the lodges here can take you fishing upriver; for fishing lodges on this coast see Barra del Colorado, above. One of the nicest places to stay and eat here is Costa Rica Expeditions' **Tortuga Lodge** (☎ 222-0333, 527-0766, fax 257-1665; Apdo. 6941, San José 1000; Dept. 235, Box 025216, Miami FL 33102-5216). Expensive ($57 and $76 s, $68 and $90 d) but comfortable, the lodge gives you everything you might want, while still being in the heart of the jungle. Three hearty meals ($7.50 breakfast, $12 lunch, and $13 dinner) are served daily, and the family-style meals include things like granola as part of the breakfast, and vegetables, rice, beans, fish, fowl or meat, and soup or salad for lunch and dinner. The trail behind the lodge has a large number of poison dart frogs, and you may see other flora and fauna as well. In front of the lodge, fishing and fruit bats fly over the docks at night and marine toads are found on the ground. Every type of excursion, from fishing to turtle walks, is offered. An unusual feature of the lodge is that none of the doors have locks because there have never been any problems with theft. There's no charge for depositing you on the other side of the river where the beach and the turtle research station are. From there, it's a long but pleasant hike down along the black sand beach to the village of Tortuguero. On the way, you walk by an open-air museum showing the multiple ways plastic has been put to use in modern society. Free admission. If you head in from the coast, there's a trail (good birdwatching) that leads to Mawamba. The mosquitoes will be overjoyed to see you, and giant silky golden web spiders line the path as well.

The **Hotel Ilán-Ilán** (☎ 255-2031/2262, fax 255-1946; Apdo. 91, 1150 San José) is downriver from the Tortuga Lodge and on the same side. They charge $225 for a three-day package. One of the newest lodges, the **El Manatí Ecological Lodge** (☎ 221-6148) offers simple cabins with fan and private bath for $40 d. Breakfast is $5; lunch and dinner are $7. Also on this side of the river, the **Jungle Lodge** (☎ 233-0155/6579, fax 233-0778) is run by Cotur, which has trips ($250 for a three-day package).

Across the river, the 12-room **Aracarí** (☎ 253-3537), which opened in 1993, is basically an annex of the Mawamba down the canal. Rates are $30 s, $45 d; food prices are also lower than the Tortuga Lodge. The 36-room **Mawamba** (☎ 223-2421, fax 255-4039), within walking distance of the village, has similar rates and a swimming pool. A library and conference center are under construction. Both are managed by naturalists. The **Laguna Lodge** (☎/fax 225-3740), situated in the same general area, offers a three-day/two-night tour for $220. Rooms have cold-water baths and ceiling fans. Basic but hearty meals are served family-style, and a variety of tours are available.

Caño Palma Biological Station

An exciting sea excursion from Tortuguero is to the Canadian-run **Estación Bíologica Caño Palma**, which covers 19 acres (40 ha) of tropical lowland forest. It's eight km to the N along the Caño Palma canal, inside the boundaries of the Colorado National Wildlife Reserve. This field station was founded by zoologist Marilyn Cole of the Canadian Organization for Tropical Education and Rainforest Conservation. The station aims to preserve the area, inform the public, and conduct research. Toward this end, it gives slide lectures on the rainforest and its preservation to schoolchildren in Toronto. The surrounding area holds an abundance of wildlife, including jaguars, margays, three species of monkeys, green parrots, toucans, anteaters, sloths, tapirs, and river otters. Studies carried out here include research on migratory birds and on the behavioral patterns of howler monkeys. Visits are free but donations are gratefully accepted. After a brief introduction, you will be taken on a short guided tour of one of the trails. Volunteers are welcome; they must be over 21 and be able to contribute financially towards their stay. The organization is currently running a campaign to purchase land adjacent to the station. Dubbed "Save An Acre," it involves purchasing a quarter-acre for $35 or a full acre for $125; all funds donated will be used for purchasing the land and not for administrative costs. For more information, call Patricio Opay on his beeper at ☎ 296-2626. In Canada ☎ 905-683-2116, fax 416-392-4979, or write COTERC, Box 335, Pickering, Ontario, Canada LIV 2R6.

VILLAGE ACCOMMODATION: If you're on a tight budget, you'll have to stay in the village, populated by a mix of African-Americans, white Ticos, and the descendants of Mosquito Indians. The peaceful environs are bordered on one side by pounding surf and rustling palms, while the other side is lined with houses facing the canal. Dogs sleep in the sun, and chickens cluck about. One disadvantage of staying here is that there's no backup generator. You all sweat together when it breaks down. The other disadvantage is that you can be relaxing and all of a sudden a group of 30 tourists will appear in your peripheral vision and march right through, video cameras in hand. **Sabina's Cabanas** (around $5, more expensive with shared bath) are a clean and pleasant alternative. The only problem with the place is that Sabina is not the friendliest of souls. Similarly priced but probably superior, the **Meryscar** is 200 m S of the information booth. Low-budget **Cabinas Brisas del Mar** is another. If Miss Junie has secured the money, she may have finished her hotel, next to her restaurant. The Aracarí management is also planning a hotel in the village, which will be in the inexpensive-moderate range. You can stay upriver at **Cabinas Tatané** (☎ 222-2175, fax 223-1609 for package tour info), whose owner (Marco Zamora) will come and get you in his boat. He can also guide you to turtles. To stay at any of these places, leave a message with Olger Riviera at the *pulpería* (☎ 710-6716); the owners should call back and confirm. Meals here are $4-$5 for what would cost you $2 in San José. Eat at **Tio Leo's** restaurant, **Comidas Miss Junie**, the **Meryscar, Soda El Dolar**, or the **Pacana Restaurante**, which entertains with natural history videos at night. You can also try **Sabina's** and the **Abastecedor Riversan**. If you're staying in town, the best things to do are to hang your hammock and relax, hike the visitor's trail behind the ranger's station (good wildlife viewing opportunities), and rent a boat or canoe to see the wildlife. This will cost around $1.50-$4 per hour and a guide is often included in the rates; it's considerably cheaper than going with the lodges and may be preferable. Everything in town is expensive, and many items are unobtainable; bring what you need with you from San José or from home.

GETTING AROUND: Locals give tours (in groups of up to 10, the maximum permitted by law) of the turtle breeding grounds. The cost is $2 pp (discounts for parties of four or more). Tickets are sold daily from 4-6 PM at the park's information kiosk. The ideal way to experience the wonder of this park is to rent a dugout canoe (*cacuya*) from a Tortuguero villager (make sure that yours has a plastic bailer). A guide will accompany you for about $10 pd. Park it beside a bank, and take in the thousands of sounds that emerge. For those accustomed to the deafening noise of the city, it is wondrous to discover these sounds of a natural world that exists and functions quite apart from the will or regulation of humanity. The best times to go are very early in the morning (when the lodge boats are not present, but the animals are) and late in the afternoon. The advantage of a smaller boat is that you can maneuver in close to shore.

night tours: All lodges and many local guides run night tours on the river. If you go with Costa Rica Expeditions, they use a giant halogen lamp. You might see a napping tiger heron, a boat billed heron, the red eyeshine of a submerged crocodile, a "rat" (opossum) on a palm, and a variety of lizards. Stop and listen to the sounds of the night and be aware that you are truly in a faraway place.

HIKING: A hike up 328-ft (100-m) **Cerro Tortuguero**, the park's highest point, affords an overview of the canal system. Local legend maintains that a turtle-shaped magnetic rock inside a cave on this mountain attracts the ferromagnetic crystals within the turtles' brains. One story has it that the rock revolves, drawing the turtles in, and then returns to its original position. Some locals raised a stink when gravel was removed from the mountain to pave the airstrip, maintaining that the mountain would be altered and the turtles would not return! A nice walk is along the beach down to or from the village of Tortuguero and on to the frequently waterlogged *El Gavilán* nature trail (or the new self-guiding trail), both of which run in back of the park headquarters. (Payment of park entrance fee is required.)

INFORMATION AND SHOPPING: The **Joshua B. Powers Information Kiosk** is in the village. The displays tell the history of the area. One of the best places to get information and recommendations is at **The Jungle Shop** (☎ 710-6716), a store run by Elvin and Antoinette Gutiérrez, which is across from the Soda El Dolar. The Caribbean Conservation Corps' fine quarterly newsletter, *Velador*, will keep you informed of developments in the park. Join as an individual for $35 or as a family for $50. Write Box 2866, Gainesville FL 32602. To join by phone, ☎ 800-678-7853. Visa/MasterCard accepted.

GREEN TURTLE RESEARCH STATION: The Caribbean Conservation Corporation, organized in 1959 by Dr. Archie Carr, operates two permanent field research facilities: one is in the Bahamas and the other is this station. Acquired in 1963, the original was built in the 1940s as temporary quarters for land surveyors with the United Fruit Company. A new biological research station opened in August 1995. Here you may visit the H. Clay Frick Natural History Visitor Center, which features full-color displays as well as information about the area's sea turtles. A video is shown and there is a gift shop that helps fund programs here. It's open daily from 10 to noon and from 2 to 5:30. **volunteering:** The Caribbean Conservation Corp offers one-and two-week packages for volunteers here. For more information, see Volunteering, page 163.

EGGLAYING: Largest of the sea turtles, leatherbacks nest on the beach primarily in March and April and hatch from May through June; they are also occasionally found through to the start of the green turtle nesting season in July. Continuing on from July to September, 1,000-4,000 green sea turtle females lay annually in Tortuguero, the largest such colony in the Americas. Solitary and rarely encountered, the hawksbill also nests here from July to September. The first recorded observation of egglaying was by the Dutch in 1592. Turtles lay eggs at night, from 8 PM to 5 AM.

You are required to go with a guide if you want to see the egglaying. Flashlight and camera flash are prohibited because you may frighten a mother arriving to nest, sending her lumbering back towards the water. After searching for a spot beyond the high tide, the mother turtle becomes totally involved in digging the nest, shoveling out the round nest with her paddle-shaped hind legs. Crouching over the nest, which may reach 164 inches (50 cm) in depth, she expels an average of 100 eggs, together with a lubricating fluid. After covering the nest with sand, she returns to the sea. During the two-hour procedure, she heaves continual sighs and her eyes tear, presumably to clear her eyes of sand. Two months later, the hatchlings face the world's greatest obstacle course as they race to the sea. Very few survive to breeding age. No turtle tagged here has been found nesting on any other beach, and genetic tests confirm that green turtles only nest on the beach where they were born. For further information about sea turtles, consult the Caribbean Conservation Corps' superbly informative brochure *Tortuguero's Sea Turtles*.

FROM TORTUGUERO: Many lodges can transport you up to Barra del Colorado at a cost. You can also charter a boat (also very expensive) or get a ride on a passing coconut barge. Besides flying back, you can take the canal route, which may be part of your tour. Because the canal to Moín became silted up after the 1991 earthquake and because of changing land use patterns, many boats use a route down to El Carmen, a banana plantation near Siquirres. If you pass through this seemingly endless plantation, you'll note the different colored ribbons securing the plastic bags to the plants. These indicate different stages of maturity and range from yellow, blue and green to red, which indicates a mature plant. If you stop at the processing center, you'll see the group of workers who sort, spray, and pack the bananas dipping their hands directly into fungicide-imbued water. The first quality (for export), second quality (for internal consumption), and third quality (for cattle feed) are separated, with the rejects being thrown in an overhead rack. The best bananas are placed on trays and fumigated with hand sprayers, labeled, and then thrown into boxes for export.

Limón

Hot and humid Limón (pop. 65,000), the first town to be successfully established in the nation's tropical lowlands, was originally founded with the intention of rivaling Puntarenas as a coffee export port. Instead, it ended up devoted mainly to banana export. Limón was founded in the 1880s in an unpopulated swampy area facing the Atlantic 104 miles (168 km) from San José. By 1927 it had 7,000 inhabitants. In its golden age, it rivaled San José as a commercial center, where North Americans, Jamaicans, Cubans, Panamaneans, Britons, Germans, and Chinese lived and traded. The nation's very first "company" town, Limón fell victim to its own slavish dependence on the banana. Despite the banana's reappearance in the 1950s, Limón never recovered after the industry's initial slump. An earthquake on April 22, 1991 hit the town hard. Frustration with slow response on the part of the government led protesters to block the streets with rickety trucks on May 18, 1992. The protests, which lasted four days, were quelled with tear gas and 90 were arrested. Although the head of the Rural Guard alleged that the protesters were "drug addicts and criminals," the protests did spur government action. In 1993, a five-day campaign was mounted to arrest drug dealers and seize contraband. "Operation Rasta" made no arrests and found no drugs. An internal investigation a month later revealed the reason: some security officials were in cahoots with traffickers and had tipped them off! Today, Limón is a small, sweaty town with atmosphere galore.

GETTING HERE: The bus leaves from San José hourly at the terminal directly across from the former train station (Av. 3 near Parque Nacional). Buy tickets in advance if traveling on a weekend or holiday. **by car:** Open since 1987, the Guápiles Highway, a toll road, has shortened driving time from San José to 165 km (102 miles) or 2¼ hours. A tunnel runs under Barva and through Parque Nacional Braulio Carrillo to Guápiles, then on to Limón. **by air:** Travelair (☎ 220-3054, 232-7883, fax 220-0413) flies three times a week.

GETTING AROUND: Limón is laid out similarly to San José, except that there is no segregation of odd and even streets, there are no street signs, and no locals are aware of the numbering system. Locations are usually given in terms of how many meters it is from the market, park, or small radio station. One positive feature amidst all of this confusion is that many residents speak English – or at least Jamaica-talk English. The main street is Av. 2 ("Market Street"), which extends E from the train station to Vargas Park near the waterfront. Av. 3, 4, and on up, run parallel and to the N. Calle 1 runs N-S along Vargas Park. The higher numbered *calles* run parallel to and W of Calle 1. To get to Moín from here, take a public bus, which runs past Portete en route. Taxis wait at the S side of the *mercado* starting in the wee hours of the morning.

SIGHTS: There's not much to see in Limón proper. Other than the bars, the best place to hang out is in **Parque Vargas**. Ask any sloth!

Mainly preoccupied with the fine arts of sleeping and tummy scratching, they occasionally descend to defecate or sip water from the fountains. Across from the park is the cream-colored, stuccoed **Alcaldía** (city hall). The **Ethnohistorical Museum**, containing historical material relevant to the area, is theoretically open Tues.-Sat., 10-5. The market, situated on Av. 2, C. 3/4, is a lively place to visit. Off the town's coast is the small island of **Uvita**, where Columbus anchored during his first voyage. The Asociación China has a Chinese shrine, with a map showing Chinese routes of emigration all over the world; vicious mahjong games – alive with the loud snap of slammed pieces – take place here at night.

Four km N of town there's a small beach at **Playa Bonita** (safe swimming only on the N end) and a rocky overlook at Portete, where local fishermen ply their trade and you can watch lobster traps being prepared. It's possible to buy fish and lobster from these fishermen. Note the dugout canoes here, which are stored under a bamboo shelter along the shore. Two bar-restaurants are here. The 31-acre (12½-ha) **Parque Cariari**, set between Bonita and Portete, has paths, where you can see toucans, parrots, sloths, iguanas, basilisks, and innumerable butterflies. A place to avoid swimming is at Playa Cieneguita, just S of town, which is reported to be the most polluted in the nation.

ACCOMMODATIONS: It's hot here, so you'll probably want to have a room with a fan. Spartan but inexpensive **Hotel Acón** (☎ 758-1010, fax 758-2924) has a/c, disco, and a communal TV; it's centrally located. Write Apdo. 528, Limón. Aged but still charming **Hotel Park** (☎ 758-3476) is at Av. 3, C. 1/2. It charges $20 d. Around the same price are the **Internacional** (☎ 758-0662) at C. 3, Av. 5, and a/c **Hotel Miami** (☎/fax 758-0490; Apdo. 2800, 7300, Limón) at Av. 2, C. 4/5.

low-budget accommodations: The **Hotel Palace** (☎ 758-0419) is across from the Instituto Nacional de Seguros. The **Hotel Cariari** (☎ 758-1395) is next door. Also try around the market (Av. 2, C. 3/4) for the cheapest places, most of which are noisy. These include the **Hotel Oriental** (☎ 758-0117), **Hotel Lincoln** (☎ 758-0074, Av. 5, C. 2/3), **Pensión Los Angeles** (Av. 7, C. 6/7), **Pensión Costa Rica** (1½ blocks E of the Parque Vargas), **Pensión El Sauce, Paraiso** (C. 5, Av. 5/6), rat-infested **Pensión Dorita** (Av. 4, C. 3/4), the **Balmoral**, the **Fung**, the **Linda Vista**, and the **Caballo Blanco**.

outside of town: Located in the port town, the **Moín Caribe** (☎ 758-2436, fax 758-1112) has rooms (around $20 s, $25 d) with fans and TVs. The more deluxe hotels are all near Portete to the N. A few km to the N, inexpensive **Hotel Las Olas** (☎ 758-1414; Apdo. 701, Limón) has fans or a/c, swimming pools, restaurant, satellite TV, and sauna. Inexpensive **Hotel Matama** (☎ 758-1123, fax 758-4499) is near Playa Bonita and has a restaurant and pool. Across the road, **Apartotel Cocorí** (☎/fax 758-2930, 257-4674, 255-3702) offers rooms for $40 d if you reserve directly. It has a reasonable restaurant, a pool, and tours to Tortuguero that leave daily. Nearby, bed and breakfast **Casa de Bamboo** (☎ 758-1653) charges $45 d. One km closer to Limón, expensive ($65 d) **Hotel Maribú Caribe** (☎ 758-4010, fax 758-3541) features round thatched bungalows with a/c, restaurant, car rental, and pools. Write Apdo. 623, 7300 Limón or ☎ 234-0193 in San José. The **Jardín Tropical Azul** (☎ 253-5424) has a/c cabins for $60 d with phone and TV, including breakfast. There are pools, tennis, a basketball cou:t, and a restaurant. Inexpensive and basic **Club Campestre Cahuita** (☎ 758-2861), 14 miles (22 km) to the S of Limón, has swimming pools and restaurants. Camping (from $3) is permitted across the road, and rooms are only available to non-members during slack times.

FOOD: Shrimp and lobster are slightly less expensive than elsewhere around here. Try the a/c dining room of the **Hotel Acón** or, two km to the N, the **Hotel Las Olas**. For Chinese food try the **Cien Kung,** across from the Texaco station at the Palacio Encantador. Inside the Internacional (C. 3, Av. 5) is the Turkeski. La Fuente is at C. 3, Av. 3/4. Also try the American Bar (C. 1, Av. 2 opposite Vargas Park), which has seafood and beef. Market food (Av. 2, C. 3/4) is the cheapest around. The **Soda Gemini** nearby has a good buffet and cakes. **Rasa's** serves international food. Also try the **Apollo Once**, around the corner from the Baptist Church. **Soda Mares** serves fine fruit drinks. **Café Verde** on Av. 3, C. 19/21, near the former train station and the bus stop for San José, offers expresso, capuccino, sandwiches, German pastries, Italian pasta dishes, and salads, as well as Tico breakfasts. Heading along the seawall up to Moín, you first come to the seafood-oriented **Arrecife,** then **Springfield**, which serves typical local food for about $5/meal. Next is the **Manchester,** the deluxe **El Zapote**, and then the **Soda Encanto.** The **Kimbandu** is a pricey and attractively located Caribbean-cuisine restaurant at Playa Bonita. **Ranchita Westphalia,** en route to Cahuita, specializes in former US President George Bush's favorite snack: fresh *chicharrones.*

SERVICES: Two blocks N of the market's E corner, the **Helenik Souvenir Shop and Tourist Information Center** (☎ 758-2086) offers laundry service and tour connections.

ENTERTAINMENT: Hookers and sailors frequent some of the bars. Opening onto the street, the **American Bar** (C. 1, Av. 2 opposite Vargas Park) is a live wire. The **Mark 15** disco is across from the Anglican Church. Also try the **Springfield** on the N outskirts or visit the **Johnny**

Dixon Bar at Playa Bonita. The **Atlantic Cinema** shows films. **note:** Be careful walking in this town at night.

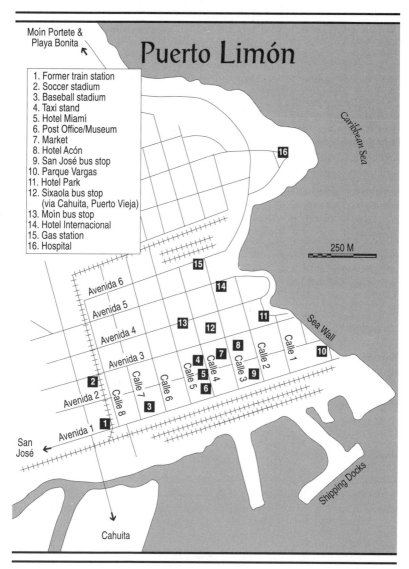

Moín Portete & Playa Bonita

Puerto Limón

1. Former train station
2. Soccer stadium
3. Baseball stadium
4. Taxi stand
5. Hotel Miamí
6. Post Office/Museum
7. Market
8. Hotel Acón
9. San José bus stop
10. Parque Vargas
11. Hotel Park
12. Sixaola bus stop
    (via Cahuita, Puerto Vieja)
13. Moín bus stop
14. Hotel Internacional
15. Gas station
16. Hospital

Caribbean Sea

250 M

Avenida 6
Avenida 5
Avenida 4
Avenida 3
Avenida 2
Avenida 1

Calle 8
Calle 7
Calle 6
Calle 5
Calle 4
Calle 3
Calle 2
Calle 1

Sea Wall

San José

Cahuita

Shipping Docks

EVENTS AND FESTIVALS: Taking place around October 12 (the former Columbus Day, now known as the *Día de las Culturas*), Limón's *carnaval* features calypso and reggae, parades, and dancing in the streets. It had its origins in 1949 when Alfred King, returning from Panama, brought the idea back with him. The celebration has its locus around the market where there are gambling and food stalls. Typically, events take place from Tues. to Sun., with bullflights, a clown parade, horse races, art exhibits, a bathing suit parade, volleyball contests, fireworks, and an eight-hour concert featuring an international selection of bands. The stretch from Escuela General Tomás Guardia to the Black Star Line Building in the center of town becomes an alcohol-free zone, with craft and food stands, art exhibitions, and a daily calypso contest. A shuttle also runs to Uvita, where there are food stands and music. (If planning to attend, be sure to book a hotel room way in advance. The *Tico Times* generally prints a schedule of events.) The Limón area celebrates **May Day** with cricket matches, picnics, quadrille dances, and domino matches. A surfing championship takes place annually at Playa Bonita, N of town.

FROM LIMON: The bus to Playa Bonita, Portete, and Moín leaves hourly from C. 4, Av. 4 in front of Radio Casino in Limón. There's no bus station, so tickets are sold in offices by the bus stops. In addition to San José, buses also run S through Cahuita and Puerto Viejo to Bribri and Sixaola, bordering Panama. There's also a direct bus (via Cahuita and Puerto Viejo) to Manzanillo. It leaves at 6 and 2:30. Buy tickets the day before (or at least several hours ahead to avoid the rush) and arrive early to secure a seat. If going to the Black Beach area of Cahuita (hotels Atlantida, Jaguar, etc.), get off at La Union stop on the main highway and walk the one km in. **by train:** The "jungle train" runs no more and all train service was halted by presidential decree in 1995.

Heading South from Limón

Aviarios del Caribe (Aviary of the Caribbean)

Set 30 km S of Limón and 10 km N of Cahuita, this small bed and breakfast and wildlife sanctuary has been established by Luis and Judy Arroyo, a Tico and *norteamericano* couple who met in Alaska. It is one of the last bastions in the area against the encroaching banana plantations. Boat tours ($25 pp) are offered from 6:30 to 3. You will see some of the 247 species of birds that have been identified so far, along with other creatures such as *caimán*s, monkeys, and river otters. There are poison dart and other frogs on display that are captured and then returned to the wild after a few days. Another exhibit shows the interior of a leafcutting ant nest. The caged birds on display were donated and/or born in captivity, so they cannot survive in the wild. You may have the opportunity to meet Buttercup, the couple's pet baby sloth. Its mother was killed on the road. The rooms are spacious and priced

moderately (at $60 d), with breakfast included. For more informa-
tion/reservations fax 758-4459 or write Apdo. 569, 7300 Limón.

Orquídeas Mundo

This nursery run by Pierre Dubois, a former botanist at Montreal's
Botanical Gardens, was established to pursue his lifelong dream of
hybridizing rare SE Asian orchids. Dubois and his wife and three
children live in a school bus, subsisting on ducks and dried bananas.
Dubois gives guided tours ($5 pp), one of which surveys his nursery
and another which explores nearby trails, where insects, birds, and
ornamentals abound. To get here cross the Río Estrella bridge and then
turn right at the sign that says Penhurst. The Dubois family lives 600 m
down the road on the right. For more information, fax 758-2818 or write
Orquídeas Mundo, Apdo. 575, Limón 7300.

Hitoy Cerere Biological Reserve
(Reserva Biológica Hitoy Cerere)

The name of this isolated 22,620-acre (9,154-ha) reserve stems from the
combination of two Native American names applied to two rivers in
the area: *Hitoy* means "woolly" in the sense of mossy or covered with
vegetation, and *cerere* means clear waters. Set between the heavily cultivated Estrella and Telirre river valleys, its rugged topography preserved the area from development. Steep peaks, which include
Bobócara (2,618 ft, 798 m) and Bitácara (3,363 ft, 1,025 m), have served
to isolate it even from the three surrounding Indian settlements.

FLORA AND FAUNA: Rising to heights of 100 ft (30 m) or more, the
reserve's lofty trees include the wild cashew, the Santa María, balsa,
and calyptrogyne or "dovetail" tree. There are also a large number of
medicinal plants and trees within the reserve, as well as over 200 species of orchids. More than 118 inches (3,000 mm) of rain fall annually,
and the average temperature is between 72.5° and 77°F (22.5-25°C).
Wildlife include three species of opossum, pizotes, sloths, anteaters,
agoutis, pacas, racoons, margays, kinkajous, otters, jaguars, tapirs,
white-faced and howler monkeys. The 115 species of birds include the
cayenne squirrel cuckoo and the blue-headed parrot.

PRACTICALITIES: It's accessible by four-wheel-drive vehicle. You
can get taxi service from Finca 16 at the Estrella Valley Standard Fruit
Co. Banana Plantation which, in turn, can be reached by the Valle de la

Estrella bus from Limón. By car, head W from Penhurst. In order to reserve meals and lodging, ☎ 233-5473 about a week beforehand. Camping is permitted. While there are no formal trails, you can follow the ones used by the rangers and the Indians who reside around the reserve's perimeter. **waterfalls:** From the ranger station, head right, cross the river, and continue upstream until you find the falls and swimming hole; a second, less impressive set are around a half-hour upstream. Look for the turnoff on the left leading to a small creek; it's about a km from the ranger station.

Cahuita National Park
(Parque Nacional Cahuita)

Cahuita – a relaxed and somnolent village of about 3,000 – is located by the entrance to Cahuita National Park, one of the nation's most popular attractions. Originally known as "The Bluff," its name was changed to Cahuita – a Spanish language transliteration of two Miskito Indian words, *kawi* (a small tree traditionally used to make dugout canoes) and *ta* (a point of land) – by a 1915 presidential decree. In recent years – following the completion of a road and the establishment of the national park – tourism in the town has grown at a phenomenal pace. Much of the popularity stems from its verdancy (in comparison to the aridity of the Pacific coast), its easy accessiblity, and the pleasant onshore breeze here. So far, however, the town retains its character and shows no signs of being transformed. Do note that theft is on the rise here (in tandem with the crack problem) so take appropriate precautions.

    flora, fauna, and the reef: While the most famed life is underwater, there's plenty to see on the ground as well. Thousands of coconut trees line the beaches, and it's easy to see monkeys as you walk along. The 593-acre (240-ha) reef is outlined by the seaward waves that break against it. It generally is less than three feet deep near the coast and in places where live coral grow, though up to 21 ft. (seven m) deep in the several channels. There are 34 species of coral, over 100 of seaweed, and 500 species of fish. The water is clearest from Feb. to April. There are also two old shipwrecks complete with cannons.

GETTING HERE: Direct buses to Sixaola (bypassing Limón) leave from Av. 4, C. Central/1 at 6, 2:30 and 4:30, passing both park entrances. From Limón, buses (one hour) leave from Av. 4, C. 3/4 at 5, 10, 1, and 4. Sixaola is about 25 minutes farther down the road. If you get a 7 AM bus from San José, there should be no problem meeting the 10 AM bus out of Limón. Sit on the left to get the best views. Along the way, you pass stands offering *pipas* (drinking coconuts), as well as vast banana plantations.

ENVIRONMENTAL PROBLEMS: Sadly, the reef is dying because of the production practices on the banana plantations. Trees are cut along river banks and replaced with banana plants. They allow the soil to float downstream. Meanwhile, the agricultural chemicals flow freely into irrigation canals, which run into the rivers. The combination of sedimentation with agrochemicals has suffocated some 60% of the reef. The fish supply is also decreasing owing to the fact that the larger fish were drawn in to feast on the smaller ones, which have now been killed off. In July 1990, in a bizarre incident, an estimated half-million fish were discovered floating belly-up in the Río Matina, apparent victims of phorate, a chemical used on the plantations. Government officials blamed the poisoning on fishermen! Results of the government lab tests and investigation remain sealed.

The Talamanca Region

Cahuita is the first area you'll visit within the area of Talamanca. Virtually inaccessible until the late 1970s, Talamanca is the poorest but greenest section of the nation. This densely forested region, shaped like a triangle, remained untouched until the end of the 19th C. Today, it retains considerable charm. Its name derives from the Miskito Indian word, *Talamalka*, which means "place of blood," referring to the end of a hunt. You can still hear such Jamaican-style phrases as "How you keeping?" and "How de morning?" The region is a relaxed melting pot of Native American, African-American, and Spanish cultures. Although this was once the place to come for those who wanted to rough it, the a/c resorts with swimming pools are moving in. Tourism as a monoculture has replaced *cacao*. *Cacao* was driven out by a virus that mysteriously appeared at the same time the banana plantations were attempting to buy up land in the area.

Most of the indigenous peoples did not make this their original home. After the Bribri, Guatuso, and Cabécar tribes burned down several missions and killed priests, they were forcibly resettled here and in Guanacaste. Although the impact of tourism has caused a shift away from traditional life for the largely African-American coastal dwellers, the Bribri and Cabécar peoples still maintain many of their customs and ancient beliefs side by side with their jeans and radios. The three indigenous peoples with reserves in the area are the Talamanca Bribri, Talamanca Cabécar, and Kékoldi. Although the tribes theoretically control what happens within their own borders, Oceana Minera, a Canadian mining multinational, was granted a permit in

1993 to prospect for copper and gold within the reserve. The tribal leaders are protesting the invasion along with attempts by the legislature to make it easier to access mineral and petroleum concessions on native reserves in the Talamanca region.

Owing largely to longstanding prejudice, the area still remains neglected by the government. The ICT's idea of doing something beneficial for visitors is to put up large and garish blue signs indicating "hotel," "*cabina*," and "restaurant" right in front of hotels, *cabinas*, and restaurants. Only the freeway and the Howard Johnsons are lacking. Meanwhile, the roads are terrible, sewage systems and running water are nonexistent, and potentially dangerous beaches with undertow remain unmarked.

ORIENTATION: The town has wide gravel streets with *cabinas* and restaurants interspersed at intervals. The bus stop is next to the miniature "park" and across from Salon Vaz. At one end of the wide gravel main street is Hotel Cahuita and the park entrance, while the Black Beach is in the other direction. The road heading towards the water leads to Cabinas Palmer and, around the corner and down to the left, to Surfside and then Edith's. The road to the Black Beach passes Miss Edith's, then the Guardia Civil and continues past sandy stretches punctuated by coral outcrops. A *verduras y frutas* stand is 300 ft (100 m) off the Black Beach road to the left; watch for the sign. A small *soda* stands across from the soccer field. This is a beautiful road to walk or cycle. On the way, you pass blooming hibiscus, birds, palms, giant green iguanas – their finned backs undulating like a pack of cards being shuffled – while the pounding surf is off to the right. **note:** Moray's Tours offers a map which lists most (but not all) of the hotels and restaurants.

HISTORY: Cahuita's name comes from the indigenous words *kawi* (mahogany) and *ta* (point). Created in 1970, it includes 2,636 acres (1,067 ha) of land and 1,483 acres (600 ha) of coral reefs that are 1,600 ft (500 m) offshore. Only 20% of the local farmers were reimbursed as promised after the park's creation. Problems here include runoff of silt from banana plantations, which is killing the reef, and poaching of turtle eggs and iguanas, which is decimating local populations. Perhaps the combined effect of years of poor attitude and insensitivity on the part of the national government caused the community to react as they did when René Castro, the Minister of Natural Resources, unilaterally acted to raise park fees for foreigners to $15 pd on September 1 1994. Almost immediately, townspeople took over the park entrances in order to prevent the new edict from being enforced. In addition,

Cahuita Tours owner Tony Mora filed a motion before the Supreme Court seeking an injunction against the fees. In response to the take-over, the ministry published a quarter-page ad in *La Nación* advising visitors against visiting the park. Minister Castro maintained that Cahuita "is a zone where the tourists who go experiment with attitudes we do not want in our country... Those types of visitors (read low-budget backpackers), unfortunately for them, will have to find them-selves another country." At press time, the park remained in the hands of locals and entrance was free of charge, but this may have changed by the time of your arrival.

VISITING THE NATIONAL PARK: Cross a bridge down past Hotel Cahuita to enter the park. Several picnic tables are near the entrance. The sandy beach stretches as far as the eye can see. Both the beach and the nature trail behind it come to a halt at a river, which must be crossed. The trail is alive with bright blue morpho (birdwing) butter-flies, land crabs, birds and, at times, monkeys. If you continue, you'll need a good pair of shoes or windsurfing sandals. Soon, you'll reach a shallow stream, the Río Perezoso, colored red from the tannic acid re-leased by decomposed vegetation. The ocean all along this stretch is smooth and translucent because the surf is breaking on the reef way offshore.

ACCOMMODATIONS: Although no longer a backpacker's rustic paradise, much of the accommodation here is fairly inexpensive (around $10 pp or less, depending upon numbers and location). Bene-fiting from a $500 million project supported by the California Coop-erative Federation and the National Union of the Development of Cooperatives, *cabinas* are flourishing and have become a veritable mom-and-pop industry. The more imaginative ones are operated by the local Italian, Swiss, and German population. The rest of the bunch all incorporate the identical concrete box design and are set in rows. If you're on a tight budget, it's better to travel in a group, which reduces the cost considerably. To contact all of these hotels, ☎ 758-1515 and ask for the extension indicated below. Some of them have one price for for-eigners and a secret lower price for locals. Most of the town's lodging is listed here, but there are still others if these are full. Look around first and bargain if you plan to stay for awhile. Taking the first diago-nal right before you get into town and heading down the road brings you to inexpensive **Cabinas Coriosos,** which is just around the corner from Restaurante Típico. Delapidated but atmospheric, inexpensive **Hotel Cahuita** (ext. 201) is conveniently located next to the park en-trance. It has a restaurant. Their *cabinas* with fans and bath are dark. Next door, low-budget/inexpensive **Cabinas Sol y Mar** (ext. 237) has rooms with private baths; the upstairs ones have balconies. Across the street from these two, **Cabinas Vaz** (ext. 218) is also in the low-budget/inexpensive range and is owned by the same strongman who operates the bar up the street. Low-budget **Cabinas Rhode Island** are set behind them. One of the superior places to stay, **Cabinas Palmer** (ext. 243) charges in the low-budget range for its room in the house and a bit more for its facing set of *cabinas*. It's down from Salon Vaz, on the way to the beach. Low-budget/inexpensive **Cabinas Jenny** (ext. 256) is just down the road by the water and has hammocks. Low-budget/inexpensive **Cabinas Brisas del Mar** (ext. 267) is across from the school and near the ocean. Another really nice place to stay is low-budget/inexpensive **Surf Side Cabinas** (ext. 246, 203) to the left behind the school; accommodation ranges from single to quad. Inexpensive **Cabinas Tito** (ext. 286) is near the Rural Guard. Inexpensive **Cabinas Colibri** (ext. 263) offers rooms with private baths, hammocks, and kitchens. The **Pastry Shop**, next door, has one *cabina*. Others in this area include inexpensive **Cabinas Sulila**, and **Cabinas Smith. note:** The problem with virtually all of these is that you have to endure the pulsations from Salon Vaz until the wee hours every single night. Those who need quiet to sleep should position themselves farther out.

Black Beach accommodations: Out of range of the pulsing nightly riddims pouring from Salon Vaz, the Black Beach area has a wide range of hostelries. More will definitely have opened by the time you arrive. Near the ball field and about a km from town, inexpensive-moderate thatched-roof **Cabinas Atlántida** (ext. 213) has fans and offers breakfast. They have a pool and a chained monkey and caged toucans on the premises. Rates are $52 s, $57 d, $64 t. Offering three quiet, large bungalows with patios, private baths, and fans, Spanish-style **El Encanto Bed and Breakfast** (fax 798-0652; Apdo. 1234, Limón) is set amidst gardens and has a patio restaurant. Rates run around $45 d with breakfast, $40 without. The **Taller de Artesanias** (Letty's) has low-budget rooms. Italian-run with two-storey stone and wood structures, inexpensive **Cabinas Black Beach** (ext. 251) hold up to four. Next door, **Jardín Rocallo** charges $30 for rooms (longer-term discount) with a kitchen and refrigerator. Write Apdo. 1152, Limón. Advertising for surfers, Soda Ciancla offers low-budget and spartan *cabinas* called **Cabinas El Ancla**. To its rear, attractive and inexpensive **Apartamiento Iguana** consists of two small houses for rent with kitchens for $50 per night. Inexpensive (about $40 pp) **Topo's Cabinas** are run by a European reptile specialist. German-run **Marion's** has three low-budget rooms, which don't have much privacy. Fairly remote is **Colibri Paradise**. One of the best places to stay for people who want peace, security, good food, and comfort, **Hotel Jaguar** (ext. 238, ☎ 226-3775, fax 226-

4693; Apdo. 7046, 1000 San José) offers very large and quite attractive rooms with queen-sized beds and attached bath with hot shower. There are no fans, but the ceilings are high, air circulation is excellent, and the rooms cool down just fine at night. It has an internationally flavored restaurant with quite innovative cuisine; breakfast is included in the price. Dietary preferences will be catered to; their vegetarian dishes are also well prepared. Owner/manager Paul Pigneaule is the brains behind the operation and his recipes are quite original. There are some short trails behind the lodge, which also faces the beach. Rooms are $30 s and $55 d.

Way up at the end of the road, low-budget/inexpensive **Cabinas Algebra** offer one *cabina* for up to three without kitchen and a second for four with kitchen. One night is free if you stay for a week. Swiss-owned and managed **Chalet Hibiscus** has two houses (each accommodates four to six) facing a coral rock beach. They rent for around $100 per night; two more with a pool in front ($80) are across the road. Less expensive *cabinas* ($45) are also available. They have a small gift shop. For reservations, write Apdo. 943, Limón. The **Magellan Inn** (fax 798-0652) is a set of *cabinas* with pool, restaurant, and bar; it is at Playa Viquez, and rates are $55 d, including continental breakfast and tax. Run by a local lady, **Ruby's** consists of five low-budget units. Just down the road towards the beach from the La Union bus stop is inexpensive 12-unit **Cabinas Arco Iris**. Also here are small and low-budget **Cabinas Margarita** (ext. 205), which have fish painted on the outside, inexpensive closely set **Cabinas Viviene**, and **Vishnu**. Run by Italians from Bologna and next to the Jaguar, **Bungalow Malú** offers three low-budget/inexpensive and very attractive *cabinas*. They contain two single beds and one queen, as well as a refrigerator. You can cook at their *ranchito*. Next down to the right, you will find **Casa Suecia**. A house for rent is also on the right. **Cabinas Piscina Natural** is another possibility in the area.

CAMPING: If you're game to camp, the only formal campgrounds are at the other park entrance at Puerto Vargas. Showers, toilets, and water are available; watch your things. There's also something of an informal campground near the edge of town on the road towards Punta Uva.

FOOD: Depending upon where you're staying, you may find yourself spending more per meal than per night. Most of the food is higher priced than in San José, but without a corresponding increase in quality. Many of the restaurants have near-identical menus and prices, offering Italian food, sandwiches, and other dishes popular with tourists. Still the least expensive place and also one of the best is **Miss Edith's**; she has some vegetarian specialties. Sadly, her restaurant is the only one around that serves local food. Be prepared for a long wait.

The standout on the gourmet side is definitely the **Hotel Jaguar** out in Black Beach. Offering seafood, **Vista del Mar** is near the park, as is the **Cahuita National Park Restaurant** and the **Hotel Cahuita**. A friendly lady sells baked goods and drinks at the park entrance. **Sol y Mar** and **Cabinas Vaz** both have restaurants, as does **Cabinas Surfside**. Near Cabinas Vaz, the **Defi** has seafood, pizza, and veggie goodies. Screened in and attractive, **El Típico** is up the road and off to the left. The **Pizza Revolution Vegetarian Restaurant**, near the park, may be revolutionary in some unknown way but it is not exclusively vegetarian. There are a number of new restaurants, including thatched **Palenque Luisa** and the **Fiesta Italian Restaurant** next to Cahuita Tours. Out down the road, **Cabinas Black Beach** has a restaurant. **Brigitte** has an inexpensive restaurant that serves a number of vegetarian dishes. On a side road, **Restaurante Vishnu** offers yogurt and other healthy food. **Bananas** is the name of Cabinas Algebra's attractive porch-top restaurant serving up local cuisine. Still farther on, **Margaritaville**, a Canadian-owned organic food restaurant, is open for dinner. A meal is about $5 and includes fresh baked bread. On the road from Black Beach to the main road is **Cafeteria Vishnu**. Offering pasta, crêpes, and pizza, **Pizzeria El Cactus** is across the road. In front of Salon Vaz, there's an old lady who sells reasonably cheap fish or chicken dinners. There are a number of stores and *pulperías*, including **Pulpería Super Kris** in Black Beach.

SERVICES: Cahuita Tours (ext. 232) changes travelers checks, offers tours (glass bottomed boat and others) and rents snorkeling equipment and bicycles. **Moray's** (☎/fax ext. 216) rents rooms, offers tours (snorkeling, to Tortuguero, horseback, and others), rents scuba and snorkeling equipment, and serves as a booking agent. Surfboards and snorkeling equipment can also be rented near El Típico. There's a book exchange near Brigitte's in Black Beach. **José McCloud** (ext. 256 or contact at Soda Vishnu) is a local tour guide who offers jungle hiking. Others include **Walter Cunningham** (ext. 229) and **Carlos Mairena** (ext. 288). At Black Beach, **Brigitte** (Apdo. 1152, Limón) rents horses and offers tours, which include lunch at her restaurant. Be sure to check out her collection of poison dart frogs. Feel free to use Cliff's tennis courts, next to the Hotel Margaritaville on the Black Beach road. Cliff may even take you on for a game. Along the Black Beach road, **Tienda de Artesanía** sells local crafts, including jewelry. Vendors sell Guatemalan goods near the park entrance, and the **Cocomico Boutique** is next to the Hotel Cahuita.

ENTERTAINMENT: The local hot spot is **Salon Vaz**, a typical bar with a large "disco" in back and lots of cool Rastaphonians hanging out. Watch the scene as the German girls flirt and often throw themselves at the guys, in pursuit of a "Caribbean experience." Condom usage is unknown; the men believe that post-coital squeezing of lime on top of their tool is sufficient to prevent AIDS and other diseases. **Bar Hannia** nearby plays reggae as well. The **Defi** has reggae on weekends.

FROM CAHUITA: Buses to Limón run at 6:30, 10:15, 12:15, 1:30, and 5. The express bus departs at 6:50, 9:15, and 4. The buses may be either early or late, so get there ahead of time. Returning buses leave at 5, 8, 10, and 3 for Limón, and for San José at 6 and 2:30. These times may change, so double-check them.

Puerto Viejo de Talamanca

This "Old Harbor," surrounds a small bay with still waters and beautiful black sand beaches. The lifestyle here gives new meaning to the term "laid back." Winding around the coast, the road unveils its beauty at every turn as you approach. Children play in front of the crashing surf. The capsized barge at the village entrance once was used to carry black sand for export. Although this is fast changing in the wake of megabuck development, the inhabitants here still have an attitude of innocence towards foreigners no longer found in places such as Jamaica. The area is relatively compact. There is a map in front of ATEC, the local Progressive Alternative Tourism Association, which shows all of the listings in this section.

GETTING HERE: Direct buses (four hours and 195 km, ☎ 221-0524) from San José depart at 6, 1:30, and 3:30; these run via Cahuita all the way to Bribri, and on to Sixaola on the Panamanian border. To arrange a ride into Puerto Viejo from El Cruce (the crossroads), where this bus leaves you, ☎ 758-3844 or 758-0854 two days in advance. Otherwise, it's a walk of a couple of miles into town, unless you stay at the outlying lodges. A direct bus leaves from the same stop in San José at 3:30. Buses from San José to Puerto Limón leave hourly from the NE corner of Parque Nacional (2½ hours). From there, buses to Sixaola that enter Puerto Viejo (1½ hours) depart at 5, 10, 1, and 4. From Limón you can also take a bus directly to Manzanillo; it leaves at 6 and 2. From La Cruce on, the road is unpaved. Plans are to pave it, which could easily flood the village with tourists.

ACCOMMODATIONS: New hotels here have been sprouting up rapidly. While the area is fast becoming overdeveloped and increasingly upscale, good values can still be found. However, you have to count on spending $8 pp, up from $3 just a few years back. Be aware that the area packs out around Christmas and Easter, as well as on certain high season weekends. The first places you come to on the way here are also two of the best.

A 49-acre (20-ha) private reserve with nature trails, **Nature Lodge Chimuri** (message: ☎/fax 798-1844) has Bribri-style cabins set 1,500 ft (500 m) from the beach. Mauricio Salazar and his Austrian wife Colocha have three two-person cabins for $23 and one four-person cabin for $33. Horseback rides, night walks ($12 pp), visits to its butterfly farm, and camping trips to the Indian reservation are also available. Bikes and rubber boots can be rented by visitors. For more information, contact Mauricio Salazar, Cabinas Chimuri, Puerto Viejo de Limón, Talamanca. **Note:** visitors not staying at the lodge must book everything directly through ATEC (☎ 798-4244). With limited facilities, but spectacularly located on the beach, low-budget **Cabinas Black Sands** was originally built by Mauricio Salazar. The new owners have preserved it intact. Both of these places have communal kitchens. Leave a message with Ana or José at ☎ 758-3844 and they will call you back collect. There is also a separately owned *cabina* for rent here.

Farther down the road towards Limón are **Cabinas Azulilla** and **Cabinas BW.** The former has shared kitchens; both are in the inexpensive range. On the way to town around the curve, moderate **Cabinas Playa Negra** (☎ 556-1132) have one nine-person unit with kitchen, TV, and private bath and two four-person units with kitchen and private bath. They have a *soda* that serves fresh fish. Closer to town, **Mr. O'Conner** have one room with private bath and fan for a low-budget rate (three persons maximum). One of the best places to stay in town, **Cabinas Casa Verde** charge around $13 s and $16 d. Write René Kessler, Apdo. 1114, Limón. The **Hotel Maritza** (☎/fax 798-1844) charges inexpensive prices for its new set of *cabinas* behind the hotel; the rooms above the hotel are among the cheapest in town. **Cabinas Ritz** and **Hotel Puerto Viejo** are towards the bottom of the low-budget scale. More expensive are **Cabinas Manuel León** (☎ 758-0854), **Cabinas Anselmo** (only one unit), **Cabinas Stanford** (fans), **Cabinas Támara**, and **Cabinas Recife. Cabinas Frederico** have two units (six persons maximum) for $15, with private bath and stove. **Cabinas Zoyla** have four units at $5 (two person maximum) with private bath. **Cabinas Grant (Bello Horizonte)** have 11 rooms ($20 s, $30 d) and two *cabinas*; for information and reservations, ☎ 758-2845 in Limón. Rates include breakfast at its restaurant. Another alternative is the inexpensive **Pensión Agaricia**, which serves breakfast to guests. Near it are

Cabinas Rico Rico, which are higher priced and feature a communal kitchen. **Cabinas Las Brisas** stand next to the Pulpería Violeta. Low-budget **Cabinas Jacaranda** are next to the Garden Restaurant. Inexpensive **Hotel Pura Vida** is across from the soccer field. About five minutes on foot from the soccer field and into the woods (look for the sign near the goalpost), the low-budget (around $4 pp) **Kiskadee** – run by a delightful retired *norteamericano* woman – offers attractive dorm-style rooms. The kitchen here is available for 50¢ pd extra. It's great for birdwatching. Up another route from the soccer field, **Cashew Jungle Lodging** has a dorm room in the basement of a fantastic house for a slightly higher rate. Amy and Mike, the owners, are a young couple who plan to make their lives here. *Cabinas* are planned. It's just isolated enough from town to be perfect. The **Cabinas La Salsa Brava** are on the beach and are low budget. **Cabinas Garibaldi**, also low budget, are nearby.

UPSCALE ACCOMMODATIONS: New Yorker Eddie Ryan has four attractive cabins for around $50 d. Breakfast, tours, and horseback rentals are also offered. Contact him at **Cabinas Maritza** (☎ 798-1844) or through the ATEC office (☎ 798-4244). The most expensive and most deluxe place to stay near town is definitely **El Pizote**, which is set back from the Black Beach as you approach town. It's named after the mischievous coatis who once inhabited a cage near the entrance. The bungalows and cabins are behind the main lodge. Tastefully designed with elegant simplicity, the lodge has screened rooms with fans, mirrors, and reading lamps, along with shared water showers and the largest shower heads you've ever seen. The rooms may not be rodent-proof; be sure to separate your toothpaste from your other belongings or a rodent may gnaw its way right into your bag to have a bite from the tube! Although the poor staff attitude needs improvement, it is still preferable to stay here than in places like Las Palmas and Punta Cocles, overdone resorts that are out of character with the area. Rates run from $22 s and $33 d to $55 s or d for the bungalows, which have private baths. Food is extra. For reservations ☎ or fax 229-1428.

FOOD: If you're planning to do your own cooking, don't miss the once-weekly vegetable truck that pulls in across from the Támara on Wed. afternoons. Other food is available at the vegetable store. Food prices have skyrocketed here in recent years, which is one reason why you don't see many locals eating out. One of the most reasonable places to eat is **Soda Priscilla**, off the main seaside road as you enter town; it opens early for breakfast. Another affordable spot is **Johnnie's Discotheque and Chinese Seafood Restaurant**, which serves Chinese and Tico food and is one of the few with prices still low enough to attract locals. One of the most popular places, **Soda Támara** has a nice patio in the back. They're open from 6:30 to 9 and closed on Tues. Another great one is **El Parquecito**, which has popular fish *casados* as well as lobster. Owner Earl here offers fishing charters. Near the Hotel Puerto Viejo, the **Soda Bela** also serves good food, including herbal tea. **Soda Marley** is juxtaposed with Cabinas Támara. Near the soccer field and very popular, the **Garden Restaurant** serves Creole, Caribbean, and Asian food. Dishes range from jungle passion salad to a range of vegetarian and seafood dishes. **Stanford's** has a balcony overlooking the sea. They serve vegetarian dishes and fish dinners. A pathetic monkey on a rope plays in a tree next door. **Soda Coral** has a large breakfast menu and serves pizza most afternoons during tourist season. Other places to try include **Salsa de Talamanca**, **Bambú**, the **Mexitico Restaurant** (at the Hotel Puerto Viejo) and the **Restaurant Maritza**.

family cooking: Out in Manzanillo, Miss Marva, Miss Alfonsina, Miss Edith, and Doña Cipriana will prepare homecooked meals if notified in advance.

baked goods: Miss Dolly, Miss Sam, and Miss Daisy sell traditional treats. Miss Sam also sometimes has food but "this isn't a restaurant." Mateo sells whole wheat bread at his home near the soccer field.

SERVICES: Most of the services and activities listed here can be found on the map in town – that is if it hasn't gotten ripped off again! Make **phone calls** from Hotel Maritza and Pulpería Manuel León. The nearest **banking** service is in Bribri. A Ministry of Health **clinic** there is open Mon. to Fri. from 7-4. In Puerto Viejo, Dr. Rosa León sees patients from 5:30-8 PM and on an emergency basis. To **rent bicycles**, contact the Soda Bela, Aldo Figueroa, Jacobo Brent at Cabinas Kaya, Petra at El Escape Caribeño, or René and Priscilla in Punta Uva. For **horseback riding**, contact Mauricio Salazar (through ATEC only!) and Antonio at "Tropical Paradise." Earl Brown can arrange **snorkeling** and **ocean fishing** expeditions. Lica at Hotel Puerto Viejo repairs **surfboards**. There is no bank here, but you can change traveler's checks at Stanford's.

An all-day tour is offered up the Sarapiquí and San Juan rivers by Miguel González (☎ 761-1056); rates are around $35-$75 pp, depending upon the number of people. Lunch and a two-hour forest hike are included. You must show your passport to Nicaraguan border authorities.

Seeing the Real Talamanca

With headquarters across from Soda Tamara in the town center, ATEC, the Association of Ecotourism and Conservation of Talamanca, is an exciting recent development on the local scene. The organization's goals are to promote ecological tourism and environmental education for the local population and for visitors. In most of Costa Rica, the situation is one of eco-exploitation rather than "ecotourism." Most guides are paid only a pittance. ATEC tours are limited to six participants and afford you the opportunity to see how Costa Ricans really live. These tours can be difficult, so make sure you choose one that suits you. In the Cahuita area, snorkeling, a bird walk, farm walks, and others are offered. In Puerto Viejo, walks are offered around farms, in the Chimuri reserve, and to the Kekoldi Indian Reserve. Snorkeling and camping can be arranged at Punta Mona. Three trips are also conducted in the Manzanillo-Gandoca Reserve, with a Gandoca/ANAI overnight hike that includes a visit to an experimental fruit farm and may allow you to spot a nesting sea turtle (for more information on ANAI, see Volunteering on page 163). Two trips are especially intriguing. One is to ASACODE, a local virgin forest and reforestation collective in San Miguel de Gandoca. Another is a horseback ride and hike to San Rafael de Bordon, a community 11 km away in the Talamanca foothills, which lets you see sustainable forest management in practice. Prices run from about $12.50 for a half-day trip to $70 for a three-night trip (not including food and lodging). A half-day of birding is $12.50 and a snorkeling trip is $17. The best way to book a tour is to stop by the ATEC office or ☎ or fax 798-4244; the best times to call are around noon or after 9 PM. For information, write ATEC, Puerto Viejo.

ENTERTAINMENT: In tourist season, the large disco below **Stanford's** has live music, as does **Bambú**, just S past the dump. Stanford's gets packed and incredibly humid – more like a sauna than a disco. On the beachside drag as you come into the village, the **Taverna Popo** is the endearing local sleaze bar. During the day, you can also watch surfers. However, keep in mind that the waters here are not for beginners. A 29-year-old US citizen drowned here in 1994 while surfing.

FROM PUERTO VIEJO: A direct bus (more expensive than changing in Limón) departs for San José daily at about 7. The bus to Limón leaves Mon. to Sat. at 6, 11, and 4 and on Sun. at 6 and 4. From Manzanillo you can take a bus directly to Limón; it leaves at 9 and 4:30. If you can get to the crossroads (*cruce*), the express bus from Sixaola to

San José passes by at around 6:30, 9:30, 11:30 and 4. The bus to Bribri leaves at 6:30, 11:30, 2:30, and 5:30, returning at 12 and 3:30.

Vicinity of Puerto Viejo de Talamanca

Punta Cocles

ACCOMMODATIONS: The long stretch from Puerto Viejo to Manzanillo, undeveloped just a few years ago, is rapidly becoming overdeveloped and environmentally degraded in the process. The development since 1990 has been phenomenal. If you want to stay here and have a car, the best procedure is to drive around and check to see what's new (indubitably a lot), and what looks like good value in line with your standards. There are a number of restaurants, including **Soda Elena, Selvyn's** (reasonable) and **Soda Naturales**. About the only truly low-budget accommodations are modest rooms ($4 pp) across from El Duende Feliz, an Italian bistro. **Bungalows Escape Caribeño** are in the area. A two-person unit is $40 and a four-person unit is $50. Both have private bath and fan. Inexpensive **Tio Lio's Resorts** are just past the bridges to the right. Luxurious **Hotel Punta Cocles** (☎ 234-0306, fax 234-0014) offers pool, a/c, and kitchens. Next is **Jardín Miraflores Lodge** (☎ 233-5127, fax 233-5390), a plantation raising heliconias for export, which offers modest – some might say overpriced – rooms with fans for $60 on up, including breakfast. The often-absent owner moved from the Bahamas to Costa Rica because of escalating labor costs. **Hotel Kashá** (☎ 288-2563, 257-4911, fax 222-2213) has large, attractive rooms (around $65), Jacuzzi, gardens, and a restaurant, the **Reef Café**. Low-budget to inexpensive, **Selvyn's Cabinas** are next to the restaurant of the same name (closed Mon.). They are near the beach and are comparatively good value. **Walaba** (☎ 224-7972/6364) has a large lodge that holds 15, as well as a set of *cabinas* that hold four to six. Inexpensive **Cabinas Punta Uva** – which have private bath and kitchen – are about a km farther. Built by Canadian multimillionaire "environmentalist" Maurice Strong, the **Villas del Caribe** (☎ 233-2200, fax 221-2801), ultra-luxury apartments housing from two to five persons, look out over the beach. These units continue to be the subject of controversy because they were constructed on Indian land. Strong – who ironically led the Earth Summit in Rio in 1992 – claims he did not know the property was part of the Keklodi reserve when he purchased it, but no compensation has been paid to date. Much of the land belongs to the Afro-Caribbean people, who have lived here for generations. However, under the 1971 Indian Law, non-Indians were granted reserves. It is not clear whether the hotel is on Indian land, part of the reserve, or both. To be fair, Strong has his defenders in the local community, and he is not the only one who has built on Indian land.

In Barra Cocles, **Cabinas Katty** have two inexpensive four-person units with private bath. Moderately priced **Cabinas DASA** at Playa Chiquita have four units, ranging from low-budget to inexpensive. For information and current rates contact Elizabeth at ☎ 220-4089 or Rosa María at ☎ 236-2631. **Maracú** (☎ 225-6215) has one house with kitchen. **Playa Chiquita** is yet another expensive hotel with paths down to the beach. A set of three bungalows with fans and a gourmet restaurant, **Kasha** (☎ 288-2563, fax 222-2213) is also at this beach. Rates are $60 d. Also along this stretch is **Yaré** (☎/fax 284-5921), a set of *cabinas* equipped with kitchenettes; there's a restaurant. **Villa Paraiso** (fax 798-4244) has eight cabins with baths and decks. There's a movie lounge, and boogie boards and bikes are available for rent. Its **Paloma Café** serves dishes ranging from vegetarian lasagna to rice pilaf to cheesecake.

Punta Uva

From Puerto Viejo, the road continues 12 km S to Manzanillo. A scarcely populated area, it is also one of the nation's most beautiful. This beach is third in line, after Playas Pirikiri and Chiquita, in the series running to the S from the village. Offshore are 650-ft (200-m) coral reefs. The Punta Uva area is part of the Gandoca-Manzanillo Reserve, but there are no funds for buying up these tracts and there is no enforcement of regulations. One of the most heinous examples of unscrupulous developers using "ecotourism" to devastate the environment can be found at the Hotel Las Palmas, which may have 80 rooms if and when construction is finished. Czech developer Jan Kalina began construction of a $3 million hotel in 1989 without obtaining the proper permits first. Permission was granted in 1990, but Kalina has been accused of filling in marshlands to construct a road, using coral material as landfill, cutting and burning forest, and excavating and dredging land in the area to build a canal. Although municipal inspectors ordered construction to cease in January 1989, building continued, and the order was ignored. The municipality complained to the Ministry of Natural Resources, Energy, and Mines (MIRINEM), but there was no response. On June 17, 1990, President Calderón and MIRINEM's director signed a permit for the project. Permission was finally revoked on March 5, 1993; Kalina has been ordered to tear down all construction in restricted areas and restore the environment's integrity. He denies having violated the permits. Although Kalina has been ordered by the ICT to demolish all but the 24 rooms initially planned, the hotel has opened and still advertises itself as an "eco-resort." Environmental devils can contact the hotel at ☎ 255-3939, fax 255-3737, or visit them in person at Edificio Crystal, First Floor, Av. 1, C. 1/3. One irony is that the Punta Uva area is known as a center of legemaniasis, a sand flea-borne viral infection that causes a cutanaceous ulcer under your skin. It can only be cured with injections, and it results in a depressed, depigmented scar.

Manzanillo & Refugio Gandoca-Manzanillo

This is a mixed-management reserve, meaning that its goal is not only preserving resources but also sustaining them through their active use by the community in the pursuit of economic development. Sadly, this covenant has been continually violated by loggers illegally operating inside and outside the reserve and by unscrupulous developers, who ignore regulations and bribe officials. Nevertheless, the portion of the reserve from Manzanillo village onwards remains relatively pristine and one of the most spectacularly beautiful places in Costa Rica, if not the world.

FLORA AND FAUNA: The reserve is the only area containing mangrove swamps along the Caribbean Coast; there's also *cativo* forest, a 741-acre (300-ha) estuary, two *jolillo* swamps, and coral reefs. Some of the mammals here are the tapir, manatee, margay, sloth, paca, and ocelot. Birds include the falcon, hawk, pelican, chestnut-mandibled toucan, and five species of parrots. Of 358 species of birds sighted, 40% are rarely seen in neighboring Panama. Crocodiles and *caimáns* are also found.

PRACTICALITIES/TOURS: Boat rides, snorkeling and trips to Playa Gandoca can be arranged through the ATEC office in Puerto Viejo. There's a public telephone at the *pulpería* in Gandoca. In Manzanillo, the low-budget **Cabinas Maxi** have five units alongside a bar, disco, and *pulpería*. The **Almonds and Corals Tent Camp** (☎ 232-3681: message) is here. Set a kilometer or so before Manzanillo, this highly unusual lodge opened in 1994. It has around 16 tents, two toilets, a reception tent, and a thatch-roofed dining pavilion. Each 16-foot-square screen tent encloses a nine-foot-square tent holding two twin beds, fan and bath. Everything is only a few meters from the beach. Walkways on stilts connect the tents to the restaurant, office, and beach. You will be awakened in the wee hours of the morning by the cries of howler monkeys. As the camp is set amidst dense tropical vegetation, the grounds are dark. Rates run around $50 s, $75 d, and $75 t.

GETTING THERE, GETTING AROUND, AND HIKING: The Limón-Manzanillo bus runs from Puerto Viejo around 7:30 to 8 AM (C. 100; beware of overcharging by driver). It returns from its afternoon run at about 3. If you wish to get here from Limón directly, the bus leaves at 6 and 2:30. The alternative is to hitch or have your own transport. A great hike runs 5½ km from Manzanillo to Punta Mona (Monkey Point). The trail is too slippery for the average video-camera-toting tourist, and Ticos generally don't come this far. So you're likely to have the area all to yourself. Offshore coral outcrops support palm trees, and surf crashes over rocks. After a couple of hours you reach Punta Mono where there's an attractive *finca* surrounded by banana plants. Another trail leads down to the island off Punta Mona, and you can then head along the beach to the right about an hour, where there's a mangrove lagoon. However, there isn't time to make it to Gandoca, see it in one day, and return to Puerto Viejo, unless you leave very early in the morning and maintain a stiff pace. From Gandoca, it's another 2½ hours along a dirt road past small *fincas*, logging trucks, and clearcuts. A stretch that has been reforested uniformly with teak contrasts dramatically with the primary growth on the other side of the road. The road runs into the enormous Noventa y Seis banana plantation, from where you can catch buses back to Puerto Viejo (50 km, 1½ hours) along the "highway." Another alternative is the "government road," a five-km route from Manzanillo to Monkey Point, passing through dense tropical forests; it's very muddy during the wet season.

ASACODE

ASACODE is the acronym for Asociación Sanmigueleña de Conservación y Desarrollo, an association of farmers in San Miguel who are conservationists investigating and practicing reforestation. Visits here are available through ATEC (see Seeing the Real Talamanca, page 519). It's an eight-hour hike to come here from Manzanillo; another route is via the trail that runs off the Bribri-Sixaola road.

Bribri

Bribri, 65 km (40 miles) from Limón, is the region's administrative center, and there's little reason to come here except to visit the bank or post office. It's also a transportation center where you can catch buses to the indigenous village of **Amubri** (stay at the **Casa de Huespedes** run by nuns there) and other indigenous villages. The village of **Watsi**, a few km away, sells handicrafts.

Leaving Costa Rica

DEPARTING BY AIR: Fluctuating with the exchange rate, the airport tax is $15 for tourists and $44 for residents and citizens – the one time that the visitor doesn't get screwed! You may wish to pay it when you reconfirm your ticket. Otherwise you'll probably have to wait in line at the airport. To get a taxi to the airport, ☎ 221-6865, ask at your hotel, or go out in the streets and search for an orange taxi well in advance of your departure. The Alajuela-bound microbus, which makes a stop at the airport, runs from Av. 2, Calles 12/14 (near Parque La Merced). You can change your remaining currency with a money changer (reliable) if the banks are closed. **note:** Don't overstay your visa! The government has dropped its formerly tolerant policy. If you overstay, you will likely find that you can't return for another 10 years! For further info, see Extending Your Visa, page 123.

SHIPPING: Orchid Alley sells orchids for export; they're upstairs next to the restaurants. Britt dispenses both free coffee samples and sells bags. They're right at the Continental departure lounge. The prices of alcohol at the duty free shops are surprisingly reasonable.

For Panama

The situation in Panama has been deteriorating for some years now, and it is not as safe as Costa Rica to visit. Check the embassy in Centro Colón to see if you need a visa (☎ 225-0667; open 8-noon) for Panama before departing. A 30-day tourist card for Canadians and US citizens can be obtained from Copa (☎ 223-7033, 221-5596; C. 1, Av. 5) in San José. You will need to show a RT ticket of some sort to enter the country. Flights are available, and *Alas Ciricanas* (☎ 255-4266) has flights from San José to downtown Panama City. **by bus:** *Ticabus* (☎ 221-9229/8954), Calle 9, Av. 4, runs to Panama City for about $20. It departs daily at 10 PM and arrives in Panama City at 5 PM. Departing daily at 7:30 AM and noon and arriving at 4:30 and 9 PM respectively, *Tracopa* bus (☎ 221-4214, 223-7685), Av. 18, C. 4, runs to David, Panama for $9. From here you can take another bus on to Panama City hourly (7 hrs.) or an *express* at noon and midnight (5½ hours). *Auto Transportes Upala* (☎ 470-0051; C. 16, Av. 3/5) and *Auto Transportes Mepe* (☎ 221-0524; Av. 11, C. Central/1) run to Changuinola. Other alternatives are to fly directly (around $130), fly *SANSA* (☎ 221-9414, 323-0397, 233-3258, fax 255-2176) to Coto 47 ($25 OW) from Mon. to Sat. and then take a taxi to Paso Canoas on the border. From there, you can catch a bus into Panama or travel overland to David and then fly to Panama City; the Paso Canoas border closes here from 12 to 2 daily.

from the Caribbean coast: The town of Sixaola (La Puente) becomes **Guabito** in Panama. The border is theoretically open daily from 7-1 and 1-5, but it may sometimes be closed on weekends. From here, minibuses run the 16 km to Changuinola, where you find the first bank and a hotel. From here, you can fly to David or travel on by train (daily) or bus to the run-down banana port of **Almirante**. It has hotels and boats ($2, 35 minutes) to **Bocas del Toro**, a set of offshore islands, where you can find still-pristine Caribbean waters and lifestyle. Stay at inexpensive and tremendously atmospheric **Hotel Bahía** (☎ 757-9626), at **Hotel Thomas** (☎ 757-9248), or at one of the low-budget *pensiones*. Diving is available. From Almirante you must take another boat to **Chiriquí Grande** (another small town with hotels) that connects by road to David. From David, you can visit the cool town of **Boquete**, about 20 km to the E; stay at **Pensión Virginia**, **Pensión Marilos**, or **Hotel Panamonte**. This town fills up for its flower festival, held annually in Jan. In short, it's much easier and faster to go via Paso Canoas, but this route is more adventurous.

information: The best current information on travel conditions in the country can be found in *Mexico and Central America Handbook*; public libraries generally have a current edition. Another alternative is David Dudenhoefer's guide, *The Panama Traveler*. If you want to learn about the history of Panamanian relations with the US and the effects of the 1989 invasion, see *The Panama Deception*. Ask your video store about it or order a copy for $54.05 postpaid from The Empowerment Project, 1653 18th St., Ste. # 3, Santa Monica CA 90404.

tours: Contact **Centro de Aventuras** (☎ 507-27-6746/8946, fax 27-6477; Box 6-4197 El Dorado, Panama, Republic of Panama). They offer various birdwatching, snorkeling, and expedition tours.

For Nicaragua

A visa is no longer required for US citizens, but you must change $60 at the border. Canadians do require a visa. Call the Nicaraguan Embassy in La California at ☎ 233-8747 to check on the latest requirements. If flying, expect to pay $100 OW. Most companies don't want their rental cars visiting Nicaragua. **by bus:** *Sirca Bus* (☎ 222-5541, 223-1464) has a 12-hour run ($9) to Managua, Nicaragua at 5 AM on Wed., Fri., and Sun. from C. 7, Av. 6/8. *Tica Bus* (☎ 221-8954, C. 9, Av. 4) also runs on Mon. Wed. and Fri. at 7 AM; it has better buses, costs less than $1 more, and arrives about the same time. Other buses from Coca Cola run to the border at Peñas Blancas. *Auto Transportes Upala* (☎ 471-0061;

C. 16, Av. 3/5) also runs. Crossing over, you pay less than a dollar for the privilege of leaving Costa Rica. Then you board a minibus and travel four km to Nicaraguan immigration. US citizens and others who do not require a visa must pay $2. Those who do need a visa must fork over $25 or pay $14 for a three-day transit visa. After the border, where you can purchase *cordobas* (the local currency) with money changers, the first town is Rivas, 37 km to the N. Inexpensive **Hotel Nicarao** is here. A number of buses per day connect Rivas with the border; cross by early afternoon to avoid getting stuck! Try to keep your luggage always in sight while in Nicaragua to deter theft. Although there is a border crossing at Los Chiles on the E coast of Costa Rica, in recent years it has been impossible for foreigners to cross from either direction. Check around in San José for any change in the situation.

tours: The **Institute for Central American Studies** runs study tours here. The 12 days ($795, ground portion only) are broken into five days of orientation in San José and a week of travel in Nicaragua. Write ICAS (☎ 224-8910), Apdo. 300, 1002 San José, Costa Rica.

☞ **Traveler's Tip.** If you're planning to cruise through Costa Rica and head on to S America, a **vehicular ferry service** runs three times a week between Cristóbal in Panamá and Cartagena, Columbia. This eliminates the need to ship your vehicle to S America. For more information, call Rodrigo Gómez or Harry Evetts in Panamá at ☎ 507-64-5564 or 64-5699.

a la tica – in the Costa Rican fashion.

apartotel – an apartment hotel with kitchen facilities. These are often suites and generally have daily, weekly, and monthly rates.

arboreal – describing a species that lives and usually feeds above ground level.

biomass – the dry weight of the plants and animals in a given ecosystem. In a tropical rainforest the biomass averages 180 tons per acre, as compared to the 120 tons found in a temperate forest.

broadleaf forest – an evergreen forest that does not contain conifers (pines).

buttress – a term used to describe the roots of rainforest trees. There are three main varieties. Often looping or undulating from side to side, serpentine buttresses extend some distance from the tree. Flying buttresses are of the stilt-root type. Plank buttresses, resembling giant wedges, are the most spectacular of the three.

bocas – Costa Rican term for late afternoon hors d'oeuvres.

bombetas – Tico fireworks whose explosive sounds may rouse you from sleep.

cabina, cabinas – literally "cabins," these are sometimes like motels and sometimes resemble apartment hotels.

cafetaleros – the wealthy coffee growers who have wielded a dominant economic and political influence.

cantina – a small local bar

cantones – counties, administrative district of a province.

carreras de caballos – horse races.

carretera – a route or highway.

cloud forest – a high-elevation forest which is kept damp most of the time through precipitation and mist. The trees are short, with heavy epiphytic growth, and there are deep mats of moss.

colón – the currency of the country; divided into 100 *centimes*.

corridas de toros – Costa Rican bull fights. (Bulls are not killed).

distritos – districts, subdivisions of a canton.

diurnal – describes an animal that is active during the day.

endemic – native to a specific region.

eyeshine – the reflection from an animal's eyes when it is hit by a light at night. Eyes do not shine on their own, and the effect may not be seen at close range.

exotic – a non-native species.

hospedaje – an inexpensive hotel usually run by a family.

iglesia – a church.

jefe politico – district political chief who is appointed by the president.

marimba – a xylophone made with gourds, traditionally found in many Latin American and African nations.

mature forest – forest that has reached its climax in terms of growth. Primary forests are often also mature.

medieria – a type of land tenure in which the landlord supplies everything except labor.

mirador – a scenic lookout point

mesa – polling place.

municipalidad – municipal council.

Nica, Nicas – nickname for Nicaraguans.

nocturnal – describes an animal that is active at night.

pensión – an inexpensive hotel.

peregrinos – pilgrimages on August 2 to the Basilica of Cartago's miraculous shrine.

precarista – a squatter on agricultural land, so named for his "precarious" position.

prehensile tail – the muscular tail of an arboreal mammal, capable of wrapping around a tree branch and supporting the animal's weight.

primary forest – undisturbed forest.

pulpería – general store.

punta guanacasteco – the national dance, performed with marimba and guitar accompaniment.

secondary forest – forest which has either been cut or destroyed by flooding. Often dense and scrubby, it harbors a changing mix of species as it matures.

sendero – a hiking trail.

soda – a small bar or snack joint.

Tico, Ticos – the nickname commonly applied to the Costa Rican people.

tugurios – urban slums, generally constructed on hills or areas subject to flooding. They promote environmental contamination, ill health, prostitution, crime, and broken families.

turno – town fiesta.

Booklist

TRAVEL & DESCRIPTION

Baker, Bill. *The Essential Road Guide for Costa Rica*. 1992. Call 800-881-8607.

Finchley, Alan. *Costa Rica: An Alternative for Americans*. New Brunswick, NJ: 1975.

Mayfield, Michael W. and Gallo, Rafael E. *The Rivers of Costa Rica: A Canoeing, Kayaking, and Rafting Guide*. Birmingham, AL: Menasha Ridge Press, 1988.

Nelson, Harold D. *Costa Rica: A Country Study*. Washington, DC: American University, 1983.

Villafranca, Richard. *Costa Rica: Gem of American Republics*. New York, 1976.

FLORA & FAUNA

The Biodiversity of Costa Rica. San José: INBio, 1995. An introduction to the nation's natural wonders and their peculiarities. Includes many color photos.

Allen, Dorothy. *The Rainforest of Gulfo Dulce*. Stanford, CA: Stanford Press, 1977.

Allen, P.H. *The Rain Forests of Golfo Dulce*. Gainesville: University of FL Press, 1956.

Berry, Fred and W. John Kress. *Heliconia: An Identification Guide*. Washington, DC, 1991. The first and only guide to this attractive ornamental which you'll often see in Costa Rica.

Boza, Mario A. and Rolando Mendoza. *The National Parks of Costa Rica*. Madrid: Industrias Graficas Alvi, S. A., 1981. A fine background guide to the parks. A new edition has just been published by Editorial Heliconia and can be purchased in Costa Rica.

Boza, Mario A. *Costa Rica National Parks*. Madrid: Infaco, S. A., 1988 and San José, Editorial Heliconia, 1992.

Carr, Archie F. *The Windward Road*. Tallahassee, FL: University Presses of Florida, 1955.

Cornelius, Stephen E. *The Sea Turtles of Santa Rosa National Park*. San José. Costa Rica: Fundación de Parques Nacionales, 1986. An excellent layman's introduction, now unfortunately out of print.

de Vries, Phillip J. *Butterflies of Costa Rica*. Princeton, NJ: Princeton University Press, 1987.

Dressler, R. L. *The Orchids*. Cambridge, England: The University Press, 1978.

Dresser, Robert L. *Field Guide to the Orchids of Costa Rica and Panama*. Ithaca, NY: Cornell University Press, 1993.

Emmons, Louse H. *Neotropical Rainforest Mammals*. Chicago, University of Chicago Press, 1990. This exceptionally fine color illustrated field guide is the finest of its kind. A must for zoologists and serious laymen alike, it contains maps showing the range of species, detailed descriptions and natural histories of the animals concerned, and references to scientific literature.

Forsyth, Adrian and Kenneth Miyata. *Tropical Nature*. New York: Scribner's, 1987. Adrian Forsyth has studied the tropical forests of Costa Rica; the late Kenneth Miyata worked in Ecuador. Working in tandem, they have sketched a brilliant portrait of the tropical rainforests, which serves as an excellent introduction for the uninitiated.

Forsyth, Adrian. *Journey through a Tropical Jungle*. Toronto: Greey de Pencier Books, 1988.

Gómez, Luis Diego. *Vegetación y Clima en Costa Rica*. San José, Costa Rica: UNED, 1987.

Hall, Carolyn. *Costa Rica, a Geographical Interpretation in Historical Perspective*. Boulder, CO: Westview Press, 1985. Possibly the best ecological guide to any nation ever published.

Head, Suzanne and Robert Heinzman, eds. *Lessons of the Rainforest*. San Francisco: Sierra Club Books, 1990. This collection of essays covers everything from activism (by Randy Hayes, founder of Rainforest Action Network) to the canopy (by Donald R. Perry) to extinction (by Anne H. and Paul Ehrlich).

Jacobs, Marius. *The Tropical Rain Forest: A First Encounter*. New York: Berlin Heidelberg, 1988. Calculated to appeal both to laymen and scientists, this comprehensive and techinical book was originally written in Dutch. It includes a chapter on Tropical America written by R. A. A. Oldeman.

Janzen, Daniel H., ed. *Costa Rica National History*. Chicago: University of Chicago Press, 1983. This superb volume is an excellent introduction to many Costa Rican species.

Owen, Dennis. *Camouflage and Mimicry*. Chicago: University of Chicago Press, 1980. Although not specifically about Costa Rica, this volume is a fascinating and beautifully illustrated study.

Perry, Donald. *Life Above the Jungle Floor*. San José, Costa Rica: Don Perro Press, 1991.

Phillips, Kathryn. *Tracking the Vanishing Frogs*. NY: St. Martin's Press, 1994. This fascinating book dramatically illustrates the mysteries surrounding the worldwide decline in amphibians. Special attention is paid to the golden toad of Monteverde.

Richards, P. W. *The Tropical Rain Forest: An Ecological Study*. Cambridge, England: University Press, 1981. First published in 1952, this is an in-depth tech nical account written more for biologists than laymen.

Sheppard, Charles R. C. *A Natural History of the Coral Reef*. Poole, Dorset: Blandford Press, 1983. If your curiosity about the reefs has been piqued by your visit, this is a fine book to read.

Skutch, Alexander F. A. *A Naturalist in Costa Rica*. Gainesville, FL: University of Florida Press, 1971.

Skutch, Alexander F. A. *A Bird Watcher's Adventures in Tropical America*. Austin: University of Texas Press, 1977.

Skutch, Alexander F. A. *A Naturalist on a Tropical Farm*. Berkeley: University of California Press, 1980

Stiles, Gary and Alexander Skutch. *A Guide to the Birds of Costa Rica*. Ithaca, NY: Cornell University Press, 1989. This suberb 477-page guide lists not only everything you might want to know about the nation's birds (including description, mating calls, habits, and range), but also illustrates them with beautiful color plates. As an added bonus, descriptions of numerous avian habitats and locations for birding are included.

Tomilson, P.B. and M. H. Zimmerman, eds. *Tropical Trees as Living Systems*. Cambridge, England: The University Press, 1978.

Wallace, David Rains. *The Quetzal and the Macaw*. San Francisco: Sierra Club Books, 1992. This well written and extremely informative history of Costa Rica's parks is a must for any visitor who wonders how and why the parks got their start. A record of what the determined will and combined efforts of a few individuals can accomplish, it is also inspirational.

Wickler, W. *Mimicry in Plants and Animals*. New York: World University Library, McGraw Hill, 1968.

Young, Allan. *Field Guide to the Natural History of Costa Rica*. San José, Costa Rica: Trejos Hermanos, 1983.

HISTORY

Creedman, Thomas S. *Historical Dictionary of Costa Rica*. NJ: Metuchen, 1977.

Hovey, Graham and Gene Brown, eds. *Central America and the Caribbean*. New York: Arno Press, 1980. This volume of clippings from *The New York Times*, one of a series in its Great Contemporary Issues books, graphically displays American activities and attitudes toward the area. A goldmine of information.

Mannix, Daniel P. and Malcolm Cooley. *Black Cargoes*. New York: Viking Press, 1982. Details the saga of the slave trade.

POLITICS & ECONOMICS

Ameringer, Charles D. *Don Pepe: A Political Biography of José Figueres of Costa Rica*. University of New Mexico Press, Albuquerque, NM 1978.

Ameringer, Charles D. *Democracy in Costa Rica*. New York: Praeger, 1982.

Barry, Tom. *Costa Rica: A Country Guide*. Albuquerque, NM: The Inter-Hemispheric Resource Center, 1989. One in a series, this superb book surveys the political and economic situation, taking in the military, environmental and social issues, and foreign influences.

Barry, Tom. *The Central America Fact Book*. New York: Grove Press, 1986. A guide to the economic and political situation in each of the region's nations, together with a list of transnationals active in the area.

Bell, John P. *Crisis in Costa Rica: The 1948 Revolution*. University of Texas Press: Austin TX, 1971.

Booth, John A. and Thomas W. Walker. *Understanding Central America*. Boulder, CO: Westview Press, 1989. A fine overview of five of its nations.

Denton, Charles F. *Patterns of Costa Rican Politics*. Allyn and Bacon: Boston, 1971.

Edelman, Marc and Joanne Kenen. *The Costa Rica Reader*. New York: Grove Weidenfield, 1989. An excellent introduction covering everything from coopera tives to contras.

English, Burt H. *Liberacion Nacional in Costa Rica*. Gainsville, FL, 1971.

Herrick, Bruce and Barclay Hudson. *Urban Poverty and Economic Development: A Case Study of Costa Rica*. NY, NY, 1980.

Interbook, Inc. *Rural Development in Costa Rica*. NY, NY 1978.

Jones, Chester Lloyd. *Costa Rica and Civilization in the Caribbean*. Russell & Russell: New York, 1967. This rather dry account, written by a University of Wisconsin economics and political science professor, was first published in 1935.

Rolbein, Seth. *Nobel Costa Rica*. New York: St. Martin's Press, 1989. A firsthand account of Costa Rican politics and its press during the late 1980s.

Saunders, John. *Rural Electrification & Development: Social and Economic Development in Costa Rica and Colombia*. Boulder, CO 1978.

Seligson, Mitchell A. *Peasants of Costa Rica and the Rise of Agrarian Capitalism*. Madison, WI, 1980.

SOCIOLOGY & ANTHROPOLOGY

Biesanz, John and Mary. *Costa Rican Life*. Westport, CT: Greenwoood Press, Inc., 1979. A portrait of sleepy Costa Rican life as it was during the 1940s.

Biesanz, Richard and Karen Zumbris Biesanz and Mavis Hiltunen Biesanz. *The Costa Ricans*. Prospect Heights, IL: Waveland, 1987 (updated edition).

Palmer, Paula. *Wa'apin Man*. Editorial Costa Rica, 1986.

Palmer, Paula. *What Happen, A Folk History of Costa Rica's Talamanca Coast*. San José, Ecodesarrollos, 1977.

Palmer, Paula with Sanchez and Mayorga. *Taking Care of Sibo's Gifts, an Environmental Treatise*. San José: Ascociacíon de Desarrollo Integral de la Reserva Indígena Cocles/Kekoldi, 1991.

ART, ARCHITECTURE & ARCHAEOLOGY

Jones, Julie, (ed.), Michael Kan and Michael J. Snarkis. *Between Continents/Between Seas: Pre-Columbian Art of Costa Rica*. Detroit: Abrams/Detroit Institute of the Arts, 1981.

LITERATURE

Pasche, Barbara and David Volpendesta. *Clamor of Innocence: Stories from Central America*. San Francisco: City Lights, 1988. Includes six stories from Costa Rica.

Ras, Barbara, ed. *Costa Rica: A Traveler's Literary Companion*. San Francisco: Whereabouts Press, 1994. This book of short stories serves as a fine introduction to the country.

Spanish Vocabulary

Days of the Week

domingo	Sunday
lunes	Monday
martes	Tuesday
miercoles	Wednesday
jueves	Thursday
viernes	Friday
sabado	Saturday

Months of the Year

enero	January
febrero	February
marzo	March
abril	April
mayo	May
junio	June
julio	July
agosto	August
septiembre	September
octubre	October
noviembre	November
diciembre	December

Numbers

uno	one
due	two
tres	three
cuatro	four
cinco	five
seis	six
siete	seven
ocho	eight
nueve	nine
diez	ten
once	eleven
doce	twelve
trece	thirteen
catorce	fourteen
quince	fifteen
dieciseis	sixteen
diecisiete	seventeen
dieciocho	eighteen
dieci nueve	nineteen
veinte	twenty
veintiuno	twenty-one
veintidos	twenty-two
treinta	thirty
cuarenta	forty
cincuenta	fifty

sesenta	sixty
setenta	seventy
ochenta	eighty
noventa	ninety
cien	one hundred
cento uno	one hundred one
doscientos	two hundred
quinientos	five hundred
mil	one thousand
mil uno	one thousand one
dos mil	two thousand
un million	one million
mil milliones	one billion
primero	first
segundo	second
tercero	third
cuarto	fourth
quinto	fifth
sexto	sixth
septimo	seventh
octavo	eighth
noveno	ninth
decimo	tenth
undecimo	eleventh
duodecimo	twelfth
ultimo	last

Conversation

¿Como esta usted?	How are you?
Bien, gracias, y usted?	Well, thanks, and you?
Buenas dias.	Good morning.
Buenas tardes.	Good afternoon.
Buenas noches.	Good evening/night.
Hasta la vista.	See you again.
Hasta luego.	So long.
¡Buen suerte!	Good luck!
Adios.	Goodbye.
Mucho gusto de conocerle.	Glad to meet you.
Felicidades.	Congratulations.
Muchas felicidades.	Happy birthday.
Feliz Navidad.	Merry Christmas.
Feliz Año Nuevo.	Happy New Year.
Gracias.	Thank you.
Por favor.	Please.
De nada/con mucho gusto.	You're welcome.
Perdoneme.	Pardon me.
¿Como se llama esto?	What do you call this?
Lo siento.	I'm sorry.
Permitame.	Permit me.
Quisiera...	I would like...
Adelante.	Come in.
Permitame presentarle...	May I introduce...

¿Como se llamo usted?	What is your name?
Me llamo...	My name is...
No se.	I don't know.
Tengo sed.	I am thirsty.
Tengo hambre.	I am hungry.
Soy norteamericano/a	I am an American.
¿Donde puedo encontrar...?	Where can I find...?
¿Que es esto?	What is this?
¿Habla usted ingles?	Do you speak English?
Hablo/entiendo un poco español.	I speak/understand a little Spanish
¿Hay alguien aqui que hable ingles?	Is there anyone here who speaks English?
Le entiendo.	I understand you.
No entiendo.	I don't understand.
Hable mas despacio por favor.	Please speak more slowly.
Repita por favor.	Please repeat.

Telling Time

¿Que hora es?	What time is it?
Son las...	It's...
... cinco.	... five o'clock.
... ocho y diez.	... ten past eight.
... seis y cuaro.	... quarter past six.
... cinco y media.	... half past five.
...siete y menos cinco.	... five of seven.
antes de ayer.	the day before yesterday.
anoche.	yesterday evening.
esta mañana.	this morning.
a mediodia.	at noon.
en la noche.	in the evening.
de noche.	at night.
a medianoche.	at midnight.
mañana en la mañana.	tomorrow morning.
mañana en la noche.	tomorrow evening.
pasado mañana.	the day after tomorrow.

Directions

¿En que direccion queda...?	In which direction is...?
Lleveme a... por favor.	Take me to... please.
Llevame alla ... por favor.	Take me there please.
¿Que lugar es este?	What place is this?
¿Donde queda el pueblo?	Where is the town?
¿Cual es el mejor camino para...?	Which is the best road to...?
De vuelta a la derecha.	Turn to the right.
De vuelta a la izquierda.	Turn to the left.
Siga derecho.	Go this way.
En esta direccion.	In this direction.
¿A que distancia estamos de...?	How far is it to...?

¿Es este el camino a...?	Is this the road to...?
¿Es...	Is it...
... cerca?	... near?
... lejos?	... far?
... norte?	... north?
... sur?	... south?
... este?	... east?
... oeste?	... west?
Indiqueme por favor.	Please point.
Hagame favor de decirme donde esta...	Please direct me to...
... el telephono.	... the telephone.
... el excusado.	... the bathroom.
... el correo.	... the post office.
... el banco.	... the bank.
... la comisaria.	... the police station.

Accommodations

Estoy buscando un hotel....	I am looking for a hotel that's...
... bueno.	... good.
... barato.	... cheap.
... cercano.	... nearby.
... limpio.	... clean.
¿Dónde hay hotel, pensión, hospedaje?	Where is a hotel, pensión, hospedaje?
Hay habitaciones libres?	Do you have available rooms?
¿Dónde están los baños/ servicios?	Where are the bathrooms?
Quisiera un...	I would like a...
... cuarto sencillo.	... single room.
... cuarto con baño.	... room with a bath.
... cuarto doble.	... double room.
¿Puedo verlo?	May I see it?
¿Cuanto cuesta?	What's the cost?
¡Es demasiado caro!	It's too expensive!

Index